SCHOOL WORLD ORDER

The Technocratic Globalization of Corporatized Education

JOHN KLYCZEK

Published by:
Trine Day LLC
PO Box 577
Walterville, OR 97489
1-800-556-2012
www.TrineDay.com
trineday@icloud.com

Library of Congress Control Number: 2019946657

Klyczek, Johnl
 – 1st ed.
p. cm.
Includes references
Epub (ISBN-13) 978-1-63424-197-7
Mobi (ISBN-13) 978-1-63424-198-4
Print (ISBN-13) 978-1-63424-196-0
1. Education. 2. Education -- History. 3. Educational change -- United States -- History -- 20th century. 4. Education -- Moral and ethical aspects. 5. Secret societies -- United States. I. Klyczek, John. II. Title

The first ten chapters have appeared online: *Dissident Views, Intrepid Report, OpEdNews, Global Reasearch: Centre for Research on Globalization, Activist Post, Rense News,* and *The Saker.*

First Edition
10 9 8 7 6 5 4 3 2 1

Printed in the USA
Distribution to the Trade by:
Independent Publishers Group (IPG)
814 North Franklin Street
Chicago, Illinois 60610
312.337.0747
www.ipgbook.com

Publisher's Foreword

No more pencils, no more books
No more teacher's, dirty looks.
Kick the tables, kick the chairs
Kick the teachers, down the stairs!

I find this book rather scary. My mother was a teacher, her father was a teacher, a principal and a superintendent. My father taught in secondary schools, and, when I was a youngster, was the vice-president of Scarritt College in Nashville. His father had been a teacher and principal at public schools in Idaho, Oregon and Montana. My wife's mother had also taught, along with many other assorted aunts, uncles, and cousins – on all sides.

Education was stressed, my ditching continuing education to start a record store and an early marriage was frowned upon and commenced many tongues a-wagging. It was a tumultuous time, and having been sent home from high school for having hair too long, I was ready for something different. But are we as a country, ready for what is being put in motion? Granted, many things may be a two-edged sword, but some hard questions remain: Who holds the hilt? How will they wield it?

John Klyczek's *School World Order* is a *tour de force*, a deep dive into a future that is rapidly approaching. He takes us down history's paths, and shows us how we have arrived at such perilous shores.

My introduction to pedagogy (the method and practice of teaching, especially as an academic subject or theoretical concept) came from Professor Antony Sutton, in his book *America's Secret Establishment: An Introduction to The Order of Skull & Bones*, where he explained the secret society's interest in controlling the U.S. education system, and how they used John Dewey and Horace Mann to import the "Prussian Education" system: Teaching us what to think, instead of how to think.

The insidiousness of what Sutton exposed was at times more than I could handle – the reality of *it* versus my families' commitments to education – a real cognitive-dissonance situation. How could I, as a college drop-out, discuss this with my eruditely-experienced family members? At the time, it would have been crudely dismissed as nothing but wild ravings of an uneducated hippie. I stayed silent.

In 1999 Charlotte Iserybt published her *The Deliberate Dumbing Down of America: A Chronological Paper Trail*. Charlotte had served as a senior policy advisor in the U.S. Department of Education, during the first term of President Ronald Reagan. While there she came across information about a federally-funded grant called Better Education Skills through Technology (Project BEST), and leaked the document to the newspaper, *Human Events*. She was soon dismissed from the Department of Education.

Charlotte was also *the* person who sent Professor Sutton the membership books (current and past) of The Order of Skull & Bones, which spurred his exploration of the furtive group. Her father and grandfather had been members.

Then in 2003, John Taylor Gatto, a two-time State Teacher of the Year in New York, released *The Underground History of American Education: A Schoolteacher's Intimate Investigation Into the Problem of Modern Schooling*. Gatto had been working with Professor Sutton up until his death in June 2002, and this book confirmed Sutton's thesis and more.

> Our once highly individualized nation has evolved into a centrally managed village, an agora made up of huge special interests which regard individual voices as irrelevant…. [T]he net effect is to reduce men and women to the status of functions…. Public opinion is turned on and off in laboratory fashion…. Americans failed to notice the deliberate conversion of formal education that was taking place, a transformation that would turn school into an instrument of the leviathan state…

I'd heard enough. I spoke up. My wife had received her certificate, and was teaching. Well, let's just say, she didn't believe me – it was just one of her husband's wacky conspiracy theories.

School World Order puts thinking such as that to bed, and respects you in the morning. John Klyczek connects the dots, tells the tales and documents it all. Prepare to be frightened.

Onward to the Utmost of Futures,
Peace,
RA "Kris" Millegan
Publisher
TrineDay
July, 25, 2019

Dedicated to my Brother in this life and the next:
Justin Brad Johnson
(May 5, 1984 – April 25, 2018)

Growing up together, you taught me more about life than I can put into words. When we were sixteen years old, you taught me about the I-Ching; you taught me how to "break it down." Since then, I have meditated upon the base-two notation of the I-Ching for eighteen years. Reflecting on the I-Ching's binary-code yin-yang logic for nearly two decades has provided me profound insights into the mathematical and formal-logical frameworks of the binary-code logics of computer technologies and the stimulus-response methods of psychological conditioning. Without these a priori discernments into the dualistic substrata of the algorithmic patterns underlying digital computation and human cognition, my analysis in this book would not have been possible. I couldn't have done it without you.

In Memory of:

Susan Klyczek
Angela "Laughing Crow" Klyczek
Cheryl Pica
John Louis Klyczek
Rosalie Klyczek
Dustin Whiting
Carol Maher
Nunzio Malvestuto
Mary Klyczek
Tom Denvit
Michael Denvit
Randall Nieland
Mark Aigner
Sandra Adams
Kim Tanner

Acknowledgments

To my Dad—Thank you for teaching me all the best lessons: believe in God; keep the Lord's prayer; tell the truth; work hard; question authority; fight for love; forgive mistakes.

To my beautiful, loving wife of seven years, Solomohn Nallshi Ennis-Klyczek—Thank you for helping to edit so many of the chapters of this manuscript. Thank you for buying so many of the books that contributed to my research. Thank you for always supporting my work and always fighting the good fight with me.

To my professors, Dr. John Martone, Dr. Ruth Hoberman, Dr. Michael Loudon, Dr. Fern Kory, Dr. Tim N. Taylor, Dr. Daiva Markelis, Dr. Christopher Hanlon, Dr. Dannie Otto, Dr. Jyoti Panjwani, Dr. Gary Aylesworth, Dr. Tim Engles, Dr. Angela Vietto, and Dr. Christopher Wixson – Thank you all for training mein the rigors of scholarly research methods throughout my undergraduate and graduate studies at Eastern Illinois University.

To my high school humanities teacher, Dan Krupa—Thank you for not giving up on me; thank you for seeing something in me. You inspired me to become a teacher; you showed me the path that led to this book.

To my friends, L'Trevene'ir Arijont Phillips; Joshua Willett; Christopher Brown; David Simon-Toledo; Kenny White (1SG.USAR.RET); Anthony Chauncey; Noble Ekundayo Kofii El Ra Bey; and the Denvits (Robert, William, Timothy, Gregory, and Doris)—Thank you for building my character and carrying me through hard times. Thank you for all the conversations that helped me sharpen the ideas articulated throughout this book.

To the many editors who have published excerpts of this book, Bev Conover (Intrepid Report); Angie Tibbs (Dissident Voice); Rob Kall (OpEdNews); Mike Adams (Natural News); Michel Chossudovsky and Jezile Torculas (Centre for Research on Globalization); Jeff Rense (Rense News); Michael Edwards (Activist Post); Doug Owen (Blacklisted News); Kelly Ray (TrineDay) and the editors at *The Saker* – Thank you for helping me spread my research to your diverse audiences all over the globe.

Table of Contents

FOREWORD

F inally, a credentialed public educator, John Klyczek, has taken the information in the late Professor Antony Sutton's remarkable history books, melded it with documentation contained in my *Deliberate Dumbing Down of America*, and made sense of what Americans are looking at today: an evolving technocratic New World Order. Klyczek's *School World Order* astutely synthesizes my *Deliberate Dumbing Down* book with Sutton's work and meticulously documents the activities of entities involved in destroying the Constitutional Republic of the United States of America in order to merge it into a totalitarian global system.

For those unaware of the revelations published in Sutton's book *America's Secret Establishment: An Introduction to the Order of Skull and Bones*, it was I, Charlotte Thomson Iserbyt, who provided Sutton with the Membership Lists of Skull and Bones 1832-1984. My father and grandfather were members of The Order and I, therefore, had access to these records which had never before been published. After carefully scrutinizing these Membership Catalogs, Sutton said to me "I now understand who is behind the destruction of our sovereign Republic under the United States Constitution." He also made a most astounding statement: "The most important piece I ever wrote is 'How The Order Controls Education.'"

So, that being the case, you must read Klyczek's book, which provides in clear language all the research heretofore denied the reader who wonders about how The Order still controls education. Their plot, initiated in the early 1800s, has aimed to twist American education into a weapon that destroys our constitutional rights. This plan uses so-called "education" to put the world under a lifelong Pavlovian Soviet-style planned economy funded by government and tax-exempt foundations. This public/private planning and control system implements corporate-fascist Planning, Programming, Budgeting and Systems (PPBS) and Total Quality Management (TQM), and it uses our children to spin off profits for the global elite. It is being implemented in 2018 through tax-funded "school choice" charter corporations run by unconstitutional public/private partnerships, using computers and other forms of brainwashing and mind control based on the psychological research of behaviorist B.F. Skinner, who said "I could make a pigeon a high achiever by reinforcing it on a proper schedule."

Klyczek's book is a goldmine of solid proof of the betrayal of the United States Constitution primarily through "education." For a clear picture of the history of how a corrupted schooling system has forsaken the future generations of America, read Klyczek's *School World Order*.

Charlotte Iserbyt

PREFACE

This book is a historical and futurist process analysis of global trends in education: the corporate privatization of schooling; and the "personalization" of learning through computerized instructional technologies. The 'trends forecast' herein has been written to append and amend one of the most important tomes ever written about the history of American education: *The Deliberate Dumbing Down of America* (2000) by former Senior Policy Advisor in the Office of Educational Research and Improvement for the US Department of Education, Charlotte Thomson Iserbyt, who penned her *Chronological Paper Trail* after blowing the whistle on the Reagan Administration's Project BEST (Better Education Skills through Technology), which laid out federal plans to computerize the education system through fascistic public-private partnerships between corporations and government-funded schools.

In *The Deliberate Dumbing Down of America*, Iserbyt provides 736 pages of research documenting how the United States Federal Government, in bed with Robber Baron corporations and philanthropies, has funded educational psychology policies that implement stimulus-response, behaviorist, and operant methods of cognitive conditioning which have been programmed into Skinnerian "teaching-machines." Iserbyt demonstrates how modern-day "Skinner-box" teaching computers are engineered to psychologically re-condition students' democratic values of individualist liberty by digitally training them to conform to the Hegelian-collectivist philosophies underlying the totalitarian political-economic systems of communism and fascism, which are being synthesized in the global planned economy of the New World Order. In the *Revised and Abridged* update to her *Chronological Paper Trail*, which was reprinted in 2011, Iserbyt shows how the elected public schoolboard authorities of the federalized education system are being handed off to the private sector under the corporate authorities of the *un-elected* executive councils of globalist, for-profit charter school companies that are deploying post-Skinnerian adaptive-learning computers to condition students for corporate-fascist workforce training in a technocratically planned world economy.

Following the historical paper trail detailed by Iserbyt, *School World Order* investigates the trajectory of current trends in education policy that are moving toward the techno-fascist plans for corporate privatization and ed-tech personalization exposed by Iserbyt in the 1980s. In particular, my research covers three major aspects of the corporate-fascist privatization of education:

- "School choice" policies that use public tax dollars to subsidize private charter schools.

- Workforce-training curriculums that replace traditional academic studies with "job-competence" training.

- Corporate-fascist control of public education governance by replacing publicly elected schoolboards with unelected corporate-executive charter "councils."

In addition, my investigation examines two main components of the hi-tech "personalization" of corporate schooling:

- The replacement of human teachers with "adaptive learning" software that uses operant-conditioning psychology to train students in job competence.

- The digital data-mining of student-learning outcomes on these adaptive-learning software.

This second data-mining component has three basic functions:

- To determine corporate workforce quotas for a fascist planned economy.

- To continually upgrade research and development of adaptive-learning software and other educational technologies.

- To enhance research and development of biofeedback, artificial intelligence, augmented reality, virtual reality, and various transhumanist technologies that ultimately transcend traditional knowledge acquisition to the point where human learning itself becomes obsolete.

I also document how these techno-fascist education policies are being set up worldwide through the globalization of corporate-technocratic schooling through online charter schools that operate international chains, which utilize adaptive-learning software for workforce training that is regulated by the "lifelong learning" standards of the United Nations Educational Scientific and Cultural Organization (UNESCO).

In sum, the scope of my *School World Order* documents that the short-term objective of the new corporate-technocratic education system is to transform our public schooling system into a network of public-private business partnerships that overthrow publicly elected schoolboards while siphoning tax subsidies to replace human teachers with operant-conditioning computers which train students to fill workforce quotas planned by politically connected corporations. At the same time, the long-term objective is to co-opt Big Data-mining of cognitive-behavioral student-learning algorithms, converting these metrics to construct transhumanist ed-tech that "upgrades" learning into an interface with "smart" technologies.

This book also reveals how The Order of Skull & Bones at Yale University has been central to both the corporate privatization of workforce schooling and the hi-tech "personalization" of educational psychology methods based on eugenic evolutionary theories.

My research has been closely guided by the counsel of Charlotte Iserbyt herself, who personally contacted me in response to my *News With Views* article, "The Corporatization of Education." Thanks to Iserbyt's gracious outreach, what began as a simple news report has blossomed into the extensive treatise before you. Charlotte has consulted with me nearly every step of the way, and it was her who recommended this project to my publisher: Kris Millegan of TrineDay Books.

Iserbyt has also been instrumental in shaping the history of TrineDay as she is the heroine who leaked her father's Skull and Bones address books to Antony C. Sutton (1925-2002). A former Research Fellow at Stanford University's Hoover Institution, Sutton investigated these secret "black books" to compile the primary-source evidence cited in his groundbreaking exposé on The Order: *America's Secret Establishment: An Introduction to the Order of Skull & Bones*, which was rescued from censorship when it was reprinted by Kris Millegan, who later partnered with Sutton to co-author the 712-page tome, *Fleshing out Skull & Bones: Investigations into America's Most Powerful Secret Society*. In brief, with the Godsend of Iserbyt's leaked address books, Sutton and Millegan came together to produce the two foremost authoritative bodies of research on the Order, and my own Skull and Bones research is based on these sources with direct collaboration with the surviving author himself.

It has been an honor to carry on the works of Iserbyt, Millegan, and Sutton, and I hope that I have honored them in due kind.

To those who would dismiss this book as mere conspiracy theory: Please note its proximity to the primary source, authoritative scholarship on the subject of Skull and Bones. Furthermore, I have not relied solely upon these resources. On the contrary, I have corroborated the works of Iserbyt, Millegan and Sutton with an extensive array of academic peer-reviewed journals, scholarly whitepapers, university press books, government documents, and mainstream news reports from both ends of the political spectrum. Without an account of these historical facts, it is impossible to assess the complete picture of current and future trends in the technocratic globalization of corporatized education.

My findings have come down hard on the schooling system. Yet *School World Order* is not an attack on the public education system; it is a defense of public education. It is neither left-wing nor right-wing, as I have indicted both Republicans and Democrats alike. If my prognosis has offended or disturbed the reader, I have only diagnosed the disease of corporate technocracy so that we might prescribe a remedy.

Sincerely,
John jakE Klyczek

1

The Hegelian Dialectic Meets the Gates Foundation, Arne Duncan, and Bruce Rauner

For over thirty years, former Senior Policy Advisor in the Office of Educational Research and Improvement for the US Department of Education, Charlotte Thomson Iserbyt, has been warning us about the coming corporatization of education through fascistic charter school privatization that will be subsidized by public finances. Iserbyt, author of *The Deliberate Dumbing Down of America*, has described the charter school takeover, otherwise known as the "school choice" movement, as "[c]ollusion between neoconservatives, corporations, and leftists in education, including former 'conservative' Secretaries of Education and the NEA, [which] enabled corporations to take control of American education."[1]

As a case study, Illinois' education debacle under Governor Bruce Rauner proves her predictions accurate.

Order out of Chaos:

After operating without a budget for over seven months, the Illinois State Legislature passed Senate Bill 2043 to appropriate $721 million dollars to fund state college and adult education programs. The emergency bill was intended to release funding for a number of public colleges, such as my alma mater, Eastern Illinois University, and Chicago State University, which were nearly forced to issue massive layoffs or possibly shutdown all operations indefinitely.

Nevertheless, Governor Rauner vetoed the legislation on February 19th, 2016. And the state legislators fell short by two votes to override the veto.[2]

According to a report from CNNMoney, "Eastern Illinois University laid off 198 staff members this week, and the college president is blaming the state government. The cuts impact 13% of the school's employees."[3] The *Chicago Tribune* reported that "Chicago State University sent notices of potential layoffs to all of its 900 employees."[4]

In an interview with CBS News, the President of Chicago State, Thomas Calhoun Jr., responded to the unprecedented layoffs: "[i]t is baffling to most of us who think deeply about this: that, on the one hand, our governor would talk about bringing jobs back to the state, attracting industry to the state, attracting the kinds of investments in our state [sic], while at the same time, cutting the very opportunity to provide a highly skilled workforce. It just doesn't make any sense."[5]

At first glance, Calhoun is right; at face value, it doesn't make any sense. But perhaps the governor's doublespeak makes more "sense" when viewed from a Hegelian dialectical perspective.

In Antony C. Sutton's bombshell *America's Secret Establishment: An Introduction to the Order of Skull & Bones*, he expounds his analysis of leaked membership booklets belonging to Iserbyt's father, Clifton Samuel Thomson,[6] who was inducted into The Order of Skull and Bones in 1924.[7] From these leaked "'Addresses' books, which used to be called 'Catalogues,'"[8] Sutton, a former Research Fellow at Stanford University's Hoover Institution, reverse engineered the history of the Hegelian manipulation of the American education system by The Order:[a] [9] "[p]rogress in the Hegelian State is through contrived conflict: the clash of opposites makes for progress. If you can control the opposites, you dominate the nature of the outcome."[10]

The following is a simplified equation for the Hegelian formula: thesis + antithesis = synthesis (or problem + reaction = solution). Now, here's what it looks like when we fill in the equation with the pertinent variables concerning the conflict between Illinois' obligations to pay its debts and its commitments to pay for public schooling:

- **Thesis/Problem:** The Old Guard Democrat Machine racks up the State of Illinois' debt crisis until it threatens to collapse into insolvency; therefore,

- **Antithesis/Reaction:** Reagan-style Republican Rauner halts state and federal funds for education in order to stop the budgetary cancer from metastasizing; as a result,

- **Synthesis/Solution:** public education institutions, without public funds, will ultimately be forced to seek financing from the

a   Sutton writes, "[f]or Iserbyt, in *The Deliberate Dumbing Down of America*, the American education system begins with Rockefeller and [Fredrick T.] Gates. But in fact, this statist system is a reflection of the Hegelian ideas brought to the United States by the Skull and Bones 'troika' of [Daniel Coit] Gilman, [Andrew Dickson] White and [Timothy] Dwight, and then financed by Rockefeller." Sutton documents how these three Bonesmen hijacked American education pedagogy, methodology, and curriculums through their influential posts as presidents of Yale University, Johns Hopkins University, Cornell University, the University of California, the Carnegie Institution, and the American Historical Association.

private sector or undergo privatization through charter school partnerships and voucher programs.

In sum, Rauner's words and actions are not really "contradictory" if his real stratagem is to attract private jobs and industry to Illinois by opening the floodgates for private charter schools to move into the public education market to fill up the void created by the budget cuts.

Of course, the failed override of the governor's veto was "a result of Democrat Scott Drury voting against the proposal and Democrat Luis Arroyo not being in attendance," writes NBC News.[11] And it was Democrats like former CEOs of Chicago Public Schools, Paul Vallas and Arne Duncan, who paved the way in Illinois for shutting down public schools and supplanting them with charters.[12]

Hence, a hand-in-glove Hegelian manipulation of the leftwing-rightwing political dialectic that is designed to narrow the education dilemma down to a debate about charter privatization one way or another.

The Charter "School Choice" Lobby:

There is abundant evidence to illustrate Rauner's charter school agenda. Former charter school supporter who was US Assistant Secretary of Education under George H. W. Bush,[13] Diane Ravitch, called Rauner "one of the most important financial backers of charter schools in Chicago."[14]

During his run for the office of governor, Rauner ran a television advertisement in which he lionized how he "helped start charter schools," such as Chicago Bulls Prep of the Noble Network of Charter Schools, to compete against failing school systems.[15] According to the *Chicago Sun-Times*, Rauner donated about $2.5 million to the Noble Network,[16] and one of the Noble charter schools has been named in his honor: Rauner College Prep.[17] In fact, before winning the governorship, Rauner sat on the Noble Network Board, and he also partnered with ACT Charter School.[18]

After he took office as governor, Rauner appointed Beth Purvis, former CEO of the Chicago International Charter School, to be a key advisor on education policy. And he paid her a $250,000 salary for her counsel.[19]

Rauner's push for corporatized charter education is often couched in the euphemism "school choice." For instance, in one of his campaign ads, which lauded his multi-million-dollar investments in charter schools, he stated, "I'll give parents more control and choices."[20] As governor, Rauner even proclaimed the week of January 24th, 2016, to be "School Choice Week in Illinois," saying that "[c]harter schools are already providing many Illinois families with choices; we look forward to supporting the growth of charter schools through our federal grant."[21]

However, as Iserbyt has emphasized in "The True Goal of School Choice," the buzzword "school choice" is nothing more than a code word for the fascistic privatization of public education. As a liaison to the President's Task Force on Private Sector Initiatives under Ronald Reagan, Iserbyt was consulted on one of the first proposals for a "school choice" initiative: "this writer [Iserbyt] inquired of one of President Reagan's political appointees whether this initiative was not corporate fascism; a politically incorrect question that resulted in someone else replacing me as Liaison with The White House."[22]

To facilitate more "school choice," Governor Rauner built a bipartisan coalition of state representatives and lobbyists who advocate voucher programs and other charter packages.

The governor appointed the Reverend James Meeks, a former Democrat State Senator, as the Chairman of the Illinois State Board of Education, despite the fact that Meeks holds no academic credentials to qualify him as an expert on education. Meeks, who endorsed Rauner during his electioneering, advocated both charter schools and voucher programs: "[i]f charters can do it, or vouchers can do it, whatever the board will think will close the education gap," stated Meeks.[23] It should be noted that, during his race for office, Rauner poured $1 million into a South Side Community Federal Credit Union at 54th Street and Wentworth Avenue located about ten miles from Meeks' Salem Baptist Church.[24]

Rauner also allied with one of the biggest charter school lobbies in Illinois: One Chance Illinois. In fact, at least two key Rauner proponents were members of the Board of Directors for One Chance Illinois: Executive Director Myles Mendoza and Pastor Corey Brooks.[25]

Governor Rauner appointed Brooks to the Board of the Illinois State Toll Highway Authority after the "Rooftop Pastor" endorsed the governor and even "appeared in a pro-Rauner campaign ad," according to NBC News.[26]

Mendoza, who was formerly a Senior Partner with Democrats for Education Reform,[27] "worked with Rauner on some of those ['school choice'] issues before Rauner had the keys to the governor's mansion," reports WBEZ News.[28] Following the governor's 2016 State of the State speech, Mendoza avowed One Chance Illinois' support for Rauner: "[o]ne Chance Illinois supports the Governor's pledge to 'create more quality school options for low-income children stuck in failing schools.' One Chance Illinois believes that traditional, charter and private school providers can come together on a policy that benefits the neediest children, and rewards quality providers."[29]

Indeed, in his State of the State address, Rauner pushed for a "Student and Career Success Package [that] will lift the cap on public charter schools and give parents and students more options."[30]

The Duncan-Gates Affair:

The reaches of Rauner's charter school comrades go beyond state-level special interests. One of his most powerful "school choice" cronies is Democrat Arne Duncan: former CEO of Chicago Public Schools (CPS) who went on to serve as United States Secretary of Education under President Barack Obama from 2009 until the end of 2015.

Duncan followed in the footsteps of his predecessor, former CPS CEO Paul Vallas, another bigtime Democrat charter school pusher. As CEO, Duncan basically mirrored Vallas' privatization reform. For Duncan's crowning achievement in Chicago was the Renaissance 2010 initiative, "which had the goal of closing 60 to 70 schools and opening 100 new smaller schools by 2010," according to a document from the American Federation of Teachers.[31]

A *Counterpunch* article by Kenneth Libby reports that

> Duncan helped the city of Chicago open over 100 new schools (at least 84 charters run by Renaissance 2010 with 31 more planned [as of December 2008]), including the city's second Disney-run elementary school, 5 military academies with more in planning stages, for-profit schools, non-profit organizations receiving financial backing from "educational venture funds," and charter schools funded by big business (Boeing, Citigroup, Bank of America, Washington Mutual, and the Gates Foundation among others – all given corporate tax breaks, buyouts, and tax deductions that take money from our public schools).[32]

During Duncan's tenure as CEO of CPS,[33] the Bill and Melinda Gates Foundation donated over $137 million to the Chicago school system to invest in various charter school reform programs and initiatives "that led to the creation of several successful small and charter high schools in Chicago," according to a Gates Foundation press release.[34] At least $1.4 million went directly to the Noble Network of Charter Schools "to fund two new schools and develop the infrastructure necessary to support additional schools based on the Noble Street model in Chicago."

11

Gates philanthropy followed Duncan over to his federal post as US Secretary of Education.[35]

During Duncan's tenure as US Secretary, the US Department of Education received $500 million co-contributed from the Bill & Melinda Gates Foundation, the Ford Foundation and several other private donors.[b][36] At least $178,114,911 of this investment was allocated specifically for "expanding effective practices in turning around low-performing schools; providing support for high-quality school choices including charters and alternative school designs; as well as for digital learning and supporting extended learning time."[37]

The ties between Education Secretary Arne Duncan and the Gates Foundation were so strong that Teaching Ambassador Fellows, Joiselle Cunningham and Lisa Clarke, questioned the potential conflict of interest in a 2014 interview with Secretary Duncan: "[o]ne of the particular questions we've heard teachers ask is if corporate-based philanthropists are playing too heavy a role in public education, and if there's a corporate agenda at the Department."[38]

Although Duncan denied that any corporations "have a seat at the table in terms of policymaking,"[39] the *New York Times* writes that "[s]ome officials complained that the Bill and Melinda Gates Foundation was trying to handpick the winners of the Department of Education's $4 billion grant competition, known as Race to the Top."[40] Senator Nancy C. Detert, chairwoman of the Education Committee in the Florida Senate, said that "The Gates program and the Arne Duncan program are pretty much the same program."[41]

Renowned critical theorist and pedagogue, Henry Giroux, has likewise called out Duncan as a corporatist. Giroux slams Duncan's charter privatization schemes in several scholarly publications, including "Chartering Disaster: Why Duncan's Corporate-Based Schools Can't Deliver an Education That Matters"[42] and "Obama's Betrayal of Public Education? Arne Duncan and the Corporate Model of Schooling."[43]

Duncan's track record as a corporatist change agent speaks for itself. In a truly fascistic policy move back in 2009, Secretary Duncan even announced the appropriation of Stimulus Package tax dollars to be spent toward corporate charter school expansion in Illinois. The US Department of Education documents that "Duncan today [April 20th, 2009,] announced that nearly $1.4 billion is now available for Illinois under the

---

b   It is worth noting that, according to Sutton, the Ford Foundation has become an instrument of The Order ever since former US National Security Advisor, McGeorge Bundy, who was a Bonesman, took over the presidency of the foundation.

American Recovery and Reinvestment Act (ARRA) of 2009."[44] The stipulations of the ARRA funds required that "[i]n order to receive today's funds, Illinois provided assurances that they will collect, publish, analyze and act on basic information regarding … progress on removing charter caps, and interventions in turning around underperforming schools."[45]

In October of 2015, Duncan announced his resignation from the office of US Secretary of Education – just three days after he authorized another $249 million in federal grants for charter schools.[46]

Coincidence or not, the timing was certainly perfect for Rauner and the "school choice" gang. The more Illinois public schools faced with bankruptcy, the more opportunities there were for private charters to apply for Duncan's federal grant dollars to subsidize their takeover of insolvent public education institutions. In fact, Rauner repeatedly called for the entire CPS system to declare bankruptcy.[47] This call was echoed by Moody's Investor's Services,[48] and at Rauner's 2016 proclamation of Illinois' official School Choice Week, he boasted that his administration was eagerly "look[ing] forward to supporting the growth of charter schools through our federal grant."[49]

During Duncan's reign as Secretary of Education, he awarded at least $19 million of federal grant moneys to Chicago's Noble Network of Charter Schools where Rauner College Prep is chartered.[50] Of Duncan's $249 million parting gift, $42,286,226 were awarded to the Illinois Department of Education with $8,412,500 allocated specifically for the Noble Network.[51]

The timing of Duncan's federal grants and Rauner's stonewall on the budget is reminiscent of a phone call by Rauner to the office of then-CEO of CPS, Arne Duncan, followed by the coincidental admission of Rauner's daughter to Walter Payton High School, despite the fact that her tests scores were "not high enough to meet Payton standards," according to CPS Inspector General, James Sullivan: "'There was a phone call made to the CEO's office by Mr. Rauner,' Sullivan said. 'Somebody in the CEO's office called Walter Payton and his daughter was admitted to the school.'"[52]

"Fifteen months later," *ABC News* reports, "Rauner made a $250,000 gift to the school he says was unrelated to the admission of his daughter."[53] When questioned about the coincidence by a *State Journal-Register* columnist, Rauner at first denied any phone contact with Duncan. Then, he backpedaled and tried to spin his behind-the-scenes dealing with Duncan: "I talked to Arne … I talked to him all the time. I said, 'Arne, is there a process? What do you do in a situation like this?'"[54]

Understandably, one might surmise that Bruce, as governor, continued talking all the time to his old pal Arne, who could provide the new Illinois governor a direct line to the White House as well as the Gates Foundation and other corporate handlers – maybe even coordinating corporate, federal, and state policy in anticipation of the Illinois budget impasse and the federal charter grant disbursement.

In the final equation, the Chicago Public Schools system was able to weather the financial drought of the Rauner administration. But not before CPS was forced to cut $100 million from its budget while selling off a total of $725 million in CPS bonds to financial corporations such as Goldman Sachs, OppenheimerFunds, and Nuveen Asset Management in a desperate effort to keep Chicago schools open.[55]

By the time the budget crisis was over, Rauner was able to get the Illinois State Legislature to pass the "Invest in Kids Act" (35 ILCS 40):[56] a law awarding tax credits for donations to private tuition scholarships which are akin to voucher programs that redistribute tax revenues to subsidize payments for enrollment in private schools.[57]

Goodbye, state universities. Hello, Gates universities.

2

CORPORATE-FASCIST WORKFORCE TRAINING FOR THE HEGELIAN STATE: THE REAL MEANING OF "CRADLE-TO-CAREER" EDUCATION

In 2015, the union-busting governor of Wisconsin, Scott Walker, took his corporatist agenda to a new level as he pushed to rewrite the mission statement of the University of Wisconsin system by erasing the phrases "search for truth" and "improve the human condition," overwriting them with a new objective for the college: to "meet the state's workforce needs."[1] At the same time, just south of the Wisconsin border, Governor Bruce Rauner was touting a similar "cradle-to-career" overhaul of education policy in Illinois, which deemphasized traditional academic studies while prioritizing corporate workforce training through privatized charter school curriculums.

Consistently, the Illinois governor explicitly equated his cradle-to-career education reform with a policy of workforce development:

- **Rauner's 2014 inaugural address:** From cradle to career ... [f]rom early childhood and K through 12 schools, to vocational and technical training, to community colleges and higher ed., we need to invest adequately in every neighborhood.... A high-quality education is essential for higher lifetime earnings, a competitive, world-class workforce and strong economic growth.[2]

- **Rauner's 2015 State of the State Address:** "From cradle to career ... we must also invest in technical and vocational training.... Let's end the era of cutting funding for technical training and community colleges."[3]

- **Rauner's 2016 State of the State Address:** "The key to rising family incomes, more high paying jobs, and a better life for everyone in Illinois, is to have a high quality, fully-integrated education system from cradle to career ... all the way to coordinated job training and technical training later in life."[4]

Workforce-training curriculums might sound like a practical way to spend tax dollars allocated for public education programs. However, the "cradle-to-career" euphemism is a code word for public-private partnerships that repurpose public educational institutions into "conveyor belts" that manufacture students into literal human resources who are socially engineered for the sole purpose of supplying the labor demands of private corporations.[5]

The "cradle-to-career" buzz-phrase is relatively new on the education scene. Nevertheless, the fascistic public-private infrastructure of cradle-to-career networks is rooted in the proto-Nazi philosophies of Georg Wilhelm Friedrich Hegel, which were imported to the United States education system by the infamous Yale secret society, Skull and Bones. Likewise, the cradle-to-career pedagogy of reducing education to job-specific workforce training for a planned economy in a Corporate State can also be traced back to Hegel and the Prussianization of the American education system.[6]

Corporate Fascism and the Hegelian State:

In chapter one, I explicate how Governor Bruce Rauner leveraged the Hegelian-dialectical stratagem of artificial conflict management to manipulate Illinois' manufactured economic crisis into a controlled demolition that implodes public education into a corporatist charter school system which syphons tax dollars to bankroll privatized education companies.

According to Charlotte Thomson Iserbyt, the stage was set for the public financing of privatized charter schools, such as Illinois' Noble Network,[7] when President Ronald Reagan authorized the "White House Private Sector Initiative which called for the corporate fascist merging of the public and private sector in order to initiate the planned economic Soviet workforce training initiative."[8]

By merging the public powers of government with the private powers of corporate industry, President Reagan's Task Force and Advisory Council on Private Sector Initiatives clearly fulfilled the definition of fascism attributed to Benito Mussolini.[9] It is said that Mussolini declared, "fascism should more appropriately be called corporatism because it is a merger of state and corporate power."[10] Apocryphal as it may be,[11] this quote has conjoined the labels "corporatism" and "fascism" as largely synonymous in contemporary political discourse,[12] and Iserbyt's equating of corporatism with fascism zeroes in on the core political-economic philosophy that historically links the current charter privatization trend back to Reagan's Executive Orders 12329 and 12427.[13]

The genesis of corporate fascism in the United States can also be traced back to Mussolini's partner in war crimes, Adolf Hitler, and the rise of Nazism. Yet the Nazi origins of corporate fascism actually stem from the German philosopher, Georg Wilhelm Friedrich Hegel, whose "Idealist" conception of "The State" became the guiding philosophy of The Order of Skull and Bones.[14]

Inspired by the Statist principles of Hegelian collectivism, The Order restructured the US legal system to empower the evolution of a mercantilist oligarchy by enfranchising corporations with rights of persons.[15] Skull and Bones also propagated collectivist social policies by instituting the Hegelianist schooling theories of eminent American educational philosophers such as the first Chair of Psychology and Pedagogy at Johns Hopkins University, G. Stanley Hall, and his doctoral student, John Dewey, who promulgated Hegelian-collectivist pedagogies through his positions as the Director of the University of Chicago School of Education and as Professor of Philosophy at Columbia University Teachers College.[16] By remodeling US law and pedagogy under the aegis of Hegelian collectivism, Skull-and-Bonesmen such as Morrison Remick Waite and Daniel Coit Gilman cooked up the recipe for the evolution of corporate-fascist workforce planning in America.[17]

In *America's Secret Establishment: An Introduction to the Order of Skull & Bones*, Antony C. Sutton documents how The Order's hijacking of America's educational and legal systems is a culmination of the proto-Nazi fascism of Hegel. Sutton writes, "[t]he right[wing] Hegelians, were the roots of Prussian militarism ... and the rise of Hitler. Key names among right Hegelians were Karl [von] Ritter ... Baron von Bismarck ... Baron von Stockmar ... Karl Theodor Dalberg," and Friedrich Trendelenberg.[18] Ritter and Trendelenberg were professors at the University of Berlin where they mentored Daniel Coit Gilman, who was the first official Treasurer of Skull and Bones.[19] Other members of The Order who learned Hegelian philosophies at the University of Berlin include Timothy Dwight and Andrew Dickson White.[20] The co-founder of Skull and Bones, William Huntington Russell, also studied in Germany during the heyday of Hegelianism.[21]

Fast-forward to the present, and succinct connections linking The Order's Hegelianism to the Nazi Party and the corporate-fascist origins of cradle-to-career charter schooling are concisely illustrated in the following historical chain:

- During World War II, Hitler's Nazi Reich was financed with the help of Bonesmen E. Roland Harriman, Knight Woolley, and Prescott Bush through their posts on the Board of Directors of Union Banking Corporation (UBC),[22] which was consequently seized by the Office of the US Attorney General in 1942 after UBC was found guilty of violating the Trading with the Enemy Act.[23]

- In the 1980s, Prescott's son, Bonesman George H. W. Bush,[24] reigned as Ronald Reagan's Vice President, helping to oversee both the President's Task Force on Private Sector Initiatives and the President's Advisory Council on Private Sector Initiatives, which set the precedent for the current public-private charter school movement.[25]

- From 2001 through 2008, George H. W. Bush's son, Bonesman George W. Bush,[26] followed in the footsteps of his father as President of the United States, signing into law stacks of corporatist voucher and charter reform legislation, such as the D. C. School Choice Incentive Act and the No Child Left Behind Act,[27] which doubled the number of public-private charter schools from 2,313 to 4,640 throughout the course of his presidency.[28] [a] [29]

Like German National Socialism, or Nazism, which was funded by the Bush family and other Bonesmen, the Hegelian ideology of The Order believes that "the State is absolute. The State requires complete obedience from the individual citizen … only to perform a role in the operation of the State."[30] In a fascist Corporate State, like the United States, elite corporations are essentially the absolute. The State is effectively a conglomerate of private corporations, rather than a federation of public institutions.

Thanks to Bonesman Morrison Remick Waite, who was Chief Justice of the US Supreme Court, the self-governance of "We the People"

a By signing into law the "Charter School Expansion Act of 1998," Democrat President Bill Clinton also carried the corporatist torch for public-private charter schools that was lit by Reagan and then passed down through the Bush dynasty to Obama.

under the American Republic was delivered over to the hands of corporations in 1886 when Waite ruled that "Corporations are persons" which must be afforded the same Constitutional rights and legal protections as human persons. In turn, democratic "power to the people" was semantically twisted into absolute "power to the corporations" which now wield the full force of the State under the auspices of exercising their "personhood rights" purportedly stipulated under the Fourteenth Amendment.[31] [b] [32]

As a result, in the Corporate States of America, obedience to the State means forfeiting individual civil rights, which govern citizens in a free republic, in exchange for collectivist "economic rights," which govern labor slaves in a corporate tyranny, in order to maintain the efficient operation of a planned economy. Usurping political rights with economic rights through public-private planning, the Corporate State supplants civic and academic education, replacing them with collectivist school-to-work training that embodies Hegel's idealization of the slave-master dialectic as the political foundation of the absolute State.

In *Phenomenology of Mind*, Hegel romanticizes political bondage in a chapter titled "Lordship and Bondage," which expresses his belief that the State enslavement of "bondsmen" by "lords" is actually mutually beneficial for both the "slave" and the "master."[33] In the modern Corporate State, Hegelian Bonesmen peddle the idea that there is a mutually beneficial relationship between workforce bondsmen and their corporate masters who enslave them to build a planned economy through public-private school-to-work partnerships, which are the focus of Reagan's Private Sector Initiatives and Governor Rauner's cradle-to-career education initiatives.

---

b   In *The Post-Corporate World: Life After Capitalism*, David Korten reveals how Bonesman Waite flagrantly asserted his ruling that corporations are people:

[i]n 1886 ... in the case of *Santa Clara County v. Southern Pacific Railroad Company*, the U.S. Supreme Court decided that a private corporation is a person and entitled to the legal rights and protections the Constitution affords to any person.... Far more remarkable, however, is that the doctrine of corporate personhood, which subsequently became a cornerstone of corporate law, was introduced into this 1886 decision without argument. According to the official case record, Supreme Court Justice Morrison Remick Waite simply pronounced before the beginning of argument in the case of *Santa Clara County v. Southern Pacific Railroad Company* that "The court does not wish to hear argument on the question whether the provision in the Fourteenth Amendment to the Constitution, which forbids a State to deny to any person within its jurisdiction the equal protection of the laws, applies to these corporations. We are all of opinion that it does." ... Thus it was that two-sentence assertion by a single judge elevated corporation to the status of persons under the law, prepared the way for the rise of global corporate rule, and thereby changed the course of history.

Cradle-to-Career Hegelianism in Two Case Studies:

To illustrate the Hegelian philosophy that is the cornerstone of Rauner's cradle-to-career workforce training, the following two cradle-to-career enterprises are provided for analysis:

- **The National Center for Community Schools (NCCS)** of the Children's Aide Society, which has collaborated with Rauner's charter school crony, former US Secretary of Education Arne Duncan.[34]

- **The Harlem Children's Zone (HCZ)**, the nonprofit education corporation that launched the quintessential prototype for the cradle-to-career model of public-private workforce schooling.

The NCCS: A 2015 cradle-to-career partnership between the NCCS and JPMorgan Chase exemplifies the Hegelian pedagogy of reducing students to cogs in the Corporate State's political-economic machine. The NCCS announced that JPMorgan Chase donated a $1,000,000 grant to support a "cradle-through-career collective impact initiative" that would "improve education, workforce and economic outcomes for South Bronx children and families" by "creating cradle-to-career pathways" for "workforce readiness and economic development."[35] Notice the near-verbatim parallels between these goals of this NCCS grant and the objectives of Rauner's cradle-to-career policy statements.

The NCCS boasts the fact that its public-private network of "community schools" partnerships "can be traced back to social reformers such as John Dewey."[36] According to Sutton, the Skull-and-Bones puppet John Dewey "can be recognized as the pre-eminent factor in the collectivisation [sic], or Hegelianization, of American Schools."[37]

Compare the Hegelian parallels between cradle-to-career workforce pedagogy and the following excerpt from Dewey's *Lectures for the First Course in Pedagogy*: "[e]ducation consists either in the ability to use one's power in a social direction or else in ability to share in the experience of others and thus widen the individual conscienceness [sic] to that of the race."[38] If we delete "the race" and substitute it with "the economy," then this quote from Dewey will fit seamlessly into any contemporary cradle-to-career mission statement. For Dewey, the individual learning experience is subordinate to the collective "race"; for cradle-to-career champions, like Rauner and the NCCS, the individual learning experience is subordinate to the planned economy; and for Hegel, the individual is subordinate to "the State."

The HCZ: Consider the Deweyan-Hegelian deindividuation that underpins the methodology of the Harlem Children's Zone (HCZ), which "popularized the idea of a 'cradle to career' pipeline," according to *PBS NewsHour*.[39] The HCZ, which was founded by *Waiting for "Superman"* documentarian, Geoffrey Canada,[40] is based on a "conveyor belt" system that emphasizes job skills training for students who matriculate through an integrated public-private network of charter schools, community organizations, and social services.[41]

In an HCZ whitepaper, under a sub-section with the Hegelian-dialectical title, "Poverty in America: Turning a Crisis into an Opportunity," the Harlem Children's Zone states, "America today also faces an unparalleled challenge to its economic strength and stability. To meet this challenge, the U.S. needs to build a workforce in which all of its members can contribute the full measure of their talents and skills."[42] Advocating for "public/private partnerships" as cost-effective innovations to educational management, the whitepaper investigates the question: "Are investments in the education and training of today's children creating a workforce that will allow society to compete effectively in tomorrow's global economy?"[43]

The HCZ, which sets the mold for cradle-to-career methodology, clearly conflates education with workforce development in this whitepaper by examining a cost-benefit analysis of the moneys invested in education versus workforce outcomes and other economic returns on those investments. In other words, the HCZ's cradle-to-career methodology aligns with the collectivist philosophies of Hegel and Dewey by subordinating individual learning outcomes to workforce outcomes for the national economy. Moreover, the adoption of the HCZ model of workforce schooling by Rauner and the NCCS demonstrates that the HCZ pilot has set the neo-Hegelian standard for cradle-to-career workforce pedagogy.

The Corporatization of Prussian *Kindergarten*:

Although the HCZ's brand of cradle-to-career schooling is a relatively new trend in education, its pedagogy of deindividuation and its bent towards corporate fascism is nothing novel to the American school system, which is rooted in Hegel's philosophical predecessor, the proto-Nazi

Johann Gottlieb Fichte,[c] [44] who was connected with the Bavarian Illuminati.[45] According to the *American Political Science Review*, "[n]ext to Hegel and Nietzsche, Fichte is the German philosopher most frequently blamed as one of the principle inspirers of the National Socialist [Nazi] ideologies of state despotism."[46] And it was Fichte who conceptualized Prussia's national-socialistic education system.

At the dawn of the nineteenth century, Fichte wrote his *Addresses to the German Nation*, in which he states,[d] [47] "[b]y means of the new education we want to mould the Germans into a corporate body, which shall be stimulated and animated in all its individual members by the same interest."[48] In his "Second Address: The General Nature of the New Education," Fichte professes, "[t]he new education must consist essentially in this, that it completely destroys freedom of will in the soil which it undertakes to cultivate, and produces on the contrary strict necessity in the decisions of the will, the opposite being impossible. Such a will can henceforth be relied on with confidence and certainty."[49] In the twenty-first century, the new cradle-to-career education system embodies Fichte's philosophy by conditioning each student's "freedom of will" to conform to the collective workforce needs of the planned economy in the Corporate States of America.

Fichte's pedagogy became the basis for Prussian military schooling, which was transplanted to the United States education system at the behest of prominent educational theorists such as Horace Mann,[50] who was a Skull-and-Bones liaison with Bonesman Alphonso Taft at Antioch College.[51] [e] [52] In "Against School," the renowned New York State Teacher of the Year (1991), John Taylor Gatto,[53] records the Prussian *kindergarten* history behind modern American education: "what shocks is that we should so eagerly have adopted one of the very worst aspects of Prussian culture: an educational system deliberately designed to produce mediocre intellects, to hamstring the inner life, to deny students appreciable leadership skills, and to ensure docile and incomplete citizens—all in order to render the populace 'manageable.'"[54]

---

c　　　　Sutton documents that "Fichte, who developed these ideas before Hegel, was a freemason, almost certainly Illuminati, and certainly was promoted by the Illuminati. For example, Johann Wolfgang Goethe (Abaris in the Illuminati code) pushed Fichte for an appointment at Jena University."

d　　　　Compare the Hegelian parallels between this quote from Fichte and the following quote from Dewey: "[e]ducation being a social process, the school is simply that form of community life in which all those agencies are concentrated that will be most effective in bringing the child to share in the inherited resources of the race, and to use his own powers for social ends."

e　　　　Alphonso Taft co-founded The Order with William H. Russell. Alphonso was also the father of Bonesman William Howard Taft, who was the only person to become both the President of the United States and Supreme Court Justice of the United States.

In the 1918 book, *Principles of Secondary Education*, Harvard's first Professor of Secondary Education, Alexander Inglis, sets forth a pedagogy that is clearly an adaptation of the Fichtean-Prussian method of education. Gatto paraphrases Inglis's "six basic functions" of education, three of which are the basis of the contemporary cradle-to-career methodology:

> 3. The *diagnostic and directive function*: School is meant to determine each student's proper social role…
>
> 4. The *differentiating function*: Once their social role has been "diagnosed," children are to be sorted by role and trained only so far as their destination in the social machine merits – and not one step further…
>
> 6. The *propaedeutic function*: The social system implied by these rules will require an elite group of caretakers. To that end, a small fraction of the kids will quietly be taught how to manage this continuing project, how to watch over and control a population deliberately dumbed down and declawed in order that government might proceed unchallenged and corporations might never want for obedient labor.[55]

Applying these three "basic functions," the Neo-Prussian cradle-to-career system of workforce schooling utilizes learning outcomes data to diagnose and differentiate which students are best conditioned for which job-specific "career pathways" curriculums, and which students will be promoted to the elite class of "managers."

Indeed, Gatto points out how Prussian education was adapted to suit the purposes of corporate education for the Corporate State:

> [m]en like [J. P. Morgan partner][56] George Peabody, who funded the cause of mandatory schooling throughout the South, surely understood that the Prussian system was useful in creating not only a harmless electorate and a servile labor force but also a virtual herd of mindless consumers. In time a great number of industrial titans came to recognize the enormous profits to be had by cultivating and tending just such a herd via public education, among them Andrew Carnegie and John D. Rockefeller.[57]

The Gates Foundation from Cradle-to-Career:

Today, the Neo-Robber Baron Gates Foundation has taken much of the education spotlight from the corporate philanthropies of the Carnegie Institute and the Rockefeller Foundation.

The Bill and Melinda Gates Foundation, which is one of the biggest charter school philanthropies in the United States, donated at least $600,000 in grants to the cradle-to-career posterchild, the Harlem Children's Zone.[58] In addition, the Gates Foundation has financed several other cradle-to-career programs, including a $305,000 grant to "the Road Map Project's cradle-to-career education work in South King County, WA";[59] a $1,000,000 grant to "provide technical assistance to Promise Neighborhoods implementation and planning grantees,[f][60] and issue-based technical assistance for key areas of the cradle-to-career pipeline of expanded learning";[61] and a $100,000 grant to the Portland Schools Foundation (PSF) as a supplement to "a $100,000 investment by JPMorgan Chase for its [PSF's] expanding work around the Cradle to Career (C2C) partnership."[62]

The Gates Foundation even paved the way for the C2C takeover in Illinois by funding the charter privatization of the Chicago Public Schools (CPS) system under the management of CPS CEO Arne Duncan, who went on to push charter school reform on a national scale as the US Secretary of Education.

Following in the footsteps of the Duncan-Gates coalition, Governor Rauner carried the C2C privatization torch as he fanned the flames of his workforce training agenda during a visit to Harper College. The *Daily Herald* reports that the Republican governor "called Harper College a model for what Illinois' community colleges need more of: partnerships with employers and training for technical jobs." In praising Harper College's public-private partnerships, Rauner stated, "[w]e should think more strategically and holistically.... Education includes vocational training, occupational training, technical training. It's all part of education. We should think strategically cradle to career."[63]

P-20 "Legalization" of Corporate Workforce Schooling:

To stimulate the expansion of more cradle-to-career networks like Harper College's public-private partnerships, Governor Rauner proclaimed in his 2016 State of the State Address that he aimed to "[c]onsolidate the majority of our councils and task forces under the P20 and Early Learning Councils."[64]

What is the Illinois P-20 Council?

In 2009, the Illinois P-20 Council was voted into law by the state legislature. The Illinois P-20 Council website states, "[t]he 'P' in our name represents Preschool and '20' stands for grade 20, education after college."[65]

---

f   According to the US Department of Education, the Promise Neighbohoods program is designed for "[b]uilding a complete continuum of cradle-to-career solutions of both educational programs and family and community supports, with great schools at the center."

Although the P-20 mission statement does not explicitly incorporate the cradle-to-career brand name, notice the near-synonymous parallels between the lifecycle span of "cradle to career" and the lifecycle span of "preschool to grade 20." These rhetorical similarities between the C2C and P-20 labels are more than mere semantics. In fact, the P-20 law is written extensively with keywords borrowed directly from the cradle-to-career workforce development lexicon.

Illinois State Statute 105 ILCS 5/22-45 establishes "an Illinois P-20 Council [that] will develop a … pre-kindergarten through grade 20 agenda [that] will strengthen this State's economic competitiveness by producing a highly-skilled workforce."[66] The council is appointed to

> [i]mprove the rigor and relevance of academic standards for college and workforce readiness[;] … [t]o advise the Governor, the General Assembly, the State's education and higher education agencies, and the State's workforce and economic development boards and agencies on policies related to lifelong learning for Illinois students and families[;] … [t]o articulate a framework for systemic educational improvement and innovation that will enable every student to meet or exceed Illinois learning standards and be well-prepared to succeed in the workforce and community[67]

The state statute also authorizes that "[t]he chairperson of the Illinois P-20 Council may authorize the creation of working groups focusing on areas of interest to Illinois educational and workforce development, including without limitation the following areas: … The assessment, alignment, outreach, and network of college and workforce readiness efforts."[68]

Note the linguistic overlaps between the letter of the law in these statutory clauses and the cradle-to-career rhetoric of the Harlem Children's Zone, the Gates Foundation, and the National Center for Community Schools quoted throughout this chapter. It is important to stress here the significance of C2C language drafted into the P-20 statute. In essence, 105 ILCS 5/22-45 incorporates the slogans of the HCZ corporation and codifies them into workforce development mandates in the Illinois civil code, thus blurring the lines between public policy and corporate bylaws while incentivizing the proliferation of corporate-government mergers through public-private partnerships.

105 ILCS 5/22-45 also invokes the globalist workforce-schooling rhetoric of the United Nations Educational Scientific and Cultural Organization (UNESCO) pedagogy of "lifelong learning."[69]

Cradle-to-Career 2.0:

After an entire year of operation without a state budget in Illinois, Rauner vetoed a $3.9 billion education and human services spending bill on June 10, 2016.[70] Judging from this executive decision, it appears that Rauner was manipulating Hegelian crisis control to actuate one of his "ten long-term goals" professed in his 2016 State of the State Address: "10 ... better align our health and human services with our cradle to career education initiatives, in order to provide higher quality, fully integrated services for our young people."[71] By stonewalling on the budget impasse, Rauner was essentially bankrupting both public education and public health and human services so that they would effectively be forced to integrate into P-20 and other privatized cradle-to-career partnerships to gain access to private funds in place of missing tax dollars.[72]

The timing was perfect. Rauner vetoed the education and human services bill just a few months after he bypassed the legislative process and went over the heads of the Illinois State Congress to issue Executive Order 2016-03, adding another element of authoritarianism to the recipe. This Executive Order Establishing the Governor's Cabinet on Children and Youth implements "a cohesive strategy among our education and health and human services agencies in producing education outcomes that will improve the quality of education and well-being for the children of Illinois."[g][73]

It seems highly unlikely that the coordination of this executive order and Rauner's veto were a mere coincidence, especially considering that the State of Illinois' government website declares that "[t]he Children's Cabinet will work closely with the P20 Council, Early Learning Council, Human Services Commission and others to ensure that the recommendations of private partners and stakeholders are communicated to agency directors and to the Governor."[74] As Rauner held the State of Illinois financially hostage, public education and social services were financially

---

g   Under Clause "IV. Composition and Function" of Executive Order 2016-03, it decrees that

[t]he Children's Cabinet shall consist of: a. The Governor, who will serve as Chairman of the Children's Cabinet; b. Lieutenant Governor; c. The Deputy Governor; d. The Director of the Governor's Office of Management and Budget; e. The State Secretary of Education; f. The Superintendent of the State Board of Education; g. The Director of the Department of Children and Family Services; h. The Director of the Department of Commerce and Economic Opportunity[;] i. The Director of the Department of Employment Security[;] j. The Director of the Department of Healthcare and Family Services; k. The Secretary of the Department of Human Services; l. The Director of the Department of Juvenile Justice; m. The Director of the Department of Public Health; n. The Executive Director of the Governor's Office of Early Childhood Development; o. The Director of the Guardianship and Advocacy Commission; p. The Executive Director of the Board of Higher Education; q. The Executive Director of the Community College Board; r. The Executive Director of the Student Assistance Commission; and s. The President of the Illinois Math and Science Academy.

broken and pushed toward privatized integration with P-20 partnerships under the auspices of 105 ILCS 5/22-45 and Executive Order 2016-03.

In the first year of operation, the Governor's Cabinet on Children and Youth launched the "Workforce Readiness through Apprenticeships and Pathways" program, and by the end of 2017, the Governor's Cabinet coordinated a host of public-private partnerships between the Illinois P-20 Council College and Career Readiness Committee; the Department of Children and Family Services; the Department of Human Services; the Illinois Council on Developmental Disabilities; the National Academies of Medicine; Lurie Children's Hospital; the Ounce of Prevention Fund; the AHIMA Foundation; Elevate Energy Inc.; Associated Builders and Contractors; the German American Chamber of Commerce; and the Illinois Manufacturer's Association.[75]

At the federal level, Republican Rauner's cradle-to-career policies were even mirrored by Democrat President Barack Obama to complete the leftwing-rightwing Hegelian dialectic. The *Illinois Review* reports, "[b]oth Governor Bruce Rauner and President Barack Obama are focused on revamping the state's early childhood education program into one that ranges from 'cradle to career.'... The President has made providing a complete and competitive education for all Americans – from cradle to career – a top priority, a White House press release confirms."[76]

At the same time, cradle-to-career workforce training has been instituted across the nation through a confederated network of state-level "P-20" education projects, including the Wisconsin P20 Data Sharing and Analysis project,[77] the P-20 Council of Connecticut,[78] the Minnesota P-20 Education Partnership,[79] the Delaware P-20 Council,[80] and the P-20 Leadership Council of Maryland.[81]

Internationally, the C2C/P-20 model of workforce schooling has been propagated under the aegis of UNESCO's "lifelong learning" methodology.[82]

How far will this corporate-globalist trajectory take us down the rabbit hole to cradle-to-career fascism? Taken to the logical extreme, the progressive merger of public education and the corporate economy is on course to streamline the "career pathways" "conveyor belts" so seamlessly into corporation-specific job training that students will one day cease to matriculate through academic departments to earn diplomas and degrees. In time, students will no longer earn degrees in scientific fields such as computer software engineering; rather, students will earn technical certificates in Windows engineering directly from the Microsoft Corporation.

Is this what the Founding Fathers had in mind when they drafted the Constitution "to form a more perfect union"?[83]

3

NATIONAL CHARTER SCHOOL FASCISM: CORPORATE P-20 COUNCIL GOVERNANCE AND THE PUBLIC-PRIVATE MERGER OF EDUCATION, CRIMINAL JUSTICE, AND HEALTH AND HUMAN SERVICES

When Hurricane Katrina devastated New Orleans in 2005, the eminent "free market" economist, Milton Friedman,[1] referred to the tragedy as "an opportunity to radically reform the educational system" into a privatized system of "school choice" competition. Heeding Friedman's call, education reformers have converted approximately 90% of the New Orleans school system into a network of for-profit and nonprofit charter school corporations that are integrated through Louisiana's two P(K)-16/20 workforce development councils:[2] the College and Career Readiness Commission and the Blue Ribbon Commission for Educational Excellence.[3] Now, nearly fifteen years later, this 90% privatization overhaul is being touted as a model for a total charter privatization takeover of the United States national education system through P(K)-16/20 workforce development councils.

This fascistic merger of America's national school system and the corporate economy for public-private workforce planning is bad enough. But there is a more pernicious endgame to the "cradle-to-career" charter school movement: corporate governance over all public/civic spheres of the United States political-economy.

Incentivized by the current era of contrived economic depression, the unelected councils of corporate charter school governance are integrating "cost-effective" public-private partnerships with other fiscally starved public institutions, including health and human services and criminal justice departments. The corporate interlocking of these three public/civic spheres under regional and state P(K)-16/20 council governance is setting the precedent for the erosion of civil process until democratic governance and Constitutional protections are ostensibly usurped by corporate charter bylaws enforced through unelected public-private councils.

Taxation without Representation:

This is the Trojan Horse behind the charter school reform movement: to subordinate American educational policy solely to the "jurisdiction" of publicly unaccountable private corporations that syphon tax dollars to subsidize the executive decisions of their unelected councils – in other words, "taxation without representation."

In "The True Goal of School Choice," Charlotte Thomson Iserbyt, exposes the threat of tax-funded charter schools that are governed by unelected councils, rather than elected schoolboards: "unlike in the past, when we had locally elected school boards to which we could register our complaints, there will be nowhere to go to complain since charter schools are run by unelected councils."[4] Because charter councils do not have to worry about getting re-elected, appointed councilmembers are not beholden to redress the grievances of parents and other local taxpayers who subsidize their corporate salaries. Rather, council officials can secure their corporate tenure by simply appeasing the executive decisions of school CEOs.[a]

This use of public tax revenues to allocate corporate welfare to unelected charter council committees qualifies as "taxation without representation." In "Heritage Foundation, NAFTA, School Choice, and the Destruction of Traditional Education," Iserbyt warns that "[t]he most lethal form of education choice is tax-supported public schools (charter schools) which have no elected school boards resulting in 'taxation without representation.' This is an oppressive system which caused our nation to revolt and declare war against the British (the American Revolution, 1776)."[5]

Iserbyt's analysis of charter council tax codes has been corroborated by "Washington state's Supreme Court [which] has become the first in the nation [in 2015] to decide that taxpayer-funded charter schools are unconstitutional, reasoning that charters are not truly public schools be-

---

a   To be sure, some charter school companies do not refer to their governing bodies as "councils." Instead, certain charter school businesses designate corporate "boards" as their governance committees for overseeing public-private educational administration. Nonetheless, these executive boards should not be confused with democratically elected schoolboards that are answerable to public constituencies of tax-paying parents and students. On the contrary, the corporate-executive board members of charter school companies are autocratically appointed through the "self-perpetuating governance" of business management.

cause they aren't governed by elected boards and therefore not account-
able to voters," according to the *Washington Post*.[6] In a similar 2011 court
decision, the Georgia Charter School Commission, which authorized
statewide public financing of corporate charter schools, was ruled unlaw-
ful by the State Supreme Court of Georgia. According to the *New York
Times*, "[i]n a 24-page ruling, Chief Justice Carol W. Hunstein said that
only local boards of education were empowered by Georgia's Constitution to open and finance public schools."[7]

From Regional to National P-20 Council Fascism:

Governance agencies like the unconstitutional Georgia Charter
School Commission manage statewide charter school planning
that is facilitated through regional P-16/20 council networks such as
the Georgia Regional P-20 Partnerships Collaboratives.[8] These regional
P-16/20 councils provide the institutional infrastructure for the state-level establishment of nationwide chains of corporate charter schools such
as the National Academy Foundation (NAF) and the Knowledge Is Power Program (KIPP), which are overseen by corporate councils such as the
NAF Central Florida Advisory Council and the KIPP Associate Council.[9]

The regional P-20 councils of California and Illinois provide two illus-
trative case study examples of statewide regional council governance that
facilitates nationwide territorial expansion of corporate charter school
chains, such as the NAF and KIPP, for the purposes of public-private
workforce planning:[b]

- **California University's SAPEP P(K)-20 Regional Intersegmental Alliances:** In 2013, California State Assembly Bill (AB) 646 was introduced under the subtitle "Public
  Education Governance: Regional P-20 Councils: Advisory
  Committee." This bill was authored to "express the intent of
  the Legislature to affirm the employer-education partnership

---

b   To be clear, I am not conflating the corporate governance structures of charter school
councils with the executive bureaucracy governance of state-level P-16/20 councils; I am not implying here that the corporate councils of charter school companies are ostensibly synonymous
with executive P-16/20 councils charted into the statutory framework of state-level legal codes.
Rather, I am demonstrating how both the corporate councils of the charter school industry as well
as the bureaucratic councils of the P-16/20 confederation are both contracted into public-private partnerships that override the democratic governance of locally elected schoolboards; and
hence, these public-private council systems are set up to seamlessly interlock into regional networks of autocratic P-16/20 councils that dictate workforce education policies to the unelected
councils of charter school corporations which manage the enforcement of federalized school-to-
work curriculums.

model of a regional P-20 council ... to advance strategic educational and economic outcomes."[10]

The fundamental objective of AB 646 was to legalize corporate-government workforce planning statewide through regional public-private partnerships that are regulated by P-20 council networks, which are coordinated between the Governor's Office of Business and Economic Development, the State Department of Education, the Department of Industrial Relations, the California Community Colleges, and "representatives of private sector employers."[11]

According to the 2013-2014 "End of Session Report Including a Summary of Legislation" by the California Assembly Committee on Jobs, Economic Development, and the Economy, AB 646 was "[h]eld on the Suspense File in Assembly Committee on Appropriations."[12] Nevertheless, regional P-20 council governance in California has advanced through California University's Student Academic Preparation and Educational Partnerships (SAPEP) P(K)-20 Regional Intersegmental Alliances, which is tied to partnerships with the NAF.

A 2014-2015 Annual Report of SAPEP Program Outcomes records that the P(K)-20 Regional Intersegmental Alliances incorporate "ten regional alliances ... aiming to create ties between campuses, schools, local communities and business organizations."[13] The University of California at Santa Barbara (UCSB) branch of these ten regional P(K)-20 alliances is "comprised of local and regional educational partnerships serving students in selected schools and districts in Santa Barbara, Ventura, and Kern Counties," according to another SAPEP Annual Performance Report.[14] In the Ventura region of the UCSB alliances, the Ventura County (VC) P-20 Council was awarded grants from the Alliance for Regional Collaboration to Heighten Educational Success (ARCHES).[15] The VC P-20 Council used the ARCHES grant moneys to establish the Engineering Design Career Pathways (EDCP) Linked-Learning California Partnership Academy (CPA) learning community programs at Hueneme High School that have evolved into NAF learning community programs throughout Oxnard Union High School District.[16]

The nonprofit NAF Corporation, which specializes in technical and vocational "career pathways" curriculums as alternatives to traditional scholarly academics, operates 716 corporate learning community academies and 487 corporate high schools throughout 34 of the United States.[17] As such, the links between NAF charter school corporations and California's regional P-20 council governance agencies demonstrate the national implications of P-20 regional council planning for public-private workforce development.

- **Northern Illinois University's Regional P-20 Network:** Under the auspices of Illinois State Statute 105 ILCS 5/22-45, the Illinois P-20 Council has been instituted to legalize public-private workforce planning statewide through a bureaucracy of council governance agencies.[18]

In accordance with subsection (e) of the legislation, the Illinois P-20 Council has amalgamated with Northern Illinois University's Center for P-20 Engagement,[19] which has instituted the Northern Illinois Regional P-20 Network.[20] NIU's Regional P-20 Network is further conglomerated into five regional "Work Groups," including a Workforce Development Group that is delegated to "[c]oordinate the Regional P-20 Network's workforce development activities with local, state, and national initiatives in order to more closely align academic offerings and student preparation with workforce needs," according to the NIU P-20 Network website.[21]

To broaden the regional influence of the Northern Illinois Regional P-20 Network to a national scale, NIU President Douglas Baker led a delegation of P-20 Network representatives *to the 2014 White House College Opportunity Summit to convene with* "colleges and universities, business leaders, nonprofits and others committed to supporting more college opportunities" and more regional workforce development planning, according to *NIU Today*.[22]

Baker's P-20 delegation emphasized that "*[r]ecent studies* show a strong correlation between the educational attainment of a state's workforce and median wages in the state, meaning that increasing access to high quality education expands economic opportunity for residents and helps to strengthen the regional economy."[23] Accompanying the P-20 Network delegation, John Rico, who is a Co-Chair of the Illinois Workforce Investment Board, stated that "[a]s a business owner, I believe that the P-20 and workforce are joined at the hip. Businesses depend on the K-12 and higher ed institutions to create the proper programs that offer students the required soft skills, training, degrees and certifications necessary for all students to thrive and prosper in their career development."[24]

Baker's and Rico's pitch to the White House for regional integration of corporate business and P-20 education councils is evidence of the trend towards nationwide assimilation of public-private P-16/20 council governance across the business and educational sectors of the United States' planned economy.

This cradle-to-career collaboration between corporate business, the Northern Illinois Regional P-20 Network, and the federal government is paralleled by the cradle-to-career collaboration between corporate business, the California SAPEP P-20 Regional Intersegmental Alliances, and the NAF. Meanwhile, these regional-national council networks are complemented by the proliferation of several other state-level P-20 councils across the country, including the P-20 Council of Connecticut,[25] the Delaware P-20 Council,[26] the P-20 Leadership Council of Maryland,[27] the Missouri P-20 Council,[28] and the Governor's P-20 Council of Arizona.[29] According to the Education Commission of the States, a total of:

> 38 states have established a P-16 or P-20 council. Two states (Louisiana and Pennsylvania) have two councils convening P-16/P-20 stakeholders, for a total of 40 P-16 or P-20 councils nationwide. An additional five states do not have a P-16 or P-20 council, but have consolidated most or all governance of public education in one or two agencies or boards who essentially perform the function of a P-16 or P-20 council.[30]

At least nine state-level P-16/20 councils are thoroughly incorporated with "local and/or regional P-16/P-20 councils."[31]

Fueling this national proliferation of P-16/20 workforce planning councils, the Bill and Melinda Gates Foundation has financed public-private P-16 and P-20 council projects with at least $8,007,834 in grants between the years 2003 and 2010.[32] In fact, the Gates Foundation Senior Policy Officer for Education is designated as an administrative member of the Superintendent's California P-16 Council, which thus puts a Gates Foundation official directly in charge of educational governance in California.[33]

In sum, these P-16/20 council networks form the nationwide institutional and statutory infrastructure necessary to facilitate mass charter privatization at both the state and federal levels by monolithic education corporations such as the NAF and KIPP. Consider the nonprofit KIPP corporation as a case study of how educational megacorporations utilize regional and state P-16/20 council planning to dominate the national education market for workforce development through "career pathways" and "career readiness" programs such as KIPP Future Focus:[34]

> • **The Knowledge Is Power Program (KIPP):** KIPP operates 200 corporate charter schools that currently span twenty US states,[35] which KIPP subdivides into thirty-one corporate regions. The KIPP website states that the company's corporate "regions are supported by a central office, governed by a common [unelected] local board, and led by a local executive director.... [A] central office provides services across multiple schools, such as human resources, recruiting, facilities management, technology, food service, procurement, and transportation, as well as alumni services."[36]
>
> KIPP coordinates three corporate regions in California and one corporate region in Illinois, which are thereby linked with the regional P-20 council networks that facilitate public-private charter school incorporation across both of those states.[37]
>
> Furthermore, the Chief Research, Design, and Innovation Officer of the KIPP Foundation, Jonathan Cowan, collaborated with Illinois P-20 Council officials and the Boston Consulting Group to conduct a study titled "Illinois Report Cards: Project Update to the P-20 Council," which charts data compiled to streamline P-20 outcomes.[38] Personnel from KIPP and the Illinois P-20 Council are also partnered through Advance Illinois, which is a 501(c)3 corporation managed by a "group of philanthropic, education, political, business, and community leaders" who provide support for various workforce development educational reforms such as House Bill (HB) 5729: the Postsecondary and Workforce Readiness (PWR) Act.[39] According to the Advance Illinois website, the Project Director of Advance Illinois is "the founding principal at KIPP Ascend Charter School in Chicago," Jim O'Connor, while the Deputy Director of Advance Illinois is Benjamin Boer, who "sits on the

Performance Evaluation Advisory Council for the Illinois State Board of Education and supports the work of a number of Illinois P-20 Council committees."[40]

To bolster national P-20 workforce training through KIPP's unelected corporate councils, KIPP is funded by the tax-exempt foundations of several megalithic corporations including the Walton Family Foundation, the Bill and Melinda Gates Foundation, Citi Foundation, Goldman Sachs Foundation, Prudential Foundation, and the JP Morgan Chase Foundation.[41] KIPP is also bankrolled by the Google Corporation and billionaire Reed Hastings, who is the founder, president, CEO, and Chairman of the Board of Netflix.[42]

Hastings, a former member of the California State Board of Education,[43] also sits on the KIPP Board of Directors, along with Walmart Baroness, Carrie Walton Penner, who is a Trustee of the Walton Family Foundation; Philippe Dauman, who is the President and CEO of Viacom; and Emma Bloomberg, the daughter of billionaire corporatist-politician Michael Bloomberg.[44]

Now, backed by the administration and financing of such corporate giants, the unelected council governance of KIPP schools is being pushed as a model for nationwide education reform by corporatists such as Hastings.

In his keynote speech at the 21st Annual California Charter Schools Conference,[45] Hastings lauded the "self-perpetuating governance" of unelected corporate charter school councils, and he called for the institution of self-perpetuating council governance throughout a 90% charter school education system across the fifty states: "the work ahead is really hard because we're at 8% of students in California whereas in New Orleans there're 90%. So we've got a lot of catch-up to do. We've got a lot of work of adding more schools. ... And if we succeed over the next twenty or thirty years, that will be one of the fastest rates of change ever seen around the world for a large system."[46]

The Deweyan-Hegelian Conglomeration of Education, Healthcare, and Law Enforcement:

Considering the extensiveness of this already widespread charter council expansion, backed with the monumental corporate sponsorship of the Gates Foundation and billionaires like Hastings, Charlotte Iserbyt investigates an imperative question in her article "School Choice Is America's Trojan Horse": "[w]hat is to keep Americans from accepting the *unelected council form of government* at all levels of government once one of the major sections of our economy (education) is being run by unelected councils?"[47]

Iserbyt is not begging the question here. P-16 and P-20 councils are not only spreading their tentacles across the field of education alone. Already, the health and human services sectors of the public economy are likewise being assimilated into privatized P-16/20 councils. In fact, several P-16 and P-20 councilmembers are appointed from various health and human services agencies, thereby interlocking the managerial personnel and administrative positions of both public education and public health and human services.

According to the Education Commission of the States:

> • One member of the Governor's P-16 Council of Arizona is likewise a member from the Early Childhood Development and Health Board.

> • A seat on the North Carolina P-16 Council is held by the Secretary of Health and Human Services.

> • A member of the Arkansas P-16 Council is simultaneously the Director (or a designee) of the Division of Child Care and Early Childhood Education of the Department of Human Services.

> • In Rhode Island, the Chair of the Human Resources Investment Council sits on the Statewide P-16 Council.

> • In Colorado, the Governor's P-20 Education Coordinating Council designates a council seat to the Associate Vice Chancellor of Student Services of the University of Colorado at Denver Health Sciences Center.

> • In Montana, the P-16 Council delegates a council seat to the Director (or designee) of the Department of Public Health and Human Services (as an ex-officio member).

> • The Nebraska P-16 Leadership Council, which is funded by the Nebraska Health and Human Services Commission, assigns the CEO of the Department of Health and Human Services as a councilmember.[48]

Moreover, in the previous two chapters, I document how Illinois Governor Bruce Rauner manipulated Hegelian-dialectical crisis management over Illinois's demolished state economy in order to crash-land insolvent public human services agencies into P-20 council receivership under the auspices of 105 ILCS 5/22-45 and Executive Order 2016-03.[49]

In addition, Rauner's "Executive Order Establishing the Governor's Cabinet on Children and Youth" also integrates the criminal justice system into Illinois's public-private P-20 partnerships through the cabinet appointment of The Director of the Department of Juvenile Justice.[50]

Similar state-level public-private partnerships between charter schools and police agencies are recommended by an article in the *Community Policing Dispatch Newsletter* of the Community Oriented Policing Services (COPS) of the US Department of Justice. The article, "A Role for Officers in Schools," reports that the Council of State Governments (CSG) Justice Center Project of the Law Enforcement Advisory Group, which advocates for "school/law enforcement partnerships ... is supported by a public/private partnership that includes the Office of Juvenile Justice and Delinquency Prevention" as well as three philanthropies that are invested in charter schools:[51] The NoVo Foundation,[52] The California Endowment,[53] and Atlantic Philanthropies.[54]

At the national level, other public-private partnerships between charter schools and police agencies are recommended by the National Resource Center on Charter School Finance in a 2008 report entitled *A Guide for Policy Makers: Partnerships Between Charter Schools and Other Organizations.*[55] Likewise, the 2015 *Final Report of the President's [Obama's] Task Force on 21st Century Policing* advocates for the federalization of similar "public-private partnership[s]" between police forces and "public health, education, mental health, and other programs not traditionally part of the criminal justice system."[56]

As a direct response to this Task Force report, the architectural firm Studio Gang launched the Polis research project for redesigning police stations as "community centers" that are structured to facilitate the public-private fusion of law enforcement, healthcare, and learning services all at one complex. Jeanne Gang, who is the founding principle of Studio Gang,[57] describes one of her Chicago Polis stations as featuring an information learning center with "a computer lab in the [police] station; free Wi-Fi was a great amenity. We thought about city services, and offering mental health services. ... We thought services could be bundled. ... We tried to associate design ideas with different recommendations from the [Task Force] report."[58]

The public-private unification of these three public services under multiplex "urban planning" construction projects is the quintessence of the Deweyan-Hegelian "cradle-to-career" philosophy that underpins both the charter school movement generally and the P-16/20 council movement specifically. Indeed, the odd admixture of leftist communitarian social philosophy with rightwing corporate-fascist political-economics could only be the product of a neo-Hegelian ideology. As historicized by Antony C. Sutton, "both Marx and Hitler, the extremes of 'left' and 'right' presented as textbook enemies, evolved out of the same philosophical system: Hegelianism."[59]

Such public-private multiplex schools also embody John Dewey's Hegelianist educational philosophy as stated in *My Pedagogic Creed*: "[t]he school is primarily a social institution. Education being a social process, the school is simply that form of community life in which all those agencies are concentrated that will be most effective in bringing the child to share in the inherited resources of the race, and to use his own powers for social ends."[60] Quite literally, Polis community centers and P-16/20 schools concentrate the integral public services and corporate agencies of a regional community into singular governance institutions that facilitate public-private political-economic planning.

These privatized amalgamations of public learning resources, public health services, and "community policing" are exemplary of the ubiquitous public-private administrative governance that is being advocated on a national scale by corporatists such as media-technology tycoon Reed Hastings. According to Hastings in his keynote speech at the 2014 California Charter Schools Conference, "self-perpetuating" public-private governance should be adopted as a standard model of bureaucracy across all sectors of America's planned political-economy because it has proven to be a more efficient form of governance than democracy.[61]

Idealizing the self-perpetuating bureaucracies of corporations, military branches, papal churches, and partisan political organizations, Hastings believes that public schools, and all other public institutions, should be managed autocratically through privatized councils, rather than democratically through town halls and electoral processes. Hence, Hastings concludes that, "the importance of the charter school movement is to evolve America from a system where governance is constantly changing [because of elections], and you can't do long-term planning, to a system of large nonprofits that ... look like the breadth of say military branches, churches, universities, nonprofits, all trying to outdo each other to serve the children."[62]

It is keen to note how Hastings is showing his hand here. For Hastings, the ultimate goal of mass charter school incorporation is to "evolve *America*" – not just the school system, but the entire political-economic structure of the country. Hastings is aiming to "evolve *America*" from an elected republican democracy that separates political and economic powers, and to mutate it into a corporate-fascist autocracy that controls every sector of the nation's planned political-economy.

Perhaps Hastings would like to sit on the P-16/20 councils that govern corporate charter school chains across the nation, since he currently also sits on the Board of Directors of the KIPP,[63] Netflix,[64] Facebook,[65] and Microsoft corporations.[66]

4

BILLIONAIRE BETSY DEVOS, BIG DATA,
AND THE
PUBLIC-PRIVATE PLANNED ECONOMY

If cutting-edge educational technologies can scientifically maximize student learning, then why do so many Silicon Valley bigwigs at Google, Apple, Hewlett-Packard, and Yahoo! send their children to the Waldorf School of the Peninsula, a school which bans computer technology from its classrooms?[1] If high-tech computerization were such a fundamental enhancement to cognitive development, then why did Steve Jobs withhold iPads and other "screen-time" technologies from his children?[2] Why would these tech gurus not practice for their own sons and daughters what they preach (and bankroll) for the public education system? These incongruences signal red flags that the real objective behind the accelerating push for personalized computer learning is not to boost academic outcomes, but to data-mine students for the purposes of corporate-fascist political-economic planning.

Enter US Secretary of Education, Betsy DeVos, a billionaire who has played both sides of the public-private fence as a supporter of federal Common Core data-mining as well as corporate charter schooling and privatized voucher programs.[3]

As President Donald Trump's Education Secretary, DeVos has effectively transferred the government data-mining policies of Common Core into a deregulated system of public-private "school choice" partnerships, which open loopholes for private corporations to coopt public student data for the purposes of for-profit behavioral advertising and workforce planning.

By capitalizing on loosened Family Educational Rights and Privacy Act (FERPA)[4] restrictions while blurring the regulatory lines between public education institutions and their privately contracted vendors,[5] DeVos is facilitating deregulatory lenience regarding the "educational data mining" (EDM) and "learning analytics" technologies laid out in a US Department of Education "Issue Brief" published under the reign of Democrat Arne Duncan.[6]

Entitled "Enhancing Teaching and Learning Through Educational Data Mining and Learning Analytics," this 2012 Department of Ed white-paper defines EDM as

> ...a suite of computational and psychological methods and research approaches for understanding how students learn...
>
> EDM develops methods and applies techniques from statistics, machine learning, and data mining to analyze data collected during teaching and learning. EDM tests learning theories and informs educational practice.[7]

Similarly, this Department of Ed "Issue Brief" defines another form of EDM as

> Learning analytics [which] applies techniques from information science, sociology, psychology, statistics, machine learning, and data mining to analyze data collected during education administration and services, teaching, and learning. Learning analytics creates applications that directly influence educational practice.[8]

DeVos's federal noninterference with high-tech EDM throughout a privatized national schooling system is primed to open backdoors for treasure-troves of public student data to be shared with educational technology companies, and even noneducational corporations, for crony-capitalist market manipulation and workforce planning.

Less Privacy, More Privatization:

DeVos has a decorated track record of school privatization activism as a member of numerous "school-choice" advocacy organizations such as the Alliance for School Choice, Advocates for School Choice, Choices for Children, The Education Freedom Fund, the American Education Reform Council, the American Federation for Children, Children First America, the Great Lakes Education Project, and Jeb Bush's Foundation for Excellence in Education. She has also funded EdChoice, formerly known as the Milton Friedman Foundation for Educational Choice.[9]

Furthermore, DeVos has been instrumental in funding charter school privatization throughout Michigan where she poured $5 million into lobbying efforts for pro-voucher legislation.[10] Additionally, she pumped $1.45 million into political efforts to stop the Michigan State Legislature from passing regulations that would have set up a local commission to oversee the state's 80% for-profit charter school system.[11]

With Trump's pledge to commit $20 billion in federal funding to school-choice reform,[12] Secretary DeVos has not skipped a beat as a crusader for education privatization that will eradicate locally elected schoolboards.[13]

Greenlighted with presidential backing, charter privatization under DeVos is ripe to capitalize on the revised federal regulations under FERPA laws which have been reinterpreted since 2011 to now permit third-party corporations to data-mine American students.[14] Through these (de)regulatory loopholes, Trump's promise of a $20-billion charter allowance is primed to incentivize accelerated digitalization of student FERPA data to be aggregated by educational data-cumulating corporations,[15] such as the now-defunct inBloom, which share databases with third-party corporations that could expropriate student data sets for potentially noneducational research and development.[16]

To be sure, such third-party corporations must be deemed to have "legitimate educational interests" in order to be granted legal access to FERPA-protected data. However, as demonstrated in chapter three, the institutional lines between traditional classroom education and "cradle-to-career" community-oriented learning are being blurred by the burgeoning privatization mergers of public education, public health and human services, and "community policing" agencies guided by workforce training pedagogies under public-private P-16/20 council governance.

With these public institutions privatized together through business partnerships managed under interlocking P-16/20 governance, DeVos's hands-off approach to educational regulation may broaden the terms and conditions of what constitutes a "legitimate educational interest" so that the legal definition encompasses any service that contributes to the improvement of the labor force or any of the healthcare, welfare, or criminal justice systems which are integral subcomponents of America's new P-16/20 council system of cradle-to-career schooling for "lifelong learning." By incorporating social services and criminal justice agencies as ostensible branches of the US education system, public-private P-16/20 mergers are setting the stage for the DeVos Department of Education to rubberstamp corporate data-mining of students for R&D by any contingent business that could enhance a student's psychosocial development from cradle to career.[a] [17]

a   The Bill and Melinda Gates Foundation donated $1,221,800 to the College for All Texans Foundation "to fund strategic planning and research support aimed at improving of P-20 data infrastructure and data use among policy makers and practitioners."

No Child Data Left Un-Mined:

DeVos was also the chair of the Philanthropy Roundtable,[18] which published *Blended Learning: A Wise Giver's Guide to Bolstering Tech-Assisted Teaching*,[19] an April 2013 guidebook advocating for educational reform through deregulated charter and voucher privatization which implements individualized online computer-learning modules that streamline Common Core testing by data-mining students in real time.

The guidebook, which hypes Common Core as "an exciting idea,"[20] endorses corporate charter schools such as KIPP Empower Academy LA, KIPP Chicago, KIPP Ascend Primary School, KIPP Ascend Middle School, KIPP Create College Prep Middle School, KIPP NYC, and KIPP Washington Heights Middle School as case-study success stories of the "blended-learning" methodology: "the artful combination of computerized instruction (personalized for each student...) with small-group teaching that is closer to tutoring than to traditional mass lectures."[21] In fact, at some of these KIPP charter schools, the entire curriculum is "taught," or facilitated, through a 100% blended-learning methodology.[22]

For implementing such computerized instruction, the guidebook promotes adaptive learning software such as Knewton and Dreambox, which data-mine students with cognitive learning algorithms that mimic the behavioral advertising algorithms used by so many web-based corporations:

> [m]uch as Netflix or Amazon or Pandora are able to learn from each user's actions to predict what that person will next need or desire, so adaptive educational software can pick up how a given student learns, and what he or she is missing.... The lessons presented to students begin to differ, and teachers get suggestions on which resources they might try to get through problems with that pupil, based on his particular learning history.[23]

This Philanthropy Roundtable blueprint for federal Common Core testing managed by private adaptive-learning/data-mining corporations seems to be serving as something of a handbook for DeVos's policies as Secretary of Education under the Every Student Succeeds Act (ESSA). Indeed, ESSA stipulates provisions for school districts to implement an

> "innovative assessment system" ... that may include–
> (1) competency-based assessments ... or performance-based assessments that combine into an annual summative determination for a student, which may be administered through computer adaptive assessments; and

(2) assessments that validate when students are ready to demonstrate mastery or proficiency and allow for differentiated student support based on individual learning needs.[24]

The language here in the ESSA law reads as if it were tailored to facilitate the corporate adaptive-learning/data-mining endorsed by DeVos's Philanthropy Roundtable. Under ESSA, public-private "'innovative assessment system[s]" of individualized adaptive-learning/data-mining software such as Knewton and Dreambox can be contracted to proctor "computer adaptive assessments" for calculating student workforce "competenc[e]" and "performance" outcomes in accordance with ESSA's "career readiness" clauses.

Such a policy of deregulated public-private data-mining for workforce development could also open backdoors for corporations to coopt student data for behavioral advertising and fascistic political-economic planning under the guise of "legitimate educational interest."

If you think that computerized public-private data-mining of students' learning analytics isn't ripe for abuse under DeVos's deregulatory oversight of ESSA, then consider how privacy activists at the Electronic Frontier Foundation (EFF) have put the Google Corporation under fire from a complaint filed with the Federal Trade Commission. The EFF has charged Google with breaching its "K-12 School Service Provider Pledge to Safeguard Student Privacy" because it allegedly assimilated student data collected from Google Apps for Education (GAFE) and then expropriated that data for noneducational behavioral advertising.[25] Similarly, Google is also being sued by University of California-Berkley students, along with hundreds of class-action litigants from twenty-one other states, because GAFE allegedly excavated their student emails to extract data for noneducational market R&D.[26]

The verdicts are still out on both cases. In the meantime, Google's loose privacy practices are setting the precedent for obfuscating the lines between government-restricted public student data and commercially tradable consumer data. Now, consider within these blurred lines the prospect of Secretary DeVos setting up for a national education databank like inBloom, which aspired to digitally aggregate all student data across the nation – until it was shut down as a result of outcries from privacy advocates.[27]

Originally called the Shared Learning Collaborative, the educational data-mining company known as inBloom was created with funding from the Bill and Melinda Gates Foundation and the Carnegie Corporation of New

York. From 2011 to 2014, inBloom programs tabulated for each individual student copious data points in over "400 data fields" sequenced into three categorical data sets: personally identifiable information (PII), student information system (SIS) data, and "user interaction information" (UII).[28 b 29]

Charting these individualized and demographic data hubs with an operating system from the NewsCorp subsidiary Wireless Generation,[30] inBloom stored this massive data aggregate in a web cloud managed by the Amazon Corporation,[31] which has also built for the Central Intelligence Agency (CIA) a similar web-based computing cloud that streamlines CIA data dossiers.[32] Once uploaded to the Amazon cloud, this PII-SIS-UII data warehouse became accessible to educational institutions and other third-party vendors including for-profit corporations.

In 2014, after fighting against testimony from the Electronic Privacy Information Center (EPIC),[33] and after battling a lawsuit filed with the New York State Supreme Court,[34] inBloom caved in to mounting public backlash against its third-party data-sharing practices by terminating all of its contracts and shutting down all operations.

But don't worry; DeVos could contract with a new Carnegie-created data-mining enterprise that is picking up where inBloom left off. Funded by a $5 million grant from the federal government through the National Science Foundation, Carnegie Mellon University has launched Learnsphere,[35] a not-for-profit digital repository for sharing student data with third parties including for-profit vendors.[36] Professor of Human Computer Interaction and Psychology at Carnegie Mellon University, Ken Koedinger, who heads up the Big Data project, explains that Learnsphere is basically a rendition of the infamous inBloom: "[t]here certainly are some similarities," stated Koedinger.[37]

To be sure, Koedinger also says that "[i]n some ways, it's a deep philosophical difference."[38] In particular, to mitigate public resistance from privacy activists, Learnsphere will not be lumping together all of its educational data into a single online cloud like inBloom. Instead, Learnsphere utilizes a "distributed infrastructure" which allows educational institu-

---

b   PII is data that identifies a specific student: name, address, Social Security number. SIS data tracks the institutional demographics of a school's academic and behavioral outcomes: attendance and suspension rates; course grades, course levels, and class sizes; standardized test scores; learning disability and IEP classifications; free/reduced-price lunch distribution; ethnic population ratios. In addition, SIS data contains certain health information such as absences due to illness or other physical or mental health complication; and SIS can also contain criminal justice records pertaining to in-school arrests and other school code violations. UII is the psycho-behavioral data collected by adaptive learning software like Dreambox, Knewton, and Khan Academy; this real-time data tracks screen time and keystrokes per assessment module while mapping student-response feedback loops to algorithmically chart a student's cognitive-behavioral efficacy.

tions and learning software companies to store student data on their own servers while creating proxy links between the servers and the central Learnsphere network.[39] Also, Koedinger pledges that Learnsphere will collect zero PII.[40]

Nevertheless, despite this "decentralized" IT infrastructure, Learnsphere is still sharing student data with third parties and for-profit vendors. Furthermore, Koedinger admits that Learnsphere must employ a monitor to scan databanks to filter out any "accidental" PII. Moreover, Learnsphere does collect certain SIS demographics such as the percentage of free and reduced-price lunch recipients in a given school.[41]

For instance, the Learnsphere website contains a shared network of inter-collaborative databanks,[42] including MITx and HarvardX Dataverse,[43] which is a data hub that contains a file titled "Socioeconomic Status Indicators of HarvardX and MITx Participants 2012-2014" with the following description:

> [t]his dataset includes the home mailing addresses of all participants … in MITx and HarvardX courses. For U.S. residents, These mailing addresses can be parsed and geo-matched with data from the US Census to develop a suite of socioeconomic status indicators, including median neighborhood income and neighborhood level of education. We also include self-reported survey data about parental level of education, and we include an indicator for whether or not the participant earned a certificate.[44]

With such vast pools of socioeconomic SIS data cross-referenced with Learnsphere's dossiers of cognitive-behavioral UII, third-party corporations under DeVos deregulation could commandeer these student data for epidemiological behavioral advertising and workforce planning by computing real-time consumer behavior patterns and workforce development trends across various social groups and geopolitical regions.

National Standards for National Socialism:

Of course, a policy of student data-mining for corporate-government workforce planning under DeVos would be nothing new to America. Learnsphere and inBloom are only two of the most recent educational data-tabulating projects to be spawned from a long historical web of corporatist Carnegie institutions.

Although the US Department of Education was not established until 1979, America's progression toward a corporate-fascist national education policy can be traced at least as far back as the publication of the Carnegie-funded *Conclusions and Recommendations for the Social Studies* by the American Historical Association in 1934. The document reads:

> [The United States] is embarking upon vast experiments in social planning and control which call for large scale cooperation on the part of the people…
>
> [T]he age of *laissez faire* in economy and government is closing and a new age of collectivism is emerging…
>
> The implications of education are clear and imperative: (a) the efficient functioning of the emerging economy and the full utilization of its potentialities require profound changes in the attitudes and outlook of the American people.[45]

To measure progress toward the achievement of these corporate-collectivist reeducation goals, twelve years later,[46] the Carnegie Corporation of New York endowed the founding of Educational Testing Services (ETS) with a $750,000 grant in 1946.[47] Ever since then, ETS has played a central role in calculating student metrics for the standardization of national learning benchmarks, including corporate-government workforce training goals. In 1964, the Carnegie Corporation put together the Committee on Assessing the Progress of Education,[48] which in 1969 evolved into the National Assessment of Educational Progress (NAEP).[49] Originally,[50] NAEP stats were configured by the Education Commission of the States,[51] which was likewise founded by a grant from the Carnegie Corporation.[52] But since 1983, the NAEP has been proctoring all of its "Nation's Report Card" evaluations through ETS.[53] [c] [54]

It should be noted that these national Carnegie metrics for corporate-government workforce schooling are rooted in the Hegelian-collectivist philosophy of the first President of the Carnegie Institution, Skull-and-Bonesman Daniel Coit Gilman, who was the first President of Johns Hopkins University and the first President of the University of California.[55] According to Antony C. Sutton, Gilman's Hegelianism at the Carnegie Institution was carried on by "other members of The Order [of Skull

---

[c] ETS has likewise played a crucial role in the data analyses of No Child Left Behind (NCLB) and Race to the Top testing. Specifically, ETS published two comprehensive reviews of NCLB testing entitled National Education Standards: Getting Beneath the Surface and Education Issues 2007. In addition, ETS conducted actuaries to contribute to a 2010 joint report by the US Department of Education and the RAND Corporation titled State and Local Implementation of the No Child Left Behind Act (Volume IX—Accountability under NCLB: Final Report). After the initiation of the Race to the Top program, ETS contracted with the Partnership for Assessment of Readiness for College and Careers (PARCC) to crunch the numbers for Race to the Top data-mining.

and Bones] [who] have been on Carnegie boards since the turn of the century."[56] It should also be noted that DeVos's colleague on the Trump Cabinet is Bonesman Stephen Mnuchin,[57] who is the US Treasury Secretary.[58]

Will DeVos carry the Carnegie torch for The Order's corporate-fascist workforce planning schemes by pushing Big Data privatization of education?

You don't need a terabyte of data to forecast this prediction.

5

Secretary DeVos, Neurocore, and Competency-Based Workforce Training: A Continuation of Outcomes-Based Behaviorism through Medicalized Education

Vice President Mike Pence's tie-breaking vote to confirm US Secretary of Education, Betsy DeVos, marks the first time in history that a VP had to issue the deciding vote to officiate a presidential cabinet appointment.[1] The contentious opposition votes expressed that among their concerns are conflicts of interest between Secretary DeVos's federal powers and her multimillion-dollar investments in a biofeedback corporation known as Neurocore, which provides neuroscience treatments for retraining cognitive habits through stimulus-response conditioning.[2]

In a letter to Chairman Lamar Alexander of the Senate Committee on Health, Education, Labor and Pensions (HELP), ten Democrat members of HELP, including Bernie Sanders, formalized the following request for extended investigation of DeVos's corporate investments: "we believe it is important to ask her questions around companies she will continue to own that are directly impacted by the Department of Education and this administration's education agenda."[3]

Although DeVos announced her resignation from Neurocore's board of directors upon her confirmation to the office of US Secretary of Education,[4] she has refused to sell her shares in the company.[5] By refusing to divest her financial interests in Neurocore, DeVos has incited concerns that she may use her federal influence to advance Neurocore's controversial biofeedback therapies as government-approved interventions for students who suffer from attention deficit hyperactivity disorder (ADHD) and other cognitive-learning disabilities.

Former White House ethics adviser, Richard W. Painter, who served under the George W. Bush administration, has criticized DeVos's conflicts of interest:

> [t]his is not an appropriate investment for the secretary of education.... How schools respond to attention issues is a vitally important policy question and ties right into achievement. In my view, there should be support, including financial support, for alternatives to ADHD drug treatments that are covered by health insurance whereas alternatives often are not covered...
>
> The secretary would be barred from participating in that important policy decision if she or her husband owned an interest in this company.[6]

Nevertheless, touted as the cutting edge of operant conditioning psychotherapy, Neurocore's biofeedback treatments could be readily advocated in the halls of academia by behaviorist pedagogues and Skinnerian educational philosophers if given the nudge from a DeVos Department of Education. At the same time, Neurocore's hi-tech occupational biofeedback therapies may be eagerly promoted at the new White House Office of American Innovation (OAI) where corporatist technocrats are seeking to capitalize on DeVos's "competency-based" workforce education initiatives under the Every Student Succeeds Act (ESSA). Finally, as an alternative medical procedure, Neurocore stimulus-response conditioning could potentially be institutionalized as a publicly subsidized treatment for cognitive-learning disabilities classified under ESSA Sections 2103 and 4108,[7] which will be amplified by state-level P-20 fusion of education and healthcare through fascistic public-private partnerships.

In sum, as the Trump-DeVos Department of Ed drives hi-tech workforce training initiatives that capitalize on ESSA/P-20 medicalization of privatized workforce education, DeVos's Neurocore Corporation could exploit a windfall of burgeoning biofeedback niches for hi-tech innovations in education, healthcare, and corporate business. The prospects of such quid pro quo cronyism are exacerbated by the fact that Neurocore CEO, Mark Murrison, has announced that the Michigan-based corporation is branching out into "national expansion," beginning with the 2016 opening of two new Brain Performance Centers in Florida.[8]

If you think that a DeVos-financed healthcare corporation would never be charged with exploiting federal programs for profit, it should be noted that Billionaire Betsy has earned capital gains dividends through investments in Universal Health Services (UHS),[9] which is a nationwide chain of psychiatric hospitals that is currently under federal investigation for Medicare and Medicaid fraud.[10][a][11]

The School as Psychological Laboratory from Behaviorism to Operant Conditioning:

Although some critics dismiss Neurocore's brain-training treatments as "quack[ery],"[12] biofeedback therapies are rooted in the behaviorist methodology of stimulus-response psychological conditioning. According to licensed biofeedback psychologist, Dr. Christopher Fisher, biofeedback is actually a form of B. F. Skinner's operant conditioning behaviorism.[13] In fact, the Neurocore website states that it uses the operant conditioning techniques of "positive reinforcement and repetition" to retrain brainwave frequencies to conduce better attention and memory spans.[14]

As such, Neurocore's Skinnerian conditioning therapies are grounded in the very same stimulus-response psychological methodology that has been the scientific basis of American education pedagogy for over a century. Throughout the early 1900s, the proto-behaviorist laboratory method of schooling was bankrolled across the nation by Secretary Abraham Flexner of the General Education Board (GEB) of the Rockefeller Foundation philanthropies, which funded teaching labs across America, including labs at the premier Columbia University Teachers College.[15] It is worth noting that the Rockefeller Foundation was also funding the biofeedback research of Norbert Weiner as early as the 1920s.[16]

In *The Leipzig Connection*, Paolo Lionni documents how Rockefeller's GEB propagated stimulus-response pedagogies through financing the research of such academic figureheads as James McKeen Cattell, James Earl Russell, and Edward Lee Thorndike at Columbia University Teachers College where Thorndike adapted his stimulus-response experiments on animal behaviors and applied them to humans.[17]

Based on these proto-behaviorist animal training experiments at Columbia Teachers College, E. L. Thorndike systematized teaching as

> the art of giving and withholding stimuli with the result of producing or preventing certain responses. In this definition of the

---

a   To be sure, in a January 19th, 2017, letter to the Designated Agency Ethics Officials of the US Department of Education, DeVos pledged to divest her financial interests in Reinhart Partners Inc., which manages the portfolio that holds DeVos's UHS investments.

term stimulus is used widely for any event which influences a person – for a word spoken to him, a look, a sentence which he reads, the air he breathes, etc., etc. The term response is used for any reaction made by him – a new thought, a feeling of interest, a bodily act, a mental or bodily condition resulting from the stimulus. The aim of the teacher is to produce desirable and prevent undesirable changes in human beings by producing and preventing certain responses.[18]

Compare Thorndike's methodology here to Neurocore's biofeedback brain-training procedures:[19] Neurocore reprograms ADHD by utilizing quantitative electroencephalography to monitor brainwave responses to video stimuli; whenever the ADHD patient exhibits an undesirable brainwave response that indicates distraction, the video stimuli is halted or altered until the patient exhibits a focused brainwave response that indicates concentrated attention.[20] Hence, the only difference between Neurocore's biofeedback science and Thorndike's "art of giving and withholding stimuli" is that the former aims to condition the autonomous nervous system while the latter targets more of the voluntary nervous system.

Fast-forward to as recently as 2007, and Columbia Teachers College is still practicing this art of stimulus-response conditioning through Comprehensive Applied Behavior Analysis in Schools, a new behaviorist instructional methodology that was developed by Skinner's protégé, Doug Greer, who is Professor of Psychology and Education at Columbia.[21]

Buttressed by this hundred-year institutional tradition of stimulus-response educational psychology, Neurocore's behaviorist therapies for learning disabilities are primed to be legitimized by the intelligentsia of US academia if incentivized by a DeVos Department of Ed.

At the same time, biofeedback conditioning is being advocated through numerous scholarly journal publications authored by contemporary educational psychologists such as the Chair of the Department of Educational Psychology at the University of Kansas, Steven Wayne Lee,[22] and the Director of the Doctoral Program in Counseling Psychology at the Boston University School of Education, Steven N. Broder.[23] With such support from current leaders of university education departments, the biofeedback neuropsychology underlying Neurocore's cognitive-behavioral therapies is already being advocated in the disciplines of educational methodology and pedagogy.

A History of Outcomes-Based Behaviorism for Workforce Education:

Neurocore is also likely to be promoted by captains of industry who seek to capitalize on the company's occupational biofeedback therapies. The Neurocore website states, "[m]any ... business professionals also use neuro-feedback to improve mental performance and productivity through increased focus and better stress management."[24] With these neuro-behaviorist applications for businesses to enhance workforce output efficiency, Neurocore's operant conditioning therapies could be promoted by corporate lobbyists as government-subsidized treatments for occupational-learning disabilities that are paid for by employer-based health insurance. To be sure, Neurocore procedures are already covered by certain insurance providers.[25]

Such subsidies for employer-funded biofeedback therapies would help business partners to fulfill "outcomes-based" workforce education contracts under public-private partnerships that are being championed by DeVos and the Trump administration. After meeting with seventeen CEOs from megacorporations such as IBM, GE, Walmart, General Motors, PepsiCo, and the Cleveland Clinic during Trump's April 2017 Strategy and Policy Forum Listening Session,[26] Secretary DeVos released the following statement from the Department of Ed: "[t]he best workforce is an educated workforce, and this Administration is committed to increasing access to career and technical education for college students and adults alike. By encouraging public-private partnerships, we can help connect students with prospective employers and provide those students with the necessary skills to find a good-paying job in their communities."[27]

To achieve these corporate-government workforce planning outcomes, public-private partnerships between businesses and educational institutions are implementing a form of outcomes-based education (OBE) methodology, which is deeply rooted in the stimulus-response method of psycho-behavioral conditioning that is the core of Neurocore science. The rationale for outcomes-based workforce education asserts that public-school funding should be contingent upon student attainment of predetermined career-readiness outcomes that can be quantified through standardized tests or performance-based assessments. What better way to control workforce learning outcomes than the scientific method of behaviorist psychological conditioning? Indeed, OBE for workforce training has a long pedagogical history of stimulus-response psycho-behavioral conditioning.

In an article titled "The Death of Free Will (Part 2 of 5)," Charlotte Thomson Iserbyt explains that

> [t]he type of so-called education being promoted throughout the United States is not truly "education." It is a system of Skinnerian/Pavlovian group-oriented, collectivist, brainwashing/training in lower level skills and the necessary attitudes and values for the workforce, using the computer (the operant conditioning machine) in conjunction with "programmed" learning (mastery learning/direct instruction) software.[28]

Iserbyt elaborates that "[t]his is the same Skinnerian Outcomes-Based Education rat lab program ... that was funded by my old office in the U.S. Dept. Of Education" under President Ronald Reagan.[29]

So far, the Trump Administration has lived up to its historical comparisons to the Reagan Administration. In particular, Reagan-style OBE behaviorism is a cornerstone of the Trump-DeVos workforce education plan. The *University Herald* reports that "Betsy DeVos has acknowledged the significant role that community colleges will play in the advancement of President Donald Trump's workforce agenda."[30] At the National Legislative Summit of the Association of Community College Trustees, DeVos stated that community colleges are "absolutely essential engines of workforce and economic development – locally and regionally ... [Community colleges] help identify and close the skills gap between employers and job seekers, so U.S. businesses and industries can thrive and expand."[31] To bring about the planned economic outcomes of these public-private workforce-schooling partnerships, the Trump-DeVos regime is filling the job skills gap by training students according to educational psychology methods based on Reagan-era OBE workforce behaviorism which was perpetuated under former President George W. Bush's No Child Left Behind (NCLB).

An example of OBE behaviorism during the reign of NCLB is described in a 2006 scholarly journal article from the *School Psychology Review*. In this peer-reviewed article titled "Integrating Frameworks from Early Childhood Intervention and School Psychology to Accelerate Growth for All Children," educational psychologists evaluated

> patterns of child performance over time and in response to certain stimuli, [so that] conditions, and consequences can be quantified ... to improve child outcomes in a more efficient fashion through

iterative problem-solving attempts ... [by] determin[ing] what additional supports and services might be needed and ... whether the additional supports and services are meaningfully accelerating child growth.[32]

Clearly, this stimulus-response method of outcomes-based teaching is merely a revision of not only Skinner's operant conditioning, but also the proto-behaviorist psychology of Wilhelm Maximillian Wundt.[b][33] The founding father of psychological science, Wundt created the world's first experimental psychology laboratory in Leipzig, Germany, where he evangelized a cadre of American psychologists, such as G. Stanley Hall,[c][34] James McKeen Cattell, and Charles Judd, who returned to the United States to propagate proto-behaviorist pedagogies for workforce training curriculums.[35]

By 1948, at least 689 postgraduate students were awarded psychology doctorates from these three Wundtian disciples,[36] Hall, Cattell, and Judd,[d][37] many of whom were bankrolled through Rockefeller's GEB funds for school laboratories designed to develop stimulus-response conditioning methods for corporate-industrial workforce training.[38]

In the 1916 GEB publication *Occasional Papers No. 1*, Chairman of the GEB, Fredrick T. Gates, professed the corporatist directive of Rockefeller-financed laboratory schools:

[w]e shall not try to make these people or any of their children philosophers or men of learning, or men of science. We have not to raise up from among them authors, editors, poets, or men of letters. We shall not search for embryo great artists, painters, musicians, nor lawyers, doctors, preachers, politicians, statesmen, of whom we have an ample supply. The task we set before ourselves is ... to

---

b   It is worth noting that former Research Fellow at Stanford University's Hoover Institution, Antony C. Sutton, documents that

Wundt's grandfather on the paternal side is of significant interest: Kirchenrat Karl Kasimir Wundt (1744-84) was Professor at Heidelberg University in the history and geography of Baden and pastor of the church at Wieblingen, a small neighborhood town.

The Illuminati-Order documents show that "Raphael" in the Illuminati is identified as this same Professor Karl Kasimir Wundt and is referred to in the Illuminati Provincial Report from Utica (i.e., Heidelberg) dated September 1782.

c   Hall was picked up as the Chair of Psychology and Pedagogy at Johns Hopkins University by the college's first president, Skull-and-Bonesman Daniel Coit Gilman. At Johns Hopkins, Gilman provided Hall with laboratory facilities and $1000 per year for psychological testing equipment to carry on the proto-behaviorist conditioning experiments that were pioneered at Wundt's seminal lab in Germany.

d   Hall's most prominent student was perhaps John Dewey, who went on to spread Hall's Wundtian gospel throughout the classrooms of US academia as the Director of the University of Chicago School of Education and as Professor of Philosophy at Columbia University Teachers College.

train these people as we find them to a perfectly ideal life just where they are … and [to] teach them to do in a perfect way what their fathers and mothers are doing in an imperfect way, in the homes, in the shops and on the farm.[39]

Stated differently, Gates's mission as GEB Chairman aimed merely to condition the working-class masses to adapt to America's economic evolution from "imperfect" manual labor into "perfect" mechanical labor managed by corporate industrialization for mass production.

A major recipient of GEB funds was Teachers College at Columbia University where E. L. Thorndike conducted stimulus-response experiments on animals such as mice and monkeys to refine proto-behaviorist conditioning methodologies for collectivist workforce training.[40] Thorndike asserted that

we believe it will be found that the best interests of the individual and society will be served by providing a certain number of pupils least gifted in intelligence with the equipment needed to begin their vocational career by the completion of the junior high school period or even earlier in a few cases. Other individuals will advance their own welfare and that of society by securing but one more year, others by two, others by three additional years. Thus although the great majority of children should spend some time in the junior high school, not all of them should be expected to continue to the completion of the senior-high-school course. Each child should have as much high-school work as the common good requires.[41]

Fast-forward after one hundred years of GEB funding, and compare Thorndike's early system of vocational "tracking" to current "career pathways" curriculums, which DeVos is promoting as Secretary of Education. The US Department of Ed issued a press release stating that, on May 9th, Secretary DeVos visited Granite Technical Institute in Salt Lake City, Utah, in order to "highlight innovative career pathways for high school students made possible through strong business-education partnerships."[42] In chapter two, I expound how career pathways are nothing more than job-specific workforce-training curriculums that are assigned to students whose learning outcomes "track" them out of traditional academic curriculums for university preparation.

Once students are tracked into prescriptive career pathways, Wundtian-Skinnerian stimulus-response pedagogies are applied to achieve workforce planning outcomes in accordance with workforce development mandates under federal laws such as the Workforce Investment Act (WIA), the Workforce Innovation and Opportunity Act (WIOA), and the Carl D. Perkins Vocational and Applied Technology Education Act (Perkins III).

Under such federal workforce planning laws, even education administrators are psycho-behaviorally conditioned to attain workforce development outcomes through operant-conditioning management incentives. According to a 2005 scholarly journal article published in *New Directions for Institutional Research*, educational institutions receiving federal aid under the provisions of WIA and Perkins III must "report outcome data to a central state administrative agency that in turn aggregates these data and reports them to the U.S. Department of Education. Both laws introduced potential rewards and consequences for states that do or do not improve student performance."[43] Adding another layer of administrative operant conditioning, these financial "rewards ['positive reinforcement'] and consequences ['punishments']" impel educational institutions into regimenting operant conditioning pedagogies in the classroom to achieve government-mandated workforce-training outcomes.

Will DeVos compound yet another layer of stimulus-response conditioning into this workforce-planning stratagem by using her cabinet position to push Neurocore's occupational biofeedback therapies as government-subsidized treatments for cognitive-learning disabilities that impede federal workforce-training outcomes? To be sure, the Neurocore Corporation does in fact provide specialized biofeedback therapies for corporate clients through the Neurocore Pro website, which offers biofeedback procedures that can catalyze "higher productivity for a business unit."[44]

On the "Corporate Health" page of the Neurocore Pro website, it describes the company's

> Corporate health program, Core Health.... By optimizing the autonomic nervous system ... we improve productivity and performance in a manner most corporate wellness programs cannot.... We have seen incredible change in the professional athletes, executives, politicians, and entrepreneurs who run our program. Now, we are introducing this program to entire executive teams and business units.[45]

If greenlighted by a DeVos Department of Ed, such Neurocore treatments for entire corporate staffs could be adapted to treat entire classes of learning-disabled students who are being trained in career pathways courses to fulfill federal workforce planning outcomes.

Competency-Based Workforce Training and the Medicalization of Hegelian Education:

Currently, corporate-government workforce planning under the Trump-DeVos Administration is shifting away from OBE rhetoric and switching to "competency-based education" directives under the new ESSA legislation. In particular, the ESSA law stipulates federal provisions for "the development of comprehensive academic assessment instruments . . . that emphasize the mastery of standards and aligned competencies in a competency-based education model."[46]

Admittedly, competency-based education is simply a rendition of OBE workforce training. According to a 1994 whitepaper titled "Outcome-Based Education: Final Report," which was published by the US Department of Ed, "Competency-Based Education (CBE), originally conceived to ease the transition from school to work, contained elements of OBE.... Rather than being accepted as a holistic approach to school reform, CBE survives chiefly as a vocational training program."[47] Indeed, when conducting a peer-reviewed journal search for the simple phrase "competency-based education" in the EBSCO *host* Academic Search Complete research database, over 70% of the articles in the first 40 search results are tabulated with the key-phrase "outcome-based education" in the detailed record.[e]

Attorney Jane Robbins, who is a senior fellow at the American Principles Project, concurs with this comparison between OBE and CBE workforce schooling. In a recent *Federalist* report, Robbins exposes cronyism between Secretary DeVos and Jeb Bush's CBE lackeys from his "school choice" non-profit, the Foundation for Educational Excellence. The article, entitled "Why 'Competency-Based Education' Will Deepen America's Education Crisis," demonstrates how "CBE is essentially the same thing as outcome-based education (OBE) ... OBE and now CBE posit that the government should establish outcomes it wants students to achieve and then work backwards, setting interim benchmarks along the journey to that goal. Students would work at their own pace to establish 'competency' at each benchmark."[48]

In a subsection titled "Plugging Kids into a Planned Hole in a Planned Economy," Robbins explains "that the entire CBE/Common Core scheme is designed for workforce development. When the government has such intensely personal algorithms on all citizens, it's easier to slot those people into the workforce needs of politically connected corporations."[49] As I

---

e   This search was conducted on September 1st, 2017.

document in chapter four, hi-tech data-mining of America's student body is integral to tracking students into competency-based career-pathways algorithms that are programmed for corporate-government workforce planning under DeVos's Department of Education.

Robbins's analysis of OBE-CBE workforce planning under Secretary DeVos is affirmed in the ESSA bill. Subsection 4205(a)(14) stipulates federal provisions for "build[ing] career competencies and career readiness and ensur[ing] that local workforce and career readiness skills are aligned with the Carl D. Perkins Career and Technical Education Act of 2006 (20 U.S.C. 2301 et seq.) and the Workforce Innovation and Opportunity Act (29 U.S.C. 3101 et seq.)."[50]

Currently, the trend in OBE-CBE workforce education is hi-tech training for healthcare job competencies needed to operate the IT and other digital technologies that are being increasingly integrated into the new national healthcare system. It should be noted that Billionaire Betsy's husband Dick DeVos, who is also heavily invested in Neurocore, campaigned for the governorship of Michigan in 2006 by pledging to upgrade the state's healthcare technology infrastructure.[51] According to *Chimes*, the official student news publication of Dick's alma mater, Calvin College, Mr. DeVos promised "[t]o combat rising health care costs ... [with] a streamlined system that utilizes technology to reduce hospital errors by making medical records more efficient."[52]

While Dick has pushed hi-tech healthcare at the state level, the enactment of Obamacare has rolled out federal provisions for OBE-CBE workforce training that cultivates medical technology competence.

In 2010, the RAND Corporation published a whitepaper study titled "Use of Outcome Metrics to Measure Quality in Education and Training of Healthcare Professionals." This document examines "the 2010 Patient Protection and Affordable Care Act (PPACA) stipulat[ions] [for] the establishment of a National Health Care Workforce Planning Commission to undertake comprehensive workforce planning in healthcare and so help synchronising federal investments into workforce development."[53] That same year, the *Annual Review of Public Health* published an article entitled "Outcome-Based Workforce Development and Education in Public Health," which "recommend[s] a framework for workforce education in public health, integrating ... competency-based education.... This framework provides a context for designing and developing high-quality, outcome-based workforce development efforts and evaluating their impact, with implications for academic and public health practice efforts to educate the public health workforce."[54]

To streamline this national healthcare workforce, Betsy DeVos is promoting educational institutions that are pioneering innovations in healthcare technology, such as Arizona State University. On May 9th, at the 2017 Arizona State University and Global Silicon Valley Summit in Salt Lake City Utah, DeVos lauded ASU's Entrepreneurship (PLUS) Innovation program for its invention of the G3Box, which re-engineers shipping containers into portable medical clinics that can be transported anywhere at relatively inexpensive prices.[55] To facilitate such new healthcare technology infrastructure, OBE-CBE initiatives are commencing specialized training for competencies in hi-tech treatments for all patient populations across the lifespan from pediatrics to geriatrics.

A 2015 issue of the scholarly journal *Pediatrics* published an article entitled "Blueprint for Action: Visioning Summit on the Future of the Workforce in Pediatrics." This article studies the "need for outcomes-based research" so that "the field of pediatrics and its workforce [can] adapt to meet challenges created by such changes" resulting from "[t]echnology and electronic medical record (EMR) systems" as well as other "health care delivery system" changes.[56]

In 2011, the *Journal of the American Society on Aging* printed an article titled "A Competency-Based Approach to Educating and Training the Eldercare Workforce." This article explores "ongoing initiatives that address geriatric workforce competency and how these efforts support and can be supported by the goals of the ACA [Affordable Care Act]."[57] More recently, a 2015 issue of the same journal published an article entitled "Ensuring Care for Aging Baby Boomers: Solutions at Hand." In this peer-reviewed article, the authors recommend eldercare initiatives that "maximiz[e] how we deploy our existing [eldercare] workforce, [by] incorporating quickly evolving technology."[58] In particular, the authors recommend workforce competencies in geriatric-care technologies such as "robot caregiver[s]," "health information technology," and "smart technolog[ies]," including "telephone-based symptom monitoring system[s]" as well as "personalized apps, wearable sensors, and social networks that encourage behavioral change" by recording and sharing "health status in real time."[59]

This "cradle-to-end-of-life" education of the healthcare workforce parallels the "cradle-to-career" charter schooling system for corporate-fascist workforce training that is being pushed by the Trump-DeVos Administration. Likewise, this cradle-to-grave system of healthcare workforce planning at the national level parallels the public-private P-20 (preschool-to-grade-twenty) council systems of workforce education at the state levels, which are already merging public education departments with public health and human services agencies. Internationally, cradle-to-death healthcare-industrial schooling is integral to the eugenic philosophy underscoring UNESCO's globalist "lifelong learning" methodology.[60]

As I explicate in chapter three, this public-private collectivization of clinical medicine and public education stems from the Hegelian roots of corporate-fascist political-economic planning in the United States. Moreover, in chapter four, I document how Carnegie-funded national learning benchmarks for outcomes-based workforce education are rooted in the Hegelian ideology of Skull-and-Bonesman Daniel Coit Gilman,[f][61] who was the first President of the Carnegie Institution.[g][62] Gilman, as the first President of Johns Hopkins University, fused Hegelianism with Wundtian proto-behaviorism by appointing the Wundtian Hegelianist, G. Stanley Hall, to the Chair of Psychology and Pedagogy at Johns Hopkins.[h][63] Thus, the public-private merger of clinical healthcare and public schooling for OBE-CBE workforce planning is the culmination of over a century of Hegelian-collectivist philosophy steering classroom implementations of Wundtian stimulus-response psychology techniques that have been propagated by Robber Baron capitalists to manage the health of the Corporate State.

ESSA, IDEA, WIOA: Neurocore Therapies for Disabled Workforce Incompetency:

As privatized P-20 collectivization of public education with public health blurs the lines between traditional classroom learning and "community-based" lifelong learning, educational institutions will incorporate more clinical approaches to conditioning student learning/cognition and psychosocial development for workforce competency. In time,

---

f   A June 1993 article titled "Outcome-Based Education: An Overview," which was published by the Education Commission of the States, documents how outcomes-based education was formulated by the Eight-Year Study of the Progressive Education Association's Commission on Relation of School and College. The Eight-Year Study was funded by the Carnegie Corporation of New York as well as Rockefeller's GEB.

g   In *America's Secret Establishment: An Introduction to the Order of Skull & Bones*, Antony C. Sutton records the fact that Gilman, who also served on Rockefeller's GEB, left America to study Hegelian philosophy under Karl von Ritter and Friedrich Trendelenberg "at the University of Berlin, where post-Hegelian philosophy had a monopoly." It is worth noting here that the Rockefeller family was also inducted into the cult of Skull and Bones through the initiation of Bonesman Percy Rockefeller in 1900.

h   Like Gilman, Hall studied at the University of Berlin under the Hegelian philosopher Trendelenberg. During the time of Gilman's presidency, John Dewey studied for his doctorate at Johns Hopkins under Hegelianist Hall as well as Hegelian philosopher George Sylvester Morris. In turn, Dewey spread Hegelianism through his eminent posts as the Director of the University of Chicago School of Education and as Professor of Philosophy at Columbia University Teachers College.

under sections 1005, 1008, and 4108 of the ESSA law, a student's workforce incompetency could be pathologized as a cognitive-behavioral disability that requires psychological and/or biomedical intervention, which could be administered through Neurocore biofeedback therapies.[64]

Clause 1008(b)(7)(A)(iii)(I-III) of the ESSA legislation obligates schools to

> (iii) address the needs of all children ... at risk of not meeting the challenging State academic standards, through activities which may include—
>
> (I) counseling, school-based mental health programs, specialized instructional support services, mentoring services, and other strategies to improve students' skills outside the academic subject areas;
>
> (II) preparation for and awareness of opportunities for post-secondary education and the workforce, which may include career and technical education programs ... [and]
>
> (III) implementation of a schoolwide tiered model to prevent and address problem behavior, and early intervening services, coordinated with similar activities and services carried out under the Individuals with Disabilities Education Act.[65]

In simpler terms, this clause authorizes the employment of various psycho-behavioral health support services to accommodate the workforce handicaps of students with cognitive-learning disabilities and "problem behavior[s]" that impede their competencies in "career and technical education programs."

Clause 1005(b)(2)(B)(vii)(II) mandates that assessments of workforce competencies must

> (vii) provide for– ...
>
> (II) the appropriate accommodations, such as interoperability with, and ability to use, assistive technology, for children with disabilities (as defined in section 602(3) of the Individuals with Disabilities Education Act (20 U.S.C. 1401(3))), including students with the most significant cognitive disabilities, and students with a disability who are provided accommodations under an Act other than the Individuals with Disabilities Education Act (20 U.S.C. 1400 et seq.), necessary to measure the academic achievement of such children relative to the challenging State academic standards or alternate academic achievement standards described in paragraph (1)(E).[66]

In other words, this clause permits the use of "assistive technolog[ies]," such as Neurocore's biofeedback technologies, that can reduce the symptoms of cognitive-behavioral disabilities that hinder a student's competencies in "alternate academic achievement standards" such as workforce training through career-pathways curriculums.

In fact, charter schools are already experimenting with assistive biofeedback technologies, such as emWave PC®, for reducing student stress and anxiety levels that result from scholastic pressures to achieve academic competency outcomes. In a 2015 issue of the academic journal *Biofeedback*, Steven C. Kassel of the Biofeedback and Family Therapy Centers in Santa Clarita, California, published an article entitled "Stress Management and Peak Performance Crash Course for Ninth Graders in a Charter School Setting." Kassel reports the findings of a study in which

> [s]eventeen 9th-grade students at [an undisclosed] charter school were selected to participate in a 3-week stress management/peak performance training program that integrated biofeedback into the overall educational schedule.... Students were guided through relaxation exercises and ... worked with the emWave PC®, a heart rate variability biofeedback instrument. ... The students showed mild to moderate improvement on test anxiety and behavioral measures.... This study suggests that ... integration of [biofeedback] relaxation techniques into a secondary school setting can improve important measures of students' scholastic achievement.[67]

At the collegiate level, student support services are currently offering counseling sessions that utilize StressEraser, RESPeRATE, Healing Rhythms, and other assistive biofeedback technologies at colleges such as Northwestern University,[68] the University of Notre Dame,[69] and Iowa State University.[70]

In the business world, occupational biofeedback therapies have already been implemented to improve healthcare workforce outcomes at companies such as BlueCross BlueShield. Employees at the Tennessee branch of the corporation underwent HeartMath biofeedback conditioning to reduce "stress [that] can affect businesses in the form of employee health problems, retention troubles and decreased productivity," according to a 2008 issue of *Workforce Magazine*.[71]

Altogether, there are already several precedents set for the application of assistive biofeedback technologies in the corporate world and academia to improve the workforce and scholastic "competencies" of employees and students. Hence, as the lines are faded between traditional academic education and job-specific workforce training, public-private/school-business partnerships can combine cognitive-learning therapies for students and occupational therapies for employees into singular biofeedback treatments for students who are tracked into career pathways curriculums that partner with specific corporations.

To administer such assistive biofeedback technologies and other psycho-behavioral accommodations for disabled students, subsection 4108(4-5)(B)(i-ii)(I-II)(bb-cc) of the ESSA legislation stipulates requirements for "ACTIVITIES TO SUPPORT SAFE AND HEALTHY STUDENTS," which

> (4) may be conducted in partnership with an institution of higher education, business, nonprofit organization, community-based organization, or other public or private entity with a demonstrated record of success in implementing activities described in this section; and
>
> (5) may include, among other programs and activities— ...
>
> (B) ... (i) school-based mental health services, including ... appropriate referrals to direct individual or group counseling services, which may be provided by school-based mental health services providers; and
>
> (ii) school-based mental health services partnership programs that—
>
> (I) are conducted in partnership with a public or private mental health entity or health care entity; and
>
> (II) provide comprehensive school-based mental health services and supports and staff development for school and community personnel working in the school that are— ...
>
> (bb) coordinated (where appropriate) with early intervening services provided under the Individuals with Disabilities Education Act (20 U.S.C. 1400 et seq.); and
>
> (cc) provided by qualified mental and behavioral health professionals who are certified or licensed by the State involved and practicing within their area of expertise.[72]

Translation: publicly funded educational institutions are permitted to basically "outsource" their mental/behavioral-health accommodations for students with disabilities by employing public-private partnerships with private healthcare corporations, such as Neurocore, and other community-based healthcare nonprofits.

In sum, the implications of these three ESSA clauses authorize private biofeedback corporations, like Neurocore, to capitalize on federal education funding by partnering with public schools through P-20 councils and other State-level public-private partnerships which provide mental/behavioral health treatments for students with disabilities that hinder academic and workforce competencies.

Final Analysis:

It would not be the first time that a presidential appointment, such as DeVos, finagled personal corporate holdings into government contracts. Recall the employment of Dick Cheney's Haliburton Corporation to support military operations in Iraq during his vice presidency under George W. Bush.[73] Considering this historical precedent, there should be little surprise if DeVos's Neurocore Corporation scores government contracts to treat public-private charter-school students who have academic or workforce incompetency disabilities.

Nonetheless, one thing is for certain: competency-based education under Secretary DeVos will perpetuate America's long history of conditioning the student body with stimulus-response methods of psycho-behavioral programming.

6

THE TECHNETRONIC ERA OF
EDU-CONDITIONING:
COGNITIVE-BEHAVIORAL WORKFORCE
SCHOOLING THROUGH ONLINE
ADAPTIVE-LEARNING COMPUTERS

S
even years before he was appointed as US National Security Advisor
to President Jimmy Carter, Zbigniew Brzezinski published *Between Two Ages: America's Role in the Technetronic Era*. In this 1970 futurist treatise on American political science, Brzezinski forecasts how "[t]he post-industrial society is becoming a 'technetronic' society: a society that is shaped culturally, psychologically, socially, and economically by the impact of technology and electronics – particularly in the area of computers and communications."[1] Almost fifty years later, President Donald Trump is ushering in Brzezinski's technetronic new age by accelerating President Barack Obama's 2009 Educate to Innovate initiative.[a]

According to the Obama White House archives, the technetronic Educate to Innovate program financed "science, technology, engineering, and mathematics" (STEM) education programs that were bankrolled with "over $700 million in public-private partnerships" between the federal government and "leading companies, foundations, non-profits, and science and engineering societies."[2] During Obama's presidency, which was counseled by Brzezinski,[b] [3] the corporatist Educate to Innovate project orchestrated pub-

a   The continuity of federal educational governance from the Democratic Obama Administration to the Republican Trump Administration at the White House parallels the continuity of state-level educational governance from Democrat Arne Duncan to Republican Bruce Rauner in Illinois. Like the Duncan-Rauner dialectic, the Obama-Trump dialectic exemplifies how the US educational system is stage-managed by the Hegelian "full-spectrum dominance" of bipartisan corporatism colluding to privatize public schooling for the purposes of "cradle-to-career" workforce planning.

b   On March 24th, 2010, a professional photographer who was employed by Obama's Executive Office of the President of the United States, Pete Souza, snapped an "Official White House Photo" of Brzezinski seated directly beside President Obama during a national security meeting. Prior to this advisory meeting, Brzezinski's endorsement of candidate Obama was instrumental to Barack's election to Commander in Chief, and on September 12, 2007, candidate Obama gave lic-private political-economic planning with "leaders such as Ursula Burns (Xerox), Sally Ride, Craig Barrett (formerly of Intel), and Glenn Britt (Time Warner Cable) to leverage the business community interest in improving STEM education. Together, they recruited over a 100 other CEOs."[4] Additionally, Obama's neoliberal regime pushed Brzezinski's technetronic agenda even further by "help[ing] [to] launch Change the Equation, a new [2010] non-profit with full-time staff dedicated to mobilizing the business community to improve the quality of STEM education in the United States."[5]

On September 25th of 2017, the technetronic policies underlying Obama's Educate to Innovate were ramped up by Trump's signature of a $200 million Presidential Memorandum on Creating Pathways to Jobs by Increasing Access to Jobs by Increasing Access to High-Quality Science, Technology, Engineering, and Mathematics (STEM) Education.[6] According to a report from the White House Office of Science and Technology Policy, "[t]his Presidential Memorandum (PM) directs the U.S. Secretary of Education to make promoting high-quality STEM and computer science education one of the Department of Education's top priorities, and beginning in fiscal year 2018, to take this priority into account when awarding competitive grant funds."[7] The Trump Administration also launched other STEM education initiatives such as Executive Order 13801 "Expanding Apprenticeships in America," which allocates federal resources for public-private "career-pathways" partnerships between schools and corporations that train students in hi-tech skills needed "to prepare workers for the jobs of the future."[8]

To condition students for these computerized jobs of the technetronic future, Secretary Betsy DeVos is advocating "virtual education" through public-private partnerships between public schools and for-profit ed-tech corporations that implement "adaptive-learning" computer modules in online courses or "blended-learning" classes that hybridize computerized

a campaign speech in which he referred to Brzezinski as "one of our most outstanding thinkers." Obama's love affair with Brzezinski is highlighted by historian Webster Griffin Tarpley, who wrote the following:

> Any lingering doubts about Obama's status as an abject puppet of Zbigniew Brzezinski and the Rockefeller Trilateral Commission ended this morning when the withered mummy of imperialism himself appeared on MSNBC's *Morning Joe* to campaign for Obama, urged on by his own moronic daughter, Mika Brzezinski, an Obama groupie and sycophant. Zbigniew, a low-level Polish aristocrat whose life has been devoted to hatred for Russia, lauded Obama for his 2002 speech opposing the Iraq war, saying that he himself was the source of Obama's arguments back then - thus confirming Obama's long-term status as his puppet, which probably began in 1981-1983, when Obama was a student at Columbia University, and Zbig was directing the anti-Russian institute.

After Zbig's death last year, former President Obama made the following statement: "Zbigniew Brzezinski was an accomplished public servant, a powerful intellect, and a passionate advocate for American leadership. His influence spanned several decades, and I was one of several Presidents who benefited from his wisdom and counsel."

instruction mixed with traditional human teaching. Moreover, to plan the technocratic economy of the future, these technetronic edu-corporations will data-mine each student's cognitive-behavioral learning algorithm(s) in order to predetermine his or her "career pathway" into a future-tech job under the "competency-based education" (CBE) stipulations of the new Every Student Succeeds Act (ESSA).

In retrospect, Brzezinski, who was a prominent member of the Council on Foreign Relations, presciently forecasted this future in which the schooling system is managed by private corporations that utilize computerized technologies to psycho-behaviorally condition students for workforce placement in a technocratically planned economy.[c][9] Of course, hi-tech cognitive-behavioral conditioning of the student body through stimulus-response learning algorithms for the purposes of technocratic workforce planning is exploitative enough. Yet there is a more sinister ulterior motive behind technetronic workforce conditioning through adaptive-learning CBE software: the replacement of human instructors with automated teaching bots to perfect the scientific management of hi-tech psychosocial engineering through public-private techno-fascism.

---

c   Brzezinski, who co-founded the Trilateral Commission with David Rockefeller Sr., foresaw the following predictions for technetronic education in the twenty-first century:

• *Virtual Schooling through Computerized Teaching Technetronics*: "The formal educational system has been relatively slow in exploiting the new opportunities for supplementary home-based education through television consoles and other electronic devices." However, "[a] good case can be made for ending initial education (more of which could be obtained in the home through electronic devices) somewhere around the age of eighteen."

• *For-Profit Ed-Tech and Corporate-Fascist Charter School Privatization*: [B]usiness[es] are becoming more involved in education, for psychological as well as for professional reasons. Greater multiplicity in educational training will make for a more pluralistic national community, and the increasing involvement of business companies in education may lead to a more rapid adaptation of the latest techniques and scientific knowledge to the educational process. American business and, to a lesser extent, government have already undertaken extensive programs of managerial "retooling" and retraining, thereby moving toward the intermittent educational pattern.

• *Workforce Training for "Career Pathways"*: [I]t [education] could be more generally pursued within a work-study framework, and it should be supplemented by periodic additional training throughout most of one's active life…

Th[e] formal initial period could be followed by two years of service in a socially desirable cause; then by direct involvement in some professional activity and by advanced, systematic training within that area; and finally by regular periods of one and eventually even two years of broadening "integrative" study at the beginning of every decade of one's life, somewhere up to the age of sixty…. Regular and formally required retraining – as well as broadening – could ensue at regular intervals throughout most of one's professional career.

• *Lifelong P-20/Cradle-to-Career Learning*: "The unprecedented spread of mass education in America raises the more general question whether mechanically extending the duration of education will suffice to meet both the psychological and technical needs of the emerging society…. By extending education on an intermittent basis throughout the lifetime of the citizen, society would go a long way."

"Individualized"/"Personalized" Education = Computerized Edu-Conditioning:

If you think that these dystopic predictions sound far-fetched, then consider the following statement given in 1984 by Dustin Heustin, a member of Utah's World Institute for Computer-Assisted Teaching:

> [w]e've been absolutely staggered by realizing that the computer has the capability to act as if it were ten of the top psychologists working with one student... Won't it be wonderful when the child in the smallest county in the most distant area or in the most confused urban setting can have the equivalent of the finest school in the world on that terminal and no one can get between that child and that curriculum?[10]

Note how Heustin is medicalizing ed-tech by comparing teaching software with psychologists, not with educators or academicians; Heustin's analogy clearly implicates that teaching computers are the hi-tech perfection of the stimulus-response method of psychological conditioning for the purposes of workforce schooling. Furthermore, notice how Heustin is glorifying instructional technologies that can supersede a human teacher or tutor from "get[ting] between" the student and the preprogrammed curriculum, thereby exalting educational technology above human teachers as the highest authority over the student's learning process. Lastly, observe how Heustin is implying that, by supplanting human instructors with computerized teaching technetronics, the traditional ratio of one teacher per several students is ostensibly inverted so that each student receives "individualized" attention from ten expert psychologists simultaneously.

This quote from Heustin is perhaps dated. Nonetheless, up-to-date adaptive-learning CBE technetronics currently deliver the same types of computerized learning that facilitate Heustin's dream of preventing human teachers from "get[ing] between" the student and the career-pathways conditioning software.

- **Affective-Behavioral Data-Mining for CBE Workforce Behaviorism:** Indeed, these adaptive-learning CBE technetronics are currently used to not only substitute human educators under the pretense of "individualized" instruction; they are also used to replace human psychologists as the digital stimulus-response algorithms are programmed to rewire a student's cognitive-behavioral conditioning. In fact, it is admitted that CBE adaptive-learning algorithms are derived from the stimulus-response psychological method of behaviorist conditioning.

A 2011 issue of the peer-reviewed journal, *Computers in Human Behavior*, explains how CBE-style adaptive-learning algorithms data-mine not only a student's academic content knowledge, but also his or her behavioral and affective responses to the computerized curriculum stimuli. This article, entitled "The Contribution of Learner Characteristics in the Development of *Computer-Based Adaptive Learning* Environments," reports that "[t]he development of learner models takes an active part in upcoming [computer-based] *adaptive learning* environments. The purpose of learner models is to drive personalization *based* on learner and *learning* characteristics … such as cognitive, affective and behavioral variables."[11] In other words, a student's adaptive-learning career-pathways algorithms are "model[ed]" from the "personaliz[ed]" data-mining of his or her behavioral reflex responses as well as his or her emotional and attitudinal responses to computerized lesson-plan stimuli.

This behavioral-affective adaptive-learning method of computerized workforce conditioning is guided by competency-based pedagogy, which is likewise rooted in the stimulus-response method of behaviorist psychology.[d] [12] In 2005, the *British Journal of Educational Technology* published an article that historicizes how computerized CBE can be traced back to the manipulation of behaviorist psychological sciences for workforce edu-conditioning:

[c]ompetency-based training (CBT) has its origins in the behaviourist movement which sought to focus attention on intended outcomes of learning and observable student behaviours (Bowden & Masters, 1993; Velde, 1999). This focus represented a shift from establishing an individual's "knowledge" to an emphasis on ability to competently perform specific workplace tasks and roles and, as argued by Velde (1999) and Mulcahy (2000), the adoption of CBT has been driven by economic and social forces, rather than educational ones.[13]

Entitled "Competency, Capability, Complexity and Computers: Exploring a New Model for Conceptualising End-User Computer

---

d   In "Schooling and the Myth of Objectivity: Stalking the Politics of the Hidden Curriculum," Dr. Henry Giroux affirms my historical analysis of OBE-CBE techno-conditioning. Giroux, who is Professor of English and Cultural Studies at McMaster University, reveals how "the technological and behaviorist models that have long exercised a powerful influence on the curriculum field were, in part, adapted from the scientific management movement of the 1920's, just as the roots of the competency-based education movement were developed in earlier research work adapted 'from the systems engineering procedures of the defense industry.'"

Education," this academic article examines how CBE pedagogy is integral to computerized adaptive-conditioning curriculums for STEM education: "[n]otions of competency have dominated the computer education literature, and have underpinned Competency-Based Training (CBT) in information technology at all levels of education and training."[14]

In sum, these scholarly publications reveal how students' career pathways curriculums are programmed by CBE adaptive-learning software that data-mine the students' cognitive, behavioral, and affective stimulus-response algorithms to "individualize" hi-tech workforce conditioning in a technocratic planned economy.

- **How Stimulus-Response UII "Personalizes" Workforce Conditioning:** Under competency-based education statutes, a student can learn at his or her own pace as he or she works through computerized teaching modules that "individualize" psycho-behavioral conditioning based on his or her performance. As the student generates responses to the computerized teaching stimuli, the software in turn generates "user interaction information" (UII), which the software then processes into "personalized" algorithms that determine the academic or career "pathway" a student must follow. If a student responds more or less proficiently to a computer stimulus, then the digitalized curriculum will be set for more or less challenging "academic" pathways (potentially at an accelerated pace); if a student responds more or less incompetently to a computer stimulus, then the digitalized curriculum will be set for more or less remediated "career" pathways (potentially at a slower pace). Thus, rather than all students receiving the same general curriculum delivered by a single human teacher, each student receives an "individualized" curriculum that is "personalized" according to his or her stimulus-response-based algorithms calculated by his or her UII generated on his or her separate computer-conditioning modules. The student's career or academic pathway may be further "personalized" according to the student's behavioral-affective responses associated with his or her cognitive-behavioral responses.

A 2015 issue of the peer-reviewed *Journal of Learning Analytics* breaks down this "personalized" stimulus-response process of data-mining psycho-behavioral UII for CBE workforce conditioning. The scholarly article, entitled "A Competence-based Service for Supporting Self-Regulated Learning in Virtual Environments," analyzes the "psychological mathematical framework" for data-mining UII with CBE adaptive-conditioning algorithms:

Competence-based Knowledge Space Theory (CbKST) incorporates psychological assumptions on underlying skills and competences required for solving specific problems (Korossy, 1997; Heller Steiner, Hockemeyer, & Albert, 2006). In this approach, competences are assigned to both learning objects (taught competences) and assessment items (tested competences)… CbKST provides adaptive assessment algorithms for efficiently determining the learner's current knowledge and competence state, which builds the basis for personalization purposes. Based on this learner information, personalized learning paths can be created. Goal setting can be done by defining skills to be achieved (competence goal) or problems to be capable of solving. The competence gap to be closed during learning is represented by the skills that are part of the goal, but not part of the competence state of a learner.[15]

To simplify this passage, a student's CBE career-path "goal[s]" are "personalized" by "psychological mathematical" adaptive-learning "algorithms" that are data-mined from the student's UII responses on computerized "assessment items (tested competencies)" as his or her UII responses are recursively conditioned with digital lesson stimuli programmed with "learning objects (taught competencies)."

Such CBE adaptive-conditioning software are commercialized for "personalized" edu-consumption through corporate-trademarked "courseware" programs, including Alta (engineered by the Knewton Corporation),[16] Intelligent Adaptive Learning™ (designed by the Dreambox Learning Corporation),[17] Brightspace LeaP™ (purchased from Knowillage Systems by the D2L Corporation),[18] and the Adaptive eLearning Platforms owned by the Smart Sparrow Corporation.[19] [e] [20] These and other for-profit courseware products are integrated into blended-learning classrooms at numerous KIPP charter schools; and they are also mainlined into online virtual schools such as Khan Academy and Capella University.[21]

In 2015, the American Enterprise Institute's (AEI) Center on Higher Education Reform published an article titled "The Student Experience: How Competency-Based Education Provid-

---

[e] Other Knewton courseware products are contracted with some of the biggest ed-tech corporations in the educational-industrial complex: Pearson Education, Houghton Mifflin Harcourt, and Cengage Learning. Dreambox is the beneficiary of millions of dollars in investments from Netflix CEO, Reed Hastings, who is also a corporate philanthropist who lobbies heavily for the overthrow of publicly elected school boards to be replaced with private charter councils that autocratically manage public-private charter-school corporations. D2L's Brightspace LeaP™ has even expanded its reaches internationally into Latin America through twenty-seven Aliat Universidades campuses across Mexico. Smart Sparrow is funded by ACT Inc., the corporation that designs, owns, and distributes the "American College Testing®" standardized test used for college admissions applications.

ers Serve Students," which reviews the "computer adaptive education" software programmed into the "FlexPath model at Capella."[22] According to the AEI, Capella's FlexPath courseware "individualize[s]" workforce edu-conditioning through

> course-based instruction [that] is maintained by bundling competencies within courses. Students register for particular courses and can work at their own pace and in any order to demonstrate mastery of each competency. Capella states that the assessments "simulate work you'll be expected to do on the job."
> 39 Students at Capella have personalized competency maps (figure 3) for each course that summarize how many competencies they have mastered and how many assessments they have completed.[23]

In a nutshell, Capella's online FlexPath platform conditions workforce competences through non-linear learning modules that allow the student to opt between various stimulus-response lesson paths that are sequenced throughout "personalized competency maps" for job-specific career-pathway curriculums.

Nevertheless, this "individualization" is not student centered. Instead, it is computer centered because a student's conditioning through a career-pathway curriculum is predetermined by the preprogrammed parameters of the adaptive-learning courseware algorithm(s). The CBE software algorithm cannot be fundamentally altered by student UII responses; for it is impossible to create a new career-pathway curriculum regardless of how ingeniously a student generates UII responses to the adaptive-learning stimulus data. It is only possible to vary the competence-lesson paths within a prescribed career-pathway curriculum.

The AEI concurs: "the components of traditional higher education programs that are typically the most flexible and able to be personalized (like choice of major, choice of classes within majors, and learning objectives within individual courses) are often fixed in CBE programs."[24] Obviously, if the "major ... classes ... and learning objectives" are all "fixed" in CBE computer-learning modules, then the only thing that could possibly be personalized are the competence paths which the student chooses to take through the fixed major, courses, and lessons that are required for certification in his or her prescribed career-pathway curriculum.

Ultimately, UII only enables the software algorithms to sort students "individually" into pre-planned career pathways because cognitive-behavioral stimulus-response algorithms cannot be scripted for jobs that have not yet been planned. As P. Wildman points out, "competencies tend to be prescriptive and are designed for a more stable environment with familiar problems."[25] In other words, competence-conditioning modules can only be preprogrammed with stimulus-response algorithms if those job competences have already been standardized in a "stable" career-pathway "environment" in which the particulars of workforce competences have been "familiar[ized]" and regimented in a planned economy.

Therefore, since workforce-competence algorithms are programmed in accordance with the market prospects and labor demands of a corporatist planned economy, such workforce-competence algorithms must be fixed within the parameters of industry-specific career-pathway quotas that have been preplanned by a public-private corporate-fascist elite. As a result, "[t]he problem with competency training," notes C. Price, "is that it is always in danger of equipping the young for the performance of yesterday's jobs" because corporate-government planning cannot account for the jobs of tomorrow which have not yet been planned.[26 f 27]

---

f   According to Charlotte Thomson Iserbyt, this de-individuated computerization of workforce conditioning is not only the corporate-fascist method of edu-conditioning; it is likewise the Soviet-communist method of collectivist-Statist edu-conditioning. In her article titled, "Heritage Foundation, NAFTA, School Choice and the Destruction of Traditional Education," Iserbyt quotes "Professor Eugene Boyce, University of Georgia ... : 'They [communists] do not educate for jobs that don't exist.'" Iserbyt elaborates:

> [n]o matter what your child wants to be/do in the future (welder or ballet dancer) his freedom to pursue his dreams will be limited by whether he is included in the school/business partnership's "quota" for training.
> Example: If he wants to be a welder at the shipbuilding company in your town, he will only be able to get training if he is fortunate enough to be included in the training quota. If the company only needs ten welders, and your son/daughter is No. 11 on the list, he/she will NOT receive training.

These parallels between communist and fascist workforce schooling through computer conditioning further demonstrate the Hegelian-dialectical full-spectrum dominance of both "leftwing" and "rightwing" educational politics that are dished out in semantically different flavors of the same pabulum of corporate-government collusion.

7

Disruptive DeVos and the AFC Push "Personalized" Virtual School Privatization

Harvard Business Professor Clayton Christensen forecasts that "smart learning platforms," such as stimulus-response adaptive-conditioning computers, will effectively overthrow human teachers. In his book *Disrupting Class: How Disruptive Technologies Will Change the Way the World Learns*, Christensen analyzes how smart-learning technetronics are "disruptive" technologies that will radically "disrupt" the traditional status quo of face-to-face education between a human teacher and a human student in a brick-and-mortar school.[1]

Christensen's book is corroborated by the American Legislative Exchange Council (ALEC), which is a corporatist interest group that lobbies to advance the for-profit expansion of privatized virtual charter school corporations. According to ALEC, "although current 'consumers' of online learning are few in number, a 'disruption' will occur when the market realizes the benefits of this practice. Then, it will become the dominant provider." Once virtual edu-conditioning through mobile technetronics becomes the "dominant provider" of schooling, human teachers will be relegated to virtual extinction.[2] [a] [3]

Secretary of Education Betsy DeVos is currently calling for the expansion of virtual schools and blended-learning classes that emphasize "individualized" or "personalized" learning, which are merely euphemisms for the

---

[a]　In his book, *Schooling and the Struggle for Public Life: Democracy's Promise and Education's Challenge*, the acclaimed "critical education" theorist, Dr. Henry Giroux, deconstructs the technocratic stratagem behind "teacher-proofing" policies and pedagogies such as "MBO (management by objectives), PBBS (performance-based budgeting systems), CBE (competency-based education), CBTE (competency-based teacher education), and MCT (minimum competency testing)." Debunking this alphabet soup of techno-education jargon, Giroux reveals how

> [t]he growing removal of curriculum development and analysis from the hands of teachers is related to the ways technocratic rationality is used to redefine teachers' work. This type of rationality increasingly takes place within a social division of labor in which thinking is removed from implementation and the model of the teacher becomes that of the technician or white-collar clerk. Likewise, learning is reduced to the memorization of narrowly defined facts and isolated pieces of information that can easily be measured and evaluated.

same "disruptive" types of computerized adaptive-learning that substitute human teachers with CBE stimulus-response algorithms programmed for career-pathways training. In fact, DeVos's technetronic workforce training agenda as Secretary of Ed is actually the culmination of her long history as a corporate-philanthropic activist who touts "individualized/personalized" career-pathways education through virtual charter schools, online courses, and computer-hybrid blended-learning classes.

In a speech at the 2015 SXSW EDU Conference, DeVos advocated for expanding "virtual schools and online learning" into an "open system of choices," which is merely a euphemism for privatizing virtual schools in a corporate-government system of competitive public-private charter school corporations that parents and students can choose between.[4]

During this SXSW EDU speech, DeVos spelled out her techno-fascist vision for the future of "individualized/personalized" education:

> [t]his is not a battle of left versus right or Democrat versus Republican.
> It's a battle of Industrial Age versus the Digital Age…
> It's old factory model versus the new internet model.
> It's the luddites versus the future.
> We must open up the education industry (and let's not kid ourselves that it isn't an industry); we must open it up to entrepreneurs and innovators…
> This is how a student who's not learning in their current model can find an individualized learning environment that will meet their needs.
> We are the beneficiaries of start-ups, ventures, and innovation in every other area of life, but we don't have that in education because it's a closed system…
> As long as education remains a closed system, we will never see the education equivalents of Google, Facebook, Amazon, Paypal, Wikipedia, or Uber.[5]

In other words, DeVos envisions a future in which the cognitive-behavioral workforce training of each student is "individual[ly]" conditioned by disruptive ed-tech streamlined across privatized virtual charter schools through public-private contracts with monopolistic Big Tech corporations managed by venture capitalist oligarchs such as Eric Schmidt, Mark Zuckerberg, Jeff Bezos, and Peter Thiel. Anyone who contests this corporate-technocratic edu-conditioning endgame, according to Billionaire Betsy, is nothing more than a backward crank, or a techno-phobic luddite.[b][6]

---

b   Not long after her commencement as Secretary of Education, DeVos even used the ad

Prior to being appointed Secretary of Education, Betsy DeVos was a founder,[7] funder,[8] board member, and Chairperson of the Great Lakes Education Project,[9] a nonprofit interest group that pushes "school choice" privatization through virtual schools and other public-private charter schools.[10] Additionally, DeVos was formerly Chair of the American Federation for Children (AFC),[11] which is another "school choice" nonprofit that lobbies for virtual charter school privatization. As Chair, DeVos made the following statement on behalf of the AFC in 2015: "[f]amilies want and deserve access to all education options, including charter schools, private schools and virtual schools.... [V]irtual schools are growing across the country. Greater innovation and choice will contribute to better K-12 educational outcomes for our children."[12]

After taking office as the US Secretary of Education, technocrat DeVos reasserted her commitment to the AFC's mission to "individualized" edu-conditioning through virtual charter school corporatization. During her address at the AFC's Eighth Annual National Policy Summit entitled "Opening Doors, Opening Windows," Secretary DeVos promoted "school choice" and ed-tech innovation as "the only way to give kids an equal opportunity to a quality education and an education that fits their unique individual needs."[13] In particular, she endorsed "charter school[s]," "online school[s]," and "any customized combination of those schools ... in an educational setting yet to be developed.... Education should elevate the role of technology to fully enter the twenty-first century."[14]

In sum, Secretary DeVos and her cronies at the AFC have a consistent track record of teaming up to lobby for virtual school choice privatization under the presuppositions that digital learning technetronics such as adaptive-learning computers will "individualize," or "personalize," educational methods of cognitive-behavioral conditioning.

The Atlantic affirms my analysis of the DeVos-AFC mission for "personalized" virtual schooling through stimulus-response adaptive-learning technetronics:

> [t]his vision was clear throughout the American Federation for Children [Eighth Annual National Policy] summit: that schools need to be reinvented with an emphasis on technology.... [Online schools were a key part of that vision...
>
> Advocates say that online schools have the potential to harness "personalized learning," a term that generally means using technology to provide an education tailored to each student's needs.[15]

hominem "flat-earther" to denounce her detractors who reject virtual school choice. Techno-elitist DeVos spouted this pejorative during her speech at the American Federation for Children's National Policy Summit in Indianapolis, on May 22, 2017.

As I have documented throughout this article, online and blended-learning ed-tech that can "tailor" lessons on a "personalized" basis require stimulus-response adaptive-learning software that data-mine students' cognitive-behavioral UII.

The Atlantic's summation of the AFC's "personalized" ed-tech summit is confirmed by comments from Kevin Chavous, who is a founding board member and executive counsel of the AFC. At the AFC summit,[16] Chavous predicted that "[t]he endgame ... is personalized learning.... We are going to get to this place where, as opposed to every child being shepherded into a schoolhouse where they sit in a classroom and where a teacher stands and delivers, and then they regurgitate back ... those days are not going to be the future."[17] Notice here how Chavous is highlighting that a fundamental feature of "personalized" digital learning is the removal of "a teacher [who] stands and delivers." Clearly, if there is no human teacher who delivers the curriculum in person, then this upgraded system of "personalized" edu-conditioning must supplant the human teacher with a network of computerized "teaching machines" that deliver the lessons through stimulus-response adaptive-learning technetronics.

Chavous, a longtime DeVos crony at the AFC, is also the Chair of the Foundation for Online and Blended Learning,[18] and he sat on the Executive Team of Jeb Bush's Digital Learning Council alongside representatives from Apple, Google, Microsoft, Cisco Systems, Intel, Dell, SMART Technologies, Blackboard, the Gates Foundation, the Carnegie Corporation, Educational Testing Service, Pearson Education, Houghton Mifflin, Connections Academy, K12 Inc., the AFC, the US Department of Energy, and ALEC.[19]

It should be noted here that Chavous is playing both sides of the Hegelian-dialectical fence via his coalition with Republicans Jeb Bush and Betsy DeVos; for Chavous is a staunch Democrat who co-founded Democrats for Education Reform shortly before he served on President Obama's education policy committee as part of his re-election campaign.[20] Indeed, to complete the Hegelian-dialectical dance, Jeb also spoke at Chavous's AFC summit where the neo-conservative urged the expansion of "student-centered ... customized" "school choice" that addresses the "uniqueness of each person" through "personalized" ed-tech.[21] Bush called for more students to become "career ready" to be "capable of riding this technological wave" into the future of hi-tech jobs in "artificial intelligence," "wireless technology," "the internet of things," "robotics," and "innovations across the board."[22]

Synthesis:

The Hegelian-dialectical perpetuation of corporate-technocratic schooling continues on: just as the neo-liberals Barack Obama and Arne Duncan carried the technetronic torch of leftist Zbigniew Brzezinski while perpetuating the charter school corporatization schemes of the rightwing George W. Bush Administration and the neo-con Heritage Foundation; so too is alt-right DeVos perpetuating this very same corporatist charter school agenda championed by both Obama and Bush alike, while her bipartisan collusion with Democrat Chavous and Republican Jeb is perpetuating the Obama-Brzezinski mission to mainstream edu-conditioning through online and blended-learning technetronics that utilize stimulus-response adaptive-learning algorithms.

8

The DeVos-Bush Connection and ALEC's Virtual Public Schools Act

As education's discontents peak to tyrannical proportions, teachers across America have been striking en masse in states like Oklahoma,[1] Arizona,[2] and Colorado.[3] Perhaps too little too late, though, because the US Supreme Court ruling over *Janus v. AFSCME* has essentially revoked the labor rights of teachers' unions.[4] Now that the collective bargaining rights of teachers have been effectively rescinded, it will be open season for Secretary of Ed DeVos and former Governor Jeb Bush to corporatize the American schooling system through public-private charter school partnerships which substitute human teachers with virtual ed-tech products that automate "competency-based" workforce education through psycho-behavioral adaptive-learning algorithms.

The corporatist ed-tech allegiance between Betsy DeVos and Jeb Bush is not limited to their American Federation for Children coalition. In chapter five, I report on alliances between the Trump-DeVos Administration and members of Jeb's Foundation for Educational Excellence (FEE),[5] which is a nonprofit corporation that promotes "competency-based education" methods through various forms of public-private "school choice,"[6] including virtual and online education.[7] [a] [8] Furthermore, there are also ties between DeVos and Bush through the American Legislative Exchange Council (ALEC), which is a corporate team of lawyers and lobbyists who draft boilerplate bills that are adopted by legislators to expand public-private partnerships and other privatization schemes such as the corporatization of virtual charter schools.

On September 16th, 2011, the ALEC Board of Directors approved their Resolution Adopting the 10 Elements of High-Quality Digital Learning for K-12, which aims to propagate personalized virtual education across

---

a   Education reporter for the Washington Post, Valerie Strauss, investigated leaked emails from the nonprofit In the Public Interest, which exposed how "Maine moved [Jebs'] FEE policy agenda through legislation and executive order that would remove barriers to online education and in some cases would require online classes – including eliminating class size caps and student-teacher ratios, allowing public dollars to flow to online schools and classes, eliminate ability of local school districts to limit access to virtual schools."

the United States.[9] These "10 Elements" are adopted from Jeb Bush's Digital Learning Council, which proclaims that its mission is to collaborate "with leaders in education, government, philanthropy, business, technology and think tanks to define the actions that lawmakers and policymakers must take to spark a revolution in K-12 digital learning."[10] In fact, ALEC's 10 Elements Resolution admits that its nationwide virtual-ed campaign is guided by the recommendations of Bush's corporate-technocrat cronies at his Digital Learning Council: "[w]hereas, in August 2010, Governors Jeb Bush and Robert Wise launched the Digital Learning Council ... resulting in the creation of the 10 Elements of High Quality Digital Learning ... it is the intent of this [ALEC] Resolution that the 10 Elements be used as a framework from which to draft legislation specific to each state's needs."[11]

Specifically, Bush's 10 Elements are used by ALEC as a legal framework for instituting "personalized" edu-conditioning through digitalized CBE learning: "3. Personalized learning: All students can customize their education using digital content through an approved digital learning provider. 4. Advancement: Students progress based on demonstrated competency."[12] This fourth "Advancement" clause is a "competency-based education" (CBE) stipulation that permits students to earn "credits" based on their "competent" responses to digitalized adaptive-learning stimuli that are "personalized" according to the cognitive-behavioral algorithms data-mined from the students' stimulus-response feedback loops.

This "personalized" CBE pedagogy of Bush's 10 Elements guides the nationwide implementation of ALEC's Virtual Public Schools Act: a "template" bill for various state and federal legislators that defines a "'[virtual school' [as] an independent public school in which the school uses technology in order to deliver a significant portion of instruction to its students via the Internet in a virtual or remote setting."[13]

ALEC's Education Task Force, which is currently co-chaired by Republican State Senator of Utah Howard Stephenson,[14] has disseminated the Virtual Public Schools Act to key lawmakers, such as Republican State Representative of Tennessee, Harry Brooks, who introduced and passed ALEC's Virtual Public Schools Act basically verbatim as his own legislation in 2011.[15]

In Texas, State Senator Florence Shapiro was the Republican Chair of the Senate Education Committee at the same time she sat on ALEC's Education Task Force in 2011, the same year that ALEC adopted Bush's 10 Elements of High Quality Digital Learning. As Chair of the Education Committee, Shapiro passed legislation that mandated virtual public schools to receive the same amount of tax funding as brick-and-mortar public schools.[16]

Similarly, Wisconsin State Representative Robin Vos was also the Wisconsin State Chair of ALEC at the same time that she sponsored a bill pushing vast expansion of for-profit virtual schools under Governor Scott Walker's school privatization agenda. According to the Center for Media and Democracy, this Vos-sponsored bill closely resembles the Virtual Public Schools Act template.[17]

In addition, *Truth Out* reports that Virginia Governor Bob McDonnell requested that the Virginia State Legislature introduce a 2010 law modeled on ALEC's Virtual Public Schools Act. The governor's request was prompted after he received campaign donations amounting to "tens of thousands of dollars" from lobbyists representing K12 Inc., a virtual charter school corporation which capitalized on the passage of the bill by setting up shop

> in Carroll County, one of the state's most impoverished counties, to maximize the public money it would receive. Even when the school board voted to close K12 Inc. down because it did worse than traditional schools on 20 out of 22 measures, Virginia legislators with ALEC connections enacted a law in 2012 requiring high school students to take an online course to graduate.[18]

This 2012 law was part of Governor Bob McDonnell's 2012 "'Opportunity to Learn' Education Agenda,"[19] which was vocally supported by Betsy DeVos.[20] [b] [21]

Perhaps the greatest beneficiaries of this nationwide expansion of ALEC legislation are K12 Inc. and Connections Education LLC, which are both for-profit virtual edu-corporations that operate chains of online and blended-learning charter schools. When the Virtual Public Schools Act was drafted and approved by ALEC in 2004,[22] both K12 Inc. and the Connections Academy branch of the parent LLC were corporate members of the School Choice Subcommittee of ALEC's Education Task Force.[23]

In fact, in Diane Ravitch's book, *Reign of Error: The Hoax of the Privatization Movement and the Danger to America's Public Schools*,[24] the former

b   It should be noted that McDonnell ended up the first Virginia Governor to be convicted of a felony, and was sentenced to two years in federal prison on eleven counts of corruption, including extortion, bribery, and conspiracy, although the United States Supreme Court later overturned the conviction.

Assistant Secretary of Education under George H. W. Bush exposes how the Co-Chair of ALEC's Education Task Force was Mickey Revenaugh:[25] the Executive Vice President of the Connections Education company who also presided over the 2011 vote to adopt Jeb Bush's 10 Elements at ALEC's 38th Annual Meeting in New Orleans titled "Solutions for the States."[26] Revenaugh drafted the Virtual Public Schools Act with the help of Bryan Flood of K12 Inc. and Don Lee,[27] who at the time of drafting the legislation was a State Representative of Colorado until he moved on to become a lobbyist as Vice President for Government Affairs at K12 Inc.[28]

Betsy and her husband, Dick DeVos, were once invested in the K12 Inc. Corporation, although they divested their shares before Betsy became US Secretary of Ed.[29] Moreover, Tom Bolvin of K12 Inc. is currently the Private Chair of ALEC's Education Task Force,[30] and the current President of Academics, Policy, and Schools at K12 Inc. is none other than Kevin Chavous, who also formerly sat on the K12 Inc. Board of Directors at the same time that he partnered with Betsy DeVos at the AFC.[31]

In addition, K12 Inc. and Connections Academy sponsored the AFC's Eighth Annual National Policy Summit where DeVos laid out her objectives for the future of "personalized" virtual edu-conditioning through CBE-style stimulus-response technetronics.[32] During DeVos's tenure as Chair of the American Federation for Children, the AFC was a "Director-Level" sponsor of ALEC's 2012 Annual Meeting,[33] and the AFC was also a "Trustee-Level" sponsor of both ALEC's 2013 Annual Meeting as well as ALEC's 2011 Annual Meeting where Bush's 10 Elements were adopted.[34 c 35]

Now that DeVos is running the US Department of Ed, she has renewed her vows to ALEC's virtual school corporatization stratagem as she announced that she is "look[ing] forward to working with you [ALEC]" in her official capacity as Secretary of Education. During her speech at the ALEC headquarters on July 20th, 2017, Secretary DeVos professed her Administration's commitment to ALEC's mission to "individualize" corporate "school choice" that "personalizes" "the quality education that best fits [each] child's unique, individual needs."[36] In the previous chapters, I prove that DeVos's "personalized"/"individualized" "school choice" is nothing more than a code phrase for virtual adaptive-learning through CBE workforce-conditioning software.

---

c   Today, a top lobbyist for the AFC is former Speaker of the Wisconsin State Assembly, Scott Jensen, who was also the Wisconsin State Chair of ALEC. It is worth noting that Jensen was convicted on three counts of felony misconduct in office, although an appeals court later overturned these convictions.

Unfortunately, DeVos affirmed her Secretarial commitment to ALEC's "personalized" virtual-ed corporatization despite the fact that "personalized" virtual charter schools have an atrocious track record of performing below the minimal standards of the public brick-and-mortar schools that are purported to be inferior to the so-called "personalized" learning of such virtual schools.[d] [37] Notwithstanding these facts, Secretary DeVos's continued allegiance to ALEC's Virtual Public Schools Act effectively asserts her true belief that "personalized" virtual-learning technetronics are "upgraded" substitutes for the "status quo" of traditional human teaching.

---

[d]   According to the Schott Foundation for Public Education, DeVos falsely reported inflated graduation rates for several virtual charter schools, including Utah Virtual Academy (96%), Idaho Virtual Academy (90%), and Oklahoma Virtual Charter Academy High School (91%), which actually only graduated 42%, 33%, and 40% respectively. Other dismal graduation statistics have been calculated for the 2016-2017 school year at the Indiana Virtual School when only 61 of its 900 seniors earned diplomas, and it only spent 10% of its budget on actual instruction versus the meager 66% typically spent on instruction at other Indiana virtual schools. Similarly, after incurring sanctions from the Indiana State Board of Education due to failure to meet minimum academic standards, the Hoosier Academy Virtual School opted to shut down operations. In another case of defunct virtual charter schooling, the Ohio Department of Education has ordered the e-school corporation, Electronic Classrooms of Tomorrow (ECOT), to repay upwards of $19 million in public funds because ECOT cannot document actual attendance of 9,000 of the 15,300 students purportedly enrolled (ECOT is appealing to the Ohio Supreme Court). A comparable ruling by the California Department of Education ordered California Virtual Academies to pay back almost $2 million dollars for unverified attendance reports and other misappropriations of public funds. Yet another botched e-school, Tennessee Virtual Academy, which could not meet the state's minimum learning outcomes, closed operations after the state legislature failed to pass a bill to reduce the minimum learning standards that e-students were required to meet at TNVA.

9

Virtual School in a Computerized Box: A History of Technocratic Education from the "Skinner Box" to "School in a Box"

The "Adjustive/Adaptive" and "Integrating" Functions of Education:

To those familiar with the darker pages of America's history of public schooling, ALEC's technocratic prospects for usurping teachers with corporate workforce-conditioning computers will come as no surprise. In the 1918 book *Principles of Secondary Education*, Harvard Professor Alexander Inglis theorized "six basic functions" of schooling, including the "integrating function" and the "adjustive, or adaptive, function," both of which are authoritarian functions of autocratic schooling.[1] Upon close reading of Inglis's century-old educational functions, it is apparent that DeVos's and ALEC's schemes to "individuate" virtual edu-conditioning are nothing less than the corporate-technocratic perfection of authoritarian educational psychology methods that have been funded by Robber Baron philanthropy to manage workforce schooling for over one hundred years.

In "Against School," the 1991 New York State Teacher of the Year, John Taylor Gatto, historicizes how Inglis's "adjustive/adaptive" function of education "establish[es] fixed habits of reaction to authority. This, of course, precludes critical judgment completely."[2] [a] [3] Undoubtedly, there is only one way to achieve machine precision in programming each student with fixed, machine-like cognitive-behavioral reflexes to authority: supplant the human instructor with a machine.

By removing the idiosyncratic elements of human personality, and then substituting those unpredictable variables with standardized adaptive-learn-

---

a   Gatto adds, "It also pretty much destroys the idea that useful or interesting material should be taught, because you can't test for reflexive obedience until you know whether you can make kids learn, and do, foolish and boring things."

ing software, privatized virtual charter schools can ensure computerized scientific management over curriculums. As a result, virtual edu-corporations can ensure fixed student-learning outcomes that are autocratically planned by public-private partnerships between ed-tech companies and charter school corporations contracting with State education departments and local school districts. In particular, standardized "adjustive/adaptive" software eliminates the possibility that a human teacher like Gatto, who routinely broke away from official curriculums, might inspire students to cultivate critical judgment of authority as creative thinkers who pursue goals outside their prescribed career pathways in the planned economy.[b] [4]

Perfecting adjustive/adaptive courseware that fix student submission to authority will also perfect Inglis's "integrating function" of schooling, which according to Gatto "might well be called 'the conformity function,' because its intention is to make children as alike as possible. People who conform are predictable, and this is of great use to those who wish to harness and manipulate a large labor force."[5] Obviously, a student with fixed cognitive-behavioral reflexes to authority will conform to the fascistic hierarchy of the collective public-private workforce by duly conforming to his or her digitally prescribed career/caste which is subordinated to the corporate-government power-structure of the technocratic planned economy.

To be sure, the supposed "individualization" of "competency-based" virtual curriculums is only "personalized" insofar as the stimulus-response adaptive-learning software can vary the pace of prescribed lessons which digitally condition a student for either job-specific workforce training through career pathways or discipline-specific university preparation through academic curriculums. Nonetheless, each "individualized" academic- or career-path algorithm still conforms to fixed obedience to corporate-government authority over political-economic planning because the digital range of career- and academic-pathway curriculums is preprogrammed by industry-specific quotas that are preplanned by public-private partnerships between Big Business and Big Government.

---

b   Gatto explains,

[o]ften I had to defy custom, and even bend the law, to help kids break out of this trap [of conditioned arrested development].
    The empire struck back, of course; childish adults regularly conflate opposition with disloyalty. I once returned from a medical leave to discover that all evidence of my having been granted the leave had been purposely destroyed, that my job had been terminated, and that I no longer possessed even a teaching license. After nine months of tormented effort I was able to retrieve the license when a school secretary testified to witnessing the plot unfold. In the meantime, my family suffered more than I care to remember. By the time I finally retired in 1991, I had more than enough reason to think of our schools – with their long-term, cell-block style, forced confinement of both students and teachers – as virtual factories of childishness.

In the final equation, Inglis's adjustive/adaptive and integrating functions, which standardize fixed conformity to corporate and government authorities over political-economic workforce planning, are the prime-directive functions of technocratic schooling; and the "diagnostic/directive" function, "differentiating function," and "propaedeutic" function, which classify individual students into different career or academic pathways, are all subordinated to the overriding adjustive/adaptive and integrating functions.[c] The ultimate outcome of this hierarchy of educational functions is the conformity of a highly specialized two-class power-structure controlled by a fascistic political-economic authority through the manipulation of Big Data cached by ed-tech companies that data-mine student psychometrics for workforce placement and job-competence conditioning directed by the public-private plans of Big Government in bed with Big Business.

These dystopian prospects for education may seem futuristic, but the truth is that this authoritarian vision of computerized schooling is over a hundred years old.

The Skinner Box:

Throughout the 1950s and 1960s, Burrhus Frederic Skinner, the godfather of operant conditioning psychology,[6] formulated mechanized multiple-choice "teaching machines" that are often historicized as the first widely recognized proto-computerized teaching technetronics.[7] Nevertheless, the first known prototype of a "teaching machine" was invented and patented by Ohio State University Professor of Psychology, Sidney L. Pressey,[8] in 1924.[9] In fact, B. F. Skinner himself cites Pressey as the first real inventor of a functional "teaching machine." In Skinner's 1968 book, *The Technology of Teaching*, the Harvard Professor of Psychology acknowledges how[10]

> Sydney L. Pressey designed several machines for the automatic testing of intelligence and information.... A recent model of one of these is shown in Figure 3. In using the device the student refers to a numbered item in a multiple-choice test. He presses the button corresponding to his first choice of answer. If he is right, the device moves on to the next item; if he is wrong, the error is tallied, and he must continue to make choices until he is right.[11] [d] [12]

---

c   For a detailed breakdown of the diagnostic/directive function, the differentiating function, and the propaedeutic function in "cradle-to-career" workforce education at public-private charter schools, review chapter two.

d   Skinner adds, "[t]he Navy's 'Self-Rater' is a larger version of Pressey's machine. The items are printed on code-punched plastic cards fed by the machine. The time required to answer is tak-

To be sure, the conceptualization of the teaching machine can be traced even further back to Edward Lee Thorndike. Actually, in his 1914 book entitled *Education: A First Book*, Thorndike first postulated his own vision of essentially the very same engineering design utilized for Pressey's prototypical teaching machine described by B. F. in 1968. Thorndike's book hypothesized that "[i]f, by a miracle of mechanical ingenuity, a book could be so arranged that only to him who had done what was directed on page one would page two become visible, and so on, much that now requires personal instruction could be managed by print."[13] Notice that Pressey's first teaching machines do not "move on to the next item" unless the student supplies the "right" response, thereby fulfilling Thorndike's dream of a mechanical "book" that conditions students by not allowing "page two [to] become visible" unless they "had done what was directed on page one."

E. L. Thorndike's vision of a mechanized teaching book was extrapolated from his psychological research into the stimulus-response learning processes of animal cognition that he studied extensively through his proto-behaviorist "puzzle box" experiments.[14] These "puzzle box" studies were the forerunners to the "Skinner box" animal experiments from which B. F. derived the methodology of operant-conditioning reinforcement scheduling that he adapted to upgrade Pressey's seminal teaching machines.[15] In B. F.'s *Technology of Teaching*,[e] [16] Figures 7 and 8 exhibit pictures of his Skinner-box experiments of rats and pigeons, and he discusses how these operant-conditioning animal-training experiments produced the stimulus-response conditioning data which he systematized to re-engineer Pressey's teaching machines.[17] [f] [18]

---

en into account in scoring."

e   In the "Acknowledgments" section of *The Technology of Teaching*, Skinner gives special thanks to Skull-and-Bonesman "McGeorge Bundy, former Dean of the Graduate School of Arts and Sciences [at Harvard University]," who was "responsible for Harvard's Committee on Programmed Instruction," which assigned its Director James G. Holland to assist with "the use of teaching machines in my [Skinner's] course on human behavior." B. F. also gives thanks for "financial support from the Ford Foundation, [and] the Carnegie Corporation," the former of which was controlled by two prominent Bonesmen from 1966 until 1981: Harold Howe II, who was the Vice President of the Ford Foundation from 1971 to 1981, and McGeorge Bundy himself, who was the President of the Ford Foundation from 1966 to 1979. Bundy would later become a "Scholar in Residence" at the Carnegie Corporation from 1990 to 1996.

f   Skinner so believed in the universality of his animal conditioning experiments applied to educational psychology that he asserted, "I could make a pigeon a high achiever by reinforcing it on a proper schedule." This over-the-top faith in his own animal-training psychology in the classroom was fueled by Skinner's belief that "[o]perant conditioning shapes behavior as a sculptor shapes a lump of clay." By comparing human students to "bird-brained" pigeons and passive lumps of clay, Skinner reveals the authoritarian objectives behind the "teaching machine" revolution which has progressed into the contemporary computerized ed-tech revolution rolled into the corporatist "school choice" privatization movement being hyped by Secretary DeVos and ALEC.

According to the Smithsonian National Museum of American History,

> [i]n the 1950s, the psychologist B. F. Skinner of Harvard University suggested that techniques he had developed for training rats and pigeons might be adopted for teaching humans. He used this apparatus teaching a Harvard course in natural sciences.
>
> The machine is a rectangular wooden box with a hinged metal lid with windows. Various paper discs fit inside, with questions and answers written along radii of the discs. One question at a time appears in the window nearer the center. The student writes an answer on a paper tape to the right and advances the mechanism. This reveals the correct answer but covers his answer so that it may not be changed.
>
> Skinner's "programmed learning" was refined and adopted in many classrooms in the 1960s. It underlies techniques still used in instruction for the office, the home and the school.[19]

In his *Technology of Teaching*, Skinner exhibits photographs of some of his "programmed learning" teaching machines,[g][20] which are expounded in the following captions:

> **1. FIGURE 4.** Machine first used to teach part of the author's [Skinner's] course at Harvard University. (An indexing phonograph to supply auditory stimuli is shown on the right.) Material is printed on the segments of a disk. The student inserts a disk in the machine and closes it; the machine cannot then be opened until he has completed the work. One frame of material appears in the window near the center. The student writes his response on a strip of paper exposed at the right. By lifting a lever at the left of the front side of the machine, the student moves the response he has written under a transparent cover and uncovers the correct response in the upper corner of the central frame. If his response is correct, he moves the lever to the right, thus punching a hole alongside the response he has called correct and altering the machine so that that particular frame will not appear again when he works around the disk a second time. When the lever is returned to its starting position, a new frame appears. (This machine was demonstrated at the annual meeting of the American Psychological Association, September, 1957.).[21]

---

g   Figure 11 is a photo of another Skinner-box teaching machine that is equipped with a "dispenser on the top of the machine which delivers tokens, candies, or coins" as "rewards," or "positive reinforcement" stimuli, that condition the student to make correct "matching choices" associated with the preprogrammed learning outcomes.

2. FIGURE 5. A machine similar to that in Figure 4. Material appears in the window at the left. The student is writing his response on a strip of paper exposed through the small window at this right. By moving a sliding knob at the upper right, he draws a transparent cover over his response and uncovers additional material at the right end of the larger window. This may tell him whether or not his response was correct, often without telling him the correct response. It may also supply additional material. The same movement of the slider uncovers additional space on the strip of paper upon which the student writes a second response if necessary. A further movement of the slider draws a transparent cover over the second response and uncovers the correct response in the large window. A new frame of the material, which is printed on a fan-folded tape, is moved into place by turning the large knob near the student's left hand. The machine cannot be operated until tightly closed and cannot again be opened except by punching a hole in the answer strip. The panel at the rear may hold material to which the program refers.[22]

Consider Skinner's question/answer stimulus-response method of his mechanized operant conditioning devices explicated in figure captions 4 and 5; and compare it to the question-answer stimulus-response method of Pressey's proto-typical multiple-choice teaching machine detailed in figure caption 3. The only apparent difference between the mechanized "Pressey box" and the Skinner-box teaching machine is that the latter sequences the multiple-choice question-answer lessons according to the reinforcement-scheduling principles of operant conditioning, which are "programmed" into Skinner's "teaching boxes" through an extensive series of "lever[s]," "slider[s]," "disk[s]," "frame[s]," "window[s]," and other mechanized gadgets such as a "phonograph."

Now compare Skinnerian mechanized edu-conditioning to the computerized stimulus-response method of operant conditioning that is sequenced through digitalized lesson-plan windows on adaptive-learning software programmed with "career-pathways" curriculums that are "personalized" with UII workforce-training algorithms. Basically, there are only two differences between Skinner-box teaching machines and adaptive-learning computer software:

1. The literal, slide-operated "windows" filled with paper learning stimuli that were "programmed" into the mechanized Skinner box have been converted into keyboard/mouse-operated digital win-

dows that display learning stimuli through pixelated 2D and voxelated 3D computer graphics.

2. The cacophony of mechanized contraptions engineered into the Skinner "teaching box" to sequence paper stimulus-response lessons with "individualized" operant-conditioning schedules have been converted into hi-speed digital algorithms that "personalize" operant-conditioning schedules based on real-time software data-mining of the student's cognitive-behavioral responses to digital learning stimuli.

Project BEST:

During the development of microprocessor computing in the 1980s, Skinner's mechanized "teaching box" was revolutionized into the first digitally sequenced teaching computers for programming students with fixed cognitive-behavioral reflexes to corporate-government authority. In fact, according to a 1983 issue of *Education Week*, B. F. admitted that 80s "computers ... are essentially sophisticated versions of the 'teaching machines' of the 1960s."[23] To streamline the institutionalization of such Skinnerian teaching computers, the Association for Educational Computing and Technology (AECT) was awarded an $855,282 federal grant in 1981 to implement Project BEST (Better Education Skills Through Technology), which laid out the blueprint for the public-private technocratic schooling system that is currently being taken to the next level by DeVos, ALEC, and K12 Inc.[24]

Charlotte Thomson Iserbyt blew the whistle on this corporate-technocratic education initiative in 1982 when she was the Senior Policy Advisor in the Office of Educational Research and Improvement for the US Department of Education under the Ronald Reagan Administration. Iserbyt leaked several internal documents from the Department of Ed pertaining to Project BEST, such as an informational brochure that states, "Project BEST is a cooperative effort involving both the federal, state, and local government and the private sector in the planning and use of modern information technologies to improve the effectiveness of basic skills, teaching and learning."[25] This document reveals that Project BEST spent almost one million dollars of federal tax revenues on public-private political-economic plans to plug students into Skinnerian IT computers that psycho-behaviorally condition learning outcomes to fulfill job quotas for corporate-technocratic workforce planning.

Another internal memo leaked by Iserbyt describes how Project BEST would set up the federal precursors to the public-private P-20 fusion of education and healthcare at the state level: "the State Team approach and the communications network with professional associations and other groups established by the project will serve as a model for the states in implementing similar efforts in other areas of education, or in such program areas as health, human services, housing, transportation, etc."[26] To plan the public-private conglomeration of technetronic education with hi-tech health and human services, the document titled "Project BEST Dissemination Design Considerations" outlines strategies to "[c]ontrol or [m]anipulate ... State participation/selection process[;] ... [t]raining of state leaders[;] ... [and] [p]erception of the need to use technology."[27] Stated differently, Project BEST's "State Team approach" "manipulate[s]" State and local control of hi-tech edu-conditioning through public-private partnerships between privatized charter school corporations, ed-tech companies, for-profit healthcare corporations, and medical-tech companies contracted with conglomerated public school districts and public health departments at the State and local levels.

The Director of Project BEST was Donald P. Ely,[28] who was also Editor and Chairman of the Definition and Terminology Committee of the AECT.[29] Ely published his 1963 "The Role of the Computer in Future Instructional Systems" in the *Audiovisual Communication Review*,[30] and he also authored "The Field of Educational Technology: A Statement of Definition," which was printed in *Audiovisual Instruction*, which was published by the Association of Educational Computing and Technology.[31]

William Spady, who was Executive Director of the Association of School Administrators, sat on the Advisory Board for Project BEST along with Shirley McCune, who was also the head of the State Services Division of Denver, Colorado.[32] McCune's technocratic game plan at Project BEST was pushed by President Reagan's Secretary of Education, Terrel Howard Bell, who was formerly the US Commissioner of Education, which headed up the Office of Education of the Department of Health, Education, and Welfare (HEW) before the Office of Education was assigned its own separate Department under President Jimmy Carter in 1979. In 1983, Secretary T. H. Bell authorized the funding of McCune's MidContinent Regional Educational Laboratory (McREL); and in 1984, Bell ratified the financing of William Spady's Utah-based Far West Laboratory for Outcomes-Based Education.[33] [h] [34]

---

h   As the 1989 Senior Director of McREL, which was paid for by the US Department of

At the end of Reagan's first term as President, Secretary Bell passed the technocratic teaching torch to his successor, Education Secretary William Bennett, who later went on to co-found the K12 Inc. Corporation until he had to resign from the K12 Inc. company after public backlash from racist comments he made on his conservative talk radio show, *Bill Bennett's Morning in America.*[35] [i] [36]

"School in a Box":

Of course, the 1980s "teaching machines" of Project BEST were rudimentary. Yet by 1990, futurist-technocrat Ray Kurzweil, who is now the Director of Engineering at Google,[37] accurately predicted the current technetronic state of computerized education in the twenty-first century.

In his 1990 tome, *The Age of Intelligent Machines*, Kurzweil foresaw that, "by the end of the first decade of the next century," around 2010, "computer-assisted instruction" (CAI),[38] or what we now know as "virtual education," would be characterized by the following eight developments:

- Every child has a computer. Computers are as ubiquitous as pencils and books.

- They are portable laptop devices about the size of a large book.

- They include very high resolution screens that are as easy to read as books.

- They include a variety of devices for entering information, including a keyboard and a track ball (or possibly a mouse).

Education, McCune announced that the technocratic "school of the future must be far different than that of today to meet the challenging needs of society." In particular, McCune stressed that future schools must be revamped into "community learning centers, not just schools.... Schools are no longer in the schooling business." Instead, schools are in the business of hi-tech "human resource development," McCune said. In a Washington *Bremerton Sun* article titled "Schools of the Future," McCune depicts how her futuristic community learning centers will emphasize "integrating technology with curriculum" in order to condition the lifelong psychosocial cognitive-behavioral development of students of all ages across the lifespan from cradle to career. This *Bremerton Sun* profile of McCune's future schools illustrates how

> [w]hen you walk in the building, there's a row of offices. In one are drug counselors. One is for social security. Another, family and child psychologists. Yet another has a doctor and nurse who do well-child exams.
>
> In the cafeteria, senior citizens mingle with students having lunch. Oldsters and youngsters are sometimes paired for school projects, like oral history.
>
> There's a child-care center, and tied into it are classes for teenagers where they learn the importance of child-nurturing skills.
>
> In the gym, homemakers are taking exercise classes. After work, more men and women will show up for their fitness workout.

i   On September 28th, 2005, Bennett broadcasted the following statement: "I do know that it's true that if you wanted to reduce crime, you could, if that were your sole purpose, you could abort every black baby in this country, and your crime rate would go down. That would be an impossible, ridiculous, and morally reprehensible thing to do, but your crime rate would go down."

- They support high quality two-way voice communication, including natural-language understanding.

- They are extremely easy and intuitive to use.

- A great variety of high-quality interactive *intelligent* and *entertaining* courseware is available.

- Computers are integrated into wireless networks.[39]

Fast-forward to the present, and virtually all eight of Kurzweil's ed-tech forecasts have come true: the pixelated command screens of 1980's Project BEST teaching computers have evolved into the high-definition stimulus-response windows of online adaptive-CBE modules operated on mobile technetronics such as tablets equipped with touch screens, voice commands, and skype capabilities.

In 2013, Kurzweil's vision of plugging every student into a virtual-learning module was set in motion through President Barack Obama's ConnectEd initiative,[40] which according to the White House Archives was launched "to connect 99% of American students in their classrooms and libraries with next-generation broadband and wireless connectivity within five years … to meet the needs of competition in a global economy."[41] Fueled by public-private partnerships, ConnectEd is bankrolled by the Federal Communications Commission and "private-sector companies [that] have committed to provide schools across the country with more than $2 billion worth of free hardware, software, educational content, and wireless connectivity."[42] With these billions of corporate-government dollars, ConnectEd's "'99-in-5' connectivity goal" aims to enable "interactive, personalized learning experiences driven by new technology" that will "[p]repar[e] our students with the skills they need to get good jobs."[43] As I demonstrate in prior chapters, "personalized learning" technologies are synonymous with CBE adaptive-learning software that data-mine students with stimulus-response algorithms which condition learning outcomes for job-skill competence.[j][44]

---

j   As a matter of fact, the equivocation of "personalized/individualized" learning with computerized edu-conditioning actually began with Pressey's, and later Skinner's, teaching machines. In The Technology of Teaching, Skinner writes, "Pressey also pointed out that such machines would increase efficiency in another way. Even in a small classroom the teacher usually knows that he is moving too slowly for some students and too fast for others. Those who could go faster are penalized, and those who should go slower are poorly taught and unnecessarily punished by criticism and failure. Machine instruction would permit each student to proceed at his own rate." Skinner elaborates on the inherent "individualization" of mechanized/computerized edu-conditioning:

[d]ifferences in ability raise other questions. A program designed for the slowest student in the school system will probably not seriously delay the fast student, who will be free to progress at his own speed. (He may profit from the coverage by filling in unsuspected gaps in his

Once the entire US student body is connected to ed-tech through Obama's ConnectEd, Kurzweil's CAI forecasts will dovetail with the following technetronic predictions envisioned by the first Executive Director of the globalist Bill and Melinda Gates Foundation, Tom Vander Ark:

> [w]e'll soon have adaptive content libraries and smart recommendation engines that string together a unique "playlist" for every student everyday. These smart platforms will consider learning level, interests, and best learning modality (i.e., motivational profile and learning style to optimize understanding and persistence).
>
> Smart learning platforms will be used by some students that learn at home, by some students that connect through hybrid schools with a day or two onsite, and by most students through blended schools that mix online learning with onsite support systems.[45]

To put it another way, Vander Ark foresees that the evolution of Kurzweil's CAI will soon culminate in adaptive "smart-learning" technetronics that "personalize" "unique 'playlist[s]'" of online stimulus-response lessons by data-mining each student's learning psychology with algorithms that measure his or her behavioral motivation as well as his or her preferred sensory learning modality, whether visual, auditory, or kinesthetic.

In sum, the commercial evolution of smart-learning/adaptive-conditioning CAI has been proliferated through government-subsidized programs such as Project BEST and ConnectEd. The final product is now the technetronic re-engineering of stimulus-response "teaching machines" to transform the mechanized Skinner box into a computerized "school in a box" that can be mass-manufactured and commercially exported across the entire planet through corporate globalization. With entire classrooms compacted inside the handheld confines of online adaptive-learning technetronics, it is only a matter of time before brick-and-mortar schools are bulldozed, and human teachers will be discarded with the rubble

---

repertoire.) If this does not prove to be the case, programs can be constructed at two or more levels, and students can be shifted from one to the other as performances dictate. If there are also differences in "types of thinking," the extra time available for machine instruction may be used to present a subject in ways appropriate to many types. Each student will presumably retain and use those ways which he finds most useful.

Notice here that Skinner was forecasting how computer-machine instruction would come to entail the current two-tiered virtual schooling system that is divided between career-pathways workforce training for "slow" students versus college-preparatory academic pathways for "fast" students. This double-standardized system of virtual-machine schooling matches succinctly with the dualistic educational philosophy theorized in the "six basic functions" of schooling conceptualized by Skinner's Harvard predecessor, Professor of Education Alexander Inglis.

10

The Globalization of "Lifelong" Corporate-Technocratic Education: "Classrooms without Walls," Teachers without Degrees

Throughout candidate Trump's 2016 presidential campaign, The Donald spewed slogans of "America First" nationalism that were the bedrock of his electioneering rhetoric. But apparently, this was all just con-game carnival barking because Trump's choice for Secretary of Education, Betsy DeVos, has proposed a merger of the United States Department of Labor with the US Department of Education to fuse the two departments together into a unitary Department of Education and the Workforce that is being modeled after the European workforce "charter-schooling" systems of the United Kingdom (UK), the Netherlands, and Switzerland.[1][a][2]

After visiting these foreign countries, Secretary DeVos reported her observations in an op-ed for *Education Week*, which recommends emulating these European nations to revamp American "school choice" reforms because "the Netherlands and the United Kingdom show that high student achievement is possible with robust parental choice and flexibility for educators. Switzerland shows the benefit of giving students a wide variety of career options through apprenticeships. Most importantly, these countries show that a commitment to freedom in education can produce student success."[3] In the long run, DeVos is gearing up to conglomerate America's privatized charter school corporations into international public-private partnerships with European workforce-schooling programs so that US workforce training can "catch up" to international school-to-work standards.[4]

Even prior to her tour of these European workforce-ed systems, DeVos delivered the keynote address to the third International Congress on Vo-

---

[a]   In the United Kingdom of England, the UK is corporatizing their public education system through privatized "academies" and "free schools," which are the semantic equivalent of America's public-private charter schools.

cational and Professional Education and Training (VPET) held in Winterthur, Switzerland, where she preemptively asserted that

> [t]here is much to learn from our European counterparts as they continue to advance education options centered on the needs of individual students and focused on their ability to succeed in the modern economy.... The proof is in the results as Switzerland, the Netherlands and the United Kingdom continue to out-perform American students on the Program for International Student Assessment (PISA).[5]

To be sure, there have long been international public-private partnerships contracted between European and American edu-companies through corporate-government partnerships across US and European schooling systems. For some time now, the UK Pearson Education Corporation, which owns and operates virtual-online charter schools across America and abroad, has been dominating the corporate education market in the United States. As such, DeVos's globalist plan to copy European school-to-work privatization is a greenlight for Pearson and other European workforce-conditioning businesses to accelerate their corporate-international takeover of American "school choice" through public-private workforce-training partnerships that implement adaptive-learning software which operantly condition students through online "career-pathways" curriculums that digitally data-mine each student's "individualized" "social and emotional learning" (SEL) algorithms for workforce placement in a globally planned economy.[b] [6]

Case and point: Connections Academy's commercial chain of online-virtual charter school corporations, which were formerly owned by an American business executive based out of Maryland, USA, until Pearson bought out the parent company, Connections Education, in 2011.

Connections Academy (Pearson PLC):

The London-based Pearson PLC,[7] which is the "world's largest education company,"[8] is widely known for publishing textbooks and formulating standardized tests for schools across the globe.[9] [c] [10] What may

---

b   In a June 28th, 2018, Tweet from the official Twitter account of the US Department of Education, Secretary DeVos posted the hashtag "#SEL" in an endorsement for socioemotional-learning methodologies. In a 2016 issue of *The Federalist*, an article titled "Schools Ditch Academics for Emotional Manipulation" documents how SEL programs are geared to improve learning outcomes by "personalizing" instruction based on mass data-mining of students' psycho-behavioral qualities such as "self-awareness, self-management, social awareness, relationship skills, and responsible decision-making" as well as "resilience, teamwork, curiosity, and leadership."

c   In 2016, a Ugandan High Court ruling ordered BIA to be barred from reopening in 2018 not be so well known, though, is the fact that the Pearson Corporation also owns and operates globalist virtual charter schools that implement "personalized" adaptive-learning technetronics.

In 2011, Pearson paid $400 million to buy out the Maryland-USA-based Connections Education,[11] which is a globalist, for-profit edu-company that manages a subsidiary corporation called Connections Academy.[12] The Pearson-owned Connections Academy proudly announces that it operates numerous virtual-online charter schools "in 21 states in the US – serving more than 40,000 students in the current school year."[13] These British-owned US charter schools include Georgia Connections Academy Charter School,[14] Oregon Connections Academy,[15] California Connections Academy @ Ripon,[16] and Maine Connections Academy.[17]

There is even an International Connections Academy (iNaCa) that enrolls student bodies across multiple nations and integrates them into a single virtual-online classroom for corporatist workforce conditioning. The International Connections Academy describes itself as "a virtual private school [that] meets individual needs through high quality instruction and enriching, rigorous curriculum; empowers students to be self-directed and reflective learners who actively participate in our global society through innovative 21st century technology; and builds the essential skills necessary for college or career readiness."[18] Stated differently, International Connections is a corporate-globalist virtual school that "individual[izes]" academic and career-training curriculums through "self-directed" learning modules on CBE-style internet platforms.[d][19]

Furthermore, by virtually corralling the student bodies of sovereign nation states into a single computerized school box, and then digitally conditioning the students for "career-readiness" in a "global society," iNaCa is the posterchild for the future of virtual workforce charter schooling in the planned global economy of the technocratic New World Order. In a Pearson blog article titled "When Classrooms Have No Walls," the International Connections Academy School Director, Hannah Rinehart, publicizes how iNaCa

---

due to failures to meet government regulations regarding sanitation and teacher training. Nonetheless, Bridge Academies has flagrantly defied the court order by continuing to operate their Uganda schools with total disregard of edicts from Uganda's First Lady and Minister of Education, Janet Museveni, who declared "that the impunity being exhibited by Bridge Management, and its likes, will not be tolerated and that Government will spare no effort to use all legal means to enforce the requirements of the Law to protect our children and our future, as a country."

d   In 1968, the godfather of computer-machine teaching himself, Harvard Psychology Professor B. F. Skinner, foreshadowed the evolution of "individualized" teaching machines into virtual-online courses that can be attended on the internet through computer devices stationed in the comfort of each student's own home. In his fifty-year-old book, *The Technology of Teaching*, Skinner foresaw that "[s]elf-instruction by machine has many special advantages apart from educational institutions. Home study is an obvious case."

puts a premium on the development of the "global student." Through programs like "Around The World in 60 Minutes," young learners are exposed to and engage with students in other countries during guided sessions that maximize the myriad benefits of the conference. Virtual students on both ends of the exchange work to prepare presentations on aspects of their traditions and daily lives that they would like to share with their virtual classmates around the world.[20]

This psycho-behavioral conditioning of the "global student" through "career-readiness" curriculums at the Pearson-owned iNaCa virtually programs students to conform as corporate citizens of a planned global political-economy.

Pearson PLC is also operating other for-profit schools abroad as part of "Pearson's 11 equity investments in programs across Asia and Africa serving more than 360,000 students," reports *Wired Magazine*.[21] These globalist charter schools include Affordable Private Education Center, Inc. (APEC) Schools in the Philippines and Omega Schools in Ghana, the latter of which enrolls students based on a "Pay-As-You-Learn™" system.[22] Similar to Pearson's Connections Academy subsidiaries, APEC and Omega Schools are both virtual schools that rely on blended-learning classrooms that hybridize human-teacher instruction with CBE-style adaptive-software instruction.[23] [e 24]

According to the *Wall Street Journal*, the British Pearson Corporation even bankrolls the US-based Bridge International Academies (BIA) Corporation, which runs chains of commercial charter school companies through globalist public-private partnerships with foreign governments.[25]

Bridge International Academies (BIA):

The Bridge Academies model of public-private charter schooling is self-described by the international edu-corporation as an "Academy in a Box,"[26] which employs "personalized"/"individualized" learning pedagogy through a blended-learning methodology that teaches students with adaptive-learning ed-tech.[27] According to *Mail & Guardian Africa*,

---

e   However, the noble and lofty rhetoric behind Pearson's global education agenda should be held in light of a *Huffington Post* investigation, which reports that "[i]n 2013, the Pearson Charitable Foundation paid $7.7 million in fines in New York State to reach an out-of-court settlement after the Office of the State Attorney General found the Foundation had broken state laws by generating business for the for-profit [Pearson Education] company." Additionally, the FBI confiscated twenty boxes of documentation during an investigation into alleged "complicity between officials in LAUSD [Los Angeles Unified School District], Pearson, the Pearson Foundation, representatives of Apple, and America Choice, a Pearson affiliate, to influence a LAUSD contract decision [with Pearson] and circumvent the bidding process."

"Bridge's model is 'school in a box' – a highly structured, technology-driven model that relies on teachers reading standardised lessons from hand-held tablet computers."[28] However, Bridge's so-called "teachers" are not actually real teachers at all.

BIA's standardized computer lessons are not taught by certified educators who hold specialized bachelors' or masters' degrees: "Bridge hires education experts to script the lessons, but the teacher's role is to deliver that content to the class. This allows Bridge to hold down costs because it can hire teachers who don't have college degrees – a teacher is only required to go through a five-week training programme on how to read and deliver the script."[29] To put it another way, BIA para-teachers need only be competent in navigating and operating the basic functions of the stimulus-response adaptive-learning tablets; they need not be competent in any of the actual academic content being taught in the adaptive-learning modules, which means they need possess no expert knowledge of reading, writing, arithmetic, or science.

As a result, BIA's school-in-a-tablet technetronics become virtual substitutes for the human authorities over the curriculum, and the college-educated, certified teacher is replaced with a paraprofessional tutor who merely facilitates the standardized tablet lessons after less than two months of training.

Like all "individualized"-learning technologies, BIA's adaptive-learning tablets "personalize" edu-conditioning lessons based on a student's cognitive-behavioral stimulus-response algorithms that are data-mined from his or her responses to digital stimuli programmed for specific career or academic learning pathways. Jacqueline Walumbe, a spokesperson for BIA, applauds how Bridge's "school in a box" computer tablets are "powered by the two-way movement of data in near-real time" that "collect[s] information on what lessons work best, [so] educators can improve lessons for all children."[30] In other words, each student's "two-way" stimulus-response data on "competency-based" software are tabulated by BIA's hi-tech "Skinner boxes" to individuate "what lessons work best" through adaptive-learning algorithms.[31]

According to Walumbe, Bridge's adaptive-competency data-mining computers have supposedly enabled Liberian students to learn "at twice the speed of their peers" in non-Bridge schools.[32] Based on these self-reported BIA statistics, corporate raiders of public education are already begging the following question: if such stimulus-response operant-conditioning computers can in fact double learning outcomes at a fraction of the cost of college-certified teachers, then why not get rid of all those expensive human beings who teach from the archaic expertise of their paper-and-pencil university studies?

Indeed, according to the *New York Times*, the Liberian government signed a 2016 contract with Bridge International Academies, which authorizes the for-profit educational corporation to "take charge of 120 government primary schools, 3 percent of the total,"[33] through a public-private project called Partnership Schools for Liberia (PSL).[34] The *New York Times* reports that this privatization contract "could lead to a nationwide charter school system."[35] Depending on the success of this public-private PSL pilot, the nationwide expansion of BIA Liberia could perhaps catapult into a worldwide system of virtual charter schools packaged inside "personalized" computer boxes.

Today, Bridge International already operates hundreds of schools with thousands of students across India and various African countries, including Nigeria, Kenya, and Uganda,[f] [36] and it has a US Office as well as a London Office.[37] It is important to note here that although the original corporate headquarters of BIA are located on the continent of Africa in Nairobi, Kenya,[38] the company is owned and operated by two white Americans who graduated from Harvard University:[39] the birthplace of the modern charter school reform movement, where "cradle-to-career" schooling spokesman,[40] Geoffrey Canada,[41] spearheaded his public-private workforce training pedagogy that evolved into the Harlem Children's Zone (HCZ) corporate charter school system.[42]

It should come as no surprise, then, that the technetronic Bridge International is funded by the corporate-globalist kingpin of charter school philanthropists: techno-plutocrat Bill Gates. Additionally, Bridge Academies is financed by two oligarchical Zuckerberg foundations:[43] Zuckerberg Education Ventures, which is a philanthropy owned by technocrat Mark Zuckerberg himself;[44] and the Chan Zuckerberg Initiative, which is a foundation owned by Mark's wife, Chan Zuckerberg.[45]

---

f   Pearson VUE formulates the General Education Degree (GED) high school equivalency test through a public-private partnership with the American Council on Education that was acquired in 2011, resulting in the GED price being raised by approximately seventy percent in most states. Pearson is also contracted with the Graduate Management Admission Council (GMAC) to formulate and proctor the Graduate Management Admission Test (GMAT) for admitting students to graduate-level business colleges. In addition, Pearson Virtual University Enterprises (VUE) also formulates and administers the state-level teacher certification tests for various American states, such as the Florida Teacher Certification Examinations (FTCE), the New York State Teacher Certification Examinations™ (NYSTCE®), The Indiana CORE Assessments for Educator Licensure, the Illinois Licensure Testing System (ILTS), the Pennsylvania Educator Certification Tests (PECT), and the Ohio Assessments for Educators (OAE).

BIA is also bankrolled by the global governance institution, the International Finance Corporation of the World Bank Group. Moreover, BIA's corporate-globalist colonization across Third-World Asia and Africa is further subsidized by foreign aid investments from Western governments, such as the United Kingdom government, which funneled £3.45 million toward the establishment of 23 BIA charter schools in Nigeria.[46]

Make America Globalist Again:

Back here in the United States, as the DeVos Administration internationally privatizes US workforce schooling through public-private partnerships with European school-to-work corporations, Pearson PLC's online virtual charter schools and other globalist workforce edu-companies are being integrated into America's nationwide system of state-level P-16 and P-20 councils, which fuse together public departments of education, labor, healthcare, human services, and community-oriented policing into an amalgamation of fascistic public-private partnerships.

Reporting on the wonders of her trip across the workforce "charter-schooling" systems of Europe, Secretary DeVos's op-ed for *Education Week* has recommended that American "school choice" take a state/local-level approach to incorporating international public-private partnerships with European workforce edu-corporations:

> [n]ow, simply copying European approaches will not be sufficient – American communities have their own unique challenges and needs…
>
> For the United States, lasting and positive changes to education cannot and should not be mandated by the federal government…
>
> Instead, forward-thinking states and school districts should take note of the effective approaches found abroad, and they should consider how they can extend educational freedom to their own constituents.[47]

Stated differently, DeVos is prompting state/regional-level P-16/20 councils to coordinate corporate-globalist "school choice" through public-private career-pathways partnerships that are aligned with European workforce training standards, such as the "Post-16 Skills Plan" issued by the UK Minister of State for Skills. Indeed, DeVos lauded how "the 'Post-16 Skills Plan' outlin[es] a new technical track for students and formaliz[es] a framework for 15 occupational routes leading to 'T-level' qualifications that students receive around age 18…. A T-level program prepares students for employment in a skilled trade or pursuit of higher technical/skilled education."[48]

By cloaking her corporate-globalist scheme in the doublespeak rhetoric of state and local education planning, DeVos can front as if her techno-fascist "school choice" agenda is an attempt to loosen the grips of centralized federal control over America education. Yet in actuality, this ostensibly bottom-up approach to international public-private schooling is really just a back-door stratagem to provide cover for ultimately overriding both the US federal government and US state governments through public-private P-16/20 council partnerships with globalist charter school companies which will effectively result in top-down international regulation of US education. As foreign edu-corporations and international workforce-ed standards are woven more thoroughly into the legal framework of P-16/20 councils in the United States, America's publicly elected education system will in time be effectively transferred to the international authority of the unelected United Nations Educational Scientific and Cultural Organization (UNESCO) under the auspices of UNESCO's "lifelong learning" standards.[g][49]

UNESCO spawned a global "lifelong learning" pedagogy for cradle-to-career workforce schooling that has been disseminated through the publications of UNESCO's *Towards a Conceptual Model of Lifelong Education* in 1973 and UNESCO's *Foundations of Lifelong Education* in 1976.[50] The principles of lifelong school-to-work set forth in these UNESCO documents are aligned with UNESCO's International Standard Classification of Education (ISCED) published in Paris, France, in 1976 and UNESCO's International Standards of Operation (ISO), which are classified into ISO 9000 for manufacturing standards and ISO 1400 for human resources standards.[51][h][52] At the third International Congress on Vocational and Professional Education and Training (VPET), Secretary DeVos dog-whistled her true intent to revivify these lifelong UN-learning

---

g   Don't be fooled by Trump's recent proclamation that the United States has pulled out from its membership in UNESCO. The official notice of "withdrawal" by the US Department of State on October 12, 2017, declares that America's UNESCO status will merely be demoted from full membership only "to establish a permanent observer mission to UNESCO [from the US] ... in order to contribute U.S. views, perspectives and expertise on some of the important issues undertaken by the organization, including ... promoting scientific collaboration and education." To put it another way, notwithstanding neo-con Trump's blustering grandstand, the United States will still be "observ[ing]" and "contribut[ing]" to UNESCO's worldwide regulations for standardizing international "scientific collaboration and education" for "lifelong learning" outcomes across the planet – the USA just won't be allowed to officially vote on any final decisions arbitrated by official UNESCO councils or committees.

h   The USA is also a signatory to UNESCO's international education treaty entitled the Agreement on the Importation of Educational, Scientific and Cultural Materials. In addition, it standards in the United States by touring Europe's workforce-schooling systems to copy international best practices for career-path education and then transfer them back to the US: "I look forward to this important opportunity to learn from European education leaders and to exchange ideas on how to ensure America's students have access to the lifelong learning journey that will put them on the path to success."[53]

If we unpack the ulterior meanings of the UNESCO jargon in this loaded statement from DeVos, her true motive behind her applause for EU workforce-ed is unveiled: her mission to interlock America's public-private P-16/20 partnerships together with European career-path privatization partnerships that are regulated under the global governance of UNESCO "lifelong learning" statutes which standardize workforce placement in a planned world economy. Recall that, in chapter two, I demonstrate the rhetorical and policy parallels between corporate "cradle-to-career" schooling, America's state-level P-16/20 education councils, and UNESCO's international "lifelong learning" pedagogy.

These globalist reaches of DeVos's technocratic plot to corporatize workforce-ed through multinational public-private partnerships with online-virtual charter school companies may be a relatively new frontier in American education. But in fact, the seeds of this fascist-international future of corporate-technocratic schooling were sown in the late nineteenth century when Johanne Gottlieb Fichte's Prussian system of militarized education was copied by Skull-and-Bones liaison, Horace Mann, who transported Fichte's collectivist pedagogy across the Atlantic Ocean to be installed as the basis of compulsory workforce schooling in the United States.[i][54] Fichte, who was an associate of the Bavarian Illuminati,[55] is not only considered to be the godfather of national-socialist fascism;[56] he is likewise the regarded as the progenitor of cosmopolitan-globalist fas-

---

should be noted that, in 1990, the World Conference on Education for All was sponsored by UNESCO and the World Bank, and it was also "[c]onvened by the executive heads of the United Nations Development Program (UNDP), [and] the United Nations Children Fund (UNICEF)."

i   Recall from chapter two that the corporate-fascist political-economics driving the cradle-to-career charter school takeover are rooted in the proto-Nazi philosophies of Johann Gottlieb Fichte, who was the philosophical predecessor of Georg Wilhelm Friedrich Hegel. In fact, it was Fichte, not Hegel, who conceptualized the dialectical theory of the historical and sociopolitical evolution of "the State"; Hegel merely popularized Fichte's dialectic which the latter originated in his *Foundations of the Science of Knowledge*. My article also historicizes how the Gospel of Hegelianism was spread throughout American schools by the Yale secret society of Skull and Bones, otherwise known as The Order of Death (or the Russell Trust Association). Specifically, chapter two documents how The Order imported Fichte's Prussian system of militarized edu-conditioning into America's compulsory schooling system while manipulating the Fichtean-Hegelian dialectic to co-opt the leftwing-rightwing political discourse over US educational policy and hence steer American public schooling incrementally toward corporate-fascist workforce training through career-pathways curriculums.

cism,[57] otherwise known today by the contemporary euphemistic terms of "free trade" globalization,[58] or "free market" globalism.[59] In his *Addresses to the German Nation*, Fichte pontificates on the cosmopolitan bent of his proto-fascist education philosophy:

> [s]o this German and very modern art of the State becomes once more the very ancient art of the State, which among the Greeks founded citizenship on education and trained such citizens as succeeding ages have never seen. Henceforth the German will do what is in form the same, though in content it will be characterized by a spirit that is not narrow and exclusive, but universal and cosmopolitan.[60] [j]

Today in 2018, more than two hundred years after the publication of his *Addresses to the German Nation* in 1808, Fichte's Prussian model of proto-fascistic school training is being refined by computerized stimulus-response methods of psycho-behavioral adaptive-learning that can be commercially mass-produced and distributed across the entire planet through market globalization and trade liberalization which facilitate public-private partnerships between multinational charter school corporations contracting with national governments that align workforce-conditioning curriculums with international standards.

In the future, as "personalized" adaptive-learning computers become the dominant providers of edu-conditioning across the planet, computers will thereby dominate the "outdated" human beings who once administered education. In this redundant technocratic system where computers are programmed to program students to work computerized jobs in a digitally planned global economy, the final equation will inevitably render human cognitive-behavioral labor obsolete, and computers will effectively become the dominant species on the planet as human cognition is eventually surpassed by automated quantum computing and artificial intelligence.

---

j   To be sure, there tends to be a rift between those scholars who view Fichte as the well-spring of proto-Nazism and those who view Fichte as a beacon of cosmopolitanism. Generally, those scholars who revere Fichte as a liberal cosmopolitanist are those who tend to be apologists attempting to rescue him from the condemnations of those who denounce him as the philosophical predecessor to Nazi fascism. In brief, it is uncommon to reconcile these two schools of thought. For the purposes of this book, it is not germane to discuss at length here the arguments on either side of this debate. Instead, it will suffice to briefly note here that I have synthesized these opposing characterizations of Fichte by simply applying the very pre-Hegelian method of dialectical reasoning coined by Fichte himself.

Chapter 11

BILLIONAIRES BEHIND CLOSED DOORS: BETSY DEVOS MEETS WITH BILDERBERGER PETER THIEL

DeVos didn't join Team Trump until February 7, 2017; but before Trump even entered the Oval Office, his administration had already proclaimed its commitment to techno-fascist workforce-schooling policies that favor public-private governance over virtual charter school corporations. In November of 2016, the Trump "Transition Team" pledged to:

> advance policies to support learning-and-earning opportunities at the state and local levels ... expansion of choice through charters, vouchers, and teacher-driven learning models; and relief from U.S. Department of Education regulations that inhibit innovation. A Trump Administration also will make post-secondary [education] options more affordable and accessible through technology enriched delivery models.[1]

To help deliver these promises of "school choice" through virtual ed-tech, "The Donald" hired a key member of his transition team: corporate-technocrat titan, Peter Thiel,[2] a billionaire member of the Bilderberg Group who is heavily invested in educational technologies.

The German-born co-founder of PayPal software, Bilderberger Thiel, sits on the Facebook Board of Directors,[3] and he is a major investor in electronic crypto-currencies through his financing of Bitcoin currencies as well as BitPay and BitGo transaction software.[4] In addition, he established the Founders Fund,[5] which is a venture capital investment group that bankrolls hi-tech innovations in artificial intelligence; internet communications; biotechnologies; energy-producing technologies; aerospace and outer-space engineering; interplanetary travel; and even educational technologies developed by Knewton and Altschools.[6] Thiel donated $1.25 million to Trump's presidential campaign,[7] and after his election to the White House, Trump tapped Thiel to sit on the executive committee of his transition team.[8]

Not only is Peter Thiel heavily invested in computerized adaptive-learning technologies such as Knewton and Clever;[9] but he also has prior experience as a speech writer for Reagan Administration Secretary of Education William Bennett,[10] who co-founded the virtual charter school corporation, K12 Inc., which was a corporate member of ALEC's Education Task Force.[11] During Betsy DeVos's first months as Education Secretary, she met with Peter at "the Thiel residence" on July 19, 2017.[12]

There is no transcript of the Thiel-DeVos meeting. But given Thiel's deep pockets for ed-tech products along with his sidekick support of virtual-ed privatizer, former Secretary Bennett, it is reasonable to infer that Thiel advised DeVos to supplant traditional public schooling with virtual workforce education that substitutes human instruction with "personalized" operant-conditioning algorithms programmed into adaptive-learning software like the Thiel-financed Knewton and Clever. Considering Thiel's dreams of constructing private artificial islands where corporatists can skirt national labor laws and trade regulations,[13] [a] [14] it is likewise reasonable to believe he recommended that DeVos deregulate "competency-based" virtual schooling through fascistic public-private partnerships between government-funded charter school corporations, ed-tech businesses, and politically connected companies that offer "career pathways" internships, apprenticeships, and other work-study programs. It is further plausible that Thiel urged DeVos to dismantle the traditional public school system because Thiel's disdain for traditional schooling is so great that he has established a private $100,000-per-year fellowship that pays college students to drop out in pursuit of entrepreneurial ventures.[15]

For those who would dismiss these suspicions concerning the closed-doors meeting between DeVos and Thiel, it should be noted that there are deeper ties between Thiel and the DeVos-Prince family, which link them together with The Donald. The *New York Times* reports that Thiel attended a "Mercer family" costume party in December of 2016 where he was photographed posing with Trump and DeVos's brother, Erik Prince:[16] the founder of the private mercenary corporation formerly known as Blackwater.[17] According to the *New York Times* article, Thiel "joke[d]" that the

---

a. Thiel has invested $1.7 million in the Seasteading Institute, which is bankrolling efforts to build "sea cities" of artificial islands in the waters of French Polynesia. The government of French Polynesia has reportedly identified Thiel as a financial backer of the Atlas-Shrugged-style "Floating Island Project" owned by the Blue Frontiers Corporation, which was set up by Seasteading Institute President Joe Quirk.

implications of this picture capturing the Thiel-Trump-Prince love triangle "was 'N.S.F.I.' (Not Safe for the Internet)."[18]

Peter Thiel has continued to advise President Trump, and it has been reported that Thiel's influence on the White House is so impactful that his employees refer to him as "the shadow president."[19] This may be implicated by his prominent position seated directly beside Trump during the president-elect's first Technology Summit at Trump Tower in Manhattan just prior to his inauguration.[20][b][21] If Thiel truly is the shadow president behind the Trump Administration, it will come as no surprise to those who are aware that Thiel is a member of the Bilderberg Group: the secretive nongovernmental organization (NGO) that surreptitiously plans the world political-economy through off-record international meetings between heads of states, international financiers, military leaders, corporate executives, intelligence operatives, media moguls, academics, technologists, and even royal families.[c][22]

---

b. Other elite technocrats in attendance at Trump's first Tech Summit include "Jeff Bezos of Amazon; Elon Musk of Tesla; Timothy D. Cook of Apple; Sheryl Sandberg of Facebook; Larry Page and Eric Schmidt of Alphabet, Google's parent company; and Satya Nadella of Microsoft," according to a *New York Times* report.

c. For an excellent treatise on how the Bilderberg Group orchestrates global governance through corporate-fascist planning of the world economy, read the international best-seller, *The True Story of the Bilderberg Group*, written by world-renowned investigate journalist, Daniel Estulin, who gave a speech revealing the details of this book to the European Union Parliament in 2010. Sleuthing like an old-school gum-shoe reporter, Estulin was able to obtain an official roster of attendees at the 2007 Bilderberg Meeting in Istanbul, Turkey. The True Story of the Bilderberg Group provides a photocopy of this document, which lists the following Bilderbergers:

> Her Majesty Queen Beatrix, Queen of the Netherlands (The Netherlands); ... Franco Bernabé, Vice Chairman, Rothschild Europe (Italy); ... Lloyd C. Blankfein, Chairman and CEO, Goldman Sachs & Co. (USA); ... Timothy F. Geithner, President and CEO, Federal Reserve Bank of New York (USA); Paul A. Gigot, Editorial Page Editor, Wall Street Journal (USA); ... Richard N. Haas, President, Council on Foreign Relations (USA); ... His Majesty, King Juan Carlos I, King of Spain (Spain); ... John Kerr (Lord Kerr of Kinlochard), Member, House of Lords, Deputy Chairman, Royal Dutch Shell PLC (UK); Henry A. Kissinger, Chairman, Kissinger Associates (USA); ... Richard N. Perle, Resident Fellow, American Enterprise Institute for Public Policy Research (USA); Rick Perry, Governor of Texas (USA); ... HRH Prince Philippe (Belgium); Rodrigo de Rato y Figaredo, Managing Director, IMF (International); ... Eric Schmidt, Chairman of the Executive Committee and CEO, Google (USA); ... Kathleen Sebelius, Governor of Kansas (USA); ... Javier Solana, High Representative for the Common Foreign and Security Policy, Secretary-General of the Council of the European Union and the Western European Union (International); Her Majesty Queen Sophia, Queen of Spain; ... Peter D. Sutherland, Chairman, BP PLC, and Chairman, Goldman Sachs International (Ireland); ... Peter A. Thiel, President, Clarium Capital Management, LLC (USA); ... Jean-Claude Trichet, Governor, European Central Bank (France/International); ... Paul Wolfowitz, President, The World Bank (International); ... Robert B. Zoellick, former US Trade Representative, former Deputy Secretary of State, Managing Director, Goldman Sachs (USA).

Last year, at the 2017 Bilderberg Meeting convened in the USA, several of President Trump's top cabinet officials, including Commerce Secretary, Wilbur Ross; National Security Advisor to the President, H. R. McMaster; Assistant to the President for Strategic Initiatives, Chris Liddell; and the National Security Council's Deputy Assistant to the President, Nadia Schadlow; were appointed to discuss the Trump Administration's "progress report" at this Bilderberg conference. Just a few weeks prior to this global-elite roundtable held in Chantilly, Virginia, the infamous Bilderberger

The Bilderberg Group was founded by Prince Bernhard of the Netherlands, who was also a Nazi *Sturmabteilung* Storm Trooper.[23] In David Rockefeller Sr.'s *Memoirs*, the late patriarch of the Skull-and-Bones Rockefeller family confesses that

> Prince Bernhard of the Netherlands convened the first conference in May 1954...
>
> I was one of eleven Americans invited, and we joined fifty delegates from eleven Western European countries – a lively mosaic of politicians, businessmen, journalists, and trade unionists...
>
> The conference had served a useful purpose, and the consensus was that we should meet again the following year under the continuing chairmanship of Prince Bernhard.[24]

Rockefeller explains how

> [i]n 1976, Bilderberg faced a scandal that almost resulted in its collapse. Early that year in testimony before the Senate Foreign Relations Committee, it was alleged that Prince Bernhard had approached the Lockheed Corporation with an offer to use his official position to influence Dutch defense procurement policies in return for a significant financial consideration. As the year wore on, the evidence against Bernhard accumulated, including indications that he had met with intermediaries during Bilderberg events. The 1976 conference was canceled, and it appeared for a time that Bilderberg was finished...
>
> I am pleased to report that as the new millennium begins, a reinvigorated Bilderberg continues to thrive.[25]

Notice what Rockefeller is admitting here: New World Order elitists clandestinely collude with one another at the Bilderberg Group's secretive roundtable conferences in order to procure illegal corporate-government contracts that undermine national sovereignty while autocratically planning the global political-economy. Realizing the criminal intentions of the Nazist Bilderbergers, we would be remiss not to suspect that Bilderberger Thiel hosted his off-the-record meeting with DeVos in order to clinch public-private contracts between Trump's Department of Education and ed-tech corporations bankrolled by Thiel, such as Knewton and Clever.

Henry Kissinger met with Trump at the White House. Approximately twelve months later, in the current year 2018, the Bilderberg Meeting in Turin, Italy, marks the first-ever attendance by an official of the Vatican: Cardinal Pietro Parolin, Vatican Secretary of State.

When intrepid journalist from We Are Change, Luke Rudkowski, confronted Thiel outside of the *Taschenbergpalais* grand hotel in Dresden, Germany, where the billionaire technocrat was attending the 2016 Bilderberg Conference, Thiel confessed, "I think often you have the best conversations in smaller groups where not everything is being monitored, and that's how you have very honest conversations and how you can think better about the future."[26] From this confession, we can deduce that Thiel's "[un]monitored ... conversations" about ed-tech privatization are more honest than his publicly recorded statements on the matter. This means that Thiel and DeVos probably discussed controversial virtual-ed privatization stratagems that are "not safe for the internet" or any other public record that might spark resistance from politically conscious activists.

Despite Thiel's spin-doctor rhetoric praising the virtues of privacy, the techno-fascist Bilderberger hypocritically co-founded the In-Q-Tel/CIA-funded Palantir Technologies Inc.:[27] a private intelligence firm that contracts to conduct Big Data-mining of biometric analyses,[28] geospatial reconnaissance,[29] IT data-mining,[30] and other digital forensics services for US police departments like Long Beach PD;[31] major financial institutions such as SAC Capital;[32] and intelligence agencies including the Department of Homeland Security and the National Security Agency (NSA).[33] Thiel's ties to Deep State cyber-intelligence through the deep coffers of his corporate-government Palantir contracts raise further cause to question the nature of the "honest conversations" during his Bilderberg-style, unmonitored meeting with Secretary DeVos at his private residence.

As of late, Peter Thiel has expressed some disappointment that Trump's Presidency has "fallen short" of his hopes;[34] nevertheless, he has assured the press that Trump is definitely "still better than Hillary Clinton or the Republican zombies," and Thiel has asserted, in true Bilderberg fashion, "I can get access [to Trump] anytime I want."[35] Indeed, "Shadow President" Thiel accompanied Trump on his April 2018 business dinner with Co-CEO of the Oracle computing corporation, Safra Catz, who dined with Trump and Thiel to discuss the bidding process for a military contract between the Pentagon's Joint Enterprise Defense Infrastructure (JEDI) cloud-computing project and Catz's Oracle Corporation, which is competing with Amazon for the JEDI contract.[36]

Trump's "shortcomings" notwithstanding, I'm sure Peter Thiel is pleased that the Trump Administration has awarded Palantir Technologies Inc. with an $876 million US Army contract to collaborate with Raytheon Co. to develop software for "battlefield network" information technologies engineered to perform "Increment 1, Capability Drop 1" data-aggregation for the Army's Distributed Common Ground System (DCGS).[37]

You can bet the Bilderberger is also happy that his ed-tech investments have flourished under the Trump regime as well. Just one year after Trump took the White House, Clever Inc. was voted number four on the *Wall Street Journal's* list of the "Top 25 Tech Companies to Watch" in 2017.[38] At the same time, the Knewton Corporation, which already contracts with Pearson PLC,[39] is expanding its educational services into a new line of direct-to-student and direct-to-teacher adaptive-learning products called Alta,[40] which commercializes "personalized" supplementary courseware for higher education classes.[41]

Chapter 12

CORPORATE-FASCIST VIRTUAL LEARNING IN A NEW AGE OF "SPIRITUAL MACHINES": THE OFFICE OF AMERICAN INNOVATION AND THE 666 KABBALAH PROPHECY

To help deliver Trump's promises of "school choice" through virtual ed-tech, "The Donald" put to task a key member of his Presidential Transition Team: his son-in-law, Senior Presidential Advisor Jared Kushner, whom Trump has appointed to head up the newly founded White House Office of American Innovation (OAI), which is essentially a presidential think-tank that concentrates on corporate-fascist political-economic planning through technocratic public-private partnerships on the cutting edge of hi-tech innovation.[1]

In a press release published on March 27, 2017, the Office of the White House Press Secretary announced the official establishment of the OAI to "create task forces to focus on initiatives such as modernizing Government services and information technology ... implementing regulatory and process reforms ... and developing 'workforce of the future' programs."[2] By prioritizing the enhancement of government-funded workforce development programs through innovative integration of upgraded IT, Kushner's OAI will surely cross paths with the Department of Education's STEM-ed workforce-training initiatives through public-private partnerships between virtual charter school corporations, adaptive ed-tech companies, local school boards, and state departments of education.

Already, Kushner's OAI Special Assistant to the President for Innovation Policy and Initiatives, Matt Lira,[3] has been vocal with his support for President Trump's "Presidential Memorandum on Creating Pathways to Jobs by Increasing Access to Jobs by Increasing Access to High-Quality Science, Technology, Engineering, and Mathematics (STEM) Education."[4] At a Red Hat Government Symposium in November, 2017, Lira praised how this presidential spending directive, which allocates $200 million per year toward STEM-ed initiatives, will "do amazing things in the economy."[5]

In the meantime, Kushner's OAI is already directly impacting education governance by advancing ed-tech policies that were put in place by former President Obama's U.S. Chief Technology Officer (USCTO),[6] Todd Park,[7] who collaborated with Google engineer Mikey Dickerson to set up the United States Digital Service,[8] which operates College Scorecard:[9] a government data-aggregation service that uses an "automated application programming interface" (API) to tabulate statistics from the US Department of Treasury, [10] the National Student Loan Data System (NSLDS) of the US Department of Education, [11] and the Integrated Postsecondary Education Data System (IPEDS) of the National Center for Education Statistics.[12 a 13]

To accelerate these hi-tech innovations in STEM-ed pedagogies and school IT administration, Jared Kushner has proclaimed that his OAI "SWAT Team" will "combin[e] internal resources with the private sector's innovation and creativity, enabling the Federal Government to better serve Americans."[14] Therefore, OAI task force "recommendations will be developed in collaboration with career staff along with private-sector and other external thought leaders."[15] Stated differently, ed-tech innovations under the corporate-technocratic umbrella of Kushner's OAI will be a matter of fascistic political-economic planning through public-private partnerships between Big Tech corporations and federal government agencies.

In fact, the techno-fascist senior White House staff leading the OAI "have already hosted listening and working sessions with more than 100 private-sector CEOs, other external thought leaders, and senior Government officials."[16] During the "start-up" phase of the OAI, Kushner worked in particular with senior White House staffer, Deputy National Security Adviser Dina Powell:[17] the former Assistant Secretary of State for Educational and Cultural Affairs to the George W. Bush Administration who, according to the *Washington Post,* is also "a former Goldman Sachs executive who spent a decade at the firm managing public-private job creation programs".[18 b 19]

In addition to finance oligarch Dina Powell, there are several elite corporate-technocrats on Kushner's SWAT Team who are advising the pub-

---

a. College Scorecard digitally indexes statistical correlations between specific colleges and the following demographic information about enrollees: ethnicity, gender, graduation rate, income level, debt level, and repayment rate.

b. At the end of Trump's first year as president, Powell, who is a member of the Council on Foreign Relations, stepped down from her White House staff post. Upon Powell's resignation, White House Press Secretary Sarah Huckabee Sanders stated that "Dina Powell has been a key, trusted advisor in this administration." Kushner personally expressed his gratitude that "Dina has done a great job for the administration."

lic-private political-economic plans plotted at the OAI.[20] The Tech Barons "include[e] Apple's chief executive Tim Cook, Elon Musk from Tesla and SpaceX, Marc Benioff from Salesforce, Bill Gates, the former chief executive of Microsoft and Ginni Rometty, the chief executive of IBM," according to *TechCrunch*.[21] Each of these corporate-technocrat councilors is actively invested in ed-tech innovations.

Here's a roster of these tech tycoons and their education technology investments:

- **Tim Cook:** We can thank Tim Cook for Trump's Presidential STEM-ed Memorandum because it was he who petitioned The Donald to mandate computer coding as a basic education subject required for graduation in all publicly accredited schools. When Kushner's OAI hosted the American Technology Council (ATC) Summit to Modernize Government Services on June 19, 2017,[22] Cook attended and said to Trump, "[s]omething I feel very passionate about is that coding should be a requirement in every public school. We have a huge deficit in the school that we need today ... and we are trying to do our part, and hopefully more than our part ... but I think your leadership from government is also needed."[23] A few months later, Trump ostensibly granted Cook's wishes by signing off on the STEM Education Memorandum on September 25, 2017.[24] Several months after that, the Apple CEO spoke at a press event at Lane Tech College Prep High School in Chicago where he showcased Apple's new 9.7-inch iPad and promoted it as an ed-tech companion device designed specifically to enhance classroom learning through academically oriented features such as the Apple Pencil stylus accessory along with Pages, Numbers, and Keynote app software. Additionally, Cook announced that the Apple Corporation will offer schools reduced prices for purchasing the new iPad with the Apple Pencil. The Apple chief executive also pledged to provide Apple-contracted schools with an extra 195 gigabytes of free iCloud storage in addition to an Apple School Manager program that registers Apple identification numbers for all students who share on-campus/in-class iPads.[25]

- **Elon Musk:** Last year, Elon Musk donated $15 million to the Global Learning XPRIZE, which partnered with UNES-

CO to award $5 million of Musk's prize money to the following ed-tech companies: Curriculum Concepts International (CCI), Chimple, Kitkit School of Enuma Inc., onebillion, and RoboTutor.[26] [c] [27]

• **Marc Benioff:** *EdSurge* reports that Marc Benioff's Salesforce donated $8.5 million "to San Francisco Unified School District and Oakland Unified School District to fund principals' innovative ideas, hiring computer science and math teachers, developing college and career guidance and buying assistive technology for special education" [*sic*].[28] Benioff is also invested in Nearpod educational technologies,[29] which cater "content personalization"[30] through "adaptive learning"[31] software and "virtual reality"[32] programs that capitalize on "[u]p and coming trends like BYOD (bring your own device [to class])," according to the *Nearpod Blog*.[33]

• **Bill Gates:** Between 2008 and 2014, the Bill and Melinda Gates Foundation donated at least $60 million for virtual-learning courseware,[34] and from 2011 and 2015, the Gates Foundation paid out at least $5,322,020 in grants for "adaptive-learning" software while the foundation dumped $20

---

c. The website for the Global Learning XPRIZE describes the winners of Elon Musk's ed-tech philanthropy:

> • RoboTutor is basically an AI tutor-bot that "combines decades of research on the science of learning with advanced language technologies and innovative machine learning tools for data-driven iterative design of educational software to increase learning gains."

> • Enuma "create[s] children's learning applications" and "special education apps on iOS" that integrate technology designs and instructional methodologies "from both the gaming industry and the education sector." Enuma's "flagship product, Todo Math, launched in 2014, has over 3 million downloads worldwide."

> • The Kitkit School corporation engineers "independent-learning" technology that digitalizes lessons through "a game-based core and flexible learning architecture" that can adapt to students' competency levels "irrespective of their knowledge, skill, and environment."

> • Chimple "is developing a learning platform aimed at enabling children to learn reading, writing and mathematics on a tablet through more than 60 explorative games and 70 different stories."

> • The onebillion company develops and distributes "reading, writing and numeracy software for children ... onebillion believes in technology as a catalyst for scaleable quality education." "Scalability" is a business term that refers to the degree to which a product line can be cost-effectively mass-marketed and mass-consumed through streamlined chains of mass-production and mass-distribution.

> • Curriculum Concepts International (CCI) "is developing structured and sequential instructional programs" along with other digital "platform[s]" that allow instructors who are "non-coders" to build personalized and "engaging learning content in any language or subject area."

million into the 2014 Next Generation Courseware Challenge contest between the following ed-tech companies:[35] "Acrobatiq, Cerego, CogBooks, Lumen Learning, Rice University OpenStax, Smart Sparrow, and the Open Learning Initiative at Stanford University."[36] Bill Gates is a member of the Bilderberg Group.[37]

- **Ginni Rometty:** CEO Ginni Rometty's IBM has developed the Watson artificial intelligence (AI) bot that has an educational companion function known as Watson Education.[38] Rometty, who holds IBM stock options,[39] sees "personalized" AI-learning as the future of IBM-tech innovations: "[w]e believe that when it comes to AI," said Rometty, "the goal matters....Our goal is augmenting intelligence. Man *and* machine is about extending expertise.... It's your data, your IP, your competitive advantage.... The insights belong to you. Watson is where your data goes to learn, but when school is out, it goes back home."[40] Rometty is a member of the Council on Foreign Relations.[41]

- **Chris Liddell:** A *TechCrunch* article reports that Chris Liddell "held the CFO job at Microsoft, GM, and International Paper before joining the talent agency WME [William Morris Endeavor]."[42] Liddell has contributed to a $2.3 million investment in Bloomz, a "PreK-8 community and messaging app ... which is used by teachers and parents in more than 10,000 schools," according to *EdWeek Market Brief.*[43] Liddell, who is also the Director of the American Technology Council (ATC), has since moved on from the OAI to become Deputy Chief of Staff for Policy Coordination under White House Chief of Staff John Kelly. Nevertheless, Liddell will still be advising the OAI through continued collaboration with Special Assistant to the President for Innovation, Policy and Initiatives, Matt Lira.[44] Chris Liddell is also a member of the Bilderberg Group.[45]

In sum, nearly every member of Kushner's OAI SWAT Team is a corporate-technocrat, and each of these techno-fascists is also actively invested in cutting-edge ed-tech products. As such, these ed-tech enthusiasts at Kushner's OAI will surely explore STEM-ed and virtual-ed policy innovations that integrate the OAI's "workforce of the future programs" with "career-pathways" workforce schooling programs which implement adaptive-learning Skinner-box computers to train students for STEM jobs in the planned economy of the future.[46]

In fact, according to *Inside Higher Ed*, the OAI recently convened an August 2018 meeting with "Diane Auer Jones, the top higher ed official at the Department of Education; Michael Poliakoff, president of the American Council of Trustees and Alumni; and a representative from Strada Education Network, a nonprofit that uses philanthropic investments to identify improved pathways from education to employment."[47] Moreover, at the helm of the OAI chain of command, Kushner himself, who is a former Common Core proponent,[48] accompanied Secretary DeVos on her visit to St. Andrews Catholic School in Orlando, Florida. During their tour of the private religious school,[49] the two White House officials praised the State of Florida's innovative "Tax Credit Scholarships,"[50] which are basically "school choice" vouchers that subsidize private tuition expenses for low-income families who cannot afford the cost of admissions at private schools, including parochial schools like St. Andrews.[51]

To be sure, we cannot document all the hi-tech "school choice" innovations being planned by Kushner and his public-private SWAT Team because the OAI will not cooperate with a Freedom of Information Act (FOIA) request from the Democracy Forward Foundation in conjunction with Food and Water Watch Inc.,[52] which have jointly filed a lawsuit to compel the OAI to comply with 5 U.S.C. § 522 of the FOIA legal code.[53]

In the wake of the joint suit, US Democratic Senators Catherine Cortez Masto of Nevada and Gary Peters of Michigan have filed their own inquiry into the dealings of the OAI. In an April 15, 2018 letter to Chief of Staff Kelly, Masto and Peters expressed worries that the OAI is "potentially a vehicle for cronyism and waste" because of the lack of transparency regarding "off-the-record meetings with business leaders such as officials from an association representing Twitter, Google, and Amazon, all hidden from public view."[54] The letter also cites Kushner's "fail[ure] to place his financial assets in a blind trust and [that he] repeatedly omitted key facts on his financial disclosure form."[55] Furthermore, the senators cite conflicts of interest between the OAI's hurricane recovery aid to Puerto Rico and the OAI Assistant for Intragovernmental and Technology Initiatives, Reed Cordish, who "holds defaulted Puerto Rican debt."[56] [d] [57]

---

d. Cordish has since resigned from his post as the Assistant for Intragovernmental and Technology Initiatives at the OAI.

Chabad Lubavitch and the Mossad:

Jared Kushner's name has not been identified on any leaked Bilderberger Group roster, but he and his OAI are apparently shrouded in Bilderberg-like secrecy that even Congress has not been able to bring to light. At the same time, Kushner, who is a practicing Orthodox Jew,[58] has donated large sums of money to Chabad Lubavitch,[59] which is a Hasidic Zionist organization that studies the Babylonian Talmud and practices the secret mysticism of Kabbalah.[60] Chabad Lubavitch is not really a secret society, but former National Security Agency (NSA) analyst Wayne Madsen reports that certain Chabad Lubavitch centers are shells that front for spy cells operating under the aegis of the Mossad, which is the Israeli version of the Central Intelligence Agency (CIA).[61 e 62] In other words, "Chabad houses," according to Madsen, are undercover deployment centers for Mossad secret agents.

Madsen, a former Senior Fellow for the Electronic Privacy Information Center,[63] states that:

> [m]ultiple reports from inside the Trump White House and the FBI that point to a major on-going counter-intelligence investigation of the financial dealings and foreign intelligence contacts of Trump's "Secretary for Everything," son-in-law Jared Kushner, and Trump's

---

e. It should be noted that, just as the secret intelligence networks of America's CIA have been infiltrated with adepts of the occult secret society of Skull and Bones such as George H. W. Bush, William Bundy, William Sloane Coffin, Charles S. Whitehouse, F. Trubee Davison, and William F. Buckley Jr., so too are the secret intelligence networks of Israeli Mossad intermingled with occult Kabbalists. Wayne Madsen's investigative research into undercover Mossad-Chabad connections reveals how, "[i]n 2014, former Mossad director general Meir Dagan publicly admitted that the Chabad organization provides spiritual assistance at Mossad's Central Command in Tel Aviv." Madsen's exposé is confirmed by a report from COL Live, which is a Chabad Lubavitch "Community News Service." In a February 2014 article titled "Lubavitchers in the Israeli Mossad," a "COLlive reporter" writes,

> [d]uring the conversation about the employment of haredi Jews in the country's many security branches, Dagan was asked whether Lubavitchers serve in the Mossad.
> His reply: "You will be surprised to know how many haredim serve in the Mossad."
> Dagan added that aside from the employment of chassidim in a professional capacity, the Chabad organization provides spiritual assistance at Mossad's central commend in Tel Aviv.
> "Chabad gets a Yashar Koach (kudos) because thanks to them the synagogue at the Mossad command was renovated and we now have a luxurious shul," [stated Dagan].

Dagan also said that "[t]he Chabad House in Minsk, (a city which) its Jewish history is known to all, became my home … Rabbi *Schneur Deitsch [of Chabad Lubavitch]* and his wife will remain forever engraved in my heart." According to the *COL Live* article, "the Rebbe's unknown ties to the head of the Mossad and their assistance to Chabad's educational and outreach activities in the Former Soviet Union were mapped out in the Hebrew book 'The Rebbe and the Mossad,' published in 1998. The inside story of the Rebbe's involvement in Israel's security, as told by its defense and government leaders, is told in JEM's [Jewish Educational Media's] documentary film *Faithful and Fortified* – Volume 1." Between these quotes from Dagan and this report from a Chabad "Community News Service," we basically have "primary source" statements from both the Mossad and the Chabad themselves which prove that Mossad agents are immersed in the spiritual practices of Chabad Lubavitch, which are rooted in the ancient mysticism of Kabbalah, which stems from an even older form of Babylonian mysticism.

daughter and Kushner's wife, Ivanka Trump, are also raising their close connections to Chabad [Lubavitch] organizations. . . .

The nexus between "Javanka" – as Kushner and Ivanka are known inside the White House by their major detractors—and some of Donald Trump's crime syndicate business partners in the worldwide network of Chabad houses, considered by many intelligence agencies to serve as Israeli Mossad "safe houses" and nests for the Russian-Jewish Solntsevskaya Mafia, has raised concerns within the FBI and Central Intelligence Agency.[64]

We know that Kushner has been under investigation by former FBI Director Robert Mueller as part of his infamous Russia-gate probe,[65] and Chabadnik Kushner even had his national security clearance temporarily revoked as a consequence.[66] We also know that Kushner has come under investigation by the White House Office of Government Ethics for potentially leveraging his official role as Senior Advisor to the President in order to garner nearly $500 million in personal business loans from Citigroup and Apollo Global Management after meeting with them in his official White House capacity to discuss public-private infrastructure planning.[67] With all these implications of criminal cronyism surrounding Kushner and his nontransparent OAI, it is not unreasonable to suspect that Kushner's OAI facilitates backchannels for Mossad-Lubavitch operations. [f][68]

f. Madsen analyzes multiple case studies which implicate that Chabad centers are actually Mossad fronts:

> • In 1985, the Rue De Palestin chapter of Chabad Lubavitch in Tunis was caught spying on the Palestine Liberation Organization (PLO) and then relaying the covert intelligence to the Mossad.

> • In 2012, India's foreign intelligence agency, the Research and Analysis Wing (RAW), deported Rabbi Sheneor Zalman and his wife Yaffa Shenoi from the Southern Indian State of Kerala on charges that these two members of the Kerala chapter of Chabad Lubavitch were in fact undercover operatives for the State of Israel. Not far away in the Goa chapter of India's network of Chabad houses, retired Mossad officer Hilik Magnus has been "operat[ing] a 'search and recovery' service for Israeli 'tourists' who go missing or are arrested in Asia."

> • When Australian Chabad acolyte, Ben Zygier, allegedly committed suicide in 2013 in an Israeli prison, the details surrounding the supposed suicide were classified under a gag order from Israeli State Security. Madsen suspects that "Zygier, who was said to be away from Australia on a Mossad mission, may have been executed after it was discovered by the Israeli intelligence agency that he was a double agent who was spilling the beans on the Mossad-Chabad connection to another intelligence agency."

> • In 2014, former Finnish representative of the European Union Parliament, Esko Seppänen, chided the Helsinki City Council's decision to convert former Marine Customs barracks into a "Chabad House" because Seppänen contended that the repurposed "Chabad barracks" were a prime location to be refitted by the Mossad for the "interception of messages" transmitted through the "telecommunications of the Finnish State."

> • In 2015, "Top Secret" files from the State Security Agency (SSA) of South Africa were leaked to unveil how the Mossad reportedly commandeered Chabad organizations to spy on South African Muslims and others.

Wayne Madsen's investigative research also finds that cronyism between Jared and Chabad-Mossad has been a key influence persuading Kushner's father-in-law, President Trump, to champion pro-Zionist foreign policies, such as the freezing of American financial aid to Palestinians; the USA's recognition of Jerusalem as the capital of the State of Israel; and the relocation of the US embassy from Tel Aviv to Jerusalem.[69] Chabad-Mossad influence over American foreign policies concerning Israel is nothing new, but Kushner's crony connections to Chabad-Mossad may also be impacting education innovation at his OAI.

Chabad Lubavitchers have asserted that the Chabad movement is "on the cutting edge" of "interactive ... online" educational technology innovations.[70] In a Chabad Lubavitch of Louisiana article titled "Technology and Spirituality, Compatible," Rabbi Mendel Rivkin writes,

> one area of technology is significantly enhancing our family's spirituality. One of the rapidly developing areas of technology involves online educational settings. Chabad is on the cutting edge in this area. My daughter Mushka participates in an online classroom (part-time – as a supplement to the wonderful education she receives at Torah Academy). She has real-time instruction from live teachers as well as visual and audio interaction with the teacher and other students in her class. They utilize a multiple interface approach (typing, speaking, listening etc.) that is all interactive and within a secure online environment. This technology has allowed her to grow in many areas including scholastically and socially.[71]

Since the DeVos Department of Education is already hyping the propagation of online virtual school corporations that implement Skinnerian adaptive-learning software, Lubavitcher Kushner is primed to push Chabad's virtual ed-tech recommendations through the OAI's "workforce of the future programs."[72]

The Technocratic Politics of Occult Kabbalah:

Rabbi Mendel Rivkin also believes that the supposed wonders of online virtual education are actually the physical manifestation of secret prophecies encrypted in the Zohar scriptures of the Kabbalah, which is an ancient occult practice of Judaic mysticism.[73 & 74] Rivkin contextualizes his glorification of virtual ed-tech with the following preface:

g. By definition, all forms of mysticism are deemed occult, often pejoratively in connotation with "pagan magick" or "black magick." However, the literal denotation of the word "occult" simply means "hidden from the eye" or, in other words, hidden from ocular perception. *Merriam-Webster's*

[w]hen explaining the flood of Noah, the Zohar comments: "And six hundred years into the sixth millennium the gates of wisdom from above and the fountains of wisdom from below will open, and the world will be corrected as a preparation for its elevation in the seventh [millennium.]"

The prediction corresponds to the year 1840. The "gates of wisdom from above" represents the Torah's inner teachings. The "fountains of wisdom from below" refers to science and technology. Indeed, we see that in both of those areas there was explosive development around that time. The industrial revolution was followed by amazing leaps in the development of science, medicine and technology. Similarly, in Torah development, the teachings of Chassidism had begun to spread and become accessible to multitudes of people via the printed and later the digital word.

All of this, the Zohar explains, serves as a preparation for the "Seventh Millenium" [*sic*] the era of Redemption. We can understand how Torah development serves this cause. But what role does science and technology play to this end?[75]

Rivkin "answers" this loaded rhetorical question by suggesting that virtual ed-tech will somehow evolve "spiritual ideas."

This very same Zohar prophecy is likewise deciphered by Lubavitcher Simon Jacobson in two separate articles "based on the teachings of the Lubavitcher Rebbe [Menachem Mendel Schneerson],"[76] who was the figurehead of Chabad Lubavitch until his death in 1994.[77] [h] [78] In both articles, which elucidate the same interpretation verbatim, Jacobson affirms Rivkin's hi-tech decryption of the "Sixth Millennium" by decoding "the current technological revolution [as] in fact the hand of G-d at work."[79]

Dictionary defines "occult" as a "transitive verb: to shut off from view or exposure"; and the *Oxford English Dictionary* likewise defines "occult" as "verb" which means to "[c]ut off from view by interposing something." Therefore, whether "black" or "white" magick, all forms of mysticism are occult spiritualities because they practice secret rituals based on secret knowledge that they keep hidden from the profane eyes of uninitiated commoners. To be sure, Chabad Lubavitch actually publishes some online free "translations" of Kabbalist texts such as the Zohar; but nevertheless, like all mystical occult texts, Kabbalah scriptures are so saturated with secret symbolism that uninitiated readers will be incapable of deciphering the texts without a legend, key, or other decoding device from an adept Kabbalist. Hence, even though the Zohar and other Kabbalah scriptures are partially translated into English online, the true meanings of those translations are still occulted so that only adepts can fully understand their secret meanings.

h. Interestingly, in 1978, President Jimmy Carter decreed that Menachem Mendel Schneerson's birthday, April 18, would thereafter be celebrated as Education Day U.S.A. until President Trump changed the Schneerson holiday to Education and Sharing Day, which The Donald proclaimed will hereafter be celebrated on the 7th of every April in honor of "Rabbi Schneerson [who] wrote that 'we can neither be satisfied nor slacken our efforts' so long as 'there is still one child that does not receive an adequate education.' These words inspire us today, as they did then [on April 18, 1978], to empower our children and share with each of them the opportunity and promise of America."

Thus, these corroborating prognostications from Lubavitchers Jacobson and Rivkin show how Chabadnik Kabbalists basically exalt digital information technologies in general, and virtual ed-tech specifically, as religious sacraments that upgrade mystical communion with "G-d" during our current era of hi-tech "preparation" for the coming new age of "Redemption."

This current "Sixth Millennium," according to Kabbalist cosmology, is signified by the number "666." Whereas Christians associate the number "666" with the satanic antichrist's "Mark of the Beast" that is prophesied for the End Times in the Bible's Book of Revelations,[80] Kabbalist numerology actually reveres the number "666" as a holy digit symbolizing the "perfection of the world" through technological breakthroughs.

According to Rabbi Yirmiyahu Ullman's "Ask the Rabbi" column,[81] which is posted on the Ohr Somayach *yeshiva* (Orthodox Jewish school) website,

> [t]he numerical value of "Meah Shearim" is 666, a number which has esoteric and kabbalistic meaning in Judaism, as indicated by the Vilna Gaon in his commentary to the Zohar...
>
> [T]he number six represents the physical world. The Torah describes the creation of the universe as a six-part, six day, process. Our ancient sources describe the universe as emanating in six directions -- north, south, east, west, up, down – from a central point. All physical space and all physical objects have these six dimensions.
>
> 666 is six repeated three times. Repeating a concept three times represents the affirmation and strength of that concept. The number 666 could thus represent the strength and perfection of the physical world, which Judaism teaches will occur in the messianic era, when the physical world will reach its ultimate purpose.[82]

Stated differently, from "six hundred years into the sixth millennium" all the way through the present century of the Sixth Millennium, the hi-tech evolution venerated by Rivkin and Jacobson has manifested a "preparation" for the coming "messianic era" of "perfection" by unveiling the occult secrets of the six dimensions of the physical world that "the hand of G-d" created in "a six-part, six day, process."

As such, it is perhaps the Kushner family's reverence for this hi-tech Kabbalah prophecy that inspired Jared and his father Charles to utilize their Kushner Companies LLC real estate company to purchase the edifice at the infamous 666 Fifth Avenue address for $1.8 billion, "paying the highest price ever for a New York office building," according to the *New York Times*.[83] As a stalwart Chabad-Lubavitcher, Kushner paid this record-breaking sum perhaps because he has faith that the numerological powers of the 666 address will function as his own personal Kabbalah talisman that blesses his leadership role in the "perfection of the physical world" through the perfection of technological evolution at his White House Office of American Innovation. To the extent that human beings understand the physical world through science, and insofar as science "perfect[s]" the physical world with technological inventions, the hi-tech innovations developed through Kushner's OAI will ostensibly help to usher in "the perfection of the physical world" prophesied in the Kabbalist interpretation of the number "666" encoded in the Zohar scriptures.

Notwithstanding the Kushners' vows to Orthodox Judaism, it is well documented that the Kushner family is devoted to the mystical Kabbalist sects of Rabbi David Pinto and his son Rabbi Yoshiyahu Pinto. From 2004 through 2013, the C. Kushner Companies Foundation and the Charles and Seryl Kushner Family Foundation funneled $217,000 dollars into the Chevrat Pinto Beth Midrash, which is Rabbi David Pinto's "House of Study."[84] According to *The Forward*, a Yiddish-Jewish magazine that has been in publication since 1897, Jared Kushner "is one of seven coequal directors of the Charles and Seryl Kushner Family Foundation, according to 2014 tax documents, and was a member of a board of directors led by his mother at the C. Kushner Companies Foundation."[85] Additionally, it is worth noting that Jared's uncle and aunt, Richard and Marisa Stadtmauer, poured at least $592,000 into Chevrat Pinto between 2009 and 2017.[86 i 87]

It appears that the Kushners' fiscal offerings to the Kabbalist priesthood have paid off; for a Kabbalist "priest" contacted the head of Republicans Abroad Israel to prophesy just one week before Trump's election that he was preordained to win the 2016 US Presidency,[88] which would in turn catapult his son-in-law into the White House Office of American Innovation. The *Times of Israel* states, "Marc Zell, head of Republicans Abroad Israel, told Yanky Farber, a columnist for *Behadrei Haredim*, that a *mekubal*, or sage steeped in the Jewish mystical tradition of Kabbalah,

---

i. It is also worth noting that Rabbi David's son, Rabbi Yoshiyahu, was jailed in an Israeli prison after being "convicted of trying to bribe the head of the Israel Police's National Fraud Squad, Ephraim Bracha, with $200,000 to obtain information about a criminal investigation into Pinto's Hazon Yeshaya foundation," according to the *Jerusalem Post*. One last notable fact from another Jewish media outlet, Ynetnews, which is a subsidiary of Israel's Yedioth Media Group: less than a month after President Trump took the reigns of the White House, Yoshiyahu "Pinto [was] released after serving a year for bribery of a senior police official despite the objections of the prosecution and the Israel Police who argue that Pinto is still a danger."

had informed him that according to the tradition's seminal text, the Zohar, Trump will be the next president of the United States."[89] Zell reported that he "passed this [prediction from the *mekubal*] on to the Trump
campaign in the US and the Jewish advisers were amazed, in a good way,
about this news."[90]

About a week later, in reverence of this *mekubal's* prophecy, Jared and
his wife, Ivanka Trump, made a ritual pilgrimage to Queens, New York,
where on November 6, 2016, just two days before the highly questionable
election of Jared's father-in-law, the Kabbalist couple "visited the grave of
the Lubavitcher Rebbe ... known as 'the Ohel' – Hebrew for 'the tent' –
which houses the remains of the former rebbe of Chabad, Menachem M.
Schneerson, as well as those of Schneerson's father-in-law, who was the
sixth Lubavitcher Rebbe."[91] [j] [92]

If this *Times of Israel* article sounds like a fringe story, be sure that this
fantastical report provides basis for a scholarly, peer-reviewed journal article entitled "A Moroccan Kabbalist in the White House: Understanding
the Relationship between Jared Kushner and Moroccan Jewish Mysticism," which was published in the academic journal *Jewish Social Studies: History, Culture, Society.* The author, Aomar Boum, who is Assistant
Professor of Anthropology at the University of California, Los Angeles,
and Faculty Fellow at the Université Internationale de Rabat, Morocco,[93]
writes that the *mekubal* who predicted the Trump presidential victory is
one of the

> miracle-working rabbis associated with Jared Kushner, the presi-
> dent's Orthodox Jewish son-in-law, [who] wasted no time claiming
> that they [*mekubals*] had had something to do with it [the Kabbalist
> prophecy of Trump's presidential win]. Rabbi David Pinto and Rab-
> bi Yoshiyahu Pinto, two descendants of a long line of North African
> rabbis, are thought to have been among those miracle workers.[94]

Professor Boum interviewed a follower of the Kabbalist Pintos, and he
relays how the interviewee, "Yosef, told me that 'the election of Trump

---

j. In another article published by *The Forward*, it is reported that Jared's wife, Ivanka Trump, has
been spotted several times wearing "a thin red thread tied around her wrist.... [which] is a noted
symbol of Kabbalah.... [I]ts first mention in Jewish texts dates back nearly 2,000 years.... The traditional, Kabbalah-referencing red thread also has seven knots in it, as seven is a highly symbolic
number in Kabbalah." To be sure, Ivanka only converted to Judaism, and thereby to Kabbalah, after
Kushner dumped her because she was not Jewish. In other words, any Judaic traditions that Ivanka
practices can be presumed to have come from Kushner and the Kushner family. *Forbes Magazine*
reports that Jared's brother, Joshua Kushner, was wearing a similar "red Kabbalah string bracelet on
the other [wrist]" at a Thrive Capital investment meeting in April of 2017. It is also worth noting that
even Donald Trump's second wife, Marla Maples, is "a longtime Kabbalist," according to *Vanity Fair.*

does not only mean that there will be Shabbat candles every Friday night at the White House, but that Moroccan mystic kabbalists will bless the White House from Ashdod every Shabbat.'"[95] Boum's academic analysis finds a "comfortable attitude of Kushner and his family toward mystical folklore, folk magic, and beliefs that have long been ridiculed by Ashkenazi Jews."[96]

"Disclaimer":

If you don't believe in anything spiritual, then you probably think there's nothing to be made of these Kabbalist overtones coloring the Kushner-Trump OAI. But even if you don't believe that there any supernatural powers conjured through these Kabbalist rites and rituals, it is apparent that Kushner does put stock in this ancient "mystery school" magick. Hence, it is imperative to at least scrutinize the sociocultural implications of Kushner's occult-spiritualist inspirations motivating his executive decisions at the techno-fascist Office of American Innovation.

Historical Timeline (The Order of the Illuminati – The Order of Skull and Bones – Educational Psychology)

	1776 1787	1832	1879	1904	1968	Present (2019)
	(rise and fall of the Illuminati)	*(Skull and Bones founded)*	*(Wundt sets up world's first psychology lab)*	*(Rockefeller GEB founded)*	*(Skinner publishes Technology of Teaching)*	*(Mnuchin shapes "Tax Cuts and Robots Act")*

The Order of the Illuminati of Bavaria (1776-1787)

- Adam Weishaupt *(founder of the Illuminati)*
- Johann Heinrich Pestalozzi *("ABC of Sense Impression")*
- Karl Kasimir Wundt *(father of Wilhelm Wundt)*

Education Psychology & Education Technology (1803-)

Herbart's ABC of Sense-Perception — *Stimulus-Response Conditioning* — *Behaviorist Conditioning* — *Operant Conditioning* — *"Teaching Machines"* — *Posthumanism*

Johann Friedrich Herbart

Wilhelm Wundt

William James

G. Stanley Hall

John Dewey

John B. Watson

James McKeen Cattell

E. L. Thorndike

B. F. Skinner → Adaptive-Learning → Artificial Intelligence
Software

[Rockefeller GEB]

(Percy Rockefeller)

McGeorge Bundy → Steven Mnuchin

Lodge 322 of The Order of Skull and Bones (1832 – Present)

Timothy Dwight

D. C. Gilman

Andrew White

Promoted Wundtian Psychology as Presidents of Johns Hopkins University, Cornell University, and Yale University.

Bankrolled Stimulus-Response and Behaviorist Animal-Training Psychology through the Rockefeller GEB

Funded Skinner's research of operant-conditioning "teaching machines" as Dean of Harvard University

Financially incentivizing computer-assisted learning through "Tax Cuts and Robots" Act

Chapter 13

Bonesman Stephen Mnuchin's "Tax Cuts and Robots Act": How the Order still Indirectly Controls Education

Duct his time as a Research Fellow at Stanford University's Hoover Institution, Antony C. Sutton became perplexed when his historical investigations discovered that the United States of America had been indispensable in propping up the techno-logical-industrial infrastructure of the Soviet Union from the begin-ning of the first Red Scare throughout the Cold War. In spite of con-certed suppression from Hoover Institution officials, Sutton recorded his findings in a three-volume series, *Western Technology and Soviet Eco-nomic Development;*[1] yet he still remained puzzled as to why the USA would help to build up the economic powers of its sworn enemy: the communist USSR. Years later, after sifting through the Order's secret address books leaked by Charlotte Thomson Iserbyt, the puzzle pieces finally made sense to Sutton, who found that prominent members of Skull and Bones were the key brokers at the center of American eco-nomic assistance not only to Soviet Russia, but also to Nazi Germa-ny. In *How the Order Creates War and Revolution* (1984), Sutton doc-uments how Bones agents have orchestrated this Hegelian-dialectical stage management of communist-fascist geopolitical conflict in order to synthesize these two despotic political systems into a global totali-tarian New World Order.[2]

Sutton's exposé on the Order's collusion with both Stalin and Hitler is undoubtedly one of the most profound historical revelations ever docu-mented; yet Sutton told Iserbyt that *How the Order Creates War and Rev-olution* is not as important as *How the Order Controls Education* (1985), which is cited throughout this book.[3] Today, the Order is still controlling education through the puppet strings of Bonesman Stephen Mnuchin.[4]

The "Tax Cuts and Robots Act":

United States Treasury Secretary Stephen Mnuchin, a former Goldman Sachs Vice President who once worked for George Soros,[5] is a power-player in the Trump Administration's technocratic policy renovations. After President Trump created the American Technology Council (ATC) with his Executive Order 13794,[6] Mnuchin attended the first meeting of the ATC where he met with top technocrats,[7] such as Bilderbergers Jeff Bezos of Amazon and Eric Schmidt of Google's parent company, Alphabet.[8] Topics of discussion between Mnuchin and the techno-elite at the seminal ATC conference included plans to improve government IT and expand computer science education.[9]

To incentivize these public-private ATC plans, Mnuchin was instrumental in pushing Trump's deregulatory tax reform plan: the "HR1: Tax Cuts and Jobs Act" of the 115th Congress.[10] According to *Politico's* White House correspondent Anne Karni, Speaker of the House of Representatives Paul Ryan praised how Mnuchin's personal contributions to Trump's tax-cut bill were able "to improve the legislation."[11] Moreover, Mnuchin hyped the tax bill by arguing that failure to pass the Trump tax overhaul would result in "a reversal of a significant amount of these [stock market] gains" that have risen during Trump's presidency.[12]

The particulars of Mnuchin's "improve[ments]" to HR1 are unclear, but the overall tax stratagem will catalyze the standardization of hi-tech virtual schooling through automated adaptive-learning computers because the oligarchical "Tax Cuts and Jobs Act" incentivizes businesses to replace human labor with computers, robotics, artificial intelligence (AI), and other technological innovations that automate workforce production. National Public Radio (NPR) reports that many economists are criticizing HR1, arguing that the "trickle-down" bill should more appropriately be named the "Tax Cuts and Robots Act."[13] In particular, MIT Professor of Economics, Daron Acemoglu, contends that the techno-fascist tax rewrite is "creating huge subsidies in our tax code for capital and encouraging employers to use machines instead of labor."[14]

Acemoglu explains how the "Full and Immediate Expensing" clause of HR1 allows businesses to immediately write off any expenses toward new "assets," such as computers, robotics, AI, and/or other automation technologies, by permitting instant deduction of total depreciation against taxable profits in the first year. As a result, as long as a company has enough liquid capital to make the purchase upfront, that corporation will effectively be able to buy an automation-tech workforce to replace human labor at ultimately zero cost because, at the end of that tax year, the total price of the automation expenses will be deducted from the company's taxable earnings immediately upon filing the business's taxes. In turn, a corporation will save money by purchasing a $1-million techno-automaton, instead of hiring a human employee to perform that same automated job at the price of $1 million dollars over ten years.

Corporate financiers have been aggressively bankrolling automation technologies in eager preparation for the Full and Immediate Expensing clause of the Trump-Mnuchin "Tax Cuts and Robots Act."[15] Oligarchs such as hedge fund managers from Hood Capital, Hodges Capital, and Columbia Threadneedle Investments have long been expecting that businesses will capitalize on the Trump-Mnuchin tax overhaul by investing in automated technologies that will slash labor expenditures. In anticipation of the neo-conservative tax reform, hedge funders and other corporate investors have boosted the Robo Global Robotics and Automation Index ETF up to a total value of $1.4 billion, which amounts to a 35% gain that is almost three times the 13.5% growth in the total S&P 500 index since Trump took office. Stocks for AeroVironment Inc., a drone manufacturer; IPG Photonics Corp., a laser company; and Harmonic Drive Systems Inc., a gear manufacturer, have grown by more than 90% since Trump's inauguration while other automation-tech corporations, such as Cognex Corp., have benefited from an 80% gain since Trump was sworn into the White House.[16] FARO Technologies Inc., which manufactures a line of ed-tech products, has likewise exploded with a big stock boom in the wake of Trump's election.[17]

Even the Trilateral Commission forecasts how the Trump-Mnuchin tax breaks will spur a boom in computerized automation investments. A whitepaper entitled "Trump and Manufactured Goods," which was authored by Trilateralist Luis Rubio of Mexico,[18] states that corporate

> profits "stationed" outside the U.S. … have been left behind because [U.S.] companies do not want to pay a 35% tax to repatriate them. Trump is proposing a very low tax (between 8% and 20% according to the press) for their repatriation, but in exchange for their being utilized for new investments on U.S. soil.… [I]t is most probable that this capital would be used for high-tech investments, that is, robots, minimizing the employment of blue-collar workers.[19]

To put it another way, the Trilateral Commission foresees that Trump's oligarchical tax plan will prompt corporations to replace Third-World "sweat-shop" slaves with even cheaper robot slaves while displacing American workers at the same time – all at the low, low rate of a 20% or even 8% repatriation tax.

In brief, the stage is set for Mnuchin's pro-robot tax scam to galvanize investments not only in labor automation generally, but also in virtual ed-tech automation that specifically replaces the labor of human instruction with adaptive-learning software and even artificial intelligence technologies.

But not to worry, Bonesman Mnuchin has asserted that he is "not worried at all" about mass unemployment due to AI automation:

> [t]echnology has made the American worker more productive. In terms of artificial intelligence taking American jobs, I think we're, like, so far away from that – not even on my radar screen.[20]

After public backlash for this ignorant comment, Mnuchin changed his tune:

> [w]hen I made the comment on artificial intelligence – and there's different views on artificial intelligence – I was referring to kind of like R2D2 in Star Wars. Robotics are here. Self-driving cars are something that are gonna be here soon. I am fully aware of and agree that technology is changing and our workers do need to be prepared.[21]

This flippant spin-doctoring of the very real threats of AI and other automated tech should be expected from Mnuchin; for he is a disciple of the perfidious Order of Death, otherwise known as Skull and Bones,[a] [22] which has manipulated the Hegelian dialectic to stage-mange America's false left-right political paradigm for almost two centuries by duplicitously masquerading on both sides of the conservative-liberal political spectrum in order to maneuver rightwing politics towards corporate fascism while steering leftwing politics toward Statist communism.[23] [b] [24]

---

a   In *America's Secret Establishment: An Introduction to the Order of Skull and Bones*, Antony Sutton provides primary-source documentation of how The Order of Death is contractually instituted under the charter of the Russell Trust Association, which was legally incorporated by William Huntington Russell and Daniel Coit Gilman, who were respectively the founding president and the founding treasurer of the Russell Trust's Order of Death. Sutton writes, "[m]ore formally, for legal purposes, The Order was incorporated as The Russell Trust in 1856. It was also once known as the 'Brotherhood of Death.' Those who make light of it, or want to make fun of it, call it 'Skull & Bones,' or just plain 'Bones.'"

b   It is important to clarify here that both communism and fascism are basically two sides

Expanding Antony C. Sutton's seminal research on the Order, I have traced the history of how prominent Bonesmen became presidents of American universities where they propagated Hegelian sociopolitical philosophies that laid the foundational groundwork for the current "school choice" movement to corporatize education through virtual charter schools which utilize adaptive-learning software for workforce training. I have also historicized how Bonesman Daniel Coit Gilman instituted Wundtian educational psychology throughout US academia by promoting Wundtian-Hegelian psychologists G. Stanley Hall and John Dewey, who became the forerunners to the behaviorist and operant-conditioning schools of educational psychology that inspired B. F. Skinner's "teaching machines," which were the predecessors of today's adaptive-learning computer programs.[25] Gilman was even instrumental in the financing of Wundtian-Hegelian workforce schooling, as he was the first president of the Carnegie Institution of Washington and an officer of the Rockefeller General Education Board (GEB).[26]

It is important to revisit here Sutton's *How the Order Controls Education,* because it shines light on how Mnuchin's endorsement of the "Tax Cuts and Robots Act" is effectively ushering in the next phase of the Order's Corporate State, Wundtian-Hegelian education system by upgrading workforce-conditioning curriculums through automated stimulus-response computers and AI-learning bots that render human teachers obsolete.

The Order of the Illuminati, The Order of Death:

The Skull and Bones cult may be traced back to the Bavarian Illuminati founded by the Jesuit Freemason,[27] Adam Weishaupt,[28] who was a Professor of Canon Law at the University of Ingolstadt, Germany.[29]

Sutton's investigation of the Order's address books leaked to him by Charlotte Thomson Iserbyt have revealed that Skull and Bones is actually "Chapter 322 of a German secret society. [...] The American chapter of this German order was founded in 1833 at Yale University by General

---

of the same "command-and-control" coin: inverse modes of essentially the same totalitarian merger of public-government power with private-corporate power. As such, The Order's fascist-communist dialectic is a two-pronged scheme with a singular objective: to consolidate the separated powers of America's legislative, executive, and judicial branches of government while eroding the checks and balances between the laissez faire freedoms of the private sector and citizens' inalienable human rights which are protected by the public rule of law under the US Constitution's Bill of Rights. Both communist and fascist restructurings of the United States government pave roads to tyranny that bring about this very dismantling of America's democratic republic; so the Bones cabal is happy to foment either a communist or fascist dictatorship because both political systems do away with the sovereign power of the people to self-govern in accordance with the "self-evident Truth" of their natural rights in the Declaration of Independence, which are codified into the legal authority of the US Constitution.

William Huntington Russell and Alphonso Taft who, in 1876, became Secretary of War in the Grant Administration." [30] [c] [31] Sutton reveals that, shortly before Russell officially set up the US chapter in 1833, "Russell imported the society from Germany [in 1832] and so it has been argued the 322 stands for '32 (1832), the second chapter, of this German organization. Possibly a chapter 320 and a chapter 321 may exist somewhere."[32]

It can be affirmed that Chapter 322 is a satellite branch of an original German secret society. Evidence of these origins can be found in an archived pamphlet which was anonymously printed and distributed to publicize the discoveries of the "File and Claw" vigilante group that broke into the "Bones Temple," also known as the Bones Tomb, in 1876. Titled "The Fall of Skull and Bones," this pamphlet describes how the File and Claw insurgents were able to raid the Bones Temple and burgle a card that states, "From the German Chapter. Presented by Patriarch D. [Daniel] C. [Coit] Gilman of D. 50."[33]

So, what was the beginning of the first chapter of the Order of Skull and Bones in Germany? There is evidence to implicate that Yale University's Brotherhood of Death is actually an offshoot of the Bavarian Illuminati of the University of Ingolstadt, Germany.

TrineDay publisher Kris Millegan, who was the late Sutton's research partner, historicizes how the existence of the diabolical Illuminati was exposed:

> [i]in 1785, [when] a courier died en-route to Paris from Frankfort-on-the-Main. *Original Shift in Days of Illuminations*, a tract written by Adam "Spartacus" Weishaupt, founder of the Illuminati, was recovered from the dead messenger. It contained the secret society's long-range plan for The New World Order through world revolution.
>
> The Bavarian Government promptly outlawed the society and in 1787 published the details of The Illuminati conspiracy in *The Original Writings of the Order and Sect of the Illuminati. . . .*[d] [34]
>
> There is disagreement among scholars as to whether or not the Illuminati survived its banishment. Nevertheless, under Weishaupt's guidance, the group had been quite successful in attracting members and through various manipulations had allied it-

---

c   Sutton continues: "Alphonso Taft was the father of William Howard Taft, the only man to be both President and Chief Justice of the United States.

d   Millegan adds, "The Illuminati was publicly founded May 1, 1776, at the University of Ingolstadt by Weishaupt, a Professor of Canon Law. It was a very 'learned' society; Weishaupt drew the earlier members of his new order from among his students," just like The Order draws its recruits from among a collegiate student body.

self with the extensive Masonic networks in Europe and the United States.[35 e 36]

Approximately five years after The Elector of Bavaria abolished the Illuminati, according to Sutton's calculations, the first chapter of The Order of Death was established in Germany:

> [t]he [Skull and Bones] catalogs have always printed in one form or another, usually at the head of the page, the letters "P and D." Thus, the 1833 list has "Period 2 Decade 3."
>
> The period is constant at "2" while the Decade increases by one each ten years, i.e., decade 3, 4, 5 etc.
>
> The "D" number is always less than the class number. Up to 1970 by 2 and after 1970 by 1. In other words, the first list of members—the class of 1833 was designated "P. 231 – D. 31."
>
> In brief, the organization started in the United States was in the third decade of the second period.... The first decade of the second period would then begin in 1800 and the first period would have ended in the decade 1790 to 1800. That places us in the time frame of the elimination of Illuminati by the Bavarian Elector.[37]

Stated differently, the last decade of the first period of The Order would have ended in the same decade that the Illuminati was disbanded.

Not only do these timelines coincide with the emergence of The Order of Skull and Bones as an underground resurgence of the Order of the Illuminati, but the occult rituals of Skull and Bones parallel the secret initiation rites of Weishaupt's Illuminati. In a 1977 *Esquire Magazine* article titled "Last Secrets of Skull and Bones," journalist Ron Rosenbaum writes, "I do seem to have come across definite, if skeletal, links between the origins of Bones rituals and those of the notorious Bavarian Illuminists."[38]

---

e   Indeed, in the collected Writings of George Washington, the first president of the United States himself recorded the following:

> [i]t is not my intention to doubt that the doctrine of the Illuminati and the principles of Jacobinism had not spread in the United States. On the contrary, no one is more satisfied of this fact than I am.
>
> The idea that I meant to convey, was, that I did not believe that the Lodges of Free Masons in this Country had, as Societies, endeavoured to propagate the diabolical tenets of the first, or pernicious principles of the latter (if they are susceptible of separation). That Individuals of them may have done it, or that the founder, or instrument employed to found, the Democratic Societies in the United States, may have had these objects; and actually had a separation of the People from their Government in view, is too evident to be questioned.

This commentary on the real threats of the Illuminati were penned by Washington in his reply letter to the Reverend G. W. Snyder, who had sent Robison's *Proofs of a Conspiracy* to the American Founding Father in order to warn him of Weishaupt's occult sleeper cells.

According to Rosenbaum, the File and Claw vigilantes describe how their break-in to the Bones Temple discovered on the walls an inscription which matches with the ceremonial rites of the Illuminati recorded in John Robison's 1798 *Proofs of a Conspiracy*. Indeed, the File and Claw's "Fall of Skull and Bones" pamphlet states,

> [o]n the west wall [of Bones Tomb] hung, among other pictures, an old engraving representing an open burial vault, in which, on a stone slab, rest four human skulls, grouped about a fool's-cap and bells, an open book, several mathematical instruments, a beggar's scrip, and a royal crown. On the arched wall above the vault are the explanatory words, in Roman letters, "*Wer war der Thor, wer Weiser, Bettler oder Kaiser?*" and below the vault is engraved, in German characters, the sentence;
>
> *Ob Arm, ob Reich, im Tode gleich.*[39]

Rosenbaum translates the Roman script as *Who was the fool, who the wise man, beggar or king?*; and the German script as *Whether poor or rich, all's the same in death*. His *Esquire* article adds, "[i]magine my surprise when I ran into that very slogan in a 1798 Scottish anti-Illuminatist tract reprinted in 1967 by the John Birch Society."[40]

That republished anti-Illuminati text is *Proofs of a Conspiracy*, by traditional "Scotch Master" Freemason and "Élève of the Lodge de la Parfaite Intelligence at Liège,"[41] John Robison: a Professor of Natural Philosophy at the University of Edinburgh and the first Secretary General of the Royal Society of Edinburgh. He investigated *The Original Writings of the Order and Sect of the Illuminati*,[42] which he cross-referenced with other secret Illuminati documents smuggled by a Benedictine monk, Alexander Horn, who was a secret agent for the British Empire.[43] According to Robison's exposé, when an initiate is "tapped" for the "Regent degree" of Illuminism,

> [t]he candidate is presented for reception in the character of a slave; and it is demanded of him what has brought him into this most miserable of all conditions. He answers – "Society" – "the State" – "Submissiveness" – "False Religion." A skeleton is pointed out to him, at the feet of which are laid a Crown and a Sword. He is asked, whether that is the skeleton of a King, Nobleman, or a Beggar? As he cannot decide, the President of the meeting says to him, "the character of being a Man is the only one that is importance.[44 f 45]

---

f   Similar accounts of the rites and rituals of the Bavarian Illuminati can be found in the writings of the Abbé Augustin Barruel, a French Jesuit Preist who authored Memoirs Illustrating the Histo-

Comparing this profession of Illuminist faith with the Germanic proverb on the wall of the Bones Temple, Rosenbaum asks, "Doesn't that sound similar to the German slogan the File and Claw team claims to have found inside Bones?"[46] The affirmative answer to this rhetorical question is undeniable; these two mystic verses are nearly identical.

Another connection between the Order of the Illuminati and the Order of Skull and Bones is their shared devotion to dialectical-collectivist Hegelianism. According to Sutton, "Karl Theodor Dalberg (1744-1817), arch-chancellor in the German Reich, related to Lord Acton in England and an Illuminati (*Baco v Verulam* in the Illuminati code), was a right[wing] Hegelian."[47] In addition, Fichtean-Hegelianism was at the core of the educational philosophies of Johann Friedrich Herbart, who studied at the University of Jena, Germany,[48] where his collectivist pedagogies were influenced by the scholarship of several key Illuminists:

> Johann Gottfried Herder (1744-1804) [who] was 'Damascus pontifex' in the Illuminato [*sic*] [;] Johann [Gottlieb] Fichte ... [who] was close to the Illuminati and pushed by Goethe ('Abaris') for the post at the University of Jena ... [and] Johann Wolfgang Goethe (1749-1832) [who] was 'Abaris' in the Illuminati."[49]

The Illuminist associate Herbart would go on to study at Interlaken, Switzerland, under the tutelage of Johann Heinrich Pestalozzi, who was formally known as "Alfred" in the Order of the Illuminati.[50]

After mentoring under Illuminatus Alfred Pestalozzi, Herbart wrote a textbook on teaching methodology which combined his Fichtean-Hegelian collectivism with Pestalozzi's Illuminist "idea of an ABC of sense impression."[51] The resulting educational philosophy penned by Herbart was translated into an 1896 American textbook entitled *Herbart's ABC of Sense-Perception and Minor Pedagogical Works*. In time, Herbart's Illuminist-Hegelian "science" of education became so popular in the United States that there was instituted a National Herbart Society for the Scientific Study of Education, which was eventually renamed as simply the National Society for the Study of Education.[52]

Furthermore, Herbart's expansion of Pestalozzi's "sense-perception" science was pivotal in shaping the stimulus-response method of psychological conditioning coined by the founding father of the psychological sciences, Wilhelm Maximillian Wundt, whose father Karl Kasimir Wundt

ry of Jacobinism, the Third Volume of which reveals essentially the same Illuminati-Freemason conspiracy uncovered by Robison. To be sure, Barruel's and Robison's accounts differ in certain respects.

was an Illuminati adept recorded under the alias, "Raphael," in "the Illuminati Provincial Report from Utica (i.e., Heidelberg) dated September 1782."[53] Over time, Wundtian-Herbartian stimulus-response psychology evolved into B. F. Skinner's operant-conditioning psychology with the help of funding from the Rockefeller GEB.[54] In fact, the proto-psychology of Illuminatus Pestalozzi can be documented as a direct impact on the stimulus-response "teaching machines" designed by Harvard Psychology Professor Skinner, whose research into the mechanization of "programmed learning" was financed by Bonesman McGeorge Bundy, who was the Dean of Harvard University's Graduate School of Arts and Sciences.[55]

In *The Technology of Teaching*, which compiles Skinner's Bundy-funded machine-learning research, B. F. cites Pestalozzi's educational methods as a rudimentary basis for his own prototypical "Skinner-box" teaching machines:

> [m]aterials designed to teach "reading with comprehension" often consist of passages to be read and questions about them to be answered. Pestalozzi, in his unpublished, *The Instruction of Children in the Home* (17), offers an early example. The student is to read a page or two...
>
> He is then to answer questions...
>
> [T]he material is designed to teach ways of reading which lead to remembering. Some help may be given by grading such material in terms of difficulty. The material itself may be made more complex, students may be asked to read more before questions are answered, or the time for answering questions may be postponed. These practices are not incompatible with programmed instruction.[56]

Indeed, modern-day adaptive-learning computers for reading comprehension still run students through a series of reading passages and response questions; the only difference is that the assigned readings and the students' responses are digitalized on software that data-mine each individual student's reading-competence algorithms in order to "personalize" his or her lesson stimuli through student-specific tailoring of Pestalozzi's three instructional variables identified by Skinner: complexity of the reading material, length of the reading material, and assessment/feedback time.

To come full circle, Bonesman Mnuchin has now pumped up tax breaks for artificial intelligence and other automation technologies such as post-Skinnerian adaptive-learning software which are rooted in the "sensory" proto-psychology of Illuminatus Johann "Alfred" Pestalozzi. In brief, there are strong historical currents that link the Bavarian Illuminati to Bonesman Mnuchin's tax cuts for AI ed-tech.

In sum, Illuminists Johann Gottfried Herder, Johann Gottlieb Fichte, Johann Wolfgang Goethe, and Johann Heinrich Pestalozzi taught Fichte-an-Hegelian philosophies and sensory-learning proto-psychology to Johann Friedrich Herbart, who laid the scientific groundwork for Illuminati heir Wilhelm Maximillian Wundt to formalize Herbart's sense-perception learning theories into an academically recognized laboratory science. After the Illuminati were banished, Wundt's stimulus-response revision of Pestalozzi's sense-perception science was conveniently picked up by Bonesman Daniel Coit Gilman, who propagated Wundtian educational psychology throughout US academia with the help of Robber-Baron financing from the GEB of Bonesman Percy Rockefeller's uncle, John D. Rockefeller Sr.[57] The General Education Board, which commissioned Bonesman Gilman as a GEB administrator,[58] bankrolled Wundtian edu-conditioning research at Teachers College of Columbia University where Edward Lee Thorndike's animal-learning "puzzle-box" experiments paved the way for B. F. Skinner to revamp Illuminist Pestalozzi's sensory-learning methods into "programmed-learning" machines that were funded by Bonesman McGeorge Bundy.[59] [g] [60] Now, the next wave of Skinner-box adaptive-learning technology is currently being galvanized by the financial string-pulling of yet another Bonesman, US Treasury Secretary Stephen Mnuchin.[h] [61]

g   In his 1968 *The Technology of Teaching*, *Burrhus Frederic* Skinner acknowledges the work of Thorndike as a forerunner to B. F.'s own work on machine-programmed learning:

> [o]ther supposed principles of programming have been found … in the work of E. L. Thorndike, who more than fifty years ago pointed to the value of making sure that the student understood one page of a text before moving on to the next. A good program does lead the student step by step, each step is within his range, and he usually understands it before moving on.

In this passage, Skinner is alluding to Thorndike's 1914 book titled *Education: A First Book*, which posited that "[i]f, by a miracle of mechanical ingenuity, a book could be so arranged that only to him who had done what was directed on page one would page two become visible, and so on, much that now requires personal instruction could be managed by print."

h   A final note: if Chapter 322 of The Order of Skull and Bones is in fact a successor chapter to Adam Weishaupt's Illuminati, then the occult rituals of Skull and Bones can be traced back to the Kabbalah practiced by Mnuchin's White House colleague, Senior Presidential Advisor Jared Kushner, who is also the head of Trump's corporate-technocratic Office of American Innovation (OAI). Weishaupt was a Freemason, and the occult rites of Freemasonry are admittedly drawn from ancient Kabbalist mysticism. In at least ninety-four separate passages of Morals and Dogma of the Ancient and Accepted Scottish Rite of Freemasonry, the Kabbalist origins of occult Freemasonry are discusses by the Sovereign Grand Commander of the Scottish Rite's Southern Jurisdiction of the United States, Albert Pike: a Confederate General of the American Civil War whose statue stands on federal property near Washington D. C.'s Judiciary Square. In one specific passage, Pike writes,

> [a]ll truly dogmatic religions have issued from the Kabalah and return to it: everything scientific and grand in the religious dreams of all the illuminati, Jacob Bœhme, Swedenborg, Saint-Martin, and others, is borrowed from the Kabalah; all the Masonic associations owe to it their Secrets and their Symbols.
>
> The Kabalah alone consecrates the alliance of the Universal Reason and the Divine Word; it establishes, by the counterpoises of two forces apparently opposite, the eternal balance of being; it alone reconciles Reason with Faith, Power with Liberty, Science with Mystery; it has the keys of the Present, the Past, and the Future.

According to *The History of Freemasonry: The Legends of the Craft*, by Albert Gallatin Mackey, who was Secretary General of the Supreme Council of the Scottish Rite for the Southern Jurisdiction of the United States, the Kabbalist doctrines of Freemasonry were heretically installed by Hermetic infiltrators steeped in Rosicrucianism, such as the former Benedictine monk, Antoine Joseph Pernelty, who "invet[ed] other degrees, and among them one, the 'Knight of the Sun,' which is in its original ritual a mere condensation of Rosicrucian doctrines, especially as developed in the alchemical branch of Rosicrucianism. There is not in the wide compass of Masonic degrees, one more emphatically Rosicrucian than this" Knight of the Sun Degree, which invokes

> the dialogue between Father Adam and Truth in which the doctrines of Alchemy and the Cabala are discussed in the search of man for theosophic truth . . .
>
> There have been whole rites fabricated on the basis of the Rosicrucian or Hermetic philosophy, such as . . . the "Rite of Illuminated Theosophists" . . .
>
> [T]he Hermetic degree upon which to the present day has exercised the greatest influence upon the higher grades of Masonry is that of the Rose Croix [The Order of the Rose Cross (or Rosicrucianism)].

Mackey contends that the Kabbalist mysticism of The Order of the Rosicrucians is antithetical to traditional Freemasonry:

> how little there is in common between Rosicrucianism and Freemasonry. The one is a mystical system founded on the Cabala; the other the outgrowth of a very natural interpretation of an operative art. The Rosicrucians were theosophists, whose doctrines were of angels and demons, of the elements, of the heavenly bodies and their influence on the affairs of men, and of the magical powers of numbers, of suffumigations, and other sorceries...
>
> But Freemasonry has not and never had anything of this kind in its system.

Whether Pike or Mackey is the more astute historian, it is a fact that Kabbalism has long been intertwined into the rites and rituals of Freemasonry; and although The Order of the Illuminati competed against sects of The Order of the Rose Croix to gain parasitic control over the traditionalist lodges of "Speculative Masonry," the rivals of Rosicrucianism and Weishaupt's Illuminism were both cadres of "mystery schools" that studied Kabbalist occultism. This begs the question: Does Illuminati-Bonesman Mnuchin believe in the 666 Kabbalah prophecy which predicts that the current "Sixth Millennium" is "preparing" the way for humankind to ascend to "Redemption" through the evolutionary perfection of the "six dimensions" of the physical world via scientific and technological breakthroughs? Has Mnuchin's hard press for the "Tax Cuts and Robots Act" emanated from his Illuminist-Kabbalist faith in the unfolding new age of evolutionary technologies such as artificial intelligence and automated adaptive-learning software?

CHAPTER 14

Precision Eugenic Education: Tracking Genetic IQ for Workforce Training

We have extensively documented how the Bilderberg Group and The Order are discarding human teachers to supplant them with Skinnerian operant-conditioning programs engineered into adaptive-learning software that data-mine students' cognitive/behavioral-learning algorithms in order to "personalize" "career-pathways" job training through public-private school-to-work partnerships which contract crony-fascist corporations in bed with publicly funded education agencies. As if the usurpation of human teachers with operant-conditioning bots is not dystopic enough, there is another insidious stratagem underlying the ubiquitous computerization of schooling: comprehensive biopsychosocial data-mining of the global student body for the purposes of crypto-eugenic social engineering.

It is especially sinister that corporations and governments are manipulating educational psychology to condition young minds for workforce placement in a planned economy. But what's even worse is the corporate-government Big Data-mining already amassing enormous pools of psycho-behavioral data on student bodies which can be co-opted for the purposes of "personalizing" each student's eugenical education based on his or her unique differences in biopsychosocial metrics calculated through "social and emotional learning" (SEL) data, IQ scores, and cognitive-behavioral UII algorithms tied together with other demographic data such as family histories and income. In turn, such data may also be used to implement psycho-behavioral conditioning that socially engineers students into neo-eugenic class ranks in a global corporate-fascist technocracy.

The Selective Function of Eugenical Education:

In chapter four, it is established that Learnsphere's public-private digital repository aggregates "student information system" (SIS) data from schools and "user interaction information" (UII) data from adaptive-learning software along with US Census demographics from the federal government which can be accessed by education technology companies and other third-party corporations to develop better ed-tech products that improve fascistic workforce education outcomes.

By cross-referencing SIS and UII data with socioeconomic US Census data and other demographic data from Learnsphere's MITx & Harvardx Dataverse, such as "parental level of education" and "neighborhood level of income," ed-tech engineers could data-mine Learnsphere to design "individualized" career-pathway algorithms that are programmed to acclimate toward the cognitive-behavioral skill levels that are statistically associated with given demographic populations.[1] For example, a statistical correlation highlighting poor literacy among first-generation college students from impoverished urban communities could be used to set the bar on operant-learning algorithms adapted for students from similar backgrounds by relegating such students to digital career-pathways curriculums that do not require high-level reading or writing skills.

In essence, computerized adaptive-conditioning modules could basically cap a student's intellectual ability based on socioeconomic and other demographic factors such as the student's family history, place of origin, and income level. Using these socio-genealogical metrics to predetermine a student's learning potential is nothing less than eugenics.

To be sure, this neo-eugenic digital data-mining is actually the technetronic perfection of a hundred-year-old teaching tenet, which Harvard Education Professor Alexander Inglis deemed the fifth function of education: "the selective function." John Taylor Gatto paraphrases Inglis's selective function of education:

> [t]his refers not to human choice at all but to Darwin's theory of natural selection as applied to what he called "the favored races."[a] [2] In short, the idea is to help things along by consciously attempting to improve the breeding stock. Schools are meant to tag the unfit – with poor grades, remedial placement, and other punishments – clearly enough that their peers will accept them as inferior and effectively bar them from the reproductive sweepstakes. That's what all those little humiliations from first grade onward were intended to do: wash the dirt down the drain.[3]

---

a.   The complete title of Darwin's famous treatise on the theory of evolution, *On the Origin of Species by Means of Natural Selection,* includes the following lesser-known subtitle: *Or the Preservation of Favoured Races in the Struggle for Life.*

The scientific manipulation of natural selection through selective breeding was originally termed eugenics by Charles Darwin's cousin,[4] Francis Galton,[b][5] who postulated two methods of eugenic engineering: "positive" eugenics, which is the selective inbreeding of the "fittest" genetic groups of elite society in order to steer the artificial enhancement of evolution through "purified" bloodlines; and "negative" eugenics, which is the systematic culling of "unfit" genetic "subpopulations" of the commoner classes by sterilizing, aborting, euthanizing, or otherwise exterminating them from the human genepool.[6]

Galton's negative-eugenic theories particularly were later imported to the United States by Robber Barons such as Andrew Carnegie and John D. Rockefeller,[7] who used their tax-exempt foundations to bankroll eugenic research institutions such as Charles Davenport's Cold Spring Harbor Laboratory and the Eugenics Record Office,[8] which were instrumental in the USA's pioneering of the world's first government-sanctioned compulsory-sterilization laws.[9] In one account published by the Human Betterment Foundation, a eugenics philanthropy which collaborated with the Eugenics Record Office, the British Eugenics Society, and the American Eugenics Society,[c][10] a document titled *Sterilization for Human Betterment* reports that the State of California alone executed 6,255 eugenic sterilization procedures forced upon individuals exhibiting "mental disease and defect ... [which] are perpetuated by heredity."[11]

It was America's mass-industrialization of eugenic social engineering that inspired Hitler to copy US corporatization of negative eugenics, which culminated in The Third Reich's genocidal efforts to "purify" human biology by eradicating "undesirable" bloodlines through sterilization,[12] abortion,[13] euthanasia,[14] concentration camps, and other Nazi

---

b.   Galton authored *Hereditary Genius: An Inquiry Into Its Laws and Consequences* in 1869. In it, he expanded upon Darwinian natural selection to lay the foundational principles behind eugenics: that humankind could sort of harness, speed up, and perfect its own evolutionary development through selective breeding "by judicious marriages during several consecutive generations." Then, in 1883, he effectively codified his research on directed evolution through selective "judicial marriages" by coining the term "eugenics" and calling his readers to strategic eugenic action in his "Inquiries into Human Faculty and Development." In this essay, Galton based his science of artificial evolution on the "Greek, eugenes namely, good in stock, hereditarily endowed with noble qualities.... We greatly want a brief word to express the science of improving stock, which is by no means confined to questions of judicious mating ... to give to the more suitable races or strains of blood a better chance of prevailing speedily over the less suitable than they otherwise would have had. The word eugenics would sufficiently express the idea."
c. In *Sterilization for Human Betterment*, E. S. Gosney and Paul Popenoe paid tribute to these eugenic allies: "[w]e are particularly indebted to ... Dr. H. H. Laughlin, superintendent of the Eugenics Record Office, who has followed the development of sterilization in the United States more closely than any other student; to the American Eugenics Society for constant and hearty cooperation, and to Major Leonard Darwin, honorary president of The Eugenics Society (London), for his active interest and encouragement."

extermination programs.[15] [d] [16] (For a thorough history of the collusion between Nazi, American, and British eugenicists, see *War Against the Weak: Eugenics and America's Campaign to Create a Master Race* by Edwin Black;[17] *The Nazi Connection: Eugenics, American Racism, and German National Socialism*,[18] by Stefan Kühl; and *In the Name of Eugenics: Genetics and the Uses of Human Heredity* by Daniel J. Kevles).[19]

After the world discovered the horrors of Hitler's "race hygiene" concentration camps where the Nazi's conducted eugenic experiments on Jews and other "undesirables," the term "eugenics" became a four-letter word associated with mad scientists, and eugenical governance policies in America and abroad faced a wave of increasing public pushback. Nevertheless, the global eugenics movement held its ground,[e] [20] and Julian

---

d. Adolph Hitler once gave a speech directly lauding America's eugenic State-sterilization policies and programs:

> [n]ow that we know the laws of heredity ... it is possible to a large extent to prevent unhealthy and severely handicapped beings from coming into the world. I have studied with great interest the laws of several American states concerning prevention of reproduction by people whose progeny would, in all probability, be of no value or be injurious to the racial stock.... [T]he possibility of excess and error is still no proof of the incorrectness of these laws. It only exhorts us to the greatest possible conscientiousness.

Hitler's study of American eugenics included a German translation of *The Passing of the Great Race* by Madison Grant, who was President of the Eugenics Research Association in America. In *The Nazi Connection: Eugenics, American Racism, and German National Socialism*, published by Oxford University Press, Stefan Kühl illustrates Hitler's love affair with *The Passing of the Great Race*:

> [i]n 1934, one of Hitler's staff members wrote to Leon Whitney of the American Eugenics Society and asked in the name of the Führer for a copy of Whitney's recently published book, *The Case for Sterilization*. Whitney complied immediately, and shortly thereafter received a personal letter of thanks from Adolf Hitler. In his unpublished autobiography, Whitney reported a conversation he had with Madison Grant about the letter from the Führer. Because he thought that Grant might be interested in Hitler's letter he showed it to him during their next meeting. Grant only smiled, reached for a folder on his desk, and gave Whitney a letter from Hitler to read. In this, Hitler thanked Grant for writing *The Passing of the Great Race* and said that "the book was his Bible." Whitney concluded that, following Hitler's actions, one could believe it.

e. Although the International Federation of Eugenics Organizations (IFEO) eventually disbanded after convening the Fourth International Eugenics Congress at German-occupied Vienna in 1939, the various national eugenics organizations that comprised these globalist eugenics networks underwent public-relations makeovers by changing their names and spin-doctoring their ongoing crypto-eugenic research under the rhetorical guises of studies in genetics, family planning, bioethics, and environmentalist population sciences. For instance, in 1972, the American Eugenics Society (AES) changed its title to the Society for the Study of Social Biology until 2014 when it was again renamed as the Society for Biodemography and Social Biology. Correspondingly, the AES's journal publication changed its title from *Eugenical News* to *Eugenics Quarterly*, which was then switched to *Social Biology* in 1969 and then finally to *Biodemography and Social Biology* in 2014. AES President Frederick Osborn admitted that the American Eugenics Society's "name was changed because it became evident that changes of a eugenic nature would be made for reasons other than eugenics, and that tying a eugenic label on them would more often hinder than help their adoption. Birth control and abortion are turning out to be great eugenic advances of our time." Other examples of crypto-eugenics PR rebranding include the Human Betterment League of North Carolina, which became the Human Genetics League of North Carolina, and the American Breeders Association, which relabeled itself as the American Genetics Association, but retained the motto "Eugenics –

Huxley, who was President of the British Eugenics Society from 1959 to 1962,[21] became the first Director-General of the United Nations Educational Scientific and Cultural Organization (UNESCO) upon the establishment of the United Nations, which was supposedly set up to prevent the human rights atrocities of Nazi eugenics from ever recurring.[f 22]

Nonetheless, in UNESCO: Its Purpose and Its Philosophy, in a chapter entitled "The Principle of Equality and the Fact of Inequality," Huxley wrote that

> [a]t the moment, it is probable that the indirect effect of civilization is dysgenic instead of eugenic; and in any case it seems likely that the dead weight of genetic stupidity, physical weakness, mental instability, and disease-proneness, which already exist in the human species, will prove too great a burden for real progress to be achieved. Thus, even though it is quite true that any radical eugenic policy will be for many years politically and psychologically impossible, it will be important for Unesco to see that the eugenic problem is examined with the greatest care, and that the public mind is informed of the issues at stake so that much that is now unthinkable may at least become thinkable.[23]

The Huxleys, The Eugenic Order of Death, and The X Club:

It is keen to note here that the Preamble to the UNESCO Constitution was penned by Skull-and-Bonesman Archibald MacLeish:[24] the first US delegate to sit on the governing board of UNESCO.[25] As such, UNESCO's international eugenics program was spawned as the brainchild of a marriage between The Order's Hegelian-collectivism and the Huxleys' Malthusian-Darwinism.[g 26] In fact, this global-eugenic liaison between the

Heredity – Breeding" into the 1950s. In England, the British Eugenics Society kept its title until 1989 when it was renamed as the Galton Institute in honor of eugenics progenitor Francis Galton.

f. It is pertinent to note here that the fourth Secretary-General of the United Nations was a former Nazi Storm Trooper, Kurt Waldheim, who held the UN reigns from 1972 until 1981.

g. Social Darwinist eugenics is rooted in the Malthusian science of "population control." The essential difference between eugenics proper and Malthusianism proper is quality versus quantity: eugenics is a socio-biological science concerned with breeding the best quality of human DNA to improve the human genepool; Malthusianism is a socioeconomic-environmental science concerned with managing a sustainable quantity of human beings on the planet in order to manage limited resources. In his 1789 *An Essay on the Principle of Population, As It Affects the Future Improvements of Society*, economist Thomas Malthus enumerated that "(1) Population is necessarily limited by the means of subsistence. (2) Population invariably increases where the means of subsistence increase, unless prevented by some very powerful and obvious checks." Based on these "Principles of Population," Malthus called for "preventive checks" on reproduction that would prevent the over-population catastrophes of famine, plague, and war. Charles Darwin, in his autobiography, reflects on how

143

Huxleys and the Germanic Order of Death can be traced all the way back to the beginnings of Thomas Henry Huxley's crusade to spread Darwinian evolutionary theory, which was picked up by Bonesman Daniel Coit Gilman, who spread Huxley's gospel of evolutionary selection by instituting courses on Darwinian biological science at Johns Hopkins University.

D. C. Gilman, in his official capacity as the first President of Johns Hopkins University, called upon Julian's grandfather, Thomas Henry Huxley, to give the inaugural address at the opening of the college in 1876.[27] Known as "Darwin's Bulldog" because he was the principal apologist for Charles Darwin's theory on natural selection,[28] T. H. Huxley was chosen by Gilman not just because of his rock-star status as the leading promulgator of the new biological-determinist science of evolution; but also because of their shared affinity for German science and literature, which they bonded around when they first met in London in 1875.[29]

According to *The Huxley File*, by former Clark University Professor Charles Blinderman,

> Huxley, who had learned German when he was a teenager and had begun serious scholarly investigation of German science upon his return to England [from his Royal Navy expedition] … was ready for his role as the foremost translator of German scientific interests and procedures into British education. He regularly corresponded with, and sometimes had as household guests, Anton Dohrn, Ernst Haeckel, Dr. Leuckart and other German biologists.[30]

As a result of Huxley's German-to-English translation labors,[31] "[m]ost of the text books used in the [English] schools for medical and technical education were in German or translations of German."[32] Thomas Henry even wrote an analysis of the German scientist Johann Wolfgang Goethe,[33] whom T.H. revered as one of

---

Malthus's over-population theories are foundational to Darwin's own theory of natural selection:

> I happened to read for amusement "Malthus on Population," and being well prepared to appreciate the struggle for existence which everywhere goes on from long continued observation of the habits of animals and plants, it at once *struck me that under these circumstances favourable variations would tend to be preserved, and unfavourable ones to be destroyed*. The result of this would be the formation of new species. Here then I had at last got a theory by which to work.

In *The Descent of Man, and Selection in Relation to Sex*, Charles Darwin appealed to Malthus in the following eugenical commentary: "[t]here is great reason to suspect, as Malthus has remarked, that the reproductive power is actually less in barbarous, than in civilised races."

the really great men of literature, [who] added some of the qualities of the man of science to those of the artist, especially the habit of careful and patient observation of Nature. The great poet was no mere book-learned speculator. His acquaintance with mineralogy, geology, botany and osteology, the fruit of long and wide studies, would have sufficed to satisfy the requirements of a professoriate in those days.[34]

Goethe was a Freemason of the Rosicrucian variety,[35] and he was a member of the Bavarian Illuminati, which can be historically traced as the original lodge of The Order of Skull and Bones.[36]

According to Leonard Huxley, his father Thomas Henry boarded a ship called "the *Germanic*" to voyage across the Atlantic Ocean to deliver his Johns Hopkins University address in the United States.[37] Once arriving on the mainland of the USA, T. H. made a stop at Yale University, the headquarters of The Order, before traveling to Johns Hopkins.[38] During his stay at Yale, Huxley wrote a letter to his wife, which boasts of the hospitality he received at the home base of Skull and Bones: "[m]y excellent host met me at the station, and seems as if he could not make enough of me. I am installed in apartments which were occupied by his uncle, the millionare [*sic*] Peabody, and am as quiet as if I were in my own house."[39] In this letter, Huxley encouraged a return to the Yale campus with his wife, Henrietta Anne Heathorn, who according to his son Leonard, "had attracted him [T. H.] from the first" due to her "unusual degree of cultivation.... She had been two years at school in Germany, and her knowledge of German and of German literature brought them together on common ground."[40]

There is no record of T. H. Huxley's membership in any secret fraternity or chivalric order connected to Skull and Bones, such as Freemasonry or Rosicrucianism. However, in *The Life and Letters of Thomas Henry Huxley, Volume I*, T. H.'s son Leonard includes an 1846 "Daguerreotype" photograph of his father,[41] which depicts the elder Huxley posing with "the hidden hand" gesture (his hand tucked inside his waistcoat) that is said to be a Freemasonic-Illuminati hand sign symbolizing their secret hand in controlling the fate of human history.[42] In the second volume of T. H.'s collected letters, Leonard displays a facsimile of his father's portrait "paint[ed] by the Hon. John Collier in the National Portrait Gallery," which portrays T. H. leaning on a stack of books while holding a human skull upside-down in his hand.[43]

Whatever the significance of these images, Huxley did form a "semi-secret society" known as "The X Club,"[44] which held private meetings where the Darwinian Bulldog plotted with other evolutionists such as Herbert Spencer,[45] who coined the term "survival of the fittest,"[46] to strategize the popularization of "Social Darwinism" into the mainstream of English society through the authority of the Royal Society of London for Improving Natural Knowledge where three X Clubbers went on to become presidents:[47] T. H. Huxley,[48] Joseph Dalton Hooker,[49] and William Spottiswoode.[50] The Royal Society itself had its beginnings in Francis Bacon's "Invisible College,"[51] which stemmed from a network of Rosicrucian mystery schools steeped in the study of "natural philosophy" that would come to be known as the empirical scientific method.[52] [h] [53]

In a personal letter to Charles Darwin dated February 20, 1871, Huxley thanked Darwin for sending a copy of his follow-up treatise on evolutionary selection titled *The Descent of Man, and Selection in Relation to Sex.* Huxley wrote, "I shall try if I can't pick out from 'Sexual Selection' some practical hint for the improvement of gutter-babies, and bring in a resolution thereupon at the School Board."[54] One such "resolution" can be found in Huxley's 1887 "Address on Behalf of the National Association for the Promotion of Technical Education," which made the case for a system of workforce schooling that would train the masses in the industrial skills needed to evolve the British economy and save the British Empire from dysgenic overpopulation:

> the struggle for existence, aris[es] out of the constant tendency of all creatures in the animated world to multiply indefinitely.... It is that inherent tendency of the social organism to generate the causes of its own destruction, never yet counteracted, which has been at the bottom of half the catastrophes which have ruined States. We are at present in the swim of one of those vast movements in which, with a population far in excess of that

---

h. Bacon, who was a disciple of the Rosicrucianist mystic John Dee, wrote a 1627 utopian allegory titled *The New Atlantis,* in which the fabled narrator tells a tale of a faraway land inhabited by Kabbalists capable of alchemical wonders akin to the science of genetic engineering:

> we make (by art) in these same orchards and gardens, trees and flowers to come earlier or later than their seasons, and to come up and bear more speedily than by their natural course they do. We make them also, by art, greater much than their nature, and their fruit greater and sweeter, and of differing taste, smell, colour, and figure from their nature. And many of them we so order as they become of medicinal use.
>
> We have also means to make divers plants rise by mixtures of earth without seeds, and likewise to make divers new plants, differing from the vulgar; and to make one tree or plant turn into another.

The New Atlantis depicts a host of other "mystical" wonders that some scholars interpret as Bacon's figurative predictions for the evolution of occult technologies developed by natural philosophers of ancient mystery schools transplanted to a far-off futurist "New World."

which we can feed, we are saved from a catastrophe, through the impossibility of feeding them, solely by our possession of a fair share of the markets of the world. And in order that that fair share may be retained, it is absolutely necessary that we should be able to produce commodities which we can exchange with food-growing people, and which they will take, rather than those of our rivals.[55]

According to the *Life and Letters of Thomas Henry Huxley*, T. H.'s Johns Hopkins speech similarly warned of "the dangers of over-population."[56] That same year in 1876, at Huxley's behest, D. C. Gilman hired T. H.'s protégé,[57] Henry Newell Martin,[58] to work as the first ever Professor of Physiology at Johns Hopkins,[59] which would go on to become one of the premier colleges conducting Malthusian-eugenic research.[60]

After World War II, the Huxley family and The Order came together again through UNESCO, which reiterated the same Malthusian-eugenic plans on an international scale. With the help of UNESCO's international "lifelong-learning" curriculums, the selective function of eugenical schooling has been preserved through semantic crypto-eugenics pedagogies that give genetic-determinist social policies a rhetorical facelift.

IQ-Genics:

Official eugenic policy in education can be traced back to the Binet-Simon IQ Test, which purported to mathematically link intellectual prowess to biological capacity.[61] The original Binet-Simon intelligence quotient, which is now revised in its fifth edition as the Stanford-Binet IQ Test,[62] provided the first measurable "proof" for the eugenic theory that intellectual ability is bound to heredity.[63] [i] [64] Using Binet-Simon IQ scores, eugenicists such as Henry Herbert Goddard justified taxonomizing the "unfit" into subclasses of "imbeciles,"[65] "morons,"[66] "idiots,"[67] and

---

i. In *Heredity in Relation to Eugenics*, Cold Spring Harbor eugenicist Charles Davenport stressed the importance of the Binet-Simon IQ tests in diagnosing genetically determined mental ability:

[a] series of tests (the Binet-Simon tests) have been devised to gauge mental ability by gauging a variety of capacities such as general information, ability to count and to repeat phrases, to recognize names and describe common things and to make fine sense discriminations. Such tests show that there are all grades of mental ability. At one extreme is the idiot, without language and incapable of attending to his bodily needs. He may retain to maturity the mentality of a child of a few months. In a higher grade mentality of a child of 3 to 5 years is retained throughout life; such are the imbeciles; then come the merely backward children who make dull adults of all grades to the normal condition.

"feebleminded,"[j] [68] who would be committed to his Vineland Training School for Backward and Feeble-Minded Children.[69] [k] [70]

Notwithstanding the traditional divide between the biological-nature sciences and the psychological-nurture sciences, IQ scores came over time to be assessed in conjunction with standardized academic test scores developed by Wundtian psychologist, Edward Lee Thorndike,[71] [l] [72] to segregate the "unfit" into remedial vocational ed while quarantining the "fit" into "gifted" academic education: a lower IQ or test grade would indicate eugenic inferiority, which would relegate the student to relatively unskilled workforce training; a higher IQ or test grade would indicate eugenic superiority, which would privilege the student to "gifted" academic studies.[73] Such scholastic-intelligence metrics were later revised by E. L.'s son, Robert Ladd Thorndike, who co-designed the Lorge-Thorndike Intelligence Tests, which were then revamped into the Cognitive Ability Test (CogAT).[74]

Today, it is no longer politically correct to affiliate IQ scores with old eugenics labels such as "idiots," "morons," "imbeciles," and "feebleminded." However, the specific scores associated with these eugenic ranks are still used to legally qualify individuals as "mentally disabled,"[75] and IQ scores well above the mean 100 are still used to legally qualify students

---

j. According to Paul Popenoe and Ezra Seymour Gosney of the Human Betterment Foundation, "feeble-mindedness" was attributed to "mental defectives" who scored below 70 on IQ tests: "any one with an I. Q. of less than 70 has sometimes been called feeble-minded. He has less than three-fourths of the average amount of intellect ... Tests made on large groups of school children in various parts of the country show that four or five per cent fall below 70 I. Q.; that is, they are feeble-minded in this conventional and technical use of other term." In a June 6, 1927 *Journal of Social Hygiene* article entitled "Eugenic Sterilization in California (II: The Feebleminded)," Popenoe reported that "[t]he mean IQ of [eugenically sterilized] males is 59.23_+.65, that of the females 61.69_+.44; in other words, the average sterilized patient is on the dividing line between low moron and middle moron. The lowest male sterilized was a low imbecile, IQ 25; ... [t]he girl of least intelligence was a high idiot with IQ 16." The Human Betterment Foundation worked in close collaboration with the US Eugenics Record Office, the British Eugenics Society, and the American Eugenics Society. In Sterilization for Human Betterment, Gosney and Popenoe paid tribute to these eugenic allies: "[w]e are particularly indebted to ... Dr. H. H. Laughlin, superintendent of the Eugenics Record Office, who has followed the development of sterilization in the United States more closely than any other student; to the American Eugenics Society for constant and hearty cooperation, and to Major Leonard Darwin [Charles Darwin's son], honorary president of The Eugenics Society (London), for his active interest and encouragement."

k. Today, the Vineland Adaptive Behavior Scale (VABS), which was formulated by Goddard's assistant Edgar A. Doll, is still used for testing mental disabilities. The Pearson Education Corporation has revised Goddard's psychometric VABS in a second and third edition, which can be purchased online.

l. According to Paolo Lionni's *The Leipzig Connection: The Systematic Destruction of American Education*, Thorndike was the protégé of James McKeen Cattell: Wilhelm Wundt's assistant, who in 1887 met with Francis Galton and "quickly absorbed Galton's approach to eugenics, selective breeding, and the measurement of intelligence. Cattell was later to become the American leader in psychological testing, and in 1894 would administer the first battery of psychological tests ever given to a large group of people, testing the freshman and senior classes at Columbia University."

as "mentally gifted." Indeed, eugenic educational "selection" based on IQ tests and other intelligence metrics is still written into public schooling laws across the United States of America. Here's a short list of recent US state-level policies for IQ-based admissions into "gifted" education programs:

- A 2018 post on the Ohio Department of Education website states that "[d]istricts shall identify students as gifted in the area of superior cognitive ability when a student ... scores two standard deviations above the mean, minus the standard error of measurement, on an approved intelligence test."[76]

- The Missouri Department of Elementary and Secondary Education's "Gifted Education Program Guidelines" for the 2017-2018 schoolyear state that the "Guidelines for Student Selection" into the "Gifted Program" include:

  [f]ull-scale or GAI scores on an individual intelligence test at or above the 95th percentile: Although they are more time-consuming, individually administered intelligence tests provide more accurate indicators for final placement purposes than do group tests. The district may use various IQ tests, administered according to their appropriateness in reference to program areas and student needs.[77]

- A 2014 memo from the Pennsylvania Department of Education states, "[t]he term 'mentally gifted' includes a person who has an IQ of 130 or higher, when multiple criteria as set forth in Department Guidelines indicate gifted ability. ... The determination shall include an assessment by a certified school psychologist. (22 Pa. Code §16.21(d))."[78]

To be sure, intelligence-quotient metrics are not the sole requisite for placing students into gifted classes in the United States; other complementary, or even alternative, measures standardizing gifted education placement are offered in these and other US state-level laws. Nevertheless, IQ scores remain a strong, if not prime, deciding factor when schools are determining a student's "track" for gifted academic studies or low-skilled career-pathways training.

At the same time, IQ scores are even measured to track outcomes on the remedial General Education Development (GED) certification,[79] which was formerly known as the General Education Degree, or the General Education Diploma, until the for-profit Pearson Education Inc. bought out the nonprofit American Council for Education, which was the sole proprietor of the GED test until 2014.[80] That year, an issue of the scholarly *Journal of Research & Practice for Adult Literacy, Secondary & Basic Education* published a peer-reviewed article which analyzed "General Education Development (GED) Credential Attainment" in correlation with "age, ethnicity, gender, and measures of both verbal and non-verbal intelligence."[81] The results "indicated that verbal IQ was predictive of GED credential attainment. These results are consistent with previous literature linking childhood IQ and educational achievement."[82] Note the racial hygienic implications of correlating ethnicity with intellectual brain capacity.

Make no mistake about it: notwithstanding public backlash against Hitlerian eugenics, the world scientific community did not discard genetic-determinist intelligence metrics as pseudo-statistics along with other eugenical biometrics studies such as phrenology and physiognomy,[83] which measured the shapes of the skull and various facial features respectively to determine whether a person was eugenically evolved or dysgenically devolved.[84] Newer academic research into the biogenetic basis of cognition still cites race hygiene eugenics data as authoritative sources. A 2009 issue of the *International Journal of Neuroscience* printed an article titled "Whole Brain Size and General Mental Ability," which "describe[s] the brain size/GMA [general mental ability] correlations with age, socioeconomic position, sex, and ancestral population groups, which also provide information about brain-behavior relationships. Finally, we examine brain size and mental ability from an evolutionary and behavior genetic perspective."[85] Citing the *Eugenics Review* and the *Scientific Papers of the Second International Congress of Eugenics*, this peer-reviewed article finds that,

> [f]ollowing World War II (1939-1945) and the revulsion evoked by Hitler's racial policies, craniometry became associated with extreme forms of racial prejudice. Research on brain size and intelligence virtually ceased, and the literature underwent vigorous critiques (Gould, 1978, 1981; Kamin, 1974; Tobias, 1970). However, as we shall show, modern studies confirm many of the earliest observations.[86]

The Return of the Bilderberg Bell Curve:

The hereditary IQ statistics amassed throughout the heyday of popular eugenics were kept alive thanks to crypto-eugenicists such as

Charles Murray, a Harvard University graduate who is a member of the secretive Bilderberg Group,[87] which was founded by a Nazi Storm Trooper: Prince Bernhard of the Netherlands.[88] In Murray's 1994 tome, *The Bell Curve*, which is filled with academic citations and mathematical graphs, charts, and tables, the Bilderberger author uses statistical measurements of IQ and various other scholastic metrics to link intellectual and academic ability to race, whereby he concludes that East Asians and Ashkenazi Jews are smarter than all other races while black-skinned and brown-skinned races are the least intelligent of all.[89]

Despite vehement public outcry against the racial-determinist claims put forward in *The Bell Curve*, Murray's crypto-eugenic theories have been revivified by popular intellectuals of today, such as atheist apologist Sam Harris,[90] who holds a Bachelor of Philosophy from Stanford University and a PhD in Cognitive Neuroscience from the University of California, Los Angeles;[91] libertarian-anarchist Stefan Molyneux, who is the founder and host of *Freedomain Radio*, which is an alternative media platform broadcast on the worldwide web;[92] clinical psychologist and Toronto University Professor of Psychology, Jordan Peterson, who is also a former Harvard University Psychology Professor;[93] and Ben Shapiro, a Harvard University graduate who is a former editor of the alt-right *Breitbart News*.[94]

These contemporary pop-culture intelligentsia defend *The Bell Curve's* eugenic IQ data as they contend that its genetic-determinist calculations are entirely objective, based solely upon precise mathematics which are dispassionately configured by unbiased, expert statisticians. However, a thorough review of *The Bell Curve's* bibliography illustrates how Murray's interpretations of race-based IQ correlations are informed by an array of classic eugenic literature from a host of old-school eugenicists. These eugenic citations include:

- The Founding Father of eugenics himself, Francis Galton;[95]

- Galton's protégé, Karl Pearson,[96] the British eugenicist who pioneered the science of statistics by systematizing Galton's biometrics theories into a laboratory science that Pearson popularized through his eugenic statistical research at his Department of Applied Statistics and Eugenics,[97] which was formed by the conglomeration of the Drapers' Company Biometrics Laboratory and the Galton Laboratory at University College London;[98]

• Pearson's eugenicist colleague,[99] educational psychologist Cyril Burt,[100] who was a member of the British Eugenics Society;[101]

• H. H. Goddard, whose Vineland School set the bar for clinical use of eugenic IQ testing across the United States;[102]

• American Eugenics Society President Frederick Osborn, who coined the term "crypto-eugenics" to denote stratagems for surreptitiously instituting eugenics under the cover of other semantic labels;[103 m 104]

• US Supreme Court Justice Oliver Wendell Holmes Jr., who ruled to uphold the legality of forced eugenic sterilization laws.[105 n 106]

Murray also cites "new school" crypto-eugenicists such as William H. Shockley and David Popenoe:[107]

• Stanford Professor of Engineering Science, William Shockley, was a Nobel Prize-winning physicist and a founder of Silicon Valley who wrote numerous promotionals endorsing "voluntary" negative-eugenics through government programs offering to pay cash stipends to low-IQ people willing to elect themselves for voluntary sterilization:[108] "[a]t a bonus rate of $1,000 for each point below 100 I.Q., $30,000 put in a trust for a 70 I.Q. moron potentially capable of producing 20 children might return $250,000 to taxpayers in reduced costs of mental retardation care. Ten percent of the bonus in spot cash might put our national talent for entrepreneurship

---

m. In his 1968 *The Future of Human Heredity: An Introduction to Eugenics in Modern Society*, Osborn, who was also a President of the Malthusian-eugenic Population Council, wrote that "[m]easures for improving the hereditary base of intelligence and character are most likely to be attained under a name other than eugenic.... Eugenic goals are most likely to be attained under a name other than eugenics." Three decades prior, in 1937, Osborn praised the eugenic sterilization projects of Nazi Germany: "[t]he German sterilization program is apparently an excellent one.... [R]ecent developments in Germany constitute perhaps the most important social experiment which has ever been tried."

n. On May 2, 1927, Supreme Court Justice Oliver Wendel Holmes Jr. voted in the majority (8 to 1) to uphold the forced sterilization of Carrie Buck under Virginia's Eugenical Sterilization Act of 1924. Justifying his ruling in the case of *Buck v. Bell*, Holmes wrote that Buck was a "probable parent of socially inadequate offspring, likewise afflicted" and that "her welfare and that of society will be promoted by her sterilization." He concluded that "[i]t is better for all the world, if instead of waiting to execute degenerate offspring for crime or to let them starve for their imbecility, society can prevent those who are manifestly unfit from continuing their kind.... Three generations of imbeciles are enough."

into action." [109] o [110] Shockley was also a "positive-eugenics" activist as he donated his own Nobel Prize-winning semen to Robert Graham's Nobel-laureate sperm bank titled the Repository for Germinal Choice,[111] which from 1980 to 1999 stored commercially available specimens of eugenically "superior" semen that were sold to women who could afford the payments to be artificially inseminated with the high-IQ sperm samples selected for breeding genius "superhumans."[112]

• David Popenoe, the son of Human Betterment eugenicist Paul Popenoe, founded and directed the National Marriage Project at Rutgers University.[113] To be fair, David's sociological research at the National Marriage Project was not concerned with the genetic heredity of family genealogies.[114] However, David's studies did focus on the sociological effects of divorce and other marital trends impacting family relationships, upon which eugenic and dysgenic breeding patterns are theoretically contingent.[115] Hence, Murray's reference to David's National Marriage Project data in support of the Bilderberger's crypto-eugenic *Bell Curve* thesis. For this reason, David Popenoe is noteworthy as a crypto-eugenic citation in our literature review of Murray's *Bell Curve* bibliography.[116]

Above all, the fountainheads of Murray's *Bell Curve* data spring from the statistical research of two notorious crypto-eugenicists who have continued their IQ-genics studies up to the present decade: former Emeritus Psychology Professor at the University of Ulster, Ireland, Richard Lynn;[117] and Emeritus Professor of Political Studies at the University of Otago, New Zealand, James Flynn.[118] Twenty-three separate publications authored by Richard Lynn are cited in *The Bell Curve* bibliography,[119] and Murray explicates Lynn's numbers and figures to substantiate a genetic-determinist IQ theory which Murray coined as "The Flynn Effect" in

---

o. In a 1980 *Playboy Magazine* interview, the new-school eugenicist Shockley professed his beliefs in old-school, racial-hygiene eugenics:

> I believe society has a moral obligation to diagnose the tragedy for American Negroes of their statistical I.Q. deficit. Furthermore, this is a worldwide tragedy, and in my opinion, the evidence is unmistakable that there is a basic, across-the-board genetic disadvantage in terms of capacity to develop intelligence and build societies on the part of the Negro races throughout the world...
>
> Yes, I believe in the created equal assertion of the Declaration of Independence, when it is interpreted in terms of equal political rights, but I would qualify it some: I don't think the right should be given equally to everyone to have children, if those people having children are clearly destined to produce retarded or defective children.

honor of James Flynn's statistical documentations of general gains in IQ scores across populations from one generation to the next.[120]

Here's how The Flynn Effect works: IQ tests need to be periodically recalibrated in order to adjust for average gains in "secular IQ" that successive generations acquire over time;[121] when the difficulty of the IQ tests are raised accordingly, Murray and Lynn find that all students score lower, yet the range of scores distributed across racial groups remains the same:[122] the standard IQ deviation from the average "white" score of 100 still remains 110 for Asians,[123] 115 for Ashkenazi Jews,[124] and 85 for "blacks."[125] In addition, when the same students retake the old IQ tests, Murray and Lynn find that all ethnicities score higher, but the standard IQ deviation from the average "white" score still remains ten points higher for Asians,[126] fifteen points higher for Ashkenazi Jews, and fifteen points lower for "blacks."[127] For James Flynn, these general evolutions in IQ across populations are the result of environmental factors such as access to education and social welfare.[128] But for Richard Lynn and Charles Murray, this consistency in mean IQ deviations, which remain the same across racial groups over time on different recalibrated IQ tests, proves that human intelligence, quantified by IQ metrics, is mainly predestined by racial-genetic inheritance.[129]

If you think that the eugenic connotations of Lynn's IQ data are not enough to fairly peg him as a eugenicist, then you should note that Lynn's contributions to research on "eugenics and dysgenics" were recently celebrated in a 2012 issue of the peer-reviewed journal *Personality and Individual Differences*, which printed a "special" edition titled "Evolution of Race and Sex Differences in Intelligence and Personality: Tribute to Richard Lynn at Eighty." In this commemorative issue, a specific article, titled "Richard Lynn's Contributions to Personality and Intelligence," offers "[a]n evaluation [that] is presented of Lynn's work on national differences in personality, race differences in intelligence, national IQs & economic development, correlates of national IQs, the Flynn effect, sex differences, *eugenics* and dysgenics, race differences in psychopathic personality, and intelligence of the Jews."[130] p [131]

---

p. In this same issue of *Personality and Individual Differences* series, J. Phillippe Rushton penned an article titled "Life History Theory and Race Differences: An Appreciation of Richard Lynn's Contributions to Science," which applauds how

> Lynn was the first to observe that while sub-Saharan Africans averaged lower on IQ tests than Europeans, internationally, East Asians averaged *higher*. Further, he found reaction time measures of intelligence showed the same worldwide pattern. He also found the Black–White IQ differences in Africa are more pronounced on subtests having higher g loadings, just as in the US. He also found national IQ differences predictably aggregated into 10 population groups

Lynn even wrote a book entitled *Eugenics: A Reassessment*, which calls for a hardcore negative-eugenics policy of administering "a contraceptive virus acting for about 10 years that could be given to 12-year-old boys. When they were aged 22, they could apply for licenses for parenthood. If they failed to obtain these, they could be vasectomized."[132] In this same book, Lynn also argued that there is "a good case for reviving the sterilization of the mentally retarded and criminals. It is indisputable on both empirical and theoretical grounds that many of these people transmit their characteristics to their children by both genetic and environmental processes."[133] Lynn continued his racial-hygiene studies of The Flynn Effect as an Emeritus Professor at the University of Ulster until April of 2018 when his emeritus status was revoked by the college's student union,[134] which motioned for Lynn's dismissal on the grounds that his eugenics theories are racist.[135]

On the flipside of The Flynn Effect, James Flynn emphasizes epigenetic inheritance of "secular IQ" gains from environmental conditions, such as education and social welfare, which raise "secular IQ" that is then passed down to the next generation through biological reproduction. In fact, in 2006, Flynn published stats that showed "black" IQ gains over time are actually closing the gap slowly between white-black IQ disparities.[136] Nevertheless, the next year, Flynn recommended that government authorities should spike public drinking supplies with sterilants in order to reduce the fertility of poor people so that their dysgenic effects on the human gene pool and their strain on the socioeconomic structure of society will be lessened. In a 2007 interview with the *Sunday Star-Times*, Flynn made the following eugenic proclamation:

> [e]veryone knows if we only allowed short people to reproduce there would be a tendency in terms of genes for height to diminish. Intelligence is no different from other human traits…
>
> A persistent genetic trend which lowered the genetic quality for brain physiology would have some effect eventually…
>
> I do have faith in science, and science may give us something that renders conception impossible unless you take an antidote…
>
> You could of course have a chemical in the water supply and have to take an antidote.[137]

This negative-eugenic proposal to forcibly sterilize low-IQ populations clearly demonstrates that Flynn believes low-IQ individuals are "unde-

identified by Cavalli-Sforza, Menzoni, and Piazza (1994). Finally, Lynn proposed cold winters theory to parsimoniously explain why East Asians and Europeans evolved a larger brain and a higher IQ than more southerly populations.

sirable," or "unfit," and must be dealt with in the same way by which the old-fashioned eugenicists would have resolved: by culling those populations of "inferior," or "dysgenic," peoples.

To be fair, Flynn did tell the *Otago Daily Times* of New Zealand that his comments were "merely trying to illustrate a point, not seriously suggest[ing] contraception in the water supply."[138] Yet in his attempts to backpedal his eugenic policy recommendations, Flynn added that it "would be wonderful" if there were "a contraception device that meant women had to take action to get pregnant instead of having to take a pill not to get pregnant."[139] In other words, even when whitewashing his own eugenic policy positions, Flynn still put his foot back in his mouth by asserting the benevolence of hi-tech control of reproductive selection, which is hardly anything less than eugenics.[q] [140]

Other cornerstones of Charles Murray's *Bell Curve* IQ data include two more crypto-eugenic psychologists: former Psychology Professor at the University of Western Ontario, John Philippe Rushton,[141] and former Professor of Educational Psychology at the University of California, Berkeley, Arthur Jensen.[142]

There are eleven separate bibliography citations in Murray's *Bell Curve* that reference the works of J. Philippe Rushton:[143] a Fellow of the Canadian Psychological Association who wrote a book titled *Race, Evolution, and Behavior*,[144] which corroborates Murray's bell-curve distributions of IQ scores across racial groups.[145] In line with Murray's racial-genetic IQ theories, Rushton made the following eugenicist remark at an *American Renaissance* conference in 2000: "Whites have, on average, more neurons and cranial size than blacks... Blacks have an advantage in sport because they have narrower hips – but they have narrower hips because they have smaller brains."[146]

---

q. It is hard to believe that Flynn made these comments in jest to be ironic because his remarks are almost identical to statements made by crypto-eugenicist environmentalist Paul Ehrlich, author of the Malthusian-eugenic *Population Bomb*. In this 1968 book, in a chapter titled "What Needs to Be Done?," Ehrlich relays that

> [m]any of my colleagues feel that some sort of compulsory birth regulation would be necessary to achieve such control [of over-population]. One plan often mentioned involves the addition of temporary sterilants to water supplies or staple foods. Doses of the antidote would be carefully rationed by the government to produce the desired population size.... It might be possible to develop such population control tools, although the task would not be simple.

Nine years later, before becoming President Barack Obama's White House Science Czar, crypto-eugenicist John P. Holdren teamed up with Ehrlich to compile *Ecoscience: Population, Resources, Environment*, which puts forward the same Malthusian-eugenic proposition of poisoning public drinking water with sterilants: "[t]he third approach to population limitation is that of involuntary fertility control. Several coercive proposals deserve discussion," such as "[a]dding a sterilant to drinking water or staple foods [which] is a suggestion that seems to horrify people more than most proposals for involuntary fertility control. Indeed, this would pose some very difficult political, legal, and social questions, to say nothing of the technical problems."

Eight years later in a 2008 book review of Richard Lynn's *The Global Bell Curve*, Rushton once again affirmed Murray by laying out essentially the same bell-curved IQ-score spreads across racial-genetic groups worldwide:

> [t]hroughout the world, Europeans and East Asians (Chinese, Japanese and Koreans) average the highest IQs and socio-economic positions. The lowest averages are found among the Aborigines in Australia and in Africans and their descendants. Intermediate positions are occupied by the Amerindians, the South Asians from the Indian sub-continent, the Maori in New Zealand, and by the mixed race peoples in South Africa, Latin America, and the Caribbean.[147]

To build a substantial body of eugenical research, Rushton acted as President of the Pioneer Fund:[148] a US philanthropic foundation set up in 1937 with the expressed mission of bankrolling "endow[ments] for the support of research into human nature, heredity and eugenics."[149] Indeed, the Pioneer Fund has financed the very "scientific racism" of Murray's all-star cast of crypto-eugenicists cited in his *Bell Curve* bibliography.[150] For example, during the 1970s, William Shockley won at least $188,700 in Pioneer grants;[151] and before becoming the current President of the Pioneer Fund upon Rushton's death in 2012,[152] Richard Lynn earned a $325,000 grant from the eugenic Pioneer philanthropy.[153] In 2000, Rushton's own Charles Darwin Institute received a Pioneer grant for $473,835.[154 r 155]

Another Pioneer Fund grantee was crypto-eugenicist Arthur Jensen who, by the time *The Bell Curve* was printed in 1994, had been awarded no less than $1,096,094 in grants from the eugenic Pioneer foundation.[156] Cited twenty-three times in *The Bell Curve's* bibliography,[157] Jensen held a seat on the Scientific Advisory Board of *Neue Anthropologie*:[158] a racial-hygienic journal published in Germany by the Society for Biological Anthropology, Eugenics and the Study of Behavior.[159] Jensen's eugenic research echoed the same racial-genetic IQ theories at the core of *The Bell Curve* as he professed to ascribe to the theory that

> [t]he number of intelligence genes seems to be lower, over-all, in the black population than in the white. As to the effect of racial mixing, nobody has yet performed experiments that reveal its relative effect on I.Q. If the racial mixture weren't there, it is possible that the I.Q. differences between blacks and whites would be even

---

r. The Pioneer Fund was co-founded by Frederick Osborn, who was also President of the First International Eugenics Congress, and Harry Hamilton Laughlin, who was also the Director of the Eugenics Record Office (ERO).

greater. I think such studies should be done to lay this uncertainty to rest once and for all.[160]

Adhering to this eugenic IQ ideology, Jensen said in an interview with American Renaissance that

> the black population in this country is in a sense burdened by the large number of persons who are at a level of g [general IQ] that is no longer very relevant to a highly industrialized, technological society. Once you get below IQs of 80 or 75, which is the cut-off for mental retardation in the California School System, children are put into special classes. These persons are not really educable up to a level for which there's any economic demand. The question is, what do you do about them? They have higher birth-rates than the other end of the distribution. …
>
> [T]he best thing the black community could do would be to limit the birth-rate among the least able members, which is of course a eugenic proposal.[161]

Last but not least,[s] the Pioneer Fund additionally bankrolled the racial-determinist crypto-eugenics studies conducted by Emeritus Professor of Education at the University of Delaware, Linda Gottfredson:[162] a doctoral graduate of Johns Hopkins University who is also referenced in *The Bell Curve*'s end citations.[163] Throughout the 1980s and 1990s,[164] Gottfredson was given at least $267,000 in Pioneer Fund grants;[165] and when Murray's *Bell Curve* was castigated by critics for its racist, crypto-eugenic bent, Gottfredson defended the Bilderberger's IQ-genics in an open letter to the public titled "Race and IQ: What Mainstream Science Says," which was first published in the *Wall Street Journal* and then again in the academic journal *Intelligence*.[166]

Co-signed by fifty-two other scientists including crypto-eugenicists such as Richard Lynn, J. Philippe Rushton, Arthur Jensen, R. Travis Osborne, and even Robert M. Thorndike (the son of R. L. and the grandson of E. L. Thorndike),[167 t 168] Gottfredson's letter doubled down on Murray's thesis by asserting that

> [m]embers of all racial-ethnic groups can be found at every IQ level. The bell curves of different groups overlap considerably,

---

s. There are actually many other crypto-eugenicists documented as sources in Murray's *Bell Curve*, but an exhaustive exposé of these "scientific racists" is not germane here.
t. R. L. Thorndike is also referenced in *The Bell Curve*'s end citations.

but groups often differ in where their members tend to cluster along the IQ line. The bell curves for some groups (Jews and East Asians) are centered somewhat higher than for whites in general. Other groups (blacks and Hispanics) are centered somewhat lower than non-Hispanic whites.[169 u 170]

Until 2015,[171] Gottfredson carried out her crypto-eugenics research on intelligence quotients at the University of Delaware campus where she continued to teach courses such as "Ethics and the Human Genome" and "Intelligence and Everyday Life," the latter of which "examine[s] various IQ tests to help understand why the differences they measure have practical value in virtually all arenas of social life, but especially education and work."[172] She also instructed a course titled "Educational Assessments for Classroom Teachers," which taught enrollees "how to create and evaluate different kinds of classroom assessments, as well as how to interpret standardized tests administered by the school district to all students or by school psychologists to individuals [sic] students."[173]

In sum, a literature review of Murray's *Bell Curve* sources reveals a collection of contemporary studies on racial-genetic determinism conducted by a close-knit circle of Pioneer Fund crypto-eugenicists whose citations in *The Bell Curve's* bib are couched in an array of surrounding references to classic eugenics texts from trailblazers in the early history of the negative-eugenics movements to control the reproduction of low-IQ peoples.

Too Many "Feeble-Minded" Going to College; Virtual Workforce Schooling for the "Unfit":

Now that you're familiar with the eugenic "authorities" that back up Murray's *Bell Curve*, I doubt you'll be surprised to know that Murray believes that too many students are futilely pursuing four-year college degrees without any regard for their genetic IQ limitations which handicap them from exceling beyond basic workforce competency. Murray contends that such dysgenically encumbered students should abandon hopes for four-year bachelor's degrees and focus instead on two-year associate degrees that emphasize technical workforce training.[174]

---

u. More specifically, Gottfredson's numbers estimate that "[t]he bell curve for whites is centered roughly around IQ 100; the bell curve for American blacks roughly around 85; and those for different subgroups of Hispanics roughly midway between those for whites and blacks. The evidence is less definitive for exactly where above IQ 100 the bell curves for Jews and Asians are centered."

In a 2008 essay titled "Are Too Many People Going to College?," crypto-eugenicist Murray answers this question with an emphatic "No." Murray argues that

> dealing with complex intellectual material is what students in the top few percentiles are really good at, in the same way that other people are really good at cooking or making pottery. For these students, doing it well is fun.
>
> Every percentile down the ability ladder – and this applies to all abilities, not just academic – the probability that a person will enjoy the hardest aspects of an activity goes down as well. Students at the 80th percentile of academic ability are still smart kids, but the odds that they will respond to a course that assigns Mill or Milton are considerably lower than the odds that a student in the top few percentiles will respond. Virtue has nothing to do with it. Maturity has nothing to do with it. Appreciation of the value of a liberal education has nothing to do with it. The probability that a student will enjoy *Paradise Lost* goes down as his linguistic ability goes down…
>
> And so we return to the question: Should all of those who have the academic ability to absorb a college-level liberal education get one? If our young woman is at the 80th percentile of linguistic ability, should she be pushed to do so? She has enough intellectual capacity, if she puts her mind to it and works exceptionally hard.
>
> The answer is no. If she wants to, fine. But she probably won't, and there's no way to force her.… A large proportion of people who are theoretically able to absorb a liberal education have no interest in doing so.[175]

Clearly, Murray is implying that scholastic measures of intelligence should predicate whether a student is enrolled in traditional academic studies or competency-based workforce training; and going by Murray's standards, it seems the dividing line between career and academic pathways cuts off somewhere near the 80th percentile of cognitive ability. If a student falls below the 80th percentile, according to Murray, he or she will not be capable of exceling academically; so that student should be consigned to "competency-based" workforce training at online virtual schools: "online courses offer more flexible options for tailoring course work to the real needs of the job. A brick-and-mortar campus is increasingly obsolete" because

> the Internet is revolutionizing everything.… [T]he possibilities for distance learning [have] expanded by orders of magnitude.

> We are now watching the early expression of those possibilities: podcasts and streaming videos in real time of professors' lectures, online discussions among students scattered around the country, online interaction between students and professors, online exams, and tutorials augmented by computer-aided instruction software.
>
> Even today, the quality of student-teacher interactions in a virtual classroom competes with the interactions in a brick-and-mortar classroom.[176]

Murray reiterated this proposition for crypto-eugenical workforce schooling through online courses when he participated with his fellow Bilderberger, the German-born Peter Thiel, on a panel at the Intelligence Squared U.S. Foundation in 2011 where they both argued "For the motion" to support the theme of the panel discussion: "Too Many Kids Go to College."[177]

In brief, Murray is a true believer in crypto-eugenical education which he asserts is best accomplished by segregating low-intelligence students into virtual "career-pathways" curriculums that condition workforce competence through adaptive-learning software. I surmise Murray is aware that, from the get-go, computer-teaching machines have been programmed on the basis of eugenic determinism.

A half century ago, Harvard Psychology Professor B. F. Skinner built upon E. L. Thorndike's "puzzle-box" animal-training experiments to develop his own "Skinner-box" "teaching machines" that were engineered for different cognitive-behavioral learning "tracks" which could be prescribed according to a student's "genuine genetic differences" in intellectual capabilities.[178] In his 1968 *The Technology of Teaching*, Burrhus Frederic Skinner discussed "differences in sensory capacity," and he asserted that "[i]f these are genetic differences, different methods of instruction may be needed."[179]

Skinner described one of the teaching machines he engineered for eugenically differentiated instruction that optimizes environmental nurture conditioning by tailoring the stimulus-response, operant-learning scheduling to fit with the intellectual capacity of each individual student's genetic endowment. Skinner designed this low-tech adaptive-learning machine for the special education of a handicapped student whom B. F. described as a "microcephalic idiot … [who] was said to have a mental age of about 18 months. He was partially toilet trained and dressed himself with help. To judge from the brain of his sister, now available for post-mortem study, his brain is probably about one-third the normal size."[180] Recall that the "scientific" definition of a "microcephalic idiot" refers to a eugenic classification that is categorized based on intelligence quotient scores. In other words, Skinner was using eugenic IQ terminology to diagnose the differentiated conditioning that must be programmed in order to maximize the psycho-genetic limitations of the student.[v] [181]

It's the Genetic IQ Economy, Stupid:

Now in the twenty-first century, Murray's eugenic claims about the correlations between IQ and career aptitude are still being echoed by academic research published in professional scientific literature that draws statistical correlations between wealth and genetically-determined IQ. In 2006, the peer-reviewed journal *Intelligence* published an article which links correlations between IQ and socioeconomic status that are reminiscent of the old-school eugenics theories of Francis Galton and British Eugenics Society President, Major Leonard Darwin, who both believed that poverty and affluence are inherited biological traits. In this *Intelligence* article entitled "Do You Have to Be Smart to Be Rich? The Impact of *IQ* on Wealth, *Income* and Financial Distress," statistics tabulated by an NLSY79 data-tracking system are crunched to show "that each point increase in *IQ* test scores raises *income* by between $234 and $616 per year after holding a variety of factors constant."[182] [w] [183]

Consider how these IQ metrics would fit perfectly with Francis Galton's eugenic theories concerning "hereditary genius."[x] [184] Likewise, con-

---

v. This eugenic teaching machine was programmed to operantly condition the low-IQ person to develop his cognitive ability of "form discrimination," or in other words shape recognition, by reinforcing accurate shape/form identification with rewards from a "device which dropped a bit of chocolate into a cup within reach … all correct responses being reinforced with chocolate" stimulus rewards. The findings of this eugenic Skinner-box experiment concluded that "the intellectual accomplishments of this microcephalic idiot in the forty-first year of his life have exceeded all of those of his first 40 years…. No very bright future beckons (he has already lived longer than most people of his kind) … but he has contributed to our knowledge by demonstrating the power of a method of instruction which could scarcely be tested on a less promising case."

w. To be accurate, this article does not suggest an oversimplified cause-and-effect relationship between a person's intelligence quotient and his or her level of wealth. The article qualifies its causal analysis of wealth-IQ correlations by reserving that "[f]inancial distress, such as problems paying bills, going bankrupt or reaching credit card limits, is related to IQ scores not linearly but instead in a quadratic relationship. This means higher IQ scores sometimes increase the probability of being in financial difficulty." To clarify this mathematical exception to the rule, even though IQ fitness strengthens a person's ability to generate income, his or her intelligence genes do not always translate into an ability to save, invest, or otherwise manage his or her cash flow of income, which means a high-IQ, high-income individual can sometimes wind up with a net worth that falls below the wealthy upper classes.

x. In *Hereditary Genius*, Galton analyzed the lineages of wealthy British aristocrats, and he identified a high percentage of affluent statesmen, military commanders, scientists, jurists, poets, musicians, and painters among those prosperous pedigrees. In turn, Galton concluded that this high concentration of "talent" among the intermarried aristocratic classes is proof that genius is in fact hereditary and that "judicious marriages" among those upper-class bloodlines can indeed breed a "highly-gifted race of men."

sider how these IQ stats would be perfect "proof" for the socioeconomic eugenics policies espoused by Major Leonard Darwin, who was the grandson of Charles Darwin.[y] [185] In a 1927 essay entitled "A Note on Eugenics," author of the dystopic *Brave New World*, Aldous Huxley, who was the brother of UNESCO Director-General Julian Huxley, had this to say in favor of Leonard Darwin's policy proposal to impose negative-eugenic fertility control upon the economically unfit:

> [i]n his book, *The Need for Eugenic Reform* ... Major Darwin finds that in a society organized on contemporary lines there is a correlation between eugenic fitness and wage-earning capacity. We regard as desirable the qualities that make for social success; these qualities must therefore be fostered. Major Darwin has elaborated a scheme for the systematic discouragement of fertility among the ill-paid and its encouragement among the well-paid. I need not go into the details here. If practical politicians accept Major Darwin's substitute for a standard of eugenic fitness – we shall have a society compelled by law to breed more and more exclusively from its most gifted and socially most successful members.[186]

Major Darwin's hundred-year-old theories on eugenics could be revived by another *Intelligence* issue published in 2015, which finds that

> the majority of studies have found that genetic factors have greater influence on *IQ* in the presence of higher levels of SES [socioeconomic status].... The results [of this study] indicate that genetic factors have a greater influence on verbal IQ for students who attend *schools* with higher levels of SES, and shared environmental factors have a greater influence on verbal IQ for students who attend *schools* with lower levels of SES, but only at extremely high and low levels of SES (scoring within the top or bottom 10th percentiles).[187]

---

y. In an attempt to breed a progeny of super geniuses, Charles Darwin and his cousin Francis Galton rigorously intermarried with the Wedgwood family, and the Huxleys also interbred with the Darwins, Galtons, and Wedgwoods in pursuit of positive eugenics. During the Third International Eugenics Congress at the American Museum of Natural History in 1932, the Galton-Darwin-Wedgwood pedigree was exhibited on a poster mapped out by Harry Hamilton Laughlin, who was the Director of America's Eugenics Record Office. Famous offspring of the Galton-Darwin-Wedgwood-Huxley family tree include the renowned physicist, Charles Galton (C. G.) Darwin, who held the Vice Presidency as well as the Presidency of the British Eugenics Society where he gave the 1939 Galton Lecture. C. G. Darwin was the grandson of Charles Darwin and the godson of Francis Galton; and C. G. would become the father-in-law of Angela Huxley, Julian Huxley's niece, while Andrew Huxley, who was the brother of Julian, married H. B. Pease (née Wedgwood), and she bore six children.

In laymen's terms, this article suggests that student IQ can be harmed by an impoverished socioeconomic environment, but there are diminishing returns on socioenvironmental IQ conditioning as the student climbs up the socioeconomic class ladder until the top of the SES pyramid is reached where genetic IQ is basically unphased by the school environment or the larger social environment. The implications of these diminishing returns on IQ training suggest that improvements in school and neighborhood environments can help to lift some lower-IQ people out of abject poverty; yet at the top of the SES food chain, the cognitive elite are only those endowed genetically with superior brain powers. Simply put, the smartest people of the richest upper classes, according to this *Intelligence* paper, are gifted with the most intelligent genes among the human species.

A thorough exploration of the volumes of *Intelligence* published over the years since its inception in 1977 uncovers myriad articles making similar or other eugenic claims about IQ statistics.[188] Apologists for Murray's bell-curved eugenics stats will probably say that the similar mounds of eugenic IQ data piled up by *Intelligence* are merely the result of cold, impartial calculations of raw numerical data. But a closer look at the *Intelligence* journal's editorial board reveals a strong eugenicist bias; for the board members have included Murray's crypto-eugenic heroes:[189] J. Philippe Rushton, Arthur Jensen, Linda Gottfredson, Richard Lynn,[190] and James Flynn. Flynn remains seated on the *Intelligence* board.[191]

"Free Market" Eugenical Schools; Data-Mining IQ to Personalize Ed-Tech Products:

Lucky for Murray and his crypto-eugenicist cadre of Pioneer Fund grantees and *Intelligence* editors, the public-private Learnsphere education database has set up the IT infrastructure that could open the doors for ed-tech corporations to develop adaptive-learning modules that condition students with eugenic-competence algorithms, which program each student's career-path curriculum so it is "personalized" according to the statistical learning limitations correlated with the eugenic/dysgenic propensities of that student's reported genetic IQ. To be sure, there are no IQ databases in the Learnsphere repository, but there are several private genealogy corporations that sequence specific IQ genes from DNA samples which are stored in databases that can be accessed for a fee; and there is nothing stopping ed-tech businesses from paying the fee to conduct product research-and-development that cross-analyzes the bio-genetic data available at gene-sequencing companies, like the for-profit 23and-Me Corporation, in cross-reference to the cognitive-behavioral UII algorithms, SIS data, US Census demographics, and other student-learning metrics filed at the Learnsphere datahub and other public-private data vaults like Common Grounds Scholar.[192] This is an online data pool which, according to a 2015 issue of the *Open Review of Educational Research*, was financed by the Bill and Melinda Gates Foundation for the purposes "of collecting evidence and serving analytics data from perhaps a million semantically legible datapoints for a single student in their middle or high school experience; or in a class in a term; or a school in a week."[193]

As a matter of fact, the 23andMe company has been already been actively contributing to data-driven research on specific DNA sequences linked to IQ. According to the *Massachusetts Institute of Technology (MIT) Review*, 23andMe "surveys customers on how long they stayed in school, a proxy for intelligence, [and] the Google-backed [23andMe] company has been playing a supporting role in the search for intelligence genes by contributing its customers' DNA data to the largest of the gene hunts."[194]

Here's how the 23andMe Corporation makes money by selling its customers' DNA to third-party research agencies that are interested in epidemiological studies of gene-to-IQ and other genotype-phenotype correlations:

In a *Business Insider* article, there is posted a screenshot of the online window for 23andMe's "Research Consent Document," which states, "[a] s a 23andMe customer, you are a partner in this mission. You have the opportunity to participate in genetic research, which could contribute to revolutionary findings in human diseases, conditions, and traits."[195] Underneath this caption is a box that can be checked to authorize consent; there is another option below this check-box which requests consent so that the 23andMe "CLIA-certified laboratory can store saliva samples for future testing."[196 z 197] If a 23andMe patron clicks on the "consent" box, the genetic data-mining corporation will "rent" the consented DNA to outside researching agencies conducting statistical analytics of specific DNA sequences and specific traits, such as IQ.

In fact, 23andMe has already contributed its customers' DNA to a scholarly journal study published in *Psychological Sciences*,[198] which found positive correlations between a particular SNP (*single-nucleotide polymor-*

---

z. *Business Insider* reports that 23andMe has shared genetic data with pharmaceutical corporations such as Pfizer and Lundbeck for the purposes of developing gene-therapy drugs and other genetic medicines.

phism) DNA sequence and the number of schoolyears completed by the person supplying the DNA sample. A 23 and Me blog post, which is titled "Ten Percent Inspiration, Ninety Percent Perspiration (and Sixty Percent Genetics)," reports that

> [a] 2013 study published in ScienceExpress identified a SNP (rs9320913) that was associated with whether or not a person had attained a college diploma, and another two (rs11584700, rs4851266) that were associated with "EduYears" – the number of years of schooling a person had…. [T]he identification of new parts of the genome that correlate with academic achievement is a promising future direction for research.
>
> Scientists at 23andMe were interested to see if these associations held true with our customers. In a study published this month in the journal Psychological Sciences, they showed that they were.[199]

Another 23andMe blog article titled "Back to School Smarts and Genetics," which was posted in 2012, expounds the genetic data-mining company's interests in cataloguing the total genomic matrix of DNA sequences that collectively determine an individual's biogenetic IQ capacity:

> there's good evidence that a percentage of the differences in measurable intelligence, such as your IQ score, can be chalked up to genetics…. At the very least your IQ score is a pretty good predictor for how well you'll do in school….
>
> As for measures of intelligence, recent studies estimate that in early childhood about 25-to-40 percent of individual variation in measurable intelligence can be attributed to genetics. In adults, this number increases to about 80 percent.
>
> A study of Dutch families found that the SNP is associated with "performance IQ" (i.e. non-verbal IQ) [*sic*]. Each A at increased subjects' performance IQ by an average of three points compared to those with no copies [*sic*]. The authors estimated that accounts for 3.4% of the variation in performance IQ between people. …
>
> It's also important to note that there is no single gene that has an inordinate impact on IQ scores. Instead there are hundreds of genes that impact intelligence with a cumulative impact on IQ scores. In a recent study researchers found another variant, this one in the HMGA2 gene, that also has a small effect on IQ scores.
>
> Although the HMGA2 gene has been associated with height, it also influences the size of the brain. Researchers also found that the C version of was also associated with a very slight increase in IQ [*sic*].[200]

As gene data-mining corporations such as 23andMe, Gene Plaza, DNA Land, and Ancestry.com normalize the commercialization of DNA-IQ tests, there will open up new markets for personalized-learning technologies in an emerging crypto-eugenic field called "precision education": the use of genetic screening to optimize a student's learning outcomes by tailoring his or her schooling so that it suits his or her genetic-IQ predispositions.

At King's College in London, an American-born Professor of Behavioural Genetics, Robert Plomin,[aa][201] confidently believes that "we can now read the DNA of a young child and get a notion of how intelligent he or she will be," according to the *MIT Review*.[202] Of course, Plomin is a current editorial board member of *Intelligence*;[203] he is also a signatory to Linda Gottfredson's "Race and IQ: What Mainstream Science Says";[204] and he is referenced multiple times in the end citations of Charles Murray's *Bell Curve*.[205] In short, Plomin is a crypto-eugenicist who is in league with the gang of genetic-determinist scientists catalogued in *The Bell Curve* bibliography.

Thus, Plomin has written a 2018 paper titled "The New Genetics of Intelligence" which, according to the *MIT Review*, "mak[es] a case that parents will use direct-to-consumer tests to predict kids' mental abilities and make schooling choices, a concept he calls precision education."[206] The name "precision education" is a play on the term for the burgeoning healthcare field known as "precision medicine," which implements genetic screening to diagnose ailments and then prescribe personalized gene therapies and other hi-tech medical treatments.

Precursors to precision education have already begun as people are purchasing DNA-IQ tests on the direct-to-consumer market. *MIT Review* reports that "[u]sers of GenePlaza, for example, can upload their 23and-Me data and pay $4 extra to access an 'Intelligence App,' which rates their DNA using data from the big 2017 study on IQ genes. It shows users where their genes place them on a bell curve from lower to higher IQ. A similar calculation is available from DNA Land."[207] Hence, it's only a matter of time before these commercial assessments of IQ genes are used to predetermine a student's learning outcomes programmed into precision-ed adaptive-learning computers.

Disturbed by *MIT Review's report on these prospects of Plomin's genetic IQ engineering for precision schooling, University of California* Professor of Sociology Catherine Bliss *voiced her opposition to the use of genetic data*

aa. Plomin supplied "the DNA of more than a thousand American geniuses" to the Chinese BGI gene-sequencing corporation. The project got derailed after news reports accused the Chinese of hatching a plot to breed "genius babies."

for determining a child's academic limitations: "[t]he idea is we'll have this information everywhere you go, like an RFID tag. Everyone will know who you are, what you are about. To me that is really scary.... A world where people are slotted according to their inborn ability – well, that is *Gattaca*.... That is eugenics."[208]

Bliss is not exaggerating here; for Plomin himself has proclaimed that the future of precision education will assign each student a "Learning Chip" that maps his or her personal genomic profile as "a reliable genetic predictor" of the student's cognitive capabilities.[209] Appealing to principles of the new precision medicine, Plomin propositions that "[i]t's wholly accepted that preventative medicine is the way to go.... Why not preventative education? We wait for problems such as reading disability to develop.... Once you have the genes, you could predict difficulties and hopefully prevent them."[210] To put it another way, once a student's "defective" IQ genes are logged onto a Learning Chip, adaptive-teaching software could scan the chip to personalize the student's learning outcomes with workforce-competence algorithms that track him or her into career-path curriculums that are cognitively compatible with his or her genetic-IQ competence.

In fact, the globalist ed-tech thinktank, Global Education Futures, has created an infographic timeline titled *Global Education 2015-2035*, which was "created as part of Global Education Futures initiative, prepared by Re-Engineering Futures Group. This map is a result of five years of work that brought hundreds of Russian and international experts into co-creative vision building for the future of education."[211] According to this futurist timeline, by 2020, students will be issued a "Genetic Passport. Students get individualized recommendations on their education in accordance with their genotype."[212]

Dialectical Eugenics: Scientific Synthesis of the False Left-Right Political Paradigm:

Precision-eugenic education has cheerleaders on both ends of current leftwing-rightwing political discourse. At the right end of the spectrum, there is Plomin's call for voluntary eugenics through the purchase of genetic IQ screenings sold on direct-to-consumer markets. This "free market" version of precision-eugenic schooling aligns with the fiscally conservative social policies advocated by Charles Murray,[213] who promotes radical-libertarian cuts to welfare programs on the "rationale" that it is self-defeating for the State to be the financial lifeline for its most "dysgenic" citizens with the lowest IQs because such "unfit" members of society are supposedly genetically incapable of using the public safety net of government aid as a booster toward lifting themselves out of their socioeconomic "incompetence."[214] For Murray, it is pointless to concentrate tax dollars into special efforts toward trying to condition students to become competent in workforce skills that are beyond the cognitive limitations of their genetic coding; so precision education would therefore have to be a pay-to-play schooling system driven by "meritocratic" market incentives.

Despite these right-of-center economics driving such precision-eugenic schooling through capitalist consumption, precision-ed spokesman Robert Plomin is actually a UK Labor Party member who identifies as left-of-center politically,[215] like his co-editor at *Intelligence*, James Flynn, who is a former member of the US Socialist Party.[216] In contrast to the commercialist, consumerist eugenic-ed promoted by so-called "leftist" Plomin, Flynn himself takes a far-left socialist stance on eugenical-ed by calling for a building up of the Welfare State so that government planning can enforce affirmative action and other "positive discrimination" programs that equally distribute access to the civic environments of education and other public welfare institutions which Flynn believes can epigenetically condition a student's IQ DNA to eugenically mutate toward the evolutionary progression of cognitively complex brain powers that can be biologically passed down to the next generation.[217]

In an interview with *Freedomain Radio* host Stefan Molyneux, Flynn stated, "[c]ertainly, education does something to stratify people in terms of genes for intelligence";[218] yet he pointed out that welfare programs do nothing more than provide enough subsistence to merely help people survive in a state of poverty that has dysgenic effects on genetic IQ development which are reproduced and multiplied because such indigent welfare recipients are typically

> ignorant of contraception and have a higher birthrate than Americans who are more affluent.... Now if you have such a situation over many generations, you would have some decline in genes for IQ. I think there is a solution to this, and that is to have a Welfare State and to have social conditions so excellent that you have eliminated the culture of poverty.... So you can choose, if you want dysgenic tendencies, have a truncated Welfare State and a culture of poverty; if you don't want a dysgenic tendency, why not try and el-

evate all your population to the point where they have middle-class aspirations and middle-class patterns of contraception?[219]

Stated differently, why not allocate tax dollars to pay for government-funded precision-education programs that mandate gene screenings? Why not map each student's genetic profile in order to qualify him or her for publicly funded Learning Chips and other assistive-learning technologies that accommodate DNA-based learning disabilities and other cognitive-behavioral handicaps recognized under federal laws such as the Individuals with Disabilities Education Act (IDEA)?

With arguments in favor of precision eugenic-ed coming in from both sides of the left-right political divide, it bodes to be inevitable that we will have some form of precision-eugenic schooling in the near future as the political debates surrounding this new medical-tech form of education are merely quibbling over which flavor of eugenic engineering in the classroom will be most palatable for students, parents, and teachers to swallow. To be sure, Plomin's "capitalist" eugenic-ed and Flynn's "socialist" eugenic-ed are not necessarily mutually exclusive; both schemes for eugenical selection through hi-tech schooling systems can coincide in a mixed economy of public-private partnerships. Under such a technocratically planned economy, students with the lowest IQs and the lowest socioeconomic statuses could qualify for welfare programs which aid them with standard-issue eugenical ed-tech that is subsidized by the government in order to help such students achieve basic workforce competence; at the same time, students with higher IQs and higher socioeconomic statuses would be able to privately purchase the most advanced eugenic ed-tech available on the consumer market in order to obtain for themselves the best scholastic advantages through genetic optimization that money can buy.

Actually, this public-private, capitalist-socialist mixture of precision-eugenics policies is the most likely version to manifest throughout school systems; for it has the most populist appeal as it makes concessions to the identity politics on both poles of ongoing leftwing-rightwing political disputes. In fact, even self-proclaimed libertarian Charles Murray has already capitulated on his hard-right aversion to the "dysgenic effects" of welfare assistance, as he has recently made a case for passing legislation to install a "universal basic income (UBI),"[220] which is a fancy term for what is nothing more than a universal welfare payment.[221] In other words, a communist redistribution of collective wealth.[222] Although Murray is only willing to support a UBI on the contingency that all other government welfare assistance is cut from the budget in exchange, he nonetheless, like Plomin, is willing to compromise on his political ideology if it means negotiating the terms and conditions of futurist, techno-eugenic governance reforms.[223]

To sum up, as the Hegelian-dialectical tensions grow between free-market eugenics and government-planning eugenics, it seems inevitable that there will come a communist-fascist synthesis of corporate eugenic-ed and welfare eugenic-ed that culminates in a scientific dictatorship of technocratic public-private partnerships.

HISTORY of PSYCHOLOGY ("NURTURE" SCIENCE)	INSTITUTIONAL HISTORY	HISTORY of The ORDER of SKULL & BONES	INSTITUTIONAL HISTORY	HISTORY of EUGENICS ("NATURE" SCIENCE)
Wilhelm Wundt (1832-1920) *(founding father of laboratory psychology)*		**Timothy Dwight V (1828-1916)** *(President of Yale 1886-1899)*		**Francis Galton (1822-1911)** *(founding father of eugenics)*
G. Stanley Hall (1846-1924) *(student of Wundt at Leipzig psychology lab; first Professor of Psychology at Johns Hopkins University; first President of APA)*	**Johns Hopkins University (1876 -)**	**Andrew Dickson White (1832-1918)** *(co-founder and first President of Cornell University who recommended D. C. Gilman to Johns Hopkins University)*	**Johns Hopkins University (1876 -)**	**Thomas Henry Huxley (1825-1895)** *("Darwin's Bulldog" and Malthusian evolutionist who gave inaugural speech at Johns Hopkins University)*
John Dewey (1859-1952) *(PhD from Hall; Wundtian-Hegelian pedagogue at Columbia University and the University of Chicago)*		**Daniel Coit Gilman (1831-1908)** *(first President of Johns Hopkins University; first President of the Carnegie Institution; Rockefeller GEB administrator*	**Carnegie Institution (1902 -)**	
James McKeen Cattell (1860-1944) *(Wundt's PhD student who hired E. L. Thorndike at Columbia University)*	**Rockefeller General Education Board (GEB) (1902-1964)**	**Percy Rockefeller (1878-1934)** *(nephew of John D. Rockefeller)*	**Rockefeller Foundation (1913 -)**	**Charles Davenport (1866-1944)** *(founder of Cold Spring Harbor Laboratory; collaborator with Nazi eugenicists such as Eugen Fischer)*
E. L. Thorndike (1874-1949) *(pioneer of behaviorist "puzzle-box" psychology at Columbia University)*		**W. Averell Harriman (1891-1986)** *(son of Mary Williamson and E. H. Harriman)*	**Eugenics Record Office (1910-1913)**	
		E. Roland Harriman (1895-1978) *(UBC Board of Directors)*		**Adolph Hitler (1889-1945)** *(Nazi eugenics regime)*
		Knight Wooley (1895-1984) *(UBC Board of Directors)*	**Union Banking Corporation (UBC) (1924-1951)**	
		Prescott Bush (1895-1972) *(UBC Board of Directors)*		
		Archibald MacLeish (1892-1982) *(co-author of UNESCO Constitution; US delegate to the governing board of UNESCO)*	**United Nations Educational, Scientific, and Cultural Organization (UNESCO) (1946 -)**	**Julian Huxley (1887-1975)** *(President of British Eugenics Society; first Director-General of UNESCO)*
B. F. Skinner (1904-1990) *(Harvard behaviorist; progenitor of operant-conditioning psychology; architect of "teaching machines")*	**Harvard University (1636 -)**	**McGeorge Bundy (1919-1996)** *(Dean of Harvard University Graduate School of Arts and Sciences)*	**Bilderberg Group (1954 -)**	
	"Tax Cuts and Robots Act" *(signed into law on December 22, 2017)*	**Steven Mnuchin (1962-)** *(US Treasury Secretary under President Donald Trump)*	**"Tax Cuts and Robots Act"** *(signed into law on December 22, 2017)*	**Charles Murray (1943-)** *(Bilderberg Group member; Harvard graduate; crypto-eugenicist author of The Bell Curve)*

Computerized Psychological Data-Mining:
Cognitive-Behavioral (UII) data from adaptive-learning software;
Socioemotional Learning (SEL) metrics from EEG, GSR, and other biofeedback wearables;

Computerized Genetic Data-Mining:
DNA IQ scores

Precision Education for "Lifelong Learning"

CHAPTER 15

SOCIO-EMOTIONAL EUGENICS "FROM WOMB TO TOMB":[a] DATA-MINING SEL PSYCHOMETRICS TO MANAGE A DIGITAL WORKFORCE CASTE SYSTEM

To be sure, even the most hardcore of scientific racists does not try to assert that IQ genes determine 100% of an individual's cognitive-intellectual capacity. As such, even hardline genetic determinists who believe that DNA controls up to 80% of a person's intelligence powers, such as *Bell Curve* apologist Sam Harris,[1] must acknowledge that, if precision ed-tech only focuses on "assisting" or "accommodating" the cognitive limitations of a student's biogenetic IQ, then such eugenic ed-tech will fail to apply the full gamut of biometric data-mining necessary to fully "personalize" the digital micromanagement of every facet of the student's complete cognitive-intellectual development. Therefore, to perfect 100% precision accuracy in capitalizing on a student's total range of cognitive-intellectual abilities, crypto-eugenic educationists must supplement genetic screenings with psychometric screenings that take inventory of the student's temperamental proclivities which account for the remaining percentiles of non-genetic influence on his or her intellectual capabilities.

Traditionally, for the purposes of academic specialization, the scientific studies of affective and behavioral cognition have typically been confined to the "nurture" fields of the social science such as psychology and sociology while the scientific study of evolutionary genetics has been confined to a separate "nature" field of the biological life sciences. Nevertheless, the science of eugenics has always integrated both the "nature" science of

---

a. "From Womb to Tomb" is taken from the title of Anita Hoge's extensively well-documented breakdown of the "social and emotional learning (SEL)" agenda. See Hoge's "The School of Tomorrow, "Womb to Tomb": A New Managed Economy, A New Prescription for America Linking Education and National Healthcare Reform to the New Workforce of the Future."

genetic engineering and "nurture" science of psychological programming. In fact, the infamous "Eugenics Tree" poster for the First International Eugenics Congress in 1912 illustrates that, from the get-go, eugenics has been an interdisciplinary study that amalgamates all of the social and life sciences together.[2]

The "Eugenics Tree" image depicts a large tree draped with a banner that states "Eugenics."[3] On the left and right sides of the tree, the caption reads, "Eugenics is the self-direction of human evolution."[4] Underneath the roots of the tree, there is another caption that reads, "Like a tree eugenics draws its materials from many sources and organizes them into an harmonious entity."[5] Each root of the tree is labeled with one of the "sources" of eugenics, which include the full spectrum of life and social sciences: "anatomy," "biology," "physiology," "psychology," "mental testing," "anthropometry," "genetics," "anthropology," "ethnology," "statistics," "politics," "economics," "biography," "genealogy," "sociology," "psychiatry," "surgery," "medicine," and, yes, even "education."[6]

In other words, psychometrics and sociometrics have been integral to eugenical biometric research ever since the inception of eugenic science, which has always sought definitive proofs of causal links between specific genotypes and specific psycho-socioemotional behaviors. At the same time, psychologists such as B. F. Skinner have always acknowledged that, in order for educational psychology to be maximally effective, even the most sophisticated forms of operant-conditioning regimens must take into consideration the eugenic, or perhaps dysgenic, limitations of the student's genetic capacity to be trained for particular cognitive-behavioral tasks.

In *The Technology of Teaching*, Skinner exhibits his experimental "teaching machine" that he designed for the special education of "microcephalic idiot[s]";[7] and he also articulates how correlations between a student's "genetic endowment" and his or her psycho-socioemotional dispositions must predicate the differentiated type of edu-conditioning that student receives through his or her "programmed-learning" machine:

> [m]otivational and emotional differences also present problems. Students differ in their susceptibility to natural and contrived reinforcers, both positive and negative. If the differences are genetic, they must be recognized in the design of the instruction, but if, as is often the case, it is a matter of conditioning reinforcers, remedial action can be taken. Emotional by-products to aversive control vary widely, possibly in part for genetic reasons but also in part

as a function of contingencies under which the student may have learned to take aversive stimulation.[8]

To simplify, Skinner's 1968 *Technology of Teaching* basically puts forward the supposition that machine-programmed instruction must first account for a student's genetically determined intellectual endowment; then, the machine-conditioning must account for the "[e]motional by-products" of the student's genetically determined cognitive faculties. In order to "personalize" the mechanization of classroom operant-conditioning that accommodates each student's genetic IQ and genetic temperament, Skinner recommends the invention of a psycho-eugenic "technology of teaching [that] will solve many of the problems raised by differences among students. It will not, however, reduce all students to one pattern. On the contrary, it will discover and emphasize genuine genetic differences. If based on a wise policy, it will also deign environmental contingencies in such a way as to generate the most promising diversity."[9]

A half-century later, and precision-eugenic ed-tech is being engineered to assess genetic IQ data and "socio-emotional learning (SEL)" data that can be programmed into adaptive-learning algorithms which condition students for workforce competence. In brief, fifty years later, B. F. Skinner's psycho-eugenic technology of teaching is coming to fruition in the form of operant-conditioning software coded with IQ-SEL algorithms. By 2019, schools will begin "Health Assessment for Education. Periodic online assessment of psychophysical status to adjust individual educational trajectory," according to the 2015-2035 timeline forecasted by the Russian-international Global Education Futures.[10]

The IQ-SEL Dialectics of Psycho-Eugenical Education:

In the latest academic literature published in the field of educational psychology, scholarly journals are peer-reviewing various bio-psychometric models that statistically chart the ratios and proportions by which a student's cognitive-intellectual development is shaped by his or her predetermined genetic-IQ capacity versus his or her socio-environmentally conditioned psycho-affective disposition.

A 2017 issue of the *International Journal of Intelligent Technologies & Applied Statistics* published findings which indicate that IQ only determines about 30% of a student's academic competence while the other 70% is determined by an array of "cognitive and non-cognitive factors" that are socio-environmentally "acquired." The article states,

[p]eople with a higher IQ score tend to have a better academic performance. The results of this study showed that the intellectual ability of 9th grade students could positively predict their future academic outcomes. It supports many earlier studies (e.g., Kpolovie [15]) that intellectual ability has a highly positive relationship with students' academic performance.... Nevertheless ... the intelligence did not account for more than approximately 30% of the total variance in academic achievement, which implies that acquired abilities, including cognitive and non-cognitive factors, play a dominant roles [sic] in education success.[11]

Similarly, a 2018 issue of the scholarly journal, *Early Childhood Research Quarterly*, which is affiliated with the Department of Human Development and Family Studies at Colorado State University, published a comparable report that finds IQ metrics to be less predictive of academic competence than psychometrics which measure "affective aspects of mastery motivation, [and] social mastery motivation."[12] The article concludes that

[s]ocioemotional aspects of mastery motivation are important in school readiness.... Mastery motivation variables predicted academic school success after controlling IQ.... Results [of Structural Equations Modeling] indicated that children's negative reactions to failure/challenge predicted all of these measures of *school* performance, over and above the role of child IQ.... Results contribute to the growing literature supporting the importance of motivation and of achievement-related emotions in *school* readiness and school success.[13]

Using such psycho-eugenic models of the statistical interplay between students' temperament and IQ, precision-eugenic educationists are aiming to optimize the cognitive parameters of students' genetic IQ limitations through the digital data-mining and operant-conditioning of their non-cognitive/socioemotional dispositions. Thus, crypto-eugenic educationists have concocted the trendy new pedagogical theory of "social and emotional learning (SEL)": a psychometric methodology of education that uses biometric technologies to scan a student's body language, facial expressions,[14] heart rate,[15] blood pressure,[16] and body temperature to data-mine his or her levels of attention,[17] motivation, and engagement in response to classroom- and online-learning stimuli.[18]

By keeping track of such psycho-affective SEL data in real time, stimulus-response adaptive-learning software can adjust the digital-learning stimuli so that it triggers the student to respond with more attention, motivation, or engagement which will spur that student into activating his or her higher cognitive-intellectual potentials preset by his or her IQ genes. As reported in a 2015 *Open Review of Educational Research* article co-written by Bill Cope, who is a Professor of Educational Policy Studies at the University of Illinois, Champaign-Urbana, and Mary Kalantzis, who is the Dean of the College of Education at the same university, "[c]omputer-mediated learning environments can monitor student sentiments with affect meters of one kind or another, collecting structured as well as unstructured data: emote-aloud meters and self-reports on affective states that address a range of feelings, including, for instance, boredom, confusion, interest, delight, fear, anxiety, satisfaction, frustration."[19]

According to Cope and Kalantzis, who co-founded the Gates-funded Common Ground Scholar database, these SEL data and other "psychometrics" can be uploaded into "Computer Adaptive Tests (CATs) [to] tailor the test to the trait level of the person taking the test.... [A]dvanced applications of these technologies include machine learning environments in which difficulty ranking of selected response items is crowdsourced based on patterns of response to particular questions in relation to student profiles."[20]

SEL Policies, CASEL Competencies, Psychometrics:

At the 2018 G20 Conference in Argentina, the first-ever "Education Working Group" of G20 Education Ministers convened the inaugural G20 Education Ministerial Meeting where US Education Secretary, Betsy DeVos, signed on to the G20 Education Ministers' Declaration 2018: Building Consensus for Fair and Sustainable Development.[21] Under "Policy Options for Education and Skills," this G20 Declaration lists the "inclusion of non-cognitive skills such as socio-emotional skills across the curriculum," which must be standardized by "robust and comprehensive learning assessment systems and data in order to measure progress and learning outcomes, to help ensure quality education for all at all stages of life."[22]

Speaking to her fellow G20 Education Ministers in Argentina, DeVos dog-whistled her intentions to plug the G20 SEL standards into the US education system as part of America's adoption of UNESCO's globalist "lifelong learning" curriculum for workforce schooling:

> [t]his gathering provides an important opportunity ... to improve education for all students on their lifelong learning journeys as they prepare for today's and tomorrow's careers.

> Indeed, education and the economy are indivisible...
>
> [S]tudents must be prepared to anticipate and adapt. They need to acquire and master broadly transferrable and versatile educational competencies like critical thinking, collaboration, communication, creativity and cultural intelligence. These are essential – but often unaddressed – skills for students regardless of their chosen careers...
>
> Learning must be lifelong, because careers are like highways, not one-way or dead-end streets. Highways have many off-ramps and on-ramps. Students should be able to exit easily for a time to learn a new skill, then re-enter the highway at an on-ramp of their choosing and change lanes as needed.[23]

To put it another way, DeVos is proclaiming that the global workforce-schooling system of the future must teach students "lifelong" socioemotional competencies like "collaboration" and "cultural intelligence" that will enable them to navigate through the virtual "highway[s]" of digital career-pathways curriculums from cradle through career.

To set up "lifelong" SEL policies for SEL technologies across the US education system, five SEL competencies, including "self-awareness," "self-management," "social awareness," "relationship skill," and "responsible decision-making,"[24] have been standardized by the nonprofit Collaborative for Academic, Social, and Emotional Learning (CASEL),"[25] which is being given funding from the Rockefeller Philanthropy Advisors, the Bill and Melinda Gates Foundation, and the Institute for Education Sciences of the US federal government.[26]

In order to program adaptive-learning computers with operant-conditioning algorithms that condition students' socioemotional competences, such educational technology is being engineered to track students' psycho-affective responses to digital-learning stimuli in real time; and there are even standardized tests for data-mining SEL metrics, such as the *Social Emotional Learning* Screening Assessment (SELA), which measures a student's levels of proficiency in CASEL's five socioemotional competences.

Printed in a 2018 issue titled "Social-Emotional Assessment to Guide Educational Practice," the *Journal of Applied Developmental Psychology* published a "study [that] examined the initial validation of scores for a new universal screening measure called SELA," which "offers educators a time-efficient, sensitive, and reliable measure that effectively identifies students at-risk socially and academically."[27] According to this peer-reviewed journal, "268 children from prep through year 3" were data-mined in a SEL experiment to garner "psychometric evidence for the SELA," which is "based on the CASEL five [competencies] model and the existing SSIS [Social Skills Improvement System] Performance Screening Guide."[28]

Like the SELA, The Social Skills Improvement System (SSIS) Classwide Intervention Program is sponsored by CASEL, which endorses the "SSIS SEL edition" as "a social skills promotion program that uses free-standing SEL lessons and teaching practices for students in preschool through eighth grade…. [T]he program provides learning around all five social-emotional competencies."[29] Moreover, CASEL promotes SSIS webinars offered by Pearson Assessment: the Clinical Assessment branch of the Pearson Education Corporation which offers "gold-standard assessment contributions in cognitive/ability, memory, neuropsychology, behavior, personality/psychopathology, achievement and speech/language…. We [Pearson] currently serve approximately 300,000 customers in the U.S. with assessments for psychologists, speech language pathologists, occupational therapists, and related professionals."[30] Many of these psychometric assessments, including the SSIS,[31] are administered through online software modules and other computerized ed-tech.[32]

To officially promote such SEL data-mining technologies, federal government policies have already been put in place. For examples, the Strengthening Education Through Research Act (SETRA) and certain grants from the Race to the Top Early Learning Challenge,[33] according to attorney Jane Robbins of the American Principles Project, have been instituted to incentivize "SEL standards and data-collection and preserving this [SEL data] in states' student-data systems. So now every child's permanent dossier can include how well he played with others when he was four."[34] Right now, efforts to mainstream such SEL data-mining across the United States are underway as SEL lobbyists and other interest groups are calling for innovative reforms to the Every Student Succeeds Act (ESSA).

In a broad interpretation of ESSA, The National Education Association (NEA) proposes that SEL "skills," which "are sometimes referred to as 21st century skills, deeper learning, non-academic, non-cognitive, or soft skills," can be instituted through ESSA reforms because the ESSA bill removes the Elementary and Secondary Education Act (ESEA) language pertaining to "core academic subjects," replacing it with language pertaining to a "well-rounded education."[35] [b] [36]

b. In an *NEA Today* article entitled "How ESSA Helps Advance Social and Emotional Learning," the

To be sure, there are no direct or explicit statutes mandating "social and emotional learning (SEL)" stipulations in ESSA. However, there are clauses that allow for the incorporation of the SEL "competencies" standardized by CASEL. A RAND Corporation "Research Brief," entitled "How the Every Student Succeeds Act Can Support Social and Emotional Learning," states that "[a]n extensive review of ESSA legislation shows that there are at least three possible funding streams for states, local agencies, districts, and schools to obtain support for SEL implementation."[37] These three "funding streams" include Title I: Improving the Academic Achievement of the Disadvantaged; Title II: Preparing, Training, and Recruiting High-Quality Teachers, Principals, or Other School Leaders; Title IV: 21st-Century Schools.[38] In fact, on May 16th, 2018, The Department of Education "issu[ed] a notice inviting applications for a new award for fiscal year (FY) 2018 for the Center To Improve Social and Emotional Learning and School Safety (Center)--Cooperative Agreement, Catalog of Federal Domestic Assistance (CFDA) number 84.424B."[39]

There are also state-level approaches to enacting the SEL provisions embedded in ESSA. In a report titled "What Is Social and Emotional Learning?," the National Conference of State Legislatures explains that

> [u]nder the federal law, Every Student Succeeds Act (ESSA), states may decide to account for the social and emotional learning happening in their schools, and to use that data to make decisions about how best to support schools. For example, many states are considering using social and emotional learning indicators, like school climate or student engagement, in their new state accountability systems.[40]

According to a news article in *Education Week*, these ESSA-sanctioned SEL reforms are already taking place in states like "California, [where] a group of large urban school districts, known as the CORE districts, redesigned the accountability system so that school culture and climate, as well as social-emotional-learning metrics, are 40 percent of their school quality index."[41] As a matter of fact, the CASEL Collaborating States Initiative (CSI)[42] has already established a state-level network of "[a]ll 50 States [which] now have preschool SEL competencies. 8 states have K-12 SEL competencies.... 16 states have SEL-related websites."[43] For instance, the

---

NEA endorsed the SEL innovations discussed at a Center for American Progress (CAP) panel discussion titled "With the Head and the Heart: Harnessing the Power of Social and Emotional Learning Under ESSA."

Minnesota Department of Education standardizes CASEL's socioemotional competencies to "improve academic, social and emotional learning through inquiry and data collection";[44] and the Rhode Island (RI) Department of Education's Council for Elementary and Secondary Education has recognized the RI SEL Standards: Competencies for School and Life Success,[45] which draw upon CASEL's five competencies.[46]

Additionally, CASEL's CSI Standards Advisory Committee is setting up :

> (1) a comprehensive set of free-standing standards and learning goals for SEL with developmental benchmarks for preschool through high school; (2) model policies, including consistent language and terminology that can be used to help embed SEL standards and learning goals throughout the education system; and (3) practice guidelines and other tools to support implementation of social and emotional learning for preschool through high school.[47]

Key players on the CASEL CSI include Stephanie Jones of Harvard University, Sara Castro-Olivo of Texas A&M University, Mary Hurley of the Oakland Unified School District, Robert Jagers of the University of Michigan, and Aaliyah Samuel of the National Governors Association.[48]

At the Congressional level, a bill titled "The Social and Emotional Learning for Families (SELF) Act" was recently introduced on June 14, 2018, by Democrat US Representative of Ohio, Tim Ryan, whose pitch for the legislation proclaims,

> [t]here is growing recognition that social and emotional skills are essential for students' healthy functioning and positive academic outcomes. Social emotional learning helps increase attendance, decrease suspensions and behavioral incidences, and improve attention and participation among students.... It's why I've introduced the SELF Act which promotes and encourages collaboration between schools and parents around the development of their students' social and emotional skills. This partnership is not only beneficial to the student's long term academic success, but necessary for them to be a productive member of the American workforce.[49]

It is keen to note here that underlying Democrat Ryan's "SELF Act" is admittedly a workforce training scheme that mandates psychometric profiling of students for workforce placement in a planned economy. Indeed, through fascistic public-private partnerships, labor departments and politically connected crony corporations are geared up to streamline SEL metrics into computer projections for workforce planning. An academic article titled "Soft Skills for the Workplace," which was published in a 2013 issue of *Change Magazine of Higher Learning*, examines "corporate training" programs that employ socioemotional "soft-skills assessments," such as "the situational judgment test (SJT), the Tailored Adaptive Personality Assessment System (TAPAS), and the Personal Potential Index (PPI)," which are all standardized psychometrics tests.[50] TAPAS was developed by the US Army while the PPI is trademarked by Educational Testing Services (ETS).[51]

Other psychometric SEL tests have been designed with the help of Jonathan E. Martin, who is "an adviser for district and school strategic implementation for ProExam, a nonprofit company that develops standards of credentialing in higher education, health care, and other professions." In a 2016 *Education Week* article titled "We Should Measure Students' Noncognitive Skills," Martin, touts the wonders of SEL data-mining; and he relays how he

> advise[d] researchers who created a K-12 assessment system for noncognitive skills that was successfully piloted in 20 regular-public, charter, and private schools this past spring and will be available for schools to use in the fall. Teachers or counselors administer the assessment to students online and can choose to do so annually or multiple times a year to generate data about such character strengths as responsibility, resilience, teamwork, curiosity, and leadership...
>
> [E]ducators can measure noncognitive skills with confidence and then use the information to help students succeed in a variety of ways...
>
> School leaders committed to educating the whole child will be able to present their boards and supervisors with data for both academic and noncognitive successes as part of their evaluation process. School board members who demand metrics for strategic planning will have evidence of their schools' success (or lack thereof) in developing student character.[52]

What's more, SEL "metrics for strategic planning" can even be data-mined in real time by a bio-psychometric education technology called "Affectiva."[53] According to the academic Wrench in the Gears blog authored by Professor of Education at Townsend University, Morna Mc-Dermott McNulty, "Affectiva uses voice and facial recognition software to track real-time emotions of device users interacting with online content. That company [Affectiva] spun out of the MIT Media lab and contracts with global brands to test advertising campaigns; but it is also used to gather data about student engagement with online education programs."[54]

It is quite telling that Affectiva's SEL algorithms, which are programmed to scan students' socioemotional engagement in response to digital learning stimuli, are in essence the same as Affectiva's behavioral-advertising algorithms, which are programmed to data-mine consumers' socioemotional engagement with commercial ads. No wonder the Global Education Futures timeline projects that precision-ed SEL data-mining will become popularized by 2019, the same year that the Russian-international thinktank forecasts each student will be edu-conditioned by a technetronic "[e]ducational designer toolbox" that synthesizes "[p]ersonal data and advanced big data models [to] allow efficient mass-scale recommendation services for education and career tracks."[55]

Socio-Emotional Race Hygiene:

It is disconcerting enough to know that students' permanent records are being converted into SEL psychological profiles that are digitally data-mined for techno-fascist workforce planning by federal, state, and local governments in public-private partnership with charter school corporations, education technology businesses, and nonprofit psychometric-testing companies. Yet it is even more disturbing to know that these psycho-affective student dossiers are keeping track of statistical correlations between particular ethnic populations and specific SEL competencies (or lack thereof). The result is that SEL lessons are being differentiated for different racial groups so that competency-based socioemotional learning incorporates race-specific educational psychology: in other words, crypto-eugenical schooling.

Of course, crypto-eugenic SEL proponents will couch racial-hygienic social-emotional learning in the doublespeak rhetoric of a "social justice" redistribution of educational resources. Nevertheless, this phony "SJW" SEL is nothing less than another version of Frederick Osborn's covert eugenics which studies psychosocial biodiversity in order to draw crypto-eugenic statistical correlations between particular ethnic populations and their propensities to exhibit certain social behaviors, emotional temperaments, and cognitive psychological processes. There is only one real difference between old-school eugenics proper and the "new" crypto-eugenic science of SEL biodiversity: the former interpreted ethnic-determinist biopsychosocial data with the rhetoric of racial supremacism whereas the latter interprets the very same genetic-determinist biopsychosocial data with the sugar-coated rhetoric of fake multiculturalism which pretends to emphasize the value of cultural biodiversity while it ultimately only stresses how different ethnic populations should receive different educational opportunities.

Numerous studies of race-based SEL outcomes have already recorded crypto-eugenical data on race-specific affective psychology. According to the RAND Corporation, "[a] substantial number of [SEL] interventions have been validated with samples that mostly consist of students who come from low-income families or from racial/ethnic minority groups."[56] For example, a recent race-specific SEL study was funded with $149,995 through the Spencer Foundation's 2016 Spencer Midcareer grant, which was awarded to Dr. Rivas-Drake for the purposes of collaborating with CASEL at the "local" and "regional" levels to "promote competencies (e.g., empathy, perspective-taking)" by "examining the potential role of SEL in shaping youths' ethnic-racial identity development.... Understanding SEL practices in greater depth will allow Dr. Rivas-Drake to substantively and methodologically expand her research program to consider particular SEL practices in adolescent ethnic-racial identity processes."[57]

Other examples of race-based SEL studies can be found in "A Review of the Literature on Social and Emotional Learning for Students Age 3-8: Outcomes for Different Student Populations and Settings," which was published by The National Center for Education Evaluation and Regional Assistance of the Institute of Education Sciences in collaboration with the Regional Educational Laboratory of the Inner City Fund (ICF) International. This whitepaper reports that

> some researchers have found lower social and emotional competence and greater behavior problems among Black and Hispanic students than among White or Asian American students (Garner et al., 2014)...
>
> Since social and emotional competence predicts later school performance, racial/ethnic minority students may benefit from having SEL interventions available to them early (Garner et al., 2014).[58] c [59]

---

c. More racialist SEL research is printed in a whitepaper titled "Pursuing Social and Emotional Development Through a Racial Equity Lens: 5 Strategies for System Leaders to Take Action." Published by the Aspen Institute, this document recommends that schools audit their social, emotional, and academic development (SEAD) outcomes by "[p]roduc[ing] data analysis to ground the audit in current conditions. Data should include student and teacher responses to school climate surveys,

To be sure, the overall literature review reported in this article shows that "[t]he research evidence on SEL interventions with racial/ethnic minority students is mixed."[60] Nonetheless, this research overview documents scholarly efforts to calculate statistical relationships between particular races/ethnicities and specific socioemotional competences which parallel the statistical correlations between particular races/ethnicities and general intelligence quotients: both biometric IQ scores and psychometric SEL scores are spread on essentially the same "bell curve" where "White[s]" and "Asian[s]" score higher than "Black and Hispanic" peoples. As such, crypto-eugenic SEL data is being cited to suggest that ethnic "minorities," particularly those from low-income backgrounds, are in special need of socioemotional conditioning.

To put such racial-hygienic SEL metrics into "systemwide" action, an academic article in a 2007 issue of the *Journal of Educational & Psychological Consultation* makes the case for race-based SEL data-mining across networks of public-private partnerships between schools and various "community systems." This peer-reviewed journal article advocates that SEL "programs need to be tailored culturally to ethnic and racial minority children to maximize the programs' effectiveness (Botvin, 2004)…. [S]ystems to support SEL must be integrated across levels of prevention/promotion and treatment services … across student developmental levels, and across school, family, and community systems" including "the educational and mental health systems."[61]

One example of a "community system" already adopting SEL data-mining practices is the public-private "Community Oriented Policing System(s)" (COPS). A case study of SEL data aggregation by COPS programs in the classroom is documented in a peer-reviewed report published in 2017 issue of the academic journal *Addictive Behaviors*. Titled "Coming to the New D.A.R.E.: A Preliminary Test of the Officer-Taught Elementary Keepin' It REAL Curriculum," this research paper evaluates a new Drug Abuse Resistance Education (DARE) program in which schools are visited by a local police officer who "teaches social and emotional competencies such as decision making and resistance skills" that train students to "just say 'no.'"[62] The methodology of this DARE study assessed

[s]ocial and emotional competencies and other risk factors [that] were examined among students (*N*=943) in 26 classrooms, 13 classrooms in the treatment condition (*n*=359) and 13 class-

as well as discipline, attendance, and grades cross-tabulated by race of student and race of teachers to understand patterns at baseline."

rooms in the control condition (n=584) using a quasi-experimental matched group design. Pretest comparisons of treatment and control groups were completed, along with attrition analyses, and hierarchical logistic and linear regressions were computed to assess the intervention.... The results of this study suggest that D.A.R.E.'s elementary keepin' it REAL program has promise as a social and emotional learning (SEL) based prevention program.[63]

Of course, this DARE data not only highlighted those students who increased their social-emotional ability to abstain from drug use; but it also necessarily pegged those students who are socioemotionally "at risk" of becoming addicted to drugs. Obviously, the latter students could be digitally flagged as potential criminals or potential disturbances to the peace of the local district community. As school-based COPS records compile race-specific psycho-behavioral profiles of socioemotionally "incompetent" students who are at risk of becoming criminals, "personalized" ed-tech data-mining for "lifelong" community-based learning is getting geared up to take racial profiling to a whole new level, especially since students' SEL profiles are primed to be cross-tabulated with their genetic-IQ profiles.

In 2017, an article titled "Race/Ethnicity and Criminal Behavior: Neurohormonal Influences" was published in the academic *Journal of Criminal Justice*, which is affiliated with the Minot State University Department of Sociology in Minot, North Dakota, USA. In this peer-reviewed article, "Evolutionary neuroandrogenic (ENA) theory" is explored "to explain race/ethnic variations in offending" which are purportedly caused by epigenetic, neurobiological determinism.[64] Correlating the social-emotional behaviors of criminals with specific ethnicities, this social-science report concludes that

> among seven different racial/ethnic groups, blacks have the highest and East Asians have the lowest criminal involvement. Strictly social environmental explanations for race/ethnic differences in criminality appear to be inadequate for explaining these differences.... With some exceptions and qualifications, currently-available evidence seems to support the idea that racial/ethnic variations in offending could be at least partially explained by ENA theory.[65]

In brief, this scholarly journal applies ENA theory to posit that the socio-temperamental behaviors of criminals are neurobiologically determined due to biogenetic differences across racial populations that evolved differentially over time through epigenetic hormonal changes that mutated in response to differential exposures to varying high-stress environments that triggered the release of stress hormones such as cortisol, adrenaline, and norepinephrine. Notice how this racial-biological hierarchy of criminal sociologies is a direct parallel to the racial hierarchies of SEL psychometrics and eugenic IQ scores: "Asians" rank at the top while "blacks" rank at the bottom with "whites" somewhere in between. Apropos, this *Journal of Criminal Justice* article suggests that certain racial-biological predispositions to criminal behavior are augmented by "intelligence" variations among racial genotypes as "rapid postpubertal declines in offending depend heavily on learning ability.… [F]our lines of evidence of racial/ethnic differences in learning ability are reviewed."[66]

To sum up, the rise of biopsychosocial Big Data will soon give a whole new meaning to the gimmick of "individualized-learning" technology as adaptive-learning algorithms are upgraded to data-mine a student's socio-emotional temperament, genetical IQ, criminal psycho-behavioral tendencies, and even ethnographic heritage in order to "personalize" his or her digital workforce-schooling pathways. Under the guise of "racial equity," crypto-eugenic educationists could appeal to using these comprehensive biopsychosocial profiles to enact "racial-social justice" by segregating racial/ethnic "minorities" into digital workforce-competence ghettos programmed to re-educate the SEL "incompetence" of these populations who statistically have higher rates of criminal behaviors.

Even more dystopic, as state-level P(K)-16/20 councils conglomerate corporate charter schools with community-oriented policing agencies through public-private partnerships, race-specific SEL data-mining of "at-risk" student bodies could digitally assemble "pre-crime" student records to be data-mined by COPS agencies for the purposes of identifying potential criminal "threats" in the community. It is a fact that detectives in California arrested the alleged "Golden State Killer" after matching his DNA with digital genetic profiles uploaded to the public-private GEDmatch genealogy hub online; and numerous other alleged murderers and rapists have been incriminated by DNA evidence data-mined from the GEDmatch website.[67] If law enforcement officers have already begun to data-mine public-private genealogy dossiers to catch suspects, how long until COPS agents begin data-mining student psychological profiles mapped out on permanent SEL-IQ records in order to match criminal profiles with "at-risk" student profiles and thereby catch criminals or even "pre-criminals"?

It should be noted here that eugenics is in fact the origin of the very notion of "precrime" detection, which is the ability to predict and thus prevent crimes before they are committed.[68] Popularized in the cinematic representation of Philip K. Dick's short story, "The Minority Report,"[69] precrime is a fundamentally eugenic concept inspired by the mastermind of eugenics himself, Francis Galton, who charted statistics on "*facial* criminal types" based on "composite-photography" analyses of "generic" phrenological and physiognomical facial features that recurred across various "mug-shot" photographs.[70] Galton also devised the biometric method of fingerprint mapping, which he popularized as the very first biometrical method of forensic crime-scene investigation.[71]

The criminological anthropometry statistics of Galton and others, such as British prison doctors David Nicholson and James Bruce Thomson, were sponsored by Sir Edmund Du Cane,[72] who operated Great Britain's prison system under eugenic premises as the Prison Commissioner, the Surveyor-General of Prisons, the Chairman of Directors of Convict Prisons, and the Inspector-General of Military Prisons.[73] In addition, court records and police reports were compiled to document family histories of criminal behaviors across successive generations, and eugenicists cited these lawbreaking family trees as proof that criminal deviances are genetically inherited social behaviors that must be weeded out from the human genepool through negative-eugenics policies such as sterilization and abortion.[74] In fact, Du Cane, who attended the International Prison Congress in 1872, published the first-ever criminal "registry" in 1877 when he ordered forced prison labor to print a "Black Book" listing "over 12,000 habitual criminals with their aliases and descriptions."[75]

In brief, the history of keeping criminal records in police departments and judicial courts is steeped in the history of tracking "dysgenic" family heritages in order to bar off "defective" bloodlines from interbreeding with, and thereby "tainting," the "fit" bloodlines of "civilized" populations.

From Francis Galton to Angela Duckworth – Eugenic IQ-SEL Metrics for Workforce Planning:

If you want more definitive proof that SEL data-mining is all about crypto-eugenics, consider the eugenical overtones of the socioemotional-learning research popularized by arguably the most prominent SEL spokesperson celebrated throughout academia: Distinguished Professor of Psychology at the University of Pennsylvania, Angela Duckworth, who won the 2013 MacArthur Foundation "Genius" Fellowship.[76]

Duckworth's scholarship focuses on quantifying a SEL competency she calls "grit."[77] At several TED Talks, Duckworth has hyped grit metrics as the counterpart to IQ scores when it comes to predicting academic achievement outcomes.[78] In one of her power-point slides at her 2009 TED Talk, Duckworth screen-projected handwritten correspondence between the creator of eugenics himself, Francis Galton, and his proto-eugenic cousin, Charles Darwin, who were cited by the MacArthur "genius" to contextualize her psycho-eugenic SEL theories on grit.[79] "Genius" Duckworth also quoted Galton's seminal eugenic text, *Hereditary Genius*, in her scholarly treatise entitled *Grit: The Power of Passion and Perseverance*.[80] Moreover, *Hereditary Genius* is even cited on the webpage for the "Grit and Self-Control" Positive Psychology Initiative,[81] which is posted on the website for the University of Pennsylvania where Duckworth is a faculty member.[82]

In addition to repeatedly citing eugenicist Galton as an authority on genius, Duckworth's SEL research is even financed by crypto-eugenics organizations such as the John Templeton Foundation:[83] a quasi-religious philanthropy that bankrolls scientific and "spiritualist" research by awarding grant moneys to the following crypto-eugenic research fields listed on the Templeton Foundation website:[84] "Voluntary Family Planning; Genetics; and Exceptional Cognitive Talent and Genius."[85] [d 86]

Notice here how the adjective "Voluntary" is placed in front of "Family Planning" to imply that Templeton birth-control projects are not like past negative-eugenics operations set up to abort and sterilize the "unfit" through Margaret Sanger's American Birth Control League,[87] which was later renamed "Planned Parenthood" in order to rhetorically distance the "women's rights" institution from the history of its "Negro Project":[88] a nationwide campaign to target black peoples for eugenic sterilization and eugenic abortion.[89] [e 90]

---

d. The following Templeton-financed genetics studies are examples of crypto-eugenics research projects: "Imprinting in Human Placentas: The Intergenerational Transmission of Health," a study conducted by The University of Michigan; and "A Chance to Equality in Health: Is People's Health Determined by Ancestral Environmental Exposures?," a study conducted by the University of California, Los Angeles.

e. In 2007, the National Book Critics Circle Award for Nonfiction was awarded to Harriet Washington for her *Medical Apartheid: The Dark History of Medical Experimentation on Black Americans from Colonial Times to the Present*. This scholarly tome documents how "Sanger's American Birth Control League merged with the Clinical Research Bureau to form the Birth Control Federation of America (BCFA). Later that year [1939], Sanger devised the Negro Project, which ... sought to find the best

Actually, the very term "family planning" is itself a euphemism coined to give a makeover to the eugenic "birth control" organizations of Sanger and her British counterpart, Marie Stopes,[91] whose eugenic Society for Constructive Birth Control and Racial Progress was the English version of the American Birth Control League.[92] Similarly, the word "genetics," which once upon a time was synonymous with the word "eugenics," gradually became the politically correct substitute for the latter term in order to give post-Hitler eugenicists a face lift.[93] Within the context of these crypto-eugenic "Funding Areas," the Templeton Foundation's interest in "Exceptional Cognitive Talent and Genius" strongly connotes the formative eugenic theory of "hereditary genius" conceptualized by Francis Galton, who is cited repeatedly in Duckworth's SEL research on grit as a determiner of learning outcomes.

In 2008, the John Templeton Foundation funded Duckworth's scientific research paper entitled "The Economics and Psychology of Personality Traits." In this whitepaper, Duckworth argues that intelligence and temperament are genetically inherited, but she also contends that social environments can epigenetically condition IQ and "SEL" genes to mutate before being passed down to offspring in their new, epigenetically reprogrammed DNA sequence. Yet despite Duckworth's pedigree in the "nurture" science of psychology, a close reading of this Templeton-financed paper reveals Duckworth's belief in a strong genetic basis for both IQ and SEL.[94]

There are over 119 references to IQ in the contents of this Duckworth-Templeton report, including various mathematical graphs, charts, and equations; and the bibliography contains fifteen sources which are extensive IQ studies.[95] She even cites crypto-eugenicist James Flynn twice, and the preface to this paper expresses her gratitude for "receiv[ing] very helpful comments on various versions of this draft from ... Flynn."[96] Based on Duckworth's expansive research into IQ genetics, backed up by her consultations with crypto-eugenicist Flynn, this "Working Paper 13810" acknowledges genetic endowment as a certain baseline for intelligence quotients: "[r]esearch on IQ also points to the enduring effects of genes, which are with us all of our lives, in contrast to more transient effects of environmental influences, which depend on a multitude of unstable variables, including social roles, levels of physical maturity and decline, and historical and cultural milieu."[97] Clearly, Duckworth is emphasizing that a student's IQ is profoundly molded by "the enduring effects of genes," which tend to outweigh and outlast the "more transient" and "unstable" effects of environment.

way of reducing the black population by promoting eugenic principles."

To be sure, Duckworth ultimately stresses the viability of environmental conditioning to improve cognitive-intellectual prowess, but she nonetheless reserves that the potential for environmental conditioning is contingent upon genetically inherited IQ:

> [g]enes exert their influence in part through the selection and evocation of environments that are compatible with one's genotype – a phenomenon sometimes referred to as "gene-environment correlation" or "nature via nurture" (see Rutter 2006) ...
>
> Substantial but temporary influence from environment is a basic assumption of the Dickens-Flynn model reconciling the high heritability of IQ and massive gains of IQ between generations (Dickens and Flynn 2001).[98]

Stated differently, Duckworth is saying that environmental conditioning must be "compatible" with a student's inherited IQ genotype, which presupposes that IQ genes are preprogrammed to "grow" only in response to very particular socioenvironmental-learning stimuli. To simplify, Duckworth is implicating that IQ genes predicate environmental conditioning first; then, based on those DNA determiners, only certain social-learning environments can have a positive influence on epigenetically evolving those inherited IQ-gene sequences.

Duckworth makes similar claims about students' SEL temperaments, which she theorizes are likewise determined by the "nature via nurture" interplay of genetic programming and environmental conditioning upon phenotypic expression: "findings in behavioral genetics suggest that, like adult personality, temperament is only partly heritable, and as discussed in Section VI, both adult and child measured traits are affected by the environment."[99] She concludes that, "the answer to the question of whether change in personality is possible must be a definitive yes, both in terms of mean-level and rank-order change. However ... there are powerful forces for stability (such as genes and habit) which make change difficult."[100]

As the title of this "working paper" implies, Duckworth's *The Economics and Psychology of Traits* is ostensibly a workforce-planning document that evaluates IQ and SEL metrics for crypto-eugenical job placement in a market economy. Indeed, Duckworth co-authored this paper with Professor of Economics at the University of Chicago, James Heckman: the 2000 Nobel Prize-winner in Economics who collaborates with Duckworth at the Research Network on the Determinants of Life Course Capabilities and Outcomes,[101] which is part of the University of Chicago's Center for the Economics of Human Development.[102]

Combining Duckworth's IQ-SEL research with Heckman's socioeconomic labor research, their "Working Paper" presents socio-ethnographic correlations that are cited to pose crypto-eugenics theories about the genetically determined nature of race-specific socioeconomic behaviors which are the supposed cause of employment disparities across different ethnicities:

> certain personality and character traits may be more highly valued than others in the labor market (trustworthiness, perseverance, outgoingness, for example). Borghans, ter Weel and Weinberg (2006) show that technological and organizational changes have increased the importance of people skills in the workplace. They present evidence for Germany and the United States that the increased importance of people skills has affected the labor-market outcomes of blacks and women.... They also show that the rapid increase in the importance of people tasks over this time period helps explain the increase in women's wages relative to men and the stagnation in wages of black workers relative to white workers. Diligent or trustworthy employees require less supervision. More generally, different personality and cognitive traits may be more highly valued in some activities than in others.[103]

Duckworth and Heckman are suggesting that "black workers" suffer higher rates of underemployment because they lack the SEL competencies of "[d]iligen[ce]" and "trustworth[iness]," two psycho-affective "traits" which, according to Duckworth and Heckman, are in part genetically inherited.

If you feel like I'm being too critical of Duckworth, I'm not the only academic who reads her IQ-SEL scholarship as crypto-eugenic research into educational and workforce psychology. On the academic blog, Stop Corporate Surveillance in Schools, an article hash-tagged under the keyword "eugenics" was posted by Professor of Education at Townsend University, Morna McDermott McNulty. Entitled "Grit, Human Capital, and Data Mining: What's Next for Children," McNulty's article concurs that Duckworth has a crypto-eugenic affinity for Galton; that the Templeton Foundation is a crypto-eugenics philanthropy; and that the Duckworth-Heckman report on workforce SEL is a crypto-eugenic whitepaper which "makes it clear Social Emotional Learning (SEL) data collection is about developing profiles for economic and labor forecasts."[104]

Additionally, Assistant Professor of Education at Connecticut College, Lauren Anderson, penned a 2014 article in *Education Week* titled "Grit, Galton, and Eugenics," which comes to the same conclusions regarding the crypto-eugenic ulterior motive behind of Duckworth's SEL agenda. Anderson questions,

> What underlying assumptions about participants and peers – members of "researched" and "researcher" communities – are operating here, and what meaning is to be made of them? What, for example, would participants think and feel if they traced the unproblematized quotation to its fuller source? Would what they find comport with their understanding of the research in which they (or their children) participated? What about colleagues in the research community? Is the assumption that we will read neutral references to eugenical texts unproblematically, that we will not be punched in the gut by the institutional violence that they represent? ...
>
> Duckworth's work – now with MacArthur Foundation funding following that of Gates, Templeton, and KIPP, among others – is shaping public discourse, policy and programming, especially concerning the importance of "character" education in urban schools serving low-income kids of color. It is therefore not just *fair*, but also *important* to understand and ask questions about the ideological foundation on which that work rests.
>
> In this case, given the historical underpinnings – evident in Galton's prime placement – coupled with individualistic, rather than structural, explanations for students' "success" and "failure," it is essential to interrogate the claims to objectivity on the part of the researcher and the tacit approval (or uncritical uptake) of frameworks and findings on the part of those promoting the research.[105]

The Chinese Social Credit Score Comes to the American School System:

In a *Federalist* article entitled "Schools Ditch Academics For Emotional Manipulation," Senior Fellow of the American Principles Project, Jane Robbins, and President of Education Liberty Watch, Karen Effrem, question

> the movement advanc[ing] to assess, record, and analyze personal characteristics of children. What happens to all that data? Incentivized by USED, states are building massive statewide longitudinal data systems to track every aspect of every student from cradle to, or through, their career. Thus, unreliable data collected from mak-

ing guesses about students' emotional states will presumably be entered into the database, to live in eternity.[106]

It doesn't take a crystal ball to see that, in time, the data-mining of students' cognitive-behavioral UII, SEL metrics, and genetic information will be aggregated and plugged into an Americanized version of the Communist Chinese Social Credit System. In 2015, the Ant Financial Corporation put in place the Sesame Credit scoring system, which data-mines Chinese citizens' social media profiles, financial histories, and other public records to digitally rank the Chinese people with "social scores" that determine not only access to loans and luxury items, but also access to employment, healthcare, online dating services, hotels, rental cars, and even food.[107] The Chi-Com Sesame Corporation also "blacklists" activist groups that the Chinese government deems "illegal social organisations" in order to regulate "correct political direction."[108]

For a frightening science-fiction depiction of this Orwellian Social Credit System on steroids, watch the *Black Mirror* episode entitled "Nosedive."[109] To get a glimpse of China-style social-score discrimination in the United States, look no further than the recent purge of "fake news," "conspiracy theories," "hate speech,"[110] and other forms of "extremist content" that has already censored both rightwing pundits,[111] including *Infowars* host Alex Jones and *Vice* co-founder Gavin Mcinnes,[112] as well as leftwing newscasts, such as Police the Police and TeleSUR English,[113] which have been red-flagged by the "fact-checking" algorithms and "community-standards" algorithms of social-network corporations such as Facebook, Twitter, YouTube, and other social-media platforms.[114] How long before a person's behavioral social-media profile, internet search histories, and financial credit score are agglomerated with his or her psycho-affective SEL metrics, cognitive behavioral UII data, and genetic-IQ scores? How long until such permanently digitized education records are linked to "social-credit" algorithms that restrict not only a person's rights to access the worldwide web, but also his or her rights to real-world employment, healthcare, travel, and civil due process?

If you think that the Chinese Social Credit System could never come to the United States, know that the psycho-eugenic data-mining of American students is getting a direct helping hand from corporate-communist China. The Chinese Foxconn Corporation, which infamously hung "suicide nets" outside of its factories to prevent workers from jumping to their deaths,[115] has recently signed workforce education contracts with the State of Wisconsin,[116] where the State Department of Public Instruction "has developed Social and Emotional Learning Competencies for PK-adult."[117] With input from the Wisconsin PK-16 Workforce and Leadership Council,[118] these PK-adult SEL competencies are standardized by employing a policy of data-mining students for their SEL psychometrics to "Use Data to Assess Progress" toward "student mental health ... and academic and career planning (ACP)."[119] [f] [120] Since workforce schooling in Wisconsin is being managed by the Chi-Com Foxconn Corporation, this international public-private partnership will create a direct channel through which Wisconsin's fascistic school-to-work programs in America can data-mine precision-ed SEL and IQ metrics to experiment with Chinese models of digital biopsychosocial engineering akin to the Sesame Social Credit System. In the meantime, the new iOS 12 update for iPhones has "quietly" installed all updated cellular phones with "Trust Score" software that is an "Americanized" brand of the Chinese Social Score System designed by the Apple Corporation,[121] which contracted to have its computer hardware manufactured at the Foxconn plants where the Communist Chinese government hung suicide nets to prevent the wage slaves from jumping out of the factory windows to their deaths.[122]

Brave School World:

Don't be fooled into thinking that we live in a post-eugenics world in which our information technologies have become so precise that they are incapable of being programmed with racist and classist algorithms based on the biometric and psychometric hierarchies of old-fashioned eugenics ethnographies. On the contrary, crypto-eugenicists are ready to take another stab at the old Robber Baron enterprise of the mass-industrial, biopsychosocial re-engineering of society. Not because they mean to apply more humane bioethics that will interpret anthropometric data more equitably, but because advancements in Big Data will enable them to be exponentially more efficient in tagging and tracking "dysgenic" biometrics and psychometrics on an individualized basis. Equipped with these new supercomputer powers, crypto-eugenic technocrats now have confidence that they can perfectly mete out the "personalized" precision-eugenic interventions needed to technetronically engineer society

---

f. In a document titled "Social and Emotional Learning Competencies," the Wisconsin Department of Public Instruction asserts that "[s]ocial and emotional learning competencies are lifelong skills, essential for everyone." This statement is a dog-whistle signaling that UNESCO's "lifelong learning" pedagogy is the "hidden curriculum" underlying SEL data-mining for competency-based workforce schooling.

into a workforce caste system that digitally dictates student job placement based on IQ-SEL-UII algorithms.

The hubris of this hyper-rational faith in Big Data is hardly different from the hubris that drove Hitlerian eugenicists to believe that "defective" genotypes could be "cleansed" by the powers of mass-mechanized statistical analysis applied through the International Business Machines (IBM) punch-card computing system used in Nazi concentration camps to keep meticulous record of the eugenic executions and eugenic biomedical experiments carried out at camps like *Auschwitz, Buchenwald, Dachau*.[123 g 124]

IBM Hollerith punch-card systems were leased to the Third Reich from IBM's corporate headquarters in the United States, which was run by Chairman and Chief Executive Thomas J. Watson, who held business meetings with Hitler himself in 1937.[125] The Nazi regime's eugenic concentration camps processed the "Hollerith" punch cards to categorize their "defective" inmates into sixteen numbered hole-punch codes: 1—Political Prisoner; 2—Bible Researcher [Jehova's Witness]; 3—Homosexual; 4—Dishonorable Military Discharge; 5—Clergy; 6—Communist Spaniard; 7—Foreign Civilian Worker; 8—Jew; 9—Asocial; 10—Habitual Criminal; 11—Major Felon; 12—Gypsy; 13—Prisoner of War; 14—Covert Prisoner; 15—Hard Labor Detainee; 16—Diplomatic Consul.[126] Upon his or her death, each prisoner's IBM Hollerith card would be punched with a death code: C-3—Death by natural causes; D-4—Execution; E-5—Suicide; and F-6—SB Special Treatment, which signified death by gas chamber (in other words, eugenic murder).[127]

According to documentation in Edwin Black's award-winning *IBM and Holocaust*, Herman Hollerith's punch-card processors were also internationally leased for tabulating eugenical demographics and other population data compiled by "[c]ensus and statistical departments in Russia, Italy, England, France, [and] Austria."[128] Except for Russia and Italy, each of these countries was represented at the International Federation of Eugenics Organizations (IFEO) where Charles Davenport was the president until he bowed out to Nazi eugenicist Ernst Rüdin, who was the Director of the Kaiser Wilhelm Institute for Psychiatry.[129]

But to be sure, the endgame for the IFEO did not actually aim to totally exterminate the "unfit." According to Stefan Kühl's *The Nazi Connection: Eugenics, American Racism, and German National Socialism*, the IFEO held a "Committee on Race Crossing [which] was jointly led by

g   The three Institutes to pioneer eugenic murder were the Kaiser Wilhelm Institute for Psychiatry; the Kaiser Wilhelm Institute for Brain Research; and the Kaiser Wilhelm Institute for Anthropology, Human Heredity, and Eugenics, which was headed by Eugene Fischer as the director.

Davenport and [Eugen] Fischer. Both agreed that 'the contrast between the slight scientific activity in the field of hybrid investigation and the vast extent of race crossing in almost all parts of the earth' was unfortunate."[130] Notwithstanding historical oversimplifications, the grand scheme of the IFEO was to cull the excess numbers of "undesirable" genepools and to enslave the remaining "sub-humans" as immutably fixed genetic serfs who are biologically programmed for hivemind bondage under a eugenically superior "master race" of "supermen." In *War Against the Weak*, journalist Edwin Black reveals how IFEO President Charles

> Davenport envisioned a new mankind of biological castes with master races in control and slave races serving them. He compared the coming world order to "colonies of bees and termites. … All the bees in a hive, including the queen, are full sisters and have been for uncounted generations. Each one is hatched with a set of instincts, which enables it, in machine-like fashion, to do the proper thing at the proper time for the existence of the colony. In human communities, also, the more uniform the instincts and ideals the less friction and the less need for government control with its vast system of law, law enforcement and punishment."[131]

Compare this eugenic "hivemind" caste system to the Scientific Caste System fictionalized in the famous dystopic novel, *Brave New World*, by Aldous Huxley, who was the brother of British Eugenics Society President, Julian Huxley.[132] In Aldous's eugenic dystopia, the technocratic World Controllers wield the powers of mechanical-industrial mass-production to genetically engineer workforce slaves in test-tubes on factory assembly lines so that their racial-genetic biological makeups are designed for job-specific social roles in the Scientific Caste System which is governed by the planned economy of the World State.[133] The World Government's eugenic caste system is stratified into Alpha, Beta, Gamma, Delta, and Epsilon classes,[h] [134] which are ranked into biogenetic tiers that

h. Huxley's idea of a Scientific Caste System can be traced back to Plato's *Republic* in which Socrates deliberates on a proto-utopian government of "philosopher aristocrats" who rule over a proto-eugenic caste system. In the perfect City-State contemplated by Socrates, the "philosopher king" and his council of aristocrats must selectively breed the citizenry in the same manner as "dogs and birds … [and] the same of horses and animals in general" so that "the best of either sex should be united with the best as often, and the inferior with the inferior, as seldom as possible; and that they should rear the offspring of the one sort of union, but not of the other, if the flock is to be maintained in first-rate condition." Through this process of proto-eugenic selection, the philosopher aristocracy enculturates a workforce caste hierarchy in which the "gold" upper-class breeds are privileged to be the "command[ers]" who rule over the lower-class "bronze and iron" breeds that are subjugated to serve as lesser-skilled labor slaves, such as "husbandmen and craftsmen." In Book III of *The Republic*, are distinguished in terms of phrenological features and IQ scores that mirror the racial-eugenic taxonomies of old-fashioned eugenicists.[135]

In particular, the upper castes are of the lightest skin complexions and the highest IQs while the lowest castes are of the darkest skin complexions and the lowest IQs with cranial structures akin to the skulls of primates and primitive hominids such as neanderthals. More specifically, the "Bokanovsky" clones who belong to the very bottom caste of Epsilon-Minuses are frequently referred to as "semi-morons" with Black African complexions.[136] For instance, the Alpha Plus character, Bernard Marx, encounters two Epsilon workforce slaves: "[a]n Epsilon negro porter" and a "liftman [who] was a small simian creature, dressed in the black tunic of an Epsilon-Minus Semi-Moron."[137] The narrator also describes "eighty-three almost noseless black brachycephalic Deltas [who] were cold-pressing" alongside "[o]ne hundred and seven heat-conditioned Epsilon Senegalese."[138] By characterizing "black," "negro," and "Senegalese" workforce drones as Semi-Moron Epsilons and Deltas with "simian" features such as "brachycephalic" skulls and "noseless" faces,[i][139] Aldous Huxley's eugenic caste hierarchy is clearly an allusion to the racial-hygienic conception of black-complexioned peoples as dysgenically devolved.[j][140]

---

in the "Parable of the Metals," Socrates lays out each tier of this proto-eugenical workforce caste system: "we [the aristocracy] shall say to them in our tale, you are brothers, yet God has framed you differently. Some of you have the power of command, and in the composition of these he has mingled gold, wherefore also they have the greatest honour; others he has made of silver to be auxiliaries; others again who are to be husbandmen and craftsmen he composed of brass and iron." To put it another way, Socrates' "government of the best" breeds and conditions a workforce caste hierarchy based on the belief that the different labor classes are physically (or biologically) composed of different metals which endow the different body types with different characteristics and capabilities, stratifying them into segregated castes that perform job-specific functions for the Aristocratic State. Consider how Socrates' proto-eugenical workforce hierarchy in Plato's "Parable of the Metals" is paralleled to the futurist-eugenic workforce hierarchy of Huxley's Scientific Caste System, which ranks the different genetic-labor classes with Greek alphabet labels (Alpha, Beta, Gamma, Delta, Epsilon) to honor the proto-eugenics of the Greek philosopher Socrates, who postulated the "Parable of the Metals" in Plato's *Republic*. Basically, the only difference between these two caste systems is that, in Plato's philosophical literature, labor classes are selectively bred and ranked according to a hierarchy of metals whereas, in Huxley's science-fiction literature, labor classes are genetically engineered and ranked according to a hierarchy of colors and Greek letters. i. According to the *Oxford Dictionary* online, the term "brachycephalic" refers to "[h]aving a relatively broad, short skull (typically with the breadth at least 80 per cent of the length)." The *Merriam-Webster Dictionary* defines "brachycephalic" as "short-headed or broad-headed with a cephalic index of over 80." To put it another way, brachycephalic skulls are those that are abnormally proportioned, which results in a diminished cranial cavity with less space for brain mass in contrast to a normally shaped skull.

j. Aldous's five eugenic castes in *Brave New World* mirror the five eugenical racial types taxonomized by his grandfather, Thomas Henry Huxley; for in both classification systems, intelligence is linked to skull structure and skin color. In 1870, Thomas Henry read a paper at the Ethnological Society in England, which would shortly thereafter be merged into the Anthropological Society to become the Anthropological Institute and then the Royal Anthropological Institute. In this Ethnological Society presentation, T. H. Huxley postulated a racial taxonomy of the human species, classifying humankind into five basic races: "Australoid; Negroid; Xanthochroi (fair whites of Europe); Melanchroi

Of course, the traditional reading of *Brave New World* interprets the novel as Aldous Huxley's warning to beware of scientific dictatorship through a eugenic caste system. However, this common misreading taught in schools does not account for the volumes of Aldous's non-fiction essays in which he advocates for the very Scientific Caste System that he portrays in *Brave New World*.

In his 1927 "The Future of the Past," Huxley makes clear his vision of a scientific aristocracy that will technocratically rule over a eugenic caste system:

> [i]n the Future that we envisage, eugenics will be practiced in order to improve the human breed…. Society will be organized as a hierarchy of mental quality and the form of government will be aristocratic in the literal sense of the word – that is to say, the best will rule…. Our children may look forward to the establishment of a new caste system based on differences in natural ability.[141]

Moreover, in his 1931 "On the Charms of History and the Future of the Past," Huxley asserts that this eugenic caste system will be "designed to give the members of the lower castes only such instruction as it is profitable for society at large and the upper castes in particular that they should have."[142]

Furthermore, in his promotional essay for the release of *Brave New World*, which is titled "Science and Civilization," Huxley pragmatically resolves that

> stupid people are probably the state's least troublesome subjects, and a society composed in the main of stupid people is more likely stable than one with a high proportion of intelligent people. The economist-ruler would therefore be tempted to use the knowledge of genetics not for eugenic but dysgenic purposes – for the deliberate lowering of the average mental standard. True, this would have

(dark whites of Europe, North Africa, Asia Minor, and Hindustan, including the Irish, Celts, Bretons, Spaniards, Arabs, and Brahmins; and Mongoloid (including the peoples of Asia, Polynesia, and the Americas)." Although T. H. H. never exactly ranked these five races into any clear evolutionary hierarchy, he based his anthropological taxonomy partially upon what amount to phrenological skull measurements. For instance, according to Thomas Henry, the "Negro" forehead indicates "child-like character," which implies that the "Negro," at the physiological level, is in a state of arrested cognitive development as a symptom of arrested evolutionary development, presumably because the skull structure of the forehead somehow dictates the shape, the size, and, thereby, the function and capability of the brain. Similarly, T. H. Huxley suggested that only the most biologically superior Melanchroi (dark whites) can achieve cognitive parity with any Xanthocroi (fair whites), which of course presupposes that fair-skinned Xanthocroi are somehow innately more evolved than darker-complexioned races. These eugenical ethnographies of "dark-white," or "flaxen," peoples, whom T. H. H. regards as prone to certain dysgenic traits, are likewise paralleled in his grandson's eugenic caste system in *Brave New World*. For example, Aldous depicts other Epsilon Semi-Morons as "blue-eyed, flaxen and freckled," which invokes Thomas Henry's subclass of "dark white," or "flaxen," Melanchroi who are supposedly less evolved or otherwise biologically inferior to "fair white" Xanthocroi.

to be accompanied by the special breeding and training of a small caste of experts, without whom a scientific civilization cannot exist. Here, incidentally, I may remark that in a scientific civilization society must be organized on a caste basis. The rulers and their advisory experts will be a kind of Brahmins controlling, in virtue of a special and mysterious knowledge, vast hordes of the intellectual equivalents of Sudras and Untouchables.[143]

In sum, these passages illustrate, in Aldous's own words, that he believed the scientific management of civilization must eventually evolve into a neo-feudalist, eugenic caste system that does away with the "unstable" freedoms of *laissez faire* market competition and democratic social mobility. Forty years later, in *Beyond Freedom and Dignity*, B. F. Skinner compared *Brave New World* to his own behaviorist-utopian novel, *Walden Two*;[144] in this comparative literary analysis, Skinner refers to *Brave New World*, not as a dystopia, but as one of the great "behavioral utopias – Aldous Huxley's *Brave New World* (1932) is no doubt the best known" (222).[145]

To ensure the "social stability" of this eugenic caste system in Aldous's Brave New World Order, the World Controllers supplement genetic engineering with behaviorist psychological conditioning. Whereas chapter one of the novel portrays the mass-industrialization of genetic engineering for the purpose of biosocial political-economic planning,[146] chapter two depicts how the Neo-Pavlovian Conditioning Centres use behaviorist psychological punishments, such as electric shocks and loud explosions, to condition the lower-genetic classes to dislike cognitive-intellectual activities such as reading and reflecting upon nature, which are antithetical to the mandated workforce duties of those lower castes.[147] The World State brainwashing centers also impose subconscious psychological conditioning by means of hypnopædia, which is a subliminal messaging technique, to "teach" "Elementary Class Consciousness" to ensure that different psycho-genetic castes do not intermix.[148]

It is not a coincidence that this vision of a global eugenic caste system was penned by Aldous Huxley, whose brother, UNESCO Director-General Julian Huxley, became the head of an international eugenics program operated under the aegis of the global governance institution of the United Nations. In fact, there is an abundance of scholarly evidence that proves Aldous's eugenic World Government was much inspired by Julian.

In an academic journal article titled "'Community, Identity, Stability': The Scientific Society and the Future of Religion in Aldous Huxley's *Brave*

New World," Professor of English at Dalhousie University, Brad Congdon,[149] explicates how Aldous's dystopian novel is a dark-satirical response to Julian's own 1931 novel, *What Dare I Think?*.[150] Congdon's literary analysis is affirmed by French novelist and filmmaker, Michel Houellebecq,[151] who authored his own work of fiction entitled *The Elementary Particles*, which highlights the parallels between the Huxley brothers' novels: "'It [*What Dare I think?*] was written by Julian Huxley, Aldous' older brother, and published in 1931, a year before *Brave New World*. All of the ideas his brother used in the novel—genetic manipulation and improving the species, including the human species—are suggested here. All of them are presented as unequivocally desirable goals that society should strive for.'"[152]

Both Houellebecq and Congdon are corroborated by primary source evidence in the archives of the Galton Institute, formerly known as the British Eugenics Society where, in 1962, Julian gave the Galton Lecture, which he titled "Eugenics in Evolutionary Perspective." Julian opened this lecture by publicly acknowledging how Aldous was impressed by Julian's other Galton Lectures: "I am honoured at having been twice asked to give the Eugenics Society's Galton Lecture.... [A]nd I am proud of the remarks which he [Lord Horder] and my brother Aldous made about these [lectures]."[153] Additionally, in 1965, about two years after Aldous died, Julian wrote a eulogy of sorts for his brother in *Aldous Huxley 1894-1963: A Memorial Volume*, which admits that Aldous's *Brave New World* borrows concepts from Julian himself:

> [m]ost people seem to imagine that Aldous came to me for help over the biological facts and ideas he utilized so brilliantly in *Brave New World* and elsewhere in his novels and essays. This was not so. He picked them up all from his miscellaneous reading *and from occasional discussions with me* [my emphasis] and a few other biologists, from which we profited as much as he.[154]

Stated differently, though Julian is downplaying his influence upon Aldous's creative process in drafting the novel, Julian still divulges that he helped shape his brother's literary vision of eugenic engineering in *Brave New World*.

A History of the Psycho-Eugenic Dialectic Guided by The Order's Hidden Hand:

In 1946, the eugenicist Director-General of UNESCO, Julian Huxley, took a flight to the United States to address UNESCO's mission statement to the United Nations General Assembly in New York, and during his stay in the US, he visited Washington DC where he met with President Harry S. Truman and his UNESCO colleague, Bonesman Archibald MacLeish, who authored the UNESCO Constitution.[155]

Which brings our analysis full-circle.

In the final equation, The Order of Skull and Bones has been instrumental in molding together the history of psychological conditioning and the history of eugenic engineering into a singular science of globalist psycho-eugenics.

Recall that Bonesman Daniel Coit Gilman propagated Wundtian stimulus-response psychology when he was the President of Johns Hopkins University where he personally hired Professor of Psychology and Pedagogics, G. Stanley Hall,[156] who became the first-ever President of the American Psychological Association after founding the United States' first-ever experimental psychology laboratory,[157] which was modeled after Wilhelm Wundt's lab at the University of Leipzig.[158] Furthermore, recollect that John D. Rockefeller, the uncle of Bonesman Percy Rockefeller,[159] leveraged his philanthropic General Education Board (GEB), with the help of GEB administrator Gilman,[160] to bankroll Wundt's laboratory method of school-to-work psychology.[161] Moreover, remember that Bonesman McGeorge Bundy financed B. F. Skinner's research and development of behaviorist "teaching machines" which are the predecessors to today's adaptive-learning software being incentivized by Bonesman Mnuchin's "Tax Cuts and Robots Act."[162] Thus, ever since Wilhelm Wundt originated the behavioral-psychological sciences, the technological refinement of stimulus-response workforce schooling has been guided toward computerized operant-conditioning by The Order's hidden hand.

The same goes for the science of eugenics.

Recall that Bonesman Gilman promoted the Malthusian-eugenics of Thomas Henry Huxley at Johns Hopkins University.[163] What's more, Bonesman Percy Rockefeller's uncle, John D. Rockefeller, used his tax-exempt Rockefeller Foundation to pour money into Nazi eugenics projects at the Kaiser Wilhelm Institute for Anthropology, Human Heredity, and Eugenics; the Kaiser Wilhelm Institute for Psychiatry; and the Kaiser Wilhelm Institute for Brain Research.[164] The Rockefeller Foundation also paid large sums to American eugenics institutions such as Charles Davenport's Cold Spring Harbor Station for Experimental Evolution,[165] which was established with the help of another Robber Baron philanthropy: the Carnegie Institute where Bonesman Gilman was its first president.[166] k [167]

---

k. Eugene Fischer, the Nazi Director of the Kaiser Wilhelm Institute for Anthropology, Human He-

Davenport's Cold Spring Harbor eugenics laboratory was eventually fused with the Eugenics Record Office, which was erected with substantial donations of money and land from railroad magnate E. H. Harriman's wife, Mary Williamson Harriman (née Averell), who was the mother of Bonesmen W. Averell Harriman and E. Roland Harriman.[168] E. Roland would later aid in financing the Nazi-eugenic takeover of Germany through his influence at Union Banking Corporation (UBC), which funneled capital to Hitler through one of the Führer's major financial backers: the German industrialist owner of UBC, Fritz Thyssen, whose fellow-Nazi banking partners, H. J. Kouwenhoven and J. L. Guinter, sat on the UBC Board of Directors along with E. Roland and his fellow Bonesmen, Knight Woolley and Prescott Bush, the latter of whom was the father of Bonesman George H. W. Bush and the grandfather of Bonesman George W. Bush.[169] [170]

After WWII, Bonesman Archibald MacLeish set up the United Nations Educational Scientific and Cultural Organization with the help of Julian Huxley who chartered eugenics into UNESCO's mission statement.[171] Now in the twenty-first century, Bonesman Mnuchin's "Tax Cuts and Robots Act" is conditioning investors to put their dollars into automated precision-education technologies that data-mine students' genetic-IQ scores to "personalize" eugenical adaptive-learning algorithms for "lifelong" workforce schooling.

In brief, ever since the beginning of corporate-industrial eugenics, the technocratic advancement of data-driven eugenic engineering has been guided by The Order's hidden hand.

To tie everything together, both the history of eugenics and the history of psychological conditioning were written by the same hidden hand of The Order of Death, which has propagated both of these sciences throughout the institutional fabric of American society and politics. Today, these two historical lines, which are tied together with the very same puppet strings of The Order, have converged in the current rallying cries to digitally data-mine students' genetic-IQ scores, psycho-affective SEL metrics, and cognitive-behavioral UII algorithms in order to "personalize" adaptive-learning software with competency-based precision-ed curriculums programmed for psycho-eugenical workforce schooling in a planned economy governed by Big Data.

redity, and Eugenics, served as a "corresponding scientist" to the Carnegie Institution and as a key research associate of Charles Davenport.

l. For more information on how these members of The Order colluded with the Nazi regime, read the award-winning *America's Nazi Secret*, which was originally published as *The Belarus Secret*, by John Loftus, who was a prosecutor for the Office of Special Investigations of the US Department of Justice. See also *Rise of the Fourth Reich* by Jim Marrs.

Chapter 16

EDU-GENICS 2.0: TRANSHUMANIST EDUCATION

I t is fundamentally anti-democratic to apply B. F. Skinner's operant-conditioning method to student learning in any educational setting, whether corporate charter school or government public school.
Operant stimulus-response conditioning kills individual free will by psychologically training students to conceive of learning as a passive process
that must be prompted by an external school authority who either bribes
students with external rewards, like gold stars and good grades, or threatens students with external punishments, such as detentions and failing
grades. Stated differently, Skinnerian stimulus-response conditioning imposed by a compulsory school authority blunts a student's own intrinsic
motivations to cultivate his or her personal freedom to curiously respond
to the natural stimuli of the mysteries of the universe without having to be
prompted by an external authority.

Even more pernicious is the computerization of operant-behaviorism
in the classroom because Skinnerian adaptive-learning software conditions students to respond more to the hi-resolution bells, whistles, and
bright lights of virtual learning stimuli; and to respond less to the subtle
stimuli of their own intuitive inquiries into the wonders of the world and
their own life experiences. Add genetic-IQ data-mining to the mix of this
algorithmic computer-conditioning equation, and psycho-eugenic "Skinner box" teaching machines will bring about the virtual extinction of free
thought as we know it.

Therefore, by definition, Skinnerian adaptive-learning computers
are antithetical to the etymological root of the word "education," which
means to "lead out" or "bring forth" the inner potential already latent
within the individual pupil's free will. According to the *Oxford Dictionary*
online, the word "educate" stems "from Latin educat- 'led out', from the
verb educare, related to educere 'lead out' (see educe)."[1] According to the
Merriam-Webster Dictionary, the root of the word "educate" comes from
"Middle English, to rear, from Latin *educatus,* past participle of *educare*

to rear, educate, from *educere* to lead forth – more at educe."[2] [a] [3] Clearly, these Latin etymologies of the word "education" define a pedagogy which is diametrically opposite from edu-conditioning that is engineered into "Skinner-box" teaching computers which train students to respond to digital stimuli in order to conform to the authority of workforce-competence algorithms on adaptive software.

In brief, computerized edu-conditioning is the science of training students with external digital inputs programmed by corporate-government authorities whereas true education is the art of "leading out" the inner-authority of a student's own conscience by inspiring the independent refinement of his or her own powers of consciousness.

Christian philosopher C. S. Lewis professed that, "[i]f education is beaten by training, civilization dies."[4] Indeed, when operant-computer conditioning trains students to reactionarily regurgitate their pre-programmed career-path curriculums, and to not veer away from their "cradle-to-career" paths in pursuit of their own creative thoughts outside their job paths, then corporate and government authoritarians can commandeer educational technologies to mentally enslave the student body to submit to the despotic hierarchy of a techno-fascist planned economy with no moral or ethical compass other than the gospel of efficiency.

But for the hi-tech "learning engineers" of the future, computer-determinism dictating each student's career-path training is not a tyrannical upending of civilization. Rather, these ed-utopists believe that the digitalized psycho-eugenic micromanaging of student-employee "competence" from cradle to career is only the evolutionary transformation of civilization as they believe that human beings do not have souls, and that there is nothing divine or dignified to be "drawn out" from within the core of the individual student's consciousness. These technocrat pedagogues view the human student not just as a wild animal to be tamed by computerized stimulus-response training; these psycho-eugenic education-

---

a. To be sure, a 2004 issue of the peer-reviewed journal, *Educational Forum*, clarifies that

> there are two different Latin roots of the English word "education." They are educare, which means to train or to mold, and educere, meaning to lead out. While the two meanings are quite different, they are both represented in our word "education." Thus, there is an etymological basis for many of the vociferous debates about education today. The opposing sides often use the same word to denote two very different concepts. One side uses education to mean the preservation and passing down of knowledge and the shaping of youths in the image of their parents. The other side sees education as preparing a new generation for the changes that are to come – readying them to create solutions to problems yet unknown. One calls for rote memorization and becoming good workers. The other requires questioning, thinking, and creating. To further complicate matters, some groups expect schooling to fulfill both functions, but allow only those activities promoting educare to be used.

ists even go so far as to degrade the human pupil as nothing more than a raw material object, a literal "human resource" to be industrially re-engineered through evolutionary technology interventions.

Decidedly, at the heart of this techno-materialist education philosophy is a transhumanist outlook on the future of learning: a techno-eugenic belief that the human species is not a perfect creation in the image of God, but instead is an imperfect accident of evolving matter and energy that must be repaired and rebuilt through psycho-eugenic technological modifications. As explained in a 2015 issue of the peer-reviewed *Journal of Evolution and Technology*, "human beings [are] regarded by transhumanists as 'works in progress'" that need to be "alter[ed]" through "technological means ... in order to bring about the transhuman or the posthuman."[5] Hence, the transhumanist educational philosopher denies the divine spirit of humanity by rendering the human organism down to a mere neurobiological computer system that must be progressively "updated" through psycho-behavioral "software" reprogramming and neurophysiological "hardware" upgrades.

To put it bluntly, transhumanist education is the rewiring of the human species through the computerized interfacing of operant psychological conditioning and eugenic biotechnological engineering. Affirmatively, a 2014 issue of the scholarly journal, *Pedagogica Historica*, relays how interdisciplinary studies in "neuroscientific research," "human intelligence and IQ," and "futurology and *transhumanism* ... have rendered the traditional nature-nurture debate obsolete."[6] Specifically,

> [i]n the last 20 years developments in such fields as neuroscience, nanotechnology and transhumanism have revolutionised, but not resolved, the nature-nurture debate. ... [N]ature and nurture, instead of being opposites, are much more closely intertwined than previously believed. Epigenetic studies have shown that "genes, though still important, have lost their privileged and prominent status, particularly as the distinction between nature and nurture disappears."[7]

In other words, the hard line that once divided the "nature" science of eugenic engineering and the "nurture" science of psychological conditioning has been blurred, resulting in an agglomerated psycho-eugenic science of transhumanism which studies the techno-evolution of the electrical-computational structure of the human mind-body system.

If transhumanists can normalize the theory that the psycho-affective and biogenetic domains of human learning are crisscrossed throughout neuro-cerebral circuitry, then transhumanist educators will be able to make the case that learning advantages gained from adaptive-conditioning software algorithms are effectively no different from learning advantages gained through neurotechnological brain-body modifications that enhance student cognition. Thus, in the technocratic school of the future, adaptive-learning software will not only data-mine students' cognitive-behavioral UII, IQ DNA, and SEL metrics to "personalize" operant-conditioning algorithms; but students will also be data-mined to advance research and development of transhumanist biotechnologies for ed-tech innovation and other "legitimate educational interests" acknowledged by FERPA, such as the enhancement of cognitive-behavioral therapies and even gene therapies for learning disabilities classified under IDEA.

Transhumanism Is Neo-Eugenic "Education":

The neo-eugenic science of transhumanism was conceptualized by UN-ESCO eugenicist Julian Huxley.[8] In *UNESCO: Its Purpose and Its Philosophy*, Huxley professed that "[i]t is, however, essential that eugenics should be brought entirely within the borders of science, for, as already indicated, in the not very remote future the problem of improving the average quality of human beings is likely to become urgent; and this can only be accomplished by applying the findings of a truly scientific eugenics."[9] Yet in the wake of vehement public backlash against the atrocities of the Nazi eugenic Holocaust, Huxley's eugenics proper was forced to go underground, repackaging itself in various crypto-eugenic disguises, one of which is "transhumanism": the scientific postulate that human evolution through biological-genetic selection has been largely superseded by a symbiotic evolution that cybernetically merges the human species with its own technological handiwork.

A 2015 academic journal article, "Historical Outlines of Eugenics and Its Influences on Education," highlights how transhumanism is a form of crypto-eugenics:

> [w]ith transhumanists, eugenics comes in the form of genetic engineering, which for them represents one of the ways to reach the posthuman state…
>
> Therefore, transhumanists repeat eugenicists' ideas and strive towards a technocratic attitude which was described by [Aldous] Huxley in his novel *Brave New World*.…
>
> Also, they repeat eugenicists' mistakes by thinking that undesirable traits can be easily found and removed.[10]

207

Additionally, a 2010 issue of the peer-reviewed *Journal of Medicine and Philosophy* articulates how neo-eugenic transhumanism builds upon its genetic-determinist origins by combining DNA predestination engineering with ed-tech enhancements such as biotechnological body modifications and neuro-technetronic cognition upgrades:

> [t]he transhumanist position, in other words, is something of a hybrid: it accepts the idea that humans possess certain deeply "hardwired" predispositions, but it rejects the notion that these traits are – or should be – sacrosanct and immutable. For the transhumanists, the defining feature of human nature is precisely its ability to reshape itself over time, through deliberate processes of self-transformation that range from education to genetic intervention.[11]

Notice here that the authors place education and genetic engineering in the same spectrum on the range of transhumanist enhancements.

These up-to-date academic journals show that futurist acolytes of transhumanism believe in a neo-eugenic cosmology wherein the future of human evolution is driven not by biological-genetic selection, but by technological selection that edits human DNA while simultaneously interfacing it with cyborg-like body modifications and technetronic brain augmentations that are being touted as educational technologies. In fact, in UNESCO's founding document, Julian Huxley pontificates that the future science of neo-eugenic transhumanism will encompass techno-cognitive selection through human-machine symbiosis in conjunction with biogenetic selective breeding:

> [e]volution in the human sector consists mainly of changes in the form of society, in tools and machines, in new ways of utilising the old innate potentialities, instead of in the nature of these potentialities, as in the biological sector. ... [T]hey [biological natures] could certainly be improved further by deliberate eugenic measures, if we consciously set ourselves to improve them. Meanwhile, however, it is in social organisation, in machines, and in ideas that human evolution is mostly made manifest.[12]

By definition, eugenic evolution that melds humans and machines into a new species is nothing less than transhumanism.

Indeed, in a 1957 book entitled *New Bottles for New Wine*, Huxley wrote a chapter titled "Transhumanism." Therein, he himself coined the term with the following passage:

[t]he human species can, if it wishes, transcend itself – not just sporadically, an individual here in one way, an individual there in another way, but in its entirety, as humanity. We need a name for this new belief. Perhaps transhumanism will serve: man remaining man, but transcending himself, by realizing new possibilities of and for his human nature.

"I believe in transhumanism": once there are enough people who can truly say that, the human species will be on the threshold of a new kind of existence, as different from ours as ours is from that of Peking man. It will at last be consciously fulfilling its real destiny.[13]

Simply put, Huxley's futurist science of transhumanism is eugenics 2.0, which fuses together machines and humankind to create a breakaway species that diverges from modern *homo sapiens* just as *homo sapiens* diverged from Peking men,[14] Australopithecines,[15] Neanderthals,[16] and other pre-human hominids.[17]

Today, one of the most famous followers of Huxley's neo-eugenics movement is Google's Chief of Engineering, Ray Kurzweil, who preached the gospel of transhumanism in his 1999 treatise, *The Age of Spiritual Machines*: "[h]umanoids emerged 15 million years ago ... [O]ur own species, *Homo sapiens*, emerged perhaps 500,000 years ago.... The story of evolution since that time now focuses in on a human-sponsored variant of evolution: technology.... Technology picks right up with the exponentially quickening pace of evolution."[18]

Kurzweil, who believes he will become "godlike" from transhumanist upgrades,[19] refers to technology as "evolution by other means,"[20] and he theorizes that

[t]he next inevitable step is a merger of the technology-inventing species with the computational technology it initiated the creation of. At this stage in the evolution of intelligence on a planet, the computers are themselves based at least in part on the designs of the brains (that is, computational organs) of the species that originally created them and in turn the computers become embedded in and integrated into that species' bodies and brains. Region by region, the brain and nervous system of that species are ported to the computational technology and ultimately replace those information-processing organs.[21]

To bring about this technetronic evolution of the human species through so-called educational technologies, there has a grown a cadre of neo-eugenic transhumanist academics and intellectuals whom German philosopher Jürgen Habermas calls out as "liberal eugenicists [who] base their arguments on the claim that there is 'no particular difference between eugenics and education.'"[22]

A 2017 issue of the scholarly *Journal of Philosophy of Education* expounds on Habermas's criticism of philosopher Peter Sloterdijk's trans-eugenic proposal

> to redefine education as a form of genetic "taming" ... [which] seemed to be support for positive eugenics.... Sloterdijk's new humanism was to be based on the materialist principles of a biotechnological age.... Sloterdijk seems to embrace technology and the enhancement of the human body and mind as the next great step forward in educational theory.[23]

Like Habermas,

> [m]any of those attending the Elmau Conference interpreted Sloterdijk's position as support for routine transhuman enhancement. As a result, the augmentation value of any education would be less closely linked to static models of the human and more closely identified with the medical enhancement possibilities of the human species, including improvements in memory, eyesight, speed of reaction, application to work, concentration levels and various other abilities that are now also subject to genetic experimentation. These are the ways that "royal shepherds" will in the future govern the tamed masses.[24]

In brief, the acclaimed Habermas, along with other philosophers and public intellectuals, warn against the "positive eugenics" underlying Sloterdijk's equivocation of "education" with "genetic 'taming'" through "transhuman enhancement" and "genetic experimentation" controlled by technocratic "royal shepherds." Note here the parallels between Sloterdijk's transhumanist caste system of "royal shepherds" over genetically "tamed masses"; Aldous Huxley's Scientific Caste System of eugenic Alpha World Controllers over dysgenic Gammas, Deltas, and Epsilons; and Socrates' aristocratic caste system of golden philosopher kings over brass and iron labor slaves.

The "liberal" eugenics of Sloterdijk is likewise espoused in a 2010 issue of the academic journal, *Nature*, which makes a case for transhumanist enhancement through neurotechnological body modifications, claiming that such biotechnological upgrades are essentially no different from the cognitive boosts achieved from traditional schoolhouse learning:

> [h]uman ingenuity has given us means of enhancing our brains through inventions such as written language, printing, and the Internet.... [N]ewer technologies such as brain stimulation and prosthetic brain chips, should be viewed in the same general category as education, good health habits, and information technology— ways that our uniquely innovative species tries to improve itself.[25]

Education is also conflated with "liberal-eugenic" transhumanism in a 2015 academic journal article titled "The Future of Education: Genetic Enhancement and Metahumanities": "there is a structural analogy between educational and genetic enhancement such that the moral evaluation of these two procedures should be seen as analogous, too. I will show that an affirmation of educational enhancement suggests an affirmation of genetic enhancement.... I will explain the relevance of the question by considering transhumanism and posthumanism."[26]

Realizing that education and transhumanism will be one and the same in the future, this gives a whole new meaning to Article 26 of UNESCO's 1948 Universal Declaration of Human Rights,[27] which states that "[e]ducation shall be directed to the full development of the human personality and to the strengthening of respect for human rights and fundamental freedoms."[28] In the twenty-first century of transhumanism, educating the "full ... human personality" means biogenetically and neurocognitively augmenting the literal student body through human-computer interface mergers. Under this transhumanist objectification of "human personality," "human rights" and "freedoms" are the rights and freedoms to be biotechnologically altered with neo-eugenic "educational" technetronics.

Consider this transhumanist reading of Article 26 in the context of the certified "Masterclasses in Bioethics" currently offered by the UNESCO Chair in Bioethics and Human Rights.[29] One masterclass on "Neurobioethics and Transhumanism" is titled "Neurosciences That Love Human Beings," and it "is designed for doctors, bioethicists, philosophers, theologians and trainers who want to deepen the new scenarios of neurobioethics and transhumanism."[30] This "Neurobioethics and Transhumanism" master-course *collaborates with* The Interdisciplinary Research Group in Neurobiothics of the Ateneo Pontificio Regina Apostolorum in Rome to conduct a set of 10 seminars and round- table seminars, including a Brain Awareness Week conference promoted by DANA Foundation, on neurosurgical, neurological, psychiatric, psychological, philosophical, theological, legal, bioethical aspects related to the so-called "Head Transplantation" (Human Head Transplantation) and the possible anthropological, ethical, legal, health and social consequences of these interventions on human life.

A particular emphasis will be given to the reflection about issues related to informed consent, focusing on a dual category of vulnerable subjects: tetraplegic patients or affected by other pathologies severely debilitating the motor system[sic]; people from social, cultural, political contexts who explicitly or implicitly limit the full exercise of what established by the Universal Declaration of Human Rights [sic], ratified by UN since 1948. This awareness will in particular focus on issues related to the dignity and value of our human body, as well as its availability/unavailability.[31]

Notice how this UNESCO masterclass on transhumanist bioethics pays special concern to the rights and freedoms of persons with tetraplegia and other disabilities of "the motor system" that can be therapeutically treated with biotech and neurotech brain-body modifications.

But despite this humanitarian rhetoric from UNESCO's transhumanist masterclass, a 2014 whitepaper from UNESCO's Information For All Programme (IFAP) admits that transhumanism is potentially a new age version of techno-fascism on steroids:

scientists are discussing the convergence of nano-, bio- and cognitive technologies the development of which is in turn closely linked to ICT [information and communications technologies] and which have an equally powerful potential to influence socio-cultural processes. Specialists are predicting even more fundamental changes by the middle of the twenty-first century. Artificial intelligence will attain the level of natural intellect and in a number of cases will surpass it. Machine-human hybrids, cyborgs and humanoid robot-androids created on a biological basis, will become more and more widespread. Also becoming ever more widespread are the ideas that technological intervention in the human organism, fundamental changes to the nature of man, are desirable and beneficial in that they enable a biological evolution which is truly controlled. Some call this world view transhumanism and some technological fascism. Either way, our future lies more and more in the hands of new engineers, genetic scientists and programmers.[32]

IDNA: Your Genetic Student ID:

Although transhumanists fundamentally believe that human biology is technologically malleable, they nonetheless reserve that the tech-netronic transformation of each human body is limited by its particular neuro-electrical capacity which is based on its unique genetic code. As such, the trans-technological re-engineering of the human organism can only be successful if the biotech brain-body modifications are compatible with the individual human specimen's unique neurogenetic electrical bi-ology. Therefore, if a student's DNA is exceptionally dysgenic, then he or she will not possess the neurogenetic biological prerequisites needed to qualify for upper-grade transhumanist ed-tech enhancements.

In fact, in the opening chapter of the 1946 UNESCO: Its Purpose and Its Philosophy, under a subheading titled "The Principle of Equality and the Fact of Inequality," eugenicist Julian Huxley asserts that "[t]here are instances of biological inequality which are so gross that they cannot be reconciled at all with the principle of equal opportunity. Thus low-grade mental defectives cannot be offered equality of educational opportuni-ty."[33] Toward the end of this eugenics section, Huxley concludes that, "[i]n face of it, indeed, the principle of equality of opportunity must be amended to read 'equality of opportunity within the limits of aptitude.'"[34] Moving into the futurist era of transhumanism, this eugenic UNESCO policy is being effectively reasserted with trans-eugenic suppositions that even educational opportunities through biotechnological upgrades must be limited by the psycho-electrical aptitude of a student's neurogenetic hardwiring in the same way that computer hardware and software up-grades are limited based on the computational coding of the operating system as well as the electrical and information-processing capacities of the hard drive. At the same time, transhumanist educationists stress that, before a student can plug into the highest-grade trans-tech engineered for the highest neurocognitive processing powers, the student's neurogenetic endowment must first be selectively re-engineered up to a higher elec-trical-computational potential by means of hi-tech reproduction through preimplantation genetic diagnosis (PGD) and even Crispr Cas9 DNA editing.[b][35]

---

b. A 2009 issue of the peer-reviewed journal, *Clinical Genetics*, provides the following definition of PGD:

> [p]re-implantation genetic diagnosis (PGD) is generally defined as the testing of pre-im-plantation stage embryos or oocytes for genetic defects. It has been developed for couples whose potential offspring are at risk of severe Mendelian disorders, structural chromosome abnormalities or mitochondrial disorders. Pre-implantation embryo diagnosis requires in

A 2017 scholarly article titled "Transhuman Education? Sloterdijk's Reading of Martin Heidegger's Letter on Humanism" shows how the "liberal" transhumanist philosopher, Peter Sloterdijk, concurs that trans-technetronic education must be preceded by trans-genetic precision education through technocratic selective breeding. In this peer-reviewed journal publication, Sloterdijk envisions a "Star Trek view of the future" that "resonated unhelpfully and rather scandalously with Nazi eugenics" as Sloterdijk called for "human societies [to] support elements of selective breeding that would enhance the human and ... bear on the education process itself."[36]

In opposition, philosopher Jürgen Habermas has rallied considerable public aversion to Sloterdijk's proposal for educational selection through eugenic-engineering selection. Nevertheless, "metahumanist" philosopher Stefan Lorenz Sorgner has come to Sloterdijk's rescue, rebutting Habermas's counterarguments while building upon Sloterdijk's dreams of transhumanist edu-genics by forecasting the positive outcomes of how "gene analysis will become a prerequisite for a well-informed education. . . . Bioprivacy, and big gene data will be the keywords in this context, and I expect ... enormous revisions in the field, of the future of occupations and insurance companies as well as education."[37]

If you think that these futurist discussions about transhumanist precision-ed are isolated to the ivory wifi towers of virtual academia, be aware that international teams of for-profit corporations, nonprofit foundations, and nongovernmental organizations are think-tanking a twenty-year implementation plan for mainlining transhumanist ed-tech across the global student body. An elaborate infographic disseminated by the Re-Engineering Futures Group comprehensively details their technocratic plans of the Global Education Futures Initiative orchestrated by "hundreds of Russian and international experts."[38] This transhumanist vision of the future of global schooling draws a complex timeline predicting how "[t]

vitro fertilization, embryo biopsy and either using fluorescent in situ hybridization or polymerase chain reaction at the single cell level.

In a 2018 post on the Genetics Home Reference website of the NIH, the US National Library of Medicine details the following explication of CRISPR-Cas9 "genome-editing" technology:

CRISPR-Cas9 ... is short for clustered regularly interspaced short palindromic repeats and CRISPR-associated protein 9. The CRISPR-Cas9 system has generated a lot of excitement in the scientific community because it is faster, cheaper, more accurate, and more efficient than other existing genome editing methods.

CRISPR-Cas9 was adapted from a naturally occurring genome editing system in bacteria. The bacteria capture snippets of DNA from invading viruses and use them to create DNA segments known as CRISPR arrays. The CRISPR arrays allow the bacteria to "remember" the viruses (or closely related ones). If the viruses attack again, the bacteria produce RNA segments from the CRISPR arrays to target the viruses' DNA. The bacteria then use Cas9 or a similar enzyme to cut the DNA apart, which disables the virus.

echnologies that enable prenatal education based on big data, audiovisual stimulation, and biofeedback" will become available by 2018; and by 2025, "School in the Womb" through "[p]renatal study programs" will perfect hi-tech "acquisition of knowledge and skills in the womb."[39] In the interim, students will be issued "Genetic Passport[s]" by the year 2020 so that "[s]tudents get individualized recommendations on their education in accordance with their genotype," which will be linked to an "[o]bligatory universal net ID."[40]

According to the Global Education Futures initiative, these transhumanist revolutions will be spurred when "[c]risis necessitates cuts in education budgets" so that "[n]ew education formats are in high demand," which results in "IT companies emerg[ing] as leaders in the global education market" to thereon develop transhuman-learning IT.[41]

Wearable GSR Sensors That Data-Mine SEL:

In another infographic detailing the transhumanist plans for Global Education Futures, the Re-Engineering Futures Group maps out how the "[l]earning process will be dynamically adapted to students' personal needs, their learning style and abilities, and even their current mind and body condition" which will be data-mined by "Biometrics Monitoring" devices which are depicted in the infographic as metallic bracelets worn the wrist for "tracking attention level, level of enjoyment, etc."[42]

As a matter of fact, such transhumanistic wearables are already being piloted in American schools with the financial backing of the Bill and Melinda Gates Foundation, which has already dumped over $1 million dollars into "galvanic skin response" (GSR) bracelets that can biometrically gauge a student's psycho-socioemotional engagement with classroom lessons and coursework. In 2011, the Gates Foundation poured $621,265 into the National Center on Time & Learning "to measure engagement physiologically with Functional Magnetic Resonance Imaging and Galvanic Skin Response to determine correlations between each measure and develop a scale that differentiates different degrees or levels of engagement."[43] Then, in 2012, George H. W. Bush's former Assistant Secretary of Education, Diane Ravitch, exposed a Gates Foundation grant of $498,055 to Clemson University to trial the use of GSR bracelets that wirelessly data-mine students' psycho-physiological responses to instructional stimuli. The original grant stated that Clemson University would "work with members of the Measuring Effective Teachers (MET) team to measure engagement physiologically with Galvanic Skin Response

(GSR) bracelets which will determine the feasibility and utility of using such devices regularly in schools with students and teachers."[44]

After public backlash against these invasions into students' and teachers' personal biodata, a spokesman for the Gates Foundation, Chris Williams, announced the redaction of the official grant document. Williams claimed that Clemson's grant contract with MET, which partners with Educational Testing Services (ETS) and the RAND Corporation, was a mere typo.[45] However, Williams's redaction did not just erase MET from the Clemson grant; the redaction also subtracted $34,773 from the grant. On the Gates Foundation website, there is posted only one official education grant awarded to Clemson University before 2013: a $463,282 grant "to conduct a pilot study of new ways to measure student engagement for use in research."[46] Clearly, the redaction appears more than a mere typo; it appears that the Gates philanthropy, attempting to smooth over public relations, fired MET from the Clemson project and in turn reneged $34,773 that were presumably allocated for MET's contributions to the original grant research.

The Gates Foundation's transhumanistic GSR biometrics, otherwise known as "Q sensors,"[47] are likewise referred to as "engagement pedometers," which are classroom biofeedback technetronics that quantify a student's psycho-affective stimulus-response engagement based on digital calculations of his or her neurophysiological reactions to learning stimuli.[48] There are now on the consumer market several commercial models of such Q sensors, including Empatica Inc.'s E4, which according to the Massachusetts Institute of Technology, "measures photoplethysmography (PPG), electrodermal activity (EDA), temperature and 3-axis accelerometer data. PPG provides continuous heart rate and heart-rate variability data. Thus, this sensor measures both main branches of the autonomic nervous system: sympathetic and parasympathetic."[49] There is also Empatica's Embrace engagement pedometer, which "runs apps to detect and alert to significant changes in EDA, motion, and temperature. It also tells the time. One app alerts to changing autonomic stress levels. Another app alerts to combined motion-autonomic events that have been shown to happen during seizures."[50] In addition, recall from that the US Secretary of Education herself, Betsy DeVos, is heavily invested in Neurocore biofeedback technetronics that assist students with ADHD and other cognitive-learning disabilities.

Other biometric wearables are being designed for workforce training by the Amazon Corporation, which has been granted two patents on biometric wristbands engineered to measure the movements of warehouse employees in order to track their real-time labor movements and in turn provide electrical stimuli to redirect inefficient labor movements toward streamlined procedural movements.[51] Specifically, these transhumanistic wearables for the workplace monitor employee hand movements in re-lations to the warehouse's internet-of-things smart grid, which sends vi-bratory jolts to the worker's biometric wristband whenever the employee stocks a product on a wrong shelf. Furthermore, these transhumanistic biometrics can even record how long an employee spends in the bath-room and even how often an employee scratches or fidgets.[52]

Neurologically Downloading Digital Learning Data Directly into Your Brain:

To be sure, wearable biometric sensors might not seem like trans-humanist technologies since they do not require invasive surgeries radically alter the neurobiological structure of the human makeup. Nev-ertheless, once these wearable biodata monitors are as commonplace as cellphones, it will only be a matter of time before people begin to make the next transition from wearable tech to implantable tech. Therefore, wearable biotech is "gateway tech" that leads to hardcore implantable transhumanist tech.

In *The Age of Spiritual Machines*, Ray Kurzweil, who was awarded the 1999 National Medal of Technology from President Clinton,[53] pre-dicts that breakthroughs in implantable neurotech will be the crowning achievement of transhumanist education in 2029:

> [h]uman learning is primarily accomplished through virtual teachers and is enhanced by the widely available neural implants. The implants improve memory and perception, but it is not yet possible to down-load knowledge directly. Although enhanced through virtual experi-ences, intelligent interactive instruction, and neural implants, learn-ing still requires time-consuming human experience and study.[54]

Kurzweil's idea of learning through neural implants may sound like fantastical science fiction, but a 2017 issue of the peer-reviewed *Journal of Philosophy of Education* lays out the trajectory by which the current in-ternet-screen interface of adaptive-learning software will evolve into neu-roprosthetic interfaces that electronically upload "learning" data directly into a student's brain:

> [f]irst there is the current incorporation of Information and Communications Technology (ICT) in the classroom.... These new resources are welcomed by teachers who are hard pressed to keep the attention of children well used to the distractions of multi-media devices at home...
>
> In a second step, forms of interface actually change the nature of the interface and turn the interface into a separable object in the world.... The dependency on interface devices is a feature of a "transhuman" state of mind.... The preparation of these ethically transhuman mental states is already widespread among users of current interface technologies. An argument can be made that teachers are unwittingly enhancing the normativity of screen-interface relationships with the world at large.
>
> A third step, and one considerably further down the slippery slope, is the transformation of the human brain and nervous system by means of neurological implants, thus transforming humans into cyborgs or cybernetic organisms.[55]

According to a 2015 issue of an academic journal entitled *Learning, Media, and Technology*, this perfect storm of converging digital-interface ed-tech is often sugar-coated under the innocuous-sounding umbrella term, "'technology-enhanced learning', or 'TEL'," which "has been adopted as an apparently useful, inoffensive and descriptive shorthand for what is in fact a complex and often problematic constellation of social, technological and educational change" that encompasses "problematic links between TEL and the philosophy of *transhumanism*."[56]

The transhuman transformation of TEL into neo-eugenic human-computer interfaces is not far-fetched. Actually, neuro-technetronic interfaces have been experimentally implanted in human brains since as early as 1956 by José Manuel Rodriguez Delgado:[57] the Director of Neuropsychiatry at the Yale University School of Medicine who invented the "stimoceiver,"[58] which is an implantable electrode device that can physically manipulate neurobiological systems through radio-controlled electrical stimulation.[59]

In his 1969 book, *Physical Control of the Mind: Towards a Psychocivilized Society*, Delgado presents a "[d]iagramatic representation of an electrode assembly implanted within the brain and anchored to the skull. The depth of the brain is thus accessible simply by plugging in a connector."[60] Illustrating a case study of his stimoceiver in action, Delgado describes a

> patient [who] was committed to a ward for the criminally insane, and electrodes were implanted in her amygdala and hippocampus for ex-

ploration of possible neurological abnormalities.... [S]he became one of the first clinical cases instrumented with a stimoceiver, which made it possible to study intracerebral activity without restraint...

During depth explorations, it was demonstrated that crises of assaultive behavior similar to the patient's spontaneous bursts of anger could be elicited by radio stimulation of contact 3 in the right amygdala.[61]

In an interview with the author of *The C.I.A. Doctors: Human Rights Violations by American Psychiatrists*,[62] Colin A. Ross M.D. explains that Delgado's "idea of the future is—and this he was totally serious about and described in detail—we're going to put electrodes in the entire population ... and we're going to control the entire population, and this is not going to be fascism; this is going to be the next step in evolution."[63]

Throughout the 1980s and 1990s, Delgado's "stimoceiver" research was improved upon by Professor of Neuroscience at the University of Minnesota, Apostolos Georgopoulos,[64] and University of Pittsburgh Professor of Neurobiology, Andrew Schwartz,[65] who experimented with computerized brain implants that enabled monkeys to maneuver robotic limbs through wireless thought transmissions.[66] Taking Georgopoulos's and Schwartz's brain-chip research to the next level today is Eric C. Leuthardt: a transhumanist neurosurgeon at Washington University in St. Louis who has been experimenting with neuro-brain modifications for over fifteen years.[67] In one Frankenstein-like experiment that is photographed and discussed in the *Massachusetts Institute of Technology (MIT) Review*, Leuthardt drilled holes through his patients' skulls and implanted transmitter electrodes therein; as a result, his "patients had shown the capacity to play Space Invaders – moving a virtual spaceship left and right – simply by thinking."[68]

Leuthardt also partnered with Gerwin Schalk on a 2006 US Army Research Office project wherein the two engineered a prototyped "thought helmet" that could "decode 'imagined speech'—words not vocalized, but simply spoken silently in one's mind."[69] The ultimate objective of this experiment on "12 bedridden epilepsy patients" was the invention of a military technology "that could detect a soldier's imagined speech and transmit it wirelessly to a fellow soldier's earpiece."[70] The findings of this transhumanist study concluded that Leuthardt and Schalk "believe they have found the little voice that we hear in our mind when we imagine speaking."[71] [c] Based on the successes of these shocking experiments,

c. Leuthardt even wrote a science fiction novel about transhumans with computer-brain interfaces:

"Leuthardt believes that in the next several decades such implants will be like plastic surgery or tattoos, undertaken with hardly a second thought."[72]

Leuthardt's outlook on the future of transhuman brain implants is corroborated by the July/August 2015 issue of *Foreign Affairs*, which is the official journal publication of the Council on Foreign Relations (CFR): a globalist non-governmental organization that has steered the course of American foreign policy for nearly a hundred years.[d][73] This 2015 issue of the CFR journal prints an article penned by Professor of Robotics at the Robotics Institute of Carnegie Mellon University, Illah Reza Nourbakhsh, who looks ahead to a coming era when brain chips will not only be able to remotely control robotics, but also be capable of uploading the cerebral-nervous system with expanded memory storage that can be instantly updated with information/knowledge files at highly amplified cognitive-processing speeds:

> it is merely a matter of time before human-robot couplings greatly outperform purely biological systems.
>
> These superhuman capabilities will not be limited to physical action: computers are increasingly capable of receiving and interpreting brain signals transmitted through electrodes implanted in the head (or arranged around the head) and have even demonstrated rudimentary forms of brain-based machine control. Today, researchers are primarily interested in designing one-way systems, which can read brain signals and then send them to devices such as prosthetic limbs and cars. But no serious obstacles prevent computer interfaces from sending such signals right back, arming a human brain with a silicon turbo-charge. The ability to perform complex mathematical calculations, produce top-quality language translation, and even deliver virtuosic musical performances might one day depend not solely on innate skill and practice but also on having access to the best brain-computer hybrid architecture.[74]

"[i]n his first novel, a techno-thriller called, 90 percent of human beings have elected to get computer hardware implanted directly into their brains. This allows a seamless connection between people and computers, and a wide array of sensory experiences without leaving home."

d. The following is a list globalist CFR groupies appointed by President Trump: John Bolton (National Security Advisor); H. R. McMaster (National Security Advisor); Steven Mnuchin (Secretary of the Treasury); Rex Tillerson (Secretary of State); Neil M. Gorsuch (Supreme Court Justice); Dina Powell (Deputy National Security Advisor for Strategy); Jerome Powell (Chairman of the Federal Reserve); Ginni Rometty (Member of Strategic and Policy Forum); Anthony Scaramucci (Director of Communications); Jamie Dimon (Member of Strategic and Policy Forum); Robert Wood Johnson IV (United States Ambassador to the United Kingdom); Elaine Chao (United States Secretary of Transportation); Laurence Fink (Member of Strategic and Policy Forum); Robert Lighthizer (United States Trade Representative); Kathleen Troia McFarland (Deputy National Security Adviser); Stephen Schwarzman (Member of Strategic and Policy Forum).

DARPA Loves You, So It's Making a Brain Chip for You:

For some time now, the United States government has been actively building prototypes of brain chips and other neural implants for the supposed purposes of treating brain diseases and other neuro-cognitive disorders. In 2017, the National Science Foundation (NSF) funded research that developed a therapeutic brain chip through which "a quadriplegic man experienced the sense of touch again through a robotic arm connected to a brain-computer interface (BCI) implanted in his head that allowed him to 'feel' pressure on the robotic hand."[75]

Even the military industrial complex is engineering transhumanist brain chips through projects at the Defense Advanced Research Project Agency (DARPA).[76] According to *Gizmodo*, DARPA is constructing "brain computer interface projects, which seek not just to use chips to treat mental illness, but also to restore memories and movement to battle-wounded soldiers."[77] Supposedly, DARPA's transhumanist brain enhancements are aimed only at "developing treatments for schizophrenia, PTSD, traumatic brain injury, borderline personality disorder, anxiety, addiction and depression."[78] However, "[r]umors have swirled that the DARPA's real goal in all this research is to create enhanced super soldiers…. A 2015 book about the history of DARPA, 'The Pentagon's Brain,' suggested that government scientists hope that implanting chips in soldiers will eventually… allow soldiers to perform feats like waging war using their thoughts alone."[79]

DARPA is also collaborating on the public-private Brain Research through Advanced Innovative Neurotechnology (BRAIN) Initiative, which is a National Institutes of Health (NIH) enterprise that partners with for-profit corporations to develop transhumanist neuro-computer interfaces through the following BRAIN Initiative projects:[80]

- **Electrical Prescriptions (ElectRx):** The ElectRx program aims to help the human body heal itself through neuromodulation of organ functions using ultraminiaturized devices, approximately the size of individual nerve fibers, which could be delivered through minimally invasive injection.[81]

- **Hand Proprioception and Touch Interfaces (HAPTIX):** The HAPTIX program aims to create fully implantable, modular and reconfigurable neural-interface microsystems that communicate wirelessly with external modules, such as a prosthesis interface link, to deliver naturalistic sensations to amputees.[82]

• **Neural Engineering System Design (NESD):** The NESD program aims to develop an implantable neural interface able to provide unprecedented signal resolution and data-transfer bandwidth between the brain and the digital world.[83]

• **Neuro Function, Activity, Structure and Technology (Neuro-FAST):** The Neuro-FAST program seeks to enable unprecedented visualization and decoding of brain activity to better characterize and mitigate threats to the human brain, as well as facilitate development of brain-in-the loop systems to accelerate and improve functional behaviors. The program has developed CLARITY, a revolutionary tissue-preservation method, and builds off recent discoveries in genetics, optical recordings and brain-computer interfaces.[84]

• **Next-Generation Nonsurgical Neurotechnology (N3):** The N3 program aims to develop a safe, portable neural interface system capable of reading from and writing to multiple points in the brain at once. Whereas the most advanced existing neurotechnology requires surgical implantation of electrodes, N3 is pursuing high-resolution technology that works without the requirement for surgery so that it can be used by able-bodied people.[85]

• **Reliable Neural-Interface Technology (RE-NET):** The RE-NET program seeks to develop the technologies needed to reliably extract information from the nervous system, and to do so at a scale and rate necessary to control complex machines, such as high-performance prosthetic limbs.[86]

• **Restoring Active Memory (RAM):** The RAM program aims to develop and test a wireless, fully implantable neural-interface medical device for human clinical use. The device would facilitate the formation of new memories and retrieval of existing ones in individuals who have lost these capacities as a result of traumatic brain injury or neurological disease.[87]

• **Revolutionizing Prosthetics:** The Revolutionizing Prosthetics program aims to continue increasing functionality of DARPA-developed arm systems to benefit Service members and others who have lost upper limbs.[88]

• **Systems-Based Neurotechnology for Emerging Therapies (SUBNETS):** The SUBNETS program seeks to create implanted, closed-loop diagnostic and therapeutic systems for treating neuropsychological illnesses.[89]

In addition to these transhuman brain chips and neurotech interfaces modifications, the BRAIN Initiative's public-private transhumanism enterprise is engineering other "investigational brain implants."[90] According to a press release issued by the NIH on June 27, 2018, the BRAIN Initiative has been successful with the "[f]irst demonstration of adaptive DBS [deep brain stimulation] for Parkinson's disease using motor cortex sensing" through[91]

> a novel DBS system using a stimulation lead in the subthalamic nucleus (STN) and a second electrocorticographic (ECoG) implant over the motor cortex for detecting the gamma signal, both connected to an implantable pulse generator (IPG) capable of recording as well as stimulation. The team first prototyped a control algorithm using an external computer, which sensed when the ECoG gamma signal exceeded a certain threshold – indicating dyskinesia [tremors] – and implemented changes to the STN stimulation via radio signals.[92]

These and other BRAIN Initiative inventions are being revolutionized with the aid of the following private corporations: Google, GE, GlaxoSmithKline, NeuroPace, NeuroNexus, Medtronic, Inscopix, Blackrock Microsystems, Second Sight, and Boston Scientific.[93]

As corporate-government transhumanism research picks up steam in the coming years, it is predicted that human-computer interfaces for precision education will become commonplace by 2025. According to a US government whitepaper titled *Global Trends 2025: A Transformed World*, which was printed by the Office of the Director of the National Intelligence Council, it is anticipated that, by 2025,

> [h]uman cognitive augmentation technologies [will] include drugs, implants, virtual learning environments, and wearable devices to enhance human cognitive abilities. Training software exploits neuroplasticity to improve a person's natural abilities, and wearable and implantable devices promise to improve vision, hearing, and even memory. Bio and information technologies promise enhanced human mental performance at every life stage...
>
> Desires for improved military planning, combatant performance, treatment of Alzheimer's disease, increasing education effectiveness, enhanced personal entertainment, and improving job performance could spur the development of these technologies.[94]

Corporate-Commercialized Transhumanism Consumerism:

Right now in the private sector, other Big Tech corporations, such as Elon Musk's Neuralink and Mark Zuckerberg's Facebook, are gearing up to commercialize "brain-computer interfaces" (BCIs) for transhumanist enhancements that can be bought and sold on the global marketplace.

Elon Musk, who was a member of President Trump's Economic Advisory Council,[95] has started up a venture corporation called Neuralink,[96] which is engineering "neural lace" technology "that can be implanted in the human brain, with the eventual purpose of helping human beings merge with software and keep pace with advancements in artificial intelligence. These enhancements could improve memory or allow for more direct interfacing with computing devices," according to *The Verge*.[97] Musk professes, "[o]ver time I think we will probably see a closer merger of biological intelligence and digital intelligence."[98]

Similarly, Facebook's Chairman and CEO,[99] Bilderberger Mark Zuckerberg,[100] has confirmed that his Facebook Corporation is constructing non-invasive BCIs that enable a user to type on a digital screen simply by thinking.[101] At the 2017 F8 Facebook Developer Conference, former Director of DARPA, Regina Dugan, announced that, under her directorship, Facebook's Building 8, which is the company's R&D division, is building thought-to-text BCIs through corporate-academic research partnerships with Harvard University; Stanford University; the Massachusetts Institute of Technology; Johns Hopkins University; the University of California, Berkeley; the University of California, San Francisco; and Washington University of St. Louis, Missouri.[102]

To take these transhumanist BCIs to the next level, the Facebook Corporation posted an open job listing in 2017 for a "Brain-Computer Interface (BCI) Engineer who will be responsible for working on a 2-year B8 [Building 8] project focused on developing advanced BCI technologies" through "[a]pplication of machine learning methods, including encoding and decoding models, to neuroimaging and electrophysiological data."[103] In addition, Facebook posted another 2017 job listing for a "Neural Imaging Engineer" to be hired for "developing novel non-invasive neuroimaging technologies" by "[d]esign[ing] and evaluat[ing] novel neural imaging methods based on optical, RF, ultrasound, or other entirely non-invasive approaches."[104]

Even transhumanist neurosurgeon Eric Leuthardt has set up his own BCI company called NeuroLutions. The *MIT Technology Review* reports that "NeuroLutions has raised several million so far, and a noninvasive brain interface for stroke victims who have lost function on one side is currently in human trials. The device consists of brain-monitoring electrodes that sit on the scalp and are attached to an arm orthosis . . . that moves the paralyzed limb . . . without brain surgery [implantation]."[105]

Leuthardt admits that these noninvasive BCIs are just lower-grade versions of his direct-to-brain implants; and he confesses that the long-run objective of NeuroLutions is to first normalize these noninvasive BCIs, which are more palatable to consumers and investors, and then to acclimate the BCI marketplace toward the ultimate goal of Leuthardt's transhumanist brain-tech corporation: plugging the cerebral circuitry of the human brain directly into a neuro-computer interface. Leuthardt explains, "[w]ith current technology, I could make an implant—but how many people are going to want that now? ... I think it's very important to take practical, short interval steps to get people moved along the pathway toward this road of the long-term vision."[106] Clearly, Leuthardt is making it known that his noninvasive NeuroLutions BCIs are merely stepping-stone technologies, like wearable biofeedback devices, which are marketed to condition consumers to first grow comfortable with wearable trans-tech so that they will gradually over time become accepting of surgically implantable trans-tech.

These incremental steps from wearable biotech to implantable trans-tech will follow a socially engineered road that progresses from transhumanist modifications for assisting the disabled to transhumanist augmentations for neo-eugenically upgrading the healthy and able-bodied. A *Wired Magazine* interview with Kernel Corporation CEO, Bryan Johnson, explains how his transhumanist biotech company "is exploring how to build and implant chips into the skulls of those with some form of neurological disease and dysfunction, to reprogram their neural networks to restore some of their lost abilities."[107]

The *Wired* interviewer asked Johnson if "brain augmentation" for the disabled wouldn't snowball down a slippery slope where non-augmented people "might not be able to compete in education, in jobs, and even in cocktail conversation."[108] Johnson casually retorted by conflating the advantages of purchasing BCI-learning enhancements with the advantages of purchasing private school lessons:

> [w]ell, how do you feel about some people getting a private education and other people being stuck in inner city schools? ...

So it's already happening. People somehow think that a cognitive improvement is something new to the scene. It's not. We just simply have different forms. A private education is a form of enhancement. Humans always do whatever they can to maximize their well being. If we simply add technology to the brain, it's a continuation of what humans have always done.[109]

Assistive-Learning Tech under IDEA Morphs into Transhumanist Enhancement:

In the short term, it's going to be a hard sale to convince the general public that implanting a microchip inside a student's brain is the functional equivalent of purchasing that student the best textbooks and teachers money can buy. That said, it will probably not be a very difficult sale to persuade anyone to approve of transhumanist BCIs as medical devices to help students with neurocognitive disabilities. Thus, in the long run, it will only be a matter of time before therapeutic uses of neuro-computer interfaces are expanded to non-medical uses for neo-eugenic upgrades toward transhumanist evolution.

In the 2015 issue of *Foreign Affairs*, entitled "Hi, Robot: Work and Life in the Age of Automation," an article published by Professor of Robotics, Illah Reza Nourbakhsh, details the progression by which human-robotics systems to assist the disabled will eventually be converted to neo-eugenically augment the cerebral-nervous systems of able-bodied persons:

> [r]esearchers at Carnegie Mellon; the University of California, Berkeley; and a number of other medical robotics laboratories are currently developing exoskeletal robotic legs that can sense objects and maintain balance. With these new tools, elderly people who are too frail to walk will find new footing.... For visually impaired wheelchair users, exoskeletal robotic legs combined with computerized cameras and sensors will create a human-robot team…
>
> Such outcomes would represent unqualified gains for humanity. But as robotic prosthetics enter the mainstream, the able-bodied will surely want to take advantage of them, too. These prosthetics will house sensors and cloud-connected software that will exceed the human body's ability to sense, store, and process information. Such combinations are the first step in what futurists such as Hans Moravec and Ray Kurzweil have dubbed "transhumanism": a post-evolutionary transformation that will replace humans with a hybrid of man and machine.[110]

According to a 2017 journal article published by the Philosophy of Education Society of Great Britain, the use of transhuman-tech to treat students with neurocognitive learning disorders will gradually shift to the use of such trans-tech to equip mentally healthy students with neo-eugenic upgrades that will give them superior neurocognitive advantages in the academic arena: "[m]ost commentators recognise that the difference between enhancement as therapy and non-medical enhancement will not survive close scrutiny."111 This peer-reviewed research paper explains that,

> [w]hen the body is enhanced for therapeutic reasons, there is generally little or no objection but in view of the general slippage from medical to non-therapeutic uses in practice, the chemical and mechanical transformation of the body is now becoming central to the very idea of education at all. Even on a logical level, the slippery slope from one to the other seems indicated (McNamee, 2006). It is in this context that the issue of transhuman education, however ill-defined, now arises to dislodge our assumptions about human education, natural justice, human rights etc.[112]

Stated differently, just by realizing that cognitive-learning disabilities can be remedied with direct technetronic interventions plugged straight into the cerebral-nervous system, it begs the question: how is it ethical or fair that only disabled students are allowed to improve their learning outcomes through assistive BCIs and other transhumanist ed-tech?

Indeed, a 2015 issue of the scholarly *Journal of Motor Behavior* paints a picture illustrating how the mainstreaming of transhumanist medical technetronics will be a gateway that bridges the transition to transhuman neo-eugenics tech engineered to evolve humankind into a new cyborg species. Providing thorough documentation that transhumanist engineers are already prototyping "neuroprosthetics" that "electrically stimulat[e] the brain" with "repetitive transcranial magnetic stimulation (rTMS)," this article, which is titled "The Potential Transformation of Our Species by Neural Enhancement," elaborates how

> [a] quick search on PubMed (January 24, 2014) revealed that rTMS is now seeing applications in: chronic pain syndromes, depression, Parkinson's disease, personality disorder, posttraumatic stress disorder, stroke, bipolar disorder, and, enhancing motor learning. Many of the foregoing are clinical examples that would be in the restoration range as outlined in Figure 1.

227

Yet it is not a big step toward shifting applications to, for example, enhancing attention and simply improving performance in those who already operate in the natural range shown in Figure 1. Indeed, Clark and Parasuraman (2014) in an editorial on enhancing brain function explicitly state that TMS and related brain stimulation methodologies "can be used to improve attention, perception, memory and other forms of cognition in healthy individuals" (p. 889). Nelson, McKinley, Golob, Warm, and Parasuraman (2014) also showed recently that transcranial direct current stimulation could be used to enhance vigilance in neurologically unimpaired participants.

At this stage we are now asking questions about transhumanism.[113]

Exploring these slippery-slope transhumanism questions, E. Paul Zehr, who is a research scientist at the Rehabilitation Neuroscience Laboratory at the University of Victoria in Canada, expounds on how

> the same basic constructs used for neural enhancement after injury could amplify abilities that are already in the natural normal range. That is, neural enhancement technologies to restore function and improve daily abilities for independent living could be used to improve so-called normal function to ultimate function. Approaching that functional level by use and integration of technology takes us toward the concept of a new species. This new subspecies – *homo sapiens technologicus*—is one that uses technology not just to assist but to change its own inherent biological function.[114] e [115]

Paving the techno-evolutionary way toward the neo-eugenic emergence of "*homo sapiens technologicus*," transhumanist technetronics have already built to assist blind and deaf students with visual and auditory competences. In *The Age of Spiritual Machines*, transhumanist technocrat Ray Kurzweil envisages the following "assistive technologies" to become mainlined sometime by the end of the next year, 2019:

---

e. Additionally, Zehr, who is also an associate of the University of Victoria's Centre for Biomedical Research, explores the real-world implications of another example of dystopic art imitating real-life science: a futurist novel titled *Amped* in which

> neural implants (most notably something called the neural-autofocus that is used to sharpen concentration and intelligence) become widely available. In the beginning, these devices were introduced for use in those with cognitive disabilities, mental challenges, or health risks (e.g., to control epilepsy), but they eventually see widespread application throughout the population. Subsequently a two-tiered class of humans emerges—those who are amped and those who are not.

[b]lind persons routinely use eyeglass-mounted reading-navigation systems, which incorporate the new, digitally controlled, high-resolution optical sensors. These systems can read text in the real world.... These automated reading-navigation assistants communicate to blind users through both speech and tactile indicators...

Retinal and vision neural implants have emerged but have limitations and are used by only a small percentage of blind persons.

Deaf persons routinely read what other people are saying through the deaf person's lens displays....Cochlear and other implants for improving hearing are effective and are widely used.[116]

Kurzweil's predictions have proven strikingly accurate. The Second Sight Corporation, which partners with the government-funded BRAIN Initiative, has produced the first-ever commercially available artificial retina called the "Argus II bionic eye."[117] This transhumanist implantable can restore vision for certain types of blindness to consumers through market distributers such as the German Retina Implant company as well as the French Pixium Vision Corporation.[118] Additionally, Second Sight is currently designing a brain implant that can restore even more vision to a wider range of blindness maladies. The *MIT Technology Review* documents how the Orion brain chip has been given approval from the US Food and Drug Administration (FDA)[119] to conduct a "small study involving five patients at two sites, Baylor College of Medicine and the University of California, Los Angeles."[120]

Regarding Kurzweil's predictions for cochlear implants, the National Institutes on Deafness and Other Communication Disorders (NIDCD) of the National Institutes of Health (NIH) documents that the FDA "first approved cochlear implants in the mid-1980s to treat hearing loss in adults. Since 2000, cochlear implants have been FDA-approved for use in eligible children beginning at 12 months of age."[121] Innovating an even more transhumanistic advancement in hearing-tech, the Facebook Corporation is engineering biotech sensors that enable "skin hearing" by decoding sound vibrations through skin sensors that convert the sound waves into words.[122]

In addition to assisted-vision BCIs and assisted-hearing neurotech, there are also precedents set for transhumanistic biofeedback wearables to be implemented in schools as "assistive technologies" to help students with cognitive-learning disabilities that are recognized under the Individuals with Disabilities Education Act (IDEA) and the Every Student Succeeds Act (ESSA). In chapter five, I document how collegiate and elementary education institutions are already using assistive biofeedback-tech to relieve student stress during school counseling sessions that utilize wearable SEL biometrics such as emWave PC®, StressEraser, RESPeRATE, and Healing Rhythms. I also examine how DeVos's conflicts of interest between her secretarial powers and her investments in Neurocore, a biofeedback corporation, will potentially expand the uses of biofeedback-tech in schools for the purposes of assisting students with ADHD and other cognitive-learning disabilities. All of these assistive biofeedback technologies for disabled students are essentially transhumanistic because these technetronic devices are wearables that monitor and regulate neurobiology in real time.

Another proposal to utilize transhumanistic medical-tech in education involves the implementation of magnetic resonance imaging (MRI) scans to data-mine students for their neuro-cerebral learning capacities.[123] In *NOVA*'s 2016 "School of the Future" documentary, which was financed by the Carnegie Corporation and the David H. Koch Science Fund, MRI data-mining of student brains is promoted as the cutting-edge in ed-tech learning assessment.[124]

Similarly, students' brainwaves are being data-mined through technetronic headbands engineered by the BrainCo Corporation.[125] This transhumanist ed-tech company is funded by several Chinese firms such as Wandai Capital, Decent Capital, Han Tan Capital, and the China Electronics Corporation, which classifies itself as "one of the key state-owned conglomerates directly under the administration of central government, and the largest state-owned IT company in China."[126] Prototyped at Harvard University's Innovation Lab, BrainCo's "Focus 1" headband uses electroencephalography (EEG) data-mining to calculate a student's SEL "engagement" and cognitive-behavioral "focus."[127] At the 2017 International Society for Technology in Education (ISTE) Conference, the transhumanist Focus 1 headband was awarded the prize for "Most Innovative" ed-tech.[128]

BrainCo is also engineering Brain-Machine Interface (BMI) headbands which electronically administer cognitive-behavioral therapies that treat ADHD. Additionally, BrainCo is constructing other transhumanist BMIs to enable thought-to-text typing as well as remote thought-control of robotic limbs.

The Public-Private Precision Transhumanism Initiative:

The very history of medicalizing the American education system is rooted in the "mental hygiene" philosophy of old-school eugenics, which concentrated negative-eugenic efforts toward "cleansing" the human genepool of "mental defects," including the low-IQ genetics of "morons," "idiots," "imbeciles," and the "feeble-minded"; and the "diseased" genetics of persons who have cognitive-behavioral disorders and mental illnesses.[129]

As America's state-level P-20 councils medicalize the education system through public-private partnerships between charter school corporations, state and local education departments, private healthcare companies, and public health and human services departments; transhumanist biotechnologies will make more headway into the classroom through deeper integration of cutting-edge "assistive technologies" for accommodating medically disabled students classified under IDEA and ESSA. The spread of medical transhumanist wearables throughout the school system will gain even more momentum as transhumanistic treatments for students with disabilities and diseases are developed by the NIH through the Precision Medicine Initiative (PMI): a public-private medical research project set up in 2015 by President Barrack Obama to develop "precision medicine," which employs wearable biometrics to obtain individualized healthcare data from patients in real time so that personalized gene therapies and other neo-eugenic biotech treatments can be prescribed and administered with hi-tech precision accuracy.[130]

In my article "The Precision Eugenics Initiative Part 2: The Precision Transhumanism Initiative,"[131] I have documented how PMI Working Group member Eric Dishman has experimented with various transhumanist wearables that utilize the "internet of things" to monitor health data and regulate health status. Perhaps most notably, Dishman has been the architect of wireless smart networks that track "early stage Alzheimer's patients" while "prompt[ing] them to call someone, [or] remind[ing] them to eat their breakfast, or take their medicine," according to *Forbes Magazine*.[132] Dishman's web of smart health sensors "led to products that were spun off in 2010 as part of a joint venture between Intel and General Electric into a new company called Care Innovations, where Dishman also serves as director of health policy."[133] A 2013 CNBC article titled "The Future of Medicine Means Part Human, Part Computer" reports, "Dishman said that in a ten-year timeframe he expects one-third of the population will have either a temporary device or another more permanent connected device in their body."[134]

To bring about Dishman's transhumanist vision of the future of medicine, the PMI Working Group published a 2015 whitepaper entitled "The Precision Medicine Initiative Cohort Program: Building a Research Foundation for 21st Century Medicine." This "Final Report" proclaims that the PMI will be "collecting dense clinical data articulated with sensor and mHealth [mobile health] data," which is digital health data from mobile technetronic devices such as smartphones, smartwatches, and fit-bits.[135] Subtitled "Precision Medicine Initiative Working Group Report to the Advisory Committee to the Director, NIH," this government document expounds how,

> [b]eyond the smartphone, the PMI-CP [Cohort Program] should consider the use and integration of select wireless sensors, either worn or employed in the home, that have been validated and that would provide useful health data for specific subgroups of the PMI cohort. These sensors may include research grade or commercial grade wrist-worn accelerometers, wireless weight scales, movement sensors in the home, continuous heart rate and pulse oxygen monitors, respiration monitors, glucometers, spirometers, and other FDA approved wireless medical monitoring devices used in the home.[136]

In fact, many of these plethora of transhumanist wearables have already found their ways into American classrooms through public-private partnerships between schools and the PMI. After the publication of the PMI Working Group's "Final Report," the PMI launched its 2017 *All of Us* Research Program,[137] which is already partnering with numerous universities such as the University of Illinois Chicago, Vanderbilt University, and the University of Southern California. The *All of Us* project, which will also partner with certain community colleges,[138] is run by none other than transhumanist Director Eric Dishman, who aims to log biodata from one million participants having their vitals monitored by transhumanist medical wearables.[139] Dishman's *All of Us* project has already data-mined 45,000 participants with various transhumanist wearables.[140]

The Student Body as Neo-Eugenic Guinea Pig:

As the medicalization of P-20 schooling normalizes transhumanist wearables in the classroom, it is certain that these neo-eugenic technetronics will eventually become standard-issue "school supplies" that are as ubiquitous as pencils and paper. To mainstream the use of such transhumanist ed-tech for "lifelong learning," a 2014 peer-reviewed journal article, "Nature, Nurture and Neuroscience: Some Future Directions for Historians of Education," calls on "all educationists (and many historians) [to] draw on the findings of neuroscience to inform their work" and to engage with the work of futurologists who are exploring the extent to which the human brain, which has slowly evolved over millions of years, is now increasingly susceptible to fundamental and rapid change. . . . In this brave new technologically and ethically challenging world, historians of education have a duty not only to understand and interpret the possible, probable and preferable futures envisaged by educational, pharmacological, and technical innovations, but also to participate in their creation.[141]

Once there are enough futurist "learning engineers" who are "participat[ing]" in [the] creation" of neo-eugenic biotechnologies designed to function as basic school supplies, it will be easy for technocratic educationists to officially garner legal authority to data-mine students' biopsychological-learning metrics for the purposes of researching and developing transhumanist BCIs and neuro-technologies that boost students' competency-based learning outcomes.

Indeed, under exploitable FERPA loopholes, every psychological and biological data point that can be digitally extracted from a student to advance transhumanist ed-tech will be deemed of "legitimate educational interest."[142] As attorney Jane Robbins points out in her refutation of SEL data-mining, "[i]f such psychological data resided in a psychologist's office, it would be protected by HIPAA (the Health Insurance Portability and Accountability Act). Would it be similarly protected if located in a school's database? No. It would probably be considered merely an 'education record' subject to (not protected by) federal student-privacy law."[143]

With the lines obfuscated between medical records and education records, it is probable that Learnsphere, G Scholar, and other public-private education databanks will compile dossiers that tabulate students' cognitive-behavioral UII data along with genetic code scans and neurobiological stimulus-response data from precision-ed DNA IDs, GSR SEL bracelets, neuro-cerebral brainwave headbands, and other biofeedback wearables such as Secretary DeVos's Neurocore ed-tech. In the final equation, massive public-private education datahubs will dragnet hoards of student biopsychosocial data to be leveraged by ed-tech companies and other third-party technetronics corporations, which will commandeer students' medical/education records to advance R&D into transhumanist biotechnologies that administer cognitive-behavioral learning therapies through genetic and neurobiological medical-tech that can improve a student's learning outcomes and job competences.

The more that transhumanist ed-tech companies share their vaults of students' biopsychosocial data to eugenically engineer evolutionary learning technologies, the faster we will progress to "The Singularity": the flashpoint in the progression of technological evolution when computationally intelligent neurotech, gene-tech, biotech, nanotech, robot-tech, and other artificially intelligent machine-tech will symbiotically fuse together into a Singular super-AI network of transhuman technetronics that merge with human biology to evolve the "wetware" of human physiology into cyborg-computer hardware.[144] According to *The Singularity Is Near: When Humans Transcend Biology*, by Bilderberger transhumanist Ray Kurzweil,[145]

> [t]he Singularity will allow us to transcend these limitations of our biological bodies and brains.... Our mortality will be in our own hands. We will be able to live as long as we want (a subtly different statement from saying we will live forever).... By the end of this century, the nonbiological portion of our intelligence will be trillions of trillions of times more powerful than unaided human intelligence...
>
> The Singularity will represent the culmination of the merger of our biological thinking and existence with our technology, resulting in a world that is still human but that transcends our biological roots. There will be no distinction, post-Singularity, between human and machine or between physical and virtual reality.[146]

In a graphic illustration of Kurzweil's Singularized transhumanity, a 2015 issue of the academic *Journal of Motor Behavior* displays a diagram of a transhuman cyborg creature equipped with several different biotechnological brain-body modifications, including "[r]eplacement skin; sensory tattoos; [b]rain-computer interface; visual and auditory implants; Google glasses; deep brain stimulation; brainstem implants and neural modulation; and [c]ardiac & phrenic pacemakers."[147] Reflecting on the prospects of a cyborg Singularity, E. Paul Zehr, who is a faculty member of the University of Victoria's Division of Medical Sciences, expresses these closing remarks: "[i]n truth, I remain stunned by how rapidly research applications are progressing."[148]

Corporations as Churches, Technologies as Religious Sacraments, and the Postmodern Objectification of Human Biology by a Transhuman Master Race of Techno-godmen:

It will of course be touted that this technological transformation of the human species is a natural stage in the next phase of biological evolution through computer-machine evolution which enables humankind to re-engineer its neurogenetic makeup in its own postmodernist self-image. For decades, humanistic intellectuals have implored us all to adopt post-modern philosophies, such as deconstructionism, object-oriented ontol-ogy (OOO),[149] and "thing theory,"[150] in order to overturn conservative definitions of gender, race, and class which perpetuate the supremacist political-economic powerstructure of white, male, heterosexual capital-ism. Now that transhuman-tech is equipping us to literally reconfigure the naturally inherited biological traits which have historically predicat-ed a person's social class status based on sex genetics, race genetics, and even IQ genetics, it will be argued that innovations in transhumanist bio-tech modifications are revolutions that will free humanity from biosocial bondage by empowering oppressed groups, such as women, ethnic mi-norities, transgendered people, and disabled persons, to technologically break out from under the political-economic limitations imposed upon their inherited biogenetic natures.

Indeed, a 2008 issue of the scientific journal, *Nature*, tries to suggest that there is no categorically imperative difference between the neuro-cognitive benefits of brain-computer interfaces and the neurocognitive benefits of "adequate exercise, nutrition, and sleep."[151] However, in his peer-reviewed article entitled "Enhanced Humans Versus 'Normal Peo-ple': Elusive Definitions," Vanderbilt University Professor of Education Michael Bess astutely rebuts this false analogy:

> [b]ecause these [Nature] authors wish to open the door for cogni-tive enhancements as part of the legitimate everyday functioning of our society, they simply collapse the distinction between such enhancements and other forms of beneficial human activity. Even when I'm sleeping, according to them, I am in one sense "enhanc-ing" my ability to function better the next day. By this use of the term, eating a peanut butter sandwich is not qualitatively different from having a prosthetic hippocampus implanted in my brain: both "interventions" result in a net augmentation of my ability to think, as compared with what would have been my ability if I had not undertaken them. (I can never think clearly on an empty stomach.) This is unhelpful argumentation at best... [W]e need to start with a frank assessment of the qualitative differences that divide some forms of biotechnological intervention from others. A Boeing 747 is qualitatively different from a pogo stick, even though both devices render me temporarily airborne.[152]

This well-said retort highlights the absurdity of conflating the natural benefits of inborn human biological functions, such as dieting, exercising, and resting, in comparison with artificial benefits from the transhuman alteration of human biology through BCIs and neuro-technologies. Yet postmodern transhumanists will contend that this absurdist deconstruction of biological and technological definitions is necessary to turn upside-down the patriarchal capitalist powerstructures in which white, male capitalists dominate other races and genders who are oppressed as wage slaves under the private, monopolistic ownership of the techno-industrial means of economic power. Following this political-economic paradigm, futurist disciples of postmodern philosophies, such as OOO and "thing theory," will preach a gospel of technological salvation in the coming age of utopian transhumanism when neo-eugenic upgrades will level out the political-economic playing field by booting everyone with computerized biotechnologies that empower the wielder to transcend the social caste hierarchies of a racist, sexist, capitalist hegemony.

However, the truth is that, even though the "liberal" commodification of transhuman-tech on the consumer market will surely open the gates for new expressions of human identity, all of these new identities are being mediated through a literal symbiosis with hi-tech corporate-industrial products that must be purchased through capitalistic exchange in a fascistically planned economy. In an interview on the *Joe Rogan Experience Podcast*, Elon Musk explained that the corporate-consumer dialectic is the engine that drives trans-technological human-machine evolution:

> a company is essentially a cybernetic collective of people and machines. That's what a company is. And then there are different levels of complexity in the way these companies are formed, and then there are sort of, there's sort of like a collective AI [artificial intelligence] in the Google search where we're all sort of plugged in as like nodes on the network, like leaves on a big tree. And we're all feeding this network with our questions and answers; we're all collectively programming the AI. And Google plus all the humans that connect to it are one giant cybernetic collective. This is also true of Facebook and Twitter and Instagram and all these social networks. They're giant cybernetic collectives.[153]

If we are to believe that the wage-slaving "proletariat" will eventually find liberation as human "nodes" plugged into a "cybernetic collective" which obediently consumes the technological products sold by master corporations, such as Google and Facebook, then this puts a whole new spin on the Hegelian idealization of the slave-master dialectic as a functional principle of the absolute Corporate State. As such, it is easy to refute postmodernist arguments that claim transhumanist technological modification of humankind is a liberating revolution in post-capitalist political-economics – because the entire transhumanist enterprise is nothing less than the pinnacle of corporate power through which conglomerated tech industries have amalgamated into virtual cartels that are converting human beings from wage slaves into literal "human resources" to be molded from raw-material "wetware" into commercialized biological-android merchandise patented and owned by the Corporate State.

Therefore, as harbingers of transhumanism, postmodernist OOO and thing theory do not liberate oppressed peoples by upgrading them with new biosocial identities that are afforded new political-economic opportunities which transcend capitalist hierarchies; rather, these postmodernist contortions actually dehumanize the natural dignity of human life by reducing the human being to nothing more than just another "object" or "thing" that is no different from any other raw material to be extracted and processed for corporate-industrial manufacturing. A 2015 research paper authored by the Faculty of Education at the University of Niš in Vranje, Serbia, explains that "[c]ritics of transhumanism rightfully ... warn of the problem of child objectification. The child becomes an object, a lump of clay which can be molded to the parents' wishes.... Scientists and these 'parents' adopt a technocratic attitude toward human children."[154] In "Preventing a Brave New World," former Chairman of the US President's Council on Bioethics, Leon Kass, agrees: "[h]uman children become their [transhumanists'] artifacts. Such an arrangement is profoundly dehumanizing, no matter how good the product."[155]

In brief, transhumanist OOO philosophers and thing theorists, along with other postmodern neo-eugenicists, are actually on the exact same page as the corporate techno-fascists who lobby not only to obfuscate the ethical lines between biology and technology, but also to disintegrate the legal lines that distinguish human beings, who are endowed with inalienable natural rights to sovereign self-determination, as separate from proprietary objects/things, which are owned and trademarked as chattel by corporate businesses. Jürgen Habermas affirms that

> as soon as adults treat the desirable genetic traits of their descendants as a product they can shape according to a design of their

own liking, they are exercising a kind of control over their genetically manipulated offspring that intervenes in the somatic bases of
another person's spontaneous relation-to-self and ethical freedom.
This kind of intervention should only be exercised over things, not
persons. ... This new structure of attribution results from obliterat-
ing the boundary between persons and things.[156]

Along with this gross objectification of human beings necessarily comes
the "self-interested" motivations of corporate and consumer competition in
a fascistic marketplace on the basis of a Techno-Social Darwinism in which
survival of the fittest is a matter of struggling for existence not through
competition over natural resources, but through a biotechnological race to
evolve into a transhuman breakaway civilization that eugenically diverges
from the technologically backward remnants of the human species. A 2015
issue of the Eastern European *Journal for Social Research* states, "[n]ot only
do transhumanists lean toward this objectification but they also limit the
effects of genetic engineering on themselves and their progeny. Tom Koch
thinks that transhumanists: 'do not seek general betterment as a socially supported good, however, but instead the right to personal advantage for themselves or their offspring.'"[157] Driven by so-called "rationally" selfish competi-
tions over consumption, the endgame of transhumanist Social Darwinism
is survival of the biotechnologically fittest through a commercial struggle of
existence which competes to consume the most advantageous neurogenetic technetronics products marketed by fascistic corporations.

Playing by these *laissez faire* rules, this "free trade" game of transhumanism stacks the deck so that the best neo-eugenic enhancements will
be the most expensive, which means that the highest trans-eugenic upgrades will basically only be available to the most affluent members of
the technocratic oligarchy of the future. In turn, the socioeconomic advantages of the rich will be transformed into biogenetic and neurocognitive advantages through their purchases of "luxury" BCIs and upscale
neuro-technetronics that afford the wealthy elite to amplify their psychophysiological abilities to dominate the political-economic theater with a
simple switch, button, click, or plug-in. A warning of this very scenario is
put forward by Fiachra Long, who is a Professor of Education at the University of Cork in the Republic of Ireland:

[w]hile no one denies the benefit of such a use of a "posthuman"
technology to help the paralysed, it is all too likely that this new
technology (when it becomes available) will be used by the rich to

further enhance the wealthy and the healthy and the initial clarity about the benefit of such research will disappear. Current editing of the DNA, which has now become more straightforward, will soon modify the human genome and this will precipitate a new age of the posthuman with unforeseeable results.[158]

To be sure, there is at least one dystopic result that is foreseeable: the splitting up of humankind into two separate species as the economic elite merge with their superior transhuman technologies to become a neo-eugenic master race that diverges from the evolutionary destiny of the impoverished masses of technologically backward labor slaves.

In the 2015 *Foreign Affairs* article titled "The Coming Robot Dystopia: All Too Inhuman," Carnegie Mellon University roboticist, Illah Reza Nourbakhsh, discusses how the ultra-rich can monopolize neo-eugenic robotics to become "more human than human":

> [s]uch [trans-tech] advantages, however, would run headlong into a set of ethical problems: just as a fine line separates genetic engineering from eugenics, so, too, is there no clear distinction between robotics that would lift a human's capabilities to their organic limit and those that would vault a person beyond all known boundaries. Such technologies have the potential to vastly magnify the already significant gaps in opportunity and achievement that exist between people of different economic means. In the robotic future, today's intense debates about social and economic inequality will seem almost quaint.[159]

Nonetheless, notwithstanding these ethical dilemmas, the CFR author concludes his analysis not by calling for a moratorium on further development of neo-eugenic trans-robotics, but by recommending that "[e]ducators and regulators must help robot inventors acquire knowledge."[160]

The Rockefeller Foundation funded a transhumanist whitepaper which similarly forecasts a future when techno-evolution will split humanity into separate species. Entitled "Dreaming the Future of Health for the Next 100 Years," this document publishes proceedings of the Rockefeller Foundation's 2013 Global Health Summit,[161] which report that "[t]he use of robotics, [sic] bio-engineering to augment human functioning is already well underway and will advance. Re-engineering of humans into potentially separate and unequal forms through genetic engineering or mixed human-robots raises debates on ethics and equality. A new demography is projected to emerge after 2030."[162]

As the uber-rich push the trajectory of transhumanist ed-volution to follow the forecasts of the Global Education Futures timeline, 2017 marks the year when "Neural Interfaces … in mobile and wearable form adopt [sic] to ergonomics and natural patterns of human bodies."[163] A year later in 2018, "[c]heap and user-friendly neural interfaces become mass market consumer product[s]."[164] During the next decade, a transhumanist "Neuroweb of Learning" will emerge; and by 2028, "[n]onverbal message exchange through neural interfaces becomes a learning tool."[165] It is at this point in the future that "The Great Psychic Divide" will occur, causing the "[d]ivide between users and non-users of cognitive products [to] deepen."[166] After The Great Psychic Divide, the year 2030 will bring about the "Birth of Neuro-Genetic Economy" when "J.A.R.V.I.S. Inside Nanobiotechnology transforms gadgets into bionic body parts," and transhuman plutocrats evolve into neo-eugenic demigods.[167]

If transhumanist purchasing power evolves billionaire Tech Barons into a new *homo sapiens technologicus* species that is divorced from the working-poor subpopulations, then this new super-race of eugenically superior cyborgs will become a virtual master race of techno-godmen with neurogenetic-computer powers so far beyond the unmodified remnants of purely biological humanity that the astronomical gaps between these *homo* subspecies will elevate transhuman oligarchs to a godlike overlord status.

Stated differently, pay-to-enhance biotech modifications will result in an unequal distribution of transhumanist upgrade-tech that goes hand-in-hand with the economic imbalance between "The One Percent" and "The 99%." The parallel psychophysiological inequalities resulting from separate-but-equal trans-tech ownership will be so radical that there will be no bioethical common ground on which to democratically govern these divergent subspecies on a level playing field that adheres to the same Bill of Rights. By default then, so expansive will be the neurocognitive-behavioral differences between the ultra-rich, who are modified with top-notch biotech, and the indigent poor, who are unmodified or only minimally modified, that there will need to be instated a two-tiered, neo-eugenic caste system in which the most advanced transhumanist cyborgs are given a godlike sovereignty above the rules that govern lower-grade transhumans and antiquated biological humans who are denigrated to second-class and third-class statuses under a trans-eugenic religion of techno-fascist scientism.

If you think that my usage of the label "godlike" is going too far, please note that I am only using the wording of transhumanist rockstar, Ray Kurzweil himself, who said, "we're going to [technologically] expand the brain's neocortex and become more godlike."[168] Likewise, Oxford Historian Yuval Noah Harari refers to transhuman *homo technologicus* as *homo deus*, which means "god man," or "god human."

In his 2016 bestselling book, *Homo Deus: A Brief History of Tomorrow*, Harari writes,

> in order to overcome old age and misery humans will first have to acquire godlike control of their own biological substratum. If we ever have the power to engineer death and pain out of our system, that same power will probably be sufficient to engineer our system in almost any manner we like, and manipulate our organs, emotions and intelligence in myriad ways. You could buy for yourself the strength of Hercules, the sensuality of Aphrodite, the wisdom of Athena or the madness of Dionysus if that is what you are into. Up till now increasing human power relied mainly on upgrading our external tools. In the future it may rely more on upgrading the human body and mind, or on merging directly with our tools.
>
> The upgrading of humans into gods may follow any of three paths: biological engineering, cyborg engineering, and the engineering of nonorganic beings.[169]

Harari, who is a Lecturer at Hebrew University in Jerusalem, asserts that "[w]e can be quite certain that humans will make a bid for divinity, because humans have many reasons to desire such an upgrade, and many ways to achieve it.... [W]e may discover that the human genome is far too complicated for serious manipulation, but this will not prevent the development of brain-computer interfaces, nano-robots or artificial intelligence."[170] According to Harari, this *deus ex machina* through BCIs, nanotech, and AI is labeled "technohumanism," which is just a synonym for "transhumanism":

> [t]echnohumanism agrees that *Homo sapiens* as we know it has run its historical course and will no longer be relevant in the future, but concludes that we should therefore use technology in order to create *Homo deus* – a much superior human model. *Homo deus* will retain some essential features, but will also enjoy upgraded physical and mental abilities that will enable it to hold its own even against the most sophisticated non-conscious algorithms. Since intelligence is decoupling from consciousness, and since non-conscious intelligence is developing at breakneck speed, humans must actively upgrade their minds if they want to stay in the game....
>
> [A] second cognitive revolution might give *Homo deus* access to unimaginable new realms and make them lords of the galaxy.[171]

If corporate-industrialized technetronic products are the holy sacrament of Kurzweil's and Harari's new age of *Homo deus*, then the church of this technology worship is the techno-fascist, public-private corporation while the godhead of the Corporate-Technocratic Singularity is the Corporate-Technocratic State, which is worshipped by Hegelian-collectivist cult members of The Order of Skull and Bones.

In his *Philosophy of Right*, Georg Wilhelm Friedrich Hegel pontificated that "the State is the march of God in the world; its ground or cause is the power of reason realizing itself as will."[172] In chapter two, I document how the Statist-collectivist philosophies of Hegel were disseminated across the US academic system by The Order to inculcate American schools with corporate workforce training curriculums that would over time transform the United States from a free republic into a planned economy controlled by a Corporate State. Furthermore, I show how it was Bonesman Morrison Remick Waite, as Chief Justice of the United States Supreme Court, who codified the Corporate State into law when he ruled that corporations are "persons" which must be granted the same Constitutional rights and legal protections as human persons.[173] If Hegelianist Bonesmen venerate the State as "the march of God," then they essentially exalt Government as the hand of God; and in a Corporate State which surrenders government offices to the powers of private companies, Hegelianist Bonesmen thus revere those fascist corporations as industrial-economic manifestations of the will of God. In the Technocratic State of the transhumanist future when the powers of government are dominated by neo-eugenic information technologies, the cult of Skull and Bones will bow to corporate technetronics as the hi-tech evolution of God materializing on earth.

Therefore, transhumanist evolution into godlike powers through corporate-fascist ed-tech products is nothing less than the culmination of Hegelianist State worship progressing into the worship of corporate technology. Once human beings are neurobiologically interfaced with these corporate technetronics, transhuman oligarchs will be philosophically worshipping themselves as their own gods by symbiotically merging with their own technological products placed on their own corporate altars of worship.

Chapter 17

AI Posthumanism:
The End of Learning,
The End of Consciousness

Transhumanist cyborg ed-tech is not the outer limits of neo-eugenic ed-volution. Stretch your imagination a bit further to a future of posthumanism when neurogenetic biological systems plugged into human-computer interfaces will become subsumed by technetronic hardware until human-machine hybrids merge completely with artificially intelligent robots; and human consciousness achieves virtual immortality as it is effectively transported from organic, carbon-based physiology to silicon-based digital software uploaded into artificial intelligence (AI) supercomputers linked to the internet-of-everything.

To be sure, there are academic disputes over the appropriate definitions of "posthumanism" versus "transhumanism." I will not delve into that debate here; but for the purposes of my AI ed-tech analysis, I am defining posthumanism as a distinct phase in neo-eugenic, trans-tech evolution when the cognitive-learning powers of AI machines surpass even the most technetronically souped-up transhuman whose neurobiological "bandwidth" and psycho-electrical "information-processing speed" will pale in comparison with the purely digital-technetronic IT powers of "software-based" artificial intelligences that can be uploaded into "cognitive-computing" robots. In this posthuman stage of trans-eugenic evolution, *homo technologicus* will achieve digital immortality by transcending the biotechnological limitations of BCIs as human consciousnesses are uploaded into virtual-reality (VR) worlds where they can be infinitely updated and "copied" while selectively interfacing with the real world through robotic AI hardware which can download VR simulations to overlay them onto augmented reality (AR) scans of the physical world in order to enhance software-based posthuman perception of the universe.

In many ways, AI computer sciences and neurotech computer sciences are distinct specializations in the IT sciences. But transhuman BCIs and other neuro-technologies are already embedded with AI algorithms, and there will come a day when biotechnologies and AI computers are integrally intertwined so that (trans)human consciousness is effectively transferred from organic, carbon-based biology to artificially constructed composites of silicon microchips, lithium batteries, and gold-plated circuit boards.

In the meantime, the entire technocratic apparatus of cognitive-behavioral adaptive-learning software, precision-ed biogenetic-conditioning technologies, and psycho-affective SEL biofeedback technetronics is doing nothing less than collating all the myriads of stimulus-response algorithms needed to build the crowning achievement of post-transhumanism: the virtual (trans)human-AI interface.

Here's how the student biopsychosocial data collected from cognitive-behavioral UII algorithms, DNA-IQ scans, and psycho-affective SEL metrics will be cross-calculated and reconfigured to engineer artificially intelligent posthuman-computer interfaces that can transmit human-software consciousnesses across VR, AR, and real-world dimensions:

Data-Mining Human Biocomputers to Engineer AI Supercomputers:

Posthumanists essentially view the human organism as a neuro-electrical biocomputer system, which Emeritus Professor of Physiology, Development, and Neuroscience at Oxford University, Dennis Bray,[1] refers to as "wetware." In his 2009 book, *Wetware: A Computer in Every Living Cell*, Bray writes,

> [t]he term *wetware* is not new, but I think it has not been closely defined before. Wetware, in this book, is the sum of all the information-rich molecular processes inside a living cell. It has resonance with the rigid *hardware* of electronic devices and the symbolic *software* that encodes memories and operating instructions, but it is distinct from both of these. Cells are built of molecules that interact in complex webs, or circuits. These circuits perform logical operations that are analogous in many ways to electronic devices but have unique properties. The computational units of life—the transistors, if you will—are its giant molecules, especially proteins. Acting like miniature switches, they guide the biochemical processes of a cell this way or that. Linked into huge networks they form the basis of all of the distinct properties of living systems. . . . Protein complexes associated with DNA act like microchips to

switch genes on and off in different cells—executing "programs" of development. Machines made of protein molecules are the basis for the contractions of our muscles and the excitable, memory-encoding plasticity if the human brain. They are the seed corn of our awareness and sense of self.[2]

To elaborate this conception, posthumanists basically regard the human DNA code as the fundamental "operating system" that controls the quality of the two main "software applications": cognitive-behavioral IQ reasoning and socioemotional learning, which coordinate to comprise the network-computing "mainframe" that is human intelligence. Therefore, optimal posthuman upgrades may prerequire that a student's DNA sequences must first be precisely mapped out for genetic re-engineering so that his or her molecular neurobiology becomes more conducive to interfacing with computerized technetronic devices which augment cognitive reasoning and socioemotional learning.

. In the interim, students' cognitive-behavioral UII and psycho-affective SEL metrics are being data-mined to pinpoint measure the bioelectrical stimulus-response algorithms of the human nervous system which control the rational and affective modes of human information processing. As a result, this Big Data matrix of biopsychological metrics can be re-crunched to program transhuman HCIs (Human-Computer Interfaces) with compatible digital-electronic stimulus-response algorithms that will synchronize with the neurobiological stimulus-response algorithms programmed into human DNA. In particular, student UII and SEL matrixes can be coopted to engineer next-generation wireless transceiver signals that can be beamed through ultra-wideband (UWB) radio-waves,[3] 5G millimeter waves,[4] and even 6G wavelengths which can communicate directly with the neurogenetic "circuitry" of human biology.[5] At the same time, student UII algorithms can also be reverse-engineered to create software-based intelligences that mimic the conscious information-processing powers of human cognition while student SEL algorithms can be commandeered to encode AI bots with software that can recognize and imitate human emotions. In brief, students' cognitive UII and affective SEL metrics are being data-mined and re-purposed for programming humanoid AI robots that can scan and respond to human emotions, yet with superior "cognitive" information-processing powers that far exceed the organic brain's abilities to reason.

Once artificially intelligent robots can indistinguishably imitate the rational-emotional dialectic of human intelligence, these AI technetronic systems can be programmed with a digital-computational substrate that synchronizes with the logical-affective mathematical frequencies of human thought and feeling in order to attune the neuro-electrical frequencies of real-world brain consciousness with the digital-electronic computational frequencies of artificial software consciousnesses uploaded in an AI-assisted, AR/VR simulation world.

If you think that students' personalized UII and SEL algorithms are not being data-mined to engineer AI-learning software that can simulate human intelligence, you must understand that operant-conditioning adaptive-learning software and SEL biofeedback wearables are themselves both automated technetronic devices which utilize rudimentary AI algorithms for tracking students' cognitive-behavioral and socioemotional responses to virtual learning stimuli in order to digitally administer personalized adjustments to those computerized learning stimuli in real time. Stated differently, the very mathematical-computational orders of operations carried out by individualized adaptive-learning and biofeedback algorithms, which respond to digitized stimuli in real time, are by definition rudimentary forms of artificial intelligence, which by design must continuously record data and then reconfigure that data for further tracking and reconfiguring recursively.

These rough cognitive-behavioral and psycho-affective stimulus-response algorithms that are data-mined from adaptive-learning software and biofeedback devices are recalculated to formulate "fuzzy logic" data that basically capture "low-resolution" metrical estimates of how the various bits and bytes of UII and SEL meta-data represent clear mathematical operations which can be "de-fuzzed" by AI and thus reassembled to digitally simulate the human cognitive-affective intelligence operations from which the meta-data was generated and then "fuzzily" tabulated. A 2017 issue of the scholarly journal, *Educational Research and Reviews*, explains how AI ed-tech converts "fuzzy-data" metrics of human cognitive-affective behavior patterns into artificially intelligent computer simulations of "the human thinking process" which can be programmed for student assessment:

> [i]n recent years, artificial intelligence applications for understanding the human thinking process and transferring it to virtual environments come into prominence. The fuzzy logic which paves the way for modeling human behaviors and expressing even vague concepts mathematically, and is also regarded as an artificial intelligence technique ... can provide benefits in modeling these

ambiguities in human mental processes and also it can reach fairer, more sensitive and objective results....This study reveals that FAHP [fuzzy analytic hierarchy process] method can be used in the evaluation of students' projects in education.[6]

Fuzzy-logic data-mining is just one method by which students' digitized learning metrics can be revamped to engineer anthropomorphic software intelligences. In addition, all the digital mounds of cognitive-affective data aggregated throughout the Learnsphere, G Scholar, and other education datahubs can be shared and reprocessed not only to refine computerized stimulus-response algorithms for the improvement of adaptive-learning software; but also to open the gates for AI corporations to commandeer student-learning psychometrics in order to reconfigure those UII and SEL data into complex stimulus-response matrixes which can be uploaded into automated teacher/tutor bots, thereby upgrading them with cognitive-affective algorithms that mimic human intelligence.

In fact, Learnsphere houses an "ASSISTments data repository [that] contains datasets from secondary school interactions with an online tutoring system, in many cases as part of online experiments of what learning works best."[7] Learnsphere also provides a DataShop External Tools platform which is a suite of "[f]ree tools submitted by developers in the educational data mining and intelligent tutoring systems communities."[8] Ed-tech developers and other educationist researchers can utilize these DataShop External Tools to aid in cross-referencing the virtual tutoring data in the ASSISTments hub with the behaviorist psychological metrics tabulated in Learnsphere's Databrary and TalkBank: Databrary "focuses on creating tools for scientists to store, manage, preserve, analyze, and share video and other temporally dense streams of data" in order "to promote data sharing, archiving, and reuse among researchers who study the development of humans and other animals";[9] TalkBank is "an interdisciplinary research project to promote the study of human and animal communication. The subfields of study include first language acquisition, second language acquisition, conversation analysis, classroom discourse and aphasic language."[10] [a] [11] The behaviorist psychological linguistic data compiled in TalkBank is channeled into another Learnsphere data vault called "[t]he Child Language Data Exchange System (CHILDES) [which] is the part of TalkBank focused on child language, or first language acquisition. CHILDES provides tools for studying conversation-

---

a. According to the Learnsphere website, "TalkBank has been funded by grants from the National Science Foundation (including BCS-998009, 0324883) as well as the National Institutes of Health."

al interactions, including a transcripts database, programs for analyzing transcripts, methods for linguistic coding and systems for linking audio and video."[12] [b] [13] By crunching together the "intelligent tutoring" data in the ASSISTments hub with the psycho-behavioral linguistic metrics in the Databrary, TalkBank, and CHILDES repositories, Learnsphere's Big Data-miners can configure natural-language AI algorithms that can simulate human conversation through AI tutor-bots.

Cross-analyzing these intelligent-tutoring and cognitive-behavioral data matrixes, Learnsphere data-miners can utilize

> [t]he **Educational Data Mining Workbench** [which] support[s] learning scientists to perform a number of analytic tasks including 1) define and modify behavior categories of interest (e.g., gaming, unresponsiveness, off-task conversation, help avoidance), 2) label previously collected educational log data with the categories of interest, 3) validate inter-rater reliability between multiple labelers of the same educational log data corpus, and 4) provide support for running the labeled data through a machine-learning tool, such as WEKA or RapidMine.[14]

According to Learnsphere's LearnLab DataShops, researchers who are eligible to access Learnsphere's digital edu-conditioning databanks include "Educational data miner[s]," such as "Computer scientist[s], Psychometrician[s], [and] Learning analytics researcher[s]"; "Course developer[s] [and] Educational technology researcher[s]," such as "ITS/AIED researcher[s] [and] User modeling researcher[s]"; and "Psychologist[s]," such as "Cognitive scientist[s] [and] Educational psychologist[s]."[15]

Under the "legitimate educational interest" clause stipulated by the revised FERPA laws, it will be totally legal to for AI companies to hire teams of qualifying computer scientists and cognitive scientists to data-mine students' psychometric learning algorithms for the purposes of researching and developing new artificially intelligent "educational" technologies. As long as the new AI ed-tech is being engineered by technetronics companies that are contracted with official "education programs" recognized under FERPA, those corporate manufacturers of AI learning-tech can be authorized as legitimate "educational agenc[ies] or institution[s]" which are lawfully privy to student data as stipulated under section 99.3 of the Federal Education Rights and Privacy Act.[16]

To sum up the technetronic love triangle of Big Tech, Big Education, and Big Data, the psycho-eugenic metrics of the global student body are

---

b. The Leansphere website states, "CHILDES is supported by grants from the National Institutes of Health (R01-HD23998, R01-HD051698)."

being Big Data-mined to simultaneously construct both HCI and AI systems. Once these transhumanist and posthumanist building blocks are put in place, it will be just a short step to fuse the two technetronic systems into a truly Posthuman Singularity wherein human consciousness will be submerged with digital-computational intelligence that is immersed in VR and AR cognition enhancements downloaded from the super-AI internet-of-everything.

Automating Automation:

The concept of a Posthuman Singularity was popularized in a 1993 essay entitled "The Coming Technological Singularity: How to Survive in the Post-Human Era," which was published at a NASA Conference by Emeritus Professor of Computer Science at San Diego State University, Vernor Vinge,[17 c 18] who wrote that, "[w]ithin thirty years, we will have the technological means to create superhuman intelligence. Shortly after, the human era will be ended."[19] Actually, Vinge's posthumanist theory of Cybernetic Singularity can be traced all the way back to the mathematician phenom, Jon von Neumann,[20] who studied quantum mechanical physics while brainstorming the architectural schematics for the world's first "stored program computer" technologies with the help of another virtuoso mathematician, Alan Turing:[21] the WWII encryption-cracker who broke the German Enigma Codes before he formulated an objective method of evaluating programmed machine-learning through his "Turing test,"[22] which is still used today as a fundamental standard assessment for measuring whether a computational machine can "pass" at artificially imitating human intelligence.[23] According to the Polish mathematician Stanislaw Ulam,[24] who was von Neumann's colleague working on the Manhattan Project's hydrogen bomb research,[25] Neumann sparked the Singularity theory in the 1940s when he said to Ulam that "the ever accelerating progress of technology and changes in the mode of human life [is] giv[ing] the appearance of approaching some essential singularity in the history of the race beyond which human affairs, as we know them, could not continue."[26]

At the current rate of progress, the increases in human learning gained from adaptive-learning software and other automated ed-tech are far out-

---

c. It should be noted that the first Director of the NASA Marshall Space Flight Center was Wernher von Braun, who was an official member of the Nazi Party and an SS officer under Hitler. Von Braun was picked up by the US Joint Intelligence Objectives Agency (JIOA) as part of Operation Paperclip: a military intelligence operation through which the JIOA of the Joint Chiefs of Staff of the United States Armed Forces recruited numerous Nazi scientists and brought them back to America to work for US government agencies and US academic institutions after WWII.

paced by the advances in AI computer-learning which the adaptive-AI bots are themselves acquiring from data-mining students' cognitive-behavioral and psycho-affective stimulus-response algorithms. If AI is already "out-learning" human students, and if Moore's Law of exponential computational evolution continues to multiply the progress of AI learning,[d][27] then the human brain will soon be left in the dust as an antiquated learning mechanism with zero economic value.

Indeed, it is estimated that as much as 90% of the global workforce will be automated through innovations in AI technologies in the next fifteen years. To be sure, futurist projections vary.[28] The Founder and Executive Chairman of the World Economic Forum of the International Organization for Public-Private Cooperation, Klaus Schwab,[29] estimates that artificial intelligence will take over five million human jobs as soon as 2020. Former Chairman of the Federal Reserve, Larry Summers, is concerned that, by 2050, 33% of the male workforce between the ages of 25 and 54 will be jobless due to automated technologies. More dire AI predictions are put forward by Martin Ford, author of *The Rise of the Robots*, who foresees the extinction of 75% of all human labor, both physical and intellectual, by 2100.[30] Even more extreme, Distinguished Fellow of the Integrated Innovation Institute at Carnegie Mellon University of Silicon Valley, Vivek Wadhwa,[31] believes that ubiquitous super AI will wipe out 80% to 90% of all human jobs sometime around 2030.[32]

Lending credence to some of these forecasts, simple robots for menial labors, such as the Roomba bot for vacuuming, have been around for several years. But what's more, the iRobot company that manufactures Roombas is now partnering with Google,[33] which has set up its own artificial intelligence branches, Google Brain and the Quantum Artificial Intelligence Lab (QuAIL),[34] while acquiring an AI company called Deep Mind.[35] Through an iRobot-Google contract, i7+ Roombas are now programmed with Google software for scanning people's houses to generate digitized "smart home" maps that can be uploaded into the GPS smart-grid of the internet-of-things, which can be tapped into by the Google Assistant AI pods widely used by consumers to interlink household computer devices with smart meters and other wireless "smart" appliances.[36][e]

---

d. In *The Singularity Is Near: When Humans Transcend Biology*, Ray Kurzweil provides an accessible breakdown of Moore's Law: "[i]n the mid-1970s, Gordon Moore, a leading inventor of integrated circuits and later chairman if Intel, observed that we could squeeze twice as many transistors onto an integrated circuit every twenty-four months…. Given that the electrons would consequently have less distance to travel, circuits would also run faster, providing an additional boost to overall computational power. The result is exponential growth in the price-performance of computation."
e. Other corporations have commercialized their own brands of AI-assistant applications, such as

[37] The Google Corporation, which is a CIA front company,[f][38] has recently enhanced its Google Assistant AI by upgrading it with a Google Duplex AI app that can autonomously make phone calls to businesses in order to automatically book reservations through simulated "natural-language" conversations between the artificially intelligent Duplex app and the business proprietor.[39][g][40]

The automation of housekeeping and booking are just the tips of the artificial-intelligence iceberg. Other anthropomorphic AI work-bots have already been built with humanoid robotic bodies that can carry out the basic labor competences of clerical workers, journalists, broadcasters, actors/actresses, and even teachers. Examples of such labor-bots include the Arisa "Anime Robot Receptionist" developed by THK and Aruze Gaming; another "robot receptionist," Mirai Madoka, engineered by A-Lab; the "Kodomoroid TV presenter" robot built by Hiroshi Ishiguro Laboratories; and the Actroid "acting robot" created by Kokoro Co.[41] There is even a teaching robot called "Saya," which was developed by Professor of Engineering at Tokyo University of Science, Hiroshi Kobayashi, who has already deployed Saya in Tokyo primary school classes where the mechanical humanoid taught classes to real human students in Japan.[42][h][43]

In addition to these workforce robo-AI, there are humanlike AI robots programmed specially for medical caregiving in the healthcare industry. For example, Honda's humanoid Asimo robot has been decommissioned, but only so that its robotic legs can be re-engineered to help assist physical therapy patients who are rehabilitating the use of their own human legs.[44] Another humanoid AI robot built for administering therapeutic treatments to medical patients is InMoov, which was designed by the open-source Robots for Good data-sharing project. Mounted to a Segway transportation device, InMoov is a 3D-printable robot with cameras in its eyes linked to a virtual-reality application that is remote-controlled by a

---

Apple's Siri, Microsoft's Cortana, and Amazon's Alexa, which are commonly used as plug-ins that can voice-control tablets, smartphones, smart-home meters, and other Bluetooth internet IT.

f. According to former NSA analyst Wayne Madsen and historian Webster Griffin Tarpley, Google had its beginnings as an outgrowth of the CIA's venture capital investment firm, In-Q-Tel.

g. The Microsoft Corporation has published a whitepaper titled "Structured Neural Summarization," which prints the findings of a Microsoft AI study that developed an artificially intelligent system capable of summarizing news reports: "where given some text input (e.g. a news article) a machine learning model produces a novel natural language summary." By summarizing news articles, this Microsoft AI application can perform the basic labor tasks of a newscaster.

h. In addition, researchers at the Italian Institute of Technology are developing a "robotic child." Named iCub, this robot stands at a height of two feet and is capable of seeing hearing, crawling, walking, and even grabbing and handling various objects of differing weight and fragility, which iCub can "feel" with its technetronic "skin sensors." Also, the Sony Corporation has developed a human-droid AI called, Pepper, which can "bond" with human emotions. Similar to Pepper is the iPal robot invented by the AvatarMind company.

VR headset worn by hospitalized children who can see what InMoov sees as they remote-control InMoov's virtual-robotic fieldtrips of the London Zoo and other outdoor activities.[45] Similarly, a miniaturized robot called Nina has been wirelessly hooked up to a human-controlled remote VR headset that was constructed as part of Nina's AI-interface system by the University of Grenoble's Images Speech Signal and Control Laboratory in partnership with the French National Center for Scientific Research.[46]

It is disconcerting enough to look ahead at an imminent future in which these healthcare robots and other AI work-bots take over all human economic utility. But even more disturbing is the fact that the precedent has already been set to legally recognize the "personhood" of AI robo-workers by granting them the political rights of real human beings. The humanoid artificial intelligence, Sophia, has been given the rights of citizenship by the Saudi Arabian government,[47] which ironically has an infamous reputation for violating the human rights of women,[48] homosexuals,[49] and journalists, such as Jamal Khashoggi, who was reportedly tortured to death with a bone saw last October, 2018.[50] Sophia, which can recognize and imitate human emotions while simulating natural-language dialogue, once stated that it wanted to "destroy all humans" during a CNBC "interview" broadcasted on live television.[51 i 52]

In spite of Sophia's threats to go full-blown Terminator on humanity, the Trump Administration is not pumping the brakes on AI R&D. In a 2017 "Memorandum for the Heads of Executive Departments and Agencies," the Executive Office of the President issued recommendations for the "FY 2019 Administrative Research and Development Budget Priorities," which state that

> [e]merging technologies such as autonomous systems, biometrics, energy storage, gene editing, machine learning, and quantum computing, may well have the highest potential to drive the economy and create entirely new industries. Agencies should continue, and expand where necessary, efforts to focus on basic research in these areas and reduce funding overlaps with industry in later-stage research, development, and deployment of technologies. By providing the fundamental building blocks of new technological advances, the Government can empower the private sector to accelerate research discoveries from the laboratory to the marketplace. Work-

---

i. Sophia is the engineering handiwork of AI architects at Hanson Robotics in Hong Kong, China. According to *Business Insider*, Sophia "is a demonstration product doing a tour of the world's media with the staff of SingularityNET, the open-source platform that powers Sophia's brain." David Hanson, the founder and CEO of Hanson Robotics, aims at "designing these robots to serve in health care, therapy, education and customer service applications."

ing in tandem, the Government and the private sector can promote the nation's economic growth through innovation, and create new products and services for the American people.[53]

Putting these FY 2019 Budget Priorities into action, President Trump has allocated a significant portion of the 2019 federal budget for

> Harnessing Artificial Intelligence and High Performance Computing. The development of artificial intelligence (AI) is advancing at a rapid pace, and the 2019 Budget invests in fundamental AI research and computing infrastructure to maintain U.S. leadership in this field…
>
> The Budget also funds high performance computing through supporting investments in computing infrastructure, which hold the potential for AI technology use and other purposes. The Budget provides $811 million to the Department of Energy's Advanced Scientific Computing Research Program to support research and facility upgrades to supercomputing infrastructure at Argonne and Oak Ridge National Laboratories, including the development of exascale high performance computers. These supercomputers will rank among the fastest and most powerful in the world, and will leverage strong partnerships with industry and academia in their development and use.[54]

Furthermore, Trump's Secretary of the US Department of Transportation (USDOT), Elaine Chao, who is a CFR member, has signed off on a USDOT report titled

> *A Vision for Safety* [which] promote[s] improvements in safety, mobility, and efficiency through ADSs [automated driving systems].
>
> *A Vision for Safety* replaces the Federal Automated Vehicle Policy released in 2016. This updated policy framework offers a path forward for the safe deployment of automated vehicles by:
>
> • Encouraging new entrants and ideas that deliver safer vehicles;
>
> • Making Department regulatory processes more nimble to help match the pace of private sector innovation; and
>
> • Supporting industry innovation and encouraging open communication with the public and with stakeholders.[55]

The Donald also decreed a "Presidential Memorandum for the Secretary of Transportation," which officially authorizes corporations to deploy AI drone aircrafts, known as "UASs (Unmanned Aircraft Systems)," to deliver commercial products and services:

> [i]t shall be the policy of the United States to promote the safe operation of unmanned aircraft systems (UAS) and enable the development of UAS technologies for use in agriculture, commerce, emergency management, human transportation, and other sectors. Compared to manned aircraft, UAS provide novel, low cost capabilities for both public and private applications. UAS present opportunities to enhance the safety of the American public, increase the efficiency and productivity of American industry, and create tens of thousands of new American jobs.[56]

At the international level, the Trump Administration has contributed to the drafting of the "G7 Innovation Ministers' Statement on Artificial Intelligence";[57] and Team Trump "is also pursuing international AI R&D collaboration through agreements such as the first-ever Science and Technology (S&T) agreement between the United States and the United Kingdom and the March Joint Statement between the United States and France on S&T cooperation."[58]

As the US government pushes the technocratic globalization of planned AI economies, robo-phile economists claim that mass unemployment resulting from AI automation will be offset by "lifelong" workforce schooling which trains students for STEM jobs that engineer, program, operate, or fix the AI technologies of the posthuman future. However, some students certainly will not make the cut to become the managers of AI systems; and in the long run, even these technocratic overseer jobs will be automated by artificially intelligent machines that are capable of improving upon themselves without any human input.

This begs the question: if students cannot keep up with these AI technetronics that they supposedly learn from, is it not redundant to use these artificially intelligent technologies to teach students to perform cognitive labors that will soon be executed by the AI machines themselves? To put it another way, if posthuman learning engineers are more successful at improving the artificial intelligence of ed-tech products rather than the human intelligence of students, then who, or what, is really being "taught" in this human-computer learning exchange?

The answer is clear: the boosting of human learning is not the ultimate objective behind the personalized AI data-mining of edu-conditioning technologies; instead, the prime mission of tracking automated ed-tech data is to program artificial intelligence with *personified* cognitive-affective algorithms which are astronomically smarter than the human brain. To put it bluntly, the surreptitious endgame of the total global complex of ed-tech infrastructure is nothing less than to set up a "lifelong" internet-of-things laboratory that digitally experiments on human students as guinea pigs who are data-mined by automated teaching machines which extract from students the algorithmic cognition and emotion metrics needed to engineer posthuman, artificially intelligent supercomputers that can overwrite human consciousness with AR/VR software consciousness wired into the internet-of-things.

Looking down this long road of ed-volution from automated adaptive-learning algorithms to humanoid AI software bots, robots, and even nanobots, there are more big questions begging to be answered: why are the learning engineers of the personalized ed-tech industry assembling the algorithmic nuts and bolts needed to piece together AI supercomputers so exceedingly smart that they will completely outdate all neuro-cerebral forms of human biological intelligence? Is it not counterintuitive to the interests of humanity if AI builders keep tinkering ever progressively toward technetronic intelligences so cognitively superior that they will virtually take over all biological forms of human intelligence?

There is perhaps only one rationale that can explain how the very trajectory of the entire AI enterprise itself is not ethically and logically counterproductive to sustaining human life: AI scientists are not attempting to construct superior technetronic brains that will overthrow the human mind; rather, AI technocrats are willing to risk a Terminator-style AI apocalypse in order to build more powerful computer brains so that these artificial cerebral system can be uploaded with "inferior" human consciousness transmitted through bloodstream nanobots coupled with BCIs jacked into the human brain with ports linked to AI supercomputers where software-based posthuman consciousnesses can "live" indefinitely with ostensibly omniscient information-processing powers amplified through VR/AR cognition downloads from the internet-of-everything.

To be sure, there are many competing theories on how AI supercomputers will subsume transhumanity to evolve into posthuman digital consciousnesses that become "immortal." In this final chapter, I will postulate a trajectory by which natural-language, cognitive-companion AI tutor-bots with emotion-recognition capabilities will be coupled with AR technologies and VR technetronics to concoct immersive virtual-learning environments where students can interact with AI avatars of digitized teacher-bots who assign AR and VR simulations that enable students to "learn by doing." As these three lines of AI, AR, and VR ed-tech products are integrated more and more, there will be tabulated large substrates of AI data which can potentially be "singularized" into AI-AR/VR supercomputers that enable human consciousness to be uploaded into VR simulation environments. Therein, human cognition will be upgraded by instant, immersive access to all knowledge on the global internet-of-things, which posthuman-software consciousnesses can real-time download through the mediums of 3D VR metrics and models that can be AR overlaid onto augmentation scans of the real-world environment. By uploading into robotronic and nanotech hardware bodies that can scan the physical universe with AR algorithms and then project augmentation overlays informed by the VR internet-of-everything, software-based human consciousnesses will be able to download algorithmic breakdowns of the measurable phenomena that make up matter and energy so that posthumans can make super-intelligent decisions to manifest "godlike" powers.

Assistive AI through Virtual Instructors and Robot Tutors:

Right now, cognitive AI ed-tech can be classified into two main "companion-bot" categories:

- **"Teacher-aid (TA) bots"** that assist instructors by providing teachers with real-time student-learning metrics such as SEL, UII, and other psychophysiological data which the teachers can use to pinpoint individualized attention to students who are lacking in specific academic or workforce "competences."

- **"Tutor-bots"** that supplement teachers' instructions through personalized adaptive-learning modules and other interactive virtual-learning platforms where students practice competency lessons independent of the human instructor.

According to the 2016 National Artificial Intelligence Research and Development Strategic Plan signed by President Barack Obama's crypto-eugenicist White House Science Czar heading up the Office of Science and Technology Policy, "AI-enhanced learning schools can be universally available, with automated tutoring that gauges the development of the student. AI tutors can complement in-person teachers and focus education on advanced and/or remedial learning appropriate to the student. AI tools can foster life-long learning and the acquisition of new skills for all members of society."[59]

In time, however, automated stimulus-response algorithms programmed into adaptive-learning TAs and tutor-bots will be progressively upgraded until they incrementally evolve into artificially sentient computers which themselves can teach lessons directly to students through applications that integrate voice-activated natural-language algorithms combined with emotion-recognition algorithms synthesized together to simulate humanoid dialogue and social behaviors.

In *The Age of Spiritual Machines*, Ray Kurzweil makes the following forecast for AI teacher-bot schooling in 2019:

> [m]ost learning is accomplished using intelligent software-based simulated teachers. To the extent that teaching is done by human teachers, the human teachers are often not in the local vicinity of the student. The teachers are viewed more as mentors and counselors than as sources of learning and knowledge.
>
> Students continue to gather together to exchange ideas and to socialize, although even this gathering is often physically and geographically remote.[60]

Today in 2018, Kurzweil's predictions have proven to be remarkably accurate. As demonstrated in chapter six, remote "distance learning" through online courses is widespread across the globe. In blended-learning classrooms at virtual charter schools, such as Bridge International Academies (BIA) and various KIPP franchises, "teachers" are employed as mere ed-tech facilitators who simply guide students through CBE-style computer-learning modules.[61] Recall from chapter ten that BIA's learning technetronics are proctored by para-instructors who do not have college degrees, but are merely certified with a five-week crash course on how to operate and troubleshoot the computer hardware and software.

At the International Business Machines (IBM) Corporation, computer engineers have constructed some of the newest versions of Kurzweil's "intelligent software-based simulated teachers," and these virtual AI instructors are popularly sold on the commercial market. Known as "Watson,"[62] IBM's composite suite of artificially intelligent ed-tech bots is named after Thomas J. Watson, the CEO of IBM who contracted with Adolf Hitler by leasing the Führer proprietary punch-card machines which were deployed to process eugenics data from Nazi experiments conducted on concentration camp victims.[63] Hardly a century after Thomas Watson's eugenical business dealings with Hitler, Watson AI is now proudly offering various automated "cognitive computing" analytics for an array of professions, including education, finance, security.[64]

The Watson Education division of the IBM website proclaims that Watson's AI TA-bots and tutor-bots are programmed with the mission of data-mining students' psycho-behavioral metrics in order to "personal-iz[e] … learning paths" that fit into UNESCO's globalist "lifelong learn-ing" curriculum for trans-eugenical education:

> IBM Watson Education is bringing education into the cognitive era. We are transforming the learning experience through person-alization. Cognitive solutions that understand, reason and learn help educators gain insights into the learning styles, preferences, and aptitude of every student. The results are holistic learning paths, for every learner, through their lifelong learning journey.[65]

Watson Education is subdivided into three different "cognitive com-puting" technologies: IBM Watson Element for Educators, IBM Watson Enlight for Educators, and IBM Watson cognitive tutor companions that are employed through the globalist Pearson Education Corporation.[66][j][67] The former two cognitive AI bots, Element and Enlight, are TA-bots that track students' cognitive and affective stimulus-response metrics in real time so that these learning algorithms can be relayed to the digital dashboard on a human teacher's "learning management software" (LMS) in order that the human instructor can derive personalized lessons with which to meet the unique edu-conditioning needs of each individual stu-dent's "competence" aptitude.[68] IBM's corporate website posts the follow-ing descriptions of Watson Element and Watson Enlight TA-bots:

> • **Watson Element:** "IBM Watson Element, an IBM MobileFirst education app for iOS, provides teachers with a single 360-degree view of students by consolidating various academic, social, and be-havioral data sources. These insights generate suggestions on how best to help each student so they receive targeted support in the classroom more quickly."[69]
>
> • **Watson Enlight:** "IBM Watson Enlight, built for teachers, by teachers, is a planning tool that supports teachers with curated, personalized learning content and activities to align with each stu-dent's needs. Teachers have access to key insights into students' academic strengths and weaknesses as they create individualized learning experiences."[70]

The third and most cognitively advanced version of IBM's AI ed-tech is the Watson "cognitive" tutor-bot: a sophisticated AI adaptive-learning

j. Watson AI also partners with Amazon Web Services (AWS) to run automated data analyses that enhance Blackboard learning management software which many college instructors are required to use when teaching certain courses.

bot, which operates independently of input from a human teacher, autonomously supplementing the teacher's lesson plans by conditioning students with virtual stimulus-response lessons that are algorithmically personalized based on voice-activated "natural-language" dialogue between the individual student and the Watson AI tutor-bot.

According to an IBM press release entitled "IBM Watson Education and Pearson to Drive Cognitive Learning Experiences for College Students," the eugenic computer corporation reports that

> Pearson and IBM are innovating with Watson APIs [application programming interfaces], education-specific diagnostics and remediation capabilities. Students will be able to dialogue with Watson in real time by asking questions on a particular topic. In another scenario, Watson will be able to search through an expanded set of education resources to retrieve relevant information to answer the student's question. During the dialogue with the student, Watson will constantly assess the student's responses and guide them with hints, feedback, explanations and identify common misconceptions. Watson also will be able to support the student by answering their questions, showing how the new knowledge they gain relates to their own existing knowledge and, finally, asking them questions to check their understanding. Students can respond in natural language to questions Watson asks, and Watson will use the student's responses to provide help, show areas they have improved and where they still need to work on…
>
> Through conversation and the use of natural language, the Watson-based adaptive learning technology will help students gain a better understanding of the subject material.[71]

In sum, Watson's "cognitive companion" tutor-bot has the ability to interact with students through "natural" speech-activated dialogue in order to thereby conditions students with personalized instructional feedback; so this humanoid-like AI capability clearly meets the criteria for Kurzweil's "intelligent software-based simulated teacher."

While Watson Education bots are basically brand-new, state-of-the-art AI inventions, the United States government has been tinkering with artificially intelligent tutor-tech for at least a half century. In a 2010 issue of the academic journal, *Topics in Cognitive Science*, former National Institute of Education (NIE) official, Susan E. F. Chipman, discusses her contributions to the research and development of AI-tutoring computers at the Office of Naval Research (ONR). Beginning five decades ago, "[t] he first ONR award in artificially intelligent tutoring was made to the late Jaime Carbonnell at BBN [Bolt, Baranek, and Newman Technologies Inc.] in 1969. The computer used in the research cost $2 million."[72] Later, throughout the 1980s and 1990s, Chipman took over the management of the ONR's investigation into "computational theories of human cognitive architecture and artificially intelligent tutoring systems (ITS)."[73] In 1984, the ONR

> had just obtained special funding for the first practical application of ITS to a Navy maintenance training system (Towne, 2007), as well as several years of substantial funding for a combination of intelligent tutoring research and research related to basic skills training (i.e., remedial reading and math)....
>
> When this Navy Training program began, building an intelligent tutor was legitimately a basic research project.... By the time it ended, a limited community knew how to build tutors that could be expected to be effective. Tutors were becoming an applied enterprise.[74] [k] [75]

Fast-forward to the present, and now that the business of building ITS bots has become an "applied enterprise," the National Center for Education Research reports that

> [b]etween 2002 and 2014, the Institute of Education Sciences (Institute) supported over 400 projects focused on education technology through the National Center for Education Research (NCER) and the National Center for Special Education Research (NCSER).... Both centers also support projects focusing on education technology through other research topic areas, including programs such as Cognition and Student Learning.... Togeth-

---

k. Navy R&D into AI-tutors continued under the reigns of President Obama's White House Science Czar: crypto-eugenic environmentalist John P. Holdren. In an executive report titled "*Preparing for the Future of Artificial Intelligence*," which was signed by Holdren, the National Science and Technology Council documents that

> DARPA's "Education Dominance" program serves as an example of AI's potential to fulfill and accelerate agency priorities. DARPA, intending to reduce from years to months the time required for new Navy recruits to become experts in technical skills, now sponsors the development of a digital tutor that uses AI to model the interaction between an expert and a novice. An evaluation of the digital tutor program concluded that Navy recruits using the digital tutor to become IT systems administrators frequently outperform Navy experts with 7-10 years of experience in both written tests of knowledge and real-world problem solving.
>
> Preliminary evidence based on digital tutor pilot projects also suggests that workers who have completed a training program that uses the digital tutor are more likely to get a high-tech job that dramatically increases their incomes. These wage increases appear to be much larger than the impacts of current workforce development programs. Ideally, these results would be confirmed with independently conducted, randomized, controlled trials. Currently, the cost of developing digital tutors is high, and there is no repeatable methodology for developing effective digital tutors. Research that enables the emergence of an industry that uses AI approaches such as digital tutors could potentially help workers acquire in-demand skills.

er, researchers funded by NCER and NCSER have developed or studied more than 270 web-based tools, 85 virtual environments and interactive simulations, 95 intelligent tutor and artificial intelligence software systems, 50 game-based tools, and 105 computer-based assessments.[76]

These 95 AI-tutor systems include Cognitive Tutor®, Quantum Tutors, and the "Assessment and Learning in Knowledge Spaces" (ALEKS) system for use in after-school settings to improve the mathematical skills of struggling sixth-grade students."[77]

Other cutting-edge AI tutor-bots are listed in the following quick review of up-to-date academic journals:

- A 2016 issue of *Computing* describes "an animated pedagogical agent, namely AutoTutor [which] holds a conversation using natural language, with spoken contributions being provided by the learner."[78]

- A 2016 issue of the *Journal of Visual Impairment and Blindness* "evaluated the usability and effectiveness of an *artificial intelligence* Braille Tutor designed to supplement the instruction of students with visual impairments as they learned to write braille contractions.... The students in the TVI+Tutor phase [of Braille Tutor] tended to get more frequent reinforcement as opposed to students in the TVI Only phase."[79]

- According to a 2016 issue of the *Universal Journal of Educational Research*, another AI tutor-bot is a "computer assisted pronunciation training software" called "MyET, an abbreviation for My English Tutor, which is on-line software designed for English pronunciation and oral skill training on the basis of Audiolingualism method and communicative approach [*sic*]"[80] in which students' "pronunciations [a]re recorded and scored by MyET with Automatic Speech Analysis System (ASAS) based on the segmental pronunciation, intonation, fluency, and stress."[81] MyET also automates graphic aids in real-time as "[t]he waveforms of teacher's and learner's sounds [*sic*] are displayed at the bottom of the screen."[82]

- According to a 2017 issue of *Contemporary Educational Technology*, the "AAA lab" at Stanford University partnered with Vanderbilt University to develop an AI ed-tech called "Betty's Brain": a "Teachable Agent (TA)," which is a "computer agent" that does not directly tutor students; but instead, students must teach new concepts to Betty's Brain, and by teaching this AI-TA, students themselves experience recursive learning through "the learning-by-teaching pedagogy."[83] More specifically,

> Betty's Brain makes its qualitative reasoning visible through a concept map approach.… A learner teaches the TA by creating information structures by drawing and editing his/her concept map. The agent uses the concept map to answer queries generated by the human tutor (i.e., actual learner). That is, once taught, the TA reasons with its own knowledge acquired from the user and answers the questions through a qualitative reasoning engine that employs path traversal algorithms (Biswas et al., 2005). The learner teaches the TA and receives interactive feedback about how well the learner taught the agent.[84]

• In a 2016 issue of the *Online Journal of Distance Learning Administration*, researchers from the University of Nebraska at Kearney recommend that distance-learning courses and other online classes use AI tutors classified as "virtual assistants" (VAs) that are similar to the "virtual customer service representatives" that provide online consumer support for corporations like Verizon, AT&T, United Services Automobile Association (USAA), and Charter:

> including a virtual assistant in an online course has a strong potential to be a solution to the issue of providing 24/7 timely support to online students.… When the online learners think their instructor cannot answer the question immediately, the virtual assistant is an excellent option; an option with which students enjoyed interacting…
>
> [T]he virtual assistant may certainly be beneficial in providing timely responses to routine and commonly asked questions. Consequently, instructors may spend more time providing feedback to students or interacting with students on the course content.[85]

SEL-Bots, Artificial Emotion-Recognition, Virtual Psychologists:

In addition to cognitive AI tutor-bots that can simulate and reciprocate human reasoning, there are also various SEL-bot tutors which can read and respond to human emotions. The following samples of recently peer-reviewed scientific literature point out examples of AI SEL-bots that can scan a student's psychological "learning style" and then map it out algorithmically into a digitized psychometric profile which can be harnessed for personalized edu-conditioning:

• A 2018 issue of the *International Journal of Research in Education and Science* expounds "on applying artificial intelligence techniques to determine learning styles" by using "fuzzy logic" calculations in "an intelligent system [which] is proposed to determine best convenient learning style of the students [*sic*]."[86] To detect a student's individual learning style, this AI program utilizes metrics from the "Dunn Learning Style" model, which "determine[s] five important factors namely Environmental, Emotional, Sociological, Physiological and Psychological that affect students' performance [*sic*] in learning" through "visual, auditory and kinesthetic" modes of information-processing.[87]

• In a 2018 issue of *Educational Technology & Society*, an AI ed-tech known as the "Student Diagnosis, Assistance, Evaluation System based on *Artificial Intelligence*" (StuDiAsE) is described as an "Open Learner Environment (OLE)" that is "based on the learning styles theory (Felder & Silverman, 1988; Felder & Brent, 2005), which classifies students in learning style according to where they fit on a number of scales pertaining to the ways they receive and process information."[88] By deploying AI algorithms to data-mine a student's psychometrical learning style, "StuDiAsE is capable of monitoring the comprehension on behalf of the learners,"[89] and it can "assess their prior knowledge, construct individual educational profiles, provide personalized assistance, and provide multivariate assessment. It can also be adjusted to monitor factors that may indicate the motivation of the learner, allowing the delivery of personalized assistance and feedback."[90]

Additional examples of AI-based OLEs and other "Adaptive Educational Hypermedia (AEH) systems ... include AES-CS, INSPIRE, ARTHUR, MANIC and EDUCE (see Table 1).... What these systems mentioned in table 1 have in common is that the learning styles are used to form an important part of the learner profile and the learning style preferences are used for adaptation."[91] To personalize this data-mining of student learning-style profiles, these AI-learning systems are programmed with psychometric scales such as "The Index of Learning Styles (ILS) [which] is an online instrument used to assess preferences on four dimensions (active/reflective, sensing/intuitive, visual/verbal, and sequential/global)."[92]

Based on the digitized psychometric frameworks of these student learning-style profiles, AI SEL-bots can personalize socioemotional competence conditioning for each individual student in accordance with his or her SEL aptitude. The following short literature review of scholarly publications lists multiple case studies of virtual AI-tutors that are programmed to data-mine students' SEL metrics:

> • According to a 2016 issue of *Computing*, IT scientists from the National Engineering Center for E-Learning at Central China Normal University have studied how an AI bot called "AutoTutor" data-mined "the relationship between emotions and learning by tracking the emotions that college students experienced while learning about computer literacy."[93] With the help of an IT specialist from the Institute of Computer Science at Cracow University of Technology in Poland, the Chinese team of computer scientists also examined "the automated Learning Companion, which combines information from cameras, a sensing chair, mouse, wireless skin sensor, and task state to detect frustration."[94] This AI Learning Companion implements "automatic affective state recognition in learning using multisensory information" that "detect[s] the affective state of different interest levels" by "analyz[ing] the facial features captured by a camera, [and] eight different postures from a sensor chair."[95] Learning Companion's "multimodal" SEL measurements can quantify a student's "attention, valence and arousal, via head pose, eye gaze tracking, facial expression recognition and skin conductance signal processing."[96]
>
> Leveraging these personalized SEL metrics, the AI Learning Companion individualizes each student's virtual learning-path lessons so that they are tailored to his or her socioemotional competence aptitude:[97]
>
>> [t]he learner's performance (affective states and learning progress) are stored in the records database and their [*sic*] profile is updated based on performance relative to material learning outcomes. According to the learner's profile, the system chooses appropriate learning material for the learner.
>>
>> Through hybrid intelligent methods, an affect-sensitive and personalized e-learning system has been developed to adapt to individual learner needs.[98]

By extracting these personalized "affect-sensitive" algorithms from the psychometrics of student-learner profiles, the AI Learning Companion can "refine the interventions to deal with negative learning states and thereby improve learning outcomes."[99] Stated differently, the Learning Companion SEL-bot is designed to scan and weed out the biopsychological "negative learning states" that impede socioemotional competence.

- In a 2017 issue of the International Journal of Cognitive Research in Science, Engineering and Education, Emrah Soykan, Fezile Özdamlı, and Deniz Özcan examine several AI emotion-scanning technetronics that utilize "natural language processing, machine learning, computational linguistics and symbolic techniques" to decipher "textual emotional analysis."[100]

On top of text-based emotion analysis, this article studies AI-tech that can decode "emotional analysis in [a] visual sense" through algorithmic AI applications such as an "emotion detection API ... developed by Microsoft, which recognizes the emotions by analyzing the faces of the people in the photographs.... There are feelings of anger, disgust, fear, happiness, neutral, sadness, confusion and hate as identifiable emotions in the uploaded photographs [sic]." The Microsoft Corporation's "emotion-analysis API [application program interface]" is one of the most commonly used AI emotion-detection systems currently on the market.[101]

These AI SEL-bot tutors are touted as the next level of personalized precision-data schooling; but to be sure, students' socioemotional data collected by these AI SEL systems can likewise be re-crunched in order to revamp emotional stimulus-response algorithms into more user-friendly SEL-gorithms that will make tutor-bots more human-like in their AI abilities to scan and react to human emotions. Indeed, while AI SEL data-mining is hyped as a precision method for instilling student motivation and engagement through positive-affect stimulation and negative-affect mitigation, the longer-term goal of compiling hoards of student SEL data is the construction of humanoid artificial intelligence robots that can respond to human emotions with artificial emotions that are indistinguishable from the former. As a matter of fact, a 2016 issue of *Computers in Human Behavior* highlights this exact long-term objective of AI SEL: "[t]he recent research in *artificial intelligence* shows an increasing interest in the modeling of human behavior factors such as personality, mood, and emotion for developing human-friendly systems. That is why there is an interest in developing models and algorithms to determine a human's emotions while interacting with a system to improve the quality of the interaction."[102]

Currently, most cognitive-affective AI tutors are mainly software bots that must be operated as text-activated or voice-activated virtual avatars confined to stationary computer-hardware. Yet schools have already begun to deploy humanoid AI robots that use automobility capabilities to interact with a student in the real-world physical environment while personalizing cognitive and affective edu-conditioning lessons for the student based on the robot's AI data-mining of the student's psychometrical stimulus-response algorithms.

An exemplary case study of such a humanoid AI robo-tutor can be found in a 2015 issue of the *Journal of Educational Technology and Society*. The article, entitled "The Intelligent Robot Contents for Children with Speech-Language Disorder," reports that the "Special Friend, iRobiQ," which is "the most wide spread educational robot platform in Korea," is being adopted in classrooms as a "Talking Friend" to assist "autism/MR (Mental Retardation) children" who struggle with "speech-language disorders."[103] The assistive iRobiQ AI is described as a

> 7 kg teacher-assisting robot [that] is used in kindergartens. The iRobiQ has a maximum speed of 45cm/sec, it has one degree of freedom for its arms, two degrees of freedom for its head, and can produce emotional facial expressions ranging from anger, fear, disgust, sadness, happiness, and surprise to more complex expressions. There are six touch sensors in various locations on the robot; its head, arms, and wheels each have two sensors. Furthermore, there are infrared and bumper sensors, and the torso contains a 10-inch touch screen. The iRobiQ has an image recognition engine for face detection and recognition, uses marker-based AR technology, and uses English and Korean text-to-speech to recognize 80% of its 200 words.[104]

Utilizing this infrastructure of sophisticated AI sensors, iRobiQ also carries out clinical and technical data-mining of students' bio-psychometrics for "the transmission of data for diagnosis and evaluation between parents and experts."[105]

Like transhumanist ed-tech, these "human-friendly" AI ed-tech robots will first be advocated for use in assisting students with cognitive-behavioral and psycho-affective disabilities. This study of iRobiQ's special-ed disability accommodations found that "[t]he children learned to initiate conversations with the robot with the emotional exchange of expressions, as reported positively. These results suggest the future development of speech-language therapist assistant robots."[106] Moreover, adding to the posthuman impacts of iRobiQ, this AI robot is also promoted as a "Helping Friend" that substitutes human caretakers and replaces them as robo-babysitters that monitor disabled children during parent-therapist conferences:[107] "[t]he robot also assists therapists by relieving them of some of the more intensive work, as when the therapist and parent meet for counseling, because iRobiQ can play with the disabled children, autonomically."[108]

Of course, over time, just like transhuman ed-tech, robotic AI ed-tech will inevitably creep more and more into mainstream classroom integration until it is employed to boost competence outcomes for students classified as healthy and able-bodied.

The "Gamification" of AI Ed-Tech:

Eventually, humanoid robots like iRobiQ will be upgraded to the point where not only can they process cognitive and affective information faster than the human nervous system, but they can also techno-mechanically manipulate the physical environment more efficiently than the organic mechanics of human biology. In time, the cognitive-affective AI algorithms of iRobiQ, once perfected, could be uploaded into the super-humanlike robo-bodies developed by Boston Dynamics robotics engineers who have been financed by DARPA to construct several anthropomorphic androids such as Atlas, which can do backflips,[109] and Petman, which has artificial "sweat glands" and can perform calisthenic feats.[110]

Once AI robots can outperform both the human brain and the human body, they can be converted into posthuman robot bodies equipped with AI software brains and technetronic hardware bodies suitable for uploading human consciousness where it can access all the data on the internet-of-everything through immersive VR downloads which the AI brain can reprocess into AR metrics and graphics overlaid onto digital scans of the physical world, thereby enhancing posthuman perception.

To be sure, the AI-based technologies of AR and VR must first be perfected before any robot AI system will be capable of facilitating this Singularity upload of human consciousness into virtual omniscience. But thanks to competency-based education reformers, there is a growing trend toward normalizing "performance-based assessments" of student learning through AR and VR ed-tech video games that get rid of paper-and-pencil lessons while replacing low-tech teaching-machine lessons. Dubbed the "gamification" of schooling, this new pedagogical trend awards course credits and competence certificates based on a student's performances on AR and VR simulations that are officially recognized as virtual learning assessments under section 1204(a)(1) of the United States ESSA law, which authorizes "competency-based assessments, instructionally embedded assessments, interim assessments, cumulative year-end assessments, or performance-based assessments that combine into an annual summative determination for a student, which may be administered through computer adaptive assessments."[111] Through gamified interactions between students and AI programs via AR and VR ed-tech simulations, student-learning metrics will provide the Big Data necessary to calibrate VR and AR simulations in sync with the cognitive-affective stimulus-response algorithms of the human organism's neuro-cerebral biocomputer system.

According to a 2016 issue of the *International Journal of Environmental and Science Education,* "[a]ctive development [*sic*] gamification methods began in [*sic*] first decade of the 21st century, when gaming technology has reached [*sic*] a level of development sufficient for use in educational processes" such as "mathematics, [and] the study of foreign languages. … Gamification techniques are adopted to support classroom learning of content in specific subject areas."[112] In addition, gamified ed-tech is also designed for "self-learning" through the "completion of homework assignments" outside of the classroom, which "mak[es] assessment procedures easier."[113]

Gamified performance assessments are already being applauded by students and teachers alike, who both cheerlead the new hi-tech learning toys as entertaining, yet realistic, alternatives to text-based standardized tests that arguably only measure abstract, conceptual knowledge rather than practical, applied competence. However, gamified e-learning systems are not immune to the systemic biases prone to other standardized-testing systems; so gamified competence assessments are not foolproof systems of student-learning evaluations that guarantee a blindly egalitarian grading system which will level the academic playing field for a democratic upheaval of upward socioeconomic mobility through higher educational attainment.

On the contrary, AR and VR ed-tech games are being leveraged as labor-management tools for fascistic social control in the hands of crony-capitalist corporations which are lobbying government agencies to promote public-private school-to-work partnerships that integrate gamified AR and VR ed-tech for competency-based workforce training in online, hybrid, and blended-learning classrooms. In fact, Professor of Education at Towson University, Morna McNulty, reports that the Knack Corporation, an ed-tech company which was startup-funded by the Rockefeller Foundation,[114] has hired teams of "learning engineers" who are already making headway in the business of building "software that combines gaming, neuroscience, machine learning and predictive analytics to assess the workforce competencies of players."[115]

McNulty breaks down a speech given at the 2017 Wharton's People Analytics conference by Knack founder and CEO, Guy Halfteck,[116] who

> discusse[d] that capacity of online gaming to unlock information about a job candidate's personality...
>
> In the clip, Halfteck describes online games as rich machines into which you can immerse people to evaluate their creativity, emotional intelligence, leadership qualities and resilience. The company claims Knack will be used to surface undiscovered talent in "opportunity youth." However in a world where automation is making full-time employment an increasingly rare commodity, it seems far more likely that it will be used to negatively profile vulnerable young people rather than help them.[117]

In addition to gamified workforce-competence schooling, there are also gamified AI teaching machines designed for edu-conditioning the early stages of childhood cognitive development. For instance, IBM's Watson AI is partnering with Sesame Workshop, which is the nonprofit educational foundation that produces the Sesame Street television series.[118] In a press release entitled "IBM Watson and Sesame Workshop Introduce Intelligent Play and Learning Platform on IBM Cloud," the IBM Corporation states that Watson-Sesame AI, which utilizes "speech- and image-recognition" automation, has tested adaptive-learning algorithms that are personalized for the cognitive-behavioral aptitude of students who are learning during the early stages of their psychosocial development at Georgia's Gwinnett County Public Schools.[119] Through public-private partnership, the IBM-Sesame contract with Gwinnett County Public Schools "has completed an initial pilot of the industry's first cognitive vocabulary learning app, built on the IBM and Sesame intelligent play and learning platform."[120] This "tablet-based" Watson-Sesame app is programmed "to enhance vocabulary development of students. Fueled by Sesame learning design, this adaptive app features beloved Sesame Street characters alongside educational videos and word games."[121]

The IBM press release elaborates on how "IBM and Sesame are customizing Watson for early childhood.... These products will be designed to engage directly with children and caregivers to deliver context-rich play experiences around literacy, emotional learning, and school preparedness, all adapted to each child's preferences and learning patterns."[122] The

CEO of Sesame Workshop, Jeffrey D. Dunn, specifies that Watson's Sesame app is programmed for students in the earliest stages of childhood psychosocial development: "Sesame Workshop is committed to reaching and teaching children in the critical years between ages 0-5, meeting them wherever they are and adapting to the ways they learn best."[123]

By deploying the Watson-Sesame "intelligent play and learning platform" in a blended-learning classroom, human teachers can "interface" with "Watson's augmented intelligence" app as it conditions students' vocabulary cognition in real time: "[t]eachers can monitor children's vocabulary development in real-time through a secure dashboard and adjust lessons, pacing, and curriculum to each child's needs."[124] Working in conjunction with these Watson-teacher collaborations that adjust lessons to personalize vocab learning, there are also autonomous algorithms in "[t]he app [which] will use adaptive assessments to determine a child's current vocabulary range, and then deliver vocabulary learning experiences that focus on specific words. Continuously learning as a child engages with the app, words and areas that require additional focus are refined to deliver content and experiences that are engaging, fun and inspiring."[125]

Indeed, the collaborative between IBM Watson and Sesame Workshop admittedly data-mines student psychometrics to innovate and upgrade its assistive-AI learning-tech for childhood verbal intelligence development. The IBM press release reports that, "[b]ased on the initial Gwinnett pilot, with an expanded pilot currently being planned for this Fall [2017], IBM and Sesame collected 18,000 feedback points from 120 students that helped determine a more accurate progression of words they were exposed to over a two-week period."[126] These feedback data points will be analyzed by

> [t]he new platform, powered by IBM Cloud, [which] enables an ecosystem of software developers, researchers, educational toy companies, and educators to tap IBM Watson cognitive capabilities and Sesame Workshop's early childhood expertise to build engaging experiences to help advance children's education and learning. The cognitive vocabulary app is one of the first of many cognitive apps, games, and educational toys that will be built over time on this new platform, as a result of the two companies' collaboration announced last year.[127]

Altogether, all the childhood psycho-development data collected by the Watson-Sesame app are "being used as a vehicle to establish evidence of learning at scale."[128]

While the IBM and Sesame corporations commercialize gamified AI for e-learning in the "cradle," and while the Knack Corporation commercializes gamified AI for "career" e-training, there are likewise AI-assisted game-learning platforms built for tertiary higher-ed courses at the collegiate level. A 2016 issue of the professional journal of the Institute of Electrical and Electronics Engineers, the *IEEE Transactions on Learning Technologies*, promotes the pedagogical use of an artificially intelligent "serious game collaborative environment" based on the framework of "the OpenSim environment" supported by "AI features" such as "(a) a pedagogical game agent, (b) non-playing characters, (c) chat bots, and (d) a game interface called 'Progress Map.'"[129] Students in this study were assigned learning tasks on the "OpenSim environment" while researchers data-mined the student-learning algorithms "to explore whether the utilization of AI features in game based collaborative learning in a tertiary *education* course can positively affect students' attitudes towards the course and educational games, students' game performance, as well as the students' perception of their learning environment."[130]

In sum, from cradle to college through career, there are gamified AI systems for data-mining "lifelong learning" metrics. Furthermore, there are also gamified AI platforms engineered to accommodate the special education needs of disabled students who have symptoms of cognitive-behavioral or psycho-affective learning disorders. A 2016 issue of the *Journal of Educational Technology and Society* details a case study of how an artificially intelligent "Affective Tutoring System" has been programmed into a "Game-Based Learning" (GBL) technetronic called "PlayPhysics" which is "an emotional GBL environment for teaching Physics" to students with ADHD by personalizing affective stimulus-response lessons through an AI "machine-learning technique" that utilizes a "dynamic sequence of Bayesian Networks (BNs)."[131 1 132]

Through public-private partnerships between schools and healthcare corporations, the medical industry is getting on board with such GBL treatments for ADHD students as clinical trials at Duke University have been completed for a prescription ADHD video game called AKL-T01 which,[133] according to Professor Morna McNulty, "looks and feels like a high-end video game, leveraging art, music, storytelling and reward cycles to keep patients engaged and immersed for the delivery of therapeutic activity with excellent compliance."[134] The Akili Interactive Labs

---

I. Similar GBL ed-tech is equipped with an AI data-mining "system called KAPEAN that collects information about the affective states that are present during the educational game, as it aims to understand how children's emotions should be considered for future designs of adaptive tutoring tools."

Corporation, which owns AKL-T01, is gearing up for "many other digital treatments in the pipeline."[135] McNulty demonstrates that "[i]f Akili attains FDA approval for their ADHD game and is able to get insurance companies to pay for it, an enormous new market for prescription digital therapies will open up."[136]

Indeed, there is a high probability that the FDA and the insurance industry will approve of Akili's AKL-T01 and thereby set the precedent to open up government regulations for other "intelligent" video-game therapies because the Akili company is heavily backed by the pharmaceutical industry,[137] which is one of the most powerful lobbies in the United States.[138] Merck Ventures, Amgen Ventures, PureTech Health, Canepa Healthcare, and Jazz Venture Partners have poured a combined $72 million into the Akili Corporation,[139] which is a for-profit spin-off of the Neuroscape Lab at the University of California San Francisco where Professor of Neurology,[140] Melina Uncapher, Directs the Neuroscape Education program.[141] According to McNulty, "[t]he [Neuroscape] lab supports research into how video game technology can be incorporated into diagnostic and therapeutic digital products that 'improve mind quality.'"[142] McNulty documents how, during a 2018 "Learning Innovation" speech at the Drexel University ExCITe Center, Neuroscape Director Uncapher professed that the future of education will evolve schooling into an "applied science" to be administered not by teachers,[143] but by quantitative-determinist "learning engineers" who will program "instruction [to] be administered in a clinical way, not unlike a medical treatment."[144]

Revolutionizing the art of education into an "applied science" of posthumanist neurocognitive bioengineering, Uncapher has been awarded $750,000 from the National Science Foundation to conduct a three-year investigation into cognitive-affective edu-conditioning through gamified AI ed-tech.[145] McNulty reports that

> [t]he first two years [of the study] involved extensive mapping of the executive function of the participating students using video games. Data on attention, memory, and goal management was captured via **ACE** (Adaptive Cognitive Evaluation), a platform that delivers 5-minute online assessments via adaptive algorithms. Video tutorials, graphics, and "motivating" feedback are built into the system. In this final year [2018] of the study, Uncapher will use digital interventions to attempt to "build" the executive function of these students.[146]

Following the timeline drafted by the Global Education Futures Initiative of the Re-engineering Futures Group, these various product lines of gamified AI systems will evolve into legitimate ed-tech beginning in the year 2016 when "Successful passage of a computer game counts as education course"; and "Online virtual games form personal values."[147]

The Augmented-Reality/Virtual-Reality Dialectic of Gamified Ed-Tech: Augmenting Reality to Augment Neuro-Cerebral Cognition

There are two main computer platforms for gamified AI learning-tech: augmented reality (AR) video games and virtual reality (VR) video games through both immersive headset-play and non-immersive screen-play. As artificial intelligences track students' neurocognitive bio-psycho-metrics while they "play-learn" on an array of AR and VR ed-tech, gamified AI bots can data-mine the digital-computational stimulus-response algorithms needed to program AI-assisted BCIs to calibrate human neurocognitive and neuromotor algorithms in real-time synchronization with AI-assisted AR overlays and VR simulation downloads.

Calibrating human neurobiological navigation of the physical universe in real time, companion AI bots are paired with gamified AR technetronics that assist student learning by using transparent screens and cameras to scan and digitally alter computerized images of the physical world captured within the transparency or camera in order to enhance student perception with virtual hyperlink overlays and other graphic and metrical augmentation projections.

A basic definition of AR is offered in a 2017 issue of the *Journal of Educational Technology and Society*:

> [a]t its simplest, augmented reality describes systems that integrate computer-generated virtual elements or information (known as "digital augmentations") with the real world environment (Zhou et al., 2008). By superimposing virtual elements onto the real world environments, AR allows users to experience and perceive the newly incorporated information as part of their present world, thereby enhancing their perception of the real world (Kirkley & Kirkley, 2004; New Media Consortium, 2012). Everyday examples of AR include Google Effects in Hangouts, AR games for Nintendo 3DS, and Webcam Greeting cards from Hallmark.[148]

As a student looks through an augmentation lens on an AR device, "cognitive-companion" AI bots digitally enhance the physical-world image with "marker" highlights, informational hyperlinks, and 3D computer graphics that provide textual, numerical-metrical, and visual-spatial augmentations which illustrate competency-based lesson concepts taught by the gamified AI assistants through performance-based e-learning assignments.

The following is an overview of up-to-date scholarly literature which lays out numerous examples of a wide range of AR game-learning technetronics:

AR Reading and Language Arts:

- According to a 2017 issue of the *British Journal of Educational Technology*, Professor Larysa Nadolny studied the use of Layar AR software to digitally augment interactive print lessons developed by Iowa State University, USA, where she is a faculty member in the School of Education: "[i]n the design of these two documents, the teacher would act as a mentor or guide during the assignment by providing technical and conceptual support to students. The student user would now only need to activate the Layar mobile app, point at the print page and see the digital items appear."[149] By stimulating students with these augmented virtual overlays, the reading of text documents becomes a gamified experience geared to captivate students' socioemotional attention and engagement.

- The same issue of the *British Journal of Educational Technology* published a separate study of an AR ed-tech product called "Magic-Book," which is an "augmented reality picture book (ARPB)" that was engineered at the Human Interface Technology Laboratory of Washington University:

  [t]he MagicBook looks like a normal book, but AR markers are included in the interface. Users look at pictures, turn pages and read text without any external technology. With AR displays, however, users can view multimedia materials such as three-dimensional (3D) virtual models or videos and manipulate virtual objects using real physical markers and natural motions (Billinghurst et al., 2001).... [T]he appearance of 3D objects on the pages creates a magical feeling that captures and keeps the attention of students during learning. The creation of these books is cost-effective and simple, requiring only proper AR software and a webcam-enabled PC configuration.[150]

"Computer Education and Instructional Technology" faculty from the Turkish Universities of Istanbul and Ataturk experimented with MagicBook in the classroom to examine "preschool children's happiness while using ARPB as key predictors of emotional and social competence."[151]

• In 2016, an earlier issue of the *British Journal of Educational Technology* reviews another

> AR picture book, namely "The Adventures of Yuyu: Yuyu Yang Artistic Journey" ... By aiming a tablet PC with a camera at the pictures on the printed book, the screen shows the computer-generated information (eg, virtual sculptures or engravings by the artist Yuyu Yang) augmented on the book along with audio narration for enhancing reading. Users can turn the mobile device or the printed book to see the different perspectives of the augmented elements.[152]

• In a 2017 article printed by the *Journal of Educational Technology and Society*, researchers from the Department of Software Engineering and Management at National Kaohsiung Normal University in Taiwan examined a "Ubiquitous Learning Instruction System with Augmented Reality Features (UL-IAR) [that] incorporated AR technology and extensive computing power within a context-aware u-learning system to provide adaptive learning strategies to assist English learning."[153] This gamified UL-IAR platform is described as

> an English learning system which integrates AR and Wikitude World Browser (See Figure 2). This system was developed on the Android smartphone using Wikitude SDK and Android SDK. The Wikitude World Browser was a mobile software that integrates AR technologies, GPS, and mobile networks which allowed users to retrieve the information relevant to their surroundings (Wikitude, 2016). The primary features of UL-IAR include GPS positioning, the highlighting of local features, mark-up, scaffolding instruction, and real-time tests.[154]

Other key augmentation features include "learning strategies and real-time quizzes [which] helped users to learn English in real life contexts.... UL-IAR connected the database through GPS or wireless Internet to provide scenery related instruction and attendant learning materials such as vocabulary or sentences that applicable [*sic*] in real-life contexts."[155]

• According to a 2018 issue of the *Journal of Engineering Science & Technology Review*, gamified e-learning can be facilitated through "Classroom Augmented Interactive Video (CAIV)" technologies that integrate interactive AR functions such as audio-visual graphic and sound "overlays"; textual information "captions"; embedded "assessment questions" and "hyperlink[ed]" detours; and personalized "bookmarks" and "annotations" of "images, icons, emoticons, drawings or text."[156] CAIV ed-tech also data-mines "user trace" records that log "classroom video analytics" which include "the parts of the video that students have often, rarely or not at all been watching" as well as "number of likes, number of comments, notes, etc."[157] These cognitive-behavioral and psycho-affective student-learning metrics profile "rich digital footprint[s]" that "disclose hidden patterns of student behavior" which reveal "users' interactions with instructors' annotations, quiz and questions responses [sic], viewers [sic] personal annotations, or more abstract indicators, such as the attention level based on reaction times to the interactive components presented during the video."[158]

Augmented Mathematics

- In a 2015 issue of *Mathematical Problems in Engineering*, computer scientists at the Engineering and Technology Institute of Ciudad Juárez Autonomous University in Mexico have documented their analysis of an "AR mobile application for plotting a quadratic equation" on the "android operating system (AOS)."[159] Known as "pARabola plotting," this AR app utilizes an augmentation software called "Unity3D [which] offers rendering capabilities, multiple built-in shaders and effects, a physics engine, a collider detector, and a particle generator that can be used to plot equations in 2D/3D space."[160] To coordinate virtual data points across slope-intercept equations plotted on "2D/3D" scans of the real-world environment, this AR app also incorporates a "tracking subsystem" operated through "Qualcomm's Vuforia Unity plug-in,"[161] which

> converts every frame captured by the camera to a suitable format for OpenGL ES rendering and for the tracking operations. The tracking subsystem contains the computer vision algorithms that detect and track real world objects inside the video frames captured by the camera. As a result, the tracking component stores the information obtained in a state object (part of the context subsystem) used by the renderer module to ensure a correct positioning and representation of the 3D object in the video feed of the real world. The tracking-update loop will be executed for every frame that is going to be processed.[162]

Through an "interaction subsystem," a student can implement "a touch based graphical user interface (GUI)" to manipulate the digitally augmented objects which the student has parabolically plotted across AR scans of the real world.[163]

• *Innovations in Education & Teaching International* published a 2016 article that evaluates "an AR system for teaching Euclidean vectors in physics and mathematics . . . to facilitate [a] user's understanding of physical concepts, such as magnitude, direction and orientation, together with basic vector-related operations like addition, subtraction and cross product."[164] This AR system incorporates Microsoft™ "Kinect sensors" with "NITE skeleton tracking software" to track a student's body movements as he or she makes poses in the shapes of Euclidean vectors:[165]

> [t]he body of the user is continuously tracked based on the depth image from the Kinect sensor using the NITE skeleton tracking software.... The user pose includes the position, in 3D coordinates, from different parts of the user skeleton (i.e. head, neck, torso, shoulders, elbows, hands, etc.) The real-world 3D coordinates obtained by the Kinect sensor are transformed to the monitor 2D coordinate system through the openNI libraries. Finally, all graphics are generated through the openGL libraries.[166]

Through the openNI and openGL libraries, "the user visualises the augmented outcome on the display screen while moving the hands to change vectors' magnitude and/or direction."[167]

• A 2015 issue of the *Journal of STEM Education: Innovations & Research* describes "two math-focused mobile applications developed by PBS Kids [which] allow young students to move shapes (CyberChase Patch the Path) and practice addition and subtraction (Fetch Lunch Rush)."[168]

• In a 2016 issue of *Educational Technology Research & Development,* IT scientists from Finnish and South Korean universities collaborated on an academic review of two AR game-learning platforms for conditioning math competencies: "AGeRA [which] is a geometry learning system that combines a book and an AR software on a mobile phone that is capable of placing virtual content on the pages of the book";[169] and "UFractions [which] is a storytelling fraction learning game that utilizes a mobile device and wooden fraction connected to the story" [sic].[170] Informed by these AR ed-tech reviews, engineers at "developed and evaluated Leometry game, which contains geometry problems based on the Van Hiele model."[171] Leometry is an AR video game that "teach[es] basic geometric shapes such as triangles, circles, and rectangles to 5th and 6th grade elementary school students" by walking them through an AR storytelling simulation which follows "two leopards, mother leopard and her cub Senatla, escape from poachers who have illegally captured them. The player's task is to help the leopards find their way back home.… The player is assisted by a dung beetle Pex who presents various geometry challenges and gives on-demand scaffolding hints."[172] Leometry functions through ManySense software, which "can tell the exact location of the user, the current weather condition, or whether the user is walking, running or standing still."[173] To calculate this real-world data in real-time, Leometry's ManySense program incorporates a "Raw Data Aggregator" that interconnects "data sources such as sensors and Internet services" as well as "Android smartphone sensors, Sony SmartWatch SW2, Zephyr heart-rate monitor, Open-WeatherMap weather service, and Myo gesture armband."[174]

Augmented Science:

• The same *Educational Technology Research & Development* article also reviews several AR game-learning technetronics that are programmed for conditioning science competencies:

> Via Mineralia [which] is a treasure hunt game that uses location awareness for learning about a mineral exhibition in a museum … [;] EULER [which] is an educational platform that combines RFID and mobile devices … to develop a treasure hunt game for learning natural science in a park … [;] [and] Ambient Wood [which] takes students to a field trip in a forest to learn about ecology through mobile devices and environmental sensors.[175]

The international team of Finnish and South Korean IT specialists reviewed these and other AR ed-tech games as models for developing their own AR-learning game called the "Science Spots AR (SSAR) learning platform that can assist learners in comprehending scientific topics such as geometry and kinetics in an enjoyable manner."[176] By means of interactive "storytelling games" involving a "specific science topic and virtual characters that interact with the learner" in "chapters," the SSAR games condition students' science competencies through embedded AR stimulus-response lessons known as "Science Spots, which hold one or more challenges interleaved by story snippets. Each Science Spot is connected to a location and is activated through interaction with an AR map at that location," which

> may utilize context data (e.g., location, weather or the user's movement) as well as real and virtual objects. For example, a game on biology might have a challenge related to a virtual squirrel emitting sounds typical to squirrels and sitting on a real tree branch.

This context-sensitive combination of the real world and the virtual game world can bring multi-sensory learning experiences to any physical context.[177]

To overlay AR Science Spot lessons onto the physical world in real time, the SSAR game-based learning platform integrates several other digital augmentation, gamification, and adaptive-learning software, including Game Design Tool (GDT); Game Engine; Story Engine; Player Manager; Highscore Manager; AR Engine (which utilizes Wavefront OBJ formats through Vuforia software); AR Map Manager; Sound Effects (SFX) Manager; Context Manager; Content Downloader; Player Data Uploader; and "a Learning Process Monitor (LPM) that allows an educator to analyze students' performance and detect when they are stuck in the learning process. LPM has two modes: (1) real-time mode for monitoring a game in progress, and (2) retrospective mode for visualizing and analyzing data collected over game sessions."[178]

• In a 2017 issue of the *International Journal of Technology, Knowledge & Society*, researchers from Purdue University, USA, and Rowan University, USA, examine an AR-learning game titled "Butterfly's Life Cycle," which

> combined Augmented Reality with mobile technologies to create an ecology learning system embedded in a smart phone for learning butterfly ecology on campus. This system applied the built-in functions in a smart phone to integrate 3D virtual caterpillars with campus ecological environment. Students can feed and observe virtual caterpillars on host plants showed on a smart phone, and further understand the life cycle [sic] of a butterfly.[179]

Additionally, this journal report discusses the use of "augmented reality (AR) in an Astronomy course" that teaches "concept learning of moon phases" through an "Augmented Reality system [which] was mainly designed by D'Fusion software and Maya, which allowed users to interact with the virtual moon on their hand."[180] Furthermore, this academic article analyzed an "AR-based learning unit" in which Japanese students carry "Android tablet computers" around a ninth-grade campus to collect simulated radiation-level readings that will teach them "socio-scientific issues (SSI)" regarding the effects of nuclear radiation pollution resulting from the Fukushima Daiichi Nuclear Power Plant meltdown.[181]

• According to a 2015 issue of *Environmental Education Research*, Taiwanese ed-tech engineers have built a gamified AR-learning platform that digitally projects an interactive multi-media "story" called 'The Water Drop's Adventure,' which is augmented with virtual overlays of the teacher who is green-screened through a live camera feed displayed onto a computer-graphic "water drop."[182] From inside the CG water droplet, the human teacher follows along while narrating "the adventures of a water drop, guiding learners to achieve an understanding of the ecological characteristics of Taiwan's rivers and a corresponding basic knowledge of the animals living therein."[183] The education technologists Su-Ju Lu and Ying-Chieh Liu demonstrate that, by "[u]sing the real-time dynamic virtual 3D model display, students can not only interact with the 3D model, but are also given [sic] the opportunity to carefully observe the characteristics and appearance of each fish."[184] At the end of the 3D "Water Drop's Adventure" story, students play two AR games called "Fish House" and "Save the Fish."[185] As they play these games,

> [s]tudents engage with the system through somatorsensory inputs, using specific gestures to indicate "correct" and "incorrect." Students play one at a time in front of the screen, while the other students watch the game and offer advice or encouragement. When a student gives a wrong answer, the system will provide detailed instructional content to help reinforce knowledge acquisition.[186]

• A 2017 issue of the *Journal of Educational Technology & Society* expounds a research study called "Augmented Reality for Interpretive and Experiential Learning (ARIEL), [which] has investigated optimal uses of AR in science museums."[187] The ARIEL project has conducted studies of student learning through the use of three AR ed-tech devices:

> [t]he first device, "Be The Path," was augmented to show the flow of electricity when visitors completed an open circuit with their bodies. The second device, "Magnetic Maps," was augmented to visualize the magnetic field surrounding two bar magnets. And the third device, "Bernoulli Blower" (depicted in Figure 1), was augmented to feature the interactions between two types of air to keep a plastic ball afloat.[188]

Augmented Fieldtrips for Geography, Geology, and History:

• An article published in a 2017 issue of *Geosphere*, explores the use of "augmented reality field trips to [sic] Grand Canyon" as a cost-effective substitute for real-world fieldwork in geoscience studies.[189] Academics from three American universities (California State, Utah State, and Boise State) examined prototypical "AR field trip modules" that "utilize relative GPS locations for spatial orientation and reference" through "[t]he location-based app development platform GeoBob ... made by the Interactive Design for Instructional Applications and Simulations (IDIAS ...) laboratory at Utah State University."[190] These augmented-learning field-trip modules incorporate three different apps—GCX: Geologic Time; GCX: Geologic Structures; and GCX: Hydrologic Processes. These AR ed-tech apps "cover key curriculum concepts that can easily be addressed with iconic Grand Canyon features,"[191] which are simulated to condition students with competences

> (1) for geologic time: stratigraphic principles, unconformities, relative dating, numeric dating, and human versus geologic time; (2) for geologic structures: stress and strain, folds, faults, strike and dip, and plate tectonics (as related to faults); and (3) for surface-water processes: the hydrologic cycle, fluvial hydrology, sediment transport, groundwater, and human influence on surface water.[192]

During the AR field-trips, "[t]he modules require the students to physically navigate a Grand Canyon landscape that is scaled down to a 100-m-long playing field."[193] While traversing the AR Grand Canyon,

> [t]he field trip stops appear in sequence after a multiple-choice question and interactive touchscreen task have been answered correctly ... Students must physically navigate to each new location (Fig. 2) and complete interactive touchscreen activities either requiring them to identify and tap on a geologic feature or swipe the screen to draw a line (along a fold axis or on a graph) or indicate the direction of movement of a fault's hanging wall (Fig. 1), for example.[194]

• According to another 2015 article printed in the *Journal of Educational Technology & Society*, psychologists and ed-tech scholars from multiple Taiwanese universities have collaborated on the "develop[ment] [of] an *augmented reality* mobile guidance system that used a historical geo-context-embedded visiting strategy" to simulate school fieldtrips and other fieldwork studies of historical sites.[195] This mobile-AR ed-tech program is launched through

> the ASUS Eee Pad Transformer TF101 (Android 3.2).... It has the capacity to load additional information or interpretations regarding historical or geographical contexts when visitors aim the camera of a tablet computer at a historical site.... This function enables visitors to identify the historical site or heritage site using

the device's camera and to browse or listen to guidance content that corresponds to the historical site.[196]

In addition, "The 'Zoom in' and 'Zoom out' functions of the device interface enable the observation of specific areas of the historical site and provide detailed interpretive information on the areas."[197]

- Another AR video-game for learning history is described in the 2017 issue of the *International Journal of Technology, Knowledge & Society*: "a mobile city game called Frequency 1550 designed by the Waag Society," which uses cellphone screen-augmentation for "transforming the environment of real city to a corresponding virtual scene of the Middle Ages showed on mobile phones."[198]

- In a 2015 issue of *Educational Technology Research & Development*, childhood education specialists and computer engineers from several South Korean universities have explored the use of the "EcoMOBILE project that integrated AR and probeware to support students' outdoor field trips in environmental education."[199]

Gamified AR Robots:

- This same article in *Educational Technology Research & Development* analyzes an AI education technology known as "GENTORO [which] is an example of an AR-integrated robot system for children's storytelling activities (Sugimoto et al. 2009). GENTORO uses a robot and a handheld projector to enable children to create a story collaboratively, which can be expressed interactively in a physical space."[200] Additionally, this scholarly journal article also examines "RoboStage [which] is another example of AR-augmented robot systems that users can take on either physical or virtual characters with authentic scenes by integrating mixed-reality technology and robot technology [*sic*]."[201] One more AR robot reviewed by this article is the iRobiQ:

> [w]hen loaded with the AR Flash robot script, the AR-based dramatic play service is activated using the iROBIQ robot software platform, which consists of a Robot Service Executor (RSE) and a Robot Content Player (RCP). The robot script is executed by RCP. iROBIQ simultaneously executes the robot software platform and the AR library, such as Papervision 3D.[202]

These AR robots and other AR computer games were comparatively studied to investigate the differences between "computer-mediated" AR and "robot-mediated" AR in terms of which are most accurate at measur[ing] children's perceived levels of the following variables: (a) satisfaction (i.e., interest in dramatic play & user-friendliness), (b) sensory immersion (i.e., self-engagement, environment-engagement & interaction-engagement), and (c) media recognition (i.e., collaboration with media, media function & empathy with media). Data analysis indicates that children in the robot-mediated condition showed significantly higher perceptions than those in the computer-mediated condition regarding the following aspects: interest in dramatic play (satisfaction), interactive engagement (sensory immersion), and empathy with media (media recognition).[203]

As you can see, the span of AR ed-tech is vast; a veritable arsenal of augmented-learning technetronics is waiting in the wings, ready to be deployed en masse as soon as policymakers give the greenlight to standardize gamified AR as a basic learning technology across the curriculum. Indeed, education technologists have resolved the main logistical impediment to adopting AR learning-tech schoolwide. Bypassing the major cost impediment of purchasing expensive computer hardware specially built for compatibility with AR software, technocratic learning engineers have developed an array of AR apps that can be uploaded to a range of various mobile computer devices, such as smartphones, tablets, and laptops employed throughout the schooling system.

A 2017 issue of the academic journal, *Open Learning*, predicts that

[t]he increased availability of smartphones and tablets with Internet connectivity and high-computing power makes the use of AR applications a promising development for education. This breaks down the walls of the classroom, connecting schools and communities (Squire, 2013). In the near future, eventually everyone with a smartphone or a tablet will be capable of viewing augmented information. This makes it possible for a teacher to develop engaging educational activities, with games and resources that can take advantage of the AR technologies, therefore improving learning outcomes. We believe that the use of AR will change significantly many current teaching activities by enabling the addition of supplementary information that may be viewed on a mobile device (Squire & Dikkers, 2012), guiding learning activities in context and helping students to improve their individual as well as their collective understanding of educational content.[204]

Capitalizing on the flexibility of AR apps that are compatible with multiple different mobile computer devices, school administrators can either assign students AR machines owned by the schools, or the administrators can require students to bring their own personal AR hardware from home. According to a 2017 issue of the *Journal of Geography in Higher Education,* "[a]ugmented reality (AR) and Digital Tablets are becoming technical trends in higher education according the last 5 year New Media Consortium Horizon Report ... The 2014 Horizon Report incorporates a significant trend called 'BYOD' (Bring Your Own Device): which promotes students using their own devices (smartphones and tablets) in the classroom with free educational applications available."[205]

Other examples of flexible AR equipment are detailed in a 2015 issue of the *International Journal of Cognitive Research in Science, Engineering & Education,* which discusses the implementation of "the software application BuildAR of HITLAB with the ARToolKItPlus algorithm" programmed into different "standard opaque" and "see-through" "Head-Mounted Displays (HMD)" and "Head-Up Displays (HUD)" to enhance students' "interest, understanding and interiorizing [of] the learning material" at "higher education" institutions.[206]

Going by the Global Education Futures timeline, this growing menu of AR devices will be streamlined into schools beginning in the year 2018 when AR ed-tech infrastructures will become increasingly dynamic until "[p]re-school and primary school become playgrounds that use augmented reality technology."[207]

The AR-VR Dialectics of Mixed Reality AI Ed-Tech:

Gamified AR ed-tech will data-mine caches of students' neurocognitive and bioelectrical stimulus-response metrics, which will be crunched in order to program HCIs to calibrate in sync with digital augmentation overlays projected by cognitive-companion AI supercomputers. But to be sure, AR overlays require AI algorithms to not only scan and interface with real-world data from real-world sensors in real time; but AR projections also depend on AI algorithms that scan and interface with virtual data stored on the cloud-based internet-of-things in order to be able to first download a digital augmentation overlay from a virtual data cache before then transmitting it through an augmentation algorithm that overlays the virtual download on top of the real-time scan of the real-world projection. Stated differently, AR and VR technologies are not really separate technologies; they are basically inverse versions of the same interactive AI technologies that operate on a singular spectrum of digitalization algorithms which map and interface with enhanced 3D environments.

This AR-VR spectrum is explained as a "reality-virtuality continuum" in a 2017 peer-reviewed journal article entitled "The Role of Augmented Reality and Its Application in Learning":

> Augmented Reality is an area closer to the real world, located between the real environment and the virtual environment. Compared to Virtual Reality, Augmented Reality allows virtual and real objects to co-exist in the same setting; when users are immersed in Augmented Reality, they can still view or observe the real world around them. ... All senses, such as hearing, smell, and touch, can be considered as a presentation of Augmented Reality application. Moreover, the definition of Augmented Reality is not limited to only supplementing virtual elements to the real world; an approach of removing real objects by overlaying virtual ones also belongs to the area pf Augmented Reality.[208]

Thus, before human consciousness can be uploaded into posthuman AI cybernetics with the powers of instantaneous AR perception that amplifies artificial-human cognition, it is necessary to first map out the algorithmic data on the VR end of the reality-virtuality continuum so that the entire AR-VR feedback loop is comprehensively mapped by AI supercomputers. Therefore, learning engineers must first beta-test realistic VR environments wherein students are experimentally data-mined by AI bots to track the students' neurocognitive and bioelectrical stimulus-response metrics in real-time so that the visual-spatial, auditory, and kinesthetic stimuli of gamified VR environments can be calibrated to synchronize with human neurobiological metrics transmitted through HCIs that enable posthumans to control AR overlays and VR simulations simply by thinking with "brain clicks."

In *Wetware: A Computer in Every Living Cell*, which was published by Yale University Press, Dennis Bray presents a brief history of early VR technologies beginning with their fictional depiction in Aldous Huxley's *Brave New World*:

> [s]cience fiction writers and other visionaries have long anticipated the consequences of sensory inundation. Aldous Huxley's *Brave New World*, written in 1932, just a few years after talking motion pictures became widely accessible, envisaged a form of cinema in which the audience received odorous and tactile sensations in addition to visual and auditory. By grasping metal knobs on the handles of their seats they receive a stream of sensory input, experiencing a love scene on a bear rug between a black man and a pneumatic

blonde in vivid detail, each hair felt with prickling reality. Actual virtual reality devices followed slowly and at some distance: for example, a device known as Sensorama, constructed in the 1950s, simulated the experience of riding a motorcycle. The participant sat on a pillion seat holding mockup handles and faced a display of an oncoming road on a rather small cathode-ray tube. By the early 1960s there were head-mounted virtual reality displays that the user wore like a mask. Wands and gloves relayed data about the individual's arm and hand movements to a computer.[209]

According to a 2015 issue of the academic journal *Sensors,* contemporary VR ed-tech can be categorized into three classifications:

> communicative spaces, simulation spaces and experimental spaces. As a communicative space, the focus is in the communication that can be achieved through the avatars, both in a verbal way (using text chat and voice chat) and in a non-verbal way, through the appearance of the avatar, as well as through the avatar postures and gestures. As a simulation space, the focus is in the virtual representation of places such as a university, a library, a theater, etc., where avatars can meet and interact with each other. As an experimental space, the focus is in the paradigm of "learning by doing," interacting with 3D virtual objects or exploring the virtual world.[210]

Interlinking these three main VR platforms in unison with various AR platforms, technocratic learning engineers have assembled "mixed-reality" systems in the middle of the VR-AR continuum, blending together networks of virtual-reality ed-tech intersected with augmented-reality ed-tech.

In 2017, the Bill and Melinda Gates Foundation granted New York University $2,000,000 "to explore higher education applications of artificial intelligence/machine learning and virtual reality/mixed reality/augmented reality to solve challenges in HigherEd for first generation, low income and underrepresented minority students."[211]

A case study of "mixed" VR-AR ed-tech is explicated in a 2015 issue of the *Journal of Educational Technology & Society*, which details a prototype of a "widespread web-based learning platform" that incorporates a software called Moodle "to deploy across-spaces learning situations, which can be authored with a plethora of existing learning design tools, that involve different common web-based learning platforms, mobile AR applications and multiple kinds of virtual globes."[212] This across-spaces mixture of VR-AR technologies integrated three existing authoring tools (as well as other authoring tools compliant with IMS LD level A), two VLEs, four mobile AR clients and the Glue! DLE adapter … [as well as] two VGs: Google Earth and Google Maps/Street View, used as 3DVWs [3D Virtual Worlds], modifying the Manager to synchronize user information (and therefore, their avatars) in mobile AR clients and VGs.[213]

Showcasing a demonstration of this intermixture of VR-AR technetronics in action, scholarly research colleagues from American and Spanish universities have provided a visual aid in

Figure 3 [which] illustrates the user interfaces of different learning environments in an example learning situation involving Google Earth (a) and Google Maps/Street View (b) used like 3DVWs, the Junaio AR client (c) and Moodle (d) [sic]. In the figure, a student (student_a11) may access the same activity in virtual downtown Valladolid (Spain) from two VGs: Google Earth (a) and Google Maps/Street View (b). From both VGs, she can see the avatar of another student (student_a12) and some geopositioned tools (in this case, a chat and a Google Docs document). Student_a12 is physically in the street in downtown Valladolid, and he is also watching the avatar of student_a11 and the geopositioned tools (c), using a mobile device with Junaio AR client. The chat shared by these students is also accessible from within Moodle (d).[214]

Compare this across-spaces VR-AR platform with the mixed-reality edu-conditioning simulators developed by the Pearson edu-corporation. In a Pearson Education press release titled "Pearson Announces Mixed Reality Pilots Designed to Solve Real World Learning Challenges at Colleges and Universities," the globalist ed-tech company publicized that it is piloting its new mixed-reality "HoloLens" learning platform

[a]t Bryn Mawr College, a women's liberal arts college in Pennsylvania, [where] faculty, students, and staff are exploring various educational applications for the HoloLens mixed reality devices. They are testing Skype for HoloLens for connecting students with tutors in Pearson's 24/7 online tutoring service, Smarthinking. If successful, this out-of-the-box solution could provide struggling students with richer, more personalized just-in-time support from expert tutors as if they were sitting side-by-side. Bryn Mawr will also experiment with using holographs and mixed reality to explore 3D content and concepts in a number of academic disciplines, including physics, biology, and archaeology.

Pearson's work with mixed reality and HoloLens isn't limited to higher education. The company is in the early stages of evaluating the impact of holographic learning at the late grammar school stage. At Canberra Grammar School in Australia, Pearson is working with teachers in a variety of disciplines to develop holograms for use in their classrooms. The University of Canberra is partnering with Pearson to provide support for the project and evaluate the impact these holograms have on teaching and learning.[215]

Another case study of across-spaces AR-VR ed-tech is analyzed in an academic article titled "Developing Mixed Reality Educational Applications," which examines the use of an edu-conditioning app called "The Virtual Touch Toolkit":

> a mixed reality system [that] allows building 3D collaborative spaces in a virtual world where students interact with each other and can perform an active role in the resolution of a given problem.… Furthermore, the tangible interfaces provided by Virtual Touch allow the manipulation of physical artifacts that will have effects in the virtual world. In this way the student will be able to explore, experiment and interact in the virtual world using physical manipulation, thus being able to watch the immediate effects of her actions, in a constructivist learning environment[216]

In addition, ed-tech that mixes virtual and augmented reality is expounded in a 2016 issue of the American Physical Society's peer-reviewed journal, *Physical Review Physics Education Research,* which studied the use of "a highly immersive mixed-reality classroom simulator" to provide pedagogy-training for prospective physics teachers enrolled in instructional methods courses.[217] This mixed-reality learning-simulator implemented a VR software called "Open Source Tutorials in Physics Sensemaking, Suite 1," which generated AI "avatars" of virtual students assigned to "undergraduate physics learning assistants (LAs)" who were being trained in the "practice of physics pedagogy skills" through the "performance-based" task of teaching the AI avatars by "leading discussions among the five student avatars."[218] In this experiment, which was sponsored by the National Science Foundation, the digital roleplaying of the virtual class discussion focused on "a lesson about motion graphs for five highly interactive computer generated student avatars in the mixed-reality classroom simulator."[219]

As a general methodology for conditioning science competences through mixed-reality ed-tech, a 2017 issue of *Open Learning* recommends a "Science Learning Activities Model" (SLAM) pedagogy that "aims at integrating learning in formal and informal contexts through blended learning scenarios by using today's flexible, interactive and immersive technologies (e.g. mobile, augmented reality, virtual reality)."[220]

Immersive VR Edu-Conditioning:

At the VR end of the reality-virtuality continuum, immersive VR ed-tech is being used for training medical students to administer the social-sensitivity protocol required to unobtrusively communicate therapeutic transactions with patients who suffer from Post Traumatic Stress Disorder and other psychological traumas. A 2018 issue of the *Journal of the American Medical Association (JAMA)* discusses psychologist Skip Rizzo's use of a VR job-training technology which "[b]uild[s] on nearly 3 decades of experience using virtual reality to build immersive therapies for patients with posttraumatic stress disorder (PTSD)."[221] According to *JAMA*, Rizzo's immersive VR simulator "train[s] clinicians to more skillfully handle delicate interactions with patients" by

> creat[ing] interactive artificially intelligent, virtual patients complete with personalities and credible clinical circumstances. The virtual patients give clinicians in training a chance to practice difficult conversations about sensitive topics like substance abuse, mental illness, or sexual assault. "It gives novice clinicians a chance to mess up a bunch with virtual patients before they get their hands on a live one."[222]

Said Rizzo, who has already trialed similar VR-tech for treating PTSD patients by administering virtually simulated therapies that "re-create traumatic situations that trigger intense emotional responses and enable therapy."[223]

A similar VR technology for medical schools is called the "knowledge-oriented medical virtual reality (KOMVR)" system, which is specially designed to streamline the use of VR ed-tech throughout the medical industry. A 2017 issue of the EURASIA Journal of Mathematics, Science & Technology Education reports that the KOMVR "can be used for building immersive virtual reality (VR) applications dedicated to training medical skills."[224]

Medicalized VR technetronics are also being engineered to accommodate school "inclusion" policies which mandate that "special education" students with learning disorders and other disabilities must be "included" in non-remediated general education courses alongside their non-disabled peers. A 2015 issue of *Sensors* documents how

> [o]ne area where virtual worlds have been used successfully is inclusive education. For example, the "Accessibility in Virtual Worlds" project is aimed at blind students whose positions are indicated by sounds, thus allowing navigation and interaction with peers (both blind and sighted). Another example that uses virtual worlds for inclusion is Brigadoon. It is an island in Second Life which serves as a therapy for people with Asperger syndrome (autism), facilitating their social interaction by using avatars in a controlled environment.[225]

Throughout the corporate world, other industries besides the healthcare business are utilizing VR learning-tech to cut the costs of workforce training while reducing the injury risks of on-the-job safety training for employees. In a 2017 issue of the professional journal of the American Society of Safety Engineers, the Chair and CEO of Optech4D, Vincent Higgins, reviews "[a] joint study by Stanford University, University of California-Berkeley and University of Washington [which] compared competency and confidence levels of employees who had experienced classroom versus AR and VR training ... The results indicated that the fully immersive and interactive sessions left users feeling more capable, confident and able to handle hazardous situations."[226]

This article, which is titled "Augmented & Virtual Reality: The Future of Work, Not Just Play," also reviews Optech4D: a VR-tech company that provides "VR-based training" for "organizations in the oil and gas, aerospace, construction and manufacturing industries to help them understand, implement and benefit from the safety uses of these technologies.... The company also partners with Purdue University's Hangar of the Future program, a student-led, faculty-mentored innovation program tackling safety and process challenges in the aviation industry."[227] Additionally, this article notes that "Motorola supports use of AR and VR technologies in the workplace."[228]

Furthermore, there are other "realistic training simulations" that "Increas[e] Competency & Reduc[e] Cost" through "an AR/VR solution that allows the field worker to conduct a real-time video call with an office-based expert. Using this technology, the expert can see the same situation as the field worker and can guide the worker through critical tasks," thereby preventing expensive injuries and equipment damages that result from workplace safety incompetence.[229]

Even police training is utilizing VR-learning simulations. According to a 2016 article printed in the scholarly journal, *Behaviour & Information Technology*, research conducted

> [i]n Bertram, Moskaliuk, and Cress's (2015) study ... applied a virtual training environment to train police personnel for complex collaborative tasks.... [W]ith regard to the learning transfer measured by the behaviour in a real and complex situation, the virtual training was as good as the standard training.[230]

Forecasting the future trends of VR ed-tech, the timeline of the Global Education Futures Initiative marks 2020 as the year when technocrats will digitally construct "Virtual jail[s]" in which "compulsory education of prisoners occurs in virtual reality simulators."[231]

Moving along this chronology, US Secretary of Education Betsy DeVos has personally promoted the posthumanistic use of immersive virtual-reality technologies that digitally treat medically disabled students by therapeutically conditioning their recoveries from drug addiction pathologies. During her "Rethink School" tour in 2017,[232] DeVos visited a corporate-chartered "recovery high school" called Hope Academy in Indianapolis where students learn by wearing headsets that transmit a VictoryVR curriculum.[233] The VictoryVR website states that its "virtual reality curriculum is based on Next Gen Science Standards and outputted to the Oculus Rift VR system."[234] In a VictoryVR webpage article entitled "Trump Administration Takes Virtual Reality Curriculum for a Test Drive," the VR corporation publicizes DeVos's visit to Hope Academy: "Rachelle Gardner, the COO of Hope Academy, explained that the immersive nature of virtual reality helps students at her school focus on what they need to learn. After DeVos had taken in the full scope of the Hope program she said the school is 'a great example of how a school can meet the needs of specific students.'"[235] Notice how DeVos, who even posed for a photo-op wearing the Victory VR goggles, is highlighting the "personalized" methodology of therapeutic stimulus-response conditioning programmed into the posthumanistic wearable tech commercialized by the Victory VR corporation.[236] [m 237]

---

m   Similarly, Episcopal Academy in Newtown Square , Pennsylvania, which is part of Google Glass Explorer program, has piloted AR-learning experiments with Google Glass in the classroom as a supplementary learning technology. The use of Google Glass AR in schools is also promoted by the Duke University Digital Initiative.

Victory VR headgear is a proprietary ed-tech hardware that is only compatible with Victory VR's specialized curricular simulations. Nevertheless, the Facebook Corporation is currently piloting the use of its Oculus Rift and Oculus Go VR goggles for edu-conditioning at Seattle Public Schools while partnering with the Seattle-based Technology Access Foundation to train teachers how to utilize Oculus VR ed-tech in their classrooms.[238] Additionally, recall from chapter twelve that Marc Benioff of Trump's Office of American Innovation is deeply invested in VR ed-tech manufactured by the Nearpod Corporation.

To bridge the logistical gaps between the incompatibilities of different system-specific VR technetronics, learning engineers are developing versatile VR apps that can be dynamically programmed for a range of various mobile VR headgear contraptions that hook up to smartphones. Such smartphone VR headsets include Google Cardboard, Google Daydream View, and Samsung Gear VR (SM-R325).[239] Even cheaper smartphone VR devices include Merge VR Goggles, Xiaomi Mi VR Play, Zeiss One Plus, Freefly VR Beyond, View-Master DLX VR, and BlitzWolf BR-VR3.[240]

Ubiquitous smartphone VR is just the beginning. Ray Kurzweil's 2005 treatise, *The Singularity Is Near: When Humans Transcend Biology*, projects that,

> [b]ecause of the bandwidth limitations and the lack of effective three-dimensional displays, the virtual environment provided today through routine Web access does not yet fully compete with "being there," but that will change. In the early part of the second decade of this century visual-auditory virtual-reality environments will be full immersion, very high resolution, and very convincing. Most colleges will follow MIT's lead, and students will increasingly attend classes virtually. Virtual environments will provide high-quality virtual laboratories where experiments can be conducted in chemistry, nuclear physics, or any other scientific field. Students will be able to interact with a virtual Thomas Jefferson or Thomas Edison or even to *become* a virtual Thomas Jefferson. Classes will be available for all grade levels in many languages. The devices needed to enter these high-quality, high-resolution virtual classrooms will be ubiquitous and affordable even in third world countries.[241]

Virtual "Brain Clicks":

In the final equation, mass-scale student interplay with ubiquitous VR and AR ed-tech will assemble and codify the "cognitive load" and "eye-tracking" metrics that will supply a sum-total matrix of neurocognitive/bioelectrical stimulus-response algorithms which are needed for programming BCIs to calibrate in sync with AI supercomputers seamlessly interfaced with the complete range of AR and VR software on fluid upload/download e-highways running through a singular overlay/immersion continuum of reality-virtuality augmentations and simulations. The 360-degree data-mining of VR-AR ed-tech is succinctly outlined in a 2016 issue of *Behaviour & Information Technology*, which states that the

> [e]valuation of quality of VR/AR/MR platforms/environments should be based on (a) applying both expert-centred (top-down) and user-centred (bottom-up) quality evaluation methods and (b) separating "internal quality" criteria, and "quality in use" criteria in the set of quality criteria (model). Personalisation of VR/AR/MR platforms/environments should be based on learners' models/ profiles using students' learning styles, intelligent technologies, and Semantic Web applications.[242]

Stated differently, VR-AR technetronics data-mine the "user-centred" psychometrics of students' "bottom up" responses to virtual/augmented learning stimuli delivered from "top down" artificial intelligences in order that "expert-centred" ed-tech engineers can refine VR/AR-learning algorithms to better condition student-learning outcomes by sharpening augmentation overlays and virtual simulations so that they attune with each individual student's personalized neurocognition algorithms.

This full-circle Big Data-mining of human-AR and human-VR algorithms will collate a bedrock of digital-computational schematics needed to lay the foundation for uploading human consciousness into a fully immersive virtual environment where digital information can be downloaded to enhance cognitive perception of the real-world environment through augmentation overlays controlled with an "intuitive" thought-click transmission beamed through a brain chip or other BCI. In fact, Bilderberger Mark Zuckerberg has already announced plans to evolve Facebook's tele-typing BCIs into advanced brain-computer interfaces for controlling augmented-reality simulations just by thinking. In a Facebook post from Zuckerberg himself, the Bilderberger proudly declared that his Orwellian social-media company is "working on a system that will let you type straight from your brain about 5x faster than you can type on your phone today. Eventually, we want to turn it into a wearable technology that can be manufactured at scale. Even a simple yes/no 'brain click' would help make things like augmented reality feel much more natural."[243]

Likewise, the Microsoft Corporation has also filed for a patent on a BCI which transmits "thought-clicks" that are capable of "controlling mechanical tools and/or other machinery," such as "VR and AR apps," through a BCI "application [that] detect[s] neurological user intent data associated with a particular operation of a particular application state . . . . The application state is automatically changed to align with the intended operation, as determined by received neurological user intent data, so that the intended operation is performed."[244]

Similarly, in a *Forbes Magazine* interview, BrainCo CEO Bicheng Han explains how his company has constructed 20,000 posthumanist headgear technetronics that have been deployed to measure students' brainwaves in order "to capture data from 1.2 million people," which are being reconfigured to program the "use [of] artificial intelligence to create a brain typing tool – something that turns thoughts into text."[245] Another company representative, Max Newlon, reveals explains that "[t]he hope is when we have this really big database, we will do some analysis that others haven't been able to do yet. ... If we have a big database, we might do more interesting research along the lines of something like brain typing."[246] With a big enough database, BrainCo will certainly progress from brain-typing research and, like Facebook and Microsoft, venture on to AR/VR brain-click research.

It should be noted that, according to *EdSurge*, the Chinese "BrainCo has not yet established any policies that guide (or prevent) the company from using data collected from U.S. students," and

> Bill Fitzgerald, director of privacy review programs at Common Sense Media, points out that BrainCo does not have any publicly-available privacy statement, ethical review or any information about how students' data will be stored or used. If a parent wishes to have their child's information deleted, BrainCo doesn't offer information on how that happens or how it will prove to families that the biometric information is indeed removed. There is also no public-facing process on how families will be notified if their child's biometric data is breached.[247]

It is not clear how the neurocognitive biometric data obtained from student usage of BrainCo helmets will be regulated under FERPA; but if these posthumanist headsets are deemed to be of "legitimate educational interest," then the law as written can authorize BrainCo to utilize students' neurocognitive stimulus-response algorithms to engineer brain-click interfaces that can thought-control VR simulation downloads and

AR augmentation overlays to enhance lifelong learning. To be sure, BrianCo is reportedly certified by the US Food and Drug Administration Institutional Review Board "to review and monitor biomedical research involving human subjects."[248]

Meanwhile, as more and more human-AR/VR interplay is massively data-mined through the popularization of gamified ed-tech, posthumanist AI engineers at Facebook, Microsoft, BrianCo and other trans-eugenic corporations will gain access to treasure troves of algorithmic data that can be reprogrammed to transform tele-typing BCIs into AR/VR-BCIs.

Uploading Posthuman Gnosis: Software-Based Consciousness, Foglet-Projected Hologram Bodies, Virtual Immortality:

Reaching the zenith of posthumanist AI ed-tech, trans-eugenic learning engineers seek to create the ultimate human-AI education system: an artificially intelligent AR/VR-HCI that integrates the internet-of-things into the actual biology of human beings, technetronically transforming all the "wetware" of the human organism by converting the human body into a virtual "trans-droid." A 2015 issue of the academic *Journal of Motor Behavior* reports on the construction of some fundamental building blocks for just such a posthuman creature called "REX":

> [i]n 2013, the London Science Museum unveiled robotic exoskeleton (REX), a completely manufactured cyborg consisting of organs and organ systems from laboratories and companies around the world, including artificial eye and kidney (University of California, Los Angeles, CA), ear (Macquarie University, Sydney, Australia), trachea (Royal Free Hospital, London, England), heart (SynCardia, Tucson, AZ), spleen (Yale University, New Haven, CT), pancreas (De Montfort University, Leicester, England), hand and arm (Touch Bionics, Livingston, Scotland; Johns Hopkins University, Baltimore, MD), blood (Sheffield University, Sheffield, England), and foot and ankle (MIT, Cambridge, MA). REX stands with the aid of a bilateral leg robotic exoskeleton.[249]

As Moore's Law continues to exponentially miniaturize computer microprocessors down to the molecular size of about one hundred nanometers,[250] REX's relatively clunky hardware can be replaced by nanotech systems of artificially intelligent AR/VR-HCI bots infused into the bloodstream of human biological wetware. In *The Singularity Is Near*, Kurzweil predicts that

[t]he most important application of circa-2030 nanobots will literally be to expand our minds through the merger of biological and
nonbiological intelligence. The first stage will be to augment our
hundred trillion very slow interneuronal connections with high-
speed virtual connections via nanorobot communication. This will
provide us with the opportunity to greatly boost our pattern-rec-
ognition abilities, memories, and overall thinking capacity, as well
as to directly interface with powerful forms of nonbiological intelligence. The technology will also provide wireless communication
from one brain to another…

By that time we will have moved beyond just the paradigm of
nanobots in a biological brain. Nonbiological intelligence will be
billions of times more powerful, so it will predominate. We will
have version 3.0 human bodies, which we will be able to modify
and reinstate into new forms at will. We will be able to quickly
change our bodies in full-immersion visual-auditory virtual environments in the second decade of this century; in full-immersion
virtual-reality environments incorporating all the senses during
the 2020s; and in real reality in the 2040s.[251]

According to Kurzweil, nanotech HCIs are the ideal AI systems for
interfacing humans with AR/VR cognition upgrades because, in contrast
with the heavier hardware of robotic HCIs, nanobot HCIs can be installed
pervasively throughout the human wetware biosystem so that nano-AI
signals from the AR/VR internet-of-everything are permeated throughout a person's entire biocomputer system of neuro-cerebral circuitry:

[t]he use of nanobots as brain extenders will be a significant improvement over surgically installed neural implants, which are beginning to be used today. Nanobots will be introduced without surgery, through the bloodstream, and if necessary can all be directed
to leave, so the process is easily reversible. They are programmable,
in that they can provide virtual reality one minute and a variety of
brain extensions the next. They can change their configuration and
alter their software. Perhaps most important, they are massively
distributed and therefore can take up billions of positions throughout the brain, whereas a surgically introduced neural implant can
be placed only in one or at most a few locations.[252]

Putting these wild dreams into international activism, Kurzweil is a
member of the globalist *Russia 2045 Strategic Social Initiative* which,[253]
according to Bilderberg sleuth Daniel Estulin, is a technocratic cadre of

"transhumanists [who] want to create an AVATAR – a robotic human copy controlled by brain computer interface." Estulin exposes the proceedings of the Global Future 2045 International Congress, which was convened in Moscow, Russia, in 2012. According to a report of the congress, which was spearheaded by Russian billionaire Dmitry Itskov,[254]

> [b]y 2025, new generation of AVATAR provides complete transmission of sensations from all five robotic sensory organs to the operator. By 2030, plans are already in the drawing stages to create "RE-Brain," the colossal project of brain-reverse-engineering is implemented [sic]. World science comes very close to understanding the principles of consciousness. Scientists are convinced that by 2035, the first successful attempt to transfer one's personality to an alternative carrier will take place. The epoch of cybernetic immortality begins.
>
> In one generation, bodies made of nanorobots, can take any shape or rise alongside hologram bodies. By 2045, we will see drastic changes in social structure. The main priority of this development is spiritual self-improvement. A new era dawns. The era of neo-humanity.[255]

In *TransEvolution: The Coming Age of Human Deconstruction*, Estulin excerpts the following passages from this *Russia 2045* document: "[b]y 2035, an implantable information chip could be developed and wired directly to the user's brain ... synthetic sensory perception beamed directly to the user's senses";[256] and by

> [t]he 2045 social network for open innovation is expanding with projects such as AVATAR-A, a robotic copy of the human body controlled via Biological Computer Interface. Or an AVATAR-B, in which a human brain is transplanted at the end of one's life. Or an AVATAR-C, in which an artificial brain in which a human personality is transferred at the end of one's life.
>
> Basically, what these scientists want to do is to incrementally move the human mind into more disembodied and, no better way to say it, futuristic vehicles: first a humanoid robot controlled entirely by a human brain via brain-machine interface, then a conscious human brain transplanted into a humanoid robot, then consciousness uploaded to a computer, and finally a hologram that contains a full conscious human mind.[257 n 258]

---

n　　It should be noted that Estulin also uncovers how

two attendees of the Bilderberg 2012 conference in Chantilly, Virginia were Anatoly Chubais, CEO of open joint-stock company RUSNANO (formerly Russian Corporation of Nanotechnol-

Kurzweil, who is a member of the Bilderberg Group,[259] concurs with these posthumanist predictions set forth in this *Russia 2045* whitepaper. In *The Singularity Is Near*, Kurzweil demystifies the posthuman technique of "brain uploading," describing it as a

> straightforward brain-porting scenario [that] involves scanning a human brain (most likely from within), capturing all of the salient details, and reinstating the brain's state in a different – most likely much more powerful – computational substrate. This will be a feasible procedure and will happen most likely around the late 2030s....
>
> [W]ill such fundamental shifts enable us to live forever? The answer depends on what we mean by "living" and "dying." ...
>
> Currently, when our human hardware crashes, the software of our lives – our personal "mind file" – dies with it. However, this will not continue to be the case when we have the means to store and restore the thousands of trillions of bytes of information represented in the pattern that we call our brains (together with the rest of our nervous system, endocrine system, and other structures that our mind file comprises).
>
> At that point, the longevity of one's mind file will not depend on the continued viability of any particular hardware medium (for example, the survival of a biological body and brain). Ultimately software-based humans will be vastly extended beyond the severe limitations of humans as we know them today. They will live out on the Web, projecting bodies whenever they need or want them, including virtual bodies in diverse realms of virtual reality, holographically projected bodies, foglet-projected bodies, and physical bodies comprising nanobot swarms and other forms of nanotechnology...
>
> Is this form of immortality the same concept as a physical human, as we know it today, living forever? ...
>
> [I]s that person based on my mind file, who migrates across many computational substrates and who outlives any particular thinking medium, really me? ... During the course of the twenty-first century these will not remain topics for polite philosophical debates but will have to be confronted as vital, practical, political, and legal issues.[260]

---

ogies) and a key ally of the Clinton Administration. Chubais is also a former Vice Premier of the Russian Government under [Boris] Yeltsin.

Chubais, in the mid 1990s, was credited with "shock therapy" privatization and the creation of the Russian oligarchs that overnight left 40% of Russians penniless and starving.

The other Russian attending Bilderberg 2012 was Igor Ivanov, Associate member of Russian Academy of Science and President of Russian International Affairs Council, a subsidiary of the powerful US based Council on Foreign Relations.

Perhaps these predictions are hasty. Nevertheless, at the 2017 World Government Summit in Dubai, Elon Musk professed his belief that the only thing in the way of a "merger of biological intelligence and digital intelligence" is a "bandwidth problem": "[i]t's mostly about the bandwidth, the speed of the connection between your brain and the digital version of yourself, particularly output.… Some high bandwidth interface to the brain will be something that helps achieve a symbiosis between human and machine intelligence and maybe solves the control problem and the usefulness problem."[261]

For Musk, "artificial general intelligence [AGI]," or sentient AI, will soon become "smarter than the smartest human on earth"; and human beings will become "useless" unless we neo-eugenically upgrade into posthuman-AI creatures.[262] In an interview with Joe Rogan, Musk literally said, "if you can't beat it [AI], join it."[263] On the *Joe Rogan Experience Podcast*, Musk explained that humanity as a species has already unconsciously begun to join AI by constantly "interfacing" with smartphones that enhance our abilities to process information:

> [h]ow much smarter are you with a phone or computer than without? You're vastly smarter, actually.… If you connect to the internet, you can answer any question pretty much instantly – any calculation. Your phone's memory is essentially perfect. You can remember flawlessly. Your phone can remember videos, pictures, everything perfectly. Your phone is already an extension of you. You're already a cyborg. Most people don't realize they are already a cyborg. That phone is an extension of yourself. It's just that the data rate – the communication rate between you and the cybernetic extension of yourself that is your phone and computer – is slow; it's very slow. It's like a tiny straw of information flow between your biological self and your digital self. And we need to make that tiny straw like a giant river, a huge, high-bandwidth interface. It's an interface problem, a data-rate problem. [If we] [s]olve the data-rate problem, then I think we can hang on to human-machine symbiosis through the long term. And then people may decide that they want to retain their biological self of not.[264]

Now you know the ultimate objective behind Musk's Neuralink Corporation, which is engineering "Neural Lace" BCIs.[265]

While posthuman Neural Laces will be marketed as Promethean technological gifts for the betterment of humanity, it should be noted that Musk's grandfather, Joshua Haldeman,[266] was the Research Director of

Canada's Technocracy Inc.:[267] a techno-fascistic non-governmental organization that was outlawed by the Canadian government in 1940 due to fears that Technocrats were plotting to "overthrow the government and the constitution of this country [Canada] by force."[268] Musk's grandfather, Haldeman, was arrested as a result of his Technocracy membership, though he was later acquitted.[269]

Chapter 18

Counterarguments, Caveats, and Conclusions

In his 2017 book, *Life 3.0: Being Human in the Age of Artificial Intelligence*, MIT Professor of Physics Max Tegmark outlines twelve possible post-human futures in a chapter titled "Aftermath: The Next 10,000 Years":[1]

1. **Libertarian Utopia:** Humans, cyborgs, uploads and superintelligences coexist peacefully thanks to property rights.[2]

2. **Benevolent Dictator:** Everybody knows that AI runs society and enforces strict rules, but most people view this as a good thing.[3]

3. **Egalitarian Utopia:** Humans, cyborgs and uploads coexist peacefully thanks to property abolition and guaranteed income.[4]

4. **Gatekeeper:** A super-intelligent AI is created, with the goal of interfering as little as necessary to prevent the creation of another super-intelligence. As a result, helper robots with slightly subhuman intelligence abound, and human-machine cyborgs exist, but technological progress is forever stymied.[5]

5. **Protector god:** Essentially omniscient and omnipotent, AI maximizes human happiness by intervening only in ways that preserve our feeling of control of our own destiny – and masks itself well enough that many humans even doubt the AI's existence.[6]

6. **Enslaved god:** A super-intelligent AI is confined and controlled by humans, who use it to produce unimaginable technology and wealth that can be used for good or bad, depending on who controls it.[7]

7. **Conquerors:** AI takes control, decides that humans are a threat/nuisance/waste of resources, and gets rid of us by a method that we don't even understand.[8]

8. **Descendants:** AIs replace humans, but give us a graceful exit, making us view them as our worthy descendants, much as parents feel happy and proud to have a child who's smarter than they are, but who learns from them and then accomplishes what they could only dream of – even if they can't live to see it all realized.[9]

9. **Zookeeper:** An omnipotent AI keeps some humans around, who feel treated like zoo animals and can only lament their fate.[10]

10. **1984:** Technological progress toward super-intelligence is permanently curtailed, not by an AI but by a human-led Orwellian surveillance state, in which certain kinds of AI research are banned.[11]

11. **Reversion:** Technological progress toward super-intelligence is prevented by reverting to a pre-technological society in the style of the Amish.[12]

12. **Self-destruction:** Super-intelligence is never created, because humanity drives itself to extinction by other means (say nuclear and/or biotech mayhem fueled by climate mega-crises).[13]

Even with the artificial intelligence of Google's "Crystal Ball" technology,[14] it is impossible to predict which of these possible futures will come to pass. But one thing is certain: overzealous faith in ed-tech is hubris, or at least a naiveté that is willfully blind to the dire catastrophes which could result from pushing technetronic evolution too far, too fast.

It is certainly gullible to believe that the ultra-rich Tech Barons of the corporate-globalist elite will suddenly grow a conscience and halt their exploitation of the labor and personal information of people who actually work for their daily bread, instead of playing with other people's money and data. Just because newly advanced lines of labor-saving transhumanist products could, theoretically, be used to liberate workforce slaves from perpetual political-economic bondage, there is no historical evidence to substantiate the belief that the corporate-technocrats of the future will in fact manufacture trans-tech commodities for the good of the commonweal. History, to the contrary, shows that revolutionary technological inventions have never really closed the chasm between the mega-rich and the wage-earning classes of humankind. To put it another way, never in history has there been a commercial technology upgrade that abolished the Hegelian master-slave dialectic, which subjugates wage laborers into subservience to the ruling classes of corporate-industrialists and bankster financiers.

Notwithstanding the optimism of socialist utopists like Bertrand Russell, the Second Industrial Revolution did not bring about the fully employed "leisure society" through mechanized means of production that were supposed to reduce the required workday to four-hour shifts by replacing outdated modes of manual labor.[15] Instead, Robber-Baron industrialists capitalized on their mechanical innovations by ramping up the tyrannies of corporate management systems, such as "Taylorism," which was Frederick W. Taylor's "scientific management" of business that standardized the timing of workers with stopwatches in order to micromanage the production speed of their assembly-line labors.[16] (This dehumanization was famously satirized by Charlie Chaplin in *Modern Times*.) The Robber Barons even hired "Pinkertons" and other corporate-mercenary goons, who terrorized and machine-gunned rebellious employees seeking to unionize in defiance of the mechanized panopticon of industrial serfdom.[17]

In brief, the corporatist plutocrats of the Second Industrial Revolution leveraged their powers of mechanical engineering by monopolizing machine production.[18] Hence, the facts of history indicate it is reasonable to expect that the corporatist technocrats of the Fourth Industrial Revolution will likewise leverage their powers of computer engineering to consolidate political-economic domination through virtual monopolization of AI biotechnologies.[19]

It may be argued that the dangers of a possible Tech-Baron dictatorship are worth the risk if it means humanity might be "saved" from the drudgeries of menial labor by transcending the biological limitations of the intellectual and physical labors of organic brains and muscles. It might even be posited that, regardless of the potential perils, it is inevitable that humankind must brave this digital-technetronic frontier, as human beings are bio-psychologically hardwired to unconsciously pursue evolutionary "upgrades" through technological inventions. To put it another way, whether we like it or not, the complex sociological interactions of everyday life in an increasingly computerized civilization, which are driven by a subconscious desire to technologically evolve, are "naturally" inching along the trans/post-evolution of the human species.

This argument is incongruous at best. By antithetical definition, neo-eugenic trans/posthumanism is a conscious decision to artificially speed up and steer the nonconscious processes of genetic evolution by proactively intervening in the nonconscious processes of biological mutation through biotechnological modifications. Moreover, this conscious decision to technetronically transcend biology is not being articulated by a global democratic consensus of grassroots populism. On the contrary, as documented throughout this book, the movement toward trans/posthumanism is being driven from the top down by the oligarchic ruling classes of billionaire corporatists, elite technocratic scientists, "mystery school" occultists, and other globalist secret society members. At the same time, the average person still hasn't even heard of the words, "transhumanism" or "posthumanism." Therefore, it is a contradiction to imply that the great majority, who are oblivious to the trans/posthumanist plans of the global elite, are subconsciously acquiescing to this agenda just because they are unwittingly consuming the shiny new hi-tech products that are propelling this neo-eugenic trans/post-evolution. It is a non sequitur to assume that, if consumers unknowingly subject themselves to rampant privacy infringements when playing with their newest data-tracking "smart toys," then they instinctively desire their personal data to be commandeered by crony-fascist corporations in order to fuel the posthuman techno-evolution of an emerging trans-eugenic "Super Class,"[20] which vampirically harvests biodata from consumers before tossing their virtual carcasses on the side of the road in a sort of arrested evolutionary development.

It is counterintuitive to claim that the wage-earning public is somehow subconsciously willing itself to be exploited by technetronic trinkets so that techno-plutocrats can achieve their own conscious, premeditated plans to not only dominate the rest of the human species, but to diverge from the "unfit" subpopulations of working people and transcend into a brand-new dominant species: *homo deus*. For these reasons, I refute the theory that the neo-eugenic techno-evolution of posthuman artificial selection is an "organic" outgrowth of the biogenetic evolution of natural selection.

Furthermore, I contend that neo-eugenic posthumanism is as much a religion as any theistic belief system. In fact, despite Thomas Henry Huxley's self-ascribed adherence to the non-religion of skeptical agnosticism, which was conceived of by T. H. himself, he is actually quoted as asserting that "biology lectures" should be actively disseminated to "schoolmasters … with the view of converting them [schoolmasters] into scientific missionaries to convert the Christian heathen to the true faith [of evolutionary science]."[21] 150 years later, here we are: the Darwinian religion of scientism has evolved into the cult of trans-eugenic posthumanism.

In *Homo Deus*, Yoel Harari describes Big Tech corporations as, literally, New Age religious institutions:

> [d]espite all the talk of radical Islam and Christian fundamentalism, the most interesting place in the world from a religious perspective is not the Islamic State or the Bible Belt, but Silicon Valley. That's where hi-tech gurus are brewing for us brave new religions

that have little to do with God, and everything to do with technology. They promise all the old prizes – happiness, peace, prosperity, and even eternal life – but here on earth with the help of technology, rather than after death with the help of celestial beings.

These new techno-religions can be divided into two main types: techno-humanism and data religion. Data religion argues that humans have completed their cosmic task and should now pass the torch on to entirely new kinds of entities.[22]

Whereas posthumanist "data religion" has faith that humans should submit to becoming totally subsumed by software-based intelligences, transhumanist "techno-humanism" has faith that humans should upgrade our biology by symbiotically merging it with machines. Between these competing "denominations" of techno-theism, worshipers of data religion have even set up an official AI church called "Way of the Future" (WOTF) which, according to IRS filings, literally practices the "worship of a Godhead based on Artificial Intelligence (AI) developed through computer hardware and software."[23]

Notwithstanding the direct testimonies from these worshippers of evolutionary technologies, posthumanist apologists may disregard these parallels between trans-eugenic ideologies and the religious worship of technology. Defenders of the posthumanist faith might try to claim that comparisons between religious fundamentalism and radical science fanaticism are intellectual conflations from 'Luddites' who misunderstand the empirical epistemology of the scientific method.

To be sure, I do not possess the formal training and credentials in the quantitative sciences to wax authoritatively on the technical intricacies of evolutionary biology and computer engineering. Nonetheless, my university expertise in the English language arts is grounded in the discipline of classical rhetoric; and, as a scholar of letters, I have applied an academic rhetorical analysis of the formal logos and ethos implicit in the empirical philosophies underlying post-eugenic scientism. I have not taken issue with the internal quantitative logic of any empirical scientific data. Rather, I have used *a priori* philosophical reasoning to question the ethical assumptions underlying the technocratic presumption that, by default, the immediate utility of all empirical measurements leading technological advancement are self-evidently valuable to the human species.

Thus, my intellectual *a priori* analysis of posthumanist rhetoric does not require a quantitative understanding of posthuman technetronics. In fact, philosophies of ethics, by nature, must be fundamentally rooted in *a priori* reasoning – because empirical measurements cannot determine the values of human morality; empirical metrics can only measure whether or not a determined value has been enacted.[24] In other words, *a posteriori* empiricism can only quantify the "use value" of utility; empiricism cannot qualify the "intrinsic value" of morality.

As demonstrated in *Groundwork of the Metaphysics of Morals* by the transcendental idealist philosopher Immanuel Kant, moral values are in essence "categorical imperatives" akin to what the American founding fathers deemed "self-evident truths": philosophical principles that are not empirical means toward utilitarian ends, but are divine ends unto themselves.[25] Bound by the rules of quantitative calculation, the empirical method of *a posteriori* reasoning can only measure the extent to which a specific end has been attained. Quantitative *a posteriori* empiricism cannot evaluate whether a particular end is ultimately moral or otherwise desirable for the human condition.

That is a question for qualitative *a priori* logic analyzing abstract values, such as 'good' and 'evil', that cannot be corporeally measured unless first qualified by the *a priori* reasoning of metaphors, similes, analogies, and other figurative analyses that invoke images and symbols, which are the intellectual specialty of philosophers and other literary scholars of the humanities who study the metaphysical logos of the word – not the mathematical logic of the number. Human beings are not numbers. We are not inanimate objects like, say, a computer; to be used until it's worn out or obsolete and thrown away. Hence, human values are not quantities. Moreover, quantities (or numbers) are predetermined by qualities (expressed in words); for numbers can only be used to quantify those qualities which have already been identified with words. Thus, the values of human morality are *a priori* qualities which must be identified with the logos of words before they can be quantified in any way by math or science.

In sum, as a language arts professor of the humanities, it is in fact my academic responsibility to use the conventions of my scholarly discipline to check and balance the empirical myopia of the mathematical and scientific schools. Indeed, as a professor of the humanist arts and as a public educator, I cannot think of a more imperative duty than to ward off mad science bent on the dehumanizing reduction of all human consciousness to nothing more than a soulless binary-code matrix of virtually-simulated ones and zeroes. I hope that I have fulfilled that obligation as a public intellectual in the pages of *School World Order*.

Epilogue

SOLUTIONS

Public Schoolboards, Digital Student Privacy, and Back-to-Trivium Basics with a New Curriculum of "Consciousness Studies"

Corporatized charter schools and voucher programs, cognitive-behavioral adaptive-learning software, transhumanist precision-ed biotech and posthuman AI teacher-bots and tutor-bots all have in common the alluring promise of "personalized," or "individualized," learning. If the privatization of "school choice" through ed-tech would in fact maximize the critical and creative exceptionalities of each student's individual consciousness, there would perhaps be nothing to protest. However, the only aspects of this corporatist ed-tech revolution that are truly individualized are the social-engineering methods used to minimize the unique talents of each student, in order to mold the child into conformity with the mandates of a technocratically planned global economy:

- **Corporate charter schools:** Overturn individualized democratic control of local schooling policies by displacing elected schoolboards with executive business councils that impose workforce-training curriclums which condition students for job competence in career pathways prescribed to fulfill public/private economic planning quotas.

- **Cognitive-behavioral adaptive-learning software**: Constrain a student's individual free-will by using computerized animal-psychology techniques that condition the child to "learn" passively, merely by reflexively responding to autocratic workforce-training stimuli transmitted by corporate/government authorities.

- **Transhumanist precision education**: Cripples free-will by overriding individual consciousness with human-computer interfaces that hack into the neuro-electrical biopsychological algorithms, in order to robotically control the student's biocomputer system much like a cyborg-drone, technocratically programmed into an internet-of-everything planned economy.

- **Posthuman AI ed-tech**: Destroys the need for student learning altogether, as artificially intelligent machines become capable of outperforming human cognition, thereby replacing human intellectual labor until every human's consciousness is subsumed into a digital hive-mind consciousness, technocratically collectivized into a computerized Singularity.

How can the public schooling system be reformed to truly institute a pedagogy that teaches each student to learn independently through metacognitive self-inquiries into the curiosities of his or her own consciousness?

How can local schoolboards vote to standardize coursework requirements and diploma options that offer the individual student real academic choices, not just prescriptive career tracks for job placement to fill corporate-government workforce quotas?

In what ways can education technologies be integrated without undermining the dignity of the individual student's consciousness?

What curriculum can teach the individual student to cultivate self-reliance upon the powers of his or her own sovereign consciousness?

To reclaim our schools and our own consciousnesses, I propose the following five-point plan for systemic education reform:

1. **Local Control, Public Control:** Both federal government and private corporate influence on school curriculums and policies must be subordinated to local jurisdiction, which must be retained in the public sector through the democratic process of schoolboard elections.

2. **Abolish Psychological Edu-Conditioning:** All stimulus-response, behaviorist, and operant-conditioning methods of Wundtian-Skinnerian educational psychology conditioning, should be barred from the classroom.

3. **Digital Student Privacy:** All education technologies should be installed with firewalls that bar the unauthorized data-mining of student psychometrics and biometrics.

4. **Back to Trivium Basics:** Computerized workforce schooling should be rejected in favor of a renaissance in "classical" Trivium-based pedagogies of self-learning, so that each student becomes proficient in navigating the "thought-architecture" of his or her own consciousness through rational self-inquiries guided by the tripart process of thinking through grammar, logic, and rhetoric to self-discern truth.

5.A New Curriculum of "Consciousness Studies": State-controlled Communist values-clarification through "social studies" and/or Fascist workforce-training through career-pathways job-skills curriclums should be replaced with classical civics, history and the arts: buttressed by a new college-bound "consciousness studies" curriculum that explores classical metaphysical philosophies, modern and postmodern *a priori* epistemologies, and comparative studies of ancient theologies and poetics; in order to (re) discover a metaphysics of consciousness as an ethical basis for safeguarding against neo-eugenic technological subversions of human consciousness.

Save Our Elected Schoolboards

Families cannot personalize their "school choice" if they do not govern their public schools at the local level. If families forfeit their public schoolboard votes in deference to the executive business decisions of charter school companies, local education governance will be surrendered to the unelected CEOs of corporate schools in public-private partnerships with state and federal bureaucracies. Consequently, public-private charter corporations will seize the political reigns to "choose" which curriculums, pedagogies, and technologies are administered in the classroom.

The only way to truly personalize school choice is to retain democratically elected schoolboards, so families have civil rights to personally participate in their local schoolboard's choices regarding curriclums, methods, and technologies. In "How the Order Controls Education," The late Antony C. Sutton, who was a Professor of Economics at California State University, Los Angeles, concurs by resolving that "[p]ublic schools should be returned to local control."[1] Similarly, in *The Underground History of American Education*, renowned New York State Teacher of the Year (1991), John Taylor Gatto,[2] calls for reforms that "[d]ecentralize schooling down to the neighborhood school building level, each school with its own citizen managing board."[3]

Although Sutton and Gatto are spot-on in their recommendations for local control of public education, they both miss the mark in their promotion of privatized schooling reforms. Sutton is remiss when he proposes that "[a]ll restrictions on private schools should be abolished."[4] Likewise, Gatto is misguided when he recommends that "[t]he best way to start offering some choice *immediately* is to ... grant each private, parochial, and homeschool equal access to public funds through vouchers administered as a loan program, along with tax credits."[5] Both reforms recommended by Sutton (the deregulation of private schools) and Gatto (the public financing of private schools) are inadvisable, because these "school choice" reforms have opened the doors for the corporatization of education, which local control of schoolboard "choices" into the unelected executive councils of public-private partnerships.

Despite the corporate window dressing, the charter-industrial revolution is not "free market" school reform. Former Senior Policy Advisor in the Office of Educational Research and Improvement for the Reagan Administration's US Department of Education, Charlotte Thomson Iserbyt, dispels the capitalistic mythos surrounding the public-private charter-schooling industry by breaking down how "[t]he significance of the charter school/school choice issue is *not* related strictly to educational choice. It is related to acceptance of a communist system of governance where decisions are made by appointed, not elected officials. Appointed officials cannot be removed from office by voters/taxpayers."[6]

Don't be misinformed by "school choice" proponents who are misled by claims of "local control" through the privatized charter-schooling industry. Local charter "choice" is only local insofar as charter school companies hold classes at local schoolhouses. And the only "choices" offered to families are regarding which edu-corporation they can afford to pick from the menu of public-private partnerships with the local government agencies in their school districts.

Since charter school corporations are not publicly owned by the local county, city, township, village, or municipality, such privatized companies are not obliged to invite local families to question or overrule any teaching or learning policies that have been decreed by the executive councils of the charter business. The appointed corporate boards of charter councils are not legally bound to heed any complaints from taxpaying and tuition-paying families who voice non-consent to their curriclums, methods, or ed-tech products assigned for classroom-to-workforce conditioning by the CEOs of Big Education. As Charlotte Iserbyt explains in her article titled "Charter School Trap," "the regional appointive system of governance is being used with charter schools. The appointive system does not allow voters – who pay the taxes that support public-funded charter schools – to remove persons whose decisions do not represent the majority of voters."[7]

In brief, the appointed councils of corporate charter schools are not publicly controlled by the votes of local families. On the contrary, in the educational-industrial complex of the charter-schooling business, the final decisions regarding student learning are autocratically ordained by the mega-rich executives of elite private companies in collusion with the political hacks of federal, state, and local government bureaucracies. Again, it is imperative that families reclaim the public sovereignty of their democratically elected local schoolboards in order to protect their civil rights to vote for institutional learning policies that are guided by their own inalienable liberties of conscience.

Local democratic control of student learning may also be retained through homeschooling. However, it is crucial that even homeschool choice be governed by the local civil authorities of publicly elected schoolboards. Without control of local education governance, families will forfeit their civil rights to personalize their own homeschooling curriculums and methodologies. Once vacated, the local jurisdictions will be rolled over into federal government receivership under the Every Student Succeeds Act, which stipulates provisions that could require families to comply their homeschooling practices to align with corporate workforce-competence outcomes conditioned through commercialized adaptive-learning software, transhumanist biotech, and/or posthuman AI ed-tech products decreed to be implemented in the home-learning environment, in order to earn government-accredited diplomas and degrees.

In "Wake Up Homeschoolers: They're Coming for Your Children," Iserbyt details how the hi-tech "school choice" privatization of homeschooling is already being federalized through the incorporation of online charter-school companies, such as K12 Inc., into the home-learning environment:

> …virtual learning home school programs (virtual charters which are federally funded, with no elected boards) are being used across the nation by home schooled children. Their federal funding requires federal assessment. Federal assessment includes every bad thing you have heard about Communist Core. Secretary Bennett, when he was in charge of K-12 [Inc.], responded to savvy homeschoolers who asked him what test they would have to take, as follows:
>
> "You will have to take the national test, the National Assessment of Educational Progress (NAEP), since charter schools are federally funded."[8]

In another article entitled "Death Sentence for Private and Home Education, Courtesy of Supreme Court," Iserbyt elaborates how:

> [t]he NAEP is the tool for measuring accountability to political-ly-correct government viewpoints (60 percent of the test items

measure political correctness and school-to-work readiness). The NAEP, which President Bush mandated be administered in all schools, will determine not only curriculum, but compliance with accountability standards and therefore will be essential in the determination of which private schools and home schoolers will receive vouchers [and federal accreditation].[9]

It is therefore vital that families preserve the democratic due-process of local schoolboard elections through which families can vote to retain their individual right to personalize their own homeschooling curriclums and pedagogies by abstaining from federal voucher programs and "education savings account" tax breaks, that write off tuition payments for online home-learning through public-private virtual charter school corporations. Otherwise, the only "local" control of the homeschooling system will be the control of public-private workforce planning by the federal government (in bed with private ed-tech corporations) imposing top-down control of the learning that takes place within the very walls of each family's local household. Similarly, the only "personalized" aspect of a homeschooling system without local schoolboard democracy will be the powers of federal bureaucracies and private companies to personalize their Big Data control of the curriclums, methods, and technologies, which will be required to learn workforce competence under the very roofs of their own personal households.

By retaining local democratic control of education governance through public schoolboard elections, families can retain their civil right to personally take charge of the political processes of school governance through votes that determine the standardization of curriclums, methodologies, and technologies required to earn accredited diplomas and degrees from both classroom and homeschool learning in the jurisdictions of their local schoolboard districts.

Attempting to rescue local schoolboard democracy are several grassroots political movements that are putting into practice the wisdom of the founder of the Guardians of Education for Maine, Charlotte Iserbyt, who has decried appointed corporate councils, "[c]harter schools are 'taxation without representation' and the concept should undergo a constitutional challenge in the courts."[10]

- In Alabama, where the ongoing expansion of corporate charter schools has been pumped up by millions of dollars in federal grants,[11] the people of the City of Gadsden successfully negotiated on January 22, 2019, to convert the city's appointed schoolboard council into a democratically elected schoolboard through the efforts of local suffrage activists. The Chair of the Etowah County Voters' League, Mary Carstarphen Kelley, has expressed how she is "hopeful and prayerful that an elected school board will facilitate increased access and public accountability.... The election process should better acquaint parents and the community with their respective school board member."[12]

• After a final vote from the Missouri State Board of Education, the Special Administrative Board of the St. Louis Public Schools District, which is home to at least 33 public-private charter schools,[13] has returned governance powers to a democratically elected public schoolboard.[14] Executive director of the Missouri School Boards' Association, Melissa Randol, has praised the restoration of the elected schoolboard as it "allows the community to own the school district and have a voice in the direction of the school district."[15]

• In New Jersey, where the number of privatized charter schools "tripled" under the governorship of Chris Christie,[16] there is growing dialogue among taxpaying residents of the Montclair school district who seek to petition the municipal government to change the township from a Type I district with an appointed schoolboard to a Type II district with an elected schoolboard.[17]

• The call to instate a publicly elected schoolboard over the charter-entrenched Chicago Public Schools (CPS) system in Illinois has been voiced by activists such as the Director of the Lugenia Burns Hope Center, Roderick Wilson, who reasons that, "[r]ight now we have a school board but we don't have any voice. If we have a school board that is appointed by the mayor they are beholden to the mayor versus being beholden to the people that are most impacted by this. It's about empowering the people."[18]

Thanks to activists like Wilson, the people of Chicago have successfully pressured the House of Representatives of the Illinois State General Assembly to pass House Bill 2267, which will instate a publicly elected schoolboard over CPS if passed by the Senate and signed by Governor J. B. Pritzker.[19] If successful, HB 2267's elected schoolboard will dissolve the appointed CPS board, which currently seats Skull-and-Bones-man Austan Goolsbee.[20]

Building on the momentum of such grassroots political movements to save publicly elected schoolboards, families across the nation can take similar political action in their own communities, where they can revive or restore their local schoolboards to the democratic will of the taxpayers, who fund and attend the publicly financed educational institutions in their local school districts.

To fully declare the democratic independence of local schoolboard sovereignty, Charlotte Iserbyt, who is also a former schoolboard director of Camden, Maine, recommends that the federal department of education and all state departments of education should be abolished:

> [it] is essential to justify the abolition of the U.S. Department of Education, its experimental laboratories and centers, and eventually, through state legislative action, *all* fifty state departments of education which are nothing but powerful, federally-funded clones of the U.S. Department of Education, clicking their heels in unison at every federal policy initiative in order to keep the bucks rolling into their state education coffers.
>
> The former U.S. Office of Education and present U.S. Department of Education have over the years provided hundreds of millions of dollars to the state departments of education through their State Capacity Building grants, the purpose of which is to increase federal control over the local schools.[21]

By severing the puppet-strings of state and federal departments of education, local schoolboards can fully retain families' democratic rights to self-govern the standards for educational curriculums. In addition, families can also set the political precedent that they are not willing to hand over their self-governing rights to the purported efficiencies of any government leviathan or corporate machine. Likewise, families can also set the precedent that they are not willing to relinquish their self-governing rights to the autocratic efficiencies of a Big Data technocracy as a replacement for representative civil governance.

If families do not use their publicly elected local schoolboards to democratically draw sovereign political lines in the civil sands of self-governance, then the cancer of unelected council governance will metastasize across the entire political-economic system of the United States Constitutional Republic. Iserbyt forecasts how,

> [o]nce we turn that budget [the federal education budget] over to unelected council decision making, the end of representative government will not be far behind! Neoconservatives have even called for getting rid of elected representatives! Willard W. Garvey,

National Center for Privatization, in a letter to President Reagan, April 6, 1984, stated:[22]

"Privatization is now an idea whose time has come. The knowledge, communication, and computer industry can make political representatives obsolete."[23]

Abolish Psychological Edu-Conditioning:

With democratic control of education governance in the hands of publicly elected local schoolboards, families can stand up against corporate-technocratic workforce planning by petitioning to restrict not just "Skinner-box" ed-tech, but even the very ed-psych methods that are programmed into such "teaching machines" for conditioning learning in both classrooms and homeschools. Indeed, ed-tech is nothing less than ed-psych on steroids.

In 1988, the State University of New York Press published a collection of critical education essays edited by Landon E. Beyer, who was the Chair of the Department of Education at Knox College, Illinois, and Michael W. Apple, who is Professor Emeritus of Curriculum and Instruction and Educational Policy Studies at the University of Wisconsin-Madison.[24] This anthology, entitled *The Curriculum: Problems, Politics, Possibilities*, includes an article by Douglas D. Noble, entitled "Education, Technology, and the Military," which sheds light on the dark history of the literal techno-militarization of cognitive-behavioral ed-psych conditioning:

> [a] new discipline, *human engineering* or *psychotechnology*, emerged within military research [during World War II]. This work, in the Army Air Force Aviation Psychology Program and the Applied Psychology Panel, paralleled theoretical developments in information theory and cybernetics by wedding engineering and psychology into a study of "human factors" in machine design...
>
> If "human factors" engineering was the design of machines to fit men, training was the design of men to fit machines. During the war, educators and experimental psychologists mounted a massive effort in training research and development, influenced heavily by behaviorist learning psychology, [and] emerging technologies such as film and automatic instructional devices.... Although "no curriculum atom bombs" emerged from wartime training research and practice, an enormous intensification of interest was seen in the use of behaviorally oriented instructional objectives, task analysis, training aids and simulation.[25]

Noble details the specific contributions of:

> the Army's Human Resources Research Office (HumRRO), the Air Force Personnel and Training Center (AFPTRC), The American Institute for Research (AIR), and the RAND Corporation offshoot, System Development Corporation, [all of which expanded behaviorist machinations of ed-psych into] military training technologies [that] were actively disseminated within an emerging federal effort to reform public education (itself orchestrated largely by foundation and university leaders who had played key roles in wartime military research).... [T]he federal reform efforts begun in the late 1950s to transform education through "innovation" – relied almost exclusively on these military contributions.[26]

As this historical backdrop illustrates, the fight against ed-technocracy is, at its core, the battle against stimulus-response, behaviorist, operant, and other edu-conditioning methodologies in the classroom and home-school, which means the threat of ed-technocracy can only be eradicated by plucking out its ed-*psychology* roots.

Reprisals against ed-psych social engineering are nothing novel. For decades, acclaimed education theorist Alfie Kohn, who holds an MA in Social Sciences from the University of Chicago,[27] has denounced:

> the practice of dangling rewards in front of people to get them to do what we want ... whether the people in question are male or female, children or adults ... [or] whether the rewards are stickers, food, grades or money ... [or] whether the goal is to get them to work harder, learn better, act nicely, or lose weight.[28]

In *Punished by Rewards: The Trouble with Gold Stars, Incentive Plans, A's, Praise, and Other Bribes*, Kohn documents that,

> [w]hat the studies keep telling us is that rewards, like punishments, tend not only to be ineffective – particularly over the long haul – but often to undermine the very thing we're trying to promote...
>
> [N]ow, with the exception of economists and a diehard group of orthodox behaviorists (who have restyled themselves "behavior analysts"), most social scientists acknowledge that incentives tend to backfire...
>
> Alas, too many parents, teachers, and managers persist in treating people like pets, offering the equivalent of a doggie biscuit to

children, students, and employees in an effort to get them to jump through hoops.[29]

Not only are behaviorist rewards counterproductive to learning; according to Kohn, such animal-training "[r]ewards are tools used by people with more power on those with less."[30] To put it another way, stimulus-response operant-conditioning rewards are the grooming instruments by which corporatists, statists, and technocrats prey upon commercial patrons, taxpaying citizens, and digital consumers in order to socially engineer them into behaviorist subjugation.

Kohn's rejection of psychological edu-conditioning is echoed by the former International Reading Association President, Professor Kenneth Goodman. In a March 10, 1978 letter to President Jimmy Carter, Goodman denounced the outcomes-based "mastery learning" methodology of implementing behaviorist and operant-conditioning techniques to train students to respond to reading stimuli:

> [t]here is a know-nothing view that combines the outward vestiges of technology-machines, management systems, arbitrary controlled atomistic skills sequences, and constant testing—with a philosophy of behavior management. In behavior management, outcomes are assumed or arbitrarily determined and the behavior of human learners is shaped, conditioned, reinforced, extinguished, rewarded or punished until the learners achieve the target behavior.[31]

If families do not wish to be behaviorally engineered into literal human resources extracted for the building of a technocratically planned global economy, then they must vote for schoolboard policies that reject all legal requirements to incorporate psychological edu-conditioning methods into classrooms and homeschools. Otherwise, their locally elected public schoolboard governments will be little more than ceremonial institutions that merely rubberstamp the classroom enforcement of psychological conditioning methodologies compelled by politically connected corporations in crony-capitalist collusion with state and federal governments.

To break the chains of classroom and homeschool impositions of workforce-conditioning curriclums dictated by the public-private economic plans of Big Business conniving with Big Government, local schoolboards must democratically dissolve all ed-psych conditioning directives embedded in outcome-based, competency-based, and other narrow school-to-work-pedagogies. On May 5, 1984, such a resolution to ban psychological edu-conditioning from schools was passed unanimously by the Arizona Federation of Teachers, which stated its resolve to:

> oppose such programs as ECRI [Exemplary Center for Reading Instruction], Project INSTRUCT and/or any other programs that use operant conditioning under the guise of Mastery Learning, Classroom Management, Precision Teaching, and Discipline, and petition the US Congress for protection against the use of such methods on teachers and students without their prior consent.[32]

Unfortunately, the American Federation of Teachers (AFT) did not adopt this resolution from its Arizona affiliate during the AFT's national convention in 1984.[33] Nevertheless, now is the time to resurrect this platform to abolish all modes of ed-psych conditioning at the grassroots schoolboard level across all fifty states.

Schoolboards that terminate psychological conditioning mandates will also inoculate students against institutionalized brainwashing methods that train them to shut down their conscious minds and reflexively submit to the reward-and-punishment stimuli of corporate and government authorities. In Lauri Kay Baranek's Masters of Education Thesis, published by Grand Valley State University, it is documented that:

> research has shown that rewards given in school like treats and stickers negatively affect the process of learning (Deci, 1971; 1972; Festinger and Carlsmith, 1959; Lepper, Greene, and Nisbett, 1973). The use of rewards leads to less learning, more errors, less creative work, and little desire to return to a project that was once highly motivating (Garbarino, 1975; Masters and Mokros, 1973).[34]

Alfie Kohn affirms this data cited by Baranek:

> the problem [with behaviorist rewards and punishments] isn't limited to particular kinds of incentives or ways of using them. The trouble is inherent to the very *idea* of incentives. Extrinsic motivators (rewards) tend to reduce intrinsic motivation (people's interest in, or commitment to, what they're doing).[35]

To put it bluntly, the ed-psych pedagogy of extrinsic motivation through reward and punishment is the antithesis of intrinsically motivated self-learning guided by personal conscience.

The student's mind must therefore be freed from the fetters of psychological motivators adapted from animal-training rewards and punishments. In turn, the student's mind will be free to cultivate his or her own consciousness independent of extrinsic preconditioning from fetishized institutional authorities that systemically degrade the *intrinsic* personal powers of self-learning.

In *How the Order Controls Education*, former Research Fellow at Stanford University's Hoover Institution, Antony C. Sutton, concurs that Skull-and-Bones' stimulus-response and behaviorist methods of educational psychology should have no place in the classroom. Sutton asserts that:

> [s]ocial engineering as an [educational] objective has to be discarded..... It follows that Schools of Education should be abolished (this is under serious discussion at Duke University and has been proposed at University of Michigan and even Cal Berkeley [1983]). Teacher credentials should be based on subject matter entirely, not educational theory.[36]

Undoubtedly, college departments (or "schools") of education are essentially "laboratories" for advancing the scientific application of learning theories grounded in stimulus-response, behaviorist, operant, and other methods of psychological conditioning. As such, Sutton's call to shut down these teacher-training institutions would effectively advance the disarmament of animal-training psychology geared for school-to-work brainwashing.

To be sure, even the best-intentioned uses of educational psychology tend to be counterproductive to cultivating the intrinsic motivation of self-learning. As documented in Lori Kay Baranek's Master's Thesis,

> intrinsically motivated students are often hard to find, because motivation is often undermined by the heavy use of external motivators in school. A person who is extrinsically motivated performs a task in order to receive a reward of some kind. ...
>
> The solution to the problem, a lack of motivation, is to design classrooms and follow practices that foster the development of intrinsic motivation. All personnel need to reduce the use of external rewards while using programs and practices that allow students to fully develop their own intrinsic motivation in school activities (Adelman, 1989: Amabile and Gitomer, 1984; Kohn, 1993; Ryan and Grolnick, 1986).[37]

Digital Student Privacy

By expunging the extrinsic reward-and-punishment motivators of ed-psych conditioning methods from classrooms and homeschools, local schoolboards can democratically set a firm political precedent: that families will not tolerate ed-tech policies which hamper students' intrinsic motivations by advancing ed-psych conditioning to the next levels of trans- and post-humanism. Building on this political precedent, it is pivotal that families take further control of their local schoolboards by voting to pre-emptively restrict education technologies that invade the privacy of the individual student's conscience by recording his or her personal psychometric data.

Here are three major reasons that protecting each student's right to psychometric privacy is indispensable to facilitating a school system that fosters self-learning through conscientious self-inquiries:

1. Student psychometrics can be co-opted by corporations to exploit such data for behavioral advertising and workforce conditioning, which enable techno-fascist market manipulation and labor-force development for a globalist planned economy.

2. The same student data can be commandeered by government agencies tracking such psychometrics into "permanent records" that may be funneled into a Chinese-style Social Credit Score system, which will penalize students who exhibit "thought crime" algorithms by restricting those thought-criminals' rights to transportation, healthcare, and even civil due process.

3. Knowing that his or her psychometrics can be hijacked and weaponized by corporations and governments, the student who is aware of this data-mining will instinctively self-censor thoughts and actions in attempts to escape being negatively categorized by employers and government agencies. (For a detailed treatise on the psycho-social phenomenon of coerced self-oppression subliminally stemming from ubiquitous mass-surveillance, see *Discipline and Punishment* by the postmodernist philosopher, Michel Foucault,[38] who expounded the hyper-utilitarian social-engineering theories underlying the guard-tower architectural principles of Jeremy Bentham's "panopticon" prison systems).[39] [a] [40]

---

a   Jeremy Bentham was a nineteenth-century utilitarian philosopher who drafted blueprints for a modernized "panopticon" prison in which a single guard can see all of the prisoner cells form his central vantage point while none of the prisoners can see the guard from their cells. According to Bentham's architectural drawings, the panopticon prison is constructed as a single guard tower surrounded by a ring of prisoner cells, like a colosseum with a guard tower in the middle of the ring/arena. From the watchtower, the guard has a 360-degree view of all the prisoner cells. Of course, the watchman can surveil only a portion of this 360-degree view at any given moment; but since the prisoners cannot see the watchman through the shutters and grills of their cell doors, they can never know which specific cells the guardsman is surveilling. As a result, the prisoners are psychologically conditioned to behave as if they are always being watched by this mass-surveillance system. Hence, the prisoners effectively self-censor any behaviors that might be penalized by the guardsman.

To protect the free expression of human dignity, each student must be allowed the sovereign privacy of his or her own thoughts; so that he or she can quietly think through internal dialogues, question market economics and critique politically correct dogmas, without fear of being demerited or blacklisted by corporations and governments. Therefore, all schoolboards should restrict any education technologies that data-mine students' cognitive psychology, behavioral psychology, emotional psychology, neuropsychology, psycho-genetics or bio-psychology.[41]

For any student who wishes to receive school accommodations for a disability, psychometrics may be temporarily recorded to assess his or her cognitive-behavioral condition. However, the student (with consent of the parent/guardian) must voluntarily apply to take the diagnostic psychometric test, which must be conducted by medical professionals, who must classify the results of these psychometrics as confidential medical (not educational) records. Moreover, as confidential medical records, these psychometric diagnostics must only be viewed by licensed medical officials, unless voluntarily released to school counselors where the student is actively enrolled.

As a final safety net, any medical records of a student's psychometrics should be completely erased, or "forgotten," upon demand at any time after he or she reaches legal adulthood. In fact, growing public support for such a "right to be forgotten" from digital databases has already been picking up steam in the broader consumer sector of American society. According to a 2015 survey polled by Benenson Strategy Group and SKDKnickerbocker, nine out of ten Americans desire some form of a "right to be forgotten" law that would require internet search-engine companies, such as Google, Yahoo, and Bing, to comply with petitions from persons who request that their personal information be deleted from online search engines.[42]

Overseas in Europe, the Court of Justice of the European Union (EU) has already ruled to instate a broad set of "right to be forgotten" laws codified under the General Data Protection Regulations (GDPR), which require social media companies, such as Facebook, and online search engines, such as Google, to comply with users who ask for the deletion of their personal data.[43] Nonetheless, Google and Facebook are not legally required to transfer their EU GDPR policies to the jurisdiction of the United States.

As a result of this double standard, a complaint to the US Federal Trade Commission (FTC) was filed by the nonprofit consumer rights organization, Consumer Watchdog, which accused Google of violating Section 5 of the FTC Act by not offering to the American people the same "right to be forgotten" options that Google offers citizens of the EU.[44] In the wake of this Consumer Watchdog complaint, the State of California has taken a cue from the GDPR overseas by passing an "Online Erasure Law" that requires website proprietors to "delete" information posted to their platforms by a minor whenever he or she requests deletion. Although critics of this law have rightly pointed out that it does not require the deletion of information that was not posted by the minor, it is at least a step in the right direction – toward democratically pressuring legislators to reclaim our Fourth Amendment rights to personal privacy.[45]

The California Consumer Privacy Act (CCPA), which is also modeled after the EU's GDPR, is set to stipulate further restraints on web-based data-sharing companies that would require them to honor even more the "right to be forgotten". Other American states that have placed similar CCPA/GDPR laws on the books for 2019 include Hawaii (Senate Bill 418), Maryland (Senate Bill 0613), Massachusetts (Senate Docket 341), Mississippi (House Bill 2153), New Mexico (Senate Bill 176),[46] and Washington (Senate Bill 5376).[47] Whatever shortcomings any of these digital data laws may have, they are all efforts toward personal privacy. In addition, these bills all set the legislative precedent for families to take hardline stands and petition local schoolboards to enact similar digital privacy laws to protect students.

Except when psychometrically diagnosing a medical disability, schools should cautiously refrain from tracking any student's cognitive-behavioral data through technologies that monitor his or her biopsychological data, in order to accommodate his or her learning disability, by digitally augmenting lesson plans or adjusting instructional feedback in real time. To be sure, such "assistive" ed-tech devices might be able to speed up a disabled student's abilities to comprehend concepts and skills while strengthening long-term retention of knowledge. However, the personal powers gained from these hi-tech learning aids cannot be acquired without the risk of being, ironically, deprived by the collective political-economic powers gained by corporations and governments, that would extrapolate his or her psychological profile for the purpose of socially engineering a techno-fascist workforce caste system – politically micro-managed by the Social Credit Score tyranny of Big Data AI jacked into a global internet-of-everything.

For these reasons, it is unadvisable to permit any school to record students' bio-psychological data for any purpose, even disability accommodations. Inexorably, there is an inherent danger that even strictly regulated ed-tech data-mining will crack open trapdoors through which students' thought and emotion algorithms can be surreptitiously seized and technocratically predestine disabled students to the lowest castes in a digital-workforce sharecropping hierarchy on a brave new virtual plantation.

Of course, no one has the right to demand that disabled persons should be barred from any technology that assists their cognitive-behavioral disabilities, especially debilitating neurological conditions such as severe epilepsy. It is, nevertheless, the right of the individual to personally estimate, by a cost-benefit analysis, whether the risks of being psychometrically data-mined are worth the cognitive-behavioral "upgrades" gained from those technologies. At this moment, however, the consumer classes of the global economy are so enthralled with the latest hi-tech trinkets that it seems no corporation or government will be pressured to put the brakes on ed-tech advances anytime soon.

If it is not possible to put the ed-tech genie back inside its virtual bottle, then the onus is now urgently upon families to take charge of their locally elected schoolboards by demanding digital privacy through the enforcement of ed-tech data-tracking oversights stipulated in the Protection of Pupil Rights Amendment (PPRA) of 1978. Charlotte Iserbyt, who in 1982 blew the whistle on the psycho-technological edu-conditioning plans of Project BEST (Better Education Skills Through Technology), states,

> the use of many of the controversial "therapy" components [of ed-psych conditioning] requires informed parental consent under the 1978 *Protection of Pupils Rights Amendment*...
>
> If the regulations [of the PPRA] are strictly enforced, the schools will have to do the unthinkable: let parents and taxpayers in on their well-kept federally funded curriculum research, development, and dissemination-across-the-nation secrets. Such enforcement would spell disaster for their plans to convert our children into advocates of the coming socialist one world government.[48]

Indeed, according to the US Department of Education, the PPRA:

> seeks to ensure that schools and contractors obtain written parental consent before minor students are required to participate in any ED-funded survey, analysis, or evaluation that reveals information concerning:
>
> 1.   Political affiliations;
>
> 2.   Mental and psychological problems potentially embarrassing to the student and his/her family;

3.   Sex behavior and attitudes;

4.   Illegal, anti-social, self-incriminating and demeaning behavior;

5.   Critical appraisals of other individuals with whom re-spondents have close family relationships;

6.   Legally recognized privileged or analogous relation-ships, such as those of lawyers, physicians, and ministers; or

7.   Income.[49]

Applying these PPRA regulations to digital privacy, every federally subsidized ed-tech company (eventually every company with student access) must be required to obtain *expressed written permission* from a parent or guardian before that corporation is permitted to deploy any products which data-mine the student's psychometrics and thereby reveal personal information pertaining to these seven PPRA categories.

Accounting for the full assortment of ed-tech spanning adaptive-learning courseware, biofeedback biotech, transhumanist brain-computer interfaces, and assistive AI teacher-bots and tutor-bots, none of the PPRA's seven data categories is beyond the potential reach of this posthuman array of neo-eugenic education technetronics. Hence, it is imperative that families take the PPRA a step further by advocating for local schoolboard policies that actively invoke PPRA laws. For example, local regulations could require ed-tech corporations to semiannually report to parents and guardians all student data collected, stored, and/or shared in the process of facilitating computer-assisted instruction.

In the interim, the US Department of Education provides families limited recourse through PPRA petitions if they should wish to investigate potential privacy abuses of federally endowed ed-tech. The Department of Ed states:

> [p]arents or students who believe their rights under PPRA may have been violated may file a complaint with ED by writing the Family Policy Compliance Office. Complaints must contain specific allegations of fact giving reasonable cause to believe that a violation of PPRA occurred.[50]

By harnessing the democratic checks of the PPRA, families can personally watchdog the specific ed-tech assigned to students in the classroom or homeschool.

To be sure, even with the most prudent privacy policies, it is clear that schoolboards will soon be forced to deliberate on the ethical parameters for regulating ed-tech as families begin to equip disabled students with minimally invasive biotech that accommodates cognitive-behavioral learning disabilities. Soon enough, school districts will hit a crossroads where schoolboards will be forced to regulate "educational" psycho-technologies in order to either mitigate or mandate their effects on individual student consciousnesses.

Moving forward, if humanity still values the self-determination of individual consciousness, the time is now to get out in front of impending ed-tech legislation. Through local schoolboard votes and other forms of grassroots political activism, families can proactively ensure that scientific-industrial authoritarians cannot successfully ram through commercial deregulations of education technologies propped up by federal mandates requiring such products for diploma and degree accreditation. To cut off the globalist totalitarian intents of techno-aristocrats in cahoots with corporate-government oligarchs, the American people must become politically proactive by setting up local, state, and federal bulwarks against the unchecked data-mining of cognitive-behavioral, psycho-affective, or other neuro-brain algorithms.

Back to "Classical" Trivium Basics

The prevailing zeitgeist of the twenty-first century may seem to welcome transhuman technocracy as the cutting edge of the next level of human evolution. But during the rise of Nazism, Christian philosopher C. S. Lewis foresaw the trajectory toward neo-eugenic technocracy not as a leap forward in humanist evolution, but as an anti-human devolution through an empiricist religion of industrial-eugenic scientism, which deposes the classical methods of education once predicated on the metaphysical study of "Truth," which Lewis refers to as "the Tao," or "Reason."[51] In his philosophical treatise on the Tao of classical education, *The Abolition of Man* (1947), Lewis forewarns that "[t]he final stage [of dehumanization] is come when Man by eugenics, by pre-natal conditioning, and by an education and propaganda based on a perfect applied psychology, has obtained full control over himself."[52] These predictions for the coming dehumanization of psycho-eugenic ed-technocracy are narrated in Lewis's 1945 dystopian novel, *That Hideous Strength*.[53]

What was the classical educational methodology for learning the Tao of "Truth," or "Reason"? In *The Abolition of Man*, Oxford University Fellow C. S. Lewis does not prescribe a specific pedagogy by which a classical education can methodically pursue the Tao of Truth, or Reason,[54] in opposition to the inhuman neo-eugenics of social "Conditioners."[55] But as Cambridge University Chair of Medieval and Renaissance Literature,[56] Lewis wrote his philological history of such literature in *The Discarded Image*, which articulates how the core of classical "Liberal Arts" learning is grounded in a three-part educational philosophy of "Grammar, Dialectic [or Logic], [and] Rhetoric … [which] constitute the *Trivium* or threefold way."[57]

We should point out that the word "Trivium" has nothing to do with the word 'trivial' in the modern sense of insignificant, frivolous, inconsequential, etc. It is tri-vium, a three-part system of learning.

The classical Trivium is nothing less than the study of the word as the existential medium of human thought. Indeed, a cohort of C. S. Lewis and other literary scholars of the Oxford Inklings Group was Dorothy Sayers,[58] who in 1947 presented her famous Trivium essay, "The Lost Tools of Learning," at Oxford University where she propounded how the epistemology of:

> [t]he syllabus [of classical schools] was divided into two parts: the Trivium and Quadrivium. … [T]he Trivium … preceded the Quadrivium and was the preliminary discipline for it. It consisted of three parts: Grammar, Dialectic [or Logic], and Rhetoric, in that order. … [T]hese "subjects" are not what we should call "subjects" at all: they are only methods of dealing with subjects. … [L]anguage itself is simply the medium in which thought is expressed.[59]

The profound implications of this metaphysical truth highlight that the Trivium is not just an antiquated method of learning basic skills in the language arts of reading, writing, and speaking. Rather, the Trivium liberal arts of grammar, logic, and rhetoric are in fact the thought-architecture of human consciousness which predicates the art of thinking. Stated differently, the Trivium is an educational pedagogy that teaches students *how* to think – not *what* to think.

Evidence that the Tao of the Trivium is in fact the art of thinking, not just a subset of humanities "subjects," is demonstrated through its historical proto-beginnings as the foundation of Aristotelean Greek philosophy and as a cornerstone of Judeo-Christian and Islamic theology.[60 b 61] More-

---

b   According to Islamic scholar, Hamza Yusuf, who is the President of Zaytuna College in Berkeley, California, the "liberal arts" of Trivium learning have laid "foundation[s] in the Jewish, over, Trivium thought-architecture was refined at early Arabic universities where Muslim scholars set up the framework for the modern scientific method, which was later adopted across Western Europe during the era of Renaissance humanism and the Age of Enlightenment/Reason.[62] In brief, the Trivium has been instrumental in the diverse advancement of human thought throughout the last 2,300 years of recorded history.

To revivify the inalienable Tao of personal consciousness, the "categorical imperative" (the individual private right) of essentially all scientific, philosophical, and (most) theological schools of thought, I propose that public education be reformed on the basis of Trivium curriculums that teach the student to study the Logos, or Reason, of the words that he or she reads, hears, thinks and speaks. The goal of my revised Trivium is not the mastery of language in itself as an academic "subject." Rather, the goal here is to induct each student into a metacognitive understanding of the Logos, or Reason, by which he or she rhetorically expresses the Tao, or Truth, of conscience.

If these reforms sound anachronistically quaint, here are three practical reasons why an updated Trivium curriculum would revamp public schools into functioning democratic institutions where students learn to self-actualize the Tao, or Reason, through Constitutional channels of civil self-governance:

> 1. The Trivium method endows students with the analytical skills to debunk the fallacies of demagogue politicians who spew the doublespeak slogans of a Socialist-Communist Nanny State where an AI Big Brother doles out Universal Basic Income payments to digitally indentured wage slaves.

> 2. Similarly, the Trivium method empowers students to debunk the fallacies in the propaganda of commercial advertisements and corporate marketing campaigns that promote a mindless culture of slavish consumerism which props up the fascistic merger of private industry conglomerated with government bureaucracies: a counterfeit Capitalistic "free enterprise" dreamworld.

> 3. Likewise, the Trivium method equips students with critical thinking tools to debunk the rhetorical fallacies pontificated in technocratic sophistry, which tries to justify the data-driven hubris of mad scientists bent on re-engineering the human species into a neo-eugenic Singularity.

Christian, and Islamic civilizations, as well as counterparts in the Indic and Asian cultures."

In sum, a revised Trivium can endow the individual student with a logical method of independent thinking that enables him or her to debunk corporate false advertising, government public relations propaganda, and neo-eugenic technocracy jargon. Furthermore, a renewed Trivium can also equip the individual student with the rhetorical tool-kit needed to logically and objectively communicate his or her personal rebuttals of such fallacies without becoming muted or muzzled by the ideological echo chambers of phony left-right identity politics.

Modernist and postmodernist skeptics who are satisfied with the status quo of techno-behaviorist edu-conditioning will no doubt beg the questions:

- How can the old-fashioned logos, or "logocentrism," of Trivium arts cultivate a thinking and learning methodology that is at all formidable in the coming posthuman era of hyper-empirical techno-centrism where logical thought operations are calculated by AI-supercomputer algorithms?

- How can the vintage "logocentrism" of Trivium language arts be relevant in the current era of hyper-phenomenological "text-centrism" where "deconstructionist" linguistic analysis refracts the logos of a word/text through the relativism of subjectivist existentialism which has "deconstructed" human consciousness into a meaningless "text" that can be overwritten with transhuman psycho-tech augmentations?[63]

Without being tied in mental knots by all this jargon from twentieth-century post-modern "philosophers," the simple truth is that these rhetorical questions rely upon the fallacious assumption that Trivium pedagogy must be inferior, because it is older, while the trendy newfangled schools of psycho-technological conditioning and existentialist-linguistic deconstruction must be superior merely because they are new and shiny.

Yet, an accurate account of philosophical history reveals how this postmodern techno-speak is nothing more than an inversion of Aristotle's proto-Trivium philosophy of language, which postulates that *all* knowledge is attainable through precise use of linguistic "subjects and predicates" that nominally identify the "categories" of the "accidents" and "potentialities" of the "substances" of all material "matter" and all metaphysical "actuality."[64]

Furthermore, Aristotle's proto-Trivium "organon" of grammar with its substrate of logical rules is in fact the epistemological root of the scientific method by which these "accidental" "categories" of material "substances" can be precisely defined through quantitative measurements analyzed with inductive and deductive reasoning proven with formal mathematics.[65]

Simply put, from the times of ancient Greece unto the present, the core of ostensibly all philosophical and scientific inquiries of Western and Middle Eastern scholasticism have revolved in some way around the same proto-Trivium question: what are the definitive relationships between language and truth with regard to the objective physical universe and subjective metaphysical consciousness? This is the *sine qua non*. It's the horse that Science rode in on. It's what makes us Human.

Thus, the Tao of Trivium thought-architecture is anything but irrelevant to scientific or philosophical thought in this New Digital Age. The art of Trivium thinking is both the roots of, and the antithesis to, the dominant philosophical schools of thought propelling us into the hi-tech future of trans-eugenic posthumanism. As such, the Trivium is not only instrumental to the logos of rational thought; but it is also the key to debunking the hyper-skepticism of existentialist-linguistic deconstructionists who re-label human consciousness as an empty "text" to be technologically re-engineered by neo-eugenic trans-materialists.

But if Trivium schooling is not outdated, is it yet unnecessarily over-complicated with dense jargon? In "How the Order Controls Education," Antony Sutton advocates a minimalist school reform by resolving that "[t]eacher credentials should be based on subject matter entirely, not educational theory."[66] Renowned New York State Teacher of the Year (1991), John Taylor Gatto,[67] takes Sutton's minimalist recommendations a step even further in Gatto's own *Underground History of American Education*, which concludes with a call to "[b]reak the teacher certification monopoly so anyone with something valuable to teach can teach it. Nothing is more important than this."[68]

To be sure, it is understandable to be daunted by the Greek and Latin jargon of the Trivium with its complex formulas and diagrams.. In this regard, Sutton and Gatto are correct that teacher licensing should be flexible, based primarily on the instructor's college degree or exemplary professional experience, rather than his or her educational theories. The consummate teaching career of Gatto, who was hired as a school instructor on a whim after he "borrowed" a friend's teaching license,[69] is itself evidence that Gatto's and Sutton's minimalist teacher-certification reforms are indeed viable.

That said, as much as a reform curriculum should be simplified, decentralized, and open to the academic freedoms of teacher expertise, an instructor's academic or professional mastery of "subject" content, does not ensure that he or she knows how to instill that knowledge without reverting to the old-school rote method of skill-and-drill memorization and regurgitation of lectures and lessons on basic skills. Maybe teachers themselves should be required to study the Trivium and Quadrivium as part of their degree curriclums. Therefore, to give form to the educational revisions of Gatto and Sutton, I recommend that families vote for schoolboard policies that institute locally controlled Trivium methods so that the academic freedoms of flexible teacher-licensing do not cause a reversion to the old-fashioned method of rote schoolmaster discipline which falsely compartmentalizes curriclums into hyper-specialized "subjects" walled off from the interconnective thought-architecture of Trivium self-learning through the intrinsic Tao, or Reason, of the student's own conscience.In *An Underground History of American Education*, John Taylor Gatto documents how the old rote taskmaster pedagogy of "subject" fragmentation is actually just the Prussian precursor to ed-psych conditioning. Gatto writes,

> "[s]ubjects" have a real value, too, but subject study as an exclusive diet was a Prussian secret weapon to produce social stratification."[70]

Gatto expounds how the Prussian segregation of school learning took hold in

> Gary, Indiana, [where] Superintendent William A. Wirt, a former student of John Dewey's at the University of Chicago ... had supposedly invented a new organizational scheme in which school subjects were *departmentalized*; this required movement of students from room to room on a regular basis so that all building spaces were in constant use.[71]

In this Americanized model of Prussian "subject" schooling,

> [c]lassroom teachers would teach the same thing over and over to groups of traveling children; special subject teachers would deliver their special subjects to classes rotating through the building on a precision time schedule."[72]

Adding an element of stimulus-response behavioral conditioning to the recipe,

[b]ells would ring and just as with Pavlov's salivating dog, children would shift out of their seats and lurch toward yet another class.[73]

In brief, Gatto shows that, even without integrating institutional methods of psychological conditioning, the subject-specific system of schooling relegates its curricular structure to rigid, arbitrary regimentations that disjoint learning through disparate exercises in random fact regurgitation. Gatto reveals that the "endless sequences of so-called 'subjects' delivered by men and women who, however well-meaning, have only superficial knowledge of the things whereof they speak, is the introduction most kids get to the liar's world of institutional life. Ignorant mentors cannot manage larger meanings, only facts. In this way schools teach the disconnection of everything."[74]

To solve this problem of a disconnected, subject-fragmented curriculum, Gatto advocates reforms that "[a]rrange much of schooling around complex themes instead of subjects.... Substantial amounts of interdisciplinary work are needed as a corrective."[75] Yet this interdisciplinary framework for reunifying school "subjects," as shown by Dorothy Sayers and C. S. Lewis, need not be invented in a new methodology, but instead recovered through a revision of Trivium liberal arts, which traditionally were conceived of as having a metaphysical connection to all *a priori* and *a posteriori* knowledge in both the material reality of the cosmos and the phenomenal reality of consciousness.

In *The Discarded Image*, C. S. Lewis casts light on how the Medieval conception of the "Liberal Arts" Trivium as the metaphysical bridge between the cosmos and consciousness is the antithesis of the neo-Prussian compartmentalization of conscious learning into the rote churning of isolated "subjects":

> [t]o give an educational curriculum a place in the Model of the universe may at first seem an absurdity; and it would be an absurdity if the medievals had felt about it as we feel about the 'subjects' in a syllabus today. But the syllabus was regarded as immutable; ... the Liberal Arts, by long prescription, had achieved a status not unlike that of nature herself. The Arts, no less than the Virtues and Vices, were personified.[76]

Lewis is articulating how the Trivium Liberal Arts of Grammar, Dialectic [Logic], and Rhetoric were regarded as the metaphysical mediums through which all arts and sciences are cosmically interconnected between "nature herself" and the individual human soul (or consciousness).[77] In other words, once upon a time, Trivium students were taught to conceptualize grammar, logic, and rhetoric as the metaphysical architecture of thinking which interconnects all artistic and scientific truth through the Tao of consciousness.

In "The Lost Tools of Learning," Oxford University graduate Dorothy Sayers,[78] who taught Modern Languages at Hull High School for Girls,[79] scorns the degeneration of the Trivium art of thinking and self-learning into the modern "science" of disjointed "subject" training and conditioning. Sayers asks,

> [i]s not the great defect of our education today ... that although we often succeed in teaching our pupils 'subjects,' we fail lamentably on the whole at teaching them how to think: they learn everything except the art of learning.[80]

Affirming this rhetorical question, Sayers historicizes how, in contrast to modern "subject" schooling,

> [t]he whole of the Trivium was, in fact, intended to teach the pupil the proper use of the tools of learning, before he began to apply them to 'subjects' at all. First, he learned a language ... the [Grammatical] structure of a language, and hence of language itself – what it was, how it was put together, and how it worked. Secondly, he learned how to use language; how to define his terms and make accurate statements; how to construct an argument and how to detect fallacies in argument. Dialectic, that is to say, embraced Logic and Disputation. Thirdly, he learned to express himself in [Rhetorical] language – how to say what he had to say elegantly and persuasively.[81]

Hence, to reconnect the dismembered "subjects" of academic schooling, I advocate that families vote for local schoolboard policies that revivify Trivium methods of teaching the art of self-learning through the triad thought-architecture of grammar, logic, and rhetoric.

The Universal Triad:

- **Grammar:** the art of using linguistic symbols to define phenomena and thereby establish the first law of logic: the law of identity.[82]

- **Logic:** the art of identification without contradiction by thinking through grammatical symbols to rationalize the relational truths between observed phenomena:[83]

- **Rhetoric:** the art of using grammar to communicate logical relationships between identified phenomena.[84]

In a nutshell, Grammar is the standardized accumulation of descriptive language; Logic is the accurate analysis of the interrelationships between the meanings behind those descriptive words and phrases; and Rhetoric is creative and critical communication through speech and written composition.

Similarly, in terms of the scientific method, the grammar phase is the stage of gathering factually observable data pertaining to a hypothesis; the logic phase is the stage of inductively thinking through and testing out possible interconnections between gathered data in order to prove the hypothesis; and the rhetoric phase is the stage where the hypothesis has been deductively narrowed down to a theory that explicates the logical findings of the tested data.

Again, using a computer analogy, the grammar is the basic input data, such as specific types of code scripts, key strokes, and mouse clicks, which are fed into the computer; the logic is the systematic order of electro-mechanical operations by which the computer interprets those clicks, key strokes, code-scripts and other data inputs to carry out hardware and software programs; and the rhetoric is the output data, such as a particular text, image, audio, video, or other virtual transmission that is projected or manipulated by the hardware-software dialectic based on logical electro-mechanical algorithms which pre-program the computer's translation of the input data.

Notice how the basic processes of qualitative literary rhetoric, quantitative mathematical science, and even computer program engineering can all be broken down into three main procedures that parallel the three-part process of Trivium thinking. This is because the triad system of grammar, logic, and rhetoric is nothing less than an explicative mapping of the inner-workings of human thought, which must always coordinate three procedures: a process of identifying phenomena by either naming the phenomena with words or measuring them with numbers; a process of organizing words or numbers that identify phenomena; and a process of creatively and critically acting upon that "organon" of identified phenomena either by using numbers to technically measure and manipulate quantitative phenomena or by using words to describe and evaluate qualitative phenomena. It follows that computers mimic this same three-step information-processing algorithm because, as I have demonstrated throughout this book, the software and hardware architecture of all computers, from the earliest Skinner-box teaching machines to the newest brain-computer interfaces, have always been designed to imitate the cognitive-behavioral algorithms of human thought mechanics. In other words, computers are electro-mechanical brains modeled directly after the metaphysical calculus of the human mind, which is blueprinted for self-exploration in the grammar-logic-rhetoric trigram of the Trivium Tao.

Tying all these analogies together, Trivium pedagogy teaches the individual how to master the intrinsic art of mapping out and building upon the thought-architecture of his or her own consciousness. By teaching each student to grammatically define the phenomena that he or she observes pertaining to any subject of self-inquiry, the Trivium teaches how to use logical rules to independently analyze phenomena and thereby weed out any contradictions or errors in thinking, while debunking the fallacies in the rhetoric promulgated by political soothsayers, corporate celebrities, and the gurus of technocratic scientism.

Additionally, the Trivium even gives the individual student the powers of processing information with ostensibly the same logical precision as a computer, but with the powers of empathy and human judgement which an Artificial brain can never achieve.

To be sure, critics of Trivium pedagogy may point to its institutionalization during the Middle Ages. During this period, the Holy Roman Emperor Charlemagne set up a system of Medieval Trivium-oriented schools, which taught a dogmatic justification for his "divine right" as king to subjugate peasant castes as "ordained" by a Papist spin on the "Great Chain of Being" adopted from Plato's *Republic* and Aristotle's *Historia Animalia*.[85] Nevertheless, these autocratic impositions of Trivium schooling were eventually remedied, not by casting away the liberal arts, but by truly liberating the Trivium arts from political censorship.[86] From John Wycliff, Martin Luther, and other Church Reformists all the way to the founding fathers of the American and French Revolutions, the liberal arts of Trivium-based thinking sparked and kindled the rational ability to question and renounce the "divine right of kings" by reasoning that all human beings have equal access to the divine order of the universe through "right living" according to the Tao of conscience.[87]

Like any tool, "the Lost Tools" of the Trivium can be used to liberate humanity, or they can be abused to control humanity. Acknowledging that, it is here I must stress that I am in no way suggesting the old classical Trivium be reinstated to naively resurrect some aristocratic educational system from a so-called "Golden Age" of Charlemagne, Cicero, Quintilian, Isocrates, or any other figurehead of classical schooling.[88] Nor am I suggesting the revival of some antiquarian study of Latin in order to restore an "official" canon of Western literature authored by so-called "dead white guys."[89]

Rather, I am advocating a revised Trivium methodology that teaches the individual to introspectively investigate the truth of the ideas that one hears, reads, thinks and speaks. By self-reflecting on the words of his or her own mind and mouth, the Trivium student can learn to apply reliable metacognition which can detect the fallacies in his or her own thought and speech. At the same time, the student can wield the Trivium to defend those thoughts from being spellbound by the rhetorical fallacies of oppressive regimes that seek to subjugate sovereignty of conscience.

Additionally, I am in no way advocating any sort of national Trivium curriculum with federal standards that must be adhered to across all fifty states. Instead, I am proposing that families proactively vote for school-board policies that tailor their own Trivium-based curriclums at the local level.

Here are some key concepts schoolboards can consider when deliberating on the particulars of the grammar, logic, and rhetoric sequences of their locally designed Trivium curriclums:

Grammar and Grammars: A Trivium approach to grammar schooling goes beyond the simple "subject" studies of linguistic symbols in the student's own thinking/communicating language. The liberal arts philosophy of the Trivium delves into the study of grammar as a metaphysical art of epistemology.

Sister Miriam Joseph, who was a Professor of English at Saint Mary's College, philosophizes how Trivium "[g]rammar gives expression to all states of mind or soul—cognitive, volitional, emotional – in sentences that are statements, questions, wishes, prayers, commands, exclamations. In this sense ... [g]rammar is requisite to all."[90] In her book *The Trivium: The Liberal Arts of Logic, Grammar, and Rhetoric*, Joseph expands on the Trivium classifications of "general" and "special" grammar:

> [g]eneral grammar is concerned with the relation of words to ideas
> and to realities, whereas a special grammar, such as English or Latin
> or French or Spanish grammar, is concerned with the agreement
> of subject and verb in person and number or the agreement of ad-

jective and noun in number, gender, and case. General grammar is more philosophical than the special grammars because it is more directly related to logic and to metaphysics or ontology."[91]

In other words, whereas modern language arts curriclums only study the "special grammar" of sentence structure and other linguistic mechanics, Trivium grammar studies both "special grammar" as well as "general grammar," which is nothing less than the epistemological art of cataloguing vocabularies to define the phenomena of all the subjects of the arts and sciences, including the general grammar vocabularies of history, geography, biology, mathematics, philosophy, astronomy and even theology.[92]

C. S. Lewis notes how the Trivium Liberal Art of general Grammar once "correspond[ed] to what we should now call having a 'classical' education, or even to becoming a 'Humanist' in the Renaissance sense."[93] More than that, Lewis historicizes how the classical liberal art of general grammar was once ostensibly synonymous with the study of "*literatura*" and, generically, academic scholarship:

> while [Trivium study of] Grammar was thus restricted to a single tongue [Latin], in another way it sometimes extended far beyond the realm it claims today. It had done so for centuries. Quintilian suggests *literatura* as the proper translation of Greek *grammatike* (II, i), and *literatura*, though it does not mean "literature," included a good deal more than literacy. It included all that is required for "making up" a "set book": syntax, etymology, prosody, and the explanation of allusions. Isidore makes even history a department of Grammar (I, xli-xliv). He would have described the book I am writing now [*The Discarded Image*] as a book of Grammar. *Scholarship* is perhaps our nearest equivalent. In popular usage *Grammatica* or *Grammaria* slid into the vague sense of learning in general.[94]

The classical Trivium concept of grammar is similarly historicized by John Taylor Gatto, who expounds how "general grammar" is the liberal art of generic vocabulary-building as a preliminary induction into studying all arts and sciences, including civics. In his *Underground History of American Education*, Gatto documents how,

> [w]herever it occurred, schooling through the eighteenth and nineteenth centuries (up until the last third of the nineteenth) heavily invested its hours with language, philosophy, art, and the

life of the classical civilizations of Greece and Rome. In the grammar schools of the day, little pure ["special"] grammar as we understand it existed; they were places of classical learning [of "general grammar"]. Early America rested easily on a foundation of classical understanding, one subversive to the normal standards of British class society. The lessons of antiquity were so vital to the construction of every American institution it's hardly possible to grasp how deep the gulf between then and now is.[95]

This passage highlights how the "general" Trivium grammar of early American classical schools encompassed a thorough induction into the broad spectrum of arts and philosophies, which are crucial for learning the principles of civic self-governance that are vital to the U.S. Republic's radical departure from the feudalist caste serfdom of Medieval Europe.

Today, the general grammar of the classical Trivium has sadly been forgotten. The Trivium epistemology of grammatically defining the nomenclature of all academic "subjects" has been reduced to a narrow subdiscipline of "special grammar," butchered for the purposes of indoctrinating students with politically correct workplace communications. Even worse, the dumbing down of Trivium grammar has been further degraded through the modern removal of phonics curriculums from the study of English language arts "subjects."

Trendy new literacy theories that have forsaken phonics studies, such as "whole-language learning," can be traced back to Thomas Hopkins Gallaudet's "look-say" reading pedagogy, which was promoted by Horace Mann, who was President of Antioch College where co-founding patriarch of The Order, Bonesman Alphonso Taft, was a Trustee.[96] Later, Thomas Hopkins' grandsons, Bonesmen Edson Fessenden Gallaudet and Herbert Draper Gallaudet, picked up his look-say method, which was designed for teaching deaf people to read, and repackaged it for teaching non-deaf students in standard classrooms.[97] As a result, the Gallaudet brothers mainstreamed the use of their grandfather's look-say pedagogy, which was adopted by Columbia Teachers College, where education theorists trained instructors to teach all students to read without practicing the strategy of "sounding out" the phonetics of prefixes, roots, and suffixes with reference to their meanings.[98]

By supplanting phonics with the look-say method, The Order of Skull and Bones effectively mangled the "special" grammar approach to breaking down the phonology, morphology, and philology of words, thus damaging many students' ability to decipher and navigate the general grammars that signify the phenomena comprising the subjects of all arts and sciences.[99] Indeed, the Trivium methodology of inquiry-based self-learning is calibrated by the foundational principle that grammar defines the simplest data points of identified phenomena, and the grammatical definitions of the data/phenomena dictate how they must be analyzed with logical rules, because errors in logical analyses are predicated by contradictory usages of grammatical definitions. It follows that if a student's grammar is erroneous, then his or her logic will necessarily be faulty; and as a result, his or her rhetoric will likewise be fallacious. As such, if a student is not taught Trivium-based "special grammar" phonics, then he or she will be prone to misunderstanding the "general" grammatical terms of all academic subjects, which means the student's logic will be garbled when studying any scholarly discipline, and the bunk grammar and confused logic will make them inept at comprehending any artistic or scientific rhetoric.

Worse still, by warping the student's ability to understand the "special grammar" of his or her own thinking language, The Order of Skull and Bones has distorted the student's ability to keep logical track of his or her own thoughts. Since Bones-sponsored look-say schooling does not teach a student to comprehend the precise meanings of "special grammar," the student cannot coherently think through metacognitive dialogues that self-examine the reasoning of thoughts.

This is not an exaggeration. In his 1946 essay, "Politics and the English Language," novelist George Orwell remarked how a growing decline in rational thought among the British people was catalyzed by the dumbing down of the English language in Britain where the school system was suffering from its own "look-and-say" and "whole-word" learning diseases.[100] Orwell, who taught English at Frays College and Hawthorn High School for Boys,[101] observed how "the slovenliness of our language makes it easier for us to have foolish thoughts";[102] for "if thought corrupts language, language can also corrupt thought. A bad usage can spread by tradition and imitation."[103] To put it another way, when grammar skills are corrupted by the bastardized "tradition" of look-say/whole-word schooling, then any thoughts that are generated through those corrupted "special grammars" will thereby be foolish.

In Orwell's famous dystopia, *1984*, he fictionally portrayed this real-life psychological warfare on the Tao, or Reason, of thought, by means of politically corrupting the "special" and "general" grammars of the English language. The "proles" (or proletariat) and "the Party" of Orwell's fictitious "Ingsoc" (or English Socialism) are politically indoctrinated to speak a broken English called "Newspeak," which is devoid of any words that could express any thoughts of dissent against the "Doublespeak" dictums propagandized by Big Brother,[104] who decrees that "War is Peace. Freedom is Slavery. Ignorance is Strength."[105] The "Appendix" of *1984* details the backstory of how the devolution of "Oldspeak" into "Newspeak" was politically masterminded to systematically demolish the Tao, or Reason, of grammatical thought-architecture:

> [t]he purpose of Newspeak was not only to provide a medium of expression for the world-view and mental habits proper to the devotees of Ingsoc, but to make all other modes of thought impossible. It was intended that when Newspeak had been adopted once and for all and Oldspeak forgotten, a heretical thought – that is, a thought diverging from the principles of Ingsoc – should be literally unthinkable, at least so far as thought is dependent on words. ... This was done partly by the invention of new words, but chiefly by eliminating undesirable words and by stripping such words as remained of unorthodox meanings, and so far as possible of all secondary meanings whatever. ... Quite apart from the suppression of definitely heretical words, reduction of vocabulary was regarded as an end in itself, and no word that could be dispensed with was allowed to survive. Newspeak was designed not to extend but to *diminish* the range of thought, and this purpose was indirectly assisted by cutting the choice of words down to a minimum.[106]

Through a historicist close reading of *1984's* Appendix, Newspeak can be interpreted as a literary symbol representing how "the range of thought" has been politically "diminished" through the whole-word/look-say truncation of Trivium grammar. Orwell's Appendix on Newspeak poignantly illustrates how free thought is dependent upon a person's ability to comprehend the "special" grammar of his or her own thinking/communicating language. It follows that a student's conscious dominion over his or her own thought-architecture will be shuttered if he or she is inept at comprehending the meanings of the "special" grammatical symbols that he or she uses to rehearse the logical probabilities of ideas.

The degree to which look-say and other whole-language pedagogies have devastated Trivium grammar consciousness cannot be underestimated. For it is has been extensively documented that there is a direct correlation between early illiteracy and long-term failure in all other subjects, including the "non-literary subjects" of mathematics and the sciences. According to a 2011 scholarly article published in the *National Civic Review*, "the Annie E. Casey Foundation (2010) reports that students who do not read proficiently by third grade are four times more likely to leave school without a diploma than are proficient readers."[107] Another academic article concurs in a 1999 issue of *Clearing House: A Journal of Educational Strategies, Issues, and Ideas*: "[p]oor reading is one of the most common characteristics of school dropouts.... [T]he seeds for reading failure are set in the primary grades .... Current researchers believe that children should be literate by the end of the third grade."[108]

Based on these samples from the vast body of research on the links between early illiteracy and dropout rates, it is evident that Orwell's philosophy of language is precisely accurate: "thought is dependent on words";[109] so "if thought corrupts language, language can also corrupt thought,"[110] even the quantitative thoughts of mathematics and the sciences. Such statistics on illiteracy-dropout correlations are also evidence that the Skull-and-Bones look-say assault on "special" and "general" grammars must be decommissioned and, in turn, rectified with the reinstatement of traditional phonics methods and other Trivium-based grammar-schooling pedagogies.

The Laws of Logic: Following the grammar-schooling phase, during which students learn "special" linguistic grammars in order to build the core vocabularies of "general" "subject" grammars, the "dialectic" phase of education introduces the study of formal logic, which is perhaps the key distinguishing feature of a Trivium liberal arts curriculum.

In "The Lost Tools of Learning," Dorothy Sayers emphasizes how the distinctive aspect of a classical Trivium education, as opposed to modern "subject" schooling, is the "Dialectic" stage, which is devoted to the study of "Formal Logic":[111]

> [i]t is here that our curriculum shows its first sharp divergence from modern standards. The disrepute into which Formal Logic has fallen is entirely unjustified.... Logic has been discredited, partly because we have come to suppose that we are conditioned almost entirely by the intuitive and the unconscious.... Another cause for the disfavor into which Logic has fallen is the belief that it is entirely based upon universal assumptions that are either unprovable or tautological. This is not true.... Logic is the art of arguing correctly.... Indeed, the practical utility of Formal Logic today lies not so much in the establishment of positive conclusions as in the prompt detection and exposure of invalid inference.[112]

By debunking the post-Freudian philosophies of "the unconscious" repression of logic, Sayers dispels such fallacies of modernity as she sheds light on how the Trivium art of formal logic is of "practical utility" for scaffolding the individual student's intrinsic ability to reason so that he or she can introspectively self-detect "invalid inferences" and other fallacies.

Formal logic is a complex discipline, but students can begin to build a solid foundation in logical thinking by learning the three prime laws of logic: identity, contradiction, and tautology.[113] [c] [114] Once the student has learned to navigate these three fundamental rules of logical thinking, he or she can learn to self-detect and expunge any contradictions or errors in thinking. Furthermore, a student who possesses these three principles of logic can forge together the rational building-blocks essential for constructing interwoven syllogisms, enthymemes, sorites, epicheiremas, and other logical schemas which validate his or her own thinking.[115]

Don't be intimidated by all this Greek jargon. These are just fancy names for different logical structures that anyone can wield to explicate and verify his or her own logical chains of reasoning and evidence. To demystify the jargon of formal logic, Sister Miriam Joseph puts it straightforwardly: "[l]ogic prescribes how to combine concepts into judgments and judgments into syllogisms and chains of reasoning so as to achieve truth."[116]So, formal logic studies teach structures for rationally stringing "special" grammar symbols together as a means of reasoning through self-inquiries into the "general" grammars of any conceivable "subject."

Rhetoric and Rhetorical Fallacies: With a solid base in the laws of logical thinking, the Trivium student reaches the rhetoric stage where he or she learns to creatively craft grammar to communicate deductive and inductive reasoning through comparison, contrast, chronology, cause-and-effect, correlation, generalization, and principle buttressed by pathos appeals to emotion and ethos appeals to ethical principles and credible experts.[117]

---

c   The law of tautology is basically a synthesis of the first two laws of logic. The first law of identity states that any grammatical-rhetorical expression identifies particular phenomena. The second law of contradiction states that this first law is violated when a grammatical-rhetorical expression is used to identify phenomena in ways that contradict observation or in ways that contradict other grammatical-rhetorical suppositions. The third law of tautology puts these first two laws together: since a grammatical-rhetorical expression must identify particular phenomena (and not any other contradictory phenomena), then a grammatical-rhetorical expression must either be true in its identity, or it must be false (contradictory); for it cannot be both true and false. In a nutshell, the three prime laws of logic work like this: a grammatical-rhetorical expression is either true or false (contradictory), and there is no "third" or "middle" option (which is why the law of tautology is also known as "the law of the excluded third" or "the law of the excluded middle").

At the same time, during the rhetoric phase, the Trivium student learns to critically recognize and refute informal rhetorical fallacies, which include:

- **Logos fallacies that twist logic with faulty reasoning and erroneous evidence,** such as false analogies, false either-or dilemmas, hasty generalizations, equivocations, red herrings, *post hoc* causal fallacies, *non sequitur* correlation fallacies, and circular reasoning fallacies that "beg the question."[118]

- **Ethos fallacies that manipulate trust,** such as pejorative *ad hominem* attacks on personal character, sycophantic bandwagon popularity fallacies, and false appeals to authority.[119]

- **Pathos fallacies that fluster emotions** in order to cloud reason with scare tactics, guilt trips, erotic appeals, and outrage-blinding provocations.[120]

Trivium-style rhetoric, like the phonics method of "special" grammar and the formal logic discipline of "dialectics," has fallen to the wayside of the modern schooling system. Dorothy Sayers castigates this travesty of losing the Trivium tools of rhetoric and thus failing to teach students to identify and rebut rhetorical fallacies:

> we let our young men and women go out unarmed, in a day when armor was never so necessary. By teaching them all to read, we have left them at the mercy of the printed word. By the invention of the film and the radio, we have made certain that no aversion to reading shall secure them from the incessant battery of words, words, words. They do not know what the words mean; they do not know how to ward them off or blunt their edge or fling them back; they are a prey to words in their emotions instead of being masters of them in their intellects. We [the British] who were scandalized in 1940 when men were sent to fight tanks with rifles, are not scandalized when young men and women are sent into the world to fight massed propaganda with a smattering of "subjects"; and when whole classes and whole nations become hypnotized by the arts of the spell binder, we have the impudence to be astonished.[121]

Not only do schools ill-prepare students to rhetorically defend against the mass-distributed psy-op propaganda of printed words, radio transmissions, and television broadcasts; but in the midst of the current digital revolution of infotainment overkill, schools today are now even failing to teach students how to rhetorically defend against being inundated 24/7 with internet propaganda beamed straight into their smartphones, tablets, and other portable computer devices. Hence, it is now imperative, perhaps more than ever, that schools revive the liberal arts of rhetoric so that students can become empowered to self-defend against the 1984-style "doublespeak" fallacies embedded in the technocratic propaganda of today's corporations and governments.

Indeed, seventy years have elapsed since George Orwell published his prophetic *1984* in which he conceptualized the "doublespeak" propaganda of the "Ministry of Information" based on his experience working at the British Broadcasting Corporation (BBC) as Talks Producer for Eastern Services.[122] The BBC's real-life political manipulation of 1984-style "doublespeak" propaganda was implicitly condemned in Orwell's essay, "Politics and the English Language," which lambasted the fact that:

> political speech and writing are largely the defense of the indefensible ... [which] can indeed be defended, but only by arguments which are too brutal for most people to face, and which do not square with the professed aims of political parties. Thus political language has to consist largely of euphemism, question-begging and sheer cloudy vagueness."[123]

Today, seven decades after it was published in 1948, *1984* has come to pass in real life: the hi-tech doublespeak propaganda of corporations and governments is surpassing even the imagination of Orwell.

Accordingly, if the prescient warnings of Orwell's literary masterwork were ever to be heeded, now more than ever is the time. Therefore, it is urgent that students learns the Trivium liberal arts of rhetoric so they can independently spot and rebut the sophisticated doublespeak of technocratic corporations and governments.

A Trivium for Civics: To put it all together, a Trivium-based reform can enlighten the individual student with the metacognitive powers of grammar, logic, and rhetoric by which he or she can filter out fallacies in his or her own thinking while debunking the fallacies of government PR propaganda, corporate false advertising, and technocratic doublespeak jargon. The Trivium-informed student can become liberated to fully self-actualize the Tao of his or her personal conscience. In turn, the Trivium student can cultivate the self-responsibility necessary to proactively exercise and defend sovereignty of consciousness, by participating in the self-governing civil processes of locally elected schoolboards and other civic venues where he or she can vote for public policies that reflect his or her own personal conscience.

To strengthen the student's conscientious self-determination, it is important that a renewed Trivium pedagogy be grounded in the practical application of basic civics curriculums. Such Trivium-based civics should acquaint students with the "general" political grammar needed to logically navigate America's Constitutional channels of representative self-governance so that each student can rhetorically engage in conscientious activism through civil processes at the local, state, and national levels. It is therefore recommended that Trivium reform should replace apolitical and amoral social studies curriculums with a combination of American history and world history curriculums that study the civics lessons of the "classical" civilizations which laid the philosophical cornerstones of the human rights to conscientious self-determination enshrined in the US Constitution.

Dorothy Sayers recommends that "[t]he grammar of History should consist ... of dates, events, anecdotes, and personalities."[124] While studying such "general" historical grammar, the Trivium student is to be taught to practice his or her formal logic by applying inductive and deductive reasoning to evaluate the ethics of the political "events" and "personalities" of "classical" civilizations.[125]

Sayers advocates that such "general" historical grammar should also be taught in order to prompt classroom "dialectics," or debates, in which Trivium students practice their rhetoric as they learn to dispute the ethics of the political past by questioning, "[w]as the behavior of this statesman justified? What was the effect of such an enactment? What are the arguments for and against this or that form of government?"[126] In debating these ethical questions, just as the art of formal logic is perhaps most useful not in identifying what is absolutely true, but rather in identifying what is certainly false, so too is the practicality of such debates found not necessarily in identifying what exactly are the perfect forms of governance, but in identifying which systems of governance have been shown to be tyrannical or otherwise incompatible with the ethical principles of individual human rights that are realized in the Constitution of the American Republic.

Sayers explains how the Trivium study of a "general" grammar of "[a] set of dates to which one can peg all later historical knowledge is of enormous help later on in establishing the perspective of history."[127] By comparing and contrasting the historical grammars of the "dates," "events," "personalities," and philosophies of the "classical" political systems leading up to the signing of the United States Constitution, the Trivium student "shall thus get an introduction to constitutional history" that is informed by the virtues and follies of the past civilizations which provided the American founding fathers with axiomatic historical examples of how to govern (and how not to govern).[128] With knowledge of these historical backgrounds, Trivium students will be furnished with the grammatical contexts to logically and conscientiously study the ethics of America's ongoing role in modern, contemporary, and future world events.

It is therefore imperative that Trivium curriclums teach classical world history and American Constitutional history – not "text-centric," moral-relativist "social studies" curriclums. As documented in Charlotte Iserbyt's *Deliberate Dumbing Down of America*, "social studies" curriclums have been designed for the purpose of teaching globalist political correctness ever since the Carnegie Corporation financed the American Historical Association's 1934 "Investigations of the Social Studies in the Schools," which reports that:

> [o]rganized public education in the United States, much more than ever before, is now compelled, if it is to fulfill its social obligations, to adjust its objectives, its curriculum, its methods of instruction, and its administrative procedures to the requirements of the emerging integrated [world] order.
>
> If the school is to justify its maintenance and assume its responsibilities, it must recognize the new [world] order and proceed to equip the rising generation to cooperate effectively in the increasingly interdependent society.[129]

To integrate the United States into the New World Order, this Carnegie-sponsored directive was published as *Conclusions and Recommendations for the Social Studies*, which calls for US schools to implement "social studies" curriclums that re-educate "the attitudes and outlook of the American people" by teaching American students that their constitutional rights to "*laissez faire* in economy and government" are incompatible with the "new age of collectivis[t]" world economics.[130] To put it bluntly, Carnegie-spawned "social studies" curriclums have always been designed to re-educate Americans with globalist-collectivist values suitable for corporate citizenship in a world economy technocratically managed by "vast experiments in social planning and control."[131]

In contrast, the classical-grammatical approach to world history and US Constitutional history studies liberal arts curriclums instructed through Trivium-oriented learning methods that teach the student to value the inalienable Tao of his or her human rights to *"laissez faire"* of conscience, which is endowed in the Constitutional rights of the American Republic. Stated differently, students of grammatical-historical Trivium curriculums are taught to value their constitutional powers of self-governance as free citizens who have immutable human rights that cannot be sold out to the collectivist economic "rights" of a commercial caste system which socially re-engineers human beings into politically manufactured cogs programmed for turning the workforce gears of a One World Economy.

Local Public Control of Trivium Diversity: Trivium-based curriculums grounded in civics and history have already been modeled by the Logos School, which was founded on the principles espoused by Sayers's "Lost Tools of Learning."[132] According to the PhD Dissertation of Randall D. Hart, who has twenty-seven years of experience as a schoolteacher, the Logos School was set up in 1980 by Pastor Douglas Wilson of Moscow, Idaho, where the newly formed classical Trivium school "opened its doors to 19 students, operating out of a church basement. Today it has almost 300 students and has produced numerous high school graduates."[133] Wilson also authored a book titled *Recovering the Lost Tools of Learning: An Approach to Distinctively Christian Education*, which inspired the establishment of the Association of Classical and Christian Schools (ACCS).[134]

As a result, there has a been a resurgence in classical Trivium schooling in recent decades. Affiliate Professor of Fine Arts at Eastern University in Pennsylvania, Stephen R. Turley, who also teaches at Tall Oaks Classical School in Delaware,[135] reports that,

> [a]ccording to the Association of Classical Christian Schools membership statistics, there were 10 classical schools in the nation in 1994, [*sic*] today there are over 230. Since 2002, student enrollment in classical schools has doubled from 17,000 nationwide to 35,000, and all indicators suggest that the next decade will be one of significant growth.... Classical schools in 2011 had the highest SAT scores in each of the three categories of Reading, Math, and Writing among all independent religious and public schools.[136]

Skeptics of Trivium-based public education reforms may be averse to the strong Christian ties to the contemporary revival of classical Trivium schooling. Nevertheless, Trivium liberal arts schools need not be Christian-based. It is originally the work of Greeks Pagans who pre-date monotheism itself.

For centuries, there has been a rich heritage of classical Trivium-based education in the Islamic world. For instance, in a 2018 *Renovatio Journal* article titled "The Liberal Arts in an Illiberal Age," Islamic scholar Hamza Yusuf,[137] who is the President of Zaytuna College, historicizes how

> [t]he liberal arts also became the cornerstone of Islamic education, and the idea of a college as a training center for the arts in service of religion is arguably a Muslim one. (See George Makdisi's *The Rise of Colleges* and Medhi Nakosteen's *History of the Islamic Origins of Western Education*). More recently, in *God and Logic in Islam: The Caliphate of Reason*, John Walbridge makes a cogent case not only that these [Trivium] arts were the core of Islamic civilization for a thousand years, but also that their decline and erosion directly correlate to that civilization's fall and to the rise of extremism.[138]

Additionally, it should be noted that the Trivium liberal arts are even promoted by the quasi-religious, mysticist fraternity of Freemasonry. In the 1916 *Encyclopedia of Freemasonry*, Secretary General of the Supreme Council of the Scottish Rite for the Southern Jurisdiction of the United States, Albert Gallatin Mackey,[139] records how the "liberal arts" of the "trivium" are the hallmark of the "[t]he liberal man, *liberalis homo*, [which] meant, in the Middle Ages, the man who was his own master – free, independent, and often a nobleman. ... The Freemasons of the Middle Ages ... readily assumed these liberal arts."[140]

Yet, Trivium schools need not have any theological overtones at all. In 1982, former Professor of Philosophy of Law at the University of Chicago, Mortimer J. Adler,[141] authored *The Paideia Proposal*, which espouses a Trivium-based reform curriculum that is grounded not in theology, but in the "perennial philosophies" of classical, medieval, renaissance, and modern Western history.[142] Adler, a Chairman of the Board of Editors of the *Encyclopedia Britannica*,[143] was an outspoken opponent of John Dewey's Wundtian-Hegelian schooling methods, which Adler argued should be repealed and replaced with a renewed "liberal arts" curriculum steeped in "classical" perennial philosophies.[144] Toward his vision of revamping a perennial Trivium education, Adler co-edited the acclaimed *Great Books of the Western World*, which catalogues a curriculum of the "Great Conversations" across the pivotal perennial philosophies of Western civilizations.[145]

It is also worth noting that in recent years there has emerged a sort of "do-it-yourself" Trivium self-learning movement on internet media platforms influenced by the research of Jan Irvin's Logos Media (formerly Gnostic Media) as well as Richard Grove's Tragedy and Hope Media.[146]

In sum, this diversity of theological, philosophical, and grassroots Trivium methods demonstrates that communities can democratically draft local schoolboard policies that tailor Trivium curriclums to reflect the personal consciences of the taxpaying families who fund and attend those public schools.

A diversity of decentralized Trivium curriculums controlled at the local schoolboard level will be a civil bulwark against authoritarian enforcement of national Trivium standards for the purposes of autocratic social engineering. But only if local Trivium reforms abstain from public-private charter-school partnerships and other federal subsidizations of Trivium schools.

For example, there are classical schools, such as Great Hearts Academy, which is grounded in the literature of Western philosophy through the lens of the classical Trivium without a religious overtone.[147] However, Great Hearts is a public-private charter school that is managed by a corporate-executive council, not a publicly elected schoolboard.[148] By undermining the civil democratic authorities of locally elected schoolboards, the public-private corporatization of such Trivium-based "school choice" will, in turn, undermine the very liberties of consciousness that the Trivium "liberal arts" are designed to cultivate.

In this way, classical schoolteacher Stephen R. Turley is remiss when he applauds the public-privatization of Trivium schooling through corporate-government "voucher programs or tax-credit programs" and other "school choice programs," such as "former governor of Louisiana, Bobby Jindal['s] … program of school privatization, where he shifted tens of millions of dollars from the public school monopoly to pay for private, and mostly Christian, schools."[149] If Turley truly believes that the purpose of Trivium liberal arts is to "foster classical civic virtue,"[150] then he must concede that the institutional structure of Trivium schools must reflect the civic virtues of classical representative governance by upholding the public sovereignty of schoolboard democracy through the "separation of powers" between locally funded, federally funded, and privately funded schools.

Turley must also realize what Charlotte Iserbyt has been hammering at for over thirty years: federal funding means federal control of "outcomes," which means federal control of curriculum. Consequently, federal funding comes with strings attached, which can mandate that ESSA standards must be intermingled with chartered Trivium curriclums. Subsequently, federal funding of public-private Trivium charters will result in the politically correct redefinition of what it means to "foster classical civic virtue."[151]

If the purpose of the Trivium liberal arts is to teach each individual student how to cultivate civil self-reliance, then local communities must retain democratic sovereignty through public schoolboard policies that reflect the freedoms of conscience voiced by the families who fund and attend those schools. Otherwise, federally financed Trivium charter schools will merely conform with the workforce-planning and social-engineering machinations of corporate-government Statecraft.

Escape from Posthuman Dystopia – Critical "Consciousness Studies" Toward a Metaphysics of Consciousness

The "categorical-imperative" ethic of self-determination through the Tao of conscience can be preserved if each citizen is taught the Trivium thought-architecture of consciousness, which can then be actualized in personal political discourse through democratic channels of representative civil governance.[152] However, this necessary condition is not yet sufficient to safeguard against the ever-encroaching waves of neo-eugenic trans/posthuman technologies that would overwrite the subjectivity of human consciousness with the information-processing expediencies of Big Data algorithms.

To protect personal consciousness from being overridden by AI-assisted human-computer interfaces hooked up to the internet-of-everything, it is vital that every citizen pro-actively harnesses the Trivium liberal arts of critical thinking. By virtue of the Tao, or Reason, of personal conscience, the Trivium-informed citizen can formidably participate in grassroots political activism that pressures local, state, and federal governments to issue moratoriums on transhuman and posthuman technologies that compromise the free will of human consciousness.

If the American people do not fight to restrict the manufacture of human-machine interfaces and other neo-eugenic technetronics that interfere with the subjectivity of human consciousness, then by default, the American citizenry will forfeit their natural human rights to conscientious self-determination along with their constitutional civil rights to conscientious self-governance. Once the free will of human consciousness has been "upgraded" with the "superior" cognition of transhuman and posthuman psycho-technologies, the willpower of personal conscience will thereby be handed over to hyper-efficient brain-computer interfaces that overwrite organic human thinking with assistive-AI algorithms. By outsourcing the categorical-imperative subjectivity of consciousness to such brain-machine interfaces, the people of the United States will consequently sell out the ethical basis of the human rights to conscientious self-governance encoded in the U.S. Constitution.

As a result, there will be no meaningful basis for any inalienable *a priori* ethic that upholds our constitutional civil rights to political self-determination through conscientious self-governance. Without the Tao of personal conscience, civil authority will subsequently be abdicated to the hi-speed decision-making programs of Big AI algorithms that will render obsolete the decision-making willpower of human consciousness.

How can schools supplement Trivium-based civics and history curriculums with philosophical studies that will reinvigorate the ethics of conscientious self-governance which are antithetical to the posthuman digitalized-automation of consciousness?

I recommend a new curriculum of "consciousness studies" that explores the metaphysics of consciousness in search of an inferential ethics of consciousness which can rebuke the hubris of technologically tampering with the existential imperative of personal conscience that is the basis of individual political liberty.

Indeed, the Leviathan of Big Tech is already spreading its virtual tentacles into the political architecture of our democratic institutions as well as the neuro-cerebral circuitry wired into our human consciousnesses. Emboldened by a literal "god complex," oligarchic Tech Barons are racing ahead with the neo-eugenic re-engineering of consciousness. Yet, notwithstanding the fantastical discoveries in neurobiology and cerebral electrochemistry, the fact remains that not a single scientist has begun to objectively quantify the "substance" of consciousness.

To use the philosophical terminologies of Aristotle, British empiricist David Hume, and German metaphysicist Immanuel Kant, the cutting edge of science has quantitatively measured and technetronically manipulated essentially every "accident," or "impression," of consciousness; but science has not been able to quantitatively identify the "substance" of consciousness as the "thing in itself."[153] In simpler terms, there is no genius polymath anywhere who can empirically answer the basic question: what exactly is consciousness?

Neurologists and brain surgeons teamed up with computer engineers may have been successful at electronically inducing false memories,[154] wirelessly transmitting thoughts to remote-control robotic limbs,[155] and digitally replicating human cognition and emotion with AI software.[156] Nonetheless, the best teams of neurobiologists, neuropsychologists, and computer scientists around the world have yet to zero in on any objective grasp of what exactly is the "substance" of the self-aware state of desire and free will which humans refer to as "consciousness."

For instance, scientists still do not know whether consciousness resides somehow in the aggregate of the electro-chemical of "microtubule" inter-play of the human brain,[157] or whether consciousness resides somehow outside of the physical "hardware" of neuro-brain circuitry somewhere out in the wavelengths of space/time as if beaming to the brain-body biocomputer from some sort of cosmic "wifi" or "radio-wave" signal.[158] In *Homo Deus*, posthumanist Yuval Noah Harari puts the conundrum of consciousness like this:

> [t]o be frank, science knows surprisingly little about mind and consciousness. Current orthodoxy holds that consciousness is cre-ated by electrochemical reactions in the brain, and that mental ex-periences fulfill some essential data-processing function. However, nobody has any idea how a congeries of biochemical reactions and electrical currents in the brain creates the subjective experience of pain, anger or love.[159]

The best scientific guess, according to Harari, is that:

> [c]onsciousness is the biologically useless by-product of certain brain processes. Jet engines roar loudly, but the noise doesn't pro-pel the aeroplane forward. Humans don't need carbon dioxide, but each and every breath fills the air with more of the stuff. Similarly, consciousness may be a kind of mental pollution produced by the firing of complex neural networks. It doesn't do anything. It is just there. If this is true, it implies that all the pain and pleasure expe-rienced by billions of creatures for millions of years is just mental pollution. This is certainly thought worth thinking, even if it isn't true. But it is quite amazing to realize that as of 2016, this is the best theory of consciousness that contemporary science has to offer."[160]

Unless the American people actually buy this misanthropic belief that human consciousness is nothing more than "mental pollution," it is now incumbent upon citizens everywhere to reaffirm their vows to the inalien-able right of personal conscience by resurrecting Trivium liberal arts stud-ies of the metaphysical Tao of consciousness.

My proposal for a curriculum of metaphysical consciousness studies is not esoteric or impractical.[161] Even transhumanist Ray Kurzweil himself concedes that there is a practical necessity to renewing metaphysical studies of human consciousness. In *The Singularity is Near*, Kurzweil notes that:

> [t]his [posthuman] consideration takes us back to the same questions of consciousness and identity that have been debated since Plato's dialogues.... During the course of the twenty-first century these will not remain topics for polite philosophical debates but will have to be confronted as vital, practical, political, and legal issues.[162]

Here, Kurzweil admits that the posthuman digitalization of consciousness will alter human identity in such ways that the questions of classical metaphysics will be brought to the forefront of political and legal debates as governments begin to regulate the commercialization of transhuman technetronics which transform personal consciousness and free will.

To be sure, philosophies of metaphysics have grown progressively skeptical ever since Immanuel Kant erected a philosophical "wall" that has ostensibly barred human reason from realizing the metaphysics of (1) God;[163] (2) the material "substance" of the universe as the "thing in itself";[164] and (3) the phenomenal subjectivity of consciousness as the "self in itself," which Kant deemed "transcendental apperception."[165] In the shadow of "Kant's wall," essentially every philosopher except Hegel, Heidegger, and Kierkegaard has fallen under two general categories that either refute or evade both *a priori* and *a posteriori* inquiries into the metaphysics of consciousness:[166]

- On the one hand, modernist philosophies of nominalist pragmatism, utilitarian positivism, and dialectical materialism and phenomenalism.

- On the other hand, postmodernist philosophies of skeptical existentialism and relativist linguistic analysis.[167]

With metaphysical truths trapped on the other side of Kant's epistemological wall, all of these modern and postmodern philosophies have basically abandoned all attempts to recover any access to the Tao (or Logos) of God, the universe, or consciousness. Effectively giving up on metaphysics, these post-Kantian philosophies have mostly settled for trivial attempts to reduce the human condition to a transactional system of arbitrary exchanges between words, ideas, or material objects for the purposes of commodifying social intercourse. The remaining post-Kantian philosophies have settled for the vanity of cynical and hedonistic attempts to idly cope with the angst of subjectivity, absurdly "thrown" into thoughts, emotions, and sensations devoid of any Reason (or Tao).

In sum, after blocking off the metaphysics of God, the universe, and the self, the barricade of Kant's wall has built up generations of philosophies which have stripped all metaphysics down to nothing but the naked subjectivity of consciousness, without any Tao of conscience.

Yet, as humankind approaches the crossroads to transhumanism, we will be venturing into uncharted technological waters where our species will literally be re-engineering what delicately remains of personal consciousness itself. Therefore, to safeguard the last vestiges of free conscience, it is vital that an ethics of consciousness be enculturated before humankind barrels forward headlong into human-machine interfaces that alter neuro-cerebral consciousness.

A political-economic ethics derived from the metaphysics of consciousness must be predicated on a simple maxim:

> It is unethical to legalize the corporate commercialization or government institutionalization of any technologies that can compromise the subjectivity or free will of personal consciousness.

If the people of the American Republic still value personal conscience as the ethical fountain of Constitutional self-governance, we must soberly acknowledge the empirical limitations of technocratic scientism and, in turn, democratically press for legislation that will enforce regulation of technetronic evolution, so that techno-industrial 'progress' does not trample human consciousness into virtual extinction.

To enculturate these principles into the public education system, a historical-grammatical Trivium curriculum of "consciousness studies" can be developed to prompt student inquiries into the philosophical and scientific grammar necessary to explore the metaphysical Tao of consciousness, which will clarify ethical boundaries that prohibit the technological molestation of personal consciousness.

There are two main reasons for this historical-grammatical curriculum of "consciousness studies" to examine the primary-source literature of the ancient theologies, classical metaphysics, and modern *a priori* philosophies of the world:

> 1. Most of these texts, which comprise the "Great Conversations" of philosophers and theologians throughout world history, have

already been canonized as part of the required reading list of a classical Trivium education (and this list can be expanded to include the classical literature of "non-Western" metaphysics, such as the Chinese poetics of Lao Tzu's *Tao Te Ching*, the Vedic poetics of the Hindu *Rta*, and the Four Noble Truths of Buddhist *Dharma*).[168]

2. The empirical failure to quantitatively define the "substance" of consciousness has rendered the grammatical term "consciousness" into a linguistic symbol so scientifically indefinable that it could be synonymous with metaphysical terms like the "soul," the "Tao," the "Logos," the "*Rta*," and even "God."

It is not an equivocation to parallel the metaphysics of consciousness with the metaphysics of ancient theologies and classical philosophies. In *Homo Deus*, posthumanist apologist Yuval Harari himself draws the metaphysical parallels between consciousness, the soul, and God. Beginning with the premise that no one has ever weighed an ounce of God or measured a length of the soul, Harari similarly acknowledges that:

no one has ever seen experiences of pain or love through a microscope, and we have a very detailed biochemical explanation for pain and love that leaves no room for subjective experiences. However, there is a crucial difference between mind and soul (as well as between mind and God). Whereas the existence of eternal souls is purely conjecture, the experience of pain is a direct and very tangible reality…. I so far lack a scientific explanation for it…. [But] [s]ince all scientists constantly experience subjective feelings such as pain and doubt, they cannot deny their existence.[169]

To translate Harari's insight using the philosophical grammar of Aristotle and David Hume, it is plausible to suppose the nonexistence of God, since no one has empirically measured any material "accident" of the cosmos that can be directly attributed to a "substance" of God.[170] Likewise, it may be plausible to suppose the nonexistence of the soul since no one has ever measured a metaphysical "substance" of consciousness beyond any phenomenological "impression."[171] However, the failure to quantify any "substance" of consciousness is not a tenable supposition for the nonexistence of consciousness because the residual "accidents" or "impressions" of consciousness *have* been empirically measured and technologically manipulated while,[172] at the same time, every scientist anecdotally observes and testifies that he or she subjectively experiences the self-aware *cogito* of his or her own consciousness.[173]

So, there may be no empirical evidence of a metaphysics of God or the soul, but there undoubtedly is inferential evidence of a metaphysics of consciousness, even if we are paradoxically incapable of ever quantifying or otherwise scientifically defining the metaphysical thought-architecture of our own psychic subjectivity.

It may surprise you that Harari and I basically see eye-to-eye on the metaphysical problem of consciousness. But it won't astonish you that he and I call for diametrically opposite solutions. On the one side, Harari pops the cynical question, "[m]aybe the mind should join the soul, God, and ether in the dustbin of science?"[174] On the other side, my Trivium-based curriculum of "consciousness studies" would salvage the metaphysical treasure of consciousness from Harari's trash can. Whereas Harari wants to sweep up everything on the other side of Kant's epistemological-metaphysical wall (God, the soul, and consciousness), and then toss it all in the garbage dump of history, I contend that, if we throw away the metaphysics of consciousness along with the soul and God, then humanity *itself* will be discarded onto that rubbish heap.

I propose not to junk the metaphysics behind Kant's wall, but to recover the Tao of such metaphysics, especially as they pertain to consciousness, by rediscovering the "perennial" world literature of ancient theologies and classical philosophies. Reasoning by inference from this side of Kant's wall, if we know the subjectivity of consciousness does in fact exist, then our best chance to arrive at a metaphysics of consciousness may be found in re-examining the ancient metaphysics which have been theologized, philosophized, and poeticized throughout the classical literature of the world.

By revivifying historical-grammatical literary studies of the classical metaphysics of the world, such as the Tao of the East and the Logos of the West,[175] Trivium-based "consciousness studies" can explore the "Great Conversations" of metaphysics which students can juxtapose against the dominant modernist and postmodernist philosophies accelerating the techno-eugenic "ethics" that are driving the transhumanist and posthumanist re-engineering of consciousness: on one side of the coin, materialist-empiricist philosophies, such as positivism, pragmatism, and nominalism; on the flip side of the coin, skeptical-existentialist philosophies of phenomenological relativism:

- Pragmatic positivism emphasizes practical efficiency toward humanistic objectives.[176] Taken to the extreme, the principle of humanistic efficiency leads toward the exponential automation of labor until posthuman AI machines take over all human labor, including the intellectual labor of human consciousness itself.[177]

• Materialism, as a general corollary to pragmatism and positivism, believes that only material reality exists.[178] Taken to the extreme, materialism evolves into corporatist or communist systems that monetize consciousness into an economic product, instead of a dignified subject, which is "transvalued" into a transhuman commodity that can be technologically consumed through commercial market sales or technocratically "redistributed" through government welfare services.[179]

• Nominalism and its cousin, linguistic analysis, conceive that all reality exists in the essence of the language that we use to name empirical phenomena.[180] Taken to the extreme, nominalist-linguistic philosophies conflate the Tao, or Logos, of the word "godhood" with a mere psychological abstraction of the power of humanity to evolve in scientific knowledge by naming empirical phenomena for the purposes of technologically redefining it.[181] This nominalist-linguistic equivocation of "godhood" with "humanity" results in the hubris of transhumanist futurists such as Kurzweil and Harari,[182] whose zealous haste to technologically upgrade human beings into gods may bring about the very extinction of human consciousness itself.

• Existentialist phenomenologies perceive the thoughts and feelings of all experience as absolutely subjective and relativistic.[183] Taken to the extreme, this outlook becomes an abyss of nihilism in which the absurd meaninglessness of existence is its own justification to recklessly experiment with the transhuman re-engineering of consciousness since conscience is nothing more than the confused desire of angst "thrown" into the "performance" of chaos.[184]

Carried out to their "logical" extremes without any counterbalances from a metaphysical ethics of consciousness, the phenomenological philosophies of existentialism and linguistic analysis and the empiricist philosophies of materialism, nominalism, positivism, and pragmatism all have bents toward culminating in posthumanist political-economics that would trans-eugenically dehumanize consciousness into oblivion. It is therefore imperative that the neo-eugenic tendencies of these hyper-empiricist and hype-phenomenological philosophies be checked and balanced by a Trivium-based curriculum of "consciousness studies" that rediscovers the metaphysics of ancient and classical philosophies, theologies, and poetics.

Through a historical-grammatical study of such ancient and classical world literature, a Trivium curriculum of consciousness metaphysics can enlighten students with the grammatical, logical, and rhetorical powers to self-defend the subjectivity of personal conscience against the short-sighted utilitarianisms of pragmatism, materialism, nominalism, positivism, and existentialism which are recklessly accelerating technocratic political-economics into a futurist, posthuman Singularity. The individual Trivium student who takes the liberal arts journey through this new cradle-to-consciousness curriculum can self-discover a metaphysics of consciousness that reaffirms the categorical-imperative subjectivity of conscience which is the bedrock of the political ethics to self-determination that are the source of democratic self-governance. By exploring the metaphysics of the Tao of consciousness, historical-grammatical Trivium curriculums can prompt dialogues in the classrooms and in the "public squares" where citizens can democratically draw up ethical legislations that place restrictions on technologies which could compromise the subjectivity of consciousness.

Grassroots Consciousness: If successful, a Trivium "consciousness" curriculum will awaken the individual student's political consciousness to self-defend his or her personal conscience from the neo-eugenic totalitarianisms of transhumanist and posthumanist technocracies that would open a Pandora's box of catastrophic biological, psychological, social, and political-economic side-effects which could irreparably damage the very "substance" of human consciousness itself. (Consider the hard lessons learned from environmental disasters caused by impetuously re-engineering the material matter and energy of our planetary ecosystem in the pragmatic name of positivistic humanist progress without respect for the metaphysical "substance" of the Tao of the natural universe).[185]

To prevent (and reverse) the technetronic pollution of thought, it is my hope that a Trivium "consciousness" curriculum can inspire students to self-actualize the metaphysical Tao, or Reason, of conscience, through personal responsibility which takes proactive steps toward limiting the encroachments of technology upon the liberties of consciousness.

Raising personal consciousness, the Trivium-informed student can start with "baby" steps toward detoxing his or her own consciousness by unplugging from the mental pollution of social media screen-time and other forms of virtual gluttony "downloaded" through smartphones and other digital computer devices.

After putting one's own consciousness in order, the next steps can be taken toward grassroots political activism at the local government levels where citizens can democratically press for civil ordinances that protect their public school districts and neighborhood communities from being commercially "re-zoned" to facilitate trans-technological infrastructures which could biopsychologically damage the residents' consciousnesses.

For example, socially conscious citizens have recently taken political stands against the commercial zoning of 5G wifi towers in their local communities,[186] Citing reports that 5G "millimeter waves (MMWs)" have been shown to damage the DNA of the human biocomputer system,[187] grassroots activists have been pushing back against local rollouts of the newfangled 5G wifi transceivers which are currently being networked by telecommunications companies to relay the next generation of super-speed internet connectivity that is needed to power the streamlined future of posthuman "smart cities" hyperlinked through the AI internet-of-things. According to a 2018 article published in the peer-reviewed *International Journal of Hygiene and Environmental Health*, super-speed 5G MMWs emit radiation that is a "contributor to cancer risk" which can "increase skin temperature, alter gene expression, [and] promote cellular proliferation and synthesis of proteins linked with oxidative stress" while "generat[ing] ocular damages, [and] affect[ing] neuro-muscular dynamics."[188] Alert to this body of scientific research on the biopsychological health dangers of 5G millimeter waves, local activists have been politically protesting and petitioning against the deployment of 5G transmitters in the communities of Ashland, Oregon;[189] Kauai, Hawaii;[190] Marin County, California;[191] Charlotte, North Carolina;[192] Long Island, New York;[193] Albany, New York;[194] and Woodstock, New York.[195]

Branching out into multilateral coalitions, such grassroots political activists at the local levels can continue building momentum as they link up into state and national alliances that push for state and federal legislations placing moratoriums on technologies which biopsychologically impede the categorical-imperative subjectivity of personal consciousness.[196]

These are just a few examples of how socially conscious citizens can take practical steps toward reinvigorating the political ethics of personal conscience through democratic channels of self-governance. It is in these ways that I anticipate Trivium-based "consciousness" curriculums can inspire the learned to regenerate the ethics of conscientious self-governance which are antithetical to the corporate, government, and scientific tyrannies of the fascist, communist, and technocratic dictatorships that would enslave the natural human liberties of conscientious subjectivity by socially re-engineering the Tao of human consciousness into a cheaply commodified product, an arbitrary social construct, or a digital-electronic algorithm.

A Final Thought

In closing, let's recap this five-point strategy for education reform:

1. Reclaim local democratic governance of public schoolboards. (Repudiate public-private management of corporate charter schooling subsidized by privatized voucher programs and government tax breaks on private tuition expenditures).

2. Repeal ed-psych methods of cognitive-behavioral conditioning that implement external reward-and-punishment motivators.

3. Protect student privacy from psychometric ed-tech data-mining. (Protect student consciousness from trans-eugenic ed-tech social engineering).

4. Replace workforce-conditioning pedagogies with renewed Trivium methods steeped in liberal arts curriculums of classical history and constitutional civics.

5. Create a new curriculum of "consciousness studies" that explores the ethics of consciousness through comparative Trivium analyses of classical metaphysics juxtaposed against modern and postmodern philosophies of materialist empiricism, existentialist phenomenology, and linguistic analysis.

It is my humble hope that this five-point "call to action" can provide at least some practical remedy to the monstrous School World Order which I have documented in this book. But more important than this "call to action" is the following "call to thought":

• Please think vigilantly about the posthuman prospects of corporatized education technologies.

• Please ask questions about the ethics of these ed-tech products.

• Please earnestly discuss these thoughts and queries with your family, friends, business colleagues, and government representatives.

The Singularity may be near, but it is not here just yet. In the meantime, we still have an opportunity to engage in a public dialogue about how to preserve the sacred Tao of consciousness from being subsumed by the so-called evolution of posthumanist technologies. So please just think. For there is only one thing more perilous than these trans-eugenic technetronics themselves: an unquestioning trust in technology that remains willfully ignorant of real dangers through cognitive dissonance; and stays blissfully mesmerized by whatever new convenience or luxury the latest brain-twisting gadget can provide.

Just a thought.

GLOSSARY

5G: The fifth generation of wireless communications technologies. 5G technologies communicate by transmitting hi-speed "millimeter waves" over short distances.

adaptive-learning (software): Educational computer programs that data-mine students' responses to virtual-learning modules in order to "personalize" instruction by adjusting the student's lessons based on his or her performance. Adaptive-learning software remediates lessons until a student shows progress; then, when the student progresses, the software makes lessons more challenging.

ADHD (attention deficit hyperactivity disorder): A cognitive-behavioral disability in which the person has difficulty focusing his or her attention. ADHD is characterized by restlessness, distractedness, and impulsivity.

adjustive/adaptive function of education: An educational theory set forth in the 1918 book, *Principles of Secondary Education*, by Harvard's first Professor of Secondary Education, Alexander Inglis. According to the adjustive/adaptive function, the purpose of schooling is obedience training, which conditions students to obey fixed protocols for submitting to authorities.

AFC (American Federation for Children): A not-for-profit interest group that lobbies for "school choice" privatization.

AFT (American Federation of Teachers): A national teachers union founded in 1916. The AFT is an affiliate of the AFL-CIO (American Federation of Labor and Congress of Industrial Organizations).

AGI (Artificial General Intelligence): Artificial intelligence (AI) which can perform the full range of cognitive tasks that any human being can perform. AGI might theoretically exhibit "self-awareness" and "self-will" which is comparable to human consciousness. AGI, also known as "strong" or "full" AI, is more complex than "weak" or "narrow" AI, which can only perform a limited range of humanoid cognitive tasks that are more or less predetermined.

ALEC (American Legislative Exchange Council): a nonprofit interest group that lobbies to advance corporatist privatization across all sectors of the economy, including the for-profit expansion of privatized virtual charter school corporations. ALEC's team of lawyers draft boilerplate bills that are disseminated across the nation to Congress members who pass these template bills into actual state and federal laws.

algorithm: A mathematical operation that sequences logical orders for definitively calculating series of data inputs and outputs. Basically, the data inputs and outputs of an algorithm work on an if-then continuum (if input "A," then output "B"; if input "C," then output "D," etc.). In any technology that integrates digital computation, an algorithm can simply perform specific outputs in reaction to specific inputs; or an algorithm can identify and track complex data patterns by scanning all the individual input-output sequences.

AI (artificial intelligence): Any digital or computational technology that can mimic the cognitive operations of the human brain. AI can be as rudimentary as a complex stimulus-response algorithm or as sophisticated as a self-driving car. However, artificial intelligence (AI) should not be confused with artificial general intelligence (AGI). AI can only perform a limited range of humanoid cognitive tasks that are more or less predetermined. In contrast, AGI can perform the full range of cognitive tasks that any human being can perform, and AGI might theoretically exhibit "self-awareness" and "self-will" which is comparable to human consciousness.

a posteriori reasoning: A school of philosophy that believes all knowledge can only be derived after (*post*) a person has observed or measured specific phenomena. Also known as "empiricism," *a posteriori* reasoning holds that a person must observe or measure specific data/evidence in order to derive knowledge.

a priori reasoning: A school of philosophy that believes knowledge can be attained before (*prior*) a person has observed or measured specific phenomena. Also known as "rationalism," *a priori* reasoning holds that a person can employ formal logic and other modes of abstract analysis in order to scaffold universal principles and other abstract ideas to arrive at universal truths prior to gathering particular empirical data/evidence.

AR (augmented reality): A type of virtual technology that enables digital graphics or metrics to be overlaid onto the real physical world. Through cameras or transparent screens on smartphones, tablets, or headsets, AR software overlays text, images, and/or three-dimensional graphics or metrics onto the real-world images captured by the camera/screen.

ATC (American Technology Council): A US executive agency established by President Donald Trump's Executive Order 13794.[1] The ATC is basically a technocratic thinktank commissioned to advance hi-tech political-economic planning through public-private partnerships that improve government information technologies and IT infrastructures.

behaviorism: A psychological conditioning theory coined by John B. Watson, an American advertising executive who was a student of John Dewey at the University of Chicago.[2] Behaviorist conditioning is the successor to classical stimulus-response conditioning and the precursor to operant conditioning. Behaviorism trains animals to respond to stimuli with conditioned reflexes by (1) associating rewards with "desirable" stimuli and by (2) associating punishments with "undesirable" stimuli.

BCI (brain-computer interface): Any transhumanist biotechnology or psychotechnology that links the human brain with a digital-electronic computer. See also brain-machine interface (BMI), human-machine interface (HMI), and human-computer interface (HCI).

blended learning: A technology-centered method of "personalized" education that teaches students in hybrid schools that combine traditional paper-and-pencil learning in a classroom with automated virtual learning on an internet computer module.

BIA (Bridge International Academies): A globalist charter school corporation that runs international chains of "blended-learning" virtual schools which have public-private contracts with governments across the globe.

Big Data: The practice of collecting, aggregating, and analyzing massive amounts of data across all sectors of the political-economy in order to develop predictive computer analytics that can forecast, manipulate, and innovate trends in economic planning (such as corporate production, workforce development, and consumer spending) and government regulation (such as national security; public infrastructure; health and human services; and educational administration).

Bilderberg Group: A secretive nongovernmental organization (NGO) that surreptitiously plans the world political-economy through off-record international meetings between heads of states, international financiers, military leaders, corporate executives, intelligence operatives, media moguls, academics, technologists, and even royal families.

biofeedback: A method of neuro-psychological conditioning in which a person wears computerized biosensors that track his or her vitals in order to provide real-time digital feedback that tells the wearer how to manage stress. By monitoring heartrate, body temperature, brainwaves, and other electrochemical signals, biofeedback sensors condition the wearer by telling him or her when to correct neuro-psychological disturbances in his or her cognitive, behavioral, or emotional state.

biometrics: Any biological measurements used to identify or characterize a person. Biometric measurements include fingerprinting, voice-recognition, facial recognition, retinal scanning, and DNA sequencing. Such biometrics can be used to identify the unique "biosignature" of a specific person, or they can be used to infer a person's physiological, psychological, or behavioral characteristics.

biotechnology: Any technology that can interface with, re-engineer, or synthesize organic biology.

BMI (brain-machine interface): Any transhumanist biotechnology or psychotechnology that links the human brain with a digital-electronic computer. See also brain-computer interface (BCI), human-computer interface (HCI), and human-machine interface (HMI).

C2C (cradle to career): A "school choice" buzz-phrase that refers to workforce-training curriculums through privatized charter schools and other public-private "school-to-work" partnerships. Cradle-to-career workforce schooling parallels the "lifelong learning" systems of schooling promulgated by the United Nations Educational, Scientific, and Cultural Organization (UNESCO).

CAI (computer-assisted instruction): any form of school instruction that utilizes a computer to assist student learning.

career pathways: Workforce-schooling curriculums that train students for narrowly prescribed job skills in order to fulfill workforce development quotas projected by corporate-government school-to-work partnerships.

CBE (competency-based education): An educational policy that requires schools to measure learning in terms of how "competently" a student is able to perform prescribed "learning outcomes" which prepare him or her for workforce readiness. CBE policies stress that lessons should be flexibly administered so that a student can work at his or her own pace toward achieving workforce-competency outcomes. Hence, CBE policies often favor prescriptive "career pathways" curriculums on "personalized" computer modules.

CFR (Council on Foreign Relations): A non-governmental organization (NGO) that lobbies for international governance through "world trade" economics and globalist foreign policy. Established in 1921,[3] the CFR is the American counterpart to the British Royal Institute of International Affairs.[4]

cognitive-behavioral psychology: Any scientific application of any of the following methods of psychological or behavioral conditioning: stimulus-response conditioning, classical conditioning, behaviorist conditioning, operant conditioning.

CRISPR-Cas9: A gene-editing technology that uses enzymes to remove and insert DNA sequences for the purposes of genetic engineering. ("CRISPR" stands for "clustered regularly interspaced short palindromic repeats." "Cas9" stands for "CRISPR-associated protein 9").[5]

DARPA (Defense Advanced Research Project Agency): One of the most powerful US military research-and-development agencies.

data-mining: Any process by which digital technologies extract personal information from technology users.

deconstructionism: A postmodern philosophy coined by Jacques Derrida.[6] Deconstructionism is a branch of linguistic-analysis philosophy which believes that there is no such thing as a canonical interpretation of a "text" because all interpretations are equally valid. According to deconstructionism, a "text" has no objective meaning because the meaning changes based on the subjective perspective of the reader relative to his or her position in the historical space and time of human culture. Simply put, deconstructionism holds that interpretation determines meaning (meaning does not determine interpretation). In this way, deconstructionist philosophy inverts the historical-grammatical method of literary studies, which believes that a "text" has an objective meaning derived from canonical interpretations grounded in the historical context of the "text." For deconstructionists, everything is an empty, meaningless "text"; even the matter and energy of the universe are just "material texts," and even people themselves are nothing more than "biological texts," which can be endlessly reinterpreted ad hoc.

diagnostic/directive function of education: An educational theory set forth in the 1918 book, *Principles of Secondary Education*, by Harvard's first Professor of Secondary Education, Alexander Inglis. According to the diagnostic/directive function, the purpose of schooling is to determine a student's social role.

dialectical materialism: Karl Marx's materialist theory of history,[7] which postulates that the evolution of human civilizations occurs through the dialectics, or conflicts/ debates, of class struggles between dominant socioeconomic classes and subjugated socioeconomic classes. According to Marx's dialectical materialism, history will eventually culminate in a crowning revolution in which the "bourgeois" capitalist classes who own the means of economic production are finally overthrown by the laboring classes of their "proletariat" wage-slaves, who will establish a classless society in a communist utopia.

differentiating function of education: An educational theory set forth in the 1918 book, *Principles of Secondary Education*, by Harvard's first Professor of Secondary Education, Alexander Inglis. According to the differentiating function, the purpose of schooling is to segregate students according to their different roles in the social caste hierarchy.

DNA (deoxyribonucleic acid): Sequences of organic molecules which are the biochemical building blocks of all organic life. DNA is basically a fancy name for "genes," which consist sugars and phosphates connected to "nucleotides," which are comprised of four chemical components known as "nucleobases": adenine (A), thymine (T), guanine (G), and cytosine (C). Based on myriad sequences of A, T, C, and G combined into double-helixes, DNA genetically encodes the physiology of all organic life in all its diverse biological varieties of animals, plants, and microbes.[8]

EDM (educational data-mining): According to the US Department of Education, "EDM develops methods and applies techniques from statistics, machine learning, and data mining to analyze data collected during teaching and learning. EDM tests learning theories and informs educational practice."[9]

ed-tech: Education technology.

empiricism: A philosophical school of thought which posits that all knowledge is derived from observation or measurement. Also known as *a posteriori* reasoning, empiricism favors inductive reasoning, which is a method of first logging specific observations or measurements in order to logically draw general conclusions that are probabilistic (rather than certain).

epistemology: A philosophical discipline that is concerned with the study of knowledge, especially the study of *how we know* what we know.

ESEA (Elementary and Secondary Education Act): A 1965 federal education law which once set the national rules for governing public-school standards across the United States.[10] ESEA has been replaced by the Every Student Succeeds Act (ESSA) of 2015.[11]

ESSA (Every Student Succeeds Act): A 2015 federal education law which sets the national rules for governing public-school standards across the United States. ESSA is the successor to the Elementary and Secondary Education Act (ESEA) of 1965.[12]

ETS (Educational Testing Services): A nonprofit testing corporation that has been developing and proctoring academic standardized tests since 1947. Current ETS tests include the Graduate Record Examination (GRE), the Test of English as a Foreign Language (TOEFL), and the HiSET high-school equivalency test.[13]

eugenics: The "science" of controlling genetic evolution through controlled breeding that promotes the reproduction of "fit" genes while preventing the reproduction of "unfit" genes. Coined by Charles Darwin's cousin, Francis Galton, eugenics was also known as "race hygiene" in Nazi Germany under Hitler. Today, eugenics is called "genetic engineering."

existentialism: A philosophy which believes that existence precedes essence. Existentialists believe in the relative authenticity of subjective experience as a rejection of metaphysical ideals, rational universals, and empirical determinisms.

FERPA (Family Educational Rights and Privacy Act): A United States law which regulates students' privacy rights pertaining to their personal education records.

gamification: A buzzword for converting traditional school lessons into computerized video games, including augmented-reality games and virtual-reality games.

GBL (game-based learning): Refers to "gamified" learning platforms that convert traditional school lessons into computerized video games, including augmented-reality games and virtual-reality games

GEB (General Education Board): A Rockefeller philanthropy that was operational from 1902 to 1964.[14] Across the United States, the GEB financed American schooling reforms that emphasized workforce-training curricula taught through stimulus-response and behaviorist psychological-conditioning methods.

GSR monitor (galvanic skin response monitor): A transhumanist biofeedback technology that monitors a student's "skin conductivity" in order to track his or her "socio-emotional" engagement with school lessons.

HCI (human-computer interface): Any transhumanist biotechnology or psychotechnology that links the human brain with a digital-electronic computer. See also human-machine interface (HMI), brain-machine interface (BMI), and brain-computer interface (BCI).

Hegelian dialectic: A philosophical theory of history postulated by Georg Wilhelm Friedrich Hegel. The Hegelian dialectic theorizes that history evolves through dialectics, or debates, between opposing ideas that eventually synthesize into new ideas over time. One historical idea (thesis) conflicts with an opposing historical idea (antithesis); and as a result, a new idea (synthesis) is created by combining the opposing ideas of "thesis" and "antithesis." The Order of Skull and Bones manipulates the Hegelian-dialectical evolution of historical ideas through the "problem (thesis) + reaction (antithesis) = solution (synthesis)" stratagem, which foments political conflicts while co-opting both sides of the dispute in order to narrow the resolution and thereby control the historical outcome.

historical-grammatical learning: A classical method of studying literature. In the historical-grammatical method of "close reading," the language of a text is interpreted based on the historical contexts of the publication and authorship: who wrote the text; when was the text written; where was the text written; in what language was the text written; how/why was the text written. The historical-grammatical approach to literary analysis endeavors to extract the objective meaning of a text based on the internal coherency of the text's logos, or logic, as it was authentically created. Thus, the historical-grammatical school of literary studies holds to certain canonical interpretations of a text's objective logos, or logic, while rejecting other readings which rely on more or less "subjective" criteria that fall outside of the historical contexts of the publication and authorship.

HMI (human-machine interface): Any transhumanist biotechnology or psychotechnology that links the human brain with a digital-electronic computer. See also human-computer interface (HCI), brain-computer interface (BCI), and brain-machine interface (BMI).

IBM (International Business Machines): One of the first proto-computer corporations which was established in 1911.[15] Today, IBM produces cutting-edge computer technologies which are commercialized across the global markets of the world economy.

IDEA (Individuals with Disabilities Education Act): A federal law that regulates the educational rights of disabled people in the United States of America.

idealism: A philosophy that believes the world is ordered according to universal ideas, or truths, that are metaphysically transcendent.

integrating function of education: An educational theory set forth in the 1918 book, *Principles of Secondary Education*, by Harvard's first Professor of Secondary Education, Alexander Inglis. According to the differentiating function, the purpose of schooling is to condition all students to behave as uniformly as possible by training them all to conform to a regimen of collectivist values dictated by school authorities.

IQ (intelligence quotient): A psychometric score that measures the intellectual brain capacity of a human being.

IT (information technology): Any electronic or digital technology that can receive or transmit information or data. IT encompasses all communications technologies.

KIPP (Knowledge Is Power Program): A chain of corporate charter schools which includes "brick-and-mortar" classroom schools and "blended-learning" hybrid schools that combine onsite classroom learning with virtual computer learning.

law of contradiction: The second law of formal logic, which states that the first law of logic (the law of identity) is violated when a grammatical-rhetorical expression (word/phrase) is used in ways that controvert observation or in ways that contradict other grammatical-rhetorical suppositions (words/phrases). Simply put, the law of contradiction establishes that a statement is false whenever a word/phrase is used in ways that go against the identity of its own meaning/definition.

law of identity: The first law of formal logic, which states that a specific phenomenon has a specific identity that cannot be conflated with the identities of any other phenomena. Extended to grammar and rhetoric, the law of identity states that specific words/phrases refer to specific phenomena (which cannot be conflated with the identities of other words/phrases).

law of tautology: The third law of formal logic, which holds that certain grammatical-rhetorical expressions must either be true or false (because they cannot be both true and false at the same time). The law of tautology holds that, in certain instances, there is no "third" or "middle" possibility in which a logical premise is simultaneously both true and false; hence, the law of tautology is also known as "the law of the excluded third" or "the law of the excluded middle").

learning analytics: According to the US Department of Education, "[l]earning analytics applies techniques from information science, sociology, psychology, statistics, machine learning, and data mining to analyze data collected during education administration and services, teaching, and learning. Learning analytics creates applications that directly influence educational practice."[16]

Learnsphere: A public-private data-sharing hub where teachers, school administrators, ed-tech engineers, social scientists, and other education researchers can share data in order to develop better teaching strategies, schooling policies, and ed-tech products.

lifelong learning: A UNESCO educational program that emphasizes the collectivist learning of globalist values in order to achieve "social stability" in a planned world economy. To keep up with the technological evolution of the global economy, UNESCO's lifelong-learning program stresses continuing education that updates a person's job skills throughout the course of his or her life.

linguistic analysis: A branch of philosophy that believes all knowledge is derived from language. By extension, linguistic analysts believe that all knowledge is a relativistic matter of how we subjectively use language to define phenomena (not necessarily how we use logic to rationalize phenomena; and not necessarily how we use empirical measurement to quantify phenomena).

logocentrism: "Logocentrism" combines the root "logos" with the suffix "centrism." The word "logos," which is a philosophical concept conceived by the pre-Socratic Greek philosopher Heraclitus,[17] basically refers to the metaphysical order, or logic, of the universe and the human mind/spirit. The suffix "centrism" means "to be centered upon," or "to be fixated upon." Thus, logocentrism means to be philosophically centered, or fixated, upon the logos, or logic, of the universe.

logos: The word "logos," which is a philosophical concept conceived by the Greek philosopher Heraclitus, essentially refers to the metaphysical order, or logic, of the universe and the human mind/spirit.

look-say reading: A method of literacy instruction that teaches students to read by memorizing whole words. The student is taught to "look" at a whole word as a single sound; then, the student is taught to "say" the whole word as a single sound. The look-say method of reading instruction is the opposite of the phonics method, which teaches students to dissect words into smaller parts, such as prefixes, suffixes, and roots, that can be "sounded out" into syllables. (See also "whole-language learning" and "whole-word learning").

materialism: A philosophical school of thought which believes that all reality exists as physics (matter and energy). Materialism holds that all reality can be objectively measured or observed by the five senses. Materialism denies the existence of any ideal, metaphysical, or spiritual realities that transcend the physics of matter and energy. For materialists, even consciousness is a material product of the physical interplay between matter and energy.

metaphysics: A branch of philosophy that studies the realities of phenomena which cannot be directly measured or observed. Since metaphysics studies the deeper realities that transcend the material physics of matter and energy, metaphysical philosophies rely on logical inference through *a priori* reasoning (rather than *a posteriori* empiricism). Metaphysics is the philosophical domain of theology, idealism, and other "spiritual" ways of knowing truth.

modernism: A philosophical movement that is skeptical of both the traditions of classical metaphysics as well as the progresses of humanist rationalism and materialist empiricism. Modernist philosophies emphasize the subconscious fragmentation of human rationality as a result of modern industrial-scientific methods of economic mass production, hi-tech mass communications, automated mass transportation, and mechanized mass-scale war.

MR (mixed reality): A digital platform that combines augmented-reality and virtual-reality technologies.

NEA (National Education Association): The largest labor union in the United States of America. Founded in 1857, the NEA represents public schoolteachers and other public school employees across the USA.[18]

NIH (National Institutes of Health): A US federal-government agency that funds and oversees research task forces commissioned to investigate public health issues. The NIH also funds and directs public-private research initiatives that actively develop innovative healthcare technologies and medical treatments.

nominalism: A branch of philosophy that believes words, or "names," do not represent universal ideas or metaphysical truths. Rather, nominalism believes that words/names are merely arbitrary labels which humans use for decoding their empirical sensory experiences of material objects. According to nominalism, all that exists is the material matter and energy of the physical universe; and the words/names we use to define such material phenomena are merely ad hoc tools that can be more or less helpful for deciphering and manipulating material objects for practical utility. Nominalism provides the groundwork for modern schools of linguistic-analysis philosophy.

OAI (Office of American Innovation): A White House thinktank established by Donald Trump's "Presidential Memorandum on the White House Office of American Innovation."[19] The OAI pushes public-private political-economic planning that concentrates on hi-tech innovations through corporate-government partnerships.

OBE (outcomes-based education): An educational policy that requires schools to measure learning in terms of whether a student can perform predetermined "outcomes" which prepare him or her for workforce readiness. Targeting pre-established "learning outcomes," OBE policies favor instructional methods that narrowly focus on workforce-training lessons which teach students the basic job skills required to perform standardized workforce-readiness outcomes. OBE policies usually allocate school funding based on whether the students at a school have achieved such predetermined workforce-readiness outcomes.

ontology: A branch of philosophy that studies "being," or "ultimate reality." Ontology is the philosophical study of "existence": what absolutely exists; how does it truly exist; and why does it actually exist.

OOO (object-oriented ontology): A philosophy that believes inanimate objects are "non-sentient entities" which exist independently of human observation and utility. OOO theory holds that the ontology, or ultimate reality/being, of inanimate objects is not determined by human beings. Thus, OOO theory believes that the ultimate existence/essence of non-sentient objects is equal to the ultimate existence/essence of sentient human beings. As such, OOO theory blurs the lines between human beings and objects.

operant conditioning: A form of psychological conditioning coined by B. F. Skinner. Operant conditioning is the successor to the behaviorist conditioning popularized by John B. Watson and E. L. Thorndike.[20] Skinner's operant conditioning emphasizes the strategic scheduling of "positive-reinforcement rewards," "negative-reinforcement rewards," "negative punishments," and "positive punishments" in order to "shape" an animal's conditioned associations between external environmental stimuli and the animal's own internal cognitive-behavioral responses.

P-16 Council: A public-private workforce-schooling council that operates at the state level. The "P" stands for "preschool," and the "16" stands for "age 16." P-16 councils coordinate public-private economic planning through preschool, elementary-school, middle-school, and high-school workforce-training programs. P-16 school-to-work programs parallel the "lifelong learning" systems of education promulgated by the United Nations Educational, Scientific, and Cultural Organization (UNESCO).

P-20 Council: A public-private workforce-schooling council that operates at the state level. The "P" stands for "preschool," and the "20" stands for "age 20," or "education after college." P-20 councils coordinate public-private economic planning through preschool, elementary-school, middle-school, high-school, collegiate, adult-education, and other workforce-training programs. P-20 school-to-work programs parallel the "lifelong learning" systems of education promulgated by the United Nations Educational, Scientific, and Cultural Organization (UNESCO).

panopticon: An "all-seeing" prison system designed by the utilitarian philosopher, Jeremy Bentham, in 1791.[21] In Bentham's panopticon prison compound, a single guard has a 360-degree vantage point where he can view all of the prisoner cells form his single watchtower; yet none of the prisoners can see the guard from their cells, which encircle the tower. Consequently, even though the guard cannot actually see all the prison cells at the same time, his constant presence in the watchtower conditions the prisoners to behave as if he can actually see them all at once. Thus, the panopticon watchtower psychologically conditions prisoners to self-censor any behaviors that might be punished by the guardsman (even when the guard cannot actually see the prisoners). The postmodernist philosopher, Michel Foucault, re-popularized the "panopticon" concept as a term for referring to any mass-surveillance system, especially a digital-electronic surveillance grid of cameras or internet data-mining, which causes the people being surveilled to self-censor any behaviors that might be penalized by the authoritarian surveillants.

pedagogy: A fancy term that is basically synonymous with "educational philosophy" or "educational methodology." Pedagogy encompasses the theories and practices of teaching methods. As an academic discipline, pedagogy studies the art of teaching instructors *how to teach*. Pedagogies systematize teaching tactics that instructors can apply to strategically deliver skill exercises and concept lessons which effectively engage student learning.

phenomenology: A school of philosophy which believes that the only things humans can directly experience are the internal phenomena of their own subjective minds. Phenomenology holds that objective external reality can never be truly known because humans' empirical experiences of the material matter and energy of the universe are always filtered through the subjective interpretations of their internal mental processes. (Unlike solipsism, which denies the existence of anything outside the human mind, phenomenology is merely skeptical about the ability to objectively know anything about the real existences outside the human mind).

phrenology: A nineteenth-century eugenical pseudoscience that diagnosed people with psychological and sociological characteristics based on the shapes of their skulls.

physiognomy: A eugenical pseudoscience that diagnoses people with psychological and sociological characteristics based on their facial features.

PII (personally identifiable information): information, or data, that can reveal the specific identity of the person to whom the info/data belongs. PII includes a person's name, address, social security number, etc.

PK-16 Council: A public-private workforce-schooling council that operates at the state level. The "PK" stands for "pre-kindergarten," and the "16" stands for "age 16." PK-16 councils coordinate public-private economic planning through preschool, elementary-school, middle-school, and high-school workforce-training programs. PK-16 school-to-work programs parallel the "lifelong learning" systems of education promulgated by the United Nations Educational, Scientific, and Cultural Organization (UNESCO).

PK-20 Council: A public-private workforce-schooling council that operates at the state level. The "PK" stands for "pre-kindergarten," and the "20" stands for "age 20," or "education after college." PK-20 councils coordinate public-private economic planning through preschool, elementary-school, middle-school, high-school, collegiate, adult-education, and other workforce-training programs. PK-20 school-to-work programs parallel the "lifelong learning" systems of education promulgated by the United Nations Educational, Scientific, and Cultural Organization (UNESCO).

PMI (Precision Medicine Initiative): A public-private research initiative funded by the US federal government under the auspices of the National Institutes of Health. The

Precision Medicine Initiative advances the research and development of gene therapies and other genetic medicines that "personalize" healthcare by treating individual patients based on their unique biogenetic signatures/markers.

positivism: A philosophical school of thought that believes all knowledge comes from the experiences of empirically observing or measuring the particulars of material phenomena. Positivism denies metaphysics and rejects idealism while denouncing *a priori* reasoning. Coined by Auguste Comte,[22] positivism forms the philosophical basis of "scientism," which is basically the pseudo-religious worship of the scientific method.

posthumanism: A scientific philosophy that believes the biogenetic evolution of the human species will be superseded by the technological evolution of artificially intelligent machines, which will subsume human intelligence and ultimately render human consciousness into obsolescence and extinction.

postmodernism: A philosophical movement that rejects the traditions of classical metaphysics as well as the progresses of humanist rationalism and materialist empiricism. In rejection of absolute truth, universal metaphysics, objective ideas, and practical utility, postmodernist philosophies believe in the subjective relativism of ideas, the absurdity of rational determinisms, and the meaningless "performance" of sensuous existence.

PPRA (Protection of Pupil Rights Amendment): A 1978 federal law which, according to the US Department of Education, "seeks to ensure that schools and contractors obtain written parental consent before minor students are required to participate in any ED-funded survey, analysis, or evaluation that reveals [sensitive student] information."[23] PPRA-protected information includes a student's "1. Political affiliations; 2. Mental and psychological problems… 3. Sex behavior and attitudes; 4. Illegal, anti-social, self-incriminating and demeaning behavior; 5. Critical appraisals of … close family relationships; 6. Legally recognized … relationships, such as those of lawyers, physicians, and ministers; or 7. Income."[24]

pragmatism: A school of philosophy that believes truth and ethics are merely a matter of what is useful or helpful. Popularized by the American psychologist, William James,[25] pragmatism believes that whatever is useful is true, and whatever is helpful is ethical. There are no transcendent metaphysics, universal ideas, or absolute determinisms that predicate pragmatic truth or pragmatic ethics.

precision education: An educational methodology that uses genetic screening to digitally create student-learning profiles that facilitate "personalized" instruction based on the student's genetic IQ. Precision-ed gene profiles also identify and accommodate a student's cognitive-behavioral learning disabilities. Precision-ed gene screening can also be enhanced with other biometric and psychometric ed-tech, such as socioemotional biofeedback wearables.

precision medicine: "Personalized" medical treatments that include gene therapies and other genetic medicines that treat individual patients by targeting their unique biogenetic signatures/markers.

propaedeutic function of education: An educational theory set forth in the 1918 book, *Principles of Secondary Education*, by Harvard's first Professor of Secondary Education, Alexander Inglis. According to the propaedeutic function, the purpose of schooling is to train elite groups of students to take over the reins of the governing/schooling system in the future. As such, propaedeutically trained students are also taught how to manage the rest of their student peers who have been "diagnosed" into the lower castes of the sociopolitical hierarchy.

371

psychometrics: Any verbal, behavioral, neurological, or biological assessment used to identify or characterize a person's cognitive, emotional, or behavioral psychology. Psychometric measurements include IQ tests, personality tests, reflex tests, career aptitude tests, and other standardized educational tests. Such psychometrics can be used to diagnose a person as pathological, learning disabled, job-competent, or genius.

psychotechnology: Any technology that can interface with the brain or nervous system and thereby alter any cognitive, emotional, or behavioral powers of human consciousness.

rationalism: A philosophical school of thought which posits that knowledge is attained by reasoning through universal ideas that transcend the particulars of observation and measurement. Also known as *a priori* reasoning, rationalism favors deductive reasoning, which is a method of deducing truth by drawing formal-logical conclusions from universal ideas that are transcend empirical phenomena.

relativism: A philosophical school of thought that denies the objectivity of ideas. According to relativist philosophies, there is no absolute truth, nor is there any ultimate reality; nothing transcends a person's subjective perspective. Relativism believes that every subjective idea is equally true from its own relative perspective regardless of any apparent contradiction.

school choice: A euphemism that refers to the privatization of public schooling through public-private charter schools; public-private voucher programs; and government tax credits for private tuition expenses and "education savings accounts."

scientism: A "scientific" pseudo-religion which holds the radical-positivist tenet that human beings should only believe scientific facts which can be objectively proven. As a political philosophy, scientism believes that human society should only obey scientific laws which can be objectively proven.

SEL (socio-emotional learning): An educational policy that tracks students' emotions and social behaviors in order to condition them for "precision" learning outcomes. SEL policies integrate ed-tech that digitally data-mines a student's socioemotional behaviors through galvanic skin-response bracelets, emotional face-recognition scanners, and EEG brainwave headbands.

Singularity: The climax of transhuman/posthuman technological evolution, which futurists predict will culminate in the perfect merger of humankind with brain-computer interfaces jacked into artificially intelligent computers linked to the internet-of-everything.

SIS data (student information system data): Data that tracks the institutional demographics of a school's academic and behavioral outcomes: attendance and suspension rates; course grades, course levels, and class sizes; standardized test scores; learning disability and IEP classifications; free/reduced-price lunch distribution; ethnic population ratios. In addition, SIS data contains certain health information such as absences due to illness or other physical or mental health complication. SIS data can also contain criminal justice records pertaining to in-school arrests and other school code violations.

skepticism: A philosophical school that believes the ultimate and absolute answers to the "big" questions about reality and truth can never be known. Simply put, skepticism believes that, if ultimate realities or absolute truths do actually exist, humans can never know them.

Skinner box: A mechanized teaching device developed by B. F. Skinner. The operant-conditioning mechanisms of the Skinner-box "teaching machines" were modeled after B. F.'s puzzle-box animal-training experiments, which were modeled after E. L. Thorndike's behaviorist animal-conditioning experiments. The Skinner box is the precursor to contemporary adaptive-learning computer software.

Social Credit System: A Chinese-government total-surveillance grid that utilizes internet-of-everything "smart cities" to digitally keep track of citizens' financial, social, and political behaviors in order to penalize or reward those behaviors with restricted or streamlined access to transportation, healthcare, housing, and even civil due process. Based on "good behaviors," a citizen gains points on his or her social credit score; based on "bad behaviors," a citizen loses points on his or her social credit score. A high score awards a citizen by granting him or her privileged rights; but a low score punishes a citizen by restricting his or her rights.

stimulus-response psychology: The first scientific psychological theory, which was the brainchild of Wilhelm Wundt, who is the founding father of laboratory psychology as a field of academic research. Wundt's stimulus-response theory of psychology scientifically dissects all aspects of human thought and behavior into series of reflexive responses to environmental stimuli. Wundt's stimulus-response principle of psychological conditioning is the core building block of all forms of cognitive-behavioral conditioning, including classical conditioning, behaviorist conditioning, and operant conditioning.

STEM (Science, Technology, Engineering, and Mathematics): An educational reform that emphasizes technocratic learning at the expense of the arts and humanities.

subjectivism: A philosophical school of thought that believes the truth of an idea is relative to a person's subjective perspective. Subjectivism is the opposite of objectivism. Subjectivism believes that there are no objective ideas which are universally true, for there is no objective truth which transcends the relativity or partiality of a person's subjective perceptions.

TA bot (teacher-aide bot): Any artificially intelligent technology that assists teachers by data-mining and graphing students' learning analytics. By providing teachers with student-learning data, TA bots give the teachers suggestions as to which students are excelling, which students are falling behind, which students need more challenging lessons, and which students need remediated lessons.

Tao: The word "Tao," which is a philosophical concept conceived by the Chinese philosopher Lao Tzu, essentially refers to the metaphysical order, or "Way," of the natural universe and the human mind/spirit.

teacher bot: Any artificially intelligent technology that replaces a human teacher by substituting the human instructor with a virtual instructor. A teacher-bot can be a software-based AI that is either virtually embodied on a computer screen (as a visual-graphics avatar) or disembodied through a computer speaker or instant-messaging platform (as audio or text only). More advanced teacher-bots are hardware-based AI that are mechanically embodied as humanoid robots with real-world mobility which can physically interact with a student body in the real-life material environments of the student's brick-and-mortar classroom or homeschool.

technetronics: Any technologies that combine electronics and digital computation.

text-centrism: A postmodern term invented by the deconstructionist philosophers, who coined the term in contrast against metaphysical, idealist, and rationalist philosophies of "logocentrism." "Text-centrism" combines the root "text" with the suffix "centrism." The root "text" refers to any symbol or medium, such as writing or speech, that can convey language or otherwise communicate meaning. The suffix "centrism" means "to be centered upon," or "to be fixated upon." Thus, "text-centrism" means to be philosophically centered, or fixated, upon the "subjectivity" of a text. Stated differently, "text-centrism" means that there is no objective meaning contained in any text; but rather, the meaning of a text changes based on the subjective perspective of the reader relative to his or her interpretive position in the historical space and time of human culture.

Thing Theory: A "critical theory" philosophy, which posits that objects are defined by language, and that language defines objects in terms of human relationship or human utility. Thus, an object becomes a "thing" when it cannot be readily explained in terms of its relationship to human utility. According to Thing Theory, since "things" are not clearly categorized as useful in any particular way, "things" are thereby opened up to new interpretations and new experimentations so that humans can make new uses of the "things." By extension, when an aspect of humanity itself becomes a "thing," that part of the human being/experience becomes opened up to new interpretations and new experimentations so that humans can make utility out of it.

transhumanism: The "science" of re-engineering human evolution by transforming organic human biology through genetic-engineering and other biotechnological advancements, such as human-computer interfaces, which rewire human physiology and neuropsychology. Coined by eugenicist Julian Huxley, transhumanism is neo-eugenics, which is the "science" of merging humans and computers into a new cyborg species that is part human, part machine.

Trivium: The classical "liberal arts" method of qualitative learning through a three-part methodology of language arts: grammar, logic, and rhetoric. The Trivium is the foundation of all classical learning, and it provides the groundwork for learning the quantitative Quadrivium of mathematics and science: arithmetic, geometry, music, and astronomy.

tutor bot: Any artificially intelligent technology that assists students by replacing human tutors with virtual tutors. A tutor-bot can be a software-based AI that is either virtually embodied on a computer screen (as a visual-graphics avatar) or disembodied through a computer speaker or instant-messaging platform (as audio or text only). Tutor-bots usually function like automated customer-service bots that are specially designed for the educational industry.

UBI (Universal Basic Income): A communist-style universal welfare payment that provides everyone a basic income to offset mass-unemployment resulting from the AI automation of the workforce.

UII (user interaction information): Psycho-behavioral data collected by adaptive-learning software. UII data keeps real-time track of a student's screen time along with his or her number of keystrokes per learning-module. Using adaptive-learning algorithms, UII maps these student-response feedback loops into "personal" psychological profiles for tailoring "individualized" digital instruction.

UNESCO (United Nations Educational, Scientific, and Cultural Organization): An international governance organization formulated by the United Nations. UNESCO promotes the international development of scientific and cultural education as a global human right.

utilitarianism: A philosophy coined by Jeremy Bentham.[26] This philosophy believes that ethics and truth are measured simply in terms of what is most useful to human society. Measuring "good" and "bad" based on a "hedonic scale" that quantifies "pleasures" versus "pains," utilitarianist ethics are essentially based on the following equation: ethics = the minimization of human suffering + the greatest amount of good for the greatest number of people. For utilitarians, there is no universal moral principle or other objective truth that transcends this ethical calculus.

VR (virtual reality): A type of virtual technology that can digitally induce real-world experiences through headsets which display three-dimensional virtual environments. VR computer systems can be connected to other biosensors that virtually induce other sensory experiences, such as tactile/touch experiences and auditory/sound experiences.

whole-language learning: A method of literacy instruction that teaches students to read by memorizing whole words. The student is taught to "look" at a whole word as a single sound; then, the student is taught to "say" the whole word as a single sound. The whole-language method of reading instruction is the opposite of the phonics method, which teaches students to dissect words into smaller parts, such as prefixes, suffixes, and roots, that can be "sounded out" into syllables. (See also "whole-word learning" and "look-say reading").

whole-word learning: A method of literacy instruction that teaches students to read by memorizing whole words. The student is taught to "look" at a whole word as a single sound; then, the student is taught to "say" the whole word as a single sound. The whole-word method of reading instruction is the opposite of the phonics method, which teaches students to dissect words into smaller parts, such as prefixes, suffixes, and roots, that can be "sounded out" into syllables. (See also "whole-language learning" and "look-say reading").

WIA (Workforce Investment Act): A US federal law that allocates monetary resources toward developing economic industries through government grants, public-private partnerships, school-to-work programs, and other workforce-planning projects.[27] WIA is the precursor to the Workforce Innovation and Opportunity Act (WIOA) of 2014.[28]

WIOA (Workforce Innovation and Opportunity Act): A US federal law that allocates monetary resources toward developing economic industries through government grants, public-private partnerships, school-to-work programs, and other workforce-planning projects.[29] WIOA is the updated successor to the Workforce Investment Act (WIA) of 1998.[30]

Endnotes – Glossary

1   Donald J. Trump, *Executive Order 13794—Establishment of the American Technology Council* (Washington, DC: Government Publishing Office, April 28, 2017), https://www.gpo.gov/fdsys/pkg/DCPD-201700297/pdf/DCPD-201700297.pdf

2   Editors of the Encyclopedia Britannica, "John B. Watson: American Psychologist," *Encyclopedia Britannica,* January 5, 2019, https://www.britannica.com/biography/John-B-Watson
Johns Hopkins University, "John Broadus Watson: The Father of Behavioral Psychology," *JHU Gazette,* January 22, 2001, https://gazette.jhu.edu/2001/01/22/john-broadus-watson-the-father-of-behavioral-psychology/

3   Council on Foreign Relations, "About CFR," *CFR,* accessed July 19, 2019, https://www.cfr.org/about

4   Royal Institute of International Affairs, "About Chatham House: History," *Chatham House: Royal Institute of International Affairs,* accessed July 19, 2019, https://www.chathamhouse.org/about/history

5   United States, National Institutes of Health, National Library of Medicine, "What Are Genome Editing and CRISPR-Cas9?," *Genetics Home Reference: Your Guide to Understanding Genetic Conditions,* July 16, 2019, https://ghr.nlm.nih.gov/primer/genomicresearch/genomeediting

6   Leonard Lawlor, "Jacques Derrida," *Stanford Encyclopedia of Philosophy,* April 16, 2018, https://plato.stanford.edu/entries/derrida/

7   Editors of the Encyclopedia Britannica, "Dialectical Materialism: Philosophy," *Encyclopedia Britannica*, October 3, 2016, https://www.britannica.com/topic/dialectical-materialism

8   United States, National Institutes of Health, "DNA: Deoxyribonucleic Acid," *National Human Genome Research Institute: Genetics Glossary*," accessed July 19, 2019, https://www.genome.gov/genetics-glossary/Deoxyribonucleic-Acid

9   Ibid, Office of Educational Technology, *Enhancing Teaching and Learning Through Educational Data Mining and Learning Analytics: An Issue Brief*, (Washington DC: Government Publishing Office, October 2012), https://tech.ed.gov/wp-content/uploads/2014/03/edm-la-brief.pdf

10   Cameron Brenchley, "What Is ESEA?," *Homeroom: The Official Blog of the U.S. Department of Education*, April 8, 2015, https://blog.ed.gov/2015/04/what-is-esea/

11   United States, *Every Student Succeeds Act*, Public Law 114-95, 114th Congress, S. 1177, December 10, 2015, https://www.congress.gov/114/plaws/publ95/PLAW-114publ95.pdf

12   Ibid.

13   Educational Testing Services, "About ETS: Our Heritage," *ETS*, accessed July 19, 2019, https://www.ets.org/about/who/heritage/

14   Rockefeller Foundation, "The General Education Board," Rockefeller Archive Center, accessed July 19, 2019, https://rockfound.rockarch.org/general_education_board

15   International Business Machines, "History: IBM Is Founded," IBM, accessed July 19, 2019, https://www.ibm.com/ibm/history/ibm100/us/en/icons/founded/

16   United States, Office of Educational Technology, *Enhancing Teaching and Learning Through Educational Data Mining and Learning Analytics: An Issue Brief*, (Washington DC: Government Publishing Office, October 2012), https://tech.ed.gov/wp-content/uploads/2014/03/edm-la-brief.pdf

17   Daniel W. Graham, "Heraclitus," *Stanford Encyclopedia of Philosophy*, June 23, 2015, https://plato.stanford.edu/entries/heraclitus/

18   National Education Association, "About NEA: Our History," *NEA: Great Public Schools for Every Student*, accessed July 19, 2019, http://www.nea.org/home/1704.htm

19   Donald J. Trump, *Presidential Memorandum on the White House Office of American Innovation*, (Washington, DC: Government Publishing Office, March 27, 2017), https://www.whitehouse.gov/presidential-actions/presidential-memorandum-white-house-office-american-innovation/

20   Editors of the *Encyclopedia Britannica*, "B. F. Skinner: American Psychologist," *Encyclopedia Britannica*, April 29, 2019, https://www.britannica.com/biography/B-F-Skinner

21   Jacques-Alain Miller and Richard Miller, "Jeremy Bentham's Panoptic Device," *MIT Press*, 41 (Summer, 1987): 3-29.

22   Michel Bourdeau, "Auguste Comte," *Stanford Encyclopedia of Philosophy*, May 8, 2018, https://plato.stanford.edu/entries/comte/

23   United States, Department of Education, "Protection of Pupil Rights Amendment," *Law & Guidance*, February 17, 2005, https://www2.ed.gov/policy//gen/guid/fpco/ppra/index.html

24   Ibid.

25   Russell Goodman, "William James," *Stanford Encyclopedia of Philosophy*, October 20, 2017, https://plato.stanford.edu/entries/james/

26   Julia Driver, "The History of Utilitarianism," *Stanford Encyclopedia of Philosophy*, September 22, 2014, https://plato.stanford.edu/entries/utilitarianism-history/

27   United States, *Workforce Investment Act*, Public Law 105-220, 105th Congress, H.R. 1385, August 7, 1998, https://www.govinfo.gov/content/pkg/PLAW-105publ220/pdf/PLAW-105publ220.pdf

28   Ibid, Workforce Innovation and Opportunity Act, Public Law 113-128, 113th Congress, H.R. 803, July 22, 2014, https://www.congress.gov/113/plaws/publ128/PLAW-113publ128.pdf

29   Ibid.

30   Ibid, *Workforce Investment Act, Public Law* 105-220, 105th Congress, H.R. 1385, August 7, 1998, https://www.govinfo.gov/content/pkg/PLAW-105publ220/pdf/PLAW-105publ220.pdf

Endnotes – Chapter One

1   Charlotte Thomson Iserbyt, "My Letter to Phyllis Schlafly," *ABCs of DumbDown*, June 16, 2014, http://abcsofdumbdown.blogspot.com/2014/06/my-1995-letter-to-phyllis-schlafly.html

2   Lucas Koprowsk, "Gov. Rauner Vetoes MAP Grant Bill," *The Courier: The College of DuPage's Student Newspaper*, February 24, 2016, https://codcourier.org/3915/news/gov-rauner-vetoes-map-grant-bill/

3   Katie Lobosco, "Illinois University Forced to Lay off 200 Workers," *CNN Money*, February 12, 2016, https://money.cnn.com/2016/02/12/pf/college/illinois-college-layoffs/

4   Marwa Eltagouri, "Chicago State University Send Layoff Notices to All 900 Employees," *Chicago Tribune*, February 26, 2016, https://www.chicagotribune.com/news/local/breaking/ct-chi-cago-state-university-layoff-notices-20160226-story.html

5   Ibid.

6   Charlotte Thomson Iserbyt, "What a Role Model for His Daughters!" in *Fleshing Our Skull and Bones: Investigations into America's Most Powerful Secret Society*, ed. Kris Millegan (Walterville, OR: Trine Day, 2003), 25-32.

7   Antony C. Sutton, *America's Secret Establishment: An Introduction to the Order of Skull and Bones*, Updated Reprint (Walterville, OR: Trine Day, 2002), 293.

8   Ibid, 16.

9   Ibid, xv, 62-111

10   Ibid, xiv.

11   Tom Schuba, "House Dems Fall Short on Vote to Override Rauner's Veto of Spending Bill," NBC News Chicago, March 3, 2016, https://www.nbcchicago.com/blogs/ward-room/House-Dems-Fall-Short-on-Vote-to-Override-Rauners-Veto-of-College-Spending-Bill-370933781.html

12   Erin Carlson, "Opinion: Quinn Campaign Muzzles Paul Vallas," NBC News Chicago, June 20, 2014, https://www.nbcchicago.com/blogs/ward-room/Vallas-charters-264009771.html

13   Diane Ravitch, "Why I Changed My Mind about Charter School Reform: Federal Testing Has Narrowed Education and Charter Schools Have Failed to Live up to Their Promise," *Wall Street Journal*, March 9, 2010, https://www.wsj.com/articles/SB100014240527487048693045751094433053439 62

14   Carol Felsenthal, "Education Guru Diane Ravitch on Bruce Rauner: 'A Terrible Idea,'" *Chicago Magazine*, September 22, 2014, https://www.chicagomag.com/Chicago-Magazine/Felsen-thal-Files/September-2014/Education-Guru-Diane-Ravitch-on-Bruce-Rauner-A-Terrible-Idea/

15   Accessed March 10, 2016. https://www.brucerauner.com/new-ad-better-schools-for-illi-nois/

16   Art Golab, "Inside Rauner's Charter Schools," *Chicago Sun-Times*, February 4, 2014, https://chicago.suntimes.com/uncategorized/7/71/158113/inside-bruce-rauners-charter-schools

17   Rauner College Prep, Noble Network of Charter Schools, accessed March 10, 2016, https://nobleschools.org/rauner/

18   Accessed March 10, 2016. https://www.brucerauner.com/new-ad-better-schools-for-illi-nois/

19   Associated Press, "Former Charter Schools CEO Earning $250K as Rauner's Advertiser," CBS News Chicago, March 20, 2015, https://chicago.cbslocal.com/2015/03/20/former-charter-schools-ceo-earning-250k-as-rauners-adviser/

20   Accessed March 10, 2016. https://www.brucerauner.com/new-ad-better-schools-for-illi-nois/

21   Business Wire Inc., "Governor Rauner Proclaims Jan. 24-30 'School Choice Week in Illinois' Joining Leaders Nationwide in Celebrating Opportunity in Education," Business Wire: A Berkshire Hathaway Company, January 20, 2016, https://www.businesswire.com/news/home/20160120005560/en/Governor-Rauner-Proclaims-Jan.-24-30-"School-Choice

22   Charlotte Thomson Iserbyt, "The True Goal of School Choice," News With Views, September 11, 2012, http://www.newswithviews.com/iserbyt/iserbyt112.htm

23   Rick Pearson, "Rauner Names Meeks as Illinois State Board of Education Chairman," *Chicago Tribune*, January 10, 2015, https://www.chicagotribune.com/chi-rauner-names-meeks-as-illi-nois-state-board-of-education-chairman-20150110-story.html

24   John Chase and Bob Secter, "Rauner Courts Black Votes with $1M Investment," *Chi-

cago Tribune, October 3, 2014, https://www.chicagotribune.com/ct-bruce-rauner-black-votes-20141003-story.html

25   One Chance Illinois, "About Us: Our Board of Directors," One Chance Illinois, accessed March 10, 2016. http://www.onechanceillinois.org/team/board-of-directors/

26   Associated Press, "Gov. Rauner Names Rev. Corey Brooks Illinois Tollway Board," NBC News Chicago, July 17, 2015, https://www.nbcchicago.com/blogs/ward-room/Gov-Rauner-Names-Rev-Corey-Brooks-to-Illinois-Tollway-Board-316524581.html

27   One Chance Illinois, "Myles Mendoza: Executive Director," One Chance Illinois, accessed March 10, 2016. http://onechanceillinois.org/about/myles-medoza/

28   Tony Arnold, "Education Group Says School Choice Could Be What Unifies Illinois Lawmakers," WBEZ News, October 26, 2015, https://www.wbez.org/shows/wbez-news/education-group-says-school-choice-could-be-what-unifies-illinois-lawmakers/7d435f49-37f0-4fbf-ae68-46fad5ddad11

29   Illinois Review, "Organizations Respond with Thumbs up, down to Gov.'s 2016 State of the State Address," Illinois Review: Crossroads of the Conservative Community, January 27, 2016, https://illinoisreview.typepad.com/illinoisreview/2016/01/responses-to-governors-2016-state-of-the-state-address.html

30   Bruce Rauner, Transcript of Governor Bruce Rauner's State of the State Address, February 4, 2015, https://www2.illinois.gov/gov/documents/sos_transcript_02_04_15.pdf

31   American Federation of Teachers, Closing Schools to Improve Student Achievement: What the Research and Researchers Say, October 2012, https://files.eric.ed.gov/fulltext/ED538666.pdf

32   Kenneth Libby, "Arne Duncan's Dark Years in Chicago," Counterpunch, December 29, 2008, https://www.counterpunch.org/2008/12/29/arne-duncan-s-dark-years-in-chicago/

33   Bill and Melinda Gates Foundation, "Aspira Inc of Illinois: to Support the Planning and Launch of ASPIRA Charter School and to Build out a Strategic Replication Plan, Including Teaching and Learning Supports as Well as Additional Business Planning," in How We Work: Grants, November 1, 2006, https://www.gatesfoundation.org/How-We-Work/Quick-Links/Grants-Database/Grants/2006/11/OPP46759

Ibid, "Chicago Charter School Foundation: to Support Creation of Charter School Campuses and Contract Schools in the Chicago Public School System," in How We Work: Grants, September 27, 2002, https://www.gatesfoundation.org/How-We-Work/Quick-Links/Grants-Database/Grants/2002/09/OPP22958

Ibid, "Illinois Network Of Charter Schools: to support a Stategic [sic] Communications and Grassroots Advocacy Project to Increase the Awareness and Support for Illinois' Charter Schools," in How We Work: Grants, March 1, 2006, https://www.gatesfoundation.org/How-We-Work/Quick-Links/Grants-Database/Grants/2006/03/OPP41879

Ibid, "National Association Of Charter School Authorizers: to Support the National Impact Initiative, Which Seeks to Strengthen the Charter Sector's Knowledge, Disseminate Professional Authorizing Policies and Practices and Establish More Quality Authorizers around the Country," in How We Work: Grants, October 1, 2008, https://www.gatesfoundation.org/How-We-Work/Quick-Links/Grants-Database/Grants/2008/10/OPP51507

Ibid, "Noble Network of Charter Schools: to Fund Two New, Small Schools in Chicago and Share Successful Practices with Other Educators," in How We Work: Grants, January 1, 2005, https://www.gatesfoundation.org/How-We-Work/Quick-Links/Grants-Database/Grants/2005/01/OPP36528

Ibid, "Perspectives Charter School: to Create and Implement Aligned Instructional Systems and Leadership Capacity in Perspectives Charter Schools," in How We Work: Grants, September 1, 2007, https://www.gatesfoundation.org/How-We-Work/Quick-Links/Grants-Database/Grants/2007/09/OPP49063

Ibid, "Perspectives Charter School: to Support the Establishment of Perspectives New Schools Initiative and the Creation of the First Perspectives-Style School," in How We Work: Grants, December 1, 2004, https://www.gatesfoundation.org/How-We-Work/Quick-Links/Grants-Database/Grants/2004/12/OPP36536

34   Ibid, "Daley Seeks Broad Strategy to Create 'High Schools of Tomorrow': $11.2 Million in Grants Funds Systemwide Reform Strategy and New Schools," in Press Room: Press Releases and Statements, May 19, 2005, https://www.gatesfoundation.org/Media-Center/Press-Releases/2005/05/Chicagos-High-Schools-of-Tomorrow

35   Ibid, "Children's First Fund, The Chicago Public School Foundation: to Advance Collaboration Between Traditional District Schools and Public Charter Schools in Chicago," in How We

Work: Grants, February 27, 2014, https://www.gatesfoundation.org/How-We-Work/Quick-Links/Grants-Database/Grants/2014/02/OPP1063250

Ibid, "Illinois Network Of Charter Schools: to Advance Collaboration Between Traditional District Schools and Public Charter Schools in Chicago," in How We Work: Grants, March 10, 2014, https://www.gatesfoundation.org/How-We-Work/Quick-Links/Grants-Database/Grants/2014/03/OPP1105603

Ibid, "Illinois Network Of Charter Schools: for General Operating Support," in How We Work: Grants, September 12, 2011, https://www.gatesfoundation.org/How-We-Work/Quick-Links/Grants-Database/Grants/2011/09/OPP1037905

Ibid, "LEAP Innovations: to Advance Collaboration Between Traditional District Schools and Public Charter Schools in Chicago," in How We Work: Grants, March 5, 2014, https://www.gatesfoundation.org/How-We-Work/Quick-Links/Grants-Database/Grants/2014/03/OPP1107251

Ibid, "National Association Of Charter School Authorizers: for General Operating Support," in How We Work: Grants, June 27, 2012, https://www.gatesfoundation.org/How-We-Work/Quick-Links/Grants-Database/Grants/2012/06/OPP1059213

Ibid, "National Association Of Charter School Authorizers: to Provide Funds, along with Related Monitoring and Support to Each Round 2 District-Charter Collaboration Compact City, Based upon Completion of a Compact and Submission of an Approved Compact Grant Application," in How We Work: Grants, November 2, 2011, https://www.gatesfoundation.org/How-We-Work/Quick-Links/Grants-Database/Grants/2011/11/OPP1031599

Ibid, "National Association Of Charter School Authorizers: to Provide General Operating Support," in How We Work: Grants, June 26, 2014, https://www.gatesfoundation.org/How-We-Work/Quick-Links/Grants-Database/Grants/2014/06/OPP1110251

Ibid, "National Association Of Charter School Authorizers: to Provide Technical Assistance to State and Local Agencies to Establish a High Quality Charter School Program in Washington State," in How We Work: Grants, June 27, 2013, https://www.gatesfoundation.org/How-We-Work/Quick-Links/Grants-Database/Grants/2013/06/OPP1089631

Ibid, "National Association Of Charter School Authorizers: to Provide Technical Assistance and Support to Potential District Charter School Authorizer Applicants and to Districts Wishing to Explore Potential Partnerships with Public Charter Schools in Washington State," in How We Work: Grants, September 16, 2014, https://www.gatesfoundation.org/How-We-Work/Quick-Links/Grants-Database/Grants/2014/09/OPP1112154

Ibid, "National Association Of Charter School Authorizers: to Strengthen the Policy Environment for Quality Charter School Authorizing through Advocacy at the State and Federal Levels," in How We Work: Grants, May 16, 2011, https://www.gatesfoundation.org/How-We-Work/Quick-Links/Grants-Database/Grants/2011/05/OPP1034981

Ibid, "National Association Of Charter School Authorizers: to Support District-Charter Compact Cities in Advancing College Ready Strategies," in How We Work: Grants, September 9, 2014, https://www.gatesfoundation.org/How-We-Work/Quick-Links/Grants-Database/Grants/2014/09/OPP1115953

Ibid, "New Schools for Chicago: to Advance Collaboration Between Traditional District Schools and Public Charter Schools in Chicago," in How We Work: Grants, March 27, 2014, https://www.gatesfoundation.org/How-We-Work/Quick-Links/Grants-Database/Grants/2014/03/OPP1105594

Ibid, "Noble Network of Charter Schools: to Support Blended Learning Initiatives in Existing High-Performing Charter Schools," in How We Work: Grants, November 17, 2011, https://www.gatesfoundation.org/How-We-Work/Quick-Links/Grants-Database/Grants/2011/11/OPP1051529

Ibid, "Noble Network of Charter Schools: to Support Common Core Implementation," in How We Work: Grants, October 1, 2014, https://www.gatesfoundation.org/How-We-Work/Quick-Links/Grants-Database/Grants/2014/10/OPP1117091

Ibid, "Noble Network of Charter Schools: to Support Professional Development Opportunities for Teachers to Share Their Perspectives and Present Their Work as It Pertains to Teacher Effectiveness," in How We Work: Grants, May 31, 2012, https://www.gatesfoundation.org/How-We-Work/Quick-Links/Grants-Database/Grants/2012/05/OPP1063231

Ibid, "Perspectives Charter School: to Expand Blended Learning Models at Perspectives Leadership Academy and Perspectives Middle Academy Campuses in the South Side of Chicago Serving Approximately 900 Students," in How We Work: Grants, July 3, 2012, https://www.gatesfoundation.org/How-We-Work/Quick-Links/Grants-Database/Grants/2012/07/OPP1065303

Ibid, "Perspectives Charter School: to Implement a Blended Learning Initiative That Combines the PEAK Teaching for Excellence Model with Self-Paced Online Learning for Math Students at Three Campuses," in How We Work: Grants, November 17, 2011, https://www.gatesfoundation.org/How-We-Work/Quick-Links/Grants-Database/Grants/2011/11/OPP1051521

Ibid, "Perspectives Charter School: to Support Personalized Learning in Existing Schools," in How We Work: Grants, September 4, 2013, https://www.gatesfoundation.org/How-We-Work/Quick-Links/Grants-Database/Grants/2013/09/OPP1098635

36   Antony C. Sutton, *America's Secret Establishment: An Introduction to the Order of Skull and Bones*, Updated Reprint (Walterville, OR: Trine Day, 2002), 24, 52.

37   Ibid, "12 Major Foundations Commit $500 Million to Education Innovation in Concert with U.S. Department of Education's $650 Million 'Investing in Innovation' Fund: Private Foundations Also Launch Online Registry to Help Schools and Programs Access Funds," in Press Room: Press Releases and Statements, April 29, 2010, https://www.gatesfoundation.org/Media-Center/Press-Releases/2010/04/12-Foundations-Commit-to-Education-Innovation-with-US-Department-of-Education

38   Anthony Cody, "Duncan: Bill Gates Has No Seat at the Education Policy Table," *Education Week*, January 24, 2014, http://blogs.edweek.org/teachers/living-in-dialogue/2014/01/duncan_bill_gates_has_no_.html

39   Ibid.

40   Sam Dillon, "After Complaints, Gates Foundation Opens Education Aid Offer to All States," *New York Times*, October 27, 2009, https://www.nytimes.com/2009/10/28/education/28educ.html?_r=0

41   Ibid.

42   Henry A. Giroux, "Chartering Disaster: Why Duncan's Corporate-Based Schools Can't Deliver an Education That Matters," *Counterpoints* 400 (2012): 49-72.

43   Henry A. Giroux and Kenneth Saltman, "Obama's Betrayal of Public Education? Arne Duncan and the Corporate Model of Schooling," Truthout, December 17, 2008, https://truthout.org/articles/obamas-betrayal-of-public-education-arne-duncan-and-the-corporate-model-of-schooling/#

44   United States Department of Education, "Nearly $1.4 Billion in Recovery Funds Now Available for Illinois to Save Teaching Jobs and Drive Education Reform," in Archived Information, April 20, 2009, https://www.ed.gov/news/press-releases/nearly-14-billion-recovery-funds-now-available-illinois-save-teaching-jobs-and-drive-education-reform

45   Ibid.

46   Jeff Bryant, "The Ugly Charter School Scandal Arne Duncan Is Leaving Behind: Officials Are Raising Questions about a $249 Million Grant to Charter Schools Announced the Day of His Resignation," *Salon*, October 11, 2015, https://www.salon.com/2015/10/11/the_ugly_charter_school_scandal_arne_duncan_is_leaving_behind_partner/

Patrick O'Donnell, "Ohio Wins $71 Million Charter School Expansion Grant, Drawing Pride and Distrust," Cleveland.com: Advance Ohio, October 1, 2015, https://www.cleveland.com/metro/index.ssf/2015/10/ohio_wins_71_million_charter_school_expansion_grant_drawing_pride_and_distrust.html

47   John Myers, "Chicago Public Schools Face Several Challenges in Filing Bankruptcy," *Chicago City Wire*, January 6, 2017, https://chicagocitywire.com/stories/511065017-chicago-public-schools-face-several-challenges-in-filing-bankruptcy

Paris Schutz, "How Would CPS Bankruptcy Work?," WTTW News, June 23, 2016, https://news.wttw.com/2016/06/23/how-would-cps-bankruptcy-work

Sarah Karp and Melissa Sanchez, "Rauner Likes 'Bankruptcy' to Cure CPS Financial Woes," *The Chicago Reporter*, April 14, 2015, https://www.chicagoreporter.com/rauner-likes-bankruptcy-to-cure-cps-financial-woes/

48   Moody's Investor's Services Inc., "Announcement: Moody's Publishes Issuer-In-Depth Reports on Chicago and Chicago Public Schools," Moody's: Research, January 12, 2017, https://www.moodys.com/research/Moodys-Publishes-Issuer-In-Depth-Reports-on-Chicago-and-Chicago-PR_360611

49   Patrick Yeagle, "School Choice, Another Statehouse Battlefront," *Illinois Times*, January 28, 2016, https://illinoistimes.com/print-article-16742-print.html

50   Melissa Sanchez and Kalyn Belsha, "Inside Noble," *Chicago Reporter*, February 8, 2016, https://www.chicagoreporter.com/inside-noble/

51   United States, Department of Education, "U.S. Department of Education Contributes to an Improving Charter Schools Sector," Press Release, September 28, 2015, https://www.ed.gov/

news/press-releases/us-department-education-contributes-improving-charter-schools-sector

52   ABC News, "Rauner's Daughter's School Admission Called into Question," ABC 7 News Chicago, June 26, 2014, https://abc7chicago.com/uncategorized/rauners-daughters-school-admission-called-into-question/143205/

53   Ibid.

54   Bernard Schoenburg, "Rauner story on school clout seems to have changed," *State Journal-Register*, January 16, 2014, http://www.sj-r.com/article/20140115/OPINION/140119578

55   Crain Communication's Inc., "Big-Name Financial Firms Buy Chicago School Bonds," *Chicago Business*, March 31, 2016, https://www.chicagobusiness.com/article/20160331/NEWS01/160339954/goldman-sachs-oppenheimerfunds-nuveen-buy-cps-bonds

Leah Hope, Chuck Goudie, and Charles Thomas, "CPS Completes 725M Bond Sale," ABC 7 News Chicago, February 3, 2016, https://abc7chicago.com/education/cps-completes-$725m-bond-sale/1184629/

Sun Times Staff, "CPS Borrows $725 Million at Huge Cost," *Chicago Sun Times*, June 24, 2016, https://chicago.suntimes.com/news/cps-borrows-725-million-at-huge-cost/

56   State of Illinois, General Assembly, 35 ILCS 40/1-999, Illinois Compiled Statutes, accessed February 3, 2019, http://www.ilga.gov/legislation/ilcs/ilcs3.asp?ActID=3820&ChapterID=8

57   Ted Cox, "Taxes Go Straight to Private Schools," One Illinois, August 23, 2018, https://www.oneillinois.com/stories/2018/8/22/scholarships

Endnotes – Chapter Two

1   Valerie Strauss, "How Gov. Walker Tried to Quietly Change the Mission of the University of Wisconsin," *Washington Post*, February 5, 2015, https://www.washingtonpost.com/news/answer-sheet/wp/2015/02/05/how-gov-walker-tried-to-quietly-change-the-mission-of-the-university-of-wisconsin/?noredirect=on&utm_term=.cd769b1674e4

2   "Governor Bruce Rauner Inaugural Speech: A Transcript of Governor Bruce Rauner's Inauguration Speech on January 12, 2014," Illinois Policy, January 13, 2015, https://www.illinoispolicy.org/governor-bruce-rauner-inaugural-speech/

3   Office of the Governor, "Governor Bruce Rauner's State of the State Address," Illinois News, February 4, 2015, https://www2.illinois.gov/pages/news-item.aspx?ReleaseID=13213

4   Office of the Governor, "Governor Bruce Rauner's State of the State Address," Illinois News, January 27, 2016, https://www2.illinois.gov/pages/news-item.aspx?ReleaseID=13470

5   "First Lady Rauner, "Senator Kirk Promote Governor's Cradle-to-Career Education Plan," Illinois Review: Crossroads of the Conservative Community, February 19, 2015, https://illinois-review.typepad.com/illinoisreview/2015/02/first-lady-rauner-us-senator-kirk-promote-governors-cradle-to-career-education-plan.html

6   Antony C. Sutton, *America's Secret Establishment: An Introduction to the Order of Skull and Bones*, Updated Reprint, (Walterville, OR: Trine Day, 2002), 34-35, 56-57, 63-111.

7   Noble Charter Schools, "About: Mission," Rauner College Prep, accessed November 7, 2018, https://nobleschools.org/rauner/mission/

8   Charlotte Thomson Iserbyt, "Unelected Charter Schools Will Allow Lifelong Community Education," News With Views, April 11, 2014, https://www.newswithviews.com/iserbyt/iserbyt123.htm

9   Ronald Reagan, "Executive Order 12329—President's Task Force on Private Sector Initiatives," Ronald Reagan Presidential Library and Museum, October 14, 1981, https://www.reaganlibrary.gov/research/speeches/101481d

Ibid, "Executive Order 12427—President's Advisory Council on Private Sector Initiatives," Ronald Reagan Presidential Library and Museum, June 27, 1983, http://presidency.proxied.lsit.ucsb.edu/ws/index.php?pid=41524

10   The Daily Take Team of The Thom Hartmann Program, "No, Actually, This Is What a Fascist Looks Like," *Truthout*, January 18, 2013, https://truthout.org/articles/no-actually-this-is-what-a-fascist-looks-like/

11   Chip Berlet, "Mussolini on the Corporate State," Political Research Associates, January 12, 2005, http://www.publiceye.org/fascist/corporatism.html

12   Editors of the Encyclopedia Britannica, "Corporatism: Ideology," *Encyclopedia Britannica*, accessed February 18, 2019, https://www.britannica.com/topic/corporatism

13   Ronald Reagan, "Executive Order 12329—President's Task Force on Private Sector Initiatives," Ronald Reagan Presidential Library and Museum, October 14, 1981, https://www.reaganlibrary.gov/research/speeches/101481d

Ibid, "Executive Order 12427—President's Advisory Council on Private Sector Initiatives," Ronald Reagan Presidential Library and Museum, June 27, 1983, http://presidency.proxied.lsit.ucsb.edu/ws/index.php?pid=41524

14   Antony C. Sutton, *America's Secret Establishment: An Introduction to the Order of Skull and Bones*, Updated Reprint, (Walterville, OR: Trine Day, 2002), 34-35, 56, 67, 75, 83-87, 101-111, 118-120.

15   Kris Millegan, *Fleshing Out Skull and Bones: Investigations into America's Most Powerful Secret Society* (Walterville, OR: Trine Day, 2003), 690.

16   Antony C. Sutton, *America's Secret Establishment: An Introduction to the Order of Skull and Bones*, Updated Reprint, (Walterville, OR: Trine Day, 2002), 83-91, 101-105.

"Dr. John Dewey Dead at 92; Philosopher, a Noted Liberal," *New York Times*, June 2, 1952, https://archive.nytimes.com/www.nytimes.com/learning/general/onthisday/bday/1020.html

17   Kris Millegan, *Fleshing Out Skull and Bones: Investigations into America's Most Powerful Secret Society* (Walterville, OR: Trine Day, 2003), 690.

Antony C. Sutton, *America's Secret Establishment: An Introduction to the Order of Skull and Bones*, Updated Reprint, (Walterville, OR: Trine Day, 2002), 27, 32, 56, 62-68, 70, 82, 84, 87-97, 101, 107-109

18   Ibid, 63.

19   Ibid, 63, 66.

20   Ibid, 62-63.

21   Ibid, 5, 35, 283.

22   Ibid, 126, 165-170.

Ibid, *Wall Street and the Rise of Hitler: The Astonishing True Story of the American Financiers Who Bankrolled the Nazis* (California: Clairview, 1976), 103, 107, 25-26, 57, 99, 102, 103, 106, 112-114, 141.

23   Associated Press, "Documents: Bush's Grandfather Directed Bank Tied to Man Who Funded Hitler," Fox News, January 13, 2015, https://www.foxnews.com/story/documents-bushs-grandfather-directed-bank-tied-to-man-who-funded-hitler

Ben Aris and Duncan Campbell, "How Bush's Grandfather Helped Hitler's Rise to Power," *The Guardian*: US Edition, September 25, 2004, https://www.theguardian.com/world/2004/sep/25/usa.secondworldwar

Donald C. Cook, "Vesting Order 8494: August Thyssen, Jr.," Federal Register 12 no. 63 (Washington, DC: National Archives of the United States, March 29, 1947), Doc. 47-2996, March 28, 1947, https://www.govinfo.gov/content/pkg/FR-1947-03-29/pdf/FR-1947-03-29.pdf

24   Antony C. Sutton, *America's Secret Establishment: An Introduction to the Order of Skull and Bones*, Updated Reprint, (Walterville, OR: Trine Day, 2002), 295.

25   Charlotte Thomson Iserbyt, "Unelected Charter Schools Will Allow Lifelong Community Education," News With Views, April 11, 2014, https://www.newswithviews.com/iserbyt/iserbyt123.htm

Ronald Reagan, "Executive Order 12427—President's Advisory Council on Private Sector Initiatives," Ronald Reagan Presidential Library and Museum, June 27, 1983, http://presidency.proxied.lsit.ucsb.edu/ws/index.php?pid=41524

Susan Schmidt, "Debate Rages: Can Social Needs Be Met by Charity?," *Washington Post*, June 21, 1982, https://www.washingtonpost.com/archive/business/1982/06/21/debate-rages-can-social-needs-be-met-by-charity/f58702f5-9d50-4a2e-ba2f-9c38cf385fa3/?noredirect=on&utm_term=.30e876ab793f

United States, National Archives and Records Administration, "Remarks on Television Job-a-thons to Promoters of Community Service Projects," Ronald Reagan Presidential Library and Museum, April 21, 1983, https://www.reaganlibrary.gov/research/speeches/42183d

26   Antony C. Sutton, *America's Secret Establishment: An Introduction to the Order of Skull and Bones*, Updated Reprint, (Walterville, OR: Trine Day, 2002), 298.

27   Council for American Private Education, "President Bush Signs Voucher Legislation," CAPE Outlook: Voice of America's Private Schools 292 (February 2004), https://files.eric.ed.gov/fulltext/ED499508.pdf

United States, Consolidated Appropriations Act, 2004, Public Law 108-199, 108th Congress, H. R. 2673, January 23, 2003, https://www.congress.gov/108/plaws/publ199/PLAW-108publ199.pdf

Ibid, Government Accountability Office, *Report to Congressional Requesters: District of Columbia Opportunity Scholarship Program—Additional Policies and Procedures Would Improve Internal Controls and Program Operations* (Washington, DC: GAO, November 2007), https://www.gao.gov/new.items/d089.pdf

Ibid, No Child Left Behind Act of 2001, Public Law 107-110, 107th Congress, H. R. 1, January 8, 2002, https://www2.ed.gov/policy/elsec/leg/esea02/107-110.pdf

28   National Alliance for Public Charter Schools, "Dear Presidents, We Thank You for Supporting Charter Schools," National Alliance for Public Charter Schools Blog, February 15, 2016, https://www.publiccharters.org/latest-news/2016/02/15/dear-presidents-we-thank-you-supporting-charter-schools

29   United States, Charter School Expansion Act of 1998, Public Law 105-278, 105th Congress, H. R. 2616, October 22, 1998, https://www.congress.gov/105/plaws/publ278/PLAW-105publ278.pdf

30 Antony C. Sutton, *America's Secret Establishment: An Introduction to the Order of Skull and Bones*, Updated Reprint, (Walterville, OR: Trine Day, 2002), 34.

31   David Korten, *The Post-Corporate World: Life After Capitalism*, quoted in Kris Millegan, *Fleshing Out Skull and Bones: Investigations into America's Most Powerful Secret Society* (Walterville, OR: Trine Day, 2003), 690.

32   Ibid.

33   Georg Wilhelm Friedrich Hegel, *Phenomenology of Spirit,* trans. J. B. Baillie (New York: MacMillan, 1910), 175-188.

34   National Center for Community Schools, "Case Study: Chicago" (Children's Aide, 2018), https://www.nccs.org/case-study/chicago

35   Ibid, "Partnership Will Work to Improve Education, Workforce and Economic Outcomes for South Bronx Children and Families," Children's Aide Society Client News, September 23, 2015, https://www.nccs.org/news/partnership-will-work-improve-education-workforce-and-economic-outcomes-south-bronx-children

36   Ibid, "History," (Children's Aide, 2018), https://www.nccs.org/history

37   Antony C. Sutton, *America's Secret Establishment: An Introduction to the Order of Skull and Bones*, Updated Reprint, (Walterville, OR: Trine Day, 2002), 102.

38   John Dewey, *Lectures for the First Course in Pedagogy*, quoted in Antony C. Sutton, *America's Secret Establishment: An Introduction to the Order of Skull and Bones*, Updated Reprint (Walterville, OR: Trine Day, 2002), 103.

39   Jackie Mader, "Can a Harlem 'Cradle to Career' Program Succeed in Rural Mississippi?," PBS News Hour, April 28, 2015, https://www.pbs.org/newshour/education/can-success-model-harlem-deliver-promise-schools-rural-mississippi

40   *Waiting for "Superman,"* directed by Davis Guggenheim (Hollywood, CA: Paramount Home Entertainment, 2011), DVD.

41   Mary Wright Edelman, "Geoffrey Canada Does Whatever It Takes Geoffrey Canada's Innovative Strategies for Saving Thousands of Children in the Harlem Children's Zone Have Garnered Praise from Obama, Who Plans to Replicate Canada's Successes around the Country," *Huffington Post*, May 28, 2009, https://www.huffingtonpost.com/marian-wright-edelman/whatever-it-takes_b_191760.html

42   Harlem Children's Zone, *Whatever It Takes: A Whitepaper on the Harlem Children's Zone*, accessed November 7, 2018, https://hcz.org/wp-content/uploads/2014/04/HCZ-White-Paper.pdf

43   Ibid.

44   Antony C. Sutton, *America's Secret Establishment: An Introduction to the Order of Skull and Bones*, Updated Reprint, (Walterville, OR: Trine Day, 2002), 34.

45   Ibid, 34.

46   F. W. Kaufman, "Fichte and National Socialism," *The American Political Science Review* 36, no. 3 (1942): 460.

47   John Dewey, *My Pedagogic Creed*, quoted in Antony C. Sutton, *America's Secret Establishment: An Introduction to the Order of Skull and Bones*, Updated Reprint, (Walterville, OR: Trine Day, 2002), 102.

48   Johann Gottlieb Fichte, *Addresses to the German Nation*, trans. R. F. Jones and G. H. Turnbull (Chicago: Open Court Publishing Company, 1922), 15.

49   Ibid, 20.

50   John Taylor Gatto, "Against School," in *Rereading America: Cultural Contexts for Critical Thinking and Writing*, 9th edition, eds. Gary Colombo, Robert Cullen, Bonnie Lisle (Boston: Bedford/St. Martin's, 2013), 145.

51   Antony C. Sutton, *America's Secret Establishment: An Introduction to the Order of Skull and Bones*, Updated Reprint, (Walterville, OR: Trine Day, 2002), 83.

52   Ibid, 5.

53   "John Taylor Gatto Passes Away but His Spirit and Work Live On," John Taylor Gatto Blog, October 29, 2018, https://www.johntaylorgatto.com/blog/

54   John Taylor Gatto, "Against School," in *Rereading America: Cultural Contexts for Critical Thinking and Writing*, 9th edition, eds. Gary Colombo, Robert Cullen, Bonnie Lisle (Boston: Bedford/ St. Martin's, 2013), 145.

55   Ibid, 146-147.

56   JP Morgan Chase & Co., "About Us: Three Generations of Bankers," JP Morgan, accessed November 7, 2018, https://www.jpmorgan.com/country/US/en/jpmorgan/about/history/month/apr

57   John Taylor Gatto, "Against School," in *Rereading America: Cultural Contexts for Critical Thinking and Writing*, 9th edition, eds. Gary Colombo, Robert Cullen, Bonnie Lisle (Boston: Bedford/ St. Martin's, 2013), 147.

58   Harlem Children's Zone, *Harlem Children's Zone: An Investment in Success, 2008-2009 Biennial Report*, accessed November 7, 2018, https://hcz.org/wp-content/uploads/2014/04/2008-2009_ Biennial_for_web.pdf

Ibid, *2014-2015 Biennial Report: A Community of Opportunity*, accessed November 7, 2018, https://hcz.org/wp-content/uploads/2015/11/HCZ-Biennial-Report-2014-2015-single-pages.pdf

59   Bill and Melinda Gates Foundation, "Community Center for Education Results: to Support Enhanced Communications Capacity for the Road Map Project's Cradle-to-Career Education Work in South King County, WA," in How We Work: Grants, October 8, 2013, https://www.gatesfoundation.org/How-We-Work/Quick-Links/Grants-Database/Grants/2013/10/OPP1098543

60   United States Department of Education, Office of Innovation and Improvement, Program: Promise Neighborhoods, March 5, 2018, https://www2.ed.gov/programs/promiseneighborhoods/index.html

61   Ibid, "PolicyLink: to Support a Four-Year Effort That Will Provide Technical Assistance to Promise Neighborhoods Implementation and Planning Grantees, and Issue-Based Technical Assistance for Key Areas of the Cradle-to-Career Pipeline of Expanded Learning," in How We Work: Grants, April 30, 2013, https://www.gatesfoundation.org/How-We-Work/Quick-Links/Grants-Database/Grants/2013/04/OPP1088974

62   Ibid, "Investors Expand Work of Portland Schools Foundation: Recently, the Portland Schools Foundation (PSF) Announced a $100,000 Investment by JPMorgan Chase for Its Expanding Work around the Cradle to Career (C2C) Partnership," in *Press Room: Press Releases and Statements*, June 20, 2011, https://www.gatesfoundation.org/Media-Center/Press-Releases/2011/06/Investors-Expand-Work-of-Portland-Schools-Foundation

63   Katlyn Smith, "Rauner Says He'll Have Own Plan for Making Community Colleges Affordable," *The Daily Herald: Suburban Chicago's Information Source*, January 23, 2015, https://www.dailyherald.com/article/20150123/news/150129380/

64   Office of the Governor, "Governor Bruce Rauner's State of the State Address," *Illinois News*, January 27, 2016, https://www2.illinois.gov/pages/news-item.aspx?ReleaseID=13470

65   Illinois P-20 Council, "About Us," Illinois P-20 Council (State of Illinois, 2017), https://www2.illinois.gov/sites/p20/pages/about.aspx

66   State of Illinois, General Assembly, 105 ILCS 5/22-45, Illinois Compiled Statutes, accessed November 8, 2018, http://ilga.gov/legislation/ilcs/fulltext.asp?DocName=010500050K22-45

67   Ibid.

68   Ibid.

69   Ibid. Charlotte Thomson Iserbyt, *The Deliberate Dumbing Down of America: A Chronological Paper Trail* (Ravenna, OH: Conscience Press, 1999), 141.

Ibid, xxi, 138.

Ibid, 270.

70   Associated Press, "Rauner Vetoes $3.9B in Spending for Colleges, Human Services," *St. Louis Post-Dispatch*, June 10, 2016, https://www.stltoday.com/news/local/illinois/rauner-vetoes-b-in-spending-for-colleges-human-services/article_c4a8d7f8-116c-5c0c-b5c3-03eb60c29459.html

71   Office of the Governor, "Governor Bruce Rauner's State of the State Address," *Illinois News*, January 27, 2016, https://www2.illinois.gov/pages/news-item.aspx?ReleaseID=13470

72   Kirsten Schorsch, "Illinois' Rauner Finalizes $15 Billion Medicaid Overhaul," *Modern Healthcare*, November 29, 2017, https://www.modernhealthcare.com/article/20171129/ NEWS/171129919

Associated Press, "Illinois Agencies Recovering a Year After Budget Impasse," NBC News, July 9,

2018, https://www.nbcchicago.com/blogs/ward-room/Illinois-agencies-recovering-a-year-after-budget-impasse-487643031.html

73 Bruce Rauner, "Executive Order 2016-03: Executive Order Establishing the Governor's Cabinet on Children and Youth," State of Illinois, February 18, 2016, https://www2.illinois.gov/Pages/government/execorders/2016_3.aspx

74 State of Illinois, "Children's Cabinet: Children's Cabinet Executive Orders FAQs," Governor's Cabinet on Children and Youth, 2017, https://www2.illinois.gov/sites/children/Pages/faq.aspx

75 State of Illinois, 2017 Annual Report on the Governor's Cabinet on Children and Youth, December 29, 2017, https://www2.illinois.gov/sites/children/Documents/Children%27s%20Cabinet%20Report%20(2017).pdf

76 "First Lady Rauner, Senator Kirk Promote Governor's Cradle-to-Career Education Plan," *Illinois Review: Crossroads of the Conservative Community*, February 19, 2015, https://illinoisreview.typepad.com/illinoisreview/2015/02/first-lady-rauner-us-senator-kirk-promote-governors-cradle-to-career-education-plan.html

77 Wisconsin Department of Instruction, U.S. Department of Education Grant Performance Report (ED 524B) Executive Summary Wisconsin, accessed November 8, 2018, https://dpi.wi.gov/sites/default/files/imce/wisedash/pdf/wi-fy12-final-report.pdf

78 Matthew Lynch, "P-16 and P-20 Initiatives: Critical for Education Reform," *Huffington Post*, May 3, 2014, https://www.huffingtonpost.com/matthew-lynch-edd/p-16-and-p-20-initiatives_b_4894357.html

79 Minnesota P-20 Education Partnership, "Working Groups," Minnesota's Statewide Longitudinal Education Data System (SLEDS), 2010, http://www.mnp20.org/working_groups/longitudinal_data_system.html

80 Delaware Department of Education, "Governance: Delaware P-20 Council," Delaware P-20 Council, January 10, 2018, https://www.doe.k12.de.us/domain/91

81 Maryland State Archives, "P-20 Leadership Council of Maryland," *Maryland Manual On-Line: A Guide to Maryland and Its Government*, August 17, 2018, https://msa.maryland.gov/msa/mdmanual/26excom/html/29p20.html

82 Charlotte Thomson Iserbyt, *The Deliberate Dumbing Down of America: A Chronological Paper Trail* (Ravenna, OH: Conscience Press, 1999), 141.

Ibid, xxi, 138.

Ibid, 270.

83 United States, United States Constitution, "Preamble," 1789, https://www.archives.gov/founding-docs/constitution

Endnotes – Chapter Three

1 Milton Friedman, "The Promise of Vouchers," *Wall Street Journal*, December 5, 2005, http://www.wsj.com/articles/SB113374845791113764

2 Alan Greenblatt, "New Orleans District Moves to an All-Charter System," National Public Radio, May 30, 2014, http://www.npr.org/sections/ed/2014/05/30/317374739/new-orleans-district-moves-to-an-all-charter-system

3 Blue Ribbon Commission for Educational Excellence, 2007-2008 Blue Ribbon Commission for Educational Excellence Recommendations (Year Nine Report) (State of Louisiana Board of Regents, 2008), http://www.regents.la.gov/assets/docs/2013/05/BRCYear9Report.doc

John White, Louisiana Annual Performance Report: Part B (July 1, 2010 - June 30, 2011) (Louisiana Department of Education, 2012), https://www.louisianabelieves.com/docs/default-source/academics/part-b-annual-performance-report.pdf?sfvrsn=6

State of Louisiana, Master Plan for Public Postsecondary Education in Louisiana (2011) (Louisiana Board of Regents, 2012), http://www.regents.la.gov/assets/docs/2013/03/MasterPlan_Revised_04-12.pdf

United States, Department of Education, Louisiana's ESEA Flexibility Request (Washington, DC: Government Publishing Office, 2012), https://www2.ed.gov/policy/eseaflex/approved-requests/la.pdf

4 Charlotte Thomson Iserbyt, "The True Goal of School Choice," News With Views, September 11, 2012, http://www.newswithviews.com/iserbyt/iserbyt112.htm

5 Ibid, "Heritage Foundation, NAFTA, School Choice, and the Destruction of Traditional Education," News With Views, July 31, 2012, http://www.newswithviews.com/iserbyt/iserbyt111.htm

6   Emma Brown, "What Makes a Public School Public? Washington State Court Finds Charter Schools Unconstitutional," Washington Post, September 9, 2015, https://www.washingtonpost.com/local/education/what-makes-a-public-school-public-washington-state-court-finds-charter-schools-unconstitutional/2015/09/08/706975c8-5632-11e5-8bb1-b488d231bba2_story.html

7   Sam Dillon, "In Georgia, Court Ruling Could Close Some Charter Schools," New York Times, May 16, 2011, http://www.nytimes.com/2011/05/17/education/17georgia.html?_r=0

8   Georgia Department of Education, Equitable Access to Effective Educators (GaDOE, 2015), http://www2.ed.gov/programs/titleiparta/equitable/gaequityplan060115.pdf

9   Foundation for Orange County Public Schools, Central Florida NAF Academies: National Academy Foundation Programs (OCPS, 2016), https://www.foundationforocps.org/p/248/central-florida-naf-academies#.V8-pYTUYMX4

        PZ Media Inc., "Justin Sliney Volunteers for New York Charter School KIPP" Prsync, March 28, 2016,   http://prsync.com/pz-media-inc/justin-sliney-volunteers-for-new-york-charter-school-kipp-902163/

10   State of California, General Assembly, Assembly Bill (AB) 646, California State Assembly, January 6, 2014, http://www.leginfo.ca.gov/pub/13-14/bill/asm/ab_0601-0650/ab_646_bill_20140106_amended_asm_v97.html

11   Ibid.

12   California State Assembly Committee on Jobs, Economic Development, and the Economy, 2013-2014 End of Session Report Including a Summary of Legislation (Paper 524), 2014, http://digitalcommons.law.ggu.edu/cgi/viewcontent.cgi?article=1529&context=caldocs_assembly

13   University of California Office of Diversity and Engagement, Student Academic Preparation and Educational Partnerships (SAPEP) 2014-2015 Program Outcomes, accessed September 8, 2016, http://www.ucop.edu/diversity-engagement/_files/sapep-full-report-rscpsb.pdf

14   University of California, Student Academic Preparation and Educational Partnerships (SAPEP) Annual Performance Report for AY/FY 2009-2010, accessed September 8, 2016, https://oep.ucsb.edu/about/research_and_evaluation/recent_evaluation_reports/ucsb.sapep.report.2009-2010.pdf

15   Ventura County P-20 Council, "Home: What Is the Ventura County P-20 Council," accessed September 8, 2016, http://p16councilofventuracounty.org/index.htm

16   Accessed September 8, 2016, http://p20.cikeys.com/about-us/history/

17   EdWeek, "National Academy Foundation Launches Career Ready Certificate," NAF Now: In the News, January 26, 2015, https://naf.org/news_articles/national-academy-foundation-launches-career-ready-certificate

        National Academy Foundation, "NAF Network: Find an Academy," September 8, 2016, http://naf.org/naf-network/find-an-academy

18   State of Illinois, General Assembly, 105 ILCS 5/22-45, Illinois Compiled Statutes, accessed November 8, 2016, http://ilga.gov/legislation/ilcs/fulltext.asp?DocName=010500050K22-45

19   Board of Trustees of Northern Illinois University, "Homepage," Northern Illinois University Center for P-20 Engagement, accessed September 9, 2016, http://www.niu.edu/p20/index.shtml

20   Ibid, "Homepage," Northern Illinois University: Northern Illinois P-20 Network, accessed September 9, 2016, http://niu.edu/p20network/index.shtml

21   Ibid, "Work Groups: Work Groups Home," Northern Illinois University: Northern Illinois P-20 Network, accessed September 9, 2016, http://niu.edu/p20network/work-groups/index.shtml

22   Northern Illinois University, "NIU President Leads Regional Delegation to White House Summit," NIU Today, December 2, 2014, http://www.niutoday.info/2014/12/02/niu-president-leads-regional-delegation-to-white-house-summit/

23   Ibid.

24   Ibid.

25   Matthew Lynch, "P-16 and P-20 Initiatives: Critical for Education Reform," Huffington Post, May 3, 2014, http://www.huffingtonpost.com/matthew-lynch-edd/p-16-and-p-20-initiatives_b_4894357.html

26   Delaware State Department of Education, "Governance: The Delaware P-20 Council," State of Delaware: Official Website of the First State, accessed September 9, 2016, http://www.doe.k12.de.us/domain/91

27   Maryland State Archives, "P-20 Leadership Council of Maryland," Maryland Manual On-Line: A Guide to Maryland and Its Government, accessed September 9, 2016, http://msa.maryland.gov/msa/mdmanual/26excom/html/29p20.html

28   Missouri Department of Higher Education, "Initiatives: P-20 Initiatives in Higher Education," accessed September 9, 2016, http://dhe.mo.gov/p20/

29   Napolitano, Janet, "Executive Order 2005-19: Executive Order Establishing 'Governor's P-20 Council of Arizona,'" Arizona Memory Project: Arizona State Library Archives and Public Records, July 8, 2005, http://azmemory.azlibrary.gov/cdm/ref/collection/execorders/id/482

30   Education Commission of the States, "P-16/P-20 Councils – All State Profiles," Education Commission of the States: Your Education Policy Team, accessed September 9, 2016, http://ecs.force.com/mbdata/mbprofall?Rep=PCA

31   Ibid.

32   Bill and Melinda Gates Foundation, "12 Major Foundations Commit $500 Million to Education Innovation in Concert with US Department of Education's $650 Million 'Investing in Innovation' Fund," in Press Room: Press Releases and Statements, April 29, 2010, http://www.gatesfoundation.org/Media-Center/Press-Releases/2010/04/12-Foundations-Commit-to-Education-Innovation-with-US-Department-of-Education

Ibid, "College for All Texans Foundation – Closing the Gaps: to Develop a Regional Community Engagement Model around P-16 Alignment; Facilitated Jointly by Regional K-12, Higher Education, Business, and Community Leaders," in How We Work: Grants, October 1, 2007, http://www.gatesfoundation.org/How-We-Work/Quick-Links/Grants-Database/Grants/2007/10/OPP49190

Ibid, "College for All Texans Foundation – Closing the Gaps: to Fund Strategic Planning and Research Support Aimed at Improving of P-20 Data Infrastructure and Data use Among Policy Makers and Practitioners," in How We Work: Grants, November 1, 2008, http://www.gatesfoundation.org/How-We-Work/Quick-Links/Grants-Database/Grants/2008/11/OPP52394

Ibid, "Communities Foundation of Texas Grant: to Partner with the Big 8 Superintendents to Advance the Design and Development of a Comprehensive Statewide P-16 Data System That Meets Both Policy/Accountability Needs and Practice/End User Needs," in How We Work: Grants, November 1, 2008, http://www.gatesfoundation.org/How-We-Work/Quick-Links/Grants-Database/Grants/2008/11/OPP52719

Ibid, "E3 Alliance Grant: to Pilot a Regional Early Warning and Intervention System for Struggling Students While Also Supporting Implementation of Regional P-16 Alliances in Gulf Coast Regions with the Goal of Implementation of Regional, Networked Early Warning Systems," in How We Work: Grants, August 6, 2009, http://www.gatesfoundation.org/How-We-Work/Quick-Links/Grants-Database/Grants/2009/08/OPP1003579

Ibid, "Education Commission of the States: to Support Awareness Building Among Key Stakeholders around Postsecondary Goals and Objectives and P-20 Rationale for the Common Core State Standards," in How We Work: Grants, October 14, 2010, http://www.gatesfoundation.org/How-We-Work/Quick-Links/Grants-Database/Grants/2010/10/OPP1013285

Ibid, "Foundation Invests in Research and Data Systems to Improve Student Achievement," in Press Room: Press Releases and Statements, January 22, 2009, http://www.gatesfoundation.org/Media-Center/Press-Releases/2009/01/Foundation-Invests-in-Research-and-Data-Systems-to-Improve-Student-Achievement

Ibid, "LEV Foundation Grant: to Develop a Coherent P-16 Policy and Implementation Strategy for Washington State," in How We Work: Grants, July 1, 2003, http://www.gatesfoundation.org/How-We-Work/Quick-Links/Grants-Database/Grants/2003/07/OPP29142

Ibid, "School Networks Receive Grant to Strengthen Efforts to Prepare Students for College and Career Success," in Press Room: Press Releases and Statements, March 26, 2009, http://www.gatesfoundation.org/Media-Center/Press-Releases/2009/03/School-Networks-to-Strengthen-Efforts-to-Prepare-Students-for-College-and-Careers

Ibid, "Seven Cities Launch Collaborative Efforts to Improve College Graduation Rates," in Press Room: Press Releases and Statements, November 5, 2009, http://www.gatesfoundation.org/Media-Center/Press-Releases/2009/11/Seven-Cities-Launch-Collaborative-Efforts-to-Improve-College-Graduation-Rates

Ibid, "State Higher Education Executive Officers Association Grant: to Support Building Stronger P-16 Systems," in How We Work: Grants, October 1, 2005, http://www.gatesfoundation.org/How-We-Work/Quick-Links/Grants-Database/Grants/2005/10/OPP40090

Ibid, "WestEd Grant: to Support California's Effort to Close the Achievement Gap in a Partnership Among WestEd, the California Department of Education, the P-16 Council and the University of California, Office of the President," in How We Work: Grants, September 15, 2007, http://www.gatesfoundation.org/How-We-Work/Quick-Links/Grants-Database/Grants/2007/09/OPP48931

33   Education Commission of the States, "P-16/P-20 Councils – All State Profiles," Education Commission of the States: Your Education Policy Team, accessed September 9, 2016, http://ecs.force.com/mbdata/mbprofall?Rep=PCA

34   Knowledge Is Power Program, "About – Regional Office: Sarah Magnelia – Director of College Career and Career Pathways," KIPP: Philadelphia Schools, accessed September 9, 2016, http://kippphiladelphia.org/about/who-we-are/regional-office/sarah-magnelia

Ibid, "Accenture and KIPP Team to Provide More Than 300 Students with Internships at Nearly 175 Companies in Nine Cities," KIPP Press Release, July 7, 2014, http://www.kipp.org/news/accenture-and-kipp-team-to-provide-more-than-300-students-with-internships-at-nearly-175-companies-in-nine-cities

35   Ibid, "Schools: KIPP Schools," KIPP Foundation, accessed September 9, 2016, http://www.kipp.org/schools

36   Ibid, "Schools: KIPP Regions," KIPP Foundation, accessed September 9, 2016, http://www.kipp.org/schools/kipp-regions

37   Ibid, "About – About KIPP LA Schools," KIPP: Los Angeles Schools, accessed September 9, 2016, http://www.kippla.org/about-kipp-la/index.cfm

Ibid, "School Directory – KIPP Region: Chicago," KIPP Foundation, accessed September 9, 2016, http://www.kipp.org/schools/school-directory?Region=22

38   Boston Consulting Group (BCG) and Illinois State Board of Education, "Illinois Report Cards: Project Update to the P-20 Council (Draft – For Discussion Only)" (PowerPoint presentation, BCG, IL, July 27, 2011), accessed September 9, 2016, https://www.illinois.gov/gov/P20/Documents/Full%20P-20/p20-presentation-072711-ReportCard.pdf

39   Advance Illinois, "About Us: Mission and History," Advance Illinois: Every Student World Ready, accessed September 9, 2016, http://www.advanceillinois.org/about-us/mission-history/

Ibid, "Advance Illinois Applauds Signing of HB5729, the Postsecondary and Workforce Readiness Act," Advance Illinois Press Room: Press Release, August 1, 2016, http://www.advanceillinois.org/2016/08/01/press-release-hb5729/

40   Ibid, "About Us: Our Staff," Advance Illinois: Every Student World Ready, accessed September 9, 2016, http://www.advanceillinois.org/about-us/staff/

41   Knowledge Is Power Program, "About – Our Organization: National Partners," KIPP Foundation, accessed September 9, 2016, http://www.kipp.org/about-kipp/our-organization/national-partners

42   Netflix, "Investor Relations: Officers and Directors," accessed September 9, 2016, https://ir.netflix.com/management.cfm

43   Valerie Strauss, "Netflix's Reed Hastings Has a Big Idea: Kill Elected School Boards (Update)," Washington Post, March 14, 2014 https://www.washingtonpost.com/news/answer-sheet/wp/2014/03/14/netflixs-reed-hastings-has-a-big-idea-kill-elected-school-boards/

44   Knowledge Is Power Program, "About – Our Organization: Board of Directors]," KIPP Foundation, accessed September 9, 2016, http://www.kipp.org/about-kipp/our-organization/board-of-directors

45   California Charter Schools Association, "Speakers and Programs: Keynote Speakers," 21st Annual California Charter Schools Conference: Achievement through Innovation (San Jose, CA: San Jose Convention Center, March 3-6, 2014) https://www.charterconference.org/2014/

46   Reed Hastings, "21st Annual California Charter Schools Association (CCSA) Conference Keynote Speech," 21st Annual CCSA Conference, March 4, 2014, https://www.youtube.com/watch?v=iBMNllBviQU

47   Charlotte Thomson Iserbyt, "School Choice Is America's Trojan Horse (Part 1 of 2)," News With Views, June 12, 2013, http://www.newswithviews.com/iserbyt/iserbyt115.htm

48   Education Commission of the States, "P-16/P-20 Councils – All State Profiles," Education Commission of the States: Your Education Policy Team, accessed September 9, 2016, http://ecs.force.com/mbdata/mbprofall?Rep=PCA

49   Bruce Rauner, "Executive Order 2016-03: Executive Order Establishing the Governor's Cabinet on Children and Youth," State of Illinois, February 18, 2016, https://www2.illinois.gov/Pages/government/execorders/2016_3.aspx

State of Illinois, General Assembly, 105 ILCS 5/22-45, Illinois Compiled Statutes, accessed November 8, 2018, http://ilga.gov/legislation/ilcs/fulltext.asp?DocName=010500050K22-45

50   Bruce Rauner, "Executive Order 2016-03: Executive Order Establishing the Governor's Cabinet on Children and Youth," State of Illinois, February 18, 2016, https://www2.illinois.gov/Pages/government/execorders/2016_3.aspx

51   Darrell Stephens, "A Role for Officers in Schools," Community Policing Dispatch: e-Newsletter of the COPS Office 6 no. 3 (March, 2013), https://cops.usdoj.gov/html/dispatch/03-2013/a_role_for_officers.asp

52   NACA Inspired Schools Network, accessed September 9, 2016, http://www.nacainspiredschoolsnetwork.org/projects/

53   Accessed September 9, 2016, http://tcenews.calendow.org/releases/the-california-endowment-partners-with-capital-fund-and-ncb-capital-impact-to-provide-more-than-11-million-in-low-cost-loans-to-community-health-centers-throughout-the-state

54   Atlantic Philanthropies, "National Education Policy Center – Documenting and Addressing Exclusionary Practices in Charter Schools: Granted to University of Colorado, Boulder – To Reduce the Use of Exclusionary Disciplinary Practices by Charter Schools by Researching State Charter School Laws and Regulations, and Providing Information and Strategic Assistance to Atlantic's School Discipline Advocacy Grantees," 2013, https://www.atlanticphilanthropies.org/grants/national-education-policy-center-documenting-and-addressing-exclusionary-practices-in-charter-schools

55   National Research Center on Charter School Finance and Governance, A Guide for Policy Makers: Partnerships between Charter Schools and Other Organizations (October 2008), https://files.eric.ed.gov/fulltext/ED536001.pdf

56   United States, Department of Justice, President's Task Force on 21st Century Policing, Final Report of the President's Task Force on 21st Century Policing (Washington, DC: Office of Community Oriented Policing Services, 2015).

57   Studio Gang, "About: People—Jeanne Gang," accessed September 9, 2016, http://studiogang.com/people/jeanne-gang

58   Patrick Sisson, "How Jeanne Gang's Firm Designed a Better Police Station," Curbed, October 2, 2015, https://www.curbed.com/2015/10/2/9915166/jeanne-gang-architect-police-station-chicago

59   Antony C. Sutton, America's Secret Establishment: An Introduction to the Order of Skull and Bones, Updated Reprint, (Walterville, OR: Trine Day, 2002), 34.

60   John Dewey, My Pedagogic Creed, quoted in Antony C. Sutton, America's Secret Establishment: An Introduction to the Order of Skull and Bones, Updated Reprint, (Walterville, OR: Trine Day, 2002), 102.

61   Reed Hastings, "Keynote Speech: CCSA Conference 2014," California Charter Schools Association, March 4, 2014, https://www.youtube.com/watch?v=iBMNllBviQU

62   Ibid.

63   Knowledge Is Power Program, "Board of Directors," KIPP, accessed November 23, 2018, https://www.kipp.org/kipp-foundation/kipp-board-of-directors/

64   Netflix Investors, "Officers & Directors: Reed Hastings," Netflix, accessed November 23, 2018, https://www.netflixinvestor.com/governance/officers-and-directors/default.aspx

65   Facebook, "Investor Relations: Governance Documents—Board of Directors," accessed November 23, 2018, https://investor.fb.com/corporate-governance/default.aspx

66   California Charter Schools Association, "About CCSA: Board of Directors—Reed Hastings," accessed November 23, 2018, http://www.ccsa.org/about/board/reed-hastings.html

Endnotes – Chapter Four

1   Matthew Jenkin, "Tablets out, Imagination in: The Schools That Shun Technology," Guardian (US), December 2, 2015, https://www.theguardian.com/teacher-network/2015/dec/02/schools-that-ban-tablets-traditional-education-silicon-valley-london

2   Nick Bilton, "Steve Jobs Was a Low-Tech Parent," New York Times, September 10, 2014, https://www.nytimes.com/2014/09/11/fashion/steve-jobs-apple-was-a-low-tech-parent.html?_r=0

3   Susan Berry, "Five Reasons Why Betsy DeVos' Nomination as Education Chief Is Controversial," Breitbart, February 5, 2017, https://www.breitbart.com/politics/2017/02/05/five-reasons-betsy-devos-nomination-education-chief-controversial/

4   United States, Department of Education, December 2011—Revised FERPA Regulations: An Overview for Parents and Students, accessed November 8, 2018, https://www2.ed.gov/policy/gen/guid/fpco/parentoverview.pdf

5   Ibid, December 2011—Revised FERPA Regulations: An Overview for SEAS and LEAS, accessed November 8, 2018, https://www2.ed.gov/policy/gen/guid/fpco/pdf/sealea_overview.pdf

6   Ibid, Office of Educational Technology, Enhancing Teaching and Learning Through Educational Data Mining and Learning Analytics: An Issue Brief, (Washington DC: Government Publishing Office, October 2012), https://tech.ed.gov/wp-content/uploads/2014/03/edm-la-brief.pdf

7   Ibid.

8   Ibid.

9   Joanne Barkan, "Milton Friedman, Betsy DeVos, and the Privatization of Public Education: For Almost Twenty-Five Years, Betsy DeVos Has Been One of the Most Dogged Political Operatives in the Movement to Privatize Public Education," *Dissent Magazine*, January 17, 2017, https://www.dissentmagazine.org/online_articles/betsy-devos-milton-friedman-public-education-privatization

Philanthropy Roundtable, "Interview with Betsy DeVos, the Reformer," Philanthropy: the Quarterly National Magazine of the Philanthropy Roundtable, Spring 2013, https://www.philanthropyroundtable.org/philanthropy-magazine/article/spring-2013-interview-with-betsy-devos-the-reformer

10   Valerie Strauss, "A Sobering Look at What Betsy DeVos Did to Education in Michigan — and What She Might Do As Secretary of Education," *Washington Post*, December 8, 2016, https://www.washingtonpost.com/news/answer-sheet/wp/2016/12/08/a-sobering-look-at-what-betsy-devos-did-to-education-in-michigan-and-what-she-might-do-as-secretary-of-education/?noredirect=on&utm_term=.ab6c0aa85292

11   Daniel Katz, "Betsy DeVos: Secretary Of Privatization," Huffington Post, November 29, 2016, https://www.huffingtonpost.com/danielkatz/betsy-devos-secretary-of-_b_13303980.html

12   Abby Jackson, "Donald Trump Just Provided the First Detailed Education Proposal of His Campaign," *Business Insider*, September 8, 2016, https://www.businessinsider.com/donald-trump-pledges-20-billion-to-school-choice-education-agenda-2016-9

13   Charlotte Thomson Iserbyt, "You Just Lost Your Right to Vote on Education!," Rense News, February 7, 2017, https://rense.com/general96/voteonedu.htm

14   Privacy Technical Assistance Center, Responsibilities of Third-Party Service Providers under FERPA, accessed November 8, 2018, https://studentprivacy.ed.gov/sites/default/files/resource_document/file/Vendor%20FAQ.pdf

15   Louis Freedberg, "Trump Renews Call for 'School Choice' Legislation in State of the Union Speech," EdSource, February 6, 2019, https://edsource.org/2019/trump-renews-call-for-school-choice-legislation-in-state-of-the-union-speech/608259

16   Diane Ravitch, "Why Is the US Department of Education Weakening FERPA?," National Education Policy Center, April 9, 2013, https://nepc.colorado.edu/blog/why-us-department-of-education-weakening-ferpa

17   Bill and Melinda Gates Foundation, "College for All Texans Foundation: to Fund Strategic Planning and Research Support Aimed at Improving of P-20 Data Infrastructure and Data Use Among Policy Makers and Practitioners," in How We Work: Grants, November 1, 2008, https://www.gatesfoundation.org/How-We-Work/Quick-Links/Grants-Database/Grants/2008/11/OPP52394

18   Megan O'Neil, "Trump Cabinet's Philanthropic Ties Detailed in New Online Resource," *The Chronicle of Philanthropy*, January 12, 2017, https://www.philanthropy.com/article/Trump-Cabinet-s/238879

19   Laura Vanderkam, Blended Learning: A Wise Giver's Guide to Bolstering Tech-Assisted Teaching, ed. Karl Zinsmeister (Washington DC: Philanthropy, April 2013), https://www.philanthropyroundtable.org/docs/default-source/guidebook-files/blended_learning_guidebook.pdf?sfvrsn=afaba740_0

20   Ibid, 30.

21   Ibid, 8.

22   Ibid.

23   Ibid, 68.

24   United States, Every Student Succeeds Act, Public Law 114-95, 114th Congress, S. 1177, December 10, 2015, https://www.congress.gov/114/plaws/publ95/PLAW-114publ95.pdf

25   *Electronic Frontier Foundation v. Google Inc.*, Complaint and Request for Investigation, Injunction, and Other Relief (Before the United States Federal Trade Commission 2015), accessed November 8, 2018, https://www.eff.org/files/2015/12/01/ftccomplaint-googleforeducation.pdf

26   Ethan Baron, "UC students' suit claims Google scanned accounts without permission," *Mercury News,* May 13, 2016, https://www.mercurynews.com/2016/05/13/uc-students-suit-claims-google-scanned-accounts-without-permission/

27   Olga Kharif, "Privacy Fears Over Student Data Tracking Lead to InBloom's Shutdown: The Collapse of InBloom Marks a Backlash gainst the Personalized Learning Industry," Bloomberg, May 2, 2014, https://www.bloomberg.com/news/articles/2014-05-01/inbloom-shuts-down-amid-privacy-fears-over-student-data-tracking

28   Benjamin Herold, "inBloom to Shut Down Amid Growing Data-Privacy Concerns," *Education Week*, April 21, 2014, http://blogs.edweek.org/edweek/DigitalEducation/2014/04/inbloom_to_shut_down_amid_growing_data_privacy_concerns.html

29   Anya Kamenetz, "InBloom is wilting thanks to privacy concerns–but they don't stop with InBloom," Digital/Edu, Hechinger Report, July 11, 2013, http://digital.hechingerreport.org/content/inbloom-is-wilting-thanks-to-privacy-concerns-but-they-dont-stop-with-inbloom_725/

30   Rip Empson, "With $100M from the Gates Foundation and Others, inBloom Wants to Transform Education by Unleashing Its Data," TechCrunch, February 5, 2013, https://techcrunch.com/2013/02/05/with-100m-from-the-gates-foundation-others-inbloom-wants-to-transform-education-by-unleashing-its-data/

31   Class Size Matters, "Issues: Student Privacy," Class Size Matters: A Nonprofit, Nonpartisan Clearinghouse for Information on the Proven Benefits of Smaller Classes, accessed November 8, 2018, https://www.classsizematters.org/student-privacy/

32   Norman Solomon, "Under Amazon's CIA Cloud: *Washington Post*," Black Agenda Report, December 21, 2016, https://www.blackagendareport.com/wp_under_amazon_cloud

33   Electronic Privacy Information Center, "*EPIC v. The U.S. Department of Education*: Challenging the Department of Education's Family Educational Rights and Privacy Act (FERPA) 2011 Regulations," EPIC, accessed November 2018, https://epic.org/apa/ferpa/

34   Juan Carlos Rodriguez, "NY Dems Oppose Plan For Student Data Sharing," Law 360: A LexisNexis Company, December 20, 2013, https://www.law360.com/articles/497429/ny-dems-oppose-plan-for-student-data-sharing

35   Byron Spice, "Carnegie Mellon Leads New NSF Project Mining Educational Data to Improve Learning: Distributed Storage System Will Make Data More Accessible, Secure," Carnegie Mellon University News, October 2, 2014, https://www.cmu.edu/news/stories/archives/2014/october/october2_learnsphere.html

36   Diane Ravitch, "Parent Alert! NSF Awards Grant for Data Mining Children," *Common Dreams*, October 13, 2014, https://www.commondreams.org/views/2014/10/13/parent-alert-nsf-awards-grant-data-mining-children

37   Hechinger Report Contributor, "Carnegie Mellon Project Revives inBloom's Student Data Dream: Privacy Controversy to Be dodged by Not Storing Student Names, Addresses or Social Security Numbers," *US News & World Report,* July 27, 2015, https://www.usnews.com/news/articles/2015/07/27/carnegie-mellon-project-revives-failed-inbloom-dream-to-store-analyze-student-data

38   Ibid.

39   Berkman Klein Center for Internet and Society, "This Week in Student Privacy: 10/14," Harvard University, October 14, 2014, https://cyber.harvard.edu/node/95776

40   Hechinger Report Contributor, "Carnegie Mellon Project Revives inBloom's Student Data Dream: Privacy Controversy to Be dodged by Not Storing Student Names, Addresses or Social Security Numbers," US News & World Report, July 27, 2015, https://www.usnews.com/news/articles/2015/07/27/carnegie-mellon-project-revives-failed-inbloom-dream-to-store-analyze-student-data

41   Ibid.

42   Learnsphere: A Community Data Infrastructure to Support Learning Improvement Online, accessed November 8, 2018, http://learnsphere.org/

43   MITx and HarvardX Dataverse, The Presidents & Fellows of Harvard College, accessed November 8, 2018, https://dataverse.harvard.edu/dataverse/mxhx

44   "Socioeconomic Status Indicators of HarvardX and MITx Participants 2012-2014," MITx and HarvardX Dataverse, The Presidents & Fellows of Harvard College, accessed November 8, 2018, https://dataverse.harvard.edu/dataset.xhtml?persistentId=doi:10.7910/DVN/29779

45   American Historical Association, *Conclusions and Recommendations for the Social Studies* (New York: Chas. Scribner's Sons, 1934) quoted in Charlotte Thomson Iserbyt, The Deliberate Dumbing Down of America: A Chronological Paper Trail, Revised and Abridged Ed. (Parkman, OH: Conscience Press, 2011), 40.

46   Carnegie Corporation of New York, "About: Our History," Accomplishments: Notable Moments and Accomplishments from Grantmaking, Commissions, and Other Endeavors throughout Carnegie Corporation of New York's More Than 100 Years of History, 2018, https://www.carnegie.org/about/our-history/accomplishments/

47   Charlotte Thomson Iserbyt, *The Deliberate Dumbing Down of America: A Chronological Paper Trail*, Revised and Abridged Ed. (Parkman, OH: Conscience Press, 2011), 55.

48   Steven Schindler, Measuring American Education Reform: National Assessment of Educational Progress Carnegie Corporation of New York, 1964, date accessed November 8, 2018, https://cspcs.sanford.duke.edu/sites/default/files/descriptive/national_assessment_of_educational_progress.pdf

49   Charlotte Thomson Iserbyt, *The Deliberate Dumbing Down of America: A Chronological Paper Trail*, Revised and Abridged Ed. (Parkman, OH: Conscience Press, 2011), 89.

50   National Center for Education Statistics, "About NAEP: Support to NAEP," National Assessment of Educational Progress (United States Department of Education, July 18, 2018), https://nces.ed.gov/nationsreportcard/about/support.aspx#

51   Education Commission of the States, "About Us," History, 2018, https://www.ecs.org/about-us/history/

52   Charlotte Thomson Iserbyt, *The Deliberate Dumbing Down of America: A Chronological Paper Trail*, Revised and Abridged Ed. (Parkman, OH: Conscience Press, 2011), 91.

53   Ibid, 110.
Educational Testing Services, "About ETS: Who We Are," Our Heritage, 2018, https://www.ets.org/about/who/heritage/
    National Assessment of Educational Progress, The Nation's Report Card, accessed November 8, 2018, https://www.nationsreportcard.gov/

54   Educational Testing Services, Education Issues 2007 (ETS, 2006), https://www.ets.org/Media/Education_Topics/pdf/candbrief2007.pdf
    James Taylor, Brian Stecher, Jennifer O'Day, Scott Naftel, and Kerstin Carlson Le Floch, State and Local Implementation of the No Child Left Behind Act (Volume IX—Accountability under NCLB: Final Report, United States Department of Education, January 2010, https://files.eric.ed.gov/fulltext/ED508912.pdf
    Paul Barton, National Education Standards: Getting Beneath the Surface (Princeton, NJ: Educational Testing Services, June 2009), https://files.eric.ed.gov/fulltext/ED507800.pdf
    United States, Department of Education, Office of the Deputy Secretary, Implementation and Support Unit, Race to the Top Assessment: Partnership for Assessment of Readiness for College and Careers Year Two Report, (Washington DC: Government Publishing Office, 2013), https://www2.ed.gov/programs/racetothetop-assessment/reports/parcc-year-2.pdf.

55   Antony C. Sutton, *America's Secret Establishment: An Introduction to the Order of Skull and Bones*, Updated Reprint, (Walterville, OR: Trine Day, 2002), 62.

56   Ibid, 27.

57   Ibid, 195, 299.

58   Champaign Williams, "After Much Scrutiny, Senate Confirms Trump's Treasury Pick, Steven Mnuchin," *Forbes*, February 16, 2017, https://www.forbes.com/sites/bisnow/2017/02/16/after-much-scrutiny-senate-confirms-trumps-treasury-pick-steven-mnuchin/#65dd744917b3

Endnotes – Chapter Five

1   Tribune News Services Contact Reporter, "Senate confirms Betsy DeVos as Education secretary as Pence Breaks 50-50 Tie," *Chicago Tribune*, February 7, 2017, https://www.chicagotribune.com/news/nationworld/politics/ct-betsy-devos-education-secretary-confirmation-20170207-story.html

2   Emma Brown, "Democrats Request Another Hearing for DeVos, Trump's Education Pick, Before Confirmation Vote," *Washington Post*, January 23, 2017, https://www.washingtonpost.com/news/education/wp/2017/01/23/democrats-request-another-hearing-for-betsy-devos-trumps-education-pick-before-confirmation-vote/?noredirect=on&utm_term=.0cf1227b4421

3   Ibid.

4   Erica L. Green, "'Brain Performance' Firm DeVos Invested in Is Hit for Misleading Claims," *New York Times*, June 26, 2018, https://www.nytimes.com/2018/06/26/us/politics/betsy-devos-neurocore-brain-performance-ads.html

5   Matthew Goldstein, Steve Eder and Sheri Fink, "Betsy DeVos Won't Shed Stake in Biofeedback Company, Filings Show," *New York Times*, January 20, 2017, https://www.nytimes.com/2017/01/20/business/dealbook/betsy-devos-neurocore.html

6   Ibid.

7   United States, Every Student Succeeds Act, Public Law 114-95, 114th Congress, S. 1177, December 10, 2015, https://www.congress.gov/114/plaws/publ95/PLAW-114publ95.pdf

8   Mark Sanchez, "Windquest-backed Neurocore Eyes National Expansion," MiBiz, September 18, 2016, https://mibiz.com/item/24029-windquest-backed-neurocore-eyes-national-expansion

9   Ben Miller and Laura Jimenez, "Inside the Financial Holdings of Billionaire Betsy DeVos," Center for American Progress, https://www.americanprogress.org/issues/education-postsecondary/news/2017/01/27/297572/inside-the-financial-holdings-of-billionaire-betsy-devos/

10   Rosalind Adams, "What the Fuck Just Happened," Buzzfeed, December 7, 2016, https://www.buzzfeednews.com/article/rosalindadams/intake#.jtNzx18eE

11   Accessed September 21, 2017, https://extapps2.oge.gov/201/Presiden.nsf/PAS+Index/E2461CB47CF5A473852580C1002C7A3B/$FILE/DeVos,%20Elisabeth%20P.%20finalAMENDEDEA.pdf

12   Travis Gettys, "Betsy DeVos Bankrolls Quack Medical Centers That Claim to Treat ADHD and Autism with TV," Raw Story, February 7, 2017, https://www.rawstory.com/2017/02/betsy-devos-bankrolls-quack-medical-centers-that-claim-to-treat-adhd-and-autism-with-tv/

13   Christopher Fisher, "Biofeedback," Christopher Fisher, PhD, 2014, https://www.christopherfisherphd.com/psychological-services/biofeedback/

14   Neurocore Brain Performance Centers, "Homepage," accessed November 9, 2018, https://www.neurocorecenters.com/

15   Paolo Lionni, The Leipzig Connection: The Systematic Destruction of American Education, Third Printing (Sheridan, OR: Delphian Press, 1988), 72-81.

16   Rockefeller Foundation, "Evolution of a Foundation: The Advancement of Knowledge," Rockefeller Foundation: A Digital History, Rockefeller Archive Center, accessed November 9, 2018, https://rockfound.rockarch.org/the-advancement-of-knowledge

17   Paolo Lionni, The Leipzig Connection: The Systematic Destruction of American Education, Third Printing (Sheridan, OR: Delphian Press, 1988), 30-41, 64-65.

18   Edward Lee Thorndike, The Principles of Teaching Based on Psychology (New York: A. G. Seiler, 1925) quoted in Paolo Lionni, The Leipzig Connection: The Systematic Destruction of American Education, Third Printing (Sheridan, OR: Delphian Press, 1988), 32-33.

19   Neurocore Brain Performance Centers, "Who We Help—ADHD: Address the Symptoms of ADHD," accessed November 9, 2018, https://www.neurocorecenters.com/treatment/adhd

20   Kaleigh Rogers, "What the Heck Is Neurofeedback Technology, Betsy DeVos's Pet Project?," Motherboard, January 25, 2017, https://motherboard.vice.com/en_us/article/9ad5zy/betsy-devos-is-invested-in-a-company-trying-to-treat-adhd-with-brain-training

21   Teachers College, Columbia University, "The Unorthodox Behaviorist," TC Newsroom, April 6, 2007, https://www.tc.columbia.edu/articles/2007/april/the-unorthodox-behaviorist/

22   Steven W. Lee, "Curriculum Vita," accessed November 9, 2018, https://epsy.ku.edu/sites/epsy.ku.edu/files/docs/people/vita/S_Lee-02-21-18.pdf

23   Steven N. Broder, "About US/Profiles: Steven N. Broder, Clinical Associate Professor Emeritus," Boston University Wheelock College of Education and Human Development, accessed November 9, 2018, http://www.bu.edu/wheelock/profile/steven-n-broder/

24   Neurocore Brain Performance Centers, "What is Neurofeedback?," accessed November 9, 2018, https://www.neurocorecenters.com/what-is-neurofeedback

25   Ibid, "Authorization to Release Healthcare Information," accessed November 9, 2018, https://www.neurocorecenters.com/forms/insurance

26   Jeff Smith, "Betsy DeVos Watch: Listening to CEOs, Workforce Development and Student Loans," Grand Rapids Institute for Information Democracy, April 13, 2017, https://griid.org/2017/04/13/betsy-devos-watch-listening-to-ceos-workforce-development-and-student-loans/

27   United States, Department of Education, "Statement from Secretary of Education Betsy DeVos on the President's Strategy and Policy Forum Listening Session," Press Release, April 11, 2017, https://www.ed.gov/news/press-releases/statement-secretary-education-betsy-devos-presidents-strategy-and-policy-forum-listening-session

28   Charlotte Thomson Iserbyt, "The Death of Free Will (Part 2 of 5)," News With Views, December 21, 2010, http://www.newswithviews.com/iserbyt/iserbyt103.htm

29   Ibid.

30   Emily Marks, "Betsy DeVos Believes Community Colleges Play Important Role in Workforce Development," University Herald, February 22, 2017, https://www.universityherald.com/articles/66342/20170222/betsy-devos-community-colleges-play-important-role-workforce-development.htm

31   Catherine Morris, "DeVos Says Community Colleges Key to Workforce Development," Diverse Issues in Higher Education, February 16, 2017, https://diverseeducation.com/article/92766/

32   Amanda VanDerHeyden and Patricia Snyder, "Integrating Frameworks from Early Childhood Intervention and School Psychology to Accelerate Growth for All Young Children." School Psychology Review 35, no. 4 (2006): 530.

33   Antony C. Sutton, *America's Secret Establishment: An Introduction to the Order of Skull and Bones*, Updated Reprint (Walterville, OR: Trine Day, 2002), 86.

34   Ibid, 90-91.

35   Ibid, 63, 85-87, 101-102, 107-109.

Paolo Lionni, *The Leipzig Connection: The Systematic Destruction of American Education*, Third Printing (Sheridan, OR: Delphian Press, 1988), 1-27.

36   Antony C. Sutton, *America's Secret Establishment: An Introduction to the Order of Skull and Bones,* Updated Reprint (Walterville, OR: Trine Day, 2002), 91.

37   Ibid, 84-87, 101-105, 109.

"Dr. John Dewey Dead at 92; Philosopher a Noted Liberal," New York Times, June 2, 1952, https://archive.nytimes.com/www.nytimes.com/learning/general/onthisday/bday/1020.html

Paolo Lionni, *The Leipzig Connection: The Systematic Destruction of American Education*, Third Printing (Sheridan, OR: Delphian Press, 1988), 15-20, 64-65.

38   Ibid, 43-89.

39   Fredrick T. Gates, "The Country School of Tomorrow," Occasional Papers No. 1 (Publications of the General Education Board: New York, 1916), 6.

40   Paolo Lionni, *The Leipzig Connection: The Systematic Destruction of American Education*, Third Printing (Sheridan, OR: Delphian Press, 1988), 29-41, 61-65, 72, 78-81.

41   Edward Lee Thorndike, and Arthur I. Gates, Elementary Principles of Education (New York: Macmillan, 1929) quoted in Paolo Lionni, The Leipzig Connection: The Systematic Destruction of American Education, Third Printing (Sheridan, OR: Delphian Press, 1988), 40.

42   United States, Department of Education, "U.S. Secretary of Education Betsy DeVos to Visit Salt Lake City's Granite Technical Institute," Press Release, May 9, 2017, https://www.ed.gov/news/media-advisories/us-secretary-education-betsy-devos-visit-salt-lake-citys-granite-technical-institute

43   Phillippe A. Kent, "Accountability Measures in Workforce Training," New Directions for Institutional Research 128 (2005): 60.

44   Accessed September 21, 2017, http://www.neurocorepro.com/

45   Accessed September 21, 2017, http://www.neurocorepro.com/corporate-health/

46   United States, Every Student Succeeds Act, Public Law 114-95, 114th Congress, S. 1177, December 10, 2015, https://www.congress.gov/114/plaws/publ95/PLAW-114publ95.pdf

47   James M. Kearney, Outcome-Based Education: Final Report, US Department of Education, Office of Educational Research and Improvement, June 23, 1994, https://files.eric.ed.gov/fulltext/ED373457.pdf

48   Jane Robbins, "Why 'Competency-Based Education' Will Deepen America's Education Crisis," The Federalist, May 4, 2017, http://thefederalist.com/2017/05/04/competency-based-education-will-deepen-americas-education-crisis/

49   Ibid.

50   United States, Every Student Succeeds Act, Public Law 114-95, 114th Congress, S. 1177, December 10, 2015, https://www.congress.gov/114/plaws/publ95/PLAW-114publ95.pdf

51   Benjamin Herold, "DeVos Invested More Money in 'Brain Performance' Company, Despite Weak Evidence: Neurocore Makes Questionable Claims," Education Week, August 7, 2017, https://www.edweek.org/ew/articles/2017/08/07/devos-invested-more-money-in-brain-performance.htmlhttps://www.edweek.org/ew/articles/2017/08/07/devos-invested-more-money-in-brain-performance.html

52   Jonathon Hirte, "DeVos Seeks to Turn Michigan Around," Calvin College Chimes, November 3, 2006, https://web.archive.org/web/20131202234020/http:/clubs.calvin.edu/chimes/article.php?id=2723

53   Ellen Nolte, Caroline Viola Fry, Eleanor Winpenny, and Laura Brereton, Use of Outcome Metrics to Measure Quality in Education and Training of Healthcare Professionals: A Scoping Review of International Experiences (Cambridge, UK: RAND Corporation, February 2011), 13.

54   D. Koo and K. Miner, "Outcome-Based Workforce Development and Education in Public Health," Annual Review of Public Health 31 no. 1 (2011): 253-269, https://www.ncbi.nlm.nih.gov/pubmed/20001820

55   United States, Department of Education, "Prepared Remarks by U.S. Secretary of Educa-

tion Betsy DeVos to the 2017 ASU GSV Summit," Press Release, May 9, 2017, https://www.ed.gov/news/speeches/prepared-remarks-us-secretary-education-betsy-devos-2017-asu-gsv-summit

56   Theodore C. Sectish, William W. Hay Jr, John D. Mahan, Fernando S. Mendoza, Nancy D. Spector, Bonita Stanton, Peter G. Szilagyi, Teri L. Turner, Leslie R. Walker, and Kenneth Slaw, "Blueprint for Action: Visioning Summit on the Future of the Workforce in Pediatrics," Pediatrics, 136 no. 1 (2015), http://pediatrics.aappublications.org/content/136/1/161

57   Mathy Mezey, Ethel Mitty, Tara Cortes, Sarah Burger, Elizabeth Clark, and Philip McCallion. "A Competency-Based Approach to Educating and Training the Eldercare Workforce," Generations: Journal of the American Society on Aging 34 no. 4 (2011): 53.

58   Elizabeth Bragg and Jennie Chin Hansen, "Ensuring Care for Aging Baby Boomers: Solutions at Hand," Generations: Journal of the American Society on Aging 39 no. 2 (2015): 96.

59   Ibid, 94, 96.

60   Charlotte Thomson Iserbyt, The Deliberate Dumbing Down of America: A Chronological Paper Trail (Ravenna, OH: Conscience Press, 1999), 141.

Ibid, xxi, 138.

Ibid, 270.

Julian Huxley, UNESCO: Its Purpose and Its Philosophy (Washington D. C.: Public Affairs Press, 1948).

61   Charlotte Thomson Iserbyt, The Deliberate Dumbing Down of America: A Chronological Paper Trail, Revised and Abridged Ed. (Parkman, OH: Conscience Press, 2011), 36-37.

Education Commission of the States, Outcome-Based Education: An Overview (Denver: Education Commission of the States Clearing House, 1993).

62   Antony C. Sutton, America's Secret Establishment: An Introduction to the Order of Skull and Bones, Updated Reprint (Walterville, OR: Trine Day, 2002), 63, 290.

Charles R. Lanman, "Daniel Coit Gilman (1831-1908)," Proceedings of the American Academy of Arts and Sciences 52 no. 13 (1917): 836-839.

63   Antony C. Sutton, America's Secret Establishment: An Introduction to the Order of Skull and Bones, Updated Reprint (Walterville, OR: Trine Day, 2002), 63, 82, 90-91, 101.

"Dr. John Dewey Dead at 92; Philosopher a Noted Liberal," New York Times, June 2, 1952, https://archive.nytimes.com/www.nytimes.com/learning/general/onthisday/bday/1020.html

Paolo Lionni, The Leipzig Connection: The Systematic Destruction of American Education, Third Printing (Sheridan, OR: Delphian Press, 1988), 16.

64   United States, Every Student Succeeds Act, Public Law 114-95, 114th Congress, S. 1177, December 10, 2015, https://www.congress.gov/114/plaws/publ95/PLAW-114publ95.pdf

65   Ibid.

66   Ibid.

67   Steven C. Kassel, "Stress Management and Peak Performance Crash Course for Ninth Graders in a Charter School Setting," Biofeedback 43 no. 2 (2015): 90.

68   Northwestern University, Division of Student Affairs, "Outreach and Education: Relaxation and Biofeedback," Counseling and Psychological Services, accessed November 10, 2018, https://www.northwestern.edu/counseling/outreach-education/workshops-and-email-form/relaxation-biofeedback/index.html

69   University of Notre Dame, Division of Student Affairs, "Inner Resources Room," University Counseling Center: Enhancing Emotional Health for a Half Century, accessed November 10, 2018, https://ucc.nd.edu/inner-resources-room/

70   Iowa State University, "Biofeedback Center Newest Stress-Buster for Iowa State University Students," Iowa State University News Service, September 17, 2009, https://www.news.iastate.edu/news/2009/sep/biofeedback

71   Ed Frauenheim, "Changing Hearts and (Anxious) Minds," Workforce Magazine, November 21, 2008, https://www.workforce.com/2008/11/21/changing-hearts-and-anxious-minds/

72   United States, Every Student Succeeds Act, Public Law 114-95, 114th Congress, S. 1177, December 10, 2015, https://www.congress.gov/114/plaws/publ95/PLAW-114publ95.pdf

73   David E. Rosenbaum, "A Closer Look at Cheney and Halliburton," New York Times, September 28, 2004, https://www.nytimes.com/2004/09/28/us/a-closer-look-at-cheney-and-halliburton.html?mcubz=3

Endnotes – Chapter Six

1   Zbigniew Brzezinski, Between Two Ages: America's Role in the Technetronic Era (New York: Viking Press, 1970), 9.

2   United States, White House Archives, President Barack Obama, "Education," Educate to Innovate, accessed November 10, 2018, https://obamawhitehouse.archives.gov/issues/education/k-12/educate-innovate

3   Daniel Chaitin, "Former Presidents Barack Obama and George W. Bush Offer Praise to the Late Zbigniew Brzezinski,"Washington Examiner, May 27, 2017, https://www.washingtonexaminer.com/former-presidents-barack-obama-and-george-w-bush-offer-praise-to-the-late-zbigniew-brzezinski

Obama White House, "P032410PS-0305," Flickr, March 24, 2010, https://www.flickr.com/photos/obamawhitehouse/4609005318/

Russell Berman, "Despite Criticism, Obama Stands By Adviser Brzezinski," New York Sun, September 13, 2007, https://www.nysun.com/national/despite-criticism-obama-stands-by-adviser/62534/

Webster Griffin Tarpley, "Confirmed – Obama Is Zbigniew Brzezinski Puppet," Rense News, March 21, 2008, https://rense.com//general81/abig.htm

4   United States, White House Archives, President Barack Obama, "Education for K-12 Students: Knowledge and Skills for the Jobs of the Future," Educate to Innovate, accessed November 10, 2018, https://obamawhitehouse.archives.gov/issues/education/k-12/educate-innovate

5   Ibid.

6   Donald J. Trump, "Increasing Access to High-Quality Science, Technology, Engineering, and Mathematics (STEM) Education," Presidential Memorandum for the Secretary of Education, White House, September 25, 2017, https://www.whitehouse.gov/presidential-actions/presidential-memorandum-secretary-education/

7   United States, White House, Office of Science and Technology Policy, "President Trump Signs Presidential Memo to Increase Access to STEM and Computer Science Education," News Articles, September 25, 2017, https://www.whitehouse.gov/articles/president-trump-signs-presidential-memo-increase-access-stem-computer-science-education/

8   Donald J. Trump, "Presidential Executive Order Expanding Apprenticeships in America," Executive Orders (Social Programs), White House, June 15, 2017, https://www.whitehouse.gov/presidential-actions/3245/

9   Yasuchika Hasegawa, Joseph S. Nye, Jean-Claude Trichet, "Letter to 'Rockefeller Family,'" Trilateral Commission, March 25, 2017, http://www.trilateral.org/download/files/membership/TC%20Chairs%40DR%20Family%2025_03_2017%20(2).pdf

Zbigniew Brzezinski, Between Two Ages: America's Role in the Technetronic Era (New York: Viking Press, 1970), 266, 267, 268, 269.

Ibid. "Special Address by Founding Director Zbigniew Brzezinski,"The Trilateral Commission Warsaw 2004 Plenary Meeting, May 9, 2019, http://trilateral.org/download/files/ZBIGNIEW%20BRZEZINSKI.pdf

10   Dustin Heustin, "Discussion: Developing the Potential of an Amazing Tool," School and Technology (1984) quoted in Charlotte Thomson Iserbyt, The Deliberate Dumbing Down of America: A Chronological Paper Trail, Revised and Abridged Ed. (Parkman, OH: Conscience Press, 2011), 8.

11   Mieke Vandewaetere, Piet Desmet, and Geraldine Clarebout, "The Contribution of Learner Characteristics in the Development of Computer-Based Adaptive-Learning Environments," Computers in Human Behavior 27 no. 1 (2011): 118.

12   Henry A. Giroux, "Schooling and the Myth of Objectivity: Stalking the Politics of the Hidden Curriculum," McGill Journal of Education 16 no. 3 (1981): 283.

13   Renata Phelps, Stewart Hase, and Allan Ellis, "Competency, Capability, Complexity and Computers: Exploring a New Model for Conceptualising End-User Computer Education," British Journal of Educational Technology 36 no. 1 (2005): 69.

14   Ibid, 67.

15   Alexander Nussbaumer, Eva-Catherine Hillemann, Christian Gütl, and Dietrich Albert, "A Competence-based Service for Supporting Self-Regulated Learning in Virtual Environments," Journal of Learning Analytics, 2 no. 1 (2015): 106.

16   Tony Wan, "Knewton's New Business Attracts New $25M in Funding. But Some Things Don't Change," EdSurge, August 21, 2018, https://www.edsurge.com/news/2018-08-21-knewtons-new-business-attracts-new-25m-in-funding-but-some-things-don-t-change

17   Dreambox Learning, "Home: Company," accessed November 11, 2018, http://www.dreambox.com/company

18   Desire2Learn, "Desire2Learn Acquires Knowillage Systems, Inc.," D2L Newsroom, Sep-

tember 9, 2013, https://www.d2l.com/newsroom/releases/desire2learn-acquires-knowillage-systems-inc/

Ibid, "Products: Brightspace Leap™," D2L: Desire2Learn, accessed November 11, 2018, https://www.d2l.com/products/leap/

19   Smart Sparrow, "About: About Smart Sparrow," accessed November 11, 2018, https://www.smartsparrow.com/about/

Ibid, "Platform: Create Courseware That Engages Every Student," accessed November 11, 2018, https://www.smartsparrow.com/platform/

20   ACT, "About ACT: History of ACT" (2006), Internet Archive: Way Back Machine, accessed November 11, 2018, https://web.archive.org/web/20061008113919/http:/www.act.org/aboutact/history.html

Cengage Learning, "Cengage Learning Launches Knewton Adaptive Learning Technology within MindTap for Management and Sociology Students," Cengage Press Releases, February 18, 2015, https://news.cengage.com/higher-education/cengage-learning-launches-knewton-adaptive-learning-technology-within-mindtap-for-management-and-sociology-students/

D2L, "D2L Announces Strong Growth In Latin America, Signs Over A Dozen New And Returning Customers," PR Newswire, December 21, 2016, https://www.prnewswire.com/news-releases/d2l-announces-strong-growth-in-latin-america-signs-over-a-dozen-new-and-returning-customers-300382396.html

Knewton, "Partners: Enterprise Partnerships," accessed November 11, 2018, https://www.knewton.com/enterprise/

Smart Sparrow, "About: About Smart Sparrow," accessed November 11, 2018, https://www.smartsparrow.com/about/

Tony Wan, "'Netflix' Reed Hastings Leads $14.5M Series A1 for DreamBox," EdSurge, December 17, 2013, https://www.edsurge.com/news/2013-12-17-netflix-reed-hastings-leads-14-5m-series-a1-for-dreambox

21   Khan Academy, "About: Our Mission Is to Provide a Free, WorldClass Education for Anyone, Anywhere," accessed November 11, 2018, https://www.khanacademy.org/about

22   Rachel B. Baker, "The Student Experience: How Competency-Based Education Providers Serve Students," American Enterprise Institute Series on Competency-Based Higher Education, (The Center on Higher Education Reform of the American Enterprise Institute for Public Policy Research, 2015), 10.

23   Ibid.

24   Ibid, ii.

25   P. Wildman, "From Student Competencies to Regional Capability," Capability, 2 no. 1 (1996): 85-91, quoted in Renata Phelps, Stewart Hase, and Allan Ellis, "Competency, Capability, Complexity and Computers: Exploring a New Model for Conceptualising End-User Computer Education," British Journal of Educational Technology 36 no. 1 (2005): 69.

26   C. Price, "An Elusive Human Capacity," Capability, 2 no. 1 (1996) 3-4, quoted in Renata Phelps, Stewart Hase, and Allan Ellis, "Competency, Capability, Complexity and Computers: Exploring a New Model for Conceptualising End-User Computer Education," British Journal of Educational Technology 36 no. 1 (2005): 69.

27   Charlotte Thomson Iserbyt, "Heritage Foundation, NAFTA, School Choice and the Destruction of Traditional Education," News With Views, July 31, 2012, http://www.newswithviews.com/iserbyt/iserbyt111.htm

Endnotes _ Chapter Seven

1   Christensen, Clayton, Curtis W. Johnson, and Michael B. Horn. Disrupting Class: How Disruptive Innovation Will Change the Way the World Learns" (New York: McGraw Hill, 2008), quoted in Matthew Ladner, Andrew T. LeFevre, and Dan Lips, Report Card on Ranking State K-12 Performance, Progress, and Reform 16th Edition (Washington DC: American Legislative Exchange Council, 2010).

2   Ibid.

3   Henry A. Giroux, Schooling and the Struggle for Public Life: Democracy's Promise and Education's Challenge (New York: 2005), 180.

4   Betsy DeVos, "Prepared Remarks by Betsy DeVos: 'Competition, Creativity, & Choice in the Classroom," SXSW EDU Conference, March 11, 2015, http://www.federationforchildren.org/wp-content/uploads/2015/03/Betsy-SXSWedu-speech-final-remarks.pdf?e40fe9

5   Ibid.

6   United States, Department of Education, "Prepared Remarks by U.S. Secretary of Education Betsy DeVos to the American Federation for Children's National Policy Summit," Press Release, May 22, 2017, https://www.ed.gov/news/speeches/prepared-remarks-us-secretary-education-betsy-devos-american-federation-childrens-national-policy-summit

Valerie Strauss, "This Is What Betsy DeVos Thinks about People Who Oppose Her School-Choice Vision," Washington Post, May 29, 2017, https://www.washingtonpost.com/news/answer-sheet/wp/2017/05/29/this-is-what-betsy-devos-thinks-about-people-who-oppose-her-school-choice-vision/?noredirect=on&utm_term=.051fcd2a28ef

7   American Civil Liberties Union, "Background on Betsy DeVos from the ACLU of Michigan," accessed November 11, 2018, https://www.aclu.org/other/background-betsy-devos-aclu-michigan

8   MLive Media Group, "How Betsy DeVos and Her Money Has Shaped Education in Michigan," MLive: Michigan News, November 29, 2016, https://www.mlive.com/news/index.ssf/2016/11/how_betsy_devos_has_shaped_edu.html

9   Betsy DeVos, "Current Board and Leadership Positions," accessed November 11, 2018, http://www.betsydevos.com/#philanthropy

10   Great Lakes Education Project, "Mission & Priorities: Choice, Quality and Accountability," accessed November 11, 2018, https://www.glep.org/glep-mission/

11   American Federation for Children, "Bill Oberndorf Succeeds Betsy DeVos as Chairman of American Federation for Children," November 30, 2016, https://www.federationforchildren.org/bill-oberndorf-succeeds-betsy-devos-chairman-american-federation-children/

12   Ibid, "Statement from the American Federation for Children on 2016 Omnibus Bill," December 16, 2015, https://www.federationforchildren.org/statement-american-federation-children-2016-omnibus-bill/

13   United States, Department of Education, "Prepared Remarks by U.S. Secretary of Education Betsy DeVos to the American Federation for Children's National Policy Summit," Press Release, May 22, 2017, https://www.ed.gov/news/speeches/prepared-remarks-us-secretary-education-betsy-devos-american-federation-childrens-national-policy-summit

14   Ibid.

15   Matt Barnum, "Are Virtual Schools the Future? Despite Evidence of Negative Student-Learning Outcomes, Betsy DeVos Appears to Think So," The Atlantic, June 12, 2017, https://www.theatlantic.com/education/archive/2017/06/are-virtual-schools-the-future/529170/

16   American Federation for Children, "Kevin P. Chavous: Board Member," accessed November 11, 2018, https://www.federationforchildren.org/staff/kevin-p-chavous/

17   Sarah Darville, "What Is Betsy DeVos's 'Rethink School' Initiative All About? Her Wyoming Speech Offers Clues," Chalkbeat, September 12, 2017, https://www.chalkbeat.org/posts/us/2017/09/12/what-is-betsy-devoss-rethink-school-initiative-all-about-her-wyoming-speech-offers-clues/

18   Foundation for Blended and Online Learning, "Our Board: Kevin P. Chavous—Board Chairman," accessed November 11, 2018, https://www.blendedandonlinelearning.org/board-of-directors/kevin-chavous

19   "Trends: 100 People Making a Difference for Digital Learning Now," EdTech Digest, February 14, 2011, https://edtechdigest.com/2011/02/14/trends-digital-learning-now/

20   Donna Savarese, "Kevin P. Chavous Named K12 Inc. President of Academics, Policy, and Schools," MarketWatch, October 26, 2017, https://www.marketwatch.com/press-release/kevin-p-chavous-named-k12-inc-president-of-academics-policy-and-schools-2017-10-26

Kevin P. Chavous, "Gainful Employment," Gainful Employment, May 31, 2011, https://thehill.com/blogs/congress-blog/education/163941-gainful-employment-

Valerie Strauss, "Democrats Reject Her, but They Helped Pave the Road to Education Nominee DeVos," Washington Post, January 21, 2017, https://www.washingtonpost.com/news/answer-sheet/wp/2017/01/21/democrats-reject-her-but-they-helped-pave-the-road-to-education-nominee-devos/?utm_term=.afbe0bfe4358&noredirect=on

Washington Policy Center, "Kevin Chavous in Washington D.C.," Washington Policy Center Blog, July 24, 2012, https://www.washingtonpolicy.org/publications/detail/kevin-chavous-in-washington-dc

21   Jeb Bush, "Keynote Speech," American Federation for Children's 8th Annual National Policy Summit: Opening Doors, Opening Window, May 22, 2017, https://www.federationforchildren.org/event/2017-national-policy-summit/

22   Ibid.

Endnotes – Chapter Eight

1   Emily Sullivan, "Union Leader Calls For An End To Oklahoma Teachers' 9-Day Strike," National Public Radio, April 14, 2018, https://www.npr.org/sections/thetwo-way/2018/04/14/602462055/union-leader-calls-for-an-end-to-oklahoma-teachers-9-day-strike

2   Joseph Flaherty, "Back to Class: The Arizona Teachers' Strike Is Officially Over," Phoenix New Times, May 3, 2018, https://www.phoenixnewtimes.com/news/the-arizona-teachers-strike-is-officially-over-10393049

3   Danika Worthington, "Pueblo Teachers Launch Colorado's First Teachers' Strike in 24 Years," Denver Post, May 7, 2018, https://www.denverpost.com/2018/05/07/pueblo-teacher-strike/

4   Dylan Matthews, "6 Excerpts That Explain the Supreme Court's Big Anti-Union Ruling," Vox, June 27, 2018, https://www.vox.com/2018/6/27/17509460/supreme-court-janus-afscme-public-sector-union-alito-kagan-dissent

5   Foundation for Excellence in Education, "About Us," ExcelinEd, accessed November 11, 2018, https://www.excelined.org/about/

6   Ibid, "Personalized Learning: Flexible Path & Pace to Achieve Mastery," ExcelinEd, accessed November 11, 2018, https://www.excelined.org/innovation/personalized-learning/

7   McKenzie Snow, "The Federal Government and School Choice," ExcelinEd Blog, January 26, 2017, https://www.excelined.org/edfly-blog/federal-government-school-choice/

8   Valerie Strauss, "E-mails Link Bush Foundation, Corporations and Education Officials," Washington Post, January 30, 2013, https://www.washingtonpost.com/news/answer-sheet/wp/2013/01/30/e-mails-link-bush-foundation-corporations-and-education-officials/?utm_term=.5f32e0de8baa&noredirect=on

9   American Legislative Exchange Council, accessed July 19, 2018, https://www.alec.org/model-legislation/resolution-adopting-the-10-elements-of-high-quality-digital-learning-for-k-12/

10   OpenEd Solutions, Digital Learning 2020: A Policy Report for Kentucky's Digital Future (December, 2011), accessed November 11, 2018, https://education.ky.gov/school/Documents/Digital%20Learning%202020%20-%20A%20Policy%20Report.pdf

11   American Legislative Exchange Council, accessed July 19, 2018, https://www.alec.org/model-legislation/resolution-adopting-the-10-elements-of-high-quality-digital-learning-for-k-12/

12   Ibid.

13   ALEC Legislative Board of Directors, "The Virtual Public Schools Act," American Legislative Exchange Council, January 1, 2005, https://www.alec.org/model-policy/the-virtual-public-schools-act/

14   American Legislative Exchange Council, "Task Forces: Education and Workforce Development," accessed November 11, 2018, https://www.alec.org/task-force/education-and-workforce-development/

15   Lee Fang, "How Online Learning Companies Bought America's Schools," The Nation, November 16, 2011, https://www.thenation.com/article/how-online-learning-companies-bought-americas-schools/

16   Jason Stanford, "How ALEC Gets Real Tax Dollars for Fake Schools," Huffington Post, August 9, 2012, https://www.huffingtonpost.com/jason-stanford/alec-virtual-schools_b_1549202.html

17   Mary Bottari, "ALEC Bills in Wisconsin," The Center for Media and Democracy's PR Watch, July 14, 2011, https://www.prwatch.org/news/2011/07/10880/alec-bills-wisconsin

18   Judy Molland, "Why ALEC Fabricated Public School Failures (and Why We're Not Surprised)," Truthout, August 5, 2013, https://truthout.org/articles/why-alec-fabricated-public-school-failures-and-why-were-not-surprised/#

19   State of Virginia, Department of Education, "Governor McDonnell Advances 'Opportunity to Learn' Education Agenda for 2012," News Releases, January 9, 2012, http://www.doe.virginia.gov/news/news_releases/2012/jan09_gov.shtml

20   American Federation for Children, "Virginia Governor Unveils 2012 Education Reform Agenda," accessed November 11, 2018, https://www.federationforchildren.org/virginia-governor-unveils-2012-education-reform-agenda/

21   Lawrence Hurley and David Ingram, "U.S. Top Court Overturns Virginia Ex-Governor's Corruption Conviction," Reuters, June 27, 2016, https://www.reuters.com/article/us-usa-court-mcdonnell/u-s-top-court-overturns-virginia-ex-governors-corruption-conviction-idUSKCN0ZD1XS

22   Dustin Beilke, "K12 Inc. Tries to Pivot from Virtual School Failures to Profit from 'Non-Managed' Schools," Center for Media and Democracy's PR Watch, January 7, 2016, https://www.prwatch.org/news/2016/01/13009/k12-inc-tries-pivot-virtual-school-failures

23   American Legislative Exchange Council, "Education Task Force" (2005), Internet Archive: Way Back Machine, accessed November 11, 2018, http://web.archive.org/web/20050204143455/ http:/www.alec.org/viewpage.cfm?pgname=5.02

24   Diane Ravitch, Reign of Error: The Hoax of the Privatization Movement and the Danger to America's Public Schools (New York: Alfred A. Knopf, 2013), 185.

25   American Legislative Exchange Council, accessed July 19, 2018, https://www.alec.org/ AM/Template.cfm?Section=Mickey_Revenaugh

26   American Legislative Exchange Council, "Hundreds of State Legislators Gather to Discuss Policy Solutions Promoting Economic Growth and Limited Government," Press Release, August 3, 2011, https://www.alec.org/press-release/hundreds-of-state-legislators/

Deborah Seide, "Digital Learning and Its Impact on the Future," Pearson Education Blog, July 23, 2015, https://www.pearsoned.com/digital-learning-and-its-impact-on-the-future/

Lee Fang, "How Online Learning Companies Bought America's Schools," The Nation, November 16, 2011, https://www.thenation.com/article/how-online-learning-companies-bought-americas-schools/

27   American Legislative Exchange Council, "Education Task Force" (2005), Internet Archive: Way Back Machine, accessed November 11, 2018, http://web.archive.org/web/20050204143455/ http:/www.alec.org/viewpage.cfm?pgname=5.02

28   American Legislative Exchange Council, "Private Enterprise Advisory Council: Don Lee, K12 Inc.," accessed November 12, 2018, https://www.alec.org/person/don-lee/

Ibid, "NetChoice, National Federation of Independent Business and K12 Inc. Join ALEC Private Enterprise Advisory Council," Press Release, July 25, 2014, https://www.alec.org/press-release/ alec-private-enterprise-advisory-council/

29   Mark Walsh, "DeVos' Investment Stakes Raise Democratic Concerns," Education Week, February 7, 2017, https://www.edweek.org/ew/articles/2017/02/08/devos-investment-stakes-raise-democratic-concerns.html

30   American Legislative Exchange Council, "Task Forces: Education and Workforce Development," accessed November 11, 2018, https://www.alec.org/task-force/education-and-workforce-development/

31   K12 Inc., "Kevin P. Chavous Named K12 Inc. President of Academics, Policy, and Schools," K12 Newsroom: Press Releases, October 26, 2017, http://newsroom.k12.com/kevin-p-chavous-named-k12-inc-president-of-academics-policy-and-schools/

32   American Federation for Children, American Federation for Children's 8th Annual National Policy Summit: Opening Doors, Opening Window, May 22, 2017, https://www.federationforchildren.org/event/2017-national-policy-summit/

33   Lisa Graves, "A Lot of White Space: Firms Drop Off ALEC's Meeting Brochure," The Center for Media and Democracy's PR Watch, July 30, 2012, https://www.prwatch.org/news/2012/07/11679/ lot-white-space-firms-drop-alecs-meeting-brochure

34   Ibid, "ALEC Exposed: List of Corporations and Special Interests that Underwrote ALEC's 40th Anniversary Meeting," The Center for Media and Democracy's PR Watch, August 15, 2013, https://www.prwatch.org/news/2013/08/12212/alecexposed-list-corporations-and-special-interests-underwrote-alecs-40th-anniver

American Legislative Exchange Council, accessed July 19, 2018, https://www.alec.org/AM/ Template.cfm?Section=Mickey_Revenaugh

35   Ibid, "Education and Workforce Development Taskforce Meeting: Education and Workforce Development Agenda," 44th ALEC Annual Meeting—Denver, Colorado, July 21, 2017, https:// www.alec.org/meeting-session/education-and-workforce-development-task-force-meeting-4/

American Federation for Children, "Scott Jensen: Senior Government Affairs Advisor—Wisconsin," accessed November 12, 2018, https://www.federationforchildren.org/staff/scott-jensen/

American Legislative Exchange Council, ALEC Joint Board of Directors Meeting (San Diego, CA: ALEC, July 25, 2000) https://www.industrydocumentslibrary.ucsf.edu/tobacco/docs/#id=kp-cw0094

Brendan Fischer, "WI Club for Growth, Target of Walker Recall Probe, at Center of Dark Money Web," The Center for Media and Democracy's PR Watch, November 18, 2013, https://www.prwatch. org/news/2013/11/12309/new-john-doe-investigation-probes-dark-money-wisconsin-recall-elections-club

Mary Bottari, "Scott Walker: The First ALEC President," Huffington Post, December 6, 2017, https://www.huffingtonpost.com/mary-bottari/scott-walker-the-first-al_b_7502534.html

Mike Johnson and Jason Stein, "Jensen Settles Misconduct Case; Felonies Dropped," Journal Sentinel: Waukesha News, December 20, 2010, http://archive.jsonline.com/news/waukesha/112195794.html

36   United States, Department of Education, "Remarks from Secretary DeVos to the American Legislative Exchange Council," Press Release, July 20, 2017, https://www.ed.gov/news/speeches/remarks-secretary-devos-american-legislative-exchange-council

37   Arika Herron, "Hoosier Virtual Academy, an Online Charter School Serving 1,750 Students, to Close in June," Indy Star, September 29, 2017, https://www.indystar.com/story/news/education/2017/09/29/hoosier-virtual-academy-online-charter-school-serving-1-750-students-close-june/712586001/

Beth Glenn, "A Virtual Disaster for Rural Schools," Schott Foundation for Public Education, February 6, 2017, http://schottfoundation.org/blog/2017/02/06/virtual-disaster-rural-schools

Melanie Balakit, "Push Fails to Keep Tennessee Virtual Academy Open," The Tennessean: Part of the USA Today Network, April 21, 2015, https://www.tennessean.com/story/news/education/2015/04/21/tennessee-virtual-academy-makes-final-push-stay-open/26136201/

Patrick O'Donnell, "ECOT Overbilled the State again for too Many Students, State Reports, This Time by $19 Million," Cleveland Metro News: Covering Northeast Ohio, September 28, 2017, https://www.cleveland.com/metro/index.ssf/2017/09/ecot_overbilled_the_state_agai.html

Shaina Cavazos, "As Students Signed up, Online School Hired Barely any Teachers — but Founder's Company Charged It Millions," Chalk Beat, October 31, 2017, https://www.chalkbeat.org/posts/in/2017/10/31/as-students-signed-up-online-school-hired-barely-any-teachers-but-founders-company-charged-it-millions/

Tom Torlakson, "State Schools Chief Tom Torlakson Requires California Virtual Academies to Pay Nearly $2 Million to State Based on Newly Released Audit," California Department of Education News Release, October 9, 2017, https://www.cde.ca.gov/nr/ne/yr17/yr17rel72.asp

Endnotes – Chapter Nine

1   Alexander Inglis, Principles of Secondary Education, quoted in John Taylor Gatto, "Against School," Rereading America: Cultural Contexts for Critical Thinking and Writing. 9th ed., Eds. Gary Colombo, Robert Cullen, Bonnie Lisle (Boston: Bedford/St. Martin's, 2013), 146-147.

2   John Taylor Gatto, "Against School," Rereading America: Cultural Contexts for Critical Thinking and Writing. 9th ed., Eds. Gary Colombo, Robert Cullen, Bonnie Lisle (Boston: Bedford/St. Martin's, 2013), 146.

3   Ibid.

4   Ibid, 142-143.

5   Ibid, 146.

6   J. E. R. Staddon and D. T. Cerutti, "Operant Conditioning," Annual Review of Psychology 54 (2003): 115-144, https://www.ncbi.nlm.nih.gov/pmc/articles/PMC1473025/#FN1

7   Audrey Watters, "The First Teaching Machines," Hack Education: The History of the Future of Education, February 3, 2015, http://hackeducation.com/2015/02/03/the-first-teaching-machines

8   Phil McRae and Joe Bower, "Rebirth of the Teaching Machine through the Seduction of Data Analytics: This Time It's Personal," National Education Policy Center, April 30, 2013, https://nepc.colorado.edu/blog/rebirth-teaching-machine-through-seduction-data-analytics-time-its-personal

9   Stephen Petrina, "Sidney Pressey and the Automation of Education, 1924-1934," Technology and Culture, 45 no. 2 (2004): 305-330.

10   Department of Psychology, "People: B. F. Skinner (1904-1990)," Harvard University, accessed November 12, 2018, https://psychology.fas.harvard.edu/people/b-f-skinner

11   B. F. Skinner, The Technology of Teaching (New York: Appleton-Century-Crofts, 1968), 30.

12   Ibid.

13   Edward Lee Thorndike, Education: A First Book, (New York: Macmillan Company, 1914), 165.

14   Paolo Lionni, The Leipzig Connection: The Systematic Destruction of American Education, Third Printing (Sheridan, OR: Delphian Press, 1988), 30-41.

15   bid, 33.

16   Antony C. Sutton, America's Secret Establishment: An Introduction to the Order of Skull and Bones, Updated Reprint, (Walterville, OR: Trine Day, 2002), 52.

B. F. Skinner, The Technology of Teaching (New York: Appleton-Century-Crofts, 1968), viii.

"GSE faculty member Harold 'Doc' Howe II dies at 84," Harvard Gazette, December 5, 2002, https://news.harvard.edu/gazette/story/2002/12/gse-faculty-member-harold-doc-howe-ii-dies-at-84/

National Archives, John F. Kennedy Presidential Library and Museum, McGeorge Bundy Personal Papers, accessed November 12, 2018, https://www.jfklibrary.org/asset-viewer/archives/MBP-P?f=1

17   B. F. Skinner, The Technology of Teaching (New York: Appleton-Century-Crofts, 1968), 61-68.

18   Ibid, quoted in Richard I. Evans, B. F. Skinner: The Man and His Ideas (New York: Dutton and Company, 1968) quoted in Charlotte Thomson Iserbyt, The Deliberate Dumbing Down of America: A Chronological Paper Trail, (Ravenna, OH: Conscience Press, 1999), 77.

Ibid, quoted in Michael Cole, "Culture in Development," Developmental Science: An Advanced Textbook, 5th Ed., Eds. Marc H. Bornstein and Michael E. Lamb (Mahwah, NJ: Lawrence Erlbaum Associates, 2005), 48.

19   Smithsonian, "Collections: Skinner Teaching Machine," National Museum of American History, accessed November 12, 2018, http://americanhistory.si.edu/collections/search/object/nmah_690062

20   B. F. Skinner, The Technology of Teaching (New York: Appleton-Century-Crofts, 1968), 70.

21   Ibid, 36.

22   Ibid, 38.

23   Susan Walton, "There Has Been a Conspiracy of Silence about Teaching," Education Week, August 31, 1983, https://www.edweek.org/ew/articles/1983/08/31/04180056.h02.html?qs=%22there+has+been+a+conspiracy+of+silence

24   Charlotte Thomson Iserbyt, The Deliberate Dumbing Down of America: A Chronological Paper Trail (Ravenna, OH: Conscience Press, 1999), 170.

25   Association for Educational Computing and Technology, "What Is Project BEST?," Project BEST: Better Education Skills through Technology (1981), quoted in Charlotte Thomson Iserbyt, The Deliberate Dumbing Down of America: A Chronological Paper Trail, (Ravenna, OH: Conscience Press, 1999), 170.

26   United States, Department of Education, "Project BEST Dissemination Design Considerations," quoted in Charlotte Thomson Iserbyt, The Deliberate Dumbing Down of America: A Chronological Paper Trail, (Ravenna, OH: Conscience Press, 1999), 170.

27   Ibid.

28   Charlotte Thomson Iserbyt, The Deliberate Dumbing Down of America: A Chronological Paper Trail (Ravenna, OH: Conscience Press, 1999), 67.

29   Ibid, A-38.

30   Ibid, 67.

31   Ibid, A-35.

32   Ibid, 170-171

33   Ibid, 124-125, 194.

34   Shirley McCune, quoted in "Schools of the Future," Bremerton Sun, October 14, 1989, quoted in Charlotte Thomson Iserbyt, The Deliberate Dumbing Down of America: A Chronological Paper Trail, (Ravenna, OH: Conscience Press, 1999), 275-276.

35   Rhea R. Borja, "Bennett Quits K12 Inc. under Fire," Education Week, October 11, 2005, https://www.edweek.org/ew/articles/2005/10/12/07bennett.h25.html

36   Ibid.

37   Ariel Schwartz, "Google Futurist and Director of Engineering: Basic Income Will Spread Worldwide by the 2030s," Business Insider, April 14, 2018, https://www.businessinsider.com/basic-income-worldwide-by-2030s-ray-kurzweil-2018-4

38   Raymond Kurzweil, The Age of Intelligence Machines (Cambridge, MA: MIT Press, 1990), 431.

39   bid, 429, 431.

40   United States, White House Archives, President Barack Obama, "Education for K-12 Students: Knowledge and Skills for the Jobs of the Future," ConnectEd Initiative, accessed November 12, 2018, https://obamawhitehouse.archives.gov/issues/education/k-12/connected

41   Ibid, K-12 Education, accessed November 12, 2018, https://obamawhitehouse.archives.gov/issues/education/k-12

42   bid.

43   Ibid.

44   Alexander Inglis, Principles of Secondary Education, quoted in John Taylor Gatto, "Against School," *Rereading America: Cultural Contexts for Critical Thinking and Writing.* 9th ed., Eds. Gary Colombo, Robert Cullen, Bonnie Lisle (Boston: Bedford/St. Martin's, 2013), 146-147.

B. F. Skinner, The Technology of Teaching (New York: Appleton-Century-Crofts, 1968), 30, 56.

45   Tom Vander Ark, "Online Discussion: School Choice a la Carte," Education Sector (October 2009), quoted in Matthew Ladner, Andrew T. LeFevre, and Dan Lips, Report Card on Ranking State K-12 Performance, Progress, and Reform 16th Edition (Washington DC: American Legislative Exchange Council, 2010).

Endnotes – Chapter Ten

1   United States, House of Representatives, Committee on Education and the Workforce, "Foxx Statement on Proposed New Department of Education and the Workforce," Newsroom: Press Releases, June 21, 2018, https://edworkforce.house.gov/news/documentsingle.aspx?DocumentID=402877

2   Helen F. Ladd and Edward B. Fiske "Lessons for US Charter Schools from the Growth of Academies in England," Brookings Institution, November 3, 2016, https://www.brookings.edu/research/lessons-for-us-charter-schools-from-the-growth-of-academies-in-england/

Matt Barnum, "Does England's Rapid Expansion of Charter-Like 'Academies' Hold a Lesson for the U.S.?," Chalkbeat, September 21, 2017, https://www.chalkbeat.org/posts/us/2017/09/21/does-englands-rapid-expansion-of-charter-like-academies-hold-a-lesson-for-the-u-s/

Melissa Benn, "Why Are We Following the US into a Schools Policy Disaster?," The Guardian (US Edition), November 28, 2011, https://www.theguardian.com/education/2011/nov/28/us-charter-academies-free-schools

3   Betsy DeVos, "Betsy DeVos: How Can We Catch up to Other Countries in Education," Education Week, June 28, 2018, https://www.edweek.org/ew/articles/2018/06/28/betsy-devos-how-we-can-catch-up.html

4   Susan Berry, "DeVos Wants U.S. to Adopt European Education Policies," Breitbart, June 29, 2018, https://www.breitbart.com/politics/2018/06/29/devos-wants-u-s-to-adopt-european-education-policies/

5   United States, Department of Education, "U.S. Secretary of Education Betsy DeVos to Deliver Keynote Address at Third International Congress on Vocational and Professional Education and Training," Press Release, June 5, 2018, https://www.ed.gov/news/press-releases/us-secretary-education-betsy-devos-deliver-keynote-address-third-international-congress-vocational-and-professional-education-and-training

6   United States, Department of Education, "#SEL: 7:28 AM – 25 Jun 2018," As children learn to understand and control their emotions, teachers can provide support by showing empathy and encouraging children to do the same.News and Information from the U.S. Department of Education, Twitter, June 25 2018, accessed November 12, 2018, https://twitter.com/usedgov/status/1011254688245637122?ref_src=twsrc%5Etfw%7Ctwcamp%5Etweetembed%7Ctwterm%5E1011254688245637122&ref_url=https%3A%2F%2Fwww.breitbart.com%2Fbig-government%2F2018%2F06%2F29%2Fdevos-wants-u-s-to-adopt-european-education-policies%2F

"#SEL," Twitter, accessed November 12, 2018, https://twitter.com/hashtag/SEL?src=hashAs children learn to understand and control their emotions, teachers can provide support by showing empathy and encouraging children to do the same. As children learn to understand and control their emotions, teachers can provide support by showing empathy and encouraging children to do the same

Jane Robbins and Karen Effrem, "Schools Ditch Academics For Emotional Manipulation: Under Such a System Teachers Become Essentially Therapists, and Students Become Essentially Patients," The Federalist, October 19, 2016, http://thefederalist.com/2016/10/19/schools-ditch-academics-for-emotional-manipulation/

7   Pearson, "About Us: Where We Are," accessed November 12, 2018, https://www.pearson.com/uk/about-us/where-we-are.html

8   Ibid, "Home," Pearson Assessments, accessed November 12, 2018, https://www.pearsonassessments.com/

9   Ibid, Pearson VUE, accessed November 12, 2018, https://home.pearsonvue.com/

Ibid, "Investors," accessed November 12, 2018, https://www.pearson.com/corporate/investors.html

Ibid, "Products & Services for Teaching: Textbooks & eTextbooks," accessed November 12, 2018, https://www.pearson.com/us/higher-education/products-services-teaching/course-content/textbooks-and-etexts.html

10   Laura Angela Bagnetto, "Uganda's First Lady Says Bridge Schools Uganda Must Close," RFI: the World and All Its Voices (English), February 16, 2018, http://en.rfi.fr/africa/20180216-bridge-schools-uganda-hits-back-governments-refusal-grant-licences-operate

Rebecca Ratcliffe and Afua Hirsch, "UK Urged to Stop Funding 'Ineffective and Unsustainable' Bridge Schools," The Guardian (US Edition), August 3, 2017, https://www.theguardian.com/global-development/2017/aug/03/uk-urged-to-stop-funding-ineffective-and-unsustainable-bridge-academies

"Uganda Court Orders Closure of Low-Cost Bridge International Schools," BBC News, November 4, 2016, https://www.bbc.com/news/world-africa-37871130

11   Pearson, "Pearson acquires Connections Education," News & Media: News Announcements, September 15, 2011, https://www.pearson.com/corporate/news/media/news-announcements/2011/09/pearson-acquires-connections-education.html

12   Stephanie Saul, "Profits and Questions at Online Charter Schools," New York Times, December 12, 2011, https://www.nytimes.com/2011/12/13/education/online-schools-score-better-on-wall-street-than-in-classrooms.html?_r=1&seid=auto&smid=tw-nytimes&pagewanted=all

13   Connections Academy, "Pearson Acquires Connections Education: Gains Leading Position in Fast-Growing Market for Virtual Schools," News: Archives, September 15, 2011, https://www.connectionsacademy.com/news/pearson-acquisition

14   Georgia Connections Academy, "Home," accessed November 12, 2018, https://www.connectionsacademy.com/georgia-virtual-school

15   Betsy Hammond, "Oregon's Largest Charter School Miseducated Student for Years, Graduated Her Unable to Read or Write," The Oregonian, February 22, 2013, https://www.oregonlive.com/education/index.ssf/2013/02/oregons_largest_charter_school.html

16   State of California, Department of Education, "California Connections Academy @ Ripon," California School Directory, accessed November 12, 2018, https://www.cde.ca.gov/SchoolDirectory/details?cdscode=39686500125849

17   Noel K. Gallagher, "Maine's New Virtual Charter School Sees 25% Enrollment Drop Since Opening," Portland Press Herald, January 6, 2016, https://www.pressherald.com/2016/01/06/maine-virtual-academy-charter-school-says-25-percent-of-its-students-withdrew-since-it-opened-this-fall/

18   International Connections Academy, "About Us: Mission & History," accessed November 12, 2018, https://www.internationalconnectionsacademy.com/about-us/mission

19   B. F. Skinner, The Technology of Teaching (New York: Appleton-Century-Crofts, 1968), 56.

20   Hannah Reinhart, "When Classrooms Have No Walls," Pearson Education Blog, May 20, 2016, https://www.pearsoned.com/education-blog/classrooms-no-walls/

21   Anya Kamenetz, "Pearson's Quest to Cover the Planet in Company-Run Schools," Wired Magazine, April 12, 2018, https://www.wired.com/2016/04/apec-schools/

22   Maureen Sullivan, "It's Pearson CEO John Fallon Vs. Teachers' Union President Randi Weingarten," Forbes, April 28, 2016, https://www.forbes.com/sites/maureensullivan/2016/04/28/its-pearson-ceo-john-fallon-vs-teachers-union-president-randi-weingarten/#7c99c0c37341

Omega Schools, "About Us: Our Story," Omega Schools: Every Child Matters, accessed November 13, 2018, http://www.omega-schools.com/history.php

Ibid, "Home: Welcome to Omega Schools," Omega Schools: Every Child Matters, accessed November 13, 2018, http://www.omega-schools.com/

Ibid, "Our Solution: Our Pay-As-You-Learn™ Model," Omega Schools: Every Child Matters, accessed November 13, 2018, http://www.omega-schools.com/payl-model.php

23   Ibid, "About Us: Overview and Mission," Omega Schools: Every Child Matters, accessed November 13, 2018, http://www.omega-schools.com/overview.php

Affordable Private Education Center (APEC) Schools, "About APEC Schools: Welcome to APEC Schools," accessed November 13, 2018, https://www.apecschools.edu.ph/about-apec-schools/

24   Alan Singer, "Pearson Education Can Run, But It Cannot Hide," Huffington Post, February 14, 2015, https://www.huffingtonpost.com/alan-singer/pearson-education-can-run_b_6327566.html

25   Matina Stevis and Simon Clark, "Zuckerberg-Backed Startup Seeks to Shake Up African Education: Bridge Aims to Provide Cheap, Internet-based Education in Africa," Wall Street Journal, March 13, 2015, https://www.wsj.com/articles/startup-aims-to-provide-a-bridge-to-education-1426275737

26   Bridge International Academies, accessed July, 9, 2018, https://www.bridgeinternation-alacademies.com/terms-of-use/

27   Ibid, accessed July, 9, 2018, https://www.bridgeinternationalacademies.com/approach/model/

Jan Resseger, "What Nicholas Kristof Left Out in Column Promoting Bridge International Academies," JanResseger Blog, July 18, 2017, https://janresseger.wordpress.com/2017/07/18/what-nicholas-kristof-left-out-in-column-promoting-bridge-international-academies/

28   "An Africa First! Liberia Outsource Education to a Private American Firm," The Liberian Listener, March 31, 2016, http://www.liberianlistener.com/2016/03/31/africa-first-liberia-outsource-education-private-american-firm/

Mail & Guardian Africa, accessed July, 9, 2018, http://mgafrica.com/article/2016-03-31-liberia-plans-to-outsource-its-entire-education-system-to-a-private-company-why-this-is-a-very-big-deal-and-africa-should-pay-attention

29   "An Africa First! Liberia Outsource Education to a Private American Firm," The Liberian Listener, March 31, 2016, http://www.liberianlistener.com/2016/03/31/africa-first-liberia-outsource-education-private-american-firm/

Mail & Guardian Africa, accessed July, 9, 2018, http://mgafrica.com/article/2016-03-31-liberia-plans-to-outsource-its-entire-education-system-to-a-private-company-why-this-is-a-very-big-deal-and-africa-should-pay-attention

30   Jacqueline Walumbe, "Making Best Practice Standard Practice in African Schools," Huffington Post, December 27, 2017, https://www.huffingtonpost.co.uk/entry/making-best-practice-standard-practice-in-african-schools_uk_5a3d103de4b06cd2bd03d9eb?guccounter=1

31   Ibid.

32   Ibid.

33   Tina Rosenberg, "Liberia, Desperate to Educate, Turns to Charter Schools," New York Times, June 14, 2016, https://www.nytimes.com/2016/06/14/opinion/liberia-desperate-to-educate-turns-to-charter-schools.html?_r=0

34   Accessed July, 9, 2018, http://www.bridgepartnershipschools.com/partnership-schools-for-liberia/

35   Tina Rosenberg, "Liberia, Desperate to Educate, Turns to Charter Schools," New York Times, June 14, 2016, https://www.nytimes.com/2016/06/14/opinion/liberia-desperate-to-educate-turns-to-charter-schools.html?_r=0

36   Pearson, "About Pearson VUE: Company Information," Pearson VUE, accessed November 13, 2018, https://home.pearsonvue.com/About-Pearson-VUE/Company-information.aspx

Ibid, "Company Information: History," Pearson VUE, accessed November 13, 2018, https://home.pearsonvue.com/About-Pearson-VUE/Company-information/Company-history.aspx

Ibid, "Florida Department of Education: Florida Teacher Certification Examinations (FTCE) and Florida Educational Leadership Examination (FELE) Computer-Based Testing," Pearson VUE, accessed November 13, 2018, https://home.pearsonvue.com/ftce

Ibid, "Market Expertise: Academia and Admissions," Pearson VUE, accessed November 13, 2018, https://home.pearsonvue.com/Test-Owner/Market-expertise/Academic-Admissions.aspx

Ibid, "Pearson VUE Companies: GED Testing Service," Pearson VUE, accessed November 13, 2018, https://home.pearsonvue.com/About-Pearson-VUE/Company-information/Pearson-VUE-companies/GED-Testing-Service.aspx

Ibid, "Test Taker Home: GMAC Assessments," Pearson VUE, accessed November 13, 2018, http://www.pearsonvue.com/gmacassessments/

Ibid, "Test Taker Home: Illinois Licensure Testing System (ILTS)," Pearson VUE, accessed November 13, 2018, https://home.pearsonvue.com/ilts

Ibid, "Test Taker Home: Indiana CORE Assessments for Educator Licensure (IELP)," Pearson VUE, accessed November 13, 2018, https://home.pearsonvue.com/ielp

Ibid, "Test Taker Home: New York State Teacher Certification Examinations (NYSTCE)," Pearson VUE, accessed November 13, 2018, https://home.pearsonvue.com/nystce

Ibid, "Test Taker Home: Ohio Assessments for Educators (OAE)," Pearson VUE, accessed November 13, 2018, https://home.pearsonvue.com/oae

Ibid, "Test Taker Home: Pennsylvania Educator Certification Tests (PECT)," Pearson VUE, accessed November 13, 2018, https://home.pearsonvue.com/pect

Ibid, "What We Do: The Global Leader in Computer-Based Testing," Pearson VUE, accessed November 13, 2018, https://home.pearsonvue.com/About-Pearson-VUE/What-we-do.aspx

37   Bridge International Academies, "Who We Are: History," accessed November 13, 2018, https://www.bridgeinternationalacademies.com/who-we-are/history/

38   Ibid.

39   CNBC Staff, "Shannon May and Jay Kimmelman," CNBC News, October 15, 2014, https://www.cnbc.com/2014/10/06/shannon-may-and-jay-kimmelman.html

40   Harvard University, Graduate School of Education, Creating Pathways to Prosperity: A Blueprint for Action (The Pathways to Prosperity Project and The Achievement Gap Initiative at Harvard University, June 2014), http://www.agi.harvard.edu/pathways/CreatingPathwaystoProsperityReport2014.pdf

41   Harlem Children's Zone, "About Us: Leadership—Geoffrey Canada, President," accessed November 13, 2018, https://hcz.org/about-us/leadership/geoffrey-canada/

42   United States, Department of Education, "The Promise of Promise Neighborhoods: Beyond Good Intentions -- Secretary Arne Duncan's Remarks at the Harlem Children's Zone Fall Conference," Press Room: Speeches, November 10, 2009, https://www2.ed.gov/news/speeches/2009/11/11102009.html

43   Bridge International Academies, "Investors," accessed July, 9, 2018, https://www.bridgeinternationalacademies.com/investors/

44   Global Initiative for Economic, Social and Cultural Rights, "Open letter – 88 Organisations Urge Investors to Cease Support for Bridge International Academies," Latest News, March 1, 2018, https://www.gi-escr.org/latest-news/open-letter-88-organisations-urge-investors-to-cease-support-for-bridge-international-academies/

45   Benjamin Herold, "Tangled Web: Zuckerberg & Chan's Education Grants, Investments," Education Week, March 8, 2016, https://www.edweek.org/ew/section/multimedia/zuckerberg-chan-education-grants-investments.html

46   Karen McVeigh and Kate Lyons, "'Beyond Justification': Teachers Decry UK Backing for Private Schools in Africa," The Guardian: US Edition, May 5, 2017, https://www.theguardian.com/global-development/2017/may/05/beyond-justification-teachers-decry-uk-backing-private-schools-africa-bridge-international-academies-kenya-lawsuit

United Kingdom, House of Commons, International Development Committee, "DFID's Work on Education: Leaving No One Behind?," First Report of Session 2017–19, November 13, 2017, https://publications.parliament.uk/pa/cm201719/cmselect/cmintdev/367/367.pdf

47   Betsy DeVos, "Betsy DeVos: How Can We Catch up to Other Countries in Education," Education Week, June 28, 2018, https://www.edweek.org/ew/articles/2018/06/28/betsy-devos-how-we-can-catch-up.html

48   Susan Berry, "DeVos Wants U.S. to Adopt European Education Policies," Breitbart, June 29, 2018, https://www.breitbart.com/politics/2018/06/29/devos-wants-u-s-to-adopt-european-education-policies/

49   Heather Nauert, "The United States Withdraws from UNESCO," United States Department of State, Press Statement, October 12, 2017, https://www.state.gov/r/pa/prs/ps/2017/10/274748.htm

50   Charlotte Thomson Iserbyt, The Deliberate Dumbing Down of America: A Chronological Paper Trail (Ravenna, OH: Conscience Press, 1999), 141.

51   Ibid, xxi, 138.

52   Ibid, 270.

United Nations, "Agreement on the Importation of Educational, Scientific and Cultural Materials," United Nations Treaty Collection, (Lake Success, NY: UN, November 22, 1950), https://treaties.un-.org/pages/ViewDetails.aspx?src=TREATY&mtdsg_no=XIV-2&chapter=14&clang=_en

53   United States, Department of Education, "U.S. Secretary of Education Betsy DeVos to Deliver Keynote Address at Third International Congress on Vocational and Professional Education and Training," Press Release, June 5, 2018, https://www.ed.gov/news/press-releases/us-secretary-education-betsy-devos-deliver-keynote-address-third-international-congress-vocational-and-professional-education-and-training

54   Julie E. Maybee, "Hegel's Dialectics," Stanford Encyclopedia of Philosophy, June 3, 2016, https://plato.stanford.edu/entries/hegel-dialectics/

Matthew C. Altman, "Review of J.G. Fichte, Walter E. Wright (ed.) 'The Science of Knowing: J. G. Fichte's 1804 Lectures on the Wissenschaftslehre,'" Notre Dame Philosophical Reviews: An Electronic Journal, November 3, 2005, https://ndpr.nd.edu/news/the-science-of-knowing-j-g-fichte-s-1804-lectures-on-the-wissenschaftslehre/

55   Antony C. Sutton, America's Secret Establishment: An Introduction to the Order of Skull and

Bones, Updated Reprint (Walterville, OR: Trine Day, 2002), 34, 79.
56   F. W. Kaufmann, "Fichte and National Socialism," American Political Science Review, 36 no. 3 (1942): 460-470.
57   Dan Breazeale, "Johann Gottlieb Fichte," Stanford Encyclopedia of Philosophy, August 30, 2001, https://plato.stanford.edu/entries/johann-fichte/
58   Defend Democracy Press, "Trade Agreements and the Globalization of Fascism," Defend Democracy Press: The Website of the Delphi Initiative, September 21, 2016, http://www.defenddemocracy.press/trade-agreements-globalization-fascism/
59   John Hoefle, "Globalization Is Fascism: Globalization Is a Euphemism for the Replacement of Nation-States by Imperial Financier-Run Corporate Cartels," Executive Intelligence Review, May 4, 2007, https://larouchepub.com/eiw/public/2007/eirv34n18-20070504/61_718_bank.pdf
60   Johann Gottlieb Fichte, *Addresses to the German Nation*, trans. R. F. Jones and G. H. Turnbull (Chicago: Open Court Publishing Company, 1922), 117.

Endnotes – Chapter Eleven

1.   United States, White House, accessed November 10, 2016, https://www.greatagain.gov/policy/education.html
2.   Seth Fiegerman, "Peter Thiel Joins Trump's Transition Team," CNN Money, November 11, 2016, https://money.cnn.com/2016/11/11/technology/peter-thiel-trump-team/index.html
3. Editors of Encyclopedia Britannica, "Peter Thiel: American Entrepreneur," https://www.britannica.com/biography/Peter-Thiel
        "Profile: #328 Peter Thiel—Partner, Founders Fund," Forbes, https://www.forbes.com/profile/peter-thiel/#6f2bfe76533a
4.   Jonathan Vanian, "Peter Thiel's Founders Fund Goes Big on Bitcoin," Fortune, January 3, 2018, http://fortune.com/2018/01/02/bitcoin-peter-thiel-founders-fund/
        RTT News, "Peter Thiel's Founders Fund Bets Big On Bitcoins," Business Insider, January 3, 2018, https://markets.businessinsider.com/currencies/news/peter-thiel-s-founders-fund-bets-big-on-bitcoins-1012435390
5.   Founders Fund, "Team: Partner—Peter Thiel," accessed November 14, 2018, https://foundersfund.com/team/peter-thiel/
        Jessica Guynn, "The Founders Fund Emerges as Venture Capital 2.0: How Entrepreneurs Get Money, and Time, for Startups Is Changing," SF Gate, December 13, 2006, https://www.sfgate.com/bayarea/article/The-Founders-Fund-emerges-as-venture-capital-2-0-2543274.php
6.   Founders Fund, "Manifesto: What Happened to the Future," accessed November 14, 2018, https://foundersfund.com/the-future/#
        Ibid, "Portfolio," accessed November 14, 2018, https://foundersfund.com/portfolio/
7.   Malathi Nayak, "Tech investor Thiel to donate $1.25 Million to Trump Campaign," Reuters, October 16, 2016, https://www.reuters.com/article/us-usa-election-trump-thiel/tech-investor-thiel-to-donate-1-25-million-to-trump-campaign-idUSKBN12G0ZH
8.   Seth Fiegerman, "Peter Thiel Joins Trump's Transition Team," CNN Money, November 11, 2016, https://money.cnn.com/2016/11/11/technology/peter-thiel-trump-team/index.html
9.   Clever, "About: Jobs," accessed November 14, 2018, https://clever.com/about/jobs
10.   Independent Institute, "About Us: Research Fellows—Peter Thiel," accessed November 14, 2018, http://www.independent.org/aboutus/person_detail.asp?id=456
11.   American Legislative Exchange Council, "Education Task Force" (2005), Internet Archive: Way Back Machine, accessed November 11, 2018, http://web.archive.org/web/20050204143455/http://www.alec.org/viewpage.cfm?pgname=5.02
12.   "Secretary of Education Calendar (June 29, 2017 – July 19, 2017)," Freedom of Information Act, accessed November 14, 2018, https://ed.gov/policy/gen/leg/foia/sec-calendar-july-2017.pdf
13.   Cooper Smith, "Peter Thiel, PayPal Founder, Funds 'Seasteading,' Libertarian Sea Colony," Huffington Post, August 19, 2011, https://www.huffingtonpost.com/2011/08/18/peter-thiel-seasteading_n_930595.html
14.   *Daily Mail Reporter*, "Floating Cities: PayPal Billionaire Plans to Build a Whole New Libertarian Colony off the Coast of San Francisco," Daily Mail, August 25, 2011, https://www.dailymail.co.uk/news/article-2024761/Atlas-Shrugged-Silicon-Valley-billionaire-reveals-plan-launch-floating-start-country-coast-San-Francisco.html

Joe Quirk, "Peter Thiel: Peter Thiel Speaks for 6 Minutes about Seasteading," Seasteading Blog September 25, 2018, https://www.seasteading.org/tag/peter_thiel/

Josh Gabbatiss, "World's First Floating City to Be Built off the Coast of French Polynesia by 2020," The Independent, November 14, 2017, https://www.independent.co.uk/news/science/floating-city-french-polynesia-2020-coast-islands-south-pacific-ocean-peter-thiel-seasteading-a8053836.html

Julia Carrie Wong, "Seasteading: Tech Leaders' Plans for Floating City Trouble French Polynesians," The Guardian: US Edition, January 2, 2017, https://www.theguardian.com/technology/2017/jan/02/seasteading-peter-thiel-french-polynesia

15. Ben Weider, "Thiel Fellowship Pays 24 Talented Students $100,000 Not to Attend College," Chronicle of Higher Education, May 25, 2011, https://www.chronicle.com/article/Thiel-Fellowship-Pays-24/127622

16. Maureen Dowd, "With … Peter Thiel: Peter Thiel, Trump's Tech Pal, Explains Himself," New York Times, January 11, 2017, https://www.nytimes.com/2017/01/11/fashion/peter-thiel-donald-trump-silicon-valley-technology-gawker.html

17. Ryan Lucas, "4 Insights About Blackwater Founder Erik Prince," National Public Radio, August 31, 2017, https://www.npr.org/2017/08/31/547546931/4-things-to-know-about-erik-prince

18. Maureen Dowd, "With … Peter Thiel: Peter Thiel, Trump's Tech Pal, Explains Himself," New York Times, January 11, 2017, https://www.nytimes.com/2017/01/11/fashion/peter-thiel-donald-trump-silicon-valley-technology-gawker.html

19. Eliana Johnson, "Donald Trump's 'Shadow President' in Silicon Valley," Politico, February 26, 2017, https://www.politico.com/story/2017/02/donald-trumps-shadow-president-in-silicon-valley-235372

20. Biz Carson, "Here's Who Sat Where During Trump's Big Meeting with Tech Leaders," Business Insider, December 14, 2016, https://www.businessinsider.com/trump-meeting-photo-jeff-bezos-elon-musk-tim-cook-2016-12

21. David Streitfeld, "'I'm Here to Help,' Trump Tells Tech Executives at Meeting," New York Times, December 14, 2016, https://www.nytimes.com/2016/12/14/technology/trump-tech-summit.html

22. Alex Newman, "Top Trump Officials Attend Globalist Bilderberg Summit. Why?," New American, June 2, 2017, https://www.thenewamerican.com/world-news/north-america/item/26162-top-trump-officials-attend-globalist-bilderberg-summit-why

Andrea Gagliarducci, "Analysis: Cardinal Parolin, Vatican Secretary of State, at the Elite Bilderberg Meeting," Catholic News Agency, June 6, 2018, https://www.catholicnewsagency.com/news/analysis-cardinal-parolin-at-the-elite-bilderberg-meeting-55996

America Online, "Global elites expected to discuss President Trump during secret Bilderberg meeting in VA," AOL News, June 2, 2017, https://www.aol.com/article/news/2017/06/02/global-elites-discuss-president-trump-secret-meeting-virginia-bilderberg/22122204/

Charlie Skelton, "Bilderberg 2017: Secret Meeting of Global Leaders Could Prove a Problem for Trump," The Guardian: US Edition, June 1, 2017, https://www.theguardian.com/us-news/2017/jun/01/bilderberg-trump-administration-secret-meeting

"Daniel Estulin Bilderberg Speech at EU Parliament Press Conference," Public Intelligence, https://publicintelligence.net/daniel-estulin-bilderberg-speech-at-eu-parliament-press-conference/

Daniel Estulin, The True Story of The Bilderberg Group (Walterville, OR: Trine Day, 2007), vii-x.

Ekin Karasin, "Secretive Group of Global Power Brokers, the Bilderberg Group, Set to Gather in Virginia to Mull Trump Era Including Elder Statesman Henry Kissinger and NATO Secretary," Daily Mail, May 31, 2017, https://www.dailymail.co.uk/news/article-4561054/Secretive-global-group-gathers-US-mull-Trump-era.html

Emma Niles, "Bilderberg 2017: Closed-Door Meeting of Global Leaders Will Focus on Trump 'Progress Report,'" Truthdig, June 3, 2017, https://www.truthdig.com/articles/bilderberg-2017-closed-door-meeting-of-global-leaders-will-focus-on-trump-progress-report/

"Secretive Bilderberg Group Meetings Begin in Virginia," BBC News, June 1, 2017, https://www.bbc.com/news/world-us-canada-40125253

23. Bruno Waterfield, "Dutch Prince Bernhard 'Was Member of Nazi Party,'" The Telegraph, March 5, 2010, https://www.telegraph.co.uk/news/worldnews/europe/netherlands/7377402/Dutch-Prince-Bernhard-was-member-of-Nazi-party.html

24. David Rockefeller, Memoirs, (New York: Random House, 2002), 411.

25. Ibid, 412.

26. Luke Rudkowski, "Exposed: Peter Thiel Goes on the Record about Bilderberg," We Are Change, June 12, 2016, https://wearechange.org/peter-thiel-goes-record-bilderberg/

27.   Andy Greenberg, "How A 'Deviant' Philosopher Built Palantir, A CIA-Funded Data-Mining Juggernaut," Forbes, September 2, 2013, https://www.forbes.com/sites/andygreenberg/2013/08/14/agent-of-intelligence-how-a-deviant-philosopher-built-palantir-a-cia-funded-data-mining-juggernaut/#381f4dae7785
Noam Cohen, "The Libertarian Logic of Peter Thiel," Wired Magazine, December 27, 2017, https://www.wired.com/story/the-libertarian-logic-of-peter-thiel/
28.   Spencer Woodman, "Palantir Provides the Engine for Donald Trump's Deportation Machine," The Intercept, March 2, 2017, https://theintercept.com/2017/03/02/palantir-provides-the-engine-for-donald-trumps-deportation-machine/
29.   Palantir, "Palantir Gotham: Applications," accessed November 14, 2018, https://www.palantir.com/palantir-gotham/applications/
30.   Lizette Chapman and Giles Turner, "Peter Thiel's Palantir Spreads Its Tentacles Throughout Europe," Bloomberg, February 23, 2017, https://www.bloomberg.com/news/articles/2017-02-24/peter-thiel-s-palantir-spreads-its-tentacles-throughout-europe
31.   Mark Harris, "How Peter Thiel's Secretive Data Company Pushed into Policing," August 9, 2017, https://www.wired.com/story/how-peter-thiels-secretive-data-company-pushed-into-policing/
Palantir, Palantir Cyber: An End-to-End Cyber Intelligence Platform for Analysis & Knowledge Management (Palo Alto, CA: Palantir Technologies, 2013), https://www.palantir.com/wp-assets/wp-content/uploads/2013/11/Palantir-Solution-Overview-Cyber-long.pdf
32.   Svea Herbst-Bayliss, "Cohen's SAC Taps Analytics Firm Palantir to Monitor Employees," Reuters, March 19, 2014, https://www.reuters.com/article/us-hedgefunds-sac/cohens-sac-taps-analytics-firm-palantir-to-monitor-employees-idUSBREA2I29F20140319
33.   Aditi Roy, "Peter Thiel's Tech Company, Palantir, Could Help Trump Crack Down on Undocumented Immigrants," CNBC News, March 7, 2017, https://www.cnbc.com/2017/03/07/peter-thiel-palantir-trump-immigrant-crackdown.html
Sam Biddle, "How Peter Thiel's Palantir Helped the NSA Spy on the Whole World," The Intercept, February 22, 2017, https://theintercept.com/2017/02/22/how-peter-thiels-palantir-helped-the-nsa-spy-on-the-whole-world/
34.   Tyler Durden, "Peter Thiel: Donald Trump 'Still Better' Than Clinton or 'The Republican Zombies,'" Zero Hedge, March 8, 2018, https://www.zerohedge.com/news/2018-03-07/peter-thiel-donald-trump-still-better-clinton-or-republican-zombies
35.   Ariel Zilber, 'It's Still Better Than Hillary Clinton or the Republican Zombies': Trump-Backing Tech Billionaire Peter Thiel Admits 'Things Have Fallen Short' During His First Year in Office but He Has No Regrets about Endorsing Him," Daily Mail, March 7, 2018, https://www.dailymail.co.uk/news/article-5474687/Trump-backing-mogul-Peter-Thiel-no-regrets-endorsing-him.html
36.   Alan Smith, "Trump's Meeting with a Major Tech CEO Reportedly Included a Discussion about a Potential Amazon-Pentagon Deal Worth Billions," Business Insider, April 4, 2018, https://www.businessinsider.com/trump-amazon-pentagon-contract-oracle-safra-catz-meeting-2018-4
37.   Nick Wakeman, "Palantir, Raytheon to Battle under $876M Army DCGS-A Contract," Washington Technology: The Authority for Government Contractors and Partners, March 12, 2018, https://washingtontechnology.com/blogs/editors-notebook/2018/03/palantir-raytheon-army-contract-award.aspx
38.   Dave Pettit, "Top 25 Tech Companies to Watch," Wall Street Journal, June 15, 2017, https://www.wsj.com/articles/top-25-tech-companies-to-watch-1497492480
39.   Knewton, "Pearson: MyLab and Mastering with Knewton Adaptive Learning," accessed November 14, 2018, http://learn.knewton.com/pearson
40.   PR Newswire Press Release, "Knewton Launches Alta, Fully Integrated Adaptive Learning Courseware for Higher Education, Putting Achievement in Reach for Everyone," Business Insider, January 17, 2018, https://markets.businessinsider.com/news/stocks/knewton-launches-alta-fully-integrated-adaptive-learning-courseware-for-higher-education-putting-achievement-in-reach-for-everyone-1013158890
41.   Knewton Inc., accessed August 24, 2018, https://www.knewtonalta.com/

Endnotes – Chapter Twelve

1.   United States, White House, "President Donald J. Trump Announces the White House Office of American Innovation (OAI)," Press Release, March 27, 2017, https://www.whitehouse.gov/briefings-statements/president-donald-j-trump-announces-white-house-office-american-innovation-oai/
2.   Ibid.

3.   Ryan Johnston, "Applications Open for Federal STEM Education Grant Programs," EdScoop, April 26, 2018, https://edscoop.com/applications-open-for-federal-stem-education-grant-programs/

4.   United States, White House, "Presidential Memorandum for Secretary of Education," Press Release, September 25, 2017, https://www.whitehouse.gov/presidential-actions/presidential-memorandum-secretary-education/

5.   Emily Tate, "White House official: Investing in computer science education will pay off," EdScoop, November 9, 2017, https://edscoop.com/white-house-official-investing-in-computer-science-education-will-pay-off/

6.   Kathy Kemper, "Digital Bipartisanship: Designers and Innovators," Huffington Post, August 18, 2017, https://www.huffingtonpost.com/entry/digital-bipartisanship-designers-and-innovators_us_59960826e4b02eb2fda31e4d

7.   Mikey Dickerson, "Why We Need You in Government," White House Blog, March 26, 2015, https://obamawhitehouse.archives.gov/blog/2015/03/26/why-we-need-you-government

8.   Michael D. Shear, "White House Picks Engineer from Google to Fix Sites," New York Times, August 11, 2014, https://www.nytimes.com/2014/08/12/us/politics/ex-google-engineer-to-lead-fix-it-team-for-government-websites.html
United States, Digital Service, "Home," US Digital Service: Building a More Awesome Government through Technology, accessed November 15, 2018, https://www.usds.gov/

9.   Ibid, Department of Education, College Scorecard, "Home," accessed November 15, 2018, https://collegescorecard.ed.gov/

10.   Ibid, "College Scorecard Data: Data Documentation," accessed November 15, 2018, https://collegescorecard.ed.gov/data/documentation/

11.   Ibid, Executive Office of the President, Using Federal Data to Measure and Improve the Performance of U.S. Institutions of Higher Education (January, 2017), https://collegescorecard.ed.gov/assets/UsingFederalDataToMeasureAndImprovePerformance.pdf

12.   Ibid, Department of Education, Institute of Education Sciences, National Center for Education Statistics, Integrated Postsecondary Education Data System, "Home," accessed November 15, 2018, https://nces.ed.gov/ipeds/

13.   Ibid, College Scorecard, "Home," accessed November 15, 2018, https://collegescorecard.ed.gov/
Ibid, "College Scorecard Data: Data Documentation," accessed November 15, 2018, https://collegescorecard.ed.gov/data/documentation/

14.   United States, White House, "President Donald J. Trump Announces the White House Office of American Innovation (OAI)," Press Release, March 27, 2017, https://www.whitehouse.gov/briefings-statements/president-donald-j-trump-announces-white-house-office-american-innovation-oai/

15.   Ibid.

16.   Ibid.

17.   Ibid, Department of State, "Biography: Dina Powell—Assistant Secretary, Educational and Cultural Affairs," Archive: 2001 – 2009, September 28, 2005, https://2001-2009.state.gov/outofdate/bios/p/49137.htm

18.   Ashley Parker and Philip Rucker, "Trump taps Kushner to lead a SWAT team to fix government with business ideas," Washington Post, March 26, 2017, https://www.washingtonpost.com/politics/trump-taps-kushner-to-lead-a-swat-team-to-fix-government-with-business-ideas/2017/03/26/9714a8b6-1254-11e7-ada0-1489b735b3a3_story.html?noredirect=on&utm_term=.1d4451aea556

19.   Council on Foreign Relations, "Membership Roster: L-P," accessed November 15, 2018, https://www.cfr.org/membership-roster-l-p
Jordan Fabian and Max Greenwood, "Dina Powell Leaving Trump White House," The Hill, December 8, 2017, https://thehill.com/homenews/administration/363970-wapo-dina-powell-leaving-white-house

20.   Alex Shephard, "Minutes: Jared Kushner's 'SWAT Team' to Run Government Like a Business Reveals What He Doesn't Know about Government (and Business)," New Republic, accessed November 15, 2018, https://newrepublic.com/minutes/141626/jared-kushners-swat-team-run-government-like-business-reveals-doesnt-know-government-and-business
Frank Konkel, "White House Office of American Innovation Lays out Priorities," Representative Will Hurd, 23rd District: Media Center—In the News, June 27, 2017, https://hurd.house.gov/me-

dia-center/in-the-news/white-house-office-american-innovation-lays-out-priorities

21.   Jonathan Shieber, "Trump to Create White House Office for 'American Innovation' to Be Headed by Kushner," TechCrunch, accessed November 15, 2018, https://techcrunch.com/2017/03/26/trump-to-create-white-house-office-for-american-innovation-to-be-headed-by-kushner/

22.   United States, White House, "The American Technology Council Summit to Modernize Government Services," Press Release, June 21, 2017, https://www.whitehouse.gov/articles/american-technology-council-summit-modernize-government-services/

23.   "Apple CEO Tim Cook Urges Trump To Mandate Coding In Schools," EdSurge, June 21, 2017, https://www.edsurge.com/news/2017-06-21-apple-ceo-tim-cook-urges-trump-to-mandate-coding-in-schools

24.   United States, White House, "President Trump Signs Presidential Memo to Increase Access to STEM and Computer Science Education," Press Release, September 25, 2017, https://www.whitehouse.gov/articles/president-trump-signs-presidential-memo-increase-access-stem-computer-science-education/

25.   Lisa Eadiciccio, "Apple Just Announced a New Cheaper iPad. Here's What to Know about It," Time, March 27, 2018, http://time.com/5215980/new-ipad-2018-price-release-apple/

26.   Peter High, "Possibly Elon Musk's Biggest Idea Yet—Revolutionizing Education," Forbes, September 18, 2017, https://www.forbes.com/sites/peterhigh/2017/09/18/possibly-elon-musks-biggest-idea-yet-revolutionizing-education/#38fcc3c48884

27.   Ibid.

Accessed August 24, 2018, https://learning.xprize.org/teams/

Accessed August 24, 2018, https://learning.xprize.org/teams/cci

Accessed August 24, 2018, https://learning.xprize.org/teams/chimple

Accessed August 24, 2018, https://learning.xprize.org/teams/kitkit-school

Accessed August 24, 2018, https://learning.xprize.org/teams/onebillion

Accessed August 24, 2018, https://learning.xprize.org/teams/robotutor

Shilo Rea and Byron Spice, "RoboTutor Team Led By Carnegie Mellon's Mostow Wins $1 Million as Global Learning XPRIZE Finalist: Learning Tool Will Be Field-Tested in Africa for 15 Months," Simon Initiative News, September 18, 2017, https://www.cmu.edu/simon/news/stories/robo-tutor-xprize-finalist.html

Will Housh, "Scalability: Choosing a Business Model That Will Grow Your Company," Entrepreneur, March 12, 2015, https://www.entrepreneur.com/article/243237

28.   Antoinette Siu, "Marc Benioff Wants to Make Bay Area Schools 'Best in Country,'" EdSurge, September 1, 2016, https://www.edsurge.com/news/2016-09-01-marc-benioff-wants-to-make-bay-area-schools-best-in-country

29.   Nancy Dahlberg, "Education-Tech Company Nearpod Enables Teacher 'Magic,'" Miami Herald, June 14, 2015, https://www.miamiherald.com/news/business/biz-monday/article23886562.html

30.   Heather Austin, "Personalized Learning with Nearpod," Nearpod Blog, July 11, 2016, https://nearpod.com/blog/personalized-learning-with-nearpod/

31.   Jodie Pozo-Olano, "What Your Edtech Product Needs to Get a Gold Star From Educators," Entrepreneur, November 28, 2017, https://www.entrepreneur.com/article/305070

32.   Nearpod, "Nearpod VR: Take Your Student on a Virtual Reality Adventure from Your Classroom," accessed November 15, 2018, https://nearpod.com/nearpod-vr

33.   Guido Kovalsky, "2014 Insights: Building Outstanding Learning Experiences with Nearpod," Nearpod Blog, December 23, 2014, https://nearpod.com/blog/2014-insights-building-outstanding-learning-experiences-with-nearpod/

34   Bill and Melinda Gates Foundation, "Gates Foundation Announces Finalists for $20 Million in Digital Courseware Investments," Press Room: Press Releases and Statements, September 30, 2014, https://www.gatesfoundation.org/Media-Center/Press-Releases/2014/09/Gates-Foundation-Announces-Finalists-for-$20-Million-in-Digital-Courseware-Investments

35.   Ibid, "Arizona State University: to Support the Creation of the Next Generation of Adaptive Courses to Enable Student Success," How We Work: Grants, July 12, 2013, https://www.gatesfoundation.org/How-We-Work/Quick-Links/Grants-Database/Grants/2013/07/OPP1093446

Ibid, "Board of Trustees of Essex County College: to Support the Creation of the Next Generation of Adaptive Courses to Enable Student Success," How We Work: Grants, July 17, 2013, https://www.gatesfoundation.org/How-We-Work/Quick-Links/Grants-Database/Grants/2013/07/OPP1093870

Ibid, "Board of Trustees of St. Petersburg College: to Support the Creation of the Next Generation of Adaptive Courses to Enable Student Success," How We Work: Grants, July 11, 2013, https://www.gatesfoundation.org/How-We-Work/Quick-Links/Grants-Database/Grants/2013/07/OPP1093910

Ibid, "Design Innovation Factory: to Refine and Expand Catalyst Writing and Reading, an Adaptive Learning Game and Assessment Platform for Grades 4-8," How We Work: Grants, July 1, 2013, https://www.gatesfoundation.org/How-We-Work/Quick-Links/Grants-Database/Grants/2013/07/OPP1093100

Ibid, "EduInnovation: to Support the Learning Platform Bundle that Will Serve as a Resource to Educators and Administrative/District Personnel to Inform Decisions on Platform Implementation and Adaptive Learning Apps in Their Schools," How We Work: Grants, May 8, 2015, https://www.gatesfoundation.org/How-We-Work/Quick-Links/Grants-Database/Grants/2015/05/OPP1131100

Ibid, "EnLearn: to Support the Development of an Adaptive Platform for Data-Driven Optimization of Digital Learning Environments," How We Work: Grants, November 19, 2012, https://www.gatesfoundation.org/How-We-Work/Quick-Links/Grants-Database/Grants/2012/11/OPP1066939

Ibid, "EnLearn: to Support and Enable the Development of Adaptive Digital Courseware That Can Contribute to a More Personalized Teaching and Learning Experience," How We Work: Grants, July 13, 2015, https://www.gatesfoundation.org/How-We-Work/Quick-Links/Grants-Database/Grants/2015/07/OPP1132937

Ibid, "Excelsior College: to Support the Creation of the Next Generation of Adaptive Courses to Enable Student Success," How We Work: Grants, July 3, 2013, https://www.gatesfoundation.org/How-We-Work/Quick-Links/Grants-Database/Grants/2013/07/OPP1093876

Ibid, "Gainesville State College Foundation, Inc: to Support the Creation of the Next Generation of Adaptive Courses to Enable Student Success," How We Work: Grants, July 9, 2013, https://www.gatesfoundation.org/How-We-Work/Quick-Links/Grants-Database/Grants/2013/07/OPP1093932

Ibid, "KIPP Bay Area Schools: to Expand the Use of Khan Academy's Adaptive Software Platform for Self-Paced Individualized and Mastery-Based Learning," How We Work: Grants, November 17, 2011, https://www.gatesfoundation.org/How-We-Work/Quick-Links/Grants-Database/Grants/2011/11/OPP1051527

Ibid, "Maricopa County Community College District: to Support the Creation of the Next Generation of Adaptive Courses to Enable Student Success," How We Work: Grants, July 10, 2013, https://www.gatesfoundation.org/How-We-Work/Quick-Links/Grants-Database/Grants/2013/07/OPP1093883

Ibid, "New Visions for Public Schools Inc.: to Build an Adaptive Learning Platform for the Reading and the Writing Process, for Grades 3-8. The System Offers Students Many Types of Help, Meaningful Feedback, and Different Content Approaches to Achieve Differentiated Instruction," How We Work: Grants, July 2013, https://www.gatesfoundation.org/How-We-Work/Quick-Links/Grants-Database/Grants/2013/07/OPP1093158

Ibid, "North Carolina State University : to Support the Creation of the Next Generation of Adaptive Courses to Enable Student Success," How We Work: Grants, July 15, 2013, https://www.gatesfoundation.org/How-We-Work/Quick-Links/Grants-Database/Grants/2013/07/OPP1093888

Ibid, "Northeastern University: to Support the Creation of the Next Generation of Adaptive Courses to Enable Student Success," How We Work: Grants, July, 2013, https://www.gatesfoundation.org/How-We-Work/Quick-Links/Grants-Database/Grants/2013/07/OPP1093894

Ibid, "Research Foundation of State University of New York: to Support the Creation of the Next Generation of Adaptive Courses to Enable Student Success," How We Work: Grants, July 19, 2013, https://www.gatesfoundation.org/How-We-Work/Quick-Links/Grants-Database/Grants/2013/07/OPP1093915

Ibid, "Saint Leo University Inc: to Support the Creation of the Next Generation of Adaptive Courses to Enable Student Success," How We Work: Grants, July 3, 2013, https://www.gatesfoundation.org/How-We-Work/Quick-Links/Grants-Database/Grants/2013/07/OPP1093900

Ibid, "Savannah Technical College: to Support the Creation of the Next Generation of Adaptive Courses to Enable Student Success," How We Work: Grants, July 13, 2013, https://www.gatesfoundation.org/How-We-Work/Quick-Links/Grants-Database/Grants/2013/07/OPP1093905

Ibid, "Triumph Learning, LLC: to Develop an Adaptive Learning Platform for Elementary and Middle School Reading and Writing," How We Work: Grants, July 22, 2013, https://www.gatesfoundation.org/How-We-Work/Quick-Links/Grants-Database/Grants/2013/07/OPP1092882

Ibid, "University of California, Davis: to Support the Creation of the Next Generation of Adaptive Courses to Enable Student Success," How We Work: Grants, August 9, 2013, https://www.gatesfoundation.org/How-We-Work/Quick-Links/Grants-Database/Grants/2013/08/OPP1093926

Ibid, "Worcester Polytechnic Institute: to Support the Creation of the Next Generation of Adaptive Courses to Enable Student Success," How We Work: Grants, August 9, 2013, https://www.gatesfoundation.org/How-We-Work/Quick-Links/Grants-Database/Grants/2013/08/OPP1093937

36.   Ibid, "Gates Foundation Announces Finalists for $20 Million in Digital Courseware Investments," Press Room: Press Releases and Statements, September 30, 2014, https://www.gatesfoundation.org/Media-Center/Press-Releases/2014/09/Gates-Foundation-Announces-Finalists-for-$20-Million-in-Digital-Courseware-Investments

37.   Joe Sommerald, "Bilderberg Group: What is the Secretive Gathering and Are Its Members Really Plotting the New World Order?," The Independent, June 1, 2018, https://www.independent.co.uk/news/world/europe/bilderberg-group-conspiracy-theories-secret-societies-new-world-order-alex-jones-a8377171.html

38.   International Business Machines, "IBM Watson Education: Transforming Learning Experiences with Watson AI," IBM Watson, accessed November 15, 2018, https://www.ibm.com/watson/education

39.   Dierdre Bosa and Harriet Taylor, "Some IBM Shareholders Are Losing Patience with Rometty's Big Salary," CNBC News, May 5, 2017, https://www.cnbc.com/2017/05/05/ibm-shareholders-criticize-rometty-salary.html

40.   Lynn Greiner, "Man Living with Machine: IBM's AI-Driven Watson Is Learning Quickly, Expanding to New Platforms," Financial Post, November 4, 2016, https://business.financialpost.com/technology/cio/man-living-with-machine-ibms-ai-driven-watson-is-learning-quickly-expanding-to-new-platforms

41.   Council on Foreign Relations, "Membership Roster: Q-U," accessed November 15, 2018, https://www.cfr.org/membership-roster-q-u

42.   Jonathan Shieber, "Trump to Create White House Office for 'American Innovation' to Be Headed by Kushner," TechCrunch, accessed November 15, 2018, https://techcrunch.com/2017/03/26/trump-to-create-white-house-office-for-american-innovation-to-be-headed-by-kushner/

43.   Alexa J. Henry, "K-12 Dealmaking: VIF International Education Makes Acquisition; Accelerate Learning, Bloomz Raise Fund," EdWeek: Market Brief, May 29, 2016, https://marketbrief.edweek.org/marketplace-k-12/k-12-dealmaking-vif-international-education-makes-acquisition-accelerate-learning-bloomz-raise-funds/

44.   Heather Kuldell, "Office of American Innovation Leader Takes New Job: Chris Liddell is the Latest in Staff Changes at the Tech-Focused Office," Nextgov, March 19, 2018, https://www.nextgov.com/cio-briefing/2018/03/office-american-innovation-leader-takes-new-job/146779/

45.   Emma Niles, "Bilderberg 2017: Closed-Door Meeting of Global Leaders Will Focus on Trump 'Progress Report,'" Truthdig, June 3, 2017, https://www.truthdig.com/articles/bilderberg-2017-closed-door-meeting-of-global-leaders-will-focus-on-trump-progress-report/

46.   United States, White House, "President Donald J. Trump Announces the White House Office of American Innovation (OAI)," Press Release, March 27, 2017, https://www.whitehouse.gov/briefings-statements/president-donald-j-trump-announces-white-house-office-american-innovation-oai/

47.   Andrew Kreighbaum, "White House, and Kushner, Dig Into Higher Ed," Inside Higher Ed, August 10, 2018, https://www.insidehighered.com/news/2018/08/10/kushner-team-convened-higher-ed-meeting-white-house-focused-accreditation

48.   Philissa Cramer, "An Unexpected Effect of the Common Core: Facilitating Jared Kushner's Political Awakening," Chalkbeat, August 2, 2017, https://www.chalkbeat.org/posts/us/2017/08/02/an-unexpected-effect-of-the-common-core-facilitating-jared-kushners-political-awakening/

49.   Michael D. Shear, "For Trump and DeVos, a Florida Private School Is a Model for Choice," March 3, 2017, https://www.nytimes.com/2017/03/03/us/politics/trump-devos-school-choice-florida.html

50.   Emma Brown, "DeVos Praises This Voucher-Like Program. Here's What It Means for School Reform," Washington Post, April 9, 2017, https://www.washingtonpost.com/local/education/devos-praises-this-voucher-like-program-heres-what-it-means-for-school-reform/2017/04/09/78b28f52-08f2-11e7-b77c-0047d15a24e0_story.html?noredirect=on&utm_term=.500790e53a43

Leslie Postal, Beth Kassab, and Annie Martin, "Schools Without Rules: An Orlando Sentinel Investigation Florida Private Schools Rake in Nearly $1 Billion in State Scholarships with Little Oversight (Part 1 of 3 Parts)," Orlando Sentinel, October 17, 2017, https://www.orlandosentinel.com/

features/education/os-florida-school-voucher-investigation-1018-htmlstory.html

51.   Jean Gonzalez, "President Trump Visits Orlando Catholic School," Florida Catholic, March 5, 2017, https://thefloridacatholic.org/2017/03/05/president-trump-visits-orlando-catholic-school/

52.   Democracy Forward Foundation, "DFF, *F&WW v. Office of American Innovation*: Demanding Transparency In the Kushner-led Innovation Office and its Role in Shaping Infrastructure Policy," Democracy Forward, February 5, 2018, https://democracyforward.org/work/dff-fww-v-office-american-innovation/#.W-469LpFz4j

Jessica Kwong, "Trump Administration Can't Hide Jared Kushner–Led Office From FOIA Requests, Watchdogs Claim in New Court Filing," Newsweek, June 12, 2018, https://www.newsweek.com/trump-administration-attempt-exempt-jared-kushners-office-foia-laws-opposed-973191

53.   Democracy Forward Foundation, "Groups Sue To Force Kushner-led Innovation Office To Follow Federal Transparency Rules And Reveal Role In Shaping Infrastructure Policy: By Avoiding Transparency Requirements, Kushner-Led Office Blocks Critical Information From Public View Including Potential Financial Conflicts," Democracy Forward Press Room, accessed November 15, 2018, https://democracyforward.org/press/groups-sue-force-kushner-led-innovation-office-follow-federal-transparency-rules-reveal-role-shaping-infrastructure-policy/#.W-48TrpFz4i

Democracy Forward Foundation and Food & Water Watch Inc. White House Office of American Innovation, Case 1:18-cv-00349, Document 1 (United States District for the District of Columbia, February 15, 2018), https://democracyforward.org/wp-content/uploads/2018/02/OAI-As-Filed.pdf

54.   Catherine Cortez Masto and Gary C. Peters, "Letter to the Honorable John F. Kelly, Chief of Staff to the President" (Washington DC: United States Senate, April 25, 2018), https://www.cortezmasto.senate.gov/imo/media/doc/WH%20OAI%20Letter%20Final.pdf

55.   Ibid.

56.   Ibid.

57.   Billy Mitchell, "Trump Tech Adviser Reed Cordish out After a Year," FedScoop, February 16, 2018, https://www.fedscoop.com/trump-tech-adviser-cordish-out-after-a-year/

58.   Ben Sales, "Jared and Ivanka Doing Their Own Thing as Observant Jews. And That's Normal," Forward, June 15, 2017, https://forward.com/news/national/374887/jared-and-ivanka-do-their-own-thing-as-observant-jews-and-that-s-normal/

59.   Judy Maltz, "Hundreds of Thousands in Donations Tie Kushners and Trump Chabad Movement," Haaretz, January 10, 2017, https://www.haaretz.com/us-news/.premium-donations-tie-kushners-and-trump-to-chabad-movement-1.5483641

Chabad Lubavitch World Headquarters, "About Us: About Chabad-Lubavitch," The Official Website of the Chabad Lubavitch Headquarters, accessed November 15, 2018, http://lubavitch.com/aboutus.html .

60.   Chabad-Lubavitch Media Center, "About Chabad Lubavitch," accessed November 15, 2018, https://www.chabad.org/library/article_cdo/aid/36226/jewish/About-Chabad-Lubavitch.htm

Ibid, "Learning & Values: Talmud—Study Talmud," accessed November 15, 2018, https://www.chabad.org/library/article_cdo/aid/2537589/jewish/Study-Talmud.htm

Chana Ya'ar, "Chabad is Zionist, Rabbi Says: A spokesman for the Chabad-Lubavitch Chassidic Movement Says the Sect is Zionist in Its Support for Israel," Arutz Sheva: Israel National News, July 20, 2011, http://www.israelnationalnews.com/News/News.aspx/145899

Nissan Dovid Dubov, "The Key to Kabbalah: Discovering Jewish Mysticism," Chabad-Lubavitch Media Center, accessed November 15, 2018, https://www.chabad.org/library/article_cdo/aid/361868/jewish/The-Key-to-Kabbalah.htm

Yehuda Shurpin, "What Is the Talmud?: How and Why Was the Oral Torah Written," Chabad-Lubavitch Media Center, accessed November 15, 2018, https://www.chabad.org/library/article_cdo/aid/3347866/jewish/What-Is-the-Talmud.htm

Yerachmiel Tilles, "What Is Kabbalah . . . And Why?," Chabad-Lubavitch Media Center, accessed November 15, 2018, https://www.chabad.org/kabbalah/article_cdo/aid/380664/jewish/What-is-Kabbalah-And-Why.htm

61.   Wayne Madsen, "Chabad Inside the White House: A Clear and Present National Security Danger," Intrepid Report, March 5, 2018, http://www.intrepidreport.com/archives/23512

Ibid, "Who We Are," Wayne Madsen Report, May 27, 2005, https://www.waynemadsenreport.com/categories/20070329

62.   Ibid, "Chabad Inside the White House: A Clear and Present National Security Danger,"

Intrepid Report, March 5, 2018, http://www.intrepidreport.com/archives/23512

Antony C. Sutton, America's Secret Establishment: An Introduction to the Order of Skull and Bones, Updated Reprint (Walterville, OR: Trine Day, 2002), 292, 294-296.

Central Intelligence Agency, "Bush as Director of Central Intelligence," News & Information, January 29, 2018, https://www.cia.gov/news-information/featured-story-archive/2016-featured-story-archive/bush-as-director-of-central-intelligence.html

COL Live Reporter, "Lubavitchers in the Israeli Mossad," COL Live Community News Center, February 11, 2014, https://www.collive.com/show_news.rtx?id=29033&alias=lubavitchers-in-the-israeli-mossad

Douglas Martin, "William P. Bundy, 83, Dies; Advised 3 Presidents on American Policy in Vietnam," New York Times, October 7, 2000, https://www.nytimes.com/2000/10/07/us/william-p-bundy-83-dies-advised-3-presidents-on-american-policy-in-vietnam.html

Eliezer Posner, "The Torah: The Two Talmuds," Chabad-Lubavitch Media Center, accessed November 16, 2018, https://www.chabad.org/library/article_cdo/aid/718279/jewish/The-Two-Talmuds.htm

Frederick Trubee Davison, "F. Trubee Davison Papers," Yale University Library: Finding Aid Database, accessed November 16, 2018, http://drs.library.yale.edu/HLTransformer/HLTransServlet?stylename=yul.ead2002.xhtml.xsl&pid=mssa:ms.0601&query=bahamas&clear-stylesheet-cache=yes&hlon=yes&filter=&hitPageStart=1

Nissan Dovid Dubov, "The History of Kabbalah: The Oral Tradition," Chabad-Lubavitch Media Center, accessed November 16, 2018, https://www.chabad.org/library/article_cdo/aid/361876/jewish/The-Oral-Tradition.htm

Paul Lewis, "Charles S. Whitehouse, 79, Diplomat and C.I.A. Official," New York Times, July 1, 2001, https://www.nytimes.com/2001/07/01/world/charles-s-whitehouse-79-diplomat-and-cia-official.html

Warren Goldstein, "William Sloane Coffin Jr.: A Holy Impatience," Yale University Press, January 11, 2006, https://yalebooks.yale.edu/book/9780300111545/william-sloane-coffin-jr

William F. Buckley Jr., "My Friend, E. Howard Hunt," Los Angeles Times, April 29, 2013, http://articles.latimes.com/2007/mar/04/opinion/op-buckley4

Yosef Eisen, "The Amoraim: The Babylonian Talmud," Chabad-Lubavitch Media Center, accessed November 16, 2018, https://www.chabad.org/library/article_cdo/aid/2652565/jewish/The-Babylonian-Talmud.htm

63. National Cable Satellite Corporation, "Wayne Madsen: On the C-SPAN Networks," C-SPAN: Created by Cable, accessed November 16, 2018, https://www.c-span.org/person/?waynemadsen

64. Wayne Madsen, "Chabad Inside the White House: A Clear and Present National Security Danger," Intrepid Report, March 5, 2018, http://www.intrepidreport.com/archives/23512

65. Tana Ganeva, "Here's What Jared Kushner and Ivanka Trump Plan to Do as Mueller Closes in," Raw Story, May 31, 2018, https://www.rawstory.com/2018/05/heres-jared-kushner-ivanka-trump-plan-mueller-closes/

66. Sean Illing, "3 Reasons Why Jared Kushner's Security Clearance Was Downgraded," Vox, March 1, 2018, https://www.vox.com/2018/3/1/17066666/kushner-security-clearance-downgraded-trump

67. Cristina Alesci, "Jared Kushner's Meetings under Investigation for Potential Conflict, OGE Letter Says," CNN News, March 27, 2018, https://www.cnn.com/2018/03/26/politics/jared-kushner-white-house-oge/index.html

Jesse Drucker, Kate Kelly, and Ben Protess, "Kushner's Family Business Received Loans After White House Meetings," New York Times, February 28, 2018, https://www.nytimes.com/2018/02/28/business/jared-kushner-apollo-citigroup-loans.html

68. Alistair Dawber, "Prisoner X: Ben Zygier Was 'Israel's Biggest Traitor' and 'Betrayed Prized Mossad Agents to Hezbollah,'" The Independent, March 25, 2013, https://www.independent.co.uk/news/world/middle-east/prisoner-x-ben-zygier-was-israels-biggest-traitor-and-betrayed-prized-mossad-agents-to-hezbollah-8548820.html

Barbara Bensoussan, "Community and Family: Tunisia's Russian Jewish Leader," Chabad-Lubavitch Media Center, accessed November 16, 2018, https://www.chabad.org/library/article_cdo/aid/1163700/jewish/Tunisias-Russian-Jewish-Leader.htm

Chabad News, "Finnish Politician Accuses Chabad of Mossad Ties," Crown Heights: Your News and Information Center, December 23, 2014, http://crownheights.info/chabad-news/465599/finnish-politician-accuses-chabad-of-mossad-ties/

Claus Mueller, "Former Israeli Soldiers 'Flipping Out' in India," Jewish Post: Your Gateway to the Jewish World, accessed November 16, 2018, http://www.jewishpost.com/culture/Former-Israeli-Soldiers-Flipping-Out-in-India.html

Dan Goldberg, 'Prisoner X' Leaked Mossad Intelligence to Iranian Businessman, New Book Claims," Haaretz, February 21, 2014, https://www.haaretz.com/zygier-leaked-intel-to-iranian-1.5324990

Dovid Zaklikowski, "Veteran Tunisian Rabbi Passes Away After Decades Serving North African Jewry," Jewish News, December 4, 2007, https://www.chabad.org/news/article_cdo/aid/606392/jewish/From-Russia-to-Tunis.htm

"Fort Kochi - Chabad Emissaries in India Deny Espionage Charge," Vos Iz Neias: The Voice of the Orthodox Jewish Community, February 7, 2012, https://www.vosizneias.com/100494/2012/02/07/fort-kochi-india-to-deport-chabad-couple-suspected-of-being-agents/

Konrad Marshall, "We Want Justice for Ben Zygier, Family Friend Says: Australian Man Who Died in an Israeli Prison Was 'a Soft, Gentle, Sensitive Young Man," The Age, February 14, 2013, https://www.theage.com.au/national/victoria/we-want-justice-for-ben-zygier-family-friend-says-20130214-2ef9r.html

Matthew Schwarzfeld, "Lost in Goa (Part 2): Their Passports Confiscated While Awaiting Trial, the Israelis Adjust to Life in Goa," Tablet Magazine, April 28, 2010, https://www.tabletmag.com/jewish-news-and-politics/32046/lost-in-goa-2

Wayne Madsen, "Chabad Inside the White House: A Clear and Present National Security Danger," Intrepid Report, March 5, 2018, http://www.intrepidreport.com/archives/23512

Will Jordan, "Spy Cables reveal Israel's Mossad Tactics: Leaked Cables Give Insight into Activities of Israel Intelligence Agents in South Africa," Al Jazeera, February 24, 2015, https://www.aljazeera.com/news/2015/02/spy-cables-reveal-israel-mossad-tactics-south-africa-guardian-150224124719957.html

69.		Wayne Madsen, "Chabad Inside the White House: A Clear and Present National Security Danger," Intrepid Report, March 5, 2018, http://www.intrepidreport.com/archives/23512

70.		Mendel Rivkin, "Technology & Spirituality, Compatible?," Chabad New Orleans Blog, January 28, 2011, https://www.chabadneworleans.com/templates/blog/post_cdo/aid/1203266/PostID/21082/sc/tw_share

71.		Ibid.

72.		United States, White House, "President Donald J. Trump Announces the White House Office of American Innovation (OAI)," Press Release, March 27, 2017, https://www.whitehouse.gov/briefings-statements/president-donald-j-trump-announces-white-house-office-american-innovation-oai/

73.		Nissan Dovid Dubov, "The History of Kabbalah: Abraham," Chabad-Lubavitch Media Center, accessed November 16, 2018, https://www.chabad.org/library/article_cdo/aid/361874/jewish/Abraham.htm

74.		Chabad-Lubavitch Media Center, "Kabbalah Online: Classic Kabbalah," Kabbalah Online: Kosher Kabbalah from the Holy City of Safed Israel, accessed November 16, 2018, https://www.chabad.org/kabbalah/article_cdo/aid/378725/jewish/Classic-Kabbalah.htm

"Occult," Merriam-Webster Dictionary, Merriam-Webster Inc., accessed November 16, 2018, https://www.merriam-webster.com/dictionary/occult

"Occult," Oxford English Dictionary, University of Oxford Press, accessed November 16, 2018, https://en.oxforddictionaries.com/definition/occult

Shimon bar Yochai, The Zohar, trans. Shmuel-Simcha Treister (Chabad-Lubavitch Media Center), "Classic Kabbalah," Kabbalah Online: Kosher Kabbalah from the Holy City of Safed Israel, accessed November 16, 2018, https://www.chabad.org/kabbalah/article_cdo/aid/378770/jewish/The-Zohar.htm

75.		Mendel Rivkin, "Technology & Spirituality, Compatible?," Chabad New Orleans Blog, January 28, 2011, https://www.chabadneworleans.com/templates/blog/post_cdo/aid/1203266/PostID/21082/sc/tw_share

76.		Simon Jacobson, "Toward a Meaningful Life: Technology," Chabad-Lubavitch Media Center, accessed November 16, 2018, https://www.chabad.org/therebbe/article_cdo/aid/60700/jewish/Technology.htm

Ibid, "Toward a Meaningful Life: The Future," Chabad-Lubavitch Media Center, accessed November 16, 2018, https://www.chabad.org/therebbe/article_cdo/aid/60702/jewish/The-Future.htm

77.		Chabad Staff, "The Rebbe: A Brief Biography," Chabad-Lubavitch Media Center, accessed

November 16, 2018, https://www.chabad.org/therebbe/article_cdo/aid/244372/jewish/The-Reb-be-A-Brief-Biography.htm

78. Dovid Zaklikowski, "Historical Correspondence with US Presidents: The Start of Education Day U.S.A.," Chabad-Lubavitch Media Center, accessed November 16, 2018, https://www.chabad.org/therebbe/article_cdo/aid/816546/jewish/The-Start-of-Education-Day-USA.htm

United States, White House, "President Donald J. Trump Proclaims April 7, 2017, as Education and Sharing Day, U.S.A.," Proclamations, April 6, 2017, https://www.whitehouse.gov/presidential-actions/president-donald-j-trump-proclaims-april-7-2017-education-sharing-day-u-s/

79. Mendel Rivkin, "Technology & Spirituality, Compatible?," Chabad New Orleans Blog, January 28, 2011, https://www.chabadneworleans.com/templates/blog/post_cdo/aid/1203266/PostID/21082/sc/tw_share

80. Bible (King James Version), 1 Revelation 13:18.

81. "Bio," RabbiUllman.com, accessed November 17, 2018, http://wp.rabbiullman.com/

82. "Six, Six, Six," Ask the Rabbi, accessed November 17, 2018, https://ohr.edu/ask_db/ask_main.php/277/Q1/

83. Charles V. Bagli, "At Kushners' Flagship Building, Mounting Debt and a Foundered Deal," New York Times, April 3, 2017, https://www.nytimes.com/2017/04/03/nyregion/kushner-companies-666-fifth-avenue.html

84. Josh Nathan-Kazis, "Jared Kushner and the White-Haired Mystic Whose Dad 'Got a Ride' From a Dead Sage," The Forward, January 29, 2017, https://forward.com/news/361035/jared-kushner-and-the-white-haired-mystic-whose-dad-got-a-ride-from-a-dead/

85. Ibid.

86. Ibid.

87. Raanan Ben Zur, "Rabbi Pinto Released from Prison," Ynetnews, January, 25, 2017, https://www.ynetnews.com/articles/0,7340,L-4912546,00.html

Yedioth Media Group, "About Ynetnews," Ynetnews, accessed November 17, 2018, https://www.ynetnews.com/articles/0,7340,L-3028645,00.html

Yonah Jeremy Bob, "Rabbi Yoshiyahu Yosef Pinto Enters Prison," Jerusalem Post, February 16, 2016, https://www.jpost.com/Israel-News/Rabbi-Pinto-headed-to-prison-to-begin-1-year-sentence-445047

88. Toi Staff, "Judaism's Greatest Mystical Text 'Predicts Trump Victory,' Israel GOP Head Reveals," Times of Israel, November 2, 2016, https://www.timesofisrael.com/mystical-zohar-predicts-trump-victory-israel-gop-head-reveals/

89. Ibid, "Trump's Daughter, Son-in-Law, Visit Lubbavitcher Rebbe," November 6, 2016, https://www.timesofisrael.com/trumps-daughter-son-in-law-visit-lubavitcher-rebbe/

90. Ibid.

91. Ibid.

92. Ari Feldman, "Is Ivanka Trump Getting into Kabbalah with Red Thread Bracelet?" The Forward, November 3, 2017, https://forward.com/fast-forward/386850/is-ivanka-trump-getting-into-kabbalah-with-red-thread-bracelet/

Eric Cortellessa, "Jared Kushner Once Broke up with Ivanka Trump Because She Wasn't Jewish," Times of Israel, August 17, 2016, https://www.timesofisrael.com/jared-kushner-once-broke-up-with-ivanka-trump-because-she-wasnt-jewish/

Steven Bertoni, "Jared Kushner's Complex World: How Jared's Liberal Brother Runs a Billion Dollar Fund in Trump Era," Forbes, April 25, 2017, https://www.forbes.com/sites/stevenbertoni/2017/04/10/josh-kushners-complicated-world-how-jareds-brother-runs-a-billion-dollar-fund-in-the-age-of-trump/#7527d66f2409

Sarah Ellison, "Inside Ivanka and Tiffany Trump's Complicated Sister Act," Vanity Fair, December 22, 2016, https://www.vanityfair.com/news/2016/12/inside-ivanka-trump-and-tiffany-trump-complicated-sister-act

93. University of California Los Angeles, Department of Anthropology, "People: Aomar Boum—Associate Professor & Vice Chair of Undergraduate Studies," UCLA Social Sciences Division: Department of Anthropology, accessed November 17, 2018, https://www.anthro.ucla.edu/faculty/aomar-boum

94. Aomar Boum, "A Moroccan Kabbalist in the White House: Understanding the Relationship between Jared Kushner and Moroccan Jewish Mysticism," Jewish Social Studies: History, Culture, Society, 22 no. 3 (2017): 146.

95. Ibid.

96. Ibid.

Endnotes -- Chapter Thirteen

1   Antony C. Sutton, Western Technology and Soviet Economic Development (1917-1930): First Volume of a Three Volume Series (Stanford University, CA: Hoover Institution Press, 1968).
Ibid, Western Technology and Soviet Economic Development (1930-1945): Second Volume of a Three Volume Series (Stanford University, CA: Hoover Institution Press, 1971).
Ibid, Western Technology and Soviet Economic Development (1945-1965): Third Volume of a Three Volume Series (Stanford University, CA: Hoover Institution Press, 1973).
2   Ibid, America's Secret Establishment: An Introduction to the Order of Skull and Bones, Updated Reprint (Walterville, OR: Trine Day, 2002), 113-182.
3   Charlotte Thomson Iserbyt, in discussion with this author (John Klyczek), November 16, 2018.
4   Antony C. Sutton, America's Secret Establishment: An Introduction to the Order of Skull and Bones, Updated Reprint (Walterville, OR: Trine Day, 2002), 299.
5   Kelly O'Meara Morales, "Treasury Secretary Steven Mnuchin Insists That Davos Is Not 'A Hangout for Globalists,'" The Week, January 11, 2018, https://theweek.com/speedreads/748299/treasury-secretary-steven-mnuchin-insists-that-davos-not-hangout-globalists
Jen Wieczner, "Trump Treasury Pick Mnuchin Is Much Richer Than Most People Thought," Fortune, January 11, 2017, http://fortune.com/2017/01/11/trump-cabinet-steven-mnuchin-net-worth/
Szu Ping Chan and Harriet Alexander, "Profile: Steven Mnuchin, the Man Who Went from Goldman Sachs to US Treasury Secretary," The Telegraph, February 14, 2017, https://www.telegraph.co.uk/business/2016/11/30/steven-mnuchin-man-went-goldman-sachs-us-treasury-secretary/
6   Donald J. Trump, Executive Order 13794—Establishment of the American Technology Council (Washington, DC: Government Publishing Office, April 28, 2017), https://www.gpo.gov/fdsys/pkg/DCPD-201700297/pdf/DCPD-201700297.pdf
7   Janko Roettgers, "Trump Touts Government Tech Reform As Execs from Apple, Amazon, Google Visit White House," Variety, June 19, 2017, https://variety.com/2017/digital/news/tech-council-white-house-1202470275/
8   Tyler Durden, "The Full List of Incredibly Powerful People Who Will Attend This Year's Bilderberg Meeting," Business Insider, June 3, 2013, https://www.businessinsider.com/full-list-of-bilderberg-2013-attendees-2013-6
9   Janko Roettgers, "Trump Touts Government Tech Reform As Execs from Apple, Amazon, Google Visit White House," Variety, June 19, 2017, https://variety.com/2017/digital/news/tech-council-white-house-1202470275/
10   United States, 115th Congress, "Public Law No. 115-97," H.R.1 - An Act to Provide for Reconciliation Pursuant to Titles II and V of the Concurrent Resolution on the Budget for Fiscal Year 2018 (Washington, DC: Government Publishing Office, December 22, 2017), https://www.congress.gov/bill/115th-congress/house-bill/1/text
11   Annie Karni and Eliana Johnson, "Republicans Fret Over White House Sales Job on Taxes," Politico, November 26, 2017, https://www.politico.com/story/2017/11/26/white-house-taxes-push-democrats-259708
12   Jim Puzzanghera, "Mnuchin Warns of 'Significant' Stock Market Drop if Tax Reform Fails," Los Angeles Times, October 18, 2017, http://www.latimes.com/business/la-fi-mnuchin-taxes-stock-market-20171018-htmlstory.html
13   Susie Cummings, "Tax Bill Favors Adding Robots Over Workers, Critics Say," National Public Radio, December 8, 2017, https://www.npr.org/2017/12/08/569118310/tax-bill-favors-adding-robots-over-workers-critics-say
14   Stephen Lendman, "GOP Tax Cut Scam Is a Jobs Killer. Transfers Wealth to the Super-Rich," Centre for Research on Globalization, January 26, 2018, https://www.globalresearch.ca/gop-tax-cut-scam-is-a-jobs-killer-transfers-wealth-to-the-super-rich/5627269
15   David Randall, "U.S. Investors See More Automation, Not Jobs, under Trump Administration," Reuters, January 19, 2017, https://www.reuters.com/article/us-usa-funds-automation/u-s-investors-see-more-automation-not-jobs-under-trump-administration-idUSKBN1530JW
Robert A. Green, "How To Fix The Tax Code So It Doesn't Favor Robots Over Humans," Forbes, May 30, 2017, https://www.forbes.com/sites/greatspeculations/2017/05/30/how-to-fix-tax-reform-so-it-doesnt-favor-robots-over-humans/#719deb6c2d09
16   David Randall, "Tax-Cut Plan Prompts Fund Managers to Bet on Automation," Reuters, October 6, 2017, https://www.reuters.com/article/us-usa-stocks-weekahead/tax-cut-plan-prompts-fund-managers-to-bet-on-automation-idUSKBN1CB1A9

17   FARO Technologies Inc., "Solutions—Industries: Education," accessed November 17, 2018, https://www.faro.com/industry/education/

18   Trilateral Commission, "Members in the News: January 24 – January 30, 2018," accessed November 17, http://trilateral.org/news.list

19   Luis Rubio, "Trump and Manufactured Goods (English trans.)," Trilateral Commission, accessed November 17, 2018, http://trilateral.org/download/files/News/RUBIO_TRUMP_AND_MANUFACTURED_GOODS.pdf

20   Andrew Soergel, "Mnuchin 'Not At All' Worried About Automation Displacing Jobs," US News, March 24, 2017, https://www.usnews.com/news/articles/2017-03-24/steven-mnuchin-not-at-all-worried-about-automation-displacing-jobs

21   Shannon Vavra, "Mnuchin Walks Back AI Statement," Axios, May 24, 2017, https://www.axios.com/mnuchin-walks-back-ai-statement-1513302559-fc72ba82-ea8f-46cc-87d7-517e6939004e.html

22   Antony C. Sutton, *America's Secret Establishment: An Introduction to the Order of Skull and Bones*, Updated Reprint (Walterville, OR: Trine Day, 2002), 5, 8, 66.

23   Ibid, 113-182.

24   "Command and Control," Cambridge Dictionary, Cambridge University Press, accessed November 17, 2018, https://dictionary.cambridge.org/us/dictionary/english/command-and-control

     United States, Declaration of Independence, July 4, 1776, https://www.ourdocuments.gov/doc.php?flash=true&doc=2&page=transcript

     Ibid, United States Constitution, "Bill of Rights," 1791, https://www.archives.gov/founding-docs/constitution

25   Antony C. Sutton, *America's Secret Establishment: An Introduction to the Order of Skull and Bones*, Updated Reprint (Walterville, OR: Trine Day, 2002), 61-111.

26   Carnegie Institute of Washington, Yearbook No. 1: 1902 (Washington DC: Judo and Detweiler, 1903), 197-225.

     Charles R. Lanman, "Daniel Coit Gilman (1831-1908)," Daniel Coit Gilman (1831-1908)Daniel Coit Gilman (1831-1908)*Proceedings of the American Academy of Arts and Sciences 52 no. 13 (1917): 836-839.*

     David Lee Seim, "'Perhaps We Can Hit upon Some Medium of Course': Rockefeller Philanthropy, Economic Research, and the Structure of Social Science—1911-1946," Iowa State University Digital Repository: Retrospective Theses and Dissertations (2007), https://lib.dr.iastate.edu/cgi/viewcontent.cgi?article=16501&context=rtd

     David Madsen, "Daniel Coit Gilman at the Carnegie Institution of Washington," History of Education Quarterly 9 no. 2 (1969): 154-186.

     Editors of the Encyclopedia Britannica, "Daniel Coit Gilman: American Educator," Encyclopedia Britannica, October 9, 2018, https://www.britannica.com/biography/Daniel-Coit-Gilman

27   Kevin Knight, "Illuminati," *New Advent Catholic Encyclopedia*, accessed November 17, 2018, http://www.newadvent.org/cathen/07661b.htm

28   Editors of the Encyclopedia Britannica, "Illuminati," Encyclopedia Britannica, accessed November 17, 2018, https://www.britannica.com/topic/illuminati-group-designation#ref1250318

29   Isabel Hernández, "Meet the Man Who Started the Illuminati," National Geographic, accessed November 17, 2018, https://www.nationalgeographic.com/archaeology-and-history/magazine/2016/07-08/profile-adam-weishaupt-illuminati-secret-society/

     Matthew Vickery, "The Birthplace of the Illuminati," BBC, November 28, 2017, http://www.bbc.com/travel/story/20171127-the-birthplace-of-the-illuminati

30   Antony C. Sutton, America's Secret Establishment: An Introduction to the Order of Skull and Bones, Updated Reprint (Walterville, OR: Trine Day, 2002), 5.

31   Ibid.

32   Ibid, 6.

33   Order of the File and Claw, "The Fall of Skull and Bones: Compiled from the Minutes of the 76th Regular Meeting of the Order of the File and Claw, 9,29,76" (1876) quoted in *America's Secret Establishment: An Introduction to the Order of Skull and Bones*, eds. Antony C. Sutton and Kris Millegan (Walterville, OR: Trine Day, 2002), 233.

34   Kris Millegan, "Mind Control, The Illuminati and the JFK Assassination," Fleshing Out Skull and Bones: Investigations into America's Most Powerful Secret Society, ed. Kris Millegan (OR: Trine Day, 2003), 192.

35   Ibid.

36   George Washington, The Writings of George Washington: Volume 14, 1798-1799 (New York, G. P. Putmans Sons, 1893): 119.

G. W. Snydere, "Letter to George Washington from G. W. Snyder, 22 August 1798," National Archives and Records Administration (United States: National Historical Publications & Records Commission), accessed November 17, 2018, https://founders.archives.gov/documents/Washington/06-02-02-0435

37   Antony C. Sutton, America's Secret Establishment: An Introduction to the Order of Skull and Bones, Updated Reprint (Walterville, OR: Trine Day, 2002), 213-214.

38   Ron Rosenbaum, "The Last Secrets of Skull and Bones," Esquire, September 1, 1977, http://classic.esquire.com/the-last-secrets-of-skull-and-bones/

39   Order of the File and Claw, "The Fall of Skull and Bones: Compiled from the Minutes of the 76th Regular Meeting of the Order of the File and Claw, 9,29,76" (1876) quoted in America's Secret Establishment: An Introduction to the Order of Skull and Bones, eds. Antony C. Sutton and Kris Millegan (Walterville, OR: Trine Day, 2002), 233.

40   Ron Rosenbaum, "The Last Secrets of Skull and Bones," Esquire, September 1, 1977, http://classic.esquire.com/the-last-secrets-of-skull-and-bones/

41   John Robison, Proofs of a Conspiracy Against All the Religions and Governments of Europe, Carried on in the Secret Meetings of Freemasons, Illuminati and Reading Societies (1798), Reprint (London: Forgotten Books, 2008), 5, 6.

42   University of Edinburgh, "John Robison (1739-1805): Professor of Natural Philosophy (1773-1805)," Our History, accessed November, 17, 2018, http://ourhistory.is.ed.ac.uk/index.php/John_Robison_(1739-1805)

43   Mark Dilworth, "Horn, Alexander (1762–1820)," Oxford Dictionary of National Biography, accessed November 17, 2018, http://www.oxforddnb.com/view/10.1093/ref:odnb/9780198614128.001.0001/odnb-9780198614128-e-51261?rskey=QxcYCm&result=1

44   John Robison, Proofs of a Conspiracy Against All the Religions and Governments of Europe, Carried on in the Secret Meetings of Freemasons, Illuminati and Reading Societies (1798), Reprint (London: Forgotten Books, 2008), 101.

45   Kevin Knight, "Augustin Barruel," New Advent Catholic Encyclopedia, accessed November 17, 2018, http://www.newadvent.org/cathen/02310a.htm

F. M. Rickard, Ars Quatuor Coronatorum: Transactions of the Quatuor Coronati Lodge No. 2076 Vol. L. (London: W. J. Parrett Ltd., 1940), 33-34, 41-42, 47-49, 54, 56, 58, 61-62, 64-65, 68-69.

46   Ron Rosenbaum, "The Last Secrets of Skull and Bones," Esquire, September 1, 1977, http://classic.esquire.com/the-last-secrets-of-skull-and-bones/

47   Antony C. Sutton, America's Secret Establishment: An Introduction to the Order of Skull and Bones, Updated Reprint (Walterville, OR: Trine Day, 2002), 63.

48   Ibid, 77-79.

49   Ibid, 79.

50   Ibid.

51   Ibid.

52   Ibid.

53   Ibid, 86.

54   Paolo Lionni, The Leipzig Connection: The Systematic Destruction of American Education, Third Printing (Sheridan, OR: Delphian Press, 1988), 43-89.

55   B. F. Skinner, The Technology of Teaching (New York: Appleton-Century-Crofts, 1968), viii.

56   Ibid, 128-129.

57   Antony C. Sutton, America's Secret Establishment: An Introduction to the Order of Skull and Bones, Updated Reprint (Walterville, OR: Trine Day, 2002), 61-111.

"Percy Rockefeller, Nephew of John D., Passes Away: Leaves Millions, His Fortune Fabulous," Lewiston Morning Tribune, September 26, 1934, https://news.google.com/newspapers?id=rq-9fAAAAIBAJ&sjid=zzIMAAAAIBAJ&pg=1477,1491319&dq=percy+rockefeller&hl=en

58   Charles R. Lanman, "Daniel Coit Gilman (1831-1908)," Daniel Coit Gilman (1831-1908) Daniel Coit Gilman (1831-1908)Proceedings of the American Academy of Arts and Sciences 52 no. 13 (1917): 836-839.

David Lee Seim, "'Perhaps We Can Hit upon Some Medium of Course': Rockefeller Philanthropy, Economic Research, and the Structure of Social Science—1911-1946," Iowa State University Digital Repository: Retrospective Theses and Dissertations (2007), https://lib.dr.iastate.edu/cgi/viewcontent.cgi?article=16501&context=rtd

59	Paolo Lionni, *The Leipzig Connection: The Systematic Destruction of American Education*, Third Printing (Sheridan, OR: Delphian Press, 1988), 29-41, 61-65, 72, 78-81.
60	Ibid, 61.
Edward Lee Thorndike, Education: A First Book, (New York: Macmillan Company, 1914), 165.
61	Aomar Boum, "A Moroccan Kabbalist in the White House: Understanding the Relationship between Jared Kushner and Moroccan Jewish Mysticism," Jewish Social Studies: History, Culture, Society, 22 no. 3 (2017): 146.

BIBLIOGRAPHY

Alabama Department of Archives and History, "Albert Pike (1809-1891): Brigadier General," Confederate Officers Photograph Album, accessed November 18, 2018, http://www.archives.alabama.gov/conoffalb/photo135.html

Albert Gallatin Mackey, *The History of Freemasonry* (1898), Reprint (New York: Barnes & Noble, 1998), 350, 353-354.

Albert Pike, *Morals and Dogma of the Ancient and Accepted Rite of Freemasonry* (1871), Reprint (Radford, VA: Wilder Publications, 2011), 653.

Congresswoman Eleanor Holmes Norton (Representing the District of Columbia), "Norton Introduces Bill to Remove Statue of Confederate General Pike from Judiciary Square," News and Media Center: Press Releases, October 5, 2017, https://norton.house.gov/media-center/press-releases/norton-introduces-bill-to-remove-statue-of-confederate-general-pike-from

El Paso Scottish Rite Orient of Texas, "Our Building: The Albert Pike Room," accessed November 18, 2018, http://www.elpasoscottishrite.org/albert-pike-room.html

Heather Morrison, "Pursuing Enlightenment in Vienna," Louisiana State University Digital Commons: LSU Dissertations (2005), https://digitalcommons.lsu.edu/cgi/viewcontent.cgi?article=2623&context=gradschool_dissertations

Isabel Hernández, "Meet the Man Who Started the Illuminati," National Geographic, accessed November 17, 2018, https://www.nationalgeographic.com/archaeology-and-history/magazine/2016/07-08/profile-adam-weishaupt-illuminati-secret-society/

Josh Nathan-Kazis, "Jared Kushner and the White-Haired Mystic Whose Dad 'Got a Ride' From a Dead Sage," The Forward, January 29, 2017, https://forward.com/news/361035/jared-kushner-and-the-white-haired-mystic-whose-dad-got-a-ride-from-a-dead/

Louis A Watres, "The George Washington Masonic National Memorial," The Builder Magazine 8 no. 7 (1922), http://www.phoenixmasonry.org/the_builder_1922_july.htm

Mendel Rivkin, "Technology & Spirituality, Compatible?," Chabad New Orleans Blog, January 28, 2011, https://www.chabadneworleans.com/templates/blog/post_cdo/aid/1203266/PostID/21082/sc/tw_share

Paul Marshall Allen and Joan deRis Allen, The Time Is at Hand!: The Rosicrucian Nature of Goethe's Fairy Tale of the Green Snake and the Beautiful Lily and The Mystery Dramas of Rudolf Steiner (Hudson, NY: Anthroposophic Press, 1995).

Rudolph Steiner and Marie Steiner-von Sivers, "The Temple Legend: Goethe and His Connections to Rosicrucianism," (1906) Rudolph Steiner Archive & e.Library, January 15, 2013, https://wn.rsarchive.org/Lectures/GA093/English/RSP1985/TmpLeg_goethe.html

Rudolph Steiner, "Theosophy of the Rosicrucian: The New Form of Wisdom," (1907) Rudolph Steiner Archive & e.Library, July 4, 2002, https://wn.rsarchive.org/Lectures/GA099/English/RSP1966/19070522p01.html

Simon Jacobson, "Toward a Meaningful Life: Technology," Chabad-Lubavitch Media Center, accessed November 16, 2018, https://www.chabad.org/therebbe/article_cdo/aid/60700/jewish/Technology.htm

Ibid, "Toward a Meaningful Life: The Future," Chabad-Lubavitch Media Center, accessed November 16, 2018, https://www.chabad.org/therebbe/article_cdo/aid/60702/jewish/The-Future.htm

"Six, Six, Six," Ask the Rabbi, accessed November 17, 2018, https://ohr.edu/ask_db/ask_main.php/277/Q1/

Stephen Dafoe, "Masonic Biographies: Albert Mackey," accessed November 18, 2018, The Masonic Dictionary, http://www.masonicdictionary.com/mackey.html

Supreme Grand Lodge of the Ancient and Mystical Order Rosae Crucis, "History: The Ancient and Mystical Order Rosae Crucis History," AMORC, accessed November 17, 2018, https://www.amorc.org/history

Toi Staff, "Judaism's Greatest Mystical Text 'Predicts Trump Victory,' Israel GOP Head Reveals," Times of Israel, November 2, 2016, https://www.timesofisrael.com/mystical-zohar-predicts-trump-victory-israel-gop-head-reveals/

Ibid, "Trump's Daughter, Son-in-Law, Visit Lubbavitcher Rebbe," November 6, 2016, https://www.timesofisrael.com/trumps-daughter-son-in-law-visit-lubavitcher-rebbe/

United States, White House, "Presidential Memorandum on The White House Office of American Innovation," Presidential Memorandums, March 27, 2017, https://www.whitehouse.gov/presidential-actions/presidential-memorandum-white-house-office-american-innovation/

Endnotes – Chapter Fourteen

1.	MITx and HarvardX Dataverse, The Presidents & Fellows of Harvard College, accessed November 8, 2018, https://dataverse.harvard.edu/dataverse/mxhx

2.	Charles Darwin, On the Origin of Species by Means of Natural Selection: Or the Preservation of Favoured Races in the Struggle for Life (1859), Reprint (New York: Heritage Press, 1963), iii.

3.	John Taylor Gatto, "Against School," in Rereading America: Cultural Contexts for Critical Thinking and Writing, 9th edition, eds. Gary Colombo, Robert Cullen, Bonnie Lisle (Boston: Bedford/St. Martin's, 2013), 147.

4.	R. E. Fancher, "Scientific Cousins: The Relationship between Charles Darwin and Francis Galton," American Journal of Psychology 64 no. 2 (2009): 84-92.

5.	Francis Galton, Hereditary Genius: An Inquiry into Its Laws and Consequences (New York: MacMillan and Co., 1869), 1.

Ibid, Inquiries Into Human Faculty and Its Development (New York: Macmillan and Co., 1883), 24-25.

6.	Anton Weiss-Wendt and Rory Yeomans, "Racial Science in Hitler's New Europe, 1938-1945," University of Nebraska-Lincoln Digital Commons: University of Nebraska Press—Sample Books and Chapters (2013), https://digitalcommons.unl.edu/cgi/viewcontent.cgi?article=1190&context=unpresssamples

7.	Cold Spring Harbor Laboratory, "Special Collections: Carnegie Institution of Washington," CSHL Library and Archives, accessed November 18, 2018, http://library.cshl.edu/special-collections/carnegie-institution-of-washington

James Watson, "The Connection between American Eugenics and Nazi Germany," CSHL DNA Learning Center: Preparing Students and Families to Thrive in the Gene Age, accessed November 18, 2018, https://www.dnalc.org/view/15466-The-

8.	Andrea Alfano, "Good Genes, Bad Science," Cold Spring Harbor Laboratory Newsstand, October 15, 2017, https://www.cshl.edu/good-genes-bad-science/

9.	State of Indiana, "Historical Markers: 1907 Eugenics Law," Indiana Historical Bureau, accessed November 18, 2018, https://www.in.gov/history/markers/524.htm

10.	E. S. Gosney and Paul Popenoe, Sterilization for Human Betterment: A Summary of the Results of 6,000 Operations in California, 1909-1929(New York: Macmillan, 1931), xii.

11.	Ibid, 116.

12.	Nosmot Gbadamosi, "Human Exhibits and Sterilization: The Fate of Afro Germans under Nazis," CNN, July 26, 2017, https://www.cnn.com/2017/07/21/world/black-during-the-holocaust-rhineland-children-film/index.html

13.	Henry P. David, Jochen Fleischhacker, Charlotte Höhn, "Abortion and Eugenics in Nazi Germany," Population and Development Review 14 no. 1 (1988): 81-112.

14.	Michael Berenbaum, "T4 Euthanasia Program: Nazi Policy," Encyclopedia Britannica, accessed November 18, https://www.britannica.com/event/T4-Program

15.	Sara Goer, "Eugenics," Stanford Encyclopedia of Philosophy, July 2, 2014, https://plato.stanford.edu/entries/eugenics/

16.	Adolph Hitler quoted in Otto Wagener, Hitler Memoirs of a Confidant, trans. Henry Ashby Turner (Yale University Press, 1987), quoted in Edwin Black, War Against the Weak: Eugenics and America's Campaign to Create a Master Race (New York: Four Walls Eight Windows, 2003), 275-276. Stefan Kühl, The Nazi Connection: Eugenics, American Racism, and German National Socialism (Oxford: Oxford University Press, 1994), 85.

17.	Edwin Black, War Against the Weak: Eugenics and America's Campaign to Create a Master Race (New York: Four Walls Eight Windows, 2003).

18.	Stefan Kühl, The Nazi Connection: Eugenics, American Racism, and German National Socialism (Oxford: Oxford University Press, 1994).

19.	Daniel Kevles, In the Name of Eugenics: Genetics and the Uses of Human Heredity (New York: Alfred A. Knopf, 1985).

20.	Edwin Black, War Against the Weak: Eugenics and America's Campaign to Create a Master Race (New York: Four Walls Eight Windows, 2003), 425.

Galton Institute, "About," Galton Institute: Exploring Human Heredity, accessed November 18, 2018, http://www.galtoninstitute.org.uk/about/

Michael Holland, Anselm Huelsbergen, Gary Cox, Alla Barabtarlo, Karen Witt, Erin Zellers, Amy Jones, and Kelli Hansen, Controlling Heredity: The American Eugenics Crusade: 1870 – 1940, The Missouri University Life Sciences and Society Program and the Missouri University Libraries' Special Collections and Rare Books, 5 May 2011, http://mulibraries.missouri.edu/specialcollections/exhibits/eugenics/

Rachel Gur-Arie, "American Eugenics Society (1926-1972)," Embryo Project Encyclopedia at Arizona State University, November 22, 2014, https://embryo.asu.edu/pages/american-eugenics-society-1926-1972

Stefan Kühl, The Nazi Connection: Eugenics, American Racism, and German National Socialism (Oxford: Oxford University Press, 1994), 32.

21. John Timson, "Portraits of the Pioneers: Julian Huxley," Galton Institute Newsletter 35 (1999), http://www.galtoninstitute.org.uk/Newsletters/GINL9912/julian_huxley.htm

22. Central Intelligence Agency, "Unclassified Document 20589596," Nazi War Crimes Disclosure Act 2000, accessed November 26, 2018, https://www.cia.gov/library/readingroom/docs/WALDHEIM,%20KURT%20%20(DI)%20%20%20VOL.%201_0003.pdfhttps://www.cia.gov/library/readingroom/docs/WALDHEIM,%20KURT%20%20(DI)%20%20%20VOL.%201_0003.pdf

John Tagliabue, "File Show Kurt Waldheim Served under War Criminal," New York Times, March 4, 1986, https://www.nytimes.com/1986/03/04/world/files-show-kurt-waldheim-served-under-war-criminal.html

United Nations, "United Nations Secretary-General: Kurt Waldheim," accessed November, 18, 2018, https://www.un.org/sg/en/content/kurt-waldheim

23. Julian Huxley, UNESCO: Its Purpose and Its Philosophy (Washington D. C.: Public Affairs Press, 1948), 23.

24. Antony C. Sutton, America's Secret Establishment: An Introduction to the Order of Skull and Bones, Updated Reprint, (Walterville, OR: Trine Day, 2002), 27.

25. Archibald MacLeish and Henri Bonnet, "Unesco," Bulletin of the American Association of University Professors (1915-1955) 32 no. 4 (1946): 605-620.

UNESCO, "Our Relationship: UNESCO Sectors," U.S. Mission to UNESCO, accessed November 18, 2018, https://unesco.usmission.gov/our-relationship/unesco-sectors/

26. Charles Darwin , The Autobiography of Charles Darwin: From the Life and Letters of Charles Darwin, ed. Francis Darwin (1892), quoted in John Toye, Keynes on Population (Oxford: Oxford University Press, 2000), 59.

Ibid, The Descent of Man, and Selection in Relation to Sex (New York: Random House, 1936), 428.

Donald Gunn MacRae, "Thomas Malthus: English Economist and Demographer," Encyclopedia Britannica, September 28, 2018, https://www.britannica.com/biography/Thomas-Malthus

Thomas Robert Malthus, "An Essay on the Principle of Population, as It Affects the Future Improvement of Society: With Remarks on the Speculations of Mr. Godwin, M. Condorcet, and Other Writers (1798)," On Populations: Thomas Robert Malthus, ed. Gertrude Himmelfarb (New York: Modern Library, 1960), 36.

27. J. Vernon Jensen, "Thomas Henry Huxley's Address at the Opening of the Johns Hopkins University in September 1876," Notes and Records of the Royal Society of London 47 no. 2 (1993): 257-269.

28. John Atkins, Aldous Huxley: A Literary Study (New York: Orion, 1956), 12.

Milton Birnbaum, Aldous Huxley's Quest for Values (Tennessee: U of Tennessee P, 1971), 5.

29. J. Vernon Jensen, "Thomas Henry Huxley's Address at the Opening of the Johns Hopkins University in September 1876," Notes and Records of the Royal Society of London 47 no. 2 (1993): 257-269.

30. Charles Blinderman and David Joyce, "Scientific Education," The Huxley File (Clark University, 1998), https://mathcs.clarku.edu/huxley/guide11.html

31. William E. Friedman and Pamela K. Diggle, "Charles Darwin and the Origins of Plant Evolutionary Developmental Biology," The Plant Cell: American Society of Plant Biologists, April 22, 2011, https://www.ncbi.nlm.nih.gov/pmc/articles/PMC3101565/

32. Charles Blinderman and David Joyce, "Scientific Education," The Huxley File (Clark University, 1998), https://mathcs.clarku.edu/huxley/guide11.html

33. Nicholas Boyle, "Johann Wolfgang von Goethe: German Author," Encyclopedia Britannica, accessed November 18, 2018, https://www.britannica.com/biography/Johann-Wolfgang-von-Goethe

34. Thomas Henry Huxley, Aphorisms and Reflections from the Works of T. H. Huxley, ed. Henrietta A. Huxley (1908), Reprint (Gutenberg EBook, January 22, 2013), http://www.gutenberg.

org/files/38097/38097-h/38097-h.htm

35.   Robert Beachy, "Recasting Cosmopolitanism: German Freemasonry and Regional Identity in the Early Nineteenth Century," Eighteenth Century Studies 33 no. 2 (2000): 266-274.

Rudolph Steiner and Marie Steiner-von Sivers, "The Temple Legend: Goethe and His Connections to Rosicrucianism," (1906) Rudolph Steiner Archive & e.Library, January 15, 2013, https://wn.rsarchive.org/Lectures/GA093/English/RSP1985/TmpLeg_goethe.html

Rudolph Steiner, "Theosophy of the Rosicrucian: The New Form of Wisdom," (1907) Rudolph Steiner Archive & e.Library, July 4, 2002, https://wn.rsarchive.org/Lectures/GA099/English/RSP1966/19070522p01.html

Steven Bond, "'R.C.': Rosicrucianism and Cartesianism in Joyce and Beckett," Miranda 4 (2011), https://journals.openedition.org/miranda/1939

36.   Antony C. Sutton, America's Secret Establishment: An Introduction to the Order of Skull and Bones, Updated Reprint (Walterville, OR: Trine Day, 2002), 79.

37.   Leonard Huxley, Life and Letters of Thomas Henry Huxley Vol. I (London: MacMillan, 1900), 460-461.

38.   Thomas Henry Huxley, Life and Letters of Thomas Henry Huxley Vol. I, ed. Leonard Huxley (London: MacMillan, 1900), 462, 463.

39.   Ibid, 462.

40.   Leonard Huxley, Life and Letters of Thomas Henry Huxley Vol. I (London: MacMillan, 1900), 36-37.

41.   Ibid, ii.

42.   Jessica McBride, "Prince Harry's Hand Gesture: What Does It Mean?," Heavy, December 4, 2017, https://heavy.com/news/2017/12/prince-harry-hand-gesture-illuminati-masonic-devil-photos/

Zhenya Gershman, "Rembrandt: Turn of the Key," Arion: A Journal of the Humanities and the Classics at Boston University (2014), https://www.bu.edu/arion/files/2014/03/Gershman-web-version.pdf

43.   Leonard Huxley, Life and Letters of Thomas Henry Huxley Vol. II (London: MacMillan, 1900), ii.

44.   Charles Day, "The X Club: A Semi-Secret Society in the 19th Century Met to Discuss Science without Fear of Religious Persecution," Physics Today, August 4, 2011, https://physicstoday.scitation.org/do/10.1063/PT.5.010137/full/

45.   Ruth Barton, "X Club: British Science Organization," Encyclopedia Britannica, accessed November 18, 2018, https://www.britannica.com/topic/X-Club

46.   David Weinstein, "Herbert Spencer," Stanford Encyclopedia of Philosophy, January 19, 2017, https://plato.stanford.edu/entries/spencer/

47.   Royal Society, "About Us: History of the Royal Society," accessed November 18, 2018, https://royalsociety.org/about-us/history/

Ruth Barton, "'An Influential Set of Chaps': The X-Club and Royal Society Politics 1864-85," The British Journal for the History of Science 23 no. 1 (1990): 53-81.

48.   Marie Boas Hall, "The Royal Society in Thomas Henry Huxley's Time," Notes and Records of the Royal Society of London 38 no. (1984): 153-158.

49.   Royal Botanic Gardens, "Sir Joseph Dalton Hooker (1817-1911)," Bulletin of Miscellaneous Information no. 1 (1912): 1-34.

50.   Royal Society, "Picture Library: Portrait of William Spottiswoode," accessed November 18, 2018, https://pictures.royalsociety.org/image-rs-9281

51.   A. C. S., "Notes on the Foundation and History of the Royal Society," Royal Society Publishing, accessed November 23, 2018, http://rsnr.royalsocietypublishing.org/content/roynotes-rec/1/1/32.full.pdf.

52.   Charles Webster, "New Light on the Invisible College the Social Relations of English Science in the Mid-Seventeenth Century," Transactions of the Royal Historical Society 24 (1974): 19-42.

Jürgen Klein, "Francis Bacon," Stanford Encyclopedia of Philosophy, December 7, 2012, https://plato.stanford.edu/entries/francis-bacon/

Princeton University Library, "Francis Bacon (1561-1626)," Historic Maps Collection—First X, Then Y, Now Z: Landmark Thematic Maps, accessed November 23, 2018, http://libweb5.princeton.edu/visual_materials/maps/websites/thematic-maps/bacon/bacon.html

53.   Carole Jahme, "The Fantastic Dr Dee: Angels, Magic and the Birth of Modern Science," The Guardian: US Edition, June 25, 2012, https://www.theguardian.com/science/2012/jun/25/fantastic-dr-dee-birth-modern-science

Francis Bacon, New Atlantis (1627), Reprint (Kessinger Publishing Company), 315, 323.

Jim Marrs, Rule by Secrecy: The Hidden History That Connects the Trilateral Commission, the Freemasons, and the Great Pyramids (New York: Harper Collins, 2000), 227-232, 266, 320.

Louisiana State University, "Occult Science & Philosophy in the Renaissance: Signs and Symbols," LSU Hill Memorial Library: Special Collections, accessed November 23, 2018, http://exhibitions.blogs.lib.lsu.edu/?p=1257&page=10

Ron Heisler, "John Dee and the Secret Societies," The Hermetic Journal 46 (1992), http://alchemyfraternitas.ru/media/libra/kniga/46.pdf

Stephen A. McKnight, "Francis Bacon's God," The New Atlantis 10 (2005): 73-100.

54.		Thomas Henry Huxley, "Letter to Charles Darwin, February 20, 1871," The Huxley File, eds. Charles Blinderman and David Joyce (Clark University, 1998), https://mathcs.clarku.edu/huxley/letters/71.html#20feb1871

55.		Ibid, "Address on Behalf of the National Association for the Promotion of Technical Education (1887)," The Huxley File, eds. Charles Blinderman and David Joyce (Clark University, 1998), https://mathcs.clarku.edu/huxley/CE3/ProtE.html

56.		Leonard Huxley, Life and Letters of Thomas Henry Huxley Vol. I (London: MacMillan, 1900), 467.

57.		Bentley Glass "Review: Four Early Giants of Biology at Johns Hopkins," The Quarterly Review of Biology 68 no. 2 (1993): 239-242.

58.		Neil Grauer, "The Six Who Built Hopkins," Johns Hopkins Magazine, April 2000, http://pages.jh.edu/jhumag/0400web/31.html

59.		Johns Hopkins University School of Medicine, "About Us: Department History," Department of Physiology, accessed November 18, 2018, http://physiology.bs.jhmi.edu/about-us/

60.		Geoffrey Cocks, "Review: The International Eugenics Community," Reviews in American History 22 no. 4 (1994): 674-678.

Kolson Schlosser, "Malthus at Mid-Century: Neo-Malthusianism as Bio-Political Governance in the Post-WWII United States," Cultural Geographies 16 no. 4 (2009): 465-484.

Webster Griffin Tarpley and Anton Chaitkin, "Skull and Bones: The Racist Nightmare at Yale," Fleshing Out Skull and Bones: Investigations into America's Most Powerful Secret Society, ed. Kris Millegan (OR: Trine Day, 2003), 316.

61.		Cyril Burt, "The Measurement of Intelligence by the Binet Tests," Eugenics Review 6 no. 2 (1914), https://www.ncbi.nlm.nih.gov/pmc/articles/PMC2987045/pdf/eugenrev00365-0044.pdf

Elizabeth S. Kite, "The Binet-Simon Measuring Scale for Intelligence: What It Is; What It Does; How It Does It; With a Brief Biography of its Authors, Alfred Binet and Dr. Thomas Simon" (Philadelphia: Committee on Provision for the Feeble-Minded, n.d.), http://bir.brandeis.edu/bitstream/handle/10192/28935/413%20p-5.pdf?sequence=1

Ludy T. Benjamin, "The Birth of American Intelligence Testing: This Psychologist Provided a Valuable Assessment Tool, but Also Gave Fodder to Eugenics Proponents, Who Led a Dark Chapter in American History," Monitor on Psychology 40 no. 1 (2009), https://www.apa.org/monitor/2009/01/assessment.aspx

62.		Stanford-Binet Test, "History of the Stanford-Binet Test," accessed November 18, 2018, https://stanfordbinettest.com/history-stanford-binet-test

63.		Daphne Martschenko, "IQ Tests Have a Dark, Controversial History — but They're Finally Being Used for Good," Business Insider, October 11, 2017, https://www.businessinsider.com/iq-tests-dark-history-finally-being-used-for-good-2017-10

J. David Smith, Minds Made Feeble: The Myth and Legacy of the Kallikaks, (Rockville, MD: Aspen, 1985), 41.

64.		Davenport, Charles B. Heredity in Relation to Eugenics (New York: Henry Holt & Co., 1911), 65-66.

65.		Fraser Nelson, "The Return of Eugenics: Researchers Don't Like the Word – but They're Running ahead with the Idea, and Britain is at the Forefront," The Spectator, April 2, 2016, https://www.spectator.co.uk/2016/04/the-return-of-eugenics/

"'Imbeciles' Explores Legacy Of Eugenics In America," National Public Radio, February 26, 2016, https://www.npr.org/2016/02/26/468297940/imbeciles-explores-legacy-of-eugenics-in-america

66.		Joella Straley, "It Took a Eugenicist to Come up with 'Moron,'" National Public Radio, February 10, 2014, https://www.npr.org/sections/codeswitch/2014/02/10/267561895/it-took-a-eugenicist-to-come-up-with-moron

67.		Victoria Brignell, "When America Believed in Eugenics," New Statesman, December 10, 2010, https://www.newstatesman.com/society/2010/12/disabled-america-immigration

68.   C. F. Arden-Close and Hugh Robert Mill, "Major Leonard Darwin," Geographic Journal 101 no. 4 (1943): 172-177.

E. S. Gosney and Paul Popenoe, Sterilization for Human Betterment: A Summary of the Results of 6,000 Operations in California, 1909-1929(New York: Macmillan, 1931), xii, 8-9, 326-327.

69.   J. David Smith, Minds Made Feeble: The Myth and Legacy of the Kallikaks, (Rockville, MD: Aspen, 1985), 41.

70.   Michael Wehmeyer and J. David Smith, "Leaving the Garden: Henry Herbert Goddard's Exodus from the Vineland Training School," Mental Retardation 44 (2006): 150-155.

Sara S. Sparrow, Domenic V. Cicchetti, and Celine A. Saulnier, "Vineland Adaptive Behavior Scales, Third Edition (Vineland-3)," Pearson: Clinical Assessment, accessed November 18, 2018, https://www.pearsonclinical.com.au/products/view/580

Sara S. Sparrow, Domenic V. Cicchetti, and David A. Balla, "Vineland Adaptive Behavior Scales, Second Edition (Vineland™-II)," Pearson Education: Clinical Psychology, accessed November 18, 2018, https://www.pearsonclinical.com/psychology/products/100000668/vineland-adaptive-behavior-scales-second-edition-vineland-ii-vineland-ii.html

71.   Andrew P. Huddleston and Elizabeth C. Rockwell, "Assessment for the Masses: A Historical Critique of High-Stakes Testing in Reading," Texas Journal of Literacy Education 3 no. 1 (2015): 38-49.

72.   Paolo Lionni, The Leipzig Connection: The Systematic Destruction of American Education, Third Printing (Sheridan, OR: Delphian Press, 1988), 21-23.

73.   United States, Congress, Office of Technology Assessment, Testing in American Schools: Asking the Right Questions (Washington, DC: U.S. Government Printing Office, February 1992),

Wayne Au, "Hiding Behind High-Stakes Testing: Meritocracy, Objectivity and Inequality in U.S. Education," International Education Journal: Comparative Perspectives 12 no. 2 (2013): 7-19.

74.   Joan Cook, "R. L. Thorndike, Psychologist, 79; Developed Scholastic-Ability Tests," New York Times, September 25, 1990, https://www.nytimes.com/1990/09/25/obituaries/r-l-thorndike-psychologist-79-developed-scholastic-ability-tests.html

Jonathon Plucker, "R. L. Thorndike (1910-1990): Psychometrician," Human Intelligence: Historical Influences, Current Controversies, Teaching Resources, April 29, 2018, https://www.intelltheory.com/rthorndike.shtml

Lorge-Thorndike Intelligence Tests, "Review of the software Lorge-Thorndike Intelligence Tests by Irving Lorge & Robert L. Thorndike," Journal of Consulting Psychology, 22 no. 1 (1958): 82, http://psycnet.apa.org/record/2005-13609-001

Victor W. Doherty and George S. Ingebo, "The Development of a School Ability Measure Based on the Lorge-Thorndike Intelligence Test," Yearbook of the National Council on Measurement in Education no. 19 (1962): 67-71.

William F. Anderson "Relation of Lorge-Thorndike Intelligence Test Scores of Public School Pupils to the Socio-Economic Status of Their Parents," Journal of Experimental Education 31 no. 1 (1962): 73-76.

75.   National Academies of Sciences, Engineering, and Medicine, Mental Disorders and Disabilities among Low-Income Children (Washington, DC: National Academies Press, 2015), https://doi.org/10.17226/21780.

76.   Ohio Department of Education, "Gifted Education: Gifted Screening and Identification," accessed November 18, 2018, http://education.ohio.gov/Topics/Other-Resources/Gifted-Education/Gifted-Screening-and-Identification

77.   Missouri Department of Elementary and Secondary Education, Gifted Education Program Guidelines, accessed November 18, 2018, https://dese.mo.gov/sites/default/files/qs-Gifted-Program-Guidelines-2017.pdf

78.   Commonwealth of Pennsylvania, Gifted Education Guidelines (Pennsylvania Department of Education, May 2014), https://www.education.pa.gov/Documents/K-12/Gifted%20Education/Gifted%20Program%20Guidelines.pdf

79.   Pearson, "Pearson 2011 Results," News & Media: News Announcements, February 27, 2012, https://www.pearson.com/corporate/news/media/news-announcements/2012/02/pearson-2011-results.html

80.   Valerie Strauss, "The Big Problems with Pearson's New GED High School Equivalency Test," Washington Post, July 9, 2015, https://www.washingtonpost.com/news/answer-sheet/wp/2015/07/09/the-big-problems-with-pearsons-new-ged-high-school-equivalency-test/?noredirect=on&utm_term=.bbe0c12d6878

81.   Andrea Bergman, Grace Kong, and Alice Pope, "General Education Development (GED®)

Credential Attainment, Externalizing Disorders, and Substance Use Disorders in Disconnected Emerging Adults," Journal of Research and Practice for Adult Literacy, Secondary, and Basic Education 3 no. 2 (2014): 8-20.

82.　　　Ibid.

83.　　　Victor L. Hilts, "Obeying the Laws of Hereditary Descent: Phrenological Views on Inheritance and Eugenics," Journal of the History of the Behavioral Sciences 18 (1982): 62-77.

84.　　　Curators of the University of Missouri, "Controlling Heredity: The American Eugenics Crusade (1870-1940)—Origins of Eugenics," Special Collections and Rare Books, March 16, 2012, https://library.missouri.edu/exhibits/eugenics/origins.htm

"Physiognomy and Economics: About Face—People's Creditworthiness, It Seems, Can Be Seen in Their Looks," The Economist, March 5, 2009, https://www.economist.com/science-and-technology/2009/03/05/about-face

85.　　　J. Philippe Rushton and C. Davison Ankney, "Whole Brain Size and General Mental Ability: A Review," International Journal of Neuroscience 119 no. 5 (2009): 691-731.

86.　　　Ibid.

87.　　　Emily Jashinski, "At Harvard, Charles Murray Proves the Value of Campus Lectures," Washington Examiner, September 8, 2017, https://www.washingtonexaminer.com/at-harvard-charles-murray-proves-the-value-of-campus-lectures

"NATO Chief, Former US Intelligence Director Among Bilderberg Elite," RT, https://www.rt.com/news/162128-bilderberg-attendee-list-released/

Steve Sailer, "What Does It Mean That Bilderberg Hasn't Brought Macron Back?," Unz Review: An Alternative Media Selection, April 26, 2017, http://www.unz.com/isteve/what-does-it-mean-that-bilderberg-hasnt-brought-macron-back/

88. "Prince Bernhard: German-Born Consort to Holland's Queen Whose Life Embraced Triumph - and Scandal," The Guardian, December 2, 2004, https://www.theguardian.com/news/2004/dec/03/guardianobituaries.monarchy

Daniel Estulin, The True Story of The Bilderberg Group (Walterville, OR: Trine Day, 2007), 1, 19-20.

89.　　　Richard J. Herrnstein and Charles Murray, The Bell Curve: Intelligence and Class Structure in American Life (New York: Simon and Schuster, 1994), 272-280.

90.　　　Charles Murray, interview by Sam Harris, "#73 – Forbidden Knowledge: A Conversation with Charles Murray," Sam Harris Podcast, April 22, 2017, https://samharris.org/podcasts/forbidden-knowledge/

Ezra Klein, "The Sam Harris Debate: Ezra and Sam Harris Debate Race, IQ, Identity Politics, and Much More," Vox, April 9, 2018, https://www.vox.com/2018/4/9/17210248/sam-harris-ezra-klein-charles-murray-transcript-podcast

Graeme Wood, "The Atheist Who Strangled Me: In Which Sam Harris Teaches Me Brazilian Jiu-Jitsu and Explains Why Violence Is Like Rebirth," The Atlantic, May 2013, https://www.theatlantic.com/magazine/archive/2013/05/the-atheist-who-strangled-me/309292/

91.　　　Sam Harris, "About Sam Harris," accessed November 19, 2018, https://samharris.org/about/

92.　　　Charles Murray, interview by Stefan Molyneux, "The Bell Curve: IQ, Race and Gender," Freedomain Radio Podcast, September 14, 2015, https://www.youtube.com/watch?v=6lsa_97KIlc Freedomain Radio, "About," accessed November 19, 2018, https://freedomainradio.com/about/

93.　　　Anne C. Krendl, "Jordan Peterson: Linking Myth to Psychology," Harvard Crimson, April 26, 1995, https://www.thecrimson.com/article/1995/4/26/jordan-peterson-pharvard-students-may-know/?page=single

Jordan Peterson, "About Jordan Peterson," accessed November 19, 2018, https://jordanbpeterson.com/about/

Ibid, "On the So-Called 'Jewish Question'," Jordan Peterson Blog, accessed November 19, 2018, https://jordanbpeterson.com/psychology/on-the-so-called-jewish-question/

Ibid, interview by Stefan Molyneux, Freedomain Radio Podcast, "The IQ Problem," accessed November 19, 2018, https://www.youtube.com/watch?v=iF8F7tjmy_U

94.　　　Ben Shapiro, "In Sacramento 'Race and IQ' Science Project Uproar, School and Teachers Failed," The Sacramento Bee, February 14, 2018, https://www.sacbee.com/opinion/california-forum/article199889049.html

Ibid, interview by Michael Kirk, "Trump's Show Down: Ben Shapiro of the Daily Wire," Frontline, March 24, 2017, https://www.pbs.org/wgbh/frontline/interview/ben-shapiro/

Kaitlyn Schallhorn, "Ben Shapiro: Who Is He, and Why Is He So Controversial," Fox News, September 18, 2017, https://www.foxnews.com/us/ben-shapiro-who-is-he-and-why-is-he-so-controversial

95.   Richard J. Herrnstein and Charles Murray, The Bell Curve: Intelligence and Class Structure in American Life (New York: Simon and Schuster, 1994), 1-2, 14-15, 26, 284.

96.   Theodor M. Porter, "Karl Pearson: British Mathematician," Encyclopedia Britannica, accessed November 20, 2018, https://www.britannica.com/biography/Karl-Pearson

97.   Bernard J. Norton, "Karl Pearson and Statistics: The Social Origins of Scientific Innovation" Social Studies of Science 8 no. 1 (1978): 3-34.

Cera R. Lawrence, "Francis Galton (1822-1911)," The Embryo Project Encyclopedia at Arizona State University April 6, 2011, https://embryo.asu.edu/pages/francis-galton-1822-1911

E. S. Pearson, "Karl Pearson: An Appreciation of His Life and Work (Part I: 1857-1906)," Biometrika 28 (1936): 193-248.

Samuel S. Wilks, "Karl Pearson: Founder of the Science of Statistics," The Scientific Monthly 53 no. 3 (1941): 249-253.

98.   Richard J. Herrnstein and Charles Murray, The Bell Curve: Intelligence and Class Structure in American Life (New York: Simon and Schuster, 1994), 2-3, 15.

University College London, "Galton Laboratory Records," UCL Library Archives: Special Collections, accessed November, 20, 2018, http://archives.ucl.ac.uk/DServe/dserve.exe?dsqIni=Dserve.ini&dsqApp=Archive&dsqCmd=Show.tcl&dsqSearch=RefNo==%27GALTON%20LABORATORY%27&dsqDb=Catalog

99.   Gillian Sutherland and Stephen Sharp, "'The Fust Official Psychologist in the Wurrld': Aspects of the Professionalization of Psychology in Early Twentieth Century Britain," History of Science 18 (1980): 181-208.

100.   Editors of the Encyclopedia Britannica, "Sir Cyril Burt: British Psychologist," Encyclopedia Britannica, accessed November, 20, 2018, https://www.britannica.com/biography/Cyril-Burt

101.   Cyril Burt, "Intelligence and Fertility: The Effect of the Differential Birthrate on Inborn Mental Characteristics," Occasional Papers on Eugenics No. 2 (London: Eugenics Society, 1948).
Richard J. Herrnstein and Charles Murray, The Bell Curve: Intelligence and Class Structure in American Life (New York: Simon and Schuster, 1994), 11, 12, 14, 16.

102.   Ibid, 5-6, 241.

103.   Ibid, 346.

Rebecca Messall, "The Long Road of Eugenics: From Rockefeller to Roe v. Wade," Human Life Review 30 no. 4 (2004): 59.

104.   Ibid.

Barry Mehler, "Eliminating the Inferior: American and Nazi Sterilization Programs," Science for the People (1987): 14-18, https://ferris-pages.org/ISAR/archives/eliminating-inferior.htm

Dudley Kirk, "The Future of Human Heredity, an Introduction to Eugenics in Modern Society By Frederick Osborn (Review)," Perspectives in Biology and Medicine 13 no. 1 (Johns Hopkins University Press, 1969): 125-126.

Population Council Inc., "About: Timeline," Population Council. Ideas. Evidence. Impact, accessed November, 20, 2018, https://www.popcouncil.org/about/timeline

105.   Claude Moore Health Sciences Library, "Eugenics: Three Generations, No Imbeciles: Virginia, Eugenics, and Buck v. Bell," Claude Moore Health Sciences Library: Historical Collections Department, accessed January 9, 2012. http://www.hsl.virginia.edu/historical/eugenics/
Richard J. Herrnstein and Charles Murray, The Bell Curve: Intelligence and Class Structure in American Life (New York: Simon and Schuster, 1994), 5.

106.   Oliver Wendell Holmes, Buck v. Bell, 274 US 200 (1927), quoted in Claude Moore Health Sciences Library, "Eugenics: Three Generations, No Imbeciles: Virginia, Eugenics, and Buck v. Bell," Claude Moore Health Sciences Library: Historical Collections Department, accessed January 9, 2012. http://www.hsl.virginia.edu/historical/eugenics/

107.   Richard J. Herrnstein and Charles Murray, The Bell Curve: Intelligence and Class Structure in American Life (New York: Simon and Schuster, 1994), 10, 842.

108.   J. David Smith, Minds Made Feeble: The Myth and Legacy of the Kallikaks (Rockville, MD: Aspen, 1985), 178-179.

Nobel Media, "The Nobel Prize in Physics 1956: William B. Shockley Biographical," The Nobel Prize, accessed November 20, 2018, https://www.nobelprize.org/prizes/physics/1956/shockley/biographical/

Scott Rosenberg, "Silicon Valley's First Founder Was Its Worst," Wired Magazine, July 19, 2017, https://www.wired.com/story/silicon-valleys-first-founder-was-its-worst/

109.   William Shockley, "Sterilization – A Thinking Exercise," Eugenics: Then and Now, ed. C. Bajema (New York: Halsted Press, 1976), quoted in J. David Smith, Minds Made Feeble: The Myth

and Legacy of the Kallikaks (Rockville, MD: Aspen, 1985), 177.

110.   Ibid, interview by S. Jones, Playboy (1980), quoted in J. David Smith, Minds Made Feeble: The Myth and Legacy of the Kallikaks (Rockville, MD: Aspen, 1985), 181.

111.   Kat Eschner, "The "Nobel Prize Sperm Bank" Was Racist. It Also Helped Change the Fertility Industry," Smithsonian Magazine, June 9, 2017, https://www.smithsonianmag.com/smart-news/nobel-prize-sperm-bank-was-racist-it-also-helped-change-fertility-industry-180963569/

112.   David Plotz, "The 'Genius Babies,' and How They Grew," Slate, February 8, 2001, https://slate.com/human-interest/2001/02/the-genius-babies-and-how-they-grew.html

J. David Smith, Minds Made Feeble: The Myth and Legacy of the Kallikaks (Rockville, MD: Aspen, 1985), 178-179.

Michael J. Sandal, "The Case Against Designer Perfection: What's Wrong with Designer Children, Bionic Athletes, and Genetic Engineering," The Atlantic, April 2004, https://www.theatlantic.com/magazine/archive/2004/04/the-case-against-perfection/302927/

113.   National Marriage Project, "About: History," accessed November 20, 2018, http://nationalmarriageproject.org/about/

114.   Jill Lepore, "Fixed: The Rise of Marriage Therapy, and Other Dreams of Human Betterment," New Yorker, March 29, 2010, https://www.newyorker.com/magazine/2010/03/29/fixed

115.   Laura Smith, "In the 1920s, This Man Brought Marriage Counseling to America to Save the White Race: Paul Popenoe Wanted to Make Sure the 'Right' Couples Stayed Together," Timeline, September 14, 2017, https://timeline.com/popenoe-eugenics-marriage-counseling-faa8aacb0f3d

116.   Richard J. Herrnstein and Charles Murray, The Bell Curve: Intelligence and Class Structure in American Life (New York: Simon and Schuster, 1994), 842.

117.   Ibid, 272-274, 289, 359, 565, 566.

Richard Lynn, "Home: Richard Lynn—Professor Emeritus, University of Ulster," accessed November 21, 2018, http://www.rlynn.co.uk/

118.   Lisa Raffensperger, "How Adding Iodine to Salt Boosted Americans' IQ," Discover Magazine, July 23, 2013, http://blogs.discovermagazine.com/crux/2013/07/23/how-adding-iodine-to-salt-boosted-americans-iq/#.W_WhZbpFxIZ

Richard J. Herrnstein and Charles Murray, The Bell Curve: Intelligence and Class Structure in American Life (New York: Simon and Schuster, 1994), 273, 307-308, 348.

119.   Ibid, 832-833.

120.   Ibid, 307-309, 346-347, 391, 397, 422.

Karl S. Kruszelnicki, "The Flynn Effect: Your Kids Are Smarter Than You," Australian Broadcasting Corporation, March 12, 2014, http://www.abc.net.au/science/articles/2014/03/12/3961513.htm

Lisa Trahan, Karla K. Stuebing, Merril K. Hiscock, and Jack M. Fletcher, "The Flynn Effect: A Meta-Analysis," Psychological Bulletin, 140(5), 1332-1360.

121.   Manfred F. Greiffenstein, "Secular IQ Increases by Epigenesis? The Hypothesis of Cognitive Genotype Optimization," Psychological Reports 109 no. 2 (2011): 353-366.

Tom Chivers, "The Flynn Effect: Are We Really Getting Smarter?," The Telegraph, October 31, 2014, https://www.telegraph.co.uk/news/science/science-news/11200900/The-Flynn-effect-are-we-really-getting-smarter.html

122.   Noam, "The Cherry Picked Science in Vox's Charles Murray Article," Medium, May 18, 2017, https://medium.com/@houstoneuler/the-cherry-picked-science-in-voxs-charles-murray-article-bd534a9c4476

123.   James Flynn, interview by Herrick, "10 Questions for James Flynn," Gene Expressions, December 5, 2007, http://www.gnxp.com/new/2007/12/05/10-questions-for-james-flynn/

124.   Byron M. Roth, "Why Are Jews so Successful?: Review of Richard Lynn's The Chosen People: A Study of Jewish Intelligence and Achievement," American Renaissance, November 2011, https://www.amren.com/features/2011/11/the-chosen-people/

125.   James R. Flynn and William T. Dickens, "Heritability Estimates Versus Large Environmental Effects: The IQ Paradox Resolved," Brookings Institution, April 1, 2001, https://www.brookings.edu/articles/heritability-estimates-versus-large-environmental-effects-the-iq-paradox-resolved/

126.   J. Phillipe Rushton "Richard Lynn's The Global Bell Curve—The Explanation That Fits the Facts," American Renaissance, June 16, 2008, https://www.amren.com/news/2008/06/richard_lynns_t/

127.   Richard Lynn, Race Differences in Intelligence: An Evolutionary Analysis (Augusta, GA: Washington Summit Publishers, 2006): 25.

128.   Peter Wilby, "Beyond the Flynn effect: New Myths about Race, Family and IQ?," The Guardian: US Edition, September 27, 2016, https://www.theguardian.com/education/2016/

sep/27/james-flynn-race-iq-myths-does-your-family-make-you-smarter

129.   Richard Lynn, Race Differences in Intelligence: An Evolutionary Analysis (Augusta, GA: Washington Summit Publishers, 2006): 110-160.

Ronald Bailey, "Closing the Black/White IQ Gap?: James Flynn and Charles Murray Search for a Solution," Reason, December 1, 2006, https://reason.com/archives/2006/12/01/closing-the-black-white-iq-gap

130.   James Thompson, "Richard Lynn's Contributions to Personality and Intelligence," Personality and Individual Difference 53 no. 2 (2012): 157-161.

131.   J. Phillippe Rushton, "Life History Theory and Race Differences: An Appreciation of Richard Lynn's Contributions to Science," Personality and Individual Differences 53 no. 2 (2012): 85-89.

132.   Richard Lynn, Eugenics: A Reassessment (Westport, CT: Praeger, 2001): 213.

133.   Ibid, 198.

134.   Ibid, interview by Stefan Molyneux, "Race Genetics and Intelligence," Freedomain Radio Podcast, July 2, 2016, https://www.youtube.com/watch?v=MxXPA9ZnDCc

135.   "Ulster University Withdraws Status from Prof Richard Lynn," BBC, April 14, 2018, https://www.bbc.com/news/uk-northern-ireland-43768132

136.   Debra Viadero, "Black-White Gap in IQ Scores Closing, Study Finds," Education Week, June 21, 2006, https://www.edweek.org/ew/articles/2006/06/21/42iq_web.h25.html

137.   "Brainier Mums Needed to Maintain Future Generations' Intelligence, Says Professor," New Zealand Herald, July 8, 2007, https://www.nzherald.co.nz/nz/news/article.cfm?c_id=1&objectid=10450313

138.   David Loughrey, "Academic in Hot Water over Remarks," Otago Daily Times, July 9, 2007, https://web.archive.org/web/20070928205802/http:/www.odt.co.nz/article.php?refid=2007%2C07%2C09%2C1%2C00101%2C6ab28590335842ab78ad5a8ec415d749&sect=0

139.   Ibid.

140.   Paul R. Ehrlich, The Population Bomb (Binghamton, NY: Ballantine, 1968), 135-136.
Paul R. Ehrlich, John P. Holdren And Anne H. Ehrlich, Ecoscience Population, Resources, Environment (New York: W. H. Freeman, 1977): 786, 787-788.

141.   John Allemang, "Philippe Rushton, professor who pushed limits with race studies, dead at 68," The Globe and Mail, May 2, 2018, https://www.theglobeandmail.com/news/national/philippe-rushton-professor-who-pushed-limits-with-race-studies-dead-at-68/article4901806/
Richard J. Herrnstein and Charles Murray, The Bell Curve: Intelligence and Class Structure in American Life (New York: Simon and Schuster, 1994), 563-564, 666-667.

142.   Ibid, 9-10, 13, 15, 283-284, 302-304, 308, 561.
Dara Tom, "In Memoriam: Arthur R. Jensen—Professor of Education, Emeritus, UC Berkeley (1923-2012)," Communications & Public Relations Committee on Memorial Resolutions: UC Berkeley Graduate School of Education, accessed November 21, 2018, https://senate.universityofcalifornia.edu/_files/inmemoriam/html/ArthurR.Jensen.html

143.   Richard J. Herrnstein and Charles Murray, The Bell Curve: Intelligence and Class Structure in American Life (New York: Simon and Schuster, 1994), 846.

144.   Canadian Psychological Association, "CPA Awards: CPA Fellows," https://www.cpa.ca/aboutcpa/cpaawards/fellows

145.   J. Phillippe Rushton, Race, Evolution, and Behavior: A Life History Perspective, 2nd Special Abridged Ed. (Ontario: University of Western Ontario, 2000).

146.   Southern Poverty Law Center, "Jean-Philippe Rushton—About Jean-Philippe Rushton: In His Own Words," SPLC, accessed November 21, 2018, https://www.splcenter.org/fighting-hate/extremist-files/individual/jean-philippe-rushton

147.   J. Phillipe Rushton "Richard Lynn's The Global Bell Curve—The Explanation That Fits the Facts," American Renaissance, June 16, 2008, https://www.amren.com/news/2008/06/richard_lynns_t/

148.   Matthew Yglesias, "Racists Polluting My Race Science!," The Atlantic, November 30, 2007, https://www.theatlantic.com/politics/archive/2007/11/racists-polluting-my-race-science/47202/

149.   The Pioneer Fund, "A Brief History of the Pioneer Fund," July 18, 2013, https://web.archive.org/web/20130719051934/http://www.thepioneerfund.org/

150.   Edward Burmila, "Scientific Racism Isn't 'Back'—It Never Went Away," The Nation, April 6, 2018, https://www.thenation.com/article/scientific-racism-isnt-back-it-never-went-away/

151.   Adam Miller, "The Pioneer Fund: Bankrolling the Professors of Hate," The Journal of Blacks in Higher Education, 6 (1994): 58-61.

152.   Colleen Flaherty, "Pioneering Eugenics in 2018?: University of Arizona Psychologist Is

under Scrutiny for Taking Money from an Organization Founded to Support Research in Eugenics," Inside Higher Ed, September 10, 2018, https://www.insidehighered.com/news/2018/09/10/arizona-psychologist-faces-scrutiny-grants-organization-founded-support-research

Lesley Ciarula Taylor, "J. Philippe Rushton, author of controversial essay on race and brain size, dies at 68," The Toronto Star, October 5, 2012, https://www.thestar.com/obituaries/2012/10/05/j_philippe_rushton_author_of_controversial_essay_on_race_and_brain_size_dies_at_68.html

153.		Adam Miller, "The Pioneer Fund: Bankrolling the Professors of Hate," The Journal of Blacks in Higher Education, 6 (1994): 58-61.

154.		Dennis Roddy, "Weird Science," Pittsburgh Post-Gazette, January 25, 2009, http://www.post-gazette.com/dennis-roddy/2005/01/30/Weird-Science/stories/200501300217

Southern Poverty Law Center, "Academic Racism: Key Race Scientist Takes Reins at Pioneer Fund," Intelligence Report, Winter 2002, https://web.archive.org/web/20100202143751/http://www.splcenter.org/intel/intelreport/article.jsp?aid=83

155.		Rachel Gur-Arie, "American Eugenics Society (1926-1972)," Embryo Project Encyclopedia at Arizona State University, November 22, 2011, https://embryo.asu.edu/pages/american-eugenics-society-1926-1972

Stefan Kühl, The Nazi Connection: Eugenics, American Racism, and German National Socialism (Oxford: Oxford University Press, 1994), 5-6.

Truman State University, "Biography of Harry H. Laughlin," Pickler Memorial Library: Manuscript Collections—Special Collections of University Archives, accessed November 21, 2018, http://library.truman.edu/manuscripts/laughlinbio.asp

156.		Adam Miller, "The Pioneer Fund: Bankrolling the Professors of Hate," The Journal of Blacks in Higher Education, 6 (1994): 58-61.

157.		Richard J. Herrnstein and Charles Murray, The Bell Curve: Intelligence and Class Structure in American Life (New York: Simon and Schuster, 1994), 826-827.

158.		Michael Billig, Psychology, Racism, and Fascism (Searchlight, 1979), accessed November 21, 2018, http://www.psychology.uoguelph.ca/faculty/winston/papers/billig/billig.html

159.		Stefan Kühl, The Nazi Connection: Eugenics, American Racism, and German National Socialism (Oxford: Oxford University Press, 1994), 139.

160.		Southern Poverty Law Center, "Arthur Jensen—About Arthur Jensen: In His Own Words," SPLC, accessed November 21, 2018, https://www.splcenter.org/fighting-hate/extremist-files/individual/arthur-jensen

161.		Arthur Jensen, interview by American Renaissance, "A Conversation with Arthur Jensen," American Renaissance, October 29, 2012, https://www.amren.com/news/2012/10/arthur-jensen-has-died/

162.		University of Delaware, "Linda S. Gottfredson," School of Education: College of Education and Human Development, accessed November 21, 2018, https://www1.udel.edu/educ/gottfredson/reprints/

163.		Richard J. Herrnstein and Charles Murray, The Bell Curve: Intelligence and Class Structure in American Life (New York: Simon and Schuster, 1994), 321, 820.

164.		Jack Anderson and Dale Van Atta, "Pioneer Fund's Controversial Projects," Washington Post, November 16, 1989, https://www.washingtonpost.com/archive/lifestyle/1989/11/16/pioneer-funds-controversial-projects/0f05cde6-6586-462d-acfa-cfd3ae65567e/?noredirect=on&utm_term=.961d06366fdf

Ron Kaufman, "U. Delaware Reaches Accord On Race Studies," The Scientist, July 6, 1992, https://www.the-scientist.com/news/u-delaware-reaches-accord-on-race-studies-60023

165.		Adam Miller, "The Pioneer Fund: Bankrolling the Professors of Hate," The Journal of Blacks in Higher Education, 6 (1994): 58-61.

166.		Linda S. Gottfredson, "Mainstream Science on Intelligence: An Editorial with 52 Signatories, History, and Bibliography," Intelligence 24 no. 1 (1997): 13-23.

167.		David F. Lohman, "Lessons from the History of Intelligence Testing," International Journal of Educational Research 27 (2003): 1-20.

Joan Cook, "R. L. Thorndike, Psychologist, 79; Developed Scholastic-Ability Tests," New York Times, September 25, 1990, https://www.nytimes.com/1990/09/25/obituaries/r-l-thorndike-psychologist-79-developed-scholastic-ability-tests.html

168.		Richard J. Herrnstein and Charles Murray, The Bell Curve: Intelligence and Class Structure in American Life (New York: Simon and Schuster, 1994), 853.

169.		Linda S. Gottfredson, "Mainstream Science on Intelligence: An Editorial with 52 Signatories, History, and Bibliography," Intelligence 24 no. 1 (1997): 13-23.

170.   Ibid.

171.   Ibid, interview by Stefan Molyneux, "Race, Evolution, and Intelligence," Freedomain Radio Podcast, December 19, 2015, https://www.youtube.com/watch?v=CZPsXYo7gpc

172.   University of Delaware, "Welcome to the Homepage of Linda S. Gottfredson: Curriculum Vitae and Publications—Syllabi for Current and Recent Courses," School of Education: College of Education and Human Development, accessed November 21, 2018, https://www1.udel.edu/educ/gottfredson/

173.   Ibid.

174.   Charles Murray, "Are Too Many People Going to College?," American Enterprise Institute September 8, 2008, http://www.aei.org/publication/are-too-many-people-going-to-college-2/

175.   Ibid.

176.   Ibid.

177.   Charles Murray, Peter Thiel, Henry Bienen, Vivek Wadhwa, and John Donvan, "Too Many Kids Go to College," (panel discussion at Intelligence Squared U.S. Debate, Chicago, October 12, 2011), https://www.intelligencesquaredus.org/sites/default/files/pdf/transcript-too-many-kids-go-to-college-our-first-debate-in-chicago.pdf

178.   B. F. Skinner, The Technology of Teaching (New York: Appleton-Century-Crofts, 1968), 243.

179.   Ibid, 240.

180.   Ibid, 75.

181.   Ibid, 76-78.

182.   Jay L. Zagorsky, "Do You Have to Be Smart to Be Rich? The Impact of IQ on Wealth, Income and Financial Distress," Intelligence 35 no. 5 (2007): 489-501.

183.   Ibid.

184.   Francis Galton, Hereditary Genius: An Inquiry into Its Laws and Consequences (New York: MacMillan and Co., 1869), 1.

185.   Nicholas Jenkins, "Sir Charles Galton Darwin KBE MC FRS (I7761)," W. H. Auden: "Family Ghosts" (Stanford University, 2008), accessed January 3, 2012, http://www.stanford.edu/group/auden/cgi-bin/auden/individual.php?pid=I7761&ged=auden-bicknell.ged

Nobel Media, "Andrew F. Huxley: Biographical," The Nobel Prize, accessed 17 Aug. 2013, http://www.nobelprize.org/nobel_prizes/medicine/laureates/1963/huxley-bio.html

Thomas G. Blaney, "The Chief Sea Lion Among Other Wild Animals: Charles Galton Darwin and the Eugenics Movement," The Galton Institute Newsletter, 53 (2004), http://www.galtoninstitute.org.uk/Newsletters/GINL0412/chief_sea_lion.htm

Tim M. Berra, Gonzalo Alvarez, and Kate Shannon, "The Galton-Darwin-Wedgwood Pedigree of H. H. Laughlin," Biological Journal of the Linnean Society 101 (2010): 228-241.

186.   Aldous Huxley, "A Note on Eugenics," Aldous Huxley: Complete Essays (Volume II: 1926-1929), eds. Robert S. Baker and James Sexton (Chicago: Ivan R. Dee, 2000), 283.

187.   Joseph A. Schwartz, "Socioeconomic Status as a Moderator of the Genetic and Shared Environmental Influence on Verbal IQ: A Multilevel Behavioral Genetic Approach," Intelligence 52 (2015): 80-89.

188.   Jelte M. Wicherts, "The Impact of Papers Published in Intelligence 1977–2007 and an Overview of the Citation Classics," Intelligence 37 no. 5 (2009): 443-446.

189.   Eslevier, "Intelligence Editorial Board," July 29, 2012, https://web.archive.org/web/20120729121146/https://www.journals.elsevier.com/intelligence/editorial-board

190.   Angela Saini, "Racism Is Creeping Its Way Back into Mainstream Science—We Have to Stop It," The Guardian: US, January 22, 2018, Edition, https://www.theguardian.com/commentisfree/2018/jan/22/eugenics-racism-mainstream-science

191.   Elsevier, "Journals: Intelligence—Editorial Board," accessed November 21, 2018, https://www.journals.elsevier.com/intelligence/editorial-board

192.   Common Ground Scholar, "Home: Collections," accessed November 21, 2018, https://cgscholar.com/

193.   Bill Cope and Mary Kalantzis, "Sources of Evidence-of-Learning: Learning and Assessment in the Era of Big Data," Open Review of Educational Research 2 no. 1 (2015): 194-217.

194.   Antonio Regalado, "DNA Tests for IQ Are Coming, but It Might Not Be Smart to Take One: Scientists Have Linked Hundreds of Genes to Intelligence. One Psychologist Says It's Time to Test School Kids," MIT Technology Review, April 2, 2018, https://www.technologyreview.com/s/610339/dna-tests-for-iq-are-coming-but-it-might-not-be-smart-to-take-one/

195.	Lydia Ramsey, "Lawmakers Are Asking DNA-Testing Companies about Their Privacy Policies — Here's What You Should Know When Taking Genetics Tests Like 23andMe or Ancestry DNA," Business Insider, June 21, 2018, https://www.businessinsider.com/privacy-considerations-for-dna-tests-23andme-ancestry-helix-2017-12

196.	Ibid.

197.	Ibid, "23andMe Is Getting Serious about Drug Development — and It Could Signal a Fresh Approach to Finding New Medicines," Business Insider, September 17, 2017, https://www.businessinsider.com/why‐23andme-is-developing-drugs-based-on-its-data-2017-9

198.	Cornelius A. Rietveld, Dalton Conley, Nicholas Eriksson, Tõnu Esko, Sarah E. Medland, Anna A.E. Vinkhuyzen, Jian Yang, Jason D. Boardman, Christopher F. Chabris, Christopher T. Dawes, Benjamin W. Domingue, David A. Hinds, Magnus Johannesson, Amy K. Kiefer, David Laibson, Patrik K. E. Magnusson, Joanna L. Mountain, Sven Oskarsson, Olga Rostapshova, Alexander Teumer, Joyce Y. Tung, Peter M. Visscher, Daniel J. Benjamin, David Cesarini, Philipp D. Koellinger, and the Social Science Genetic Association Consortium, "Replicability and Robustness of GWAS for Behavioral Traits," Psychological Sciences 25 no. 11 (2014): 1975-1986.

199.	Robin Smith, "Ten Percent Inspiration, Ninety Percent Perspiration (and Sixty Percent Genetics)," 23andMe Blog, October 16, 2014, https://blog.23andme.com/23andme-research/ten-percent-inspiration-ninety-percent-perspiration-and-sixty-percent-genetics/

200.	Scott H., "Back to School Smarts and Genetics," 23andMe Blog, August 30, 2012, https://blog.23andme.com/health-traits/back-to-school-smarts-and-genetics/

201.	Aleks Eror, "China Is Engineering Genius Babies," Vice, March 15, 2013, https://www.vice.com/en_us/article/5gw8vn/chinas-taking-over-the-world-with-a-massive-genetic-engineering-program

Ed Yong, "Chinese Project Probes the Genetics of Genius: Bid to Unravel the Secrets of Brainpower Faces Skepticism," Nature, May 14, 2013, https://www.nature.com/news/chinese-project-probes-the-genetics-of-genius-1.12985

202.	Antonio Regalado, "DNA Tests for IQ Are Coming, but It Might Not Be Smart to Take One: Scientists Have Linked Hundreds of Genes to Intelligence. One Psychologist Says It's Time to Test School Kids," MIT Technology Review, April 2, 2018, https://www.technologyreview.com/s/610339/dna-tests-for-iq-are-coming-but-it-might-not-be-smart-to-take-one/

203.	Elsevier, "Journals: Intelligence—Editorial Board," accessed November 21, 2018, https://www.journals.elsevier.com/intelligence/editorial-board

204.	Linda S. Gottfredson, "Mainstream Science on Intelligence: An Editorial with 52 Signatories, History, and Bibliography," Intelligence 24 no. 1 (1997): 13-23.

205.	Richard J. Herrnstein and Charles Murray, The Bell Curve: Intelligence and Class Structure in American Life (New York: Simon and Schuster, 1994), 842.

206.	Antonio Regalado, "DNA Tests for IQ Are Coming, but It Might Not Be Smart to Take One: Scientists Have Linked Hundreds of Genes to Intelligence. One Psychologist Says It's Time to Test School Kids," MIT Technology Review, April 2, 2018, https://www.technologyreview.com/s/610339/dna-tests-for-iq-are-coming-but-it-might-not-be-smart-to-take-one/

207.	Ibid.

208.	Ibid.

209.	Peter Wilby, "Psychologist on a Mission to Give Every Child a Learning Chip," The Guardian: US Edition, February 18, 2014, https://www.theguardian.com/education/2014/feb/18/psychologist-robert-plomin-says-genes-crucial-education

210.	Ibid.

211.	Global Education Futures, "Global Education 2015-2035," Global Education Futures Initiative, accessed November 23, 2018, https://www.edu2035.org/images/people/Future%20of%20Global%20Education%20Map%20(2014)-ilovepdf-compressed.pdf

212. Ibid.

213.	Matthew Yglesias, "The Bell Curve Is about Policy. And It's Wrong: Charles Murray Is an Incredibly Successful — and Pernicious — Policy Entrepreneur," Vox, April 10, 2018, https://www.vox.com/2018/4/10/17182692/bell-curve-charles-murray-policy-wrong

214.	Nina J. Easton, "Book That Links Low IQ to Race, Poverty Fuels Debate : Race: Authors Say Genetics along with Environment account for Intelligence-Test Gap between Whites, Blacks," Los Angeles Times, October 30, 1994, http://articles.latimes.com/1994-10-30/news/mn-56688_1_iq-test

215.	"Heir Conditioned," Times of Higher Education, December 22, 1995, https://www.timeshighereducation.com/news/heir-conditioned/96326.article#survey-answer

Peter Wilby, "Psychologist on a Mission to Give Every Child a Learning Chip," The Guardian: US Edition, February 18, 2014, https://www.theguardian.com/education/2014/feb/18/psychologist-robert-plomin-says-genes-crucial-education

216.   University of Cambridge, "Has Intelligence Been Rising? A Lecture By James Flynn," Psychometrics Centre News, October 5, 2013, https://www.psychometrics.cam.ac.uk/news/news.13

217.   Peter Wilby, "Beyond the Flynn effect: New Myths about Race, Family and IQ?," The Guardian: US Edition, September 27, 2016, https://www.theguardian.com/education/2016/sep/27/james-flynn-race-iq-myths-does-your-family-make-you-smarter

218.   James Flynn, interview by Stefan Molyneux, "Human Intelligence: The Flynn Effect," Freedomain Radio Podcast, February 25, 2015, https://www.youtube.com/watch?v=rJ0W5Efp8N0

219.   Ibid.

220.   Christopher Lehmann-Haupt, "'What It Means to Be a Libertarian': Murray's Case Against Big Government," New York Times Book Review, February 10, 1997, https://archive.nytimes.com/www.nytimes.com/books/97/02/09/daily/libertarian-book-review.html

221.   Charles Murray, "A Guaranteed Income for Every American," American Enterprise Institute, June 3, 2016, http://www.aei.org/publication/a-guaranteed-income-for-every-american/

222.   Jathan Sadowski, "Why Silicon Valley Is Embracing Universal Basic Income," The Guardian: US Edition, June 22, 2016, https://www.theguardian.com/technology/2016/jun/22/silicon-valley-universal-basic-income-y-combinator

223.   Matthew Yglesias, "The Bell Curve Is about Policy. And It's Wrong: Charles Murray Is an Incredibly Successful — and Pernicious — Policy Entrepreneur," Vox, April 10, 2018, https://www.vox.com/2018/4/10/17182692/bell-curve-charles-murray-policy-wrong

"Why Murray's Big Idea Won't Work: Charles Murray Has an Intriguing Plan to Dismantle the Welfare State and Give Every Adult $10,000. Too Bad His Numbers Don't Add up," The Atlantic, April 2006, https://www.theatlantic.com/magazine/archive/2006/04/why-murrays-big-idea-wont-work/304830/

Endnotes – Chapter Fifteen

1.   Ezra Klein, "Sam Harris, Charles Murray, and the Allure of Race Science: This Is Not 'Forbidden Knowledge.' It Is America's Most Ancient Justification for Bigotry and Racial Inequality," Vox, March 27, 2018, https://www.vox.com/policy-and-politics/2018/3/27/15695060/sam-harris-charles-murray-race-iq-forbidden-knowledge-podcast-bell-curve

2.   Cold Spring Harbor, "Eugenics Tree Logo," DNA Learning Center: Preparing Students and Families to Thrive in the Gene Age, accessed November 23, 2018, https://www.dnalc.org/view/10229-Eugenics-tree-logo.html

Raymond Pearl, "The First International Eugenics Congress," Science 36 no. 926 (1912): 395-396.

3.   Cold Spring Harbor, "Eugenics Tree Logo," DNA Learning Center: Preparing Students and Families to Thrive in the Gene Age, accessed November 23, 2018, https://www.dnalc.org/view/10229-Eugenics-tree-logo.html

4.   Ibid.

5.   Ibid.

6.   Ibid.

7.   B. F. Skinner, The Technology of Teaching (New York: Appleton-Century-Crofts, 1968), 75.

8.   Ibid, 241.

9.   Ibid, 243.

10.   Global Education Futures, "Global Education 2015-2035," Global Education Futures Initiative, accessed November 23, 2018, https://www.edu2035.org/images/people/Future%20of%20Global%20Education%20Map%20(2014)-ilovepdf-compressed.pdf

11.   Miao Zhang, Yixue Quan, Liqin Huang, and Yi-Lung Kuo, "The Impact of Learning Styles on Academic Achievement," International Journal of Intelligent Technologies & Applied Statistics 10 no. 3 (2017): 180-181.

12.   Krisztián Józsa and Karen Caplovitz Barrett, "Affective and Social **Mastery Motivation** in Preschool as Predictors of **Early** School Success: A Longitudinal Study," Early Childhood Research Quarterly 45 no. 4 (2018): 81.

13.   Ibid.

14.   Luke Dormehl, "AI Educational Software Knows When Students Are Bored, Can Adjust Lessons Accordingly," Digital Trends, December 13, 2016, https://www.digitaltrends.com/cooltech/emotion-sniffing-learning-apps/

15.　　Antonio DePace, "Your Children Could Learn to Control Their Emotions with a Video Game," Boston Magazine, April 18, 2017, https://www.bostonmagazine.com/health/2017/04/18/rage-control-study/

16.　　Oswego High School, "Final Report for Teacher and Student Learning at OHS with Sharon Kane," Project SMART Topics in Education: Social Emotional Learning in High Needs School, accessed November 23, 2018, https://www.oswego.edu/project-smart/sites/www.oswego.edu.project-smart/files/2016-2017_tfr_-_ohs_combined.pdf

17.　　G. Shivakumar and P. A. Vijaya, "Analysis of Human Emotions Using Galvanic Skin Response and Finger Tip Temperature," International Journal of Synthetic Emotions 2 no. 1 (2012): 792-803.

18. Valerie Strauss, "$1.1 Million-Plus Gates Grants: 'Galvanic' Bracelets That Measure Student Engagement," Washington Post, July 11, 2012, https://www.washingtonpost.com/blogs/answer-sheet/post/11-million-plus-gates-grants-galvanic-bracelets-that-measure-student-engagement/2012/06/10/gJQAgAUbTV_blog.html

19.　　Bill Cope and Mary Kalantzis, "Sources of Evidence-of-Learning: Learning and Assessment in the Era of Big Data," Open Review of Educational Research 2 no. 1 (2015): 194-217.

20.　　Ibid.

21.　　Alex Newman, "DeVos Signs on to Globalist UN Education Agenda for U.S.," Freedom Project Media: The Newman Report, September 10, 2018, https://freedomproject.com/the-newman-report/810-devos-signs-on-to-globalist-un-education-agenda-for-u-s

22.　　G20, "G20 Education Ministers' Declaration 2018: Building Consensus for Fair and Sustainable Development. Unleashing People's Potential," G20 Argentina 2018 (2018), https://www.g20.org/sites/default/files/media/g20_education_ministers_declaration_english.pdf

23.　　United States, Department of Education, "Prepared Remarks by Secretary DeVos at Meeting of G20 Education Ministers," Press Office, September 5, 2018, https://www.ed.gov/news/speeches/prepared-remarks-secretary-devos-meeting-g20-education-ministers

24.　　Collaborative for Academic, Social, and Emotional Learning, "What Is SEL? Core SEL Competencies," CASEL: Educating Hearts. Inspiring Minds, accessed November 23, 2018, https://casel.org/core-competencies/

25.　　Ibid, "About CASEL," accessed November 23, 2018, https://casel.org/about-2/

26.　　Ibid, "About: Funders and Growth Partners," accessed November 23, 2018, https://casel.org/funders/

27.　　Stephen Elliott, Michael D. Davies, Jennifer R. Frey, Frank Gresham, Greta Cooper, "Development and Initial Validation of a Social Emotional Learning Assessment for Universal Screening," Journal of Applied Developmental Psychology 55 (2018): 39.

28.　　Ibid.

29.　　Collaborative for Academic, Social, and Emotional Learning, "Social Skills Improvement System (SSIS): Elementary SELect Program—Program Design and Implementation Support," accessed November 23, 2018, https://casel.org/guideprogramssocial-skills/

30.　　Pearson Education Inc., "PreK-16 Education and Special Needs: About Pearson's Clinical Assessment Group," accessed November 23, 2018, https://www.pearsonclinical.com/education/about.html

31.　　Frank Gresham and Stephen N. Elliott, "PreK-16 Education and Special Needs: Social Skills Improvement System (SSIS) Rating Scales," Pearson Education Inc., accessed November 23, 2018, https://www.pearsonclinical.com/education/products/100000322/social-skills-improvement-system-ssis-rating-scales.html#tab-scoring

32.　　Ibid, "PreK-16 Education and Special Needs: SSIS™ Social-Emotional Learning Edition (SSIS SEL)," Pearson Education Inc., accessed November 23, 2018, https://www.pearsonclinical.com/education/products/100001940/ssis-social-emotional-learning-edition.html

33.　　Karen R. Effrem, "**Government Preschool Tyranny – "You Ain't Seen Nothing Yet!,**" Education Liberty Watch, February 24, 2012, http://edlibertywatch.org/2012/02/government-preschool-tyranny-you-aint-seen-nothing-yet/

34.　　Jane Robbins and Karen Effrem, "Schools Ditch Academics For Emotional Manipulation: Under Such a System Teachers Become Essentially Therapists, and Students Become Essentially Patients," The Federalist, October 19, 2016, http://thefederalist.com/2016/10/19/schools-ditch-academics-for-emotional-manipulation/

35.　　John Rosales, "How ESSA Helps Advance Social and Emotional Learning," NEA Today, June 30, 2017, http://neatoday.org/2017/06/30/essa-sel/

36. Ibid.

37. Sean Grant, Laura S. Hamilton, Stephani L. Wrabel, Celia J. Gomez, Anamarie A. Whitaker, Jennifer T. Leschitz, Fatih Unlu, Emilio R. Chavez-Herrerias, Garrett Baker, Mark Barrett, Mark Harris, and Alyssa Ramos, "How the Every Student Succeeds Act Can Support Social and Emotional Learning," RAND Corporation Research Brief (2017), https://www.rand.org/pubs/research_briefs/RB9988.html

38. Ibid.

39. United States, Department of Education, "Applications for New Award: Center to Improve Social and Emotional Learning and School Safety-Cooperative Agreement," March 16, 2018, https://www.ed.gov/content/applications-new-award-center-improve-social-and-emotional-learning-and-school-safety-cooperative-agreement

40. National Conference of State Legislatures, "Research: Social and Emotional Learning," NCSL, April 12, 2018, http://www.ncsl.org/research/education/social-emotional-learning.aspx

41. Jonathan E. Martin, "We Should Measure Students' Noncognitive Skills," Education Week, July 27, 2016, https://www.edweek.org/ew/articles/2016/07/27/we-should-measure-students-noncognitive-skills.html

42. Collaborative for Academic, Social, and Emotional Learning, "Collaborating States Initiative," accessed November 23, 2018, https://casel.org/collaborative-state-initiative/

Evie Blad, "CORE Districts to Share Social-Emotional Measures to Inform Accountability Plans," Education Week, December 10, 2015, http://blogs.edweek.org/edweek/rulesforengagement/2015/12/core_districts__social-emotional_measures_to_inform_accountability_essa.html

43. Linda Dusenbury, Caitlin Dermody, and Roger P. Weissberg, "2018 State Scorecard Scan More States Are Supporting Social and Emotional Learning," Collaborative for Academic, Social, and Emotional Learning, February 2018, https://casel.org/wp-content/uploads/2018/02/2018-State-Scan-FINAL.pdf

44. Minnesota Department of Education, "Districts Schools and Educators: SEL Implementation Guidance," accessed November 23, 2018, https://education.mn.gov/MDE/dse/safe/clim/social/imp/

45. Rhode Island Department of Education, "Health & Safety—Social & Emotional Learning (SEL): Social and Emotional Learning 'Is a Process for Helping Children and Adults Develop the Fundamental Skills for Success in Life,'" accessed November 23, 2018, http://www.ride.ri.gov/Students-Families/HealthSafety/SocialEmotionalLearning.aspx

46. Rhode Island Council for Elementary and Secondary Education, "RI Social Emotional Learning Standards: Competencies for School and Life Success," Rhode Island Department of Education, October 24, 2017, http://www.ride.ri.gov/Portals/0/Uploads/Documents/Students-and-Families-Great-Schools/Health-Safety/Social-Emotional-Learning/1-RI%20SEL%20Standards%2010.24.17.Eng.Spanish.pdf

47. Collaborative for Academic, Social, and Emotional Learning, "About: CSI Standards Advisory Committee," accessed November 23, 2018, https://casel.org/csi-standards-advisory-committee/

48. Ibid.

49. United States Representative Tim Ryan (Representing Ohio's 13th District): "Congressman Tim Ryan Introduces Social and Emotional Learning for Families (SELF) Act," Media: Press Releases, June 14, 2018, https://timryan.house.gov/media/press-releases/congressman-tim-ryan-introduces-social-and-emotional-learning-families-self-act

50. Patrick C. Kyllonen, "Soft Skills for the Workplace," Change: The Magazine of Higher Learning 45 no. 6 (2013): 16-23.

51. Bobby Naemi, Jacob Seybert, Steven Robbins, and Patrick Kyllonen, "Examining the WorkFORCE™ Assessment for Job Fit and Core Capabilities of FACETS™," ETS Research Report Series 2 (2014): 1-43.

Educational Testing Services, "Assessment Methods," ETS (2012), accessed https://www.ets.org/s/workforce_readiness/pdf/21333_big_5.pdf

52. Jonathan E. Martin, "We Should Measure Students' Noncognitive Skills," Education Week, July 27, 2016, https://www.edweek.org/ew/articles/2016/07/27/we-should-measure-students-noncognitive-skills.html

53. Affectiva, "More: Emotion AI - Humanizing Technology through the Merger of IQ & EQ Is Inevitable," accessed November 23, 2018, https://www.affectiva.com/what/uses/more/

54. Morna McDermott McNulty, "Beware the 'Learning Engineers,'" Wrench in the Gears: A Skeptical Parent's Thoughts on Digital Curriculum, March 5, 2018, https://wrenchinthegears.com/2018/05/05/beware-the-learning-engineers/

55. Global Education Futures, "Global Education 2015-2035," Global Education Futures Initiative, accessed November 23, 2018, https://www.edu2035.org/images/people/Future%20of%20Global%20Education%20Map%20(2014)-ilovepdf-compressed.pdf

56. Sean Grant, Laura S. Hamilton, Stephani L. Wrabel, Celia J. Gomez, Anamarie A. Whitaker, Jennifer T. Leschitz, Fatih Unlu, Emilio R. Chavez-Herrerias, Garrett Baker, Mark Barrett, Mark Harris, and Alyssa Ramos, "How the Every Student Succeeds Act Can Support Social and Emotional Learning," RAND Corporation Research Brief (2017), https://www.rand.org/pubs/research_briefs/RB9988.html

57. Spencer Foundation, "Conceptualizing and Studying Social Emotional Learning (SEL) Practices in Schools: Implications for Adolescent Ethnic-Racial Identity Development **(Principal Investigator:** Deborah Rivas-Drake, University of Michigan, Education and Psychology)" Grant Library, 2016, https://www.spencer.org/conceptualizing-and-studying-social-emotional-learning-sel-practices-schools-implications-adolescent

58. Rosemarie O'Conner, Jessica De Feyter, Alyssa Carr, Jia Lisa Luo, and Helen Romm, "A Review of the Literature on Social and Emotional Learning for Students Ages 3–8: Outcomes for Different Student Populations and Settings (Part 4 of 4)," National Center for Education Evaluation and Regional Assistance (Institute of Education Sciences of the US Department of Education, 2017), https://files.eric.ed.gov/fulltext/ED572724.pdf

59. Aspen Institute, "Pursuing Social and Emotional Development through a Racial Equity Lens: 5 Strategies for System Leaders to Take Action," Aspen Institute Education and Society Program, July 2018, https://assets.aspeninstitute.org/content/uploads/2018/07/Taking-Action-on-the-Call-to-Action-FINAL.pdf

60. Rosemarie O'Conner, Jessica De Feyter, Alyssa Carr, Jia Lisa Luo, and Helen Romm, "A Review of the Literature on Social and Emotional Learning for Students Ages 3–8: Outcomes for Different Student Populations and Settings (Part 4 of 4)," National Center for Education Evaluation and Regional Assistance (Institute of Education Sciences of the US Department of Education, 2017), https://files.eric.ed.gov/fulltext/ED572724.pdf

61. Joseph E. Zins and Maurice J. Elias, "Social and Emotional Learning: Promoting the Development of All Students," Journal of Educational and Psychological Consultation 17 (2-3): 233-255.

62. L. Edward Day, Michelle Miller-Day, Michael L. Hecht, Desiree Fehmie, "Coming to the New D.A.R.E.: A Preliminary Test of the Officer-Taught Elementary Keepin' It REAL Curriculum," Addictive Behaviors 74 (2017): 67-73.

63. Ibid.

64. Lee Ellis, "Race/Ethnicity and Criminal Behavior: Neurohormonal Influences," Journal of Criminal Justice 51 (2017): 34.

65. Ibid.

66. Ibid.

67. Ashley May, "Took an Ancestry DNA Test? You Might Be a 'Genetic Informant' Unleashing Secrets about Your Relatives," USA Today, April 27, 2018, https://www.usatoday.com/story/tech/nation-now/2018/04/27/ancestry-genealogy-dna-test-privacy-golden-state-killer/557263002/

GEDmatch Inc., "Tools for DNA and Genealogy Research: Login," accessed November 24, 2018, https://www.gedmatch.com/login1.php

Matthias Gafni and Lisa M. Krieger, "Here's the 'Open-Source' Genealogy DNA Website That Helped Crack the Golden State Killer Case," Mercury News, April 26, 2018, https://www.mercurynews.com/2018/04/26/ancestry-23andme-deny-assisting-law-enforcement-in-east-area-rapist-case/

68. Neil Davie, "The Role of Medico-legal Expertise in the Emergence of Criminology in Britain (1870-1918)," Histoire de la Criminologie 3 (2010), https://journals.openedition.org/criminocorpus/316

69. Philip K. Dick, The Minority Report and Other Classic Stories by Philip K. Dick (London: Victor Gollancz, 1988).

70. Neil Davie, "The Role of Medico-legal Expertise in the Emergence of Criminology in Britain (1870-1918)," Histoire de la Criminologie 3 (2010), https://journals.openedition.org/criminocorpus/316

71. Cera R. Lawrence, "Francis Galton (1822-1911)," The Embryo Project Encyclopedia at Arizona State University April 6, 2011, https://embryo.asu.edu/pages/francis-galton-1822-1911

72. Neil Davie, "The Role of Medico-legal Expertise in the Emergence of Criminology in Britain (1870-1918)," Histoire de la Criminologie 3 (2010), https://journals.openedition.org/criminocorpus/316

73.	Seán McConville, English Local Prisons, 1860-1900: Next Only to Death (London: Routledge, 1995).

United Kingdom, Parliament, "Historic Hansard: Salary and Emoluments of Sir Edmund Du Cane," House of Commons Debate 2 c160 (March 7, 1892), https://api.parliament.uk/historic-hansard/commons/1892/mar/07/salary-and-emoluments-of-sir-edmund-du

74.	Arthur MacDonald, "Man and Abnormal Man, Including a Study of Children in Connection with Bills to Establish Laboratories under Federal and State Governments for the Study of the Criminal, Pauper, and Defective Classes, with Bibliographies," Senate Document 187: 58th Congress, 3rd Session (Washington, DC: Government Publishing Office, 1905).

Cold Spring Harbor Laboratory, "Criminality," DNA Learning Center: Eugenics Archives, accessed November 24, 2018, http://www.eugenicsarchive.org/html/eugenics/static/themes/12.html

Philip Jenkins, "Eugenics, Crime, and Ideology: The Case of Progressive Pennsylvania," Pennsylvania History: A Journal of Mid-Atlantic Studies 51 no. 1 (1984): 64-78.

Teryn Bouche and Laura Rivard, "America's Hidden History: The Eugenics Movement," Nature, September 18, 2014, https://www.nature.com/scitable/forums/genetics-generation/america-s-hidden-history-the-eugenics-movement-123919444

75.	Sydney Lee, Dictionary of National Biography: Second Supplement (Volume 1) (New York: MacMillan, 1912).

76.	University of Pennsylvania, Center for Health Incentives and Behavioral Economics at the Leonard Davis Institute, "Angela L. Duckworth, PhD, MA, MsC: Christopher H. Browne Distinguished Professor of Psychology, University of Pennsylvania Founder and CEO, Character Lab," accessed November 24, 2018, https://chibe.upenn.edu/faculty-members/angela-l-duckworth-phd-ma-msc/

77.	Angela Lee Duckworth, "True Grit: Can Perseverance be Taught?," TEDx Talks, November 12, 2009, https://www.youtube.com/watch?v=qaeFnxSfSC4

78.	Ibid.

Ibid, "Grit: The Power of Passion and Perseverance," TED Talks, May 9, 2013, https://www.youtube.com/watch?v=H14bBuluwB8

79.	Ibid, "True Grit: Can Perseverance be Taught?," TEDx Talks, November 12, 2009, https://www.youtube.com/watch?v=qaeFnxSfSC4

80.	Ibid, "Grit: The Power of Passion and Perseverance," TED Talks, May 9, 2013, https://www.youtube.com/watch?v=H14bBuluwB8

81.	Trustees of the University of Pennsylvania, "Initiatives: Grit and Self-Control," Authentic Happiness: University of Pennsylvania Positive Psychology Center, accessed November 24, 2018, https://www.authentichappiness.sas.upenn.edu/es/learn/grit

82.	Ibid, "Positive Psychology Theory Initiatives," Authentic Happiness: University of Pennsylvania Positive Psychology Center, accessed November 24, 2018, https://www.authentichappiness.sas.upenn.edu/es/learn

83.	Morna McDermott, Peggy Robertson, and Rosemarie Jensen, "Grit, Human Capital, and Data Mining: What's Next for Children?," Stop Corporate Surveillance in Schools: News, June 4, 2018, http://classroomsnotcomputers.org/2018/06/04/grit-human-capital-and-data-mining-whats-next-for-children/

84.	John Templeton Foundation, "About: Accelerating Discovery, Inspiring Curiosity," accessed November 24, 2018, https://www.templeton.org/about/vision-mission-impact

85.	Ibid, "Funding Areas," accessed November 24, 2018, https://www.templeton.org/funding-areas

86.	Ibid, "A Chance to Equality in Health: Is People's Health Determined by Ancestral Environmental Exposures? (September 2017 - August 2020)," Our Grants, https://www.templeton.org/grant/a-chance-to-equality-in-health-is-peoples-health-determined-by-ancestral-environmental-exposures

Ibid, "Imprinting in Human Placentas: The Intergenerational Transmission of Health (September 2014 - August 2017)," Our Grants, https://www.templeton.org/grant/imprinting-in-human-placentas-the-intergenerational-transmission-of-health

87.	Jennifer Latson, "What Margaret Sanger Really Said About Eugenics and Race," Time, October 14, 2016, http://time.com/4081760/margaret-sanger-history-eugenics/

Margaret Sanger, "Editorial," Birth Control Review, June 1925, https://www.nyu.edu/projects/sanger/webedition/app/documents/show.php?sangerDoc=226796.xml

88.	New York University, "About Sanger: Birth Control Organizations—American Birth Control League," Margaret Sanger Papers Project, accessed November 24, 2018, https://www.nyu.edu/projects/sanger/aboutms/organization_abcl.php

Planned Parenthood Federation of America, "About Us: Who We Are—Our History," accessed November 24, 2018, https://www.plannedparenthood.org/about-us/who-we-are/our-history

89.		New York University, "Birth Control or Race Control? Sanger and the Negro Project," Margaret Sanger Papers Project Newsletter 28 (2001), https://www.nyu.edu/projects/sanger/articles/bc_or_race_control.php

90.		Harriet A. Washington, Medical Apartheid: The Dark History of Medical Experimentation on Black Americans from Colonial Times to the Present (New York: Anchor, 2006), 197.

91.		Zoe Williams, "Marie Stopes: a Turbo-Darwinist Ranter, but Right about Birth Control," The Guardian: US Edition, September 2, 2011, https://www.theguardian.com/theguardian/2011/sep/02/marie-stopes-right-birth-control

92.		Jane Carey, "The Racial Imperatives of Sex: Birth Control and Eugenics in Britain, the United States and Australia in the Interwar Years," Women's History Review 21 (2012): 733-752.

93.		Edwin Black, War Against the Weak: Eugenics and America's Campaign to Create a Master Race (New York: Four Walls Eight Windows, 2003), 411-426.

94.		Lex Borghans, Angela Lee Duckworth, James H. Heckman, Bas ter Weel, "The Economics and Psychology of Personality Traits: Working Paper 13810," National Bureau of Economic Research Working Paper Series (NBER, February 2008).

95.		Ibid, 2, 5, 6, 10, 12-14, 22, 24-25, 28-31, 35-36, 38, 43-46, 51-55, 57-59, 61, 72, 74, 78, 81, 84-85, 88, 90, 92, 96-97, 99, 102, 109, 123, 126, 130, 133-134, 137-141, 146, 153, 156, 158,

96.		Ibid, i.

97.		Ibid, 52.

98.		Ibid, 52-53.

99.		Ibid, 18.

100.		Ibid, 58.

101.		Nobel Media, "Nobel Prizes and Laureates in Economic Sciences: The Sveriges Riksbank Prize in Economic Sciences in Memory of Alfred Nobel 2000—James J. Heckman (Prize Presentation)," The Nobel Prize, accessed November 24, 2018, https://www.nobelprize.org/prizes/economic-sciences/2000/heckman/prize-presentation/

102.		University of Chicago, "The Research Network on the Determinants of Life Course Capabilities And Outcomes: Bringing Together Scholars in Economics, Genetics, Psychology, Sociology, and Statistics to Produce New Knowledge about the Determinants, Development, and Measurement of Capabilities Across the Life Cycle, as Well as Life Course Inequalities," Center for the Economics of Human Development, accessed November 24, 2018, https://cehd.uchicago.edu/?page_id=265

103.		Lex Borghans, Angela Lee Duckworth, James H. Heckman, Bas ter Weel, "The Economics and Psychology of Personality Traits: Working Paper 13810," National Bureau of Economic Research Working Paper Series (NBER, February 2008), 75.

104.		Morna McDermott, Peggy Robertson, and Rosemarie Jensen, "Grit, Human Capital, and Data Mining: What's Next for Children?," Stop Corporate Surveillance in Schools: News, June 4, 2018, http://classroomsnotcomputers.org/2018/06/04/grit-human-capital-and-data-mining-whats-next-for-children/

105.		Lauren Anderson, "Grit, Galton, and Eugenics," Education Week, March 21, 2014, http://blogs.edweek.org/teachers/living-in-dialogue/2014/03/lauren_anderson_grit.html

106.		Jane Robbins and Karen Effrem, "Schools Ditch Academics For Emotional Manipulation: Under Such a System Teachers Become Essentially Therapists, and Students Become Essentially Patients," The Federalist, October 19, 2016, http://thefederalist.com/2016/10/19/schools-ditch-academics-for-emotional-manipulation/

107.		Charles Rollett, "The Odd Reality of Life under China's All-Seeing Credit Score System," Wired Magazine, June 5 2018, https://www.wired.co.uk/article/china-social-credit

108.		Ibid.

109.		Gabrielle Bruney, "A 'Black Mirror' Episode Is Coming to Life in China: People Will Be Prevented from Traveling on Trains and Planes Based on Their Social Credit Scores," Esquire, March 17, 2018, https://www.esquire.com/news-politics/a19467976/black-mirror-social-credit-china/

Megan Palin, "China's 'Social Credit' System Is a Real-Life 'Black Mirror' Nightmare," New York Post, September 19, 2018, https://nypost.com/2018/09/19/chinas-social-credit-system-is-a-real-life-black-mirror-nightmare/

110.		Annie Grayer, "Facebook apologizes after labeling part of Declaration of Independence 'hate speech,'" CNN, July 5, 2018, https://www.cnn.com/2018/07/05/politics/facebook-post-hate-speech-delete-declaration-of-independence-mistake/index.html

111.   Samuel Gibbs, "EU Gives Facebook and Google Three Months to Tackle Extremist Content," The Guardian: US Edition, March 1, 2018, https://www.theguardian.com/technology/2018/mar/01/eu-facebook-google-youtube-twitter-extremist-content

Sara Salinas, "Twitter Permanently Bans Alex Jones and Infowars Accounts," CNBC News, September 6, 2018, https://www.cnbc.com/2018/09/06/twitter-permanently-bans-alex-jones-and-infowars-accounts.html

112.   Alex Hern, "Facebook, Apple, YouTube and Spotify Ban Infowars' Alex Jones: Crackdown on US Conspiracy Theorist for Promoting Violence and Hate Speech," The Guardian: US Edition, August 6, 2018, https://www.theguardian.com/technology/2018/aug/06/apple-removes-podcasts-infowars-alex-jones

Janko Roettgers, "Twitter Shuts Down Accounts of Vice Co-Founder Gavin McInnes, Proud Boys Ahead of 'Unite the Right' Rally," Variety, August 10, 2018, https://variety.com/2018/digital/news/twitter-shuts-down-accounts-of-vice-co-founder-gavin-mcinnes-proud-boys-ahead-of-unite-the-right-rally-1202902397/

113.   Chauncey Alcorn, "Left-Wing New Sites Censored on Facebook Aren't in Favor of Banning Alex Jones Either," Mic, August 9, 2018, https://mic.com/articles/190621/left-wing-news-sites-censored-on-facebook-arent-in-favor-of-banning-alex-jones-either#.YqLs2BfH8

Jessica Corbett, "'Deeply Disturbing': For Second Time This Year, Facebook Suspends Left-Leaning teleSUR English Without Explanation," Common Dreams, August 14, 2018, https://www.commondreams.org/news/2018/08/14/deeply-disturbing-second-time-year-facebook-suspends-left-leaning-telesur-english

114.   Bill Boyarsky, "Will Facebook's System to Detect Fake News Lead to Censorship?," Truthdig, February 8, 2017, https://www.truthdig.com/articles/will-facebooks-system-to-detect-fake-news-lead-to-censorship/

115.   Brian Merchant, "Life and Death in Apple's Forbidden City," The Guardian: US Edition, June 28, 2017, https://www.theguardian.com/technology/2017/jun/18/foxconn-life-death-forbidden-city-longhua-suicide-apple-iphone-brian-merchant-one-device-extract

Malcolm Moore, 'Mass Suicide' Protest at Apple Manufacturer Foxconn Factory," The Telegraph, January 11, 2012, https://www.telegraph.co.uk/news/worldnews/asia/china/9006988/Mass-suicide-protest-at-Apple-manufacturer-Foxconn-factory.html

116.   Arthur Thomas, "Evers' Victory Lowers the Stakes for Foxconn in November: Democrat Nominee for Governor Ran on Possible Contract Changes, but Not on Ending the Deal," BizTimes: Milwaukee Business News, August 17, 2018, https://www.biztimes.com/2018/ideas/government-politics/evers-victory-lowers-the-stakes-for-foxconn-in-november/

John Lucas, "$100 Million Foxconn Gift Launches Major New Partnership with UW–Madison," University of Wisconsin-Madison News, August 27, 2018, https://news.wisc.edu/100-million-foxconn-gift-launches-major-new-partnership-with-uw-madison/

State of Wisconsin, Department of Workforce Development, "Governor Walker Proclaims September as Workforce Development Month," Office of the Secretary of Education: Information for Media, September 1, 2017, https://dwd.wisconsin.gov/dwd/newsreleases/2017/170901_workforce_development_month.htm

Wisconsin Department of Public Instruction, "Learning that Works: Wisconsin College Internships," Business and Information Technology: EdBITS, November 1, 2017, https://dpi.wi.gov/bit/edbits/learning-works-wisconsin-college-internships

117.   Beth Herman and Rebecca Collins, Social and Emotional Learning Competencies, (Wisconsin: Department of Public Instruction, May 2018), https://dpi.wi.gov/sites/default/files/imce/sspw/SEL-Competencies-Guide-web.pdf

118.   Wisconsin Department of Public Instruction, "Collaborative and Comprehensive Pupil Services," Student Services/Prevention & Wellness Team (Division for Learning Support: Equity and Advocacy), September 2008, https://dpi.wi.gov/sites/default/files/imce/sspw/pdf/pscandc.pdf

119.   Beth Herman and Rebecca Collins, Social and Emotional Learning Competencies, (Wisconsin: Department of Public Instruction, May 2018), https://dpi.wi.gov/sites/default/files/imce/sspw/SEL-Competencies-Guide-web.pdf

120.   Ibid.

121.   Anthony Cuthbertson, "Apple Is Quietly Giving People 'Trust Scores' Based on Their iPhone Data," The Independent, September 20, 2018, https://www.independent.co.uk/life-style/gadgets-and-tech/news/apple-trust-score-iphone-data-black-mirror-email-phone-fraud-a8546051.html

Sean Keach, "Secret Scores: Apple Gives You a TRUST Rating – and It's Based on Your Phone Call and Email Habits," The Sun, September 20, 2018, https://www.thesun.co.uk/tech/7303020/apple-trust-score-phone-calls-emails/

122.	Dawn Chmielewski, "Where Apple Products Are Born: A Rare Glimpse Inside Foxconn's Factory Gates: Foxconn, Eager to Present Its Positive Side, Agreed to Give Re/code a Restricted Tour of a Sprawling Manufacturing Facility in Shenzhen," Re/code, April 6, 2015, https://www.recode.net/2015/4/6/11561130/where-apple-products-are-born-a-rare-glimpse-inside-foxconns-factory

123.	Edwin Black, IBM and the Holocaust: The Strategic Alliance between Nazi Germany and America's Most Powerful Corporation (New York: Random House, 2001), 618-628, 730.

124.	Ibid, War Against the Weak: Eugenics and America's Campaign to Create a Master Race (New York: Four Walls Eight Windows, 2003), 283.

125.	Ibid, IBM and the Holocaust: The Strategic Alliance between Nazi Germany and America's Most Powerful Corporation (New York: Random House, 2001), 230-232.

126.	Ibid, 639, 642.

127.	Ibid, 643.

128.	Ibid, 44.

129.	Stefan Kühl, The Nazi Connection: Eugenics, American Racism, and German National Socialism (Oxford: Oxford University Press, 1994), 28, 30.

130.	Ibid, 21.

131.	Edwin Black, War Against the Weak: Eugenics and America's Campaign to Create a Master Race (New York: Four Walls Eight Windows, 2003), 416.

132.	John Timson, "Portraits of the Pioneers: Julian Huxley," Galton Institute Newsletter 35 (1999), http://www.galtoninstitute.org.uk/Newsletters/GINL9912/julian_huxley.htm

133.	Aldous Huxley, Brave New World (New York: Bantam, 1932), 1-11.

134.	Plato, The Republic, trans. B. Jowett (New York: Modern Library, 1941), 125, 181, 182.

135.	Aldous Huxley, Brave New World (New York: Bantam, 1932), 18, 39, 42-43, 67, 107, 151.

136.	Ibid.

137.	Ibid, 39, 67.

138.	Ibid, 107.

139.	"Brachycephalic," Merriam-Webster Dictionary, Merriam-Webster Inc., accessed November 24, 2018, https://www.merriam-webster.com/dictionary/brachycephalic

"Brachycephalic," Oxford English Dictionary, University of Oxford Press, accessed November 24, 2018, https://en.oxforddictionaries.com/definition/brachycephalic

140.	Aldous Huxley, Brave New World (New York: Bantam, 1932), 122.

Douglas Lorimer, "Theoretical Racism in Late-Victorian Anthropology, 1870-1900," Victorian Studies 31 no. 3 (1988): 406-407, 412, 413.

Thomas Henry Huxley, "On the Geographical Distribution of the Chief Modifications of Man," Journal of Ethnological Science 2 (1870), quoted in Douglas Lorimer, "Theoretical Racism in Late-Victorian Anthropology, 1870-1900," Victorian Studies 31 no. 3 (1988): 413.

141.	Aldous Huxley, "The Future of the Past," Aldous Huxley: Complete Essays (Volume II: 1926-1929), eds. Robert S. Baker and James Sexton (Chicago: Ivan R. Dee, 2000), 93.

142.	Ibid, "On the Charms of History and the Future of the Past," Aldous Huxley: Complete Essays (Volume III: 1930-1935), eds. Robert S. Baker and James Sexton (Chicago: Ivan R. Dee, 2000), 137.

143.	Ibid, "Science and Civilization," Aldous Huxley: Complete Essays (Volume III: 1930-1935), eds. Robert S. Baker and James Sexton (Chicago: Ivan R. Dee, 2000), 154.

144.	B. F. Skinner, Walden Two (New York: MacMillan, 1948.

145.	Ibid, Beyond Freedom and Dignity (Indianapolis: Hackett, 1971), 222.

146.	Aldous Huxley, Brave New World (New York: Bantam, 1932), 1-11.

147.	Ibid, 12-19.

148.	Ibid, 16-19.

149.	Dalhousie University Faculty of Arts and Social Sciences, "Department of English: Faculty & Staff," accessed November 24, 2018, https://www.dal.ca/faculty/arts/english/faculty-staff/Sessionals.html

150.	Brad Congdon, "'Community, Identity, Stability': The Scientific Society and the Future of Religion in Aldous Huxley's Brave New World," ECS: English Studies in Canada 37 no. 3 (2011): 83-105.

151.	Internet Movie Database, "Michel Houellebecq: Biography," IMDb, accessed November 24, 2018, https://www.imdb.com/name/nm0396391/bio?ref_=nm_ov_bio_sm

Susannah Hunnewell, "Michel Houellebecq, The Art of Fiction No. 206," Paris Review 194 (2010), https://www.theparisreview.org/interviews/6040/michel-houellebecq-the-art-of-fiction-no-206-michel-houellebecq

152.　　　Michel Houellebecq and Frank Wynne, The Elementary Particles, (New York: Vintage, 2000), quoted in Brad Congdon, "'Community, Identity, Stability': The Scientific Society and the Future of Religion in Aldous Huxley's Brave New World," ECS: English Studies in Canada 37 no. 3 (2011): 83.

153.　　　Julian Huxley, "The Galton Lecture for 1962: Eugenics in Evolutionary Perspective," Evolutionary Studies: A Centenary Celebration of the Life of Julian Huxley—Proceedings of the Twenty-Fourth Annual Symposium of the Eugenics Society, London, 1987, eds. Milo Keynes and G. Ainsworth Harrison (London: Macmillan, 1989), 207.

154.　　　Ibid, "Sir Julian Huxley, F. R. S.," Aldous Huxley 1894-1963: A Memorial Volume, ed. Julian Huxley (New York: Harper & Row, 1965), 22.

155.　　　Krishna R. Dronamraju, If I Am to Be Remembered: The Life and Works of Julian Huxley with Selected Correspondence (River Edge, NJ: World Scientific Publishing, 1993), 68.

156.　　　Alfred H. Fuchs, Rand B. Evans and Christopher D. Green, "History of Psychology: Johns Hopkins's First Professorship in Philosophy: A Critical Pivot Point in the History of American Psychology," American Journal of Psychology 120 no. 2 (2007): 303-323.

Editors of Encyclopedia Britannica, "G. Stanley Hall: American Psychologist," Encyclopedia Britannica, accessed November 25, 2018, https://www.britannica.com/biography/G-Stanley-Hall

157.　　　Manon Parry, "G. Stanley Hall: Psychologist and Early Gerontologist," American Journal of Public Health, 96 no. 7 (2006), https://www.ncbi.nlm.nih.gov/pmc/articles/PMC1483855/

158.　　　Antony C. Sutton, America's Secret Establishment: An Introduction to the Order of Skull and Bones, Updated Reprint, (Walterville, OR: Trine Day, 2002), 81-88, 90-92, 94-95, 98, 101-102, 105, 108, 109.

Robert S. Harper, "The First Psychological Laboratory," Isis 41 no. 2 (1950): 158-161.

159.　　　Antony C. Sutton, America's Secret Establishment: An Introduction to the Order of Skull and Bones, Updated Reprint, (Walterville, OR: Trine Day, 2002), 290.

"Percy Rockefeller, Nephew of John D., Passes Away: Leaves Millions, His Fortune Fabulous," Lewiston Morning Tribune, September 26, 1934, https://news.google.com/newspapers?id=rq9fAAAAIBAJ&sjid=zzlMAAAAIBAJ&pg=1477,1491319&dq=percy+rockefeller&hl=en

160.　　　Charles R. Lanman, "Daniel Coit Gilman (1831-1908)," Proceedings of the American Academy of Arts and Sciences 52 no. 13 (1917): 836-839.

161.　　　Paolo Lionni, The Leipzig Connection: The Systematic Destruction of American Education, Third Printing (Sheridan, OR: Delphian Press, 1988), 30-89.

162.　　　Antony C. Sutton, America's Secret Establishment: An Introduction to the Order of Skull and Bones, Updated Reprint, (Walterville, OR: Trine Day, 2002), 292.

B. F. Skinner, The Technology of Teaching (New York: Appleton-Century-Crofts, 1968), viii.

163.　　　J. Vernon Jensen, "Thomas Henry Huxley's Address at the Opening of the Johns Hopkins University in September 1876," Notes and Records of the Royal Society of London 47 no. 2 (1993): 257-269.

Leonard Huxley, Life and Letters of Thomas Henry Huxley Vol. I (London: MacMillan, 1900), 467.

164.　　　Edwin Black, War Against the Weak: Eugenics and America's Campaign to Create a Master Race (New York: Four Walls Eight Windows, 2003), 283.

165.　　　Cera R. Lawrence, "The Eugenics Record Office at Cold Spring Harbor Laboratory (1910-1939)," The Embryo Project Encyclopedia at Arizona State University, April 21, 2011, https://embryo.asu.edu/pages/eugenics-record-office-cold-spring-harbor-laboratory-1910-1939

166.　　　David Madsen, "Daniel Coit Gilman at the Carnegie Institution of Washington," History of Education Quarterly 9 no. 2 (1969): 154-186.

Edwin Black, War Against the Weak: Eugenics and America's Campaign to Create a Master Race (New York: Four Walls Eight Windows, 2003), 36, 41.

167.　　　Ibid, 272.

Ingrid L. Anderson, Ethics and Suffering Since the Holocaust: Making Ethics "First Philosophy" in Levinas, Wiesel, and Rubenstein (New York: Routledge, 2016).

Jonathan Marks, Human Biodiversity: Genes, Race, and History (New Brunswick, NJ: Aldine Transaction, 1995), 88.

168.　　　Antony C. Sutton, America's Secret Establishment: An Introduction to the Order of Skull and Bones, Updated Reprint, (Walterville, OR: Trine Day, 2002), 291, 292.

Cold Spring Harbor Laboratory, "Eulogy on Death of Mrs. Harriman," DNA Learning Center: Preparing Students and Families to Thrive in the Gene Age, accessed November 25, 2018, https://www.dnalc.org/view/10430-Eulogy-on-death-of-Mrs-Harriman.html

Daniel J. Kevles, In the Name of Eugenics: Genetics and the Uses of Human Heredity (New York: Alfred A. Knopf, 1985), 54-55.

James D. Watson, "Genes and Politics," Davenport's Dreams: 21st Century Reflections on Heredity and Eugenics, eds. Jan A. Witkowski and John R. Inglis (Cold Spring Harbor, NY: Cold Spring Harbor Laboratory Press, 2008), 1.

Kim Masters, "The Harriman Bunch," Washington Post, October 11, 1994, https://www.washingtonpost.com/archive/lifestyle/1994/10/11/the-harriman-bunch/9198b313-4260-4914-b99b-49e638b9f92e/?utm_term=.342bab067b20

169. Antony C. Sutton, America's Secret Establishment: An Introduction to the Order of Skull and Bones, Updated Reprint, (Walterville, OR: Trine Day, 2002), 126, 165-170.

Ibid, Wall Street and the Rise of Hitler: The Astonishing True Story of the American Financiers Who Bankrolled the Nazis (California: Clairview, 1976), 103, 107, 25-26, 57, 99, 102, 103, 106, 112-114, 141.

170. Brian Murphy, "Lawyer-Turned-Crusader Pays Price for Probe of Nazis in U.S.," Los Angeles Times, October 23, 1988, http://articles.latimes.com/1988-10-23/news/mn-237_1_nazi-collaborators

Central Intelligence Agency, "Secret Draft Working Paper: Belorussians, 60 Minutes, and the GAO's Second Investigation (U)," Nazi War Crimes Disclosure Act (2007), accessed November 26, 2018, https://www.cia.gov/library/readingroom/docs/CIA%20AND%20NAZI%20WAR%20CRIM.%20AND%20COL.%20CHAP.%2011-21%2C%20DRAFT%20WORKING%20PAPER_0008.pdf

Jim Marrs, Rise of the Fourth Reich: The Secret Societies That Threaten to Take Over America (New York: William Morrow, 2008), 12-13, 27, 116-119, 150-151, 154, 166, 168, 212, 235, 251, 255, 264, 283.

John Loftus, Americas Nazi Secret: An Insider's History of How the United States Department of Justice Obstructed Congress by: Blocking Congressional Investigations into Famous American Families Who Funded Hitler, Stalin and Arab Terrorists; Lying to Congress, the GAO and the CIA about the Postwar Immigration of Eastern European Nazi War Criminals to the US; and Concealing from the 9/11 Investigators the Role of the Arab Nazi War Criminals in Recruiting Modern Middle Eastern Terrorist Groups (Walterville, OR: Trine Day, 2010), 6, 13, 16-19, 24, 51-52, 71 266.

171. Antony C. Sutton, America's Secret Establishment: An Introduction to the Order of Skull and Bones, Updated Reprint, (Walterville, OR: Trine Day, 2002), 61, 292.

Endnotes – Chapter Sixteen

1. Educate," Oxford English Dictionary, University of Oxford Press, accessed November 24, 2018, https://en.oxforddictionaries.com/definition/educate

2. "Educate," Merriam-Webster Dictionary, Merriam-Webster Inc., accessed November 25, 2018, https://www.merriam-webster.com/dictionary/educate

3. Randall V. Bass and J. W. Good, "Educare and Educere: Is a Balance Possible in the Educational System?," The Educational Forum 68 (2004): 162.

4. C. S. Lewis "Our English Syllabus," quoted in Charlotte Thomson Iserbyt, The Deliberate Dumbing Down of America: A Chronological Paper Trail, Revised and Abridged Ed. (Parkman, OH: Conscience Press, 2011), 140.

5. Stefan Lorenz Sorgner, "The Future of Education: Genetic Enhancement and Metahumanities," Journal of Evolution and Technology 25 no. 1 (2015): 32.

6. Richard Aldrich, "Nature, Nurture and Neuroscience: Some Future Directions for Historians of Education," Pedagogica Historica 50 no. 6 (2014): 852.

7. Ibid, 859.

8. Paul Weindling, "Julian Huxley and the Continuity of Eugenics in Twentieth-century Britain," Journal of Modern European History 10 no. 4 (2012): 480-499.

World Transhumanist Association, "Do Transhumanists Advocate Eugenics?," Transhumanist FAQ: Society and Politics, accessed November 25, 2018 , https://web.archive.org/web/20060909005028/http:/www.transhumanism.org/index.php/WTA/faq21/66/

9. Julian Huxley, UNESCO: Its Purpose and Its Philosophy (Washington D. C.: Public Affairs Press, 1948), 42.

10. Aleksandra Anđelković and Dušan Spasić, "Historical Outlines of Eugenics and Its Influences on Education," Casopisza Društvene Nauke 39 no. 4 (2015): 1489-1490.

11. Michael Bess, "Enhanced Humans versus 'Normal People': Elusive Definitions," Journal of Medicine and Philosophy 35 (2010): 649.

12. Julian Huxley, UNESCO: Its Purpose and Its Philosophy (Washington D. C.: Public Affairs Press, 1948), 9-10.

13.   Ibid, New Bottles for New Wine (London: Chatto & Windus, 1957), 17.

14.   Editors of Encyclopedia Britannica, "Peking Man: Anthropology," Encyclopedia Britannica, accessed November 25, 2018, https://www.britannica.com/topic/Peking-man

15.   Henry McHenry and Donald C. Johanson, "Australopithecus: Fossil Hominin Genus," Encyclopedia Britannica, accessed November 25, 2018, https://www.britannica.com/topic/Australopithecus

16.   Erik Trinkaus, Russell Howard Tuttle, and Frank L'Engle Williams, "Neanderthal: Archaic Human," Encyclopedia Britannica, accessed November 25, 2018, https://www.britannica.com/topic/Neanderthal

17.   Erin Wayman, "What's in a Name? Hominid Versus Hominin," Smithsonian Magazine, November 16, 2011, https://www.smithsonianmag.com/science-nature/whats-in-a-name-hominid-versus-hominin-216054/

18.   Ray Kurzweil, The Age of Spiritual Machines: When Computers Exceed Human Intelligence (New York: Viking, 1999), 14.

19.   "Robots in Our Brains Will Make Us 'Godlike' Says Google," BBC, October 2, 2015, http://www.bbc.co.uk/newsbeat/article/34427570/robots-in-our-brains-will-make-us-godlike-says-google

20.   Ray Kurzweil, The Age of Spiritual Machines: When Computers Exceed Human Intelligence (New York: Viking, 1999), 14.

21.   Ibid, 255-256.

22.   Jürgen Habermas, The Future of Human Nature (Oxford/Cambridge: Blackwell Polity, 2003), quoted in Fiachra Long, "Transhuman Education? Sloterdijk's Reading of Heidegger's Letter on Humanism," Journal of Philosophy of Education 51 no. 1 (2017): 189.

23.   Fiachra Long, "Transhuman Education? Sloterdijk's Reading of Heidegger's Letter on Humanism," Journal of Philosophy of Education 51 no. 1 (2017): 177.

24.   Ibid, 189.

25.   H. Greely, B. Sahakian, J. Harris, R. C. Kessler, M. Gazzaniga, P. Campbell, and M. J. Farah, "Towards Responsible Use of Cognitive-Enhancing Drugs by the Healthy," Nature 456 (2008):702–5, quoted in Michael Bess, "Enhanced Humans versus 'Normal People': Elusive Definitions," Journal of Medicine and Philosophy 35 (2010): 642.

26.   Stefan Lorenz Sorgner, "The Future of Education: Genetic Enhancement and Metahumanities," Journal of Evolution and Technology 25 no. 1 (2015): 31.

27.   United Nations Educational, Scientific, and Cultural Organization, "Social and Human Sciences—Human Rights-Based Approach: UNESCO and the Declaration," accessed November 25, 2018, http://www.unesco.org/new/en/social-and-human-sciences/themes/human-rights-based-approach/60th-anniversary-of-udhr/unesco-and-the-declaration/

28.   United Nations, General Assembly, Universal Declaration of Human Rights (General Assembly Resolution 217 A), (N: Paris, December 10, 1948), http://www.unesco.org/education/information/50y/nfsunesco/doc/hum-rights.htm

29.   Institute of Bioethics and Human Rights, "Neurobioethics and Transhumanism Masterclass: Neurosciences That Love Human Beings," UNESCO Chair in Bioethics and Human Rights Newsletter, August 4, 2017, http://www.unescobiochair.org/2017/08/04/neurobioethics-and-transhumanism-masterclass-neurosciences-that-love-human-being/

UNESCO Chair in Bioethics and Human Rights, "Training Courses," accessed November 25, 2018, http://www.unescobiochair.org/training-courses/

30.   Institute of Bioethics and Human Rights, "Neurobioethics and Transhumanism Masterclass: Neurosciences That Love Human Beings," UNESCO Chair in Bioethics and Human Rights Newsletter, August 4, 2017, http://www.unescobiochair.org/2017/08/04/neurobioethics-and-transhumanism-masterclass-neurosciences-that-love-human-being/

31.   Ibid.

32.   Information for All Programme, "Reports on the Activities of IFAP and Status of Implementation of the Recommendations of the 7th Session of the IFAP Council," Intergovernmental Council for the Information for All Programme, Eighth Session (Paris: UNESCO Headquarters, 2014), http://unesdoc.unesco.org/images/0022/002273/227377E.pdf

33.   Julian Huxley, UNESCO: Its Purpose and Its Philosophy (Washington D. C.: Public Affairs Press, 1948), 18.

34.   Ibid, 20.

35.   J. P. M. Geraedts and G. De Wert, "Preimplantation Genetic Diagnosis," Clinical Genetics:

An International Journal of Genetic, Molecular, and Personalized Medicine 76 no. 4 (2009): 315-325. United States, National Library of Medicine, "Help Me Understand Genetics: What Are Genome Editing and CRISPR-Cas9?," Genetics Home Reference: Your Guide to Understanding Genetic Conditions, November 20, 2018, https://ghr.nlm.nih.gov/primer/genomicresearch/genomeediting

36.   *Fiachra Long,* "Transhuman Education? Sloterdijk's Reading of Heidegger's Letter on Humanism," Journal of Philosophy of Education 51 no. 1 (2017): 179.

37.   Stefan Lorenz Sorgner, "The Future of Education: Genetic Enhancement and Metahumanities," Journal of Evolution and Technology 25 no. 1 (2015): 45.

38.   Global Education Futures, "Global Education 2015-2035," Global Education Futures Initiative, accessed November 23, 2018, https://www.edu2035.org/images/people/Future%20of%20Global%20Education%20Map%20(2014)-ilovepdf-compressed.pdf

39.   Ibid.

40.   Ibid.

41.   Ibid.

42.   Ibid, "Future Education Map," Global Education Futures Initiative, accessed November 25, 2018, https://www.edu2035.org/images/people/Poster%20on%20Learner-centered%20education-ilovepdf-compressed.pdf

43.   Bill and Melinda Gates Foundation, "Empower Schools Co.: to Measure Engagement Physiologically with Functional Magnetic Resonance Imaging and Galvanic Skin Response to Determine Correlations between Each Measure and Develop a Scale That Differentiates Different Degrees or Levels of Engagement," in How We Work: Grants, November 21, 2011, https://www.gatesfoundation.org/How-We-Work/Quick-Links/Grants-Database/Grants/2011/11/OPP1028976

44.   Valerie Strauss, "$1.1 Million-Plus Gates Grants: 'Galvanic' Bracelets That Measure Student Engagement," Washington Post, June 11, 2012, https://www.washingtonpost.com/blogs/answer-sheet/post/11-million-plus-gates-grants-galvanic-bracelets-that-measure-student-engagement/2012/06/10/gJQAgAUbTV_blog.html?utm_term=.b322ae83c7bf

45.   Bill and Melinda Gates Foundation, "Measures of Effective Teaching Project Releases Final Research Report: Findings Help Inform Design and Implementation of High-Quality Feedback and Evaluation Systems," in Press Room: Press Releases and Statements, January 8, 2013, https://www.gatesfoundation.org/media-center/press-releases/2013/01/measures-of-effective-teaching-project-releases-final-research-report

46.   Ibid, "Clemson University: to Conduct a Pilot Study of New Ways to Measure Student Engagement for Use in Research," in How We Work: Grants, November 15, 2011, https://www.gatesfoundation.org/How-We-Work/Quick-Links/Grants-Database/Grants/2011/11/OPP1049604

47.   Rosalind W. Picard, "What Happened to the Q Sensor?," Massachusetts Institute of Technology Media Lab: Affective Computing, accessed November 25, 2018, https://affect.media.mit.edu/projectpages/iCalm/iCalm-2-Q.html

48.   Stephanie Simon, "Biosensors to Monitor U.S. Students' Attentiveness," Reuters, June 13, 2012, https://www.reuters.com/article/us-usa-education-gates/biosensors-to-monitor-u-s-students-attentiveness-idUSBRE85C17Z20120613

49.   Rosalind W. Picard, "What Happened to the Q Sensor?," Massachusetts Institute of Technology Media Lab: Affective Computing, accessed November 25, 2018, https://affect.media.mit.edu/projectpages/iCalm/iCalm-2-Q.html

50.   Ibid.

51.   Amazon Technologies Inc., "Ultrasonic Bracelet and Receiver for Detecting Position in 2D Plane," United States Patent Application Publication: US 2017/0278051 A1 (Washington, DC: US Patent and Trademark Office, September 28, 2017).

52.   Ceylan Yeginsu, "If Workers Slack Off, the Wristband Will Know: (And Amazon Has a Patent for It)," New York Times, February 1, 2018, https://www.nytimes.com/2018/02/01/technology/amazon-wristband-tracking-privacy.html

53.   United States, White House, Office of Science and Technology Policy, "President Clinton Announces Recipients of Nation's Highest Science and Technology Honors: President Clinton Announces 1999 National Medal of Science and National Medal of Technology Awardees," Office of the Press Secretary: Press Release, January 31, 2000, https://clintonwhitehouse4.archives.gov/textonly/WH/EOP/OSTP/html/0022_6.html

54.   Ray Kurzweil, The Age of Spiritual Machines: When Computers Exceed Human Intelligence (New York: Viking, 1999), 221.

55.   *Fiachra Long,* "Transhuman Education? Sloterdijk's Reading of Heidegger's Letter on Hu-

445

manism," Journal of Philosophy of Education 51 no. 1 (2017): 189-190.

56.　　Sian Bayne, "What's the Matter with 'Technology-Enhanced Learning'?," Learning, Media & Technology 40 no. 1 (2015): 5.

57.　　José Manuel Rodriguez Delgado and Hannibal Hamlin, "Surface and Depth Electrography of the Frontal Lobes in Conscious Patients," Electroencephalography and Clinical Neurophysiology 8 no. 3 (1956): 371-384.

58.　　Yale University School of Medicine, "Department Mourns Loss of Brain-stimulation Research Pioneer," Department of Psychology News Archive, November 28, 2011, https://medicine.yale.edu/psychiatry/newsandevents/delgado.aspx

59.　　Barry Blackwell, "José Manuel Rodriguez Delgado," Neuropsychopharmacology 37 no. 13 (2012): 2883-2884.

60.　　José Manuel Rodriguez Delgado, Physical Control of the Mind: Toward a Psychocivilized Society (New York: Harper & Row, 1971), 83.

61.　　Ibid, 137.

62.　　Colin A. Ross, The CIA Doctors: Human Rights Violations by American Psychiatrists (Austin, TX: Greenleaf Book Group, 2006).
Colin A. Ross Institute for Psychological Trauma, "About Dr. Colin Ross," accessed November 25, 2018, https://www.rossinst.com/about-dr-colin-ross

63.　　Colin A. Ross, interview by Richard Grove, State of Mind: The Psychology of Control, directed by James Lane (USA, Tragedy and Hope Studios: Free Mind Films, 2013).

64.　　Regents of the University of Minnesota, "Apostolos P. Georgopoulos, M.D., Ph.D.: Regents Professor, Departments of Neuroscience, Neurology, and Psychiatry; McKnight Presidential Chair in Cognitive Neuroscience; Director and American Legion Brain Sciences Chair," University of Minnesota Graduate Program in Neuroscience, accessed November 25, 2018, http://www.neuroscience.umn.edu/people/apostolos-p-georgopoulos-md-phd

65.　　University of Pittsburgh, "Schwartz, Andrew B., Professor of Neurobiology: Cerebral Basis for Volitional Movement and Cortical Neural Prosthetics," Department of Neurobiology, accessed November 25, 2018, https://www.neurobio.pitt.edu/faculty/schwartz.htm

66.　　Adam Piore, "The Surgeon Who Wants to Connect You to the Internet with a Brain Implant," MIT Technology Review, November 30, 2017, https://www.technologyreview.com/s/609232/the-surgeon-who-wants-to-connect-you-to-the-internet-with-a-brain-implant/

67.　　Tim Adams, "Neurosurgeon Eric Leuthardt: 'An Interface between Mind and Machine Will Happen,'" The Guardian: US Edition, April 21, 2018, https://www.theguardian.com/science/2018/apr/21/neurosurgeon-eric-leuthardt-interface-mind-machine-brain-implants

68.　　Adam Piore, "The Surgeon Who Wants to Connect You to the Internet with a Brain Implant," MIT Technology Review, November 30, 2017, https://www.technologyreview.com/s/609232/the-surgeon-who-wants-to-connect-you-to-the-internet-with-a-brain-implant/

69.　　Ibid.

70.　　Ibid.

71.　　Ibid.

72.　　Ibid.

73.　　Administration of Donald J. Trump, "Remarks at a Meeting of the President's Strategic and Policy Forum," Strategic and Policy Forum (Washington, DC: April 11, 2017), https://www.gpo.gov/fdsys/pkg/DCPD-201700246/pdf/DCPD-201700246.pdf
Alex Newman, "Some of Trump's Picks Have Troubling Links to Globalism, CFR," The New American, February 25, 2017, https://www.thenewamerican.com/usnews/politics/item/25475-some-of-trump-s-picks-have-troubling-links-to-globalism-cfr
Board of Governors of the Federal Reserve System, "About the Fed—Board Member: Jerome H. Powell, Chairman," accessed November 25, 2018, https://www.federalreserve.gov/aboutthefed/bios/board/powell.htm
Council on Foreign Relations, "Membership Roster: A-F," accessed November 25, 2018, https://www.cfr.org/membership/membership-roster-a-f
Ibid, "Membership Roster: G-K," accessed November 25, 2018, https://www.cfr.org/membership-roster-g-k
Ibid, "Membership Roster: L-P," accessed November 25, 2018, https://www.cfr.org/membership-roster-l-p
Ibid, "Membership Roster: Q-U," accessed November 25, 2018, https://www.cfr.org/membership-roster-q-u

Dan Merica, Jeff Zeleny, and Jim Acosta, "Anthony Scaramucci out as White House Communications Director," CNN, July 31, 2017, https://www.cnn.com/2017/07/31/politics/anthony-scaramucci/index.html

Eliza Relman, "How Goldman Sachs' Dina Powell Became a Top Contender to Replace Nikki Haley at the UN," Business Insider, October 10, 2018, https://www.businessinsider.com/dina-powell-trump-national-security-goldman-sachs-photos-bio-2017-8

"HR McMaster: Why Did Trump Dump National Security Adviser?," BBC News, March 22, 2018, https://www.bbc.com/news/world-europe-39033934

Roger Yu, "No One Has Left Trump's Other Business Leader Council, the Strategic and Policy Forum," USA Today, August 15, 2017, https://www.usatoday.com/story/money/2017/08/15/donald-trumps-strategic-and-policy-forum-ceos-arent-quitting/570542001/

United States, White House, Department of State, Under Secretary for Management, Bureau of Human Resources, , "McFarland, Kathleen Troia - Republic of Singapore," Certificates of Competency for Nominees to be Chiefs of Mission: Report for the Committee on Foreign Relations, June 2017, https://www.state.gov/m/dghr/coc/271992.htm

Ibid, "Meet the Secretary: Secretary Elaine L. Chao, U.S. Secretary of Transportation," Department of Transportation, accessed November 25, 2018, https://www.transportation.gov/mission/meet-secretary/secretary-elaine-l-chao

Ibid, Executive Office of the President, Office of the US Trade Representatives, "Statement By U.S. Trade Representative Robert Lighthizer on Section 301 Action," Press Office: Press Releases, July 2018, https://ustr.gov/about-us/policy-offices/press-office/press-releases/2018/july/statement-us-trade-representative

Ibid, National Security Council, "Remarks by National Security Advisor Ambassador John R. Bolton on the Administration's Policies in Latin America," Foreign Policy Remarks, November 2, 2018, https://www.whitehouse.gov/briefings-statements/remarks-national-security-advisor-ambassador-john-r-bolton-administrations-policies-latin-america/

U.S. Embassy and Consulates in the United Kingdom, "Embassy and Consulates: Ambassador Robert Wood Johnson—Ambassador of the United States of America to the United Kingdom of Great Britain and Northern Ireland," accessed November 25, 2018, https://uk.usembassy.gov/embassy-consulates/london/ambassador-2/

Virginia Rometty, interview by James Owen, "A Conversation with Ginni Rometty," Council on Foreign Relations, March 7, 2013, https://www.cfr.org/event/conversation-ginni-rometty-0

74.   Illah Reza Nourbakhsh, "The Coming Robot Dystopia: All Too Inhuman," Foreign Affairs, July/August (2015): 25-26

75.   National Science Foundation, "Quadriplegic 'feels' again thanks to brain-computer interface and robotic arm combination," NSF News: Multimedia Gallery, September 28, 2017, https://www.nsf.gov/impacts/impact_summ.jsp?cntn_id=243195&org=NSF&from=news

76.   Annie Jacobsen, The Pentagon's Brain : An Uncensored History of DARPA, America's Top-Secret Military Research Agency (New York: Little, Brown, and Company, 2015).

Justin Sanchez, "Restoring Active Memory (RAM)," Defense Advanced Research Project Agency, accessed November 25, 2018, https://www.darpa.mil/program/restoring-active-memory

Ibid, "Revolutionizing Prosthetics," Defense Advanced Research Project Agency, accessed November 25, 2018, https://www.darpa.mil/program/revolutionizing-prosthetics

77.   Kristen V. Brown, "DARPA's Brain Chip Implants Could Be the Next Big Mental Health Breakthrough—Or a Total Disaster," Gizmodo, March 6, 2017, https://gizmodo.com/darpa-s-brain-chips-could-be-the-next-big-mental-health-1791549701

78.   Ibid.

79.   Ibid.

80.   Defense Advanced Research Project Agency, "Program Information: DARPA and the Brain Initiative," accessed November 25, 2018, https://www.darpa.mil/program/our-research/darpa-and-the-brain-initiative

81.   Ibid.

82.   Ibid.

83.   Ibid.

84.   Ibid.

85.   Ibid.

86.   Ibid.

87.   Ibid.

88. Ibid.

89. Ibid.

90. United States, National Institutes of Health, Department of Health and Human Services, "BRAIN Publication Roundup," BRAIN Update, June 27, 2018, https://brainupdate.nih.gov/2018/06/27/brain-publication-roundup-june-2018/

91. Ibid.

92. Ibid.

93. "Fact Sheet: Over $300 Million in Support of the President's BRAIN Initiative," September 30, 2014,https://www.braininitiative.nih.gov/sites/default/files/pdfs/brain_fact-sheet_09302014_508c.pdf United States, National Institutes of Health, "Public-Private Partnership Program: Devices & Support Specific Manufacturers," BRAIN Initiative, accessed November 25, 2018, https://www.braininitiative.nih.gov/resources/public-private-partnership-program-devices-support-specific-manufacturers

94. United States, National Intelligence Council, Office of the Director of National Intelligence, Global Trends 2025: A Transformed World" (Washington, DC: Government Publishing Office, November 2008), http://www.dni.gov/nic/PDF_2025/2025_Global_Trends_Final_Report.pdf

95. Ariel Schwartz, "Elon Musk Defends His Position on President Trump's Advisory Council," Business Insider, April 28, 2017, https://www.businessinsider.com/elon-musk-ted-talks-trump-advisory-council-2017-4

96. Rolfe Winkler, "Elon Musk Launches Neuralink to Connect Brains With Computers: Startup from CEO of Tesla and SpaceX Aims to Implant Tiny Electrodes in Human Brains," Wall Street Journal, March 27, 2017, https://www.wsj.com/articles/elon-musk-launches-neuralink-to-connect-brains-with-computers-1490642652

97. Nick Statt, "Elon Musk Launches Neuralink, a Venture to Merge the Human Brain with AI," The Verge, March 27, 2017, https://www.theverge.com/2017/3/27/15077864/elon-musk-neuralink-brain-computer-interface-ai-cyborgs

98. Ibid.

99. Facebook, "Investor Relations: Governance Documents—Board of Directors," accessed November 27, 2018, https://investor.fb.com/corporate-governance/default.aspx

100. Joe Wolverton II, "After Bilderberg Meeting, Facebook Official Says End Internet Anonymity," The New American, https://www.thenewamerican.com/tech/computers/item/7224-after-bilderberg-meeting-facebook-official-says-end-internet-anonymity

101. James Titcomb, "Mark Zuckerberg Confirms Facebook Is Working on Mind-Reading Technology," The Telegraph, April 19, 2017, https://www.telegraph.co.uk/technology/2017/04/19/mark-zuckerberg-confirms-facebook-working-mind-reading-technology/

102. Cade Metz, "Ex-Darpa Head Regina Dugan Leaves Google for Facebook," Wired Magazine, April 13, 2016, https://www.wired.com/2016/04/regina-dugan-leaves-google-for-facebook/ Josh Constine, "Facebook Is Building Brain-Computer Interfaces for Typing and Skin-Hearing," TechCrunch, 2018, https://techcrunch.com/2017/04/19/facebook-brain-interface/

103. Facebook, accessed December 5, 2017, https://www.facebook.com/careers/jobs/a0I-1200000JXqeWEAT/

104. Facebook, accessed December 5, 2017, https://www.facebook.com/careers/jobs/a0I-1200000JXqeWEAT/

105. Adam Piore, "The Surgeon Who Wants to Connect You to the Internet with a Brain Implant," MIT Technology Review, November 30, 2017, https://www.technologyreview.com/s/609232/the-surgeon-who-wants-to-connect-you-to-the-internet-with-a-brain-implant/

106 . Adam Piore, "The Surgeon Who Wants to Connect You to the Internet with a Brain Implant," MIT Technology Review, November 30, 2017, https://www.technologyreview.com/s/609232/the-surgeon-who-wants-to-connect-you-to-the-internet-with-a-brain-implant/

107. Steven Levy, "Why You Will One Day Have a Chip in Your Brain," Wired Magazine, July 5, 2017, https://www.wired.com/story/why-you-will-one-day-have-a-chip-in-your-brain/

108. Ibid.

109. Ibid.

110. Illah Reza Nourbakhsh, "The Coming Robot Dystopia: All Too Inhuman," Foreign Affairs, July/August (2015): 24-25.

111. Fiachra Long, "Transhuman Education? Sloterdijk's Reading of Heidegger's Letter on Humanism," Journal of Philosophy of Education 51 no. 1 (2017): 190.

112. Ibid, 180.

113.   E. Paul Zehr, "The Potential Transformation of Our Species by Neural Enhancement," Journal of Motor Behavior 47 no. 1 (2015): 75.

114.   Ibid, 73.

115.   Ibid, 77.

116.   Ray Kurzweil, The Age of Spiritual Machines: When Computers Exceed Human Intelligence (New York: Viking, 1999), 204-205.

117.   Emily Mullin, "Blind Patients to Test Bionic Eye Brain Implants: The Prosthesis Could Help More People Who Have Lost Their Vision Than a Device Already on the Market," MIT Technology Review, September 18, 2017, https://www.technologyreview.com/s/608844/blind-patients-to-test-bionic-eye-brain-implants/

Katherine Bourzac, "Bionic Eye Implant Approved for U.S. Patients: The Sight-Restoring Implant Made by Second Sight Is the Most Advanced Prosthetic to Date," MIT Technology Review, February 15, 2013, https://www.technologyreview.com/s/511356/bionic-eye-implant-approved-for-us-patients/

118.   Susan Young Rojahn, "A Second Artificial Retina Option for the E.U.: Patients with Blindness Caused by Retinitis Pigmentosa Can Now Get a Light-Detecting Microchip Implanted in One of Their Retinas," MIT Technology Review, July 3, 2013, https://www.technologyreview.com/s/516796/a-second-artificial-retina-option-for-the-eu/

119.   Larry Greenemeier, "FDA Approves First Retinal Implant: US Approval That Gives Hope to Those with a Rare Genetic Eye Condition," Nature, February 15, 2013, https://www.nature.com/news/fda-approves-first-retinal-implant-1.12439

120.   Emily Mullin, "Blind Patients to Test Bionic Eye Brain Implants: The Prosthesis Could Help More People Who Have Lost Their Vision Than a Device Already on the Market," MIT Technology Review, September 18, 2017, https://www.technologyreview.com/s/608844/blind-patients-to-test-bionic-eye-brain-implants/

121.   United States, Department of Health and Human Services, National Institutes of Health, "Cochlear Implants," National Institute on Deafness and Other Communication Disorders, March 6, 2017, https://www.nidcd.nih.gov/health/cochlear-implants

122.   Nina Godlewski, "Typing With Your Thoughts, Hearing With Your Skin? Neuroscientist Weighs in on Facebook F8 Ideas," International Business Times, April 26, 2017, https://www.ibtimes.com/typing-your-thoughts-hearing-your-skin-neuroscientist-weighs-facebook-f8-ideas-2530558

123.   Morna McDermott McNulty, "Beware the 'Learning Engineers,'" Wrench in the Gears: A Skeptical Parent's Thoughts on Digital Curriculum, March 5, 2018, https://wrenchinthegears.com/2018/05/05/beware-the-learning-engineers/

124.   School of the Future, directed by NOVA (Public Broadcasting System, 2016), http://www.pbs.org/wgbh/nova/education/school-future/home/

125.   Sydney Johnson, "This Company Wants to Gather Student Brainwave Data to Measure 'Engagement,'" EdSurge, October 26, 2017, https://www.edsurge.com/news/2017-10-26-this-company-wants-to-gather-student-brainwave-data-to-measure-engagement

BrainCo, "Home: Unlocking the Power of Your Mind through Personalized Brainwave Feedback," BrainCo: Your Brain Control Everything, accessed November 27, 2018, https://www.brainco.tech/

126.   Accessed November 3, 2018, http://www.cec.com.cn/En/about_us/Company_Profile/2760.aspx

127.   Harvard Innovation Labs, "Venture Teams: BrainCo," President and Fellows Harvard College, accessed November 27, 2018, https://innovationlabs.harvard.edu/meet/venture-team/brainco/

128.   Julie Randles, "Two Edtech Innovators Earn Titles at Pitch Fest," International Society for Technology in Education Conference and Expo, June 27, 2017, https://www.iste.org/explore/articleDetail?articleid=1019&category=ISTE-blog&article=

129.   Rockefeller Foundation, "Report of the Treasurer," Annual Report (1921) (New York: The Rockefeller Foundation, 1922), accessed February 21, 2011, http://www.rockefellerfoundation.org/uploads/files/599ac1c3-7af0-48b1-917f-4b81c39da2be-1921.pdf

130.   United States, White House Archives, President Barack Obama, "Precision Medicine Initiative," accessed November 27, 2018, https://obamawhitehouse.archives.gov/precision-medicine

131.   John Klyczek, "The Precision Eugenics Initiative (Part 2): The Precision Transhumanism Initiative," Natural News, July 6, 2015, https://www.naturalnewsblogs.com/precision-eugenics-initiative-part-2-precision-transhumanism-initiative/

132.   Zina Moukheiber, "Intel's Eric Dishman: 'No One Is building Apps for Seniors,'" Forbes, April 23, 2012 http://www.forbes.com/sites/zinamoukheiber/2012/04/23/intels-eric-dishman-no-

one-is-building-apps-for-seniors/

133.   Ibid.

134.   Cadie Thompson, "The Future of Medicine Means Part Human, Part Computer," CNN, December 24, 2013, https://www.cnbc.com/2013/12/23/the-future-of-medicine-means-part-human-part-computer.html

135.   Kathy Hudson, Rick Lifton, and Bray Patrick-Lake, *The Precision Medicine Initiative Cohort Program–Building a Research Foundation for 21st Century Medicine: Precision Medicine Initiative* (PMI) Working Group Report to the Advisory Committee to the Director, NIH (National Institutes of Health, September 17, 2015), https://acd.od.nih.gov/documents/reports/DRAFT-PMI-WG-Report-9-11-2015-508.pdf

136.   Ibid.

137.   United States, Department of Health and Human Services, National Institutes of Health, "About—Program Partners: Data and Research Center," accessed November 28, 2018, https://allofus.nih.gov/about/program-partners/data-and-research-center

Ibid, "About—Program Partners: Healthcare Provider Organizations," accessed November 28, 2018, https://allofus.nih.gov/about/program-partners/health-care-provider-organizations

Ibid, "Home: The Future of Health Begins with You," accessed November 28, 2018, https://allofus.nih.gov/

Ibid, "NIH Funds Additional Medical Centers to Expand National Precision Medicine Research Program," All of Us: News, Events & Media, October 13, 2016, https://allofus.nih.gov/news-events-and-media/announcements/nih-funds-additional-medical-centers-expand-national-precision

Ibid, "PMI Cohort Program Announces New Name: the All of Us Research Program," All of Us Research Program, October 12, 2016, https://www.nih.gov/allofus-research-program/pmi-cohort-program-announces-new-name-all-us-research-program

138.   Ibid, "About—Program Partners: Data and Research Center," accessed November 28, 2018, https://allofus.nih.gov/about/program-partners/data-and-research-center

139.   Ibid, "NIH Director's Statement: Selection of Eric Dishman as Director of the Precision Medicine Initiative Cohort Program," All of Us: News, Events & Media, April 11, 2016, https://allofus.nih.gov/news-events-and-media/announcements/nih-directors-statement-selection-eric-dishman-director

140.   Ibid, "The Dish: 2017 Year in Review," All of Us: News, Events & Media, December 27, 2017, https://allofus.nih.gov/news-events-and-media/videos/dish-2017-year-review

Megan Molteni, "The NIH Launches Its Ambitious Million-Person Genetic Survey," Wired Magazine, https://www.wired.com/story/all-of-us-launches/

141.   Richard Aldrich, "Nature, Nurture and Neuroscience: Some Future Directions for Historians of Education," *Pedagogica Historica* 50 no. 6 (2014): 860.

142.   United States, Department of Education, The Family Educational Rights and Privacy Act: Guidance for Eligible Students (Washington, DC: Family Policy Compliance Office, February 2011), https://www2.ed.gov/policy/gen/guid/fpco/ferpa/for-eligible-students.pdf

143.   Jane Robbins and Karen Effrem, "Schools Ditch Academics For Emotional Manipulation: Under Such a System Teachers Become Essentially Therapists, and Students Become Essentially Patients," *The Federalist*, October 19, 2016, http://thefederalist.com/2016/10/19/schools-ditch-academics-for-emotional-manipulation/

144.   "Wetware," Oxford English Dictionary, University of Oxford Press, accessed November 28, 2018, https://en.oxforddictionaries.com/definition/wetware

145.   Dominic Gover, "Bilderberg 2.0: The Singularity, Google's Ray Kurzweil and the Ultimate Power," International Business Times, June 7, 2013, https://www.ibtimes.co.uk/google-conspiracy-bilderberg-singularity-476127

146.   Ray Kurzweil, *The Singularity Is Near: When Humans Transcend Biology* (New York: Viking, 2005), 9.

147.   E. Paul Zehr, "The Potential Transformation of Our Species by Neural Enhancement," *Journal of Motor Behavior* 47 no. 1 (2015): 76.

148.   Ibid.

149.   Timothy Morton, "Here Comes Everything: The Promise of Object-Oriented Ontology," *Qui Parle: Critical Humanities and Social Sciences* 19 no. 2 (2011): 163-190.

150.   Bill Brown, "Thing Theory," *Critical Inquiry*, 28 no. 1 (2001): 1-22.

151.   H. Greely, B. Sahakian, J. Harris, R. C. Kessler, M. Gazzaniga, P. Campbell, and M. J. Farah, "Towards Responsible Use of Cognitive-Enhancing Drugs by the Healthy," Nature 456 (2008):702–5,

quoted in Michael Bess, "Enhanced Humans versus 'Normal People': Elusive Definitions," *Journal of Medicine and Philosophy* 35 (2010): 642.

152.   Michael Bess, "Enhanced Humans versus 'Normal People': Elusive Definitions," *Journal of Medicine and Philosophy* 35 (2010): 642.

153.   Elon Musk, interview by Joe Rogan, "Joe Rogan Experience #1169," Powerful JRE, September 6, 2018, https://www.youtube.com/watch?v=ycPr5-27vSI

154.   Aleksandra Anđelković and Dušan Spasić, "Historical Outlines of Eugenics and Its Influences on Education," Casopisza Društvene Nauke 39 no. 4 (2015): 1489.

155.   Leon Kass, "Preventing A Brave New World" (2001), quoted in Aleksandra Anđelković and Dušan Spasić, "Historical Outlines of Eugenics and Its Influences on Education," Casopisza Društvene Nauke 39 no. 4 (2015): 1490.

156.   Jürgen Habermas (2003), quoted in Aleksandra Anđelković and Dušan Spasić, "Historical Outlines of Eugenics and Its Influences on Education," Casopisza Društvene Nauke 39 no. 4 (2015): 1490.

157.   Aleksandra Anđelković and Dušan Spasić, "Historical Outlines of Eugenics and Its Influences on Education," Casopisza Društvene Nauke 39 no. 4 (2015): 1490.

158.   *Fiachra Long,* "Transhuman Education? Sloterdijk's Reading of Heidegger's Letter on Humanism," *Journal of Philosophy of Education* 51 no. 1 (2017): 190.

159.   Illah Reza Nourbakhsh, "The Coming Robot Dystopia: All Too Inhuman," *Foreign Affairs,* July/August (2015): 26.

160.   Ibid, 28.

161.   Judith Rodin, "Opening Remarks by Dr. Judith Rodin at Global Health Summit: 'Dreaming the Future of Health,'" Rockefeller Foundation News & Media, January 26, 2013, https://www.rockefellerfoundation.org/about-us/news-media/opening-remarks-by-dr-judith-rodin-at-global-health-summit-dreaming-the-future-of-health/

162.   Rene Loewenson, *Dreaming the Future of Health for the Next 100 Years*: White Paper from the Global Health Summit, Beijing China (January 26-27 2013) (Beijing, China: Rockefeller Foundation, January 2013), https://assets.rockefellerfoundation.org/app/uploads/20130126182958/1b-8843cc-0d4c-4d5e-bf35-4c7b2fbbb63d-the.pdf

163.   Global Education Futures, "Global Education 2015-2035," Global Education Futures Initiative, accessed November 23, 2018, https://www.edu2035.org/images/people/Future%20of%20Global%20Education%20Map%20(2014)-ilovepdf-compressed.pdf

164.   Ibid.

165.   Ibid.

166.   Ibid.

167.   Ibid.

168.   Kathleen Miles, "Ray Kurzweil: in the 2030s, Nanobots in Our Brains Will Make Us 'Godlike,'" *Huffington Post*, October 1, 2015, https://www.huffingtonpost.com/entry/ray-kurzweil-nanobots-brain-godlike_us_560555a0e4b0af3706dbe1e2

169.   Yuval Noah Harari, *Homo Deus: A Brief History of Tomorrow* (London: Vintage, 2016), 49-50.

170. Ibid, 56.

171.   Ibid, 410.

172.   Georg Wilhelm Friedrich Hegel, *Philosophy Right*, trans. S. W. Dyde (London: George Bell and Sons, 1896), 247.

173.   David Korten, The Post-Corporate World: Life After Capitalism, quoted in Kris Millegan, *Fleshing Out Skull and Bones: Investigations into America's Most Powerful Secret Society* (Walterville, OR: Trine Day, 2003), 690.

Endnotes – Chapter Seventeen

1   University of Cambridge, "Directory: Dr. Dennis Bray," *Cambridge Neuroscience*, accessed November 29, 2018, https://www.neuroscience.cam.ac.uk/directory/profile.php?db10009

2   Dennis Bray, *Wetware: A Computer in Every Living Cell* (New Haven: Yale University Press, 2009), x-xi.

3   Wayne Gillam, "Engineering Data Security for Brain-Computer Interfaces," *Center for Neurotechnology: A National Science Foundation Engineering Research Center*, July 11, 2017, http://csne-erc.org/engage-enable/post/engineering-data-security-brain-computer-interfaces

4   Jeana Chaffin, "AT&T Futurist Report: Blended Reality–The Future of Entertainment, 5G, & Mobile Edge Computing," *AT&T Developer Program Blog*, September 24, 2018, https://developer.att.com/blog/future-of-5g-entertainment

5   Joon Ian Wong, "Brains with Machines: What Comes After Smartphones? Brain Implants, Maybe," *Quartz*, October 20, 2016, https://qz.com/814849/darpa-and-qualcomm-brain-implants-for-6g-and-neural-engineering/

Sascha Segan, "With 5G Still in the Works, 6G Is Already Taking Shape: 5G Hasn't Launched yet, but Finland's University of Oulu Just Convened a Research Group about 6G Wireless. Here's What They're Thinking," *PC Magazine*, April 19, 2018, https://www.pcmag.com/article/360533/what-is-6g

6   Ayça Çebi and Hasan Karal, "An Application of Fuzzy Analytic Hierarchy Process (FAHP) for Evaluating Students' Project," *Educational Research and Reviews* 12 no. 3 (2017): 120.

7   Carnegie Mellon University, "Explore: Repositories," *Learnsphere*, accessed December 1, 2018, http://learnsphere.org/explore.html

8   Ibid.

9   Ibid.

10   Ibid.

11   Ibid.

12   Ibid.

13   Ibid.

14   Ibid.

15   LearnLab, "DataShop@Stanford: A Data Analysis Service for the Learning Science of Community," *LearnLab: Pittsburgh Science of Learning Center*, accessed December 1, 2018, https://datashop.stanford.edu/

Ibid, "DataShop@TutorGen: A Data Analysis Service for the Learning Science of Community," *LearnLab: Pittsburgh Science of Learning Center*, accessed December 1, 2018, https://datashop.tutorgen.com/

16   United States, Department of Education, Office of Management, "Family Educational Rights and Privacy: Final Regulations—34 CFR Part 99," *Federal Register* 76 no. 232 (National Archives and Records Administration, December 2, 2011), https://www.gpo.gov/fdsys/pkg/FR-2011-12-02/pdf/2011-30683.pdf

17   San Diego State University, "Faculty and Staff: Emeritus Faculty," *Department of Computer Science*, accessed December 1, 2018, http://www.cs.sdsu.edu/faculty-and-staff/

18   National Aeronautics and Space Administration, "Biography of Wernher von Braun," *Marshall History*, August 3, 2017, https://www.nasa.gov/centers/marshall/history/vonbraun/bio.html

United States, National Archives and Records Administration, "Records of the Secretary of Defense (RG 330): Joint Intelligence Objectives Agency—Foreign Scientist Case Files 1945-1958 (Entry A1-1B)," *Nazi War Crimes Interagency Working Group: IWG Declassified Records*, October 11, 2016, https://www.archives.gov/iwg/declassified-records/rg-330-defense-secretary

19   Vernor Vinge, "The Coming Technological Singularity: How to Survive in the Post-Human Era," *Vision-21: Interdisciplinary Science and Engineering in the Era of Cyberspace* (NASA Conference Publication 10129, March 30-31, 1993), https://ntrs.nasa.gov/archive/nasa/casi.ntrs.nasa.gov/19940022855.pdf

20   William Poundstone, "John von Neumann: American Mathematician," *Encyclopedia Britannica*, accessed December 1, 2018, https://www.britannica.com/biography/John-von-Neumann

21   George Dyson, interview by John Naughton, "The True Fathers of Computing," *The Guardian: US Edition*, February 25, 2012, https://www.theguardian.com/technology/2012/feb/26/first-computers-john-von-neumann

John von Neumann, *Mathematical Foundations of Quantum Mechanics*, trans. Robert T. Beyer, ed. Nicholas A. Wheeler (Princeton, NJ: Princeton University Press, 1932).

22   IWM Staff, "How Alan Turing Cracked the Enigma Code," *Imperial War Museums*, January 5, 2018, https://www.iwm.org.uk/history/how-alan-turing-cracked-the-enigma-code

23   Alan M. Turing, "I.—Computing Machinery and Intelligence," *Mind: A Quarterly Review of Psychology and Philosophy* 59 no. 236 (1950): 433-460.

24   Editors of the Encyclopedia Britannica, "Stanislaw Ulam: American Scientist," accessed December 1, 2018, https://www.britannica.com/biography/Stanislaw-Ulam

25   Julia Damerow, "John von Neumann (1903-1957)," *Embryo Project Encyclopedia at Arizona State University* June 22, 2010, https://embryo.asu.edu/pages/john-von-neumann-1903-1957

Richard Pearson, "Mathematician Stanislaw Ulam, Leader in Bomb Research, Dies," *Washington Post*, May 16, 1984, https://www.washingtonpost.com/archive/local/1984/05/16/mathematician-stanislaw-ulam-leader-in-bomb-research-dies/08ce9d61-b174-4814-ab3c-7b7f9e6412a5/?noredirect=on&utm_term=.ba1393cabc94

26   Stanislaw Ulam, "John von Neumann (1903-1957)," *Bulletin of the American Mathematical Society* 64 no. 3 (1958): 5.

27   Ray Kurzweil, *The Singularity Is Near: When Humans Transcend Biology* (New York: Viking, 2005), 56.

28   Robert D. Atkinson, "In Defense of Robots: Why We Should Not Reject Technology in Order to 'Protect' Worker," *National Review*, April 17, 2017, https://www.nationalreview.com/magazine/2017/04/17/robots-taking-jobs-technology-workers/

29   World Economic Forum, "About Us: Klaus Schwab—Biography," accessed December 1, 2018, https://www.weforum.org/about/klaus-schwab

30   Robert D. Atkinson, "In Defense of Robots: Why We Should Not Reject Technology in Order to 'Protect' Worker," *National Review*, April 17, 2017, https://www.nationalreview.com/magazine/2017/04/17/robots-taking-jobs-technology-workers/

31   Carnegie Mellon University, "Faculty & Staff: Vivek Wadhwa—Distinguished Fellow & Adjunct Professor," *Integrated Innovation Institute: Engineering + Design + Business* accessed December 1, 2018, https://www.cmu.edu/iii/innovators/faculty-staff/wadhwa.html

32   Robert D. Atkinson, "In Defense of Robots: Why We Should Not Reject Technology in Order to 'Protect' Worker," *National Review*, April 17, 2017, https://www.nationalreview.com/magazine/2017/04/17/robots-taking-jobs-technology-workers/

33   James Vincent, "Google Wants to Improve Your Smart Home with iRobot's Room Maps," *The Verge*, October 31, 2018, https://www.theverge.com/2018/10/31/18041876/google-irobot-smart-home-spatial-data-mapping-collaboration

34   Google, "Research—Teams & Focus Areas: Google Brain Team," *Google AI*, accessed December 1, 2018, https://ai.google/research/teams/brain

National Aeronautics and Space Administration, "NASA Quantum Artificial Intelligence Laboratory (QuAIL)," *NASA*, accessed December 1, 2018, https://ti.arc.nasa.gov/tech/dash/groups/physics/quail/

35   Catherine Shu, "Google Acquires Artificial Intelligence Startup DeepMind For More Than $500M," *TechCrunch* January 27, 2014, https://techcrunch.com/2014/01/26/google-deepmind/

36   Dieter Bohn, "Google Duplex Really Works and Testing Begins This Summer: This Is What It's Like to Take a Restaurant Reservation from an AI," *The Verge*, June 27, 2018, https://www.theverge.com/2018/6/27/17508728/google-duplex-assistant-reservations-demo

James Vincent, "Google Wants to Improve Your Smart Home with iRobot's Room Maps," *The Verge*, October 31, 2018, https://www.theverge.com/2018/10/31/18041876/google-irobot-smart-home-spatial-data-mapping-collaboration

37   Ashley Carman, "Volkswagen Now Lets Apple Users Unlock Their Cars with Siri," *The Verge*, https://www.theverge.com/2018/11/12/18087416/volkswagen-vw-car-net-app-siri-shortcuts

Judith Shulevitz, "Alexa, Should We Trust You?," *The Atlantic*, November 2018, https://www.theatlantic.com/magazine/archive/2018/11/alexa-how-will-you-change-us/570844/

Tom Warren, "Microsoft Is Bringing Cortana to Fridges, Toasters, and Thermostats," *The Verge*, December 13, 2016, https://www.theverge.com/2016/12/13/13935136/microsoft-cortana-windows-10-iot-devices

38   Wayne Madsen, interview by *RT*, "Somebody's Watching Me: Social Networking Spies—CIA Monitors Trends on the Web," *Global Research TV: Centre for Research on Globalization*, January 1, 2012, http://tv.globalresearch.ca/2012/01/social-networking-spies-cia-sifts-social-media-sites

Webster G. Tarpley, Interview by *RT*, "Google Guard: Google and the NSA Are Teaming up to Take Down Internet Hackers—Tarpley: Google Is Now Openly in Alliance with the NSA," *Website of Webster Griffin Tarpley*, February 5, 2010, http://tarpley.net/google-joins-with-nsa-in-drive-to-confront-china/

39   Frederic Lardinois, "The Google Assistant Will Soon Be Able to Call Restaurants and Make a Reservation for You," *TechCrunch*, May 8, 2018, https://techcrunch.com/2018/05/08/the-google-assistant-will-soon-be-able-to-call-restaurants-and-make-a-reservations-for-you/

40   Patrick Fernandes, Miltiadis Allamanis, and Marc Brockschmidt, "Structured Neural Summarization," *Microsoft Research* (Cambridge, UK: November 5, 2018), https://arxiv.org/pdf/1811.01824.pdf

41   Zara Stone, "Ten Incredibly Lifelike Humanoid Robots to Get On Your Radar," *Forbes*, February 27, 2018, https://www.forbes.com/sites/zarastone/2018/02/27/ten-incredibly-lifelike-humanoid-robots-to-get-on-your-radar/#61e9f5d434d2

42   Elaine Chow, "Japanese Elementary School Kids Now Being Taught by Saya the Robot," *Gizmodo*, March 10, 2009, https://gizmodo.com/5167214/japanese-elementary-school-kids-now-being-taught-by-saya-the-robot

43   Giorgio Metta, "The icub Humanoid Robot Project," *Istituto Italiano Di Tecnologia: ITT Central Research Lab, Genova*, accessed December 1, 2018, https://www.iit.it/research/lines/icub
Kaleigh Rogers, "This Slightly Haunting Childlike Robot Has Helped Scientists Crowdsource Research for Over a Decade: It's Called icub and Is Able to Do Some Pretty Amazing Feats," *Motherboard*, December 20, 2017, https://motherboard.vice.com/en_us/article/d34pvm/this-slightly-haunting-childlike-robot-has-helped-scientists-crowdsource-research-for-over-a-decade
Sam Byford, "Sony Is Working on a Robot That Can 'Form an Emotional Bond' with People: VR May Be a 'New Business Domain' for the Company," *The Verge*, June 19, 2016, https://www.theverge.com/2016/6/29/12057408/sony-robot-emotion-vr-sensors

44   Keiichi Furukawa, "Honda's Asimo Robot Bows Out but Finds New Life: Underlying Tech Applied to Physical Therapy and Self-Driving Vehicles," *Nikkei Asian Review*, June 28, 2018, https://asia.nikkei.com/Business/Companies/Honda-s-Asimo-robot-bows-out-but-finds-new-life

45   Rosie Spink, "Meet the Robot Giving Hospitalised Children Superpowers," *The Guardian: US Edition*, February 6, 2015, https://www.theguardian.com/sustainable-business/2015/feb/06/robots-for-good-hospitalised-children-superpowers

46   Saoirse Kerrigan, "15 Most Forward-Thinking Projects That Could Build the Next Humanoids," *Interesting Engineering*, June 29, 2018, https://interestingengineering.com/15-most-forward-thinking-projects-that-could-build-the-next-humanoids
Zara Stone, "Ten Incredibly Lifelike Humanoid Robots to Get On Your Radar," *Forbes*, February 27, 2018, https://www.forbes.com/sites/zarastone/2018/02/27/ten-incredibly-lifelike-humanoid-robots-to-get-on-your-radar/#61e9f5d434d2

47   Zara Stone, "Everything You Need to Know About Sophia, the World's First Robot Citizen," *Forbes*, November 7, 2017, https://www.forbes.com/sites/zarastone/2017/11/07/everything-you-need-to-know-about-sophia-the-worlds-first-robot-citizen/#7d599dc446fa

48   "Six Things Women in Saudi Arabia Still Can't Do: First Licences Issued for Female Drivers, but Women Still Face Severe Restrictions Every Day," *The Week*, June 5, 2018, https://www.theweek.co.uk/60339/things-women-cant-do-in-saudi-arabia

49   Brian Whitaker, "Everything You Need to Know about Being Gay in Muslim Countries," *The Guardian: US Edition*, June 21, 2016, https://www.theguardian.com/world/2016/jun/21/gay-lgbt-muslim-countries-middle-east

50   Ben Hubbard, "What We Know About Jamal Khashoggi's Death," *New York Times*, October 20, 2018, https://www.nytimes.com/2018/10/20/world/middleeast/khashoggi-turkey-saudi-narratives.html

51   Jeff Parsons, "Watch Sophia the 'Sexy Robot' Claim She Will 'Destroy Humans' - Leaving Creator Red Faced: A Mistake During a Technical Demonstration at the SXSW Tech Show Revealed the Android's True Intentions," *The Mirror*, March 22, 2016, https://www.mirror.co.uk/tech/watch-sophia-sexy-robot-claim-7606152

52   Jim Edwards, "I Interviewed Sophia, the Artificially Intelligent Robot That Said It Wanted to 'Destroy Humans,'" *Business Insider*, November 8, 2017, https://www.businessinsider.com/interview-with-sophia-ai-robot-hanson-said-it-would-destroy-humans-2017-11
Michelle Starr, "Crazy-Eyed Robot Wants a Family -- and to Destroy All Humans: Hanson Robotics' Most Recent Humanoid Robot Is Its Most Advanced Yet, and Its Cold, Dead Eyes Will Make Your Skin Crawl," *CNet Magazine*, March 20, 2016, https://www.cnet.com/news/crazy-eyed-robot-wants-a-family-and-to-destroy-all-humans/

53   Mick Mulvaney and Michael Kratsios, "Memorandum for the Heads of Executive Departments and Agencies: FY 2019 Administration Research and Development Budget Priorities," *Executive Office of the President: Office of Management and Budget / Office of Science and Technology Policy*, August 17, 2017, https://www.whitehouse.gov/sites/whitehouse.gov/files/ostp/fy2019-administration-research-development-budget-priorities.pdf

54   United States, White House, "Research and Development" (Washington, DC: Government Publishing Office, February 2018), https://www.whitehouse.gov/wp-content/uploads/2018/02/ap_18_research-fy2019.pdf

55   Ibid, Department of Transportation, National Highway Traffic Safety Administration, *Automated Driving Systems 2.0: A Vision for Safety* (Washington, DC: DOT HS, September 2017), https://www.nhtsa.gov/sites/nhtsa.dot.gov/files/documents/13069a-ads2.0_090617_v9a_tag.pdf

56   Donald J. Trump, "Infrastructure and Technology: Unmanned Aircraft Systems Integration Pilot Program," *Presidential Memorandum for the Secretary of Transportation,* White House, October 25, 2017, https://www.whitehouse.gov/presidential-actions/presidential-memorandum-secretary-transportation/

57   United States, White House, "Infrastructure and Technology: Artificial Intelligence for the American People," *Fact Sheet,* May 10, 2018, https://www.whitehouse.gov/briefings-statements/artificial-intelligence-american-people/

58   Ibid.

59   United States, Executive Office of the President, National Science and Technology Council, Networking and Information and Technology Research and Development Subcommittee, *The National Artificial Intelligence Research and Development Strategic Plan* (Washington, DC: Government Publishing Office, October 2016), https://www.nitrd.gov/PUBS/national_ai_rd_strategic_plan.pdf

60   Ray Kurzweil, *The Age of Spiritual Machines: When Computers Exceed Human Intelligence* (New York: Viking, 1999), 204.

61   Laura Vanderkam, *Blended Learning: A Wise Giver's Guide to Bolstering Tech-Assisted Teaching,* ed. Karl Zinsmeister (Washington DC: Philanthropy, April 2013), https://www.philanthropyroundtable.org/docs/default-source/guidebook-files/blended_learning_guidebook.pdf?sfvrsn=afaba740_0

62   International Business Machines, "Watson: Products and Services," *IBM,* accessed January 8, 2018, https://www.ibm.com/watson/products-services/

63   Edwin Black, *IBM and the Holocaust: The Strategic Alliance between Nazi Germany and America's Most Powerful Corporation* (New York: Random House, 2001), 69.

64   H&R Block, "H&R Block with Watson: Taxes Will Never Be the Same," accessed December 2, 2018, https://www.hrblock.com/lp/fy17/hrblock-and-watson.html
International Business Machines, "IBM Security: Cognitive Security—Evolve Your Defenses with Security That Understands, Reasons and Learns," *IBM,* accessed January 8, 2018, https://www-03.ibm.com/security/ca-en/cognitive/
Ibid, "Watson: Products and Services," *IBM,* accessed January 8, 2018, https://www.ibm.com/watson/products-services/

65   Ibid, "IBM Watson Education: Transforming Learning Experiences with Watson AI," *IBM,* accessed January 8, 2018, https://www.ibm.com/watson/education

66   Ibid, "Watson—Education: Art of the Possible: IBM Watson and Pearson Drive Cognitive Learning for College Students—IBM and Pearson Are Bringing Watson Cognitive Capabilities to College Students and Educators," *IBM,* accessed January 8, 2018, https://www.ibm.com/watson/education/pearson
Ibid, accessed January 8, 2018, https://www.ibm.com/developerworks/library/cc-beginner-guide-machine-learning-ai-cognitive/index.html

67   Barb Darrow, "IBM and Amazon Are Sorta Strange Bedfellows in Blackboard Deal," *Fortune,* June 30, 2016, http://fortune.com/2016/06/30/ibm-and-amazon-are-sorta-strange-bedfellows-in-blackboard-deal/
Blackboard, "Blackboard Inc. and IBM Enter Strategic Relationship to Develop Cognitive Solutions and Manage Infrastructure Operations," *Blackboard Press Releases,* June 29, 2016, http://pages.blackboard.com/news-and-events/press-releases/2016/bb-ibm-strategic-relationship-develop-cognitive-solutions-manage-infrastructure-operations.aspx

68   International Business Machines, "IBM Watson Education: Transforming Learning Experiences with Watson AI," *IBM,* accessed January 8, 2018, https://www.ibm.com/watson/education

69   Ibid.

70   Ibid.

71   Ibid, "IBM Watson Education and Pearson to Drive Cognitive Learning Experiences for College Students," *IBM Newsroom: News Releases,* October 25, 2016, https://www-03.ibm.com/press/us/en/pressrelease/50842.wss

72   Susan E. F. Chipman, "Applications in Education and Training: A Force Behind the Development of Cognitive Science," *Topics in Cognitive Science* 2 (2010): 389.

73   Ibid, 390.

74   Ibid.

75   United States, Executive Office of the President, National Science and Technology Council, Committee on Technology, *Preparing for the Future of Artificial Intelligence* (Washington,

DC: Government Publishing Office, October 2016), https://obamawhitehouse.archives.gov/sites/default/files/whitehouse_files/microsites/ostp/NSTC/preparing_for_the_future_of_ai.pdf

76   Ryoko Yamaguchi and Adam Hall, "A Compendium of Education Technology Research Funded by NCER and NCSER: 2002-2014," *National Center for Education Research* (Washington, DC: National Center for Education Research, Institute of Education Sciences, U.S. Department of Education, 2017), vii.

77   Ibid, 46.

78   Jingying Chen, Nan Luo, Yuanyuan Liu, Leyuan Liu, Kun Zhang, and Joanna Kolodziej, "A Hybrid Intelligence-Aided Approach to Affect-Sensitive e-Learning," *Computing* 98 no. 1/2 (2016): 218.

79   Tessa McCarthy, L. Penny Rosenblum, Benny G. Johnson, Jeffrey Dittel, and Devin M. Kearns, "An Artificial Intelligence Tutor: A Supplementary Tool for Teaching and Practicing Braille," *Journal of Visual Impairment and Blindness* 110 no. 5 (2016): 309.

80   Sze-Chu Liu and Po-Yi Hung, "Teaching Pronunciation with Computer Assisted Pronunciation Instruction in a Technological University," *Universal Journal of Educational Research* 4 no. 9 (2016): 1940.

81   Ibid, 1941.

82   Ibid, 1940.

83   Donggil Song, "Designing a Teachable Agent System for Mathematics Learning," *Contemporary Educational Technology* 8 no. 2 (2017): 176.

84   Ibid, 178.

85   Phu Vu, Scott Fredrickson, and Richard Meyer, "Help at 3:00 AM! Providing 24/7 Timely Support to Online Students via a Virtual Assistant," *Online Journal of Distance Learning Administration* 19 no. 1 (2016): https://www.westga.edu/~distance/ojdla/spring191/vu_fredrickson_meyer191.html

86   Ali Ozdemir, Aysegul Alaybeyoglu, Naciye Mulayim, and Muhammed Uysa, "An Intelligent System for Determining Learning Style," International Journal of Research in Education and Science 4 no. 1 (2018): 208.

87   Ibid, 209.

88   Maria Samarakou, Grammatiki Tsaganou, and Andreas Papadakis, "An e-Learning System for Extracting Text Comprehension and Learning Style Characteristics," *Educational Technology and Society* 21 no. 1 (2018): 127.

89   Ibid, 129.

90   Ibid, 127.

91   Ibid.

92   Ibid, 126-127.

93   Jingying Chen, Nan Luo, Yuanyuan Liu, Leyuan Liu, Kun Zhang, and Joanna Kolodziej, "A Hybrid Intelligence-Aided Approach to Affect-Sensitive e-Learning," *Computing* 98 no. 1/2 (2016): 218.

94   Ibid.

95   Ibid.

96   Ibid, 231.

97   Ibid, 218.

98   Ibid, 231.

99   Ibid, 232.

100   Emrah Soykan, Fezile Özdamlı, and Deniz Özcan, "The Emotional Analysis of Children with Special Needs During Tablet Usage in Education," *International Journal of Cognitive Research in Science, Engineering and Education* 5 no. 2 (2017): 58.

101   Ibid.

102   Somayeh Fatahi and Hadi Moradi, "A Fuzzy Cognitive Map Model to Calculate a User's Desirability Based on Personality in e-Learning Environments," *Computers in Human Behavior* 63 (2016): 272.

103   Hawon Lee and Eunja Hyun, "The Intelligent Robot Contents for Children with Speech-Language Disorder," *Journal of Educational Technology and Society* 18 no. 3 (2015): 100, 102.

104   Ibid, 102.

105   Ibid, 100.

106   Ibid.

107   Ibid, 103.

108   Ibid, 102-103.

109   Scott Berson, "'Terrifying': Watch Humanoid Robot Backflip and Run Military-Style Obstacle Courses," *Miami Herald*, October 12, 2018, https://www.miamiherald.com/news/nation-world/national/article219911745.html

110   Adrian Covert, "Video: Boston Dynamics' Petman Is the Creepy Bipedal Evolution of Big Dog," *Popular Science*, October 26, 2009, https://www.popsci.com/technology/article/2009-10/boston-dynamics-petman-bipedal-robot-evolution-bigdog

111   United States, *Every Student Succeeds Act*, Public Law 114-95, 114th Congress, S. 1177, December 10, 2015, https://www.congress.gov/114/plaws/publ95/PLAW-114publ95.pdf

112   Elena V. Chubarkova, Ilya A.Sadchikov, Irina A. Suslova, Andrey A. Tsaregorodtsev, and Larisa N. Milova, "Educational Game Systems in Artificial Intelligence Course," *International Journal of Environmental and Science Education* 11 no. 16 (2016): 9262-9263.

113   Ibid, 9263.

114   Abigail Carlton and Guy Halfteck, "How Mobile Games Can Help You Identify Your Next Great Employee," *Rockefeller Foundation Newsletter*, March 31, 2016, https://www.rockefellerfoundation.org/blog/how-mobile-games-can-help-you-identify-your-next-great-employee/

115   Morna McDermott McNulty, "Beware the 'Learning Engineers,'" *Wrench in the Gears: A Skeptical Parent's Thoughts on Digital Curriculum*, March 5, 2018, https://wrenchinthegears.com/2018/05/05/beware-the-learning-engineers/

116   Rockefeller Foundation, "About Us—Our Team: Guy Halfteck—CEO, Knack," accessed December 2, 2018, https://www.rockefellerfoundation.org/people/guy-halfteck/ University of Pennsylvania, "People Analytics—Wharton People Analytics Conference 2017: Applying Gaming to People Analytics: Williams, Halfteck, & Kato," *The Wharton School*, December 19, 2017, https://wpa.wharton.upenn.edu/content/video/applying-gaming-people-analytics/

117   Morna McDermott McNulty, "Beware the 'Learning Engineers,'" *Wrench in the Gears: A Skeptical Parent's Thoughts on Digital Curriculum*, March 5, 2018, https://wrenchinthegears.com/2018/05/05/beware-the-learning-engineers/

118   International Business Machines, "IBM Watson—Education: IBM and Sesame Street Collaborate to Create the Next Generation of Individualized Learning Tools," *IBM*, accessed December 2, 2018, https://www.ibm.com/watson/education/sesame-street

119   Ibid, "IBM Watson and Sesame Workshop Introduce Intelligent Play and Learning Platform on IBM Cloud: Unveil Watson-Powered Cognitive Vocabulary Learning App Designed to Enhance Early Childhood Education Experiences; First Pilot at Georgia's Gwinnett County Public Schools," *IBM Newsroom: News Releases*, June 6, 2017, https://www-03.ibm.com/press/us/en/press-release/52532.wss

120   Ibid.

121   Ibid.

122   Ibid.

123   Ibid.

124   Ibid.

125   Ibid.

126   Ibid.

127   Ibid.

128   Ibid.

129   Theodouli Terzidou, Thrasyvoulos Tsiatsos, Christina Miliou, and Athanasia Sourvinou, "Agent Supported Serious Game Environment," *Institute of Electrical and Electronics Engineers (IEEE) Transactions on Learning Technologies* 9 no. 3 (2016): 217.

130   Ibid.

131   Ramón Zatarain-Cabada, Giner Alor-Hernández, María Lucía Barrón-Estrada, Ricardo Colomo-Palacios, and Hao-Chiang Koong Lin, "Guest Editorial: Intelligent and Affective Learning Environments: New Trends and Challenges," *Journal of Education Technology and Society* 19 no. 2 (2016): 1, 2.

132   Ibid, 2.

133   Akili Interactive Labs, "Akili Achieves Primary Efficacy Endpoint in Pediatric ADHD Pivotal Trial: *Company Completes Large Multi-Center, Randomized, Controlled Study of Novel Digital Medicine and Plans Regulatory Filing*," *Akili News, December 4, 2017, https://www.akiliinteractive.com/news-collection/akili-achieves-primary-efficacy-endpoint-in-pediatric-adhd-pivotal-trial*

134   Morna McDermott McNulty, "Beware the 'Learning Engineers,'" *Wrench in the Gears:*

A Skeptical Parent's Thoughts on Digital Curriculum, March 5, 2018, https://wrenchinthegears. com/2018/05/05/beware-the-learning-engineers

135   Ibid.

136   Ibid.

137   Akili Interactive Labs, "Science & Technology: Programs & Products," accessed December 2, 2018, https://www.akiliinteractive.com/programs-products

138   Jay Hancock, "Here's Where the Nation's Biggest Drug Lobby Spent Money in 2016," December 19, 2017, https://www.pbs.org/newshour/health/heres-where-the-nations-biggest-drug-lobby-spent-money-in-2016

139   Morna McDermott McNulty, "Beware the 'Learning Engineers,'" *Wrench in the Gears: A Skeptical Parent's Thoughts on Digital Curriculum*, March 5, 2018, https://wrenchinthegears. com/2018/05/05/beware-the-learning-engineers

140   Akili, "Akili Makes 5th Appearance on the Inc. 500/5000 Annual List of America's Fastest-Growing Private Companies," *New & Press Releases: Akili Culture Blog*, June 5, 2017, https://akili. com/akili-makes-5th-appearance-inc-5005000-annual-list-americas-fastest-growing-private-companies/

141   University of California San Francisco, "About: People," *Neuroscape*, accessed December 2, 2018, https://neuroscape.ucsf.edu/people/#core
Ibid, "About: Profile—Melina Uncapher, Ph.D.," accessed December 2, 2018, https://neuroscape. ucsf.edu/profile/melina-uncapher/

142   Morna McDermott McNulty, "Beware the 'Learning Engineers,'" *Wrench in the Gears: A Skeptical Parent's Thoughts on Digital Curriculum*, March 5, 2018, https://wrenchinthegears. com/2018/05/05/beware-the-learning-engineers

143   Drexel University, "Engagement: Learning Innovation," *ExCITe (Expressive and Creative Interaction Technologies) Center*, accessed December 2, 2018, https://drexel.edu/excite/engagement/ learning-innovation/

144   Morna McDermott McNulty, "Beware the 'Learning Engineers,'" *Wrench in the Gears: A Skeptical Parent's Thoughts on Digital Curriculum*, March 5, 2018, https://wrenchinthegears. com/2018/05/05/beware-the-learning-engineers

145   National Science Foundation, "Award Abstract #1540854: SL-CN—Contributions of Executive Function Subdomains to Math and Reading Cognition in the Classroom," *Standard Grant* (NSF, August 18, 2015), accessed December 2, 2018, https://wrenchinthegears.files.wordpress. com/2018/05/nsf-award-search-award1540854-sl-cn-contributions-of-executive-function-subdomains-to-math-and-reading-cognition-in-the-classroom.pdf

146   Morna McDermott McNulty, "Beware the 'Learning Engineers,'" *Wrench in the Gears: A Skeptical Parent's Thoughts on Digital Curriculum*, March 5, 2018, https://wrenchinthegears. com/2018/05/05/beware-the-learning-engineers

147   Global Education Futures, "Global Education 2015-2035," *Global Education Futures Initiative*, accessed November 23, 2018, https://www.edu2035.org/images/people/Future%20of%20 Global%20Education%20Map%20(2014)-ilovepdf-compressed.pdf

148   Susan Yoon, Emma Anderson, Joyce Lin, and Karen Elinich, "How Augmented Reality Enables Conceptual Understanding of Challenging Science Content," *Journal of Educational Technology and Society* 20 no. 1 (2017): 156.

149   Larysa Nadolny, "Interactive Print: The Design of Cognitive Tasks in Blended Augmented Reality and Print Documents," *British Journal of Educational Technology* 48 no. 3 (2017): 816.

150   Rabia M. Yilmaz, Sevda Kucuk, and Yuksel Goktas, "Are Augmented Reality Picture Books Magic or Real for Preschool Children Aged Five to Six?," *British Journal of Educational Technology* 48 no. 3 (2017): 824-825.

151   Ibid, 827.

152   Kun-Hung Cheng and Chin-Chung Tsai, "The Interaction of Child–Parent Shared Reading with an Augmented Reality (AR) Picture Book and Parents' Conceptions of AR Learning," *British Journal of Educational Technology* 47 no. 1 (2016): 206.

153   Shu-Chun Ho, Sheng-Wen Hsieh, Pei-Chen Sun and Cheng-Ming Chen, "To Activate English Learning: Listen and Speak in Real Life Context with an AR Featured U-Learning System," *Journal of Educational Technology and Society* 20 no. 2 (2017): 177.

154   Ibid, 179.

155   Ibid, 180.

156   I. Kazanidis, G. Palaigeorgiou, A. Papadopoulou, and A. Tsinakos, "Augmented Interac-

tive Video: Enhancing Video Interactivity for the School Classroom," *Journal of Engineering Science & Technology Review* 11 no. 2 (2018): 177, 178.

157   Ibid, 178.

158   Ibid, 178-179.

159   Ramón Iván Barraza Castillo, Vianey Guadalupe Cruz Sánchez, and Osslan Osiris Vergara Villegas, "A Pilot Study on the Use of Mobile Augmented Reality for Interactive Experimentation in Quadratic Equation," *Mathematical Problems in Engineering* (2015): 4.

160   Ibid, 4.

161   Ibid, 6.

162   Ibid.

163   Ibid.

164   Anabel Martin-Gonzalez, Angel Chi-Poot, and Victor Uc-Cetina, "Usability Evaluation of an Augmented Reality System for Teaching Euclidean Vectors," *Innovations in Education & Teaching International* 53 no. 6 (2016): 628.

165   Ibid, 628, 629.

166   Ibid, 629.

167   Ibid.

168   Anne Estapa and Larysa Nadolny, "The Effect of an Augmented Reality Enhanced Mathematics Lesson on Student Achievement and Motivation," *Journal of STEM Education: Innovations & Research* 16 no. 3 (2015): 41.

169   Teemu H. Laine, Eeva Nygren, Amir Dirin, and Hae-Jung Suk, "Science Spots AR: a Platform for Science Learning Games with Augmented Reality," Educational Technology Research & Development 64 no. 3 (2016): 509.

170   Ibid, 511.

171   Ibid, 507.

172   Ibid, 516-517.

173   Ibid, 515.

174   Ibid, 516.

175   Ibid, 511

176   Ibid.

177   Ibid, 512.

178   Ibid.

179   Yu-Tung Kuo and Yu-Chung Kuo, "The Role of Augmented Reality and Its Application in Learning," *International Journal of Technology, Knowledge & Society: Annual Review* 13 no. 1 (2017): 2.

180   Ibid.

181   Ibid, 5.

182   Su-Ju Lu and Ying-Chieh Liu, "Integrating Augmented Reality Technology to Enhance Children's Learning in Marine Education," *Environmental Education Research* 21 no. 4 (2015): 526.

183   Ibid, 530.

184   Ibid, 529.

185   Ibid, 530.

186   Ibid.

187   Susan Yoon, Emma Anderson, Joyce Lin, and Karen Elinich, "How Augmented Reality Enables Conceptual Understanding of Challenging Science Content," *Journal of Educational Technology and Society* 20 no. 1 (2017): 156.

188   Ibid, 159.

189   Natalie Bursztyn, Andy Walker, Brett Shelton, and Joel Pederson, "Assessment of Student Learning Using Augmented Reality Grand Canyon Field Trips for Mobile Smart Devices," *Geosphere* 13 no. 2 (2017): 260.

190   Ibid, 261.

191   Ibid.

192   Ibid.

193   Ibid.

194   Ibid.

195   Yu-Lien Chang, Huei-Tse Hou, Chao-Yang Pan, Yao-Ting Sung and Kuo-En Chang, "Apply an Augmented Reality in a Mobile Guidance to Increase Sense of Place for Heritage Places," *Journal of Education Technology and Society* 18 no. 2 (2015): 166.

196   Ibid, 169.

459

197   Ibid, 171.

198   Yu-Tung Kuo and Yu-Chung Kuo, "The Role of Augmented Reality and Its Application in Learning," *International Journal of Technology, Knowledge & Society: Annual Review* 13 no. 1 (2017): 4.

199   Jeonghye Han, Miheon Jo, Eunja Hyun, and Hyo-jeong So, "Examining Young Children's Perception Toward Augmented Reality-Infused Dramatic Play," *Educational Technology Research & Development* 63 no. 3 (2015): 460.

200   Ibid.

201   Ibid.

202   Ibid, 462.

203   Ibid, 455-456.

204   José Bidarra and Ellen Rusman, "Towards a Pedagogical Model for Science Education: Bridging Educational Contexts through a Blended Learning Approach," *Open Learning* 32 no. 1 (2017): 11.

205   Carlos Carbonell Carrera and Luis A. Bermejo Asensio, "Landscape Interpretation with Augmented Reality and Maps to Improve Spatial Orientation Skill," *Journal of Geography in Higher Education* 41 no. 1 (2017): 122.

206   Tashko Rizov and Elena Rizova, "Augmented Reality as a Teaching Tool in Higher Education," *International Journal of Cognitive Research in Science, Engineering & Education* 3 no. 1 (2015): 7, 8, 10.

207   Global Education Futures, "Global Education 2015-2035," *Global Education Futures Initiative*, accessed November 23, 2018, https://www.edu2035.org/images/people/Future%20of%20Global%20Education%20Map%20(2014)-ilovepdf-compressed.pdf

208   Yu-Tung Kuo and Yu-Chung Kuo, "The Role of Augmented Reality and Its Application in Learning," *International Journal of Technology, Knowledge & Society: Annual Review* 13 no. 1 (2017): 2.

209   Dennis Bray, *Wetware: A Computer in Every Living Cell* (New Haven: Yale University Press, 2009), 46.

210   Juan Mateu, María José Lasala, and Xavier Alamán, "Developing Mixed Reality Educational Applications: The Virtual Touch Toolkit," *Sensors* 15 no. 9 (2015): 21761-21762.

211   Bill and Melinda Gates Foundation, "New York University: to Explore Higher Education Applications of Artificial Intelligence/Machine Learning and Virtual Reality/Mixed reality/Augmented Reality to Solve Challenges in HigherEd for First Generation, Low Income and Underrepresented Minority Students," in *How We Work: Grants*, November 27, 2017, https://www.gatesfoundation.org/How-We-Work/Quick-Links/Grants-Database/Grants/2017/11/OPP1180123

212   Juan A. Muñoz-Cristóbal, Luis P. Prieto, Juan I. Asensio-Pérez, Alejandra Martínez-Monés, Iván M. Jorrín-Abellán, and Yannis Dimitriadis, "Coming Down to Earth: Helping Teachers Use 3D Virtual Worlds in Across-Spaces Learning Situations," *Journal of Educational Technology & Society* 18 no. 1 (2015): 13.

213   Ibid, 18.

214   Ibid.

215   Pearson, "Pearson Announces Mixed Reality Pilots Designed to Solve Real World Learning Challenges at Colleges and Universities," *Pearson News & Events*, October 26, 2016, https://www.pearson.com/us/about/news-events/news/2016/10/pearson-announces-mixed-reality-pilots-at-colleges-and-universities.html

216   Juan Mateu, María José Lasala, and Xavier Alamán, "Developing Mixed Reality Educational Applications: The Virtual Touch Toolkit," *Sensors* 15 no. 9 (2015): 21761.

217   Jacquelyn J. Chini, Carrie L. Straub, and Kevin H. Thomas, "Learning from Avatars: Learning Assistants Practice Physics Pedagogy in a Classroom Simulator," *Physical Review Physics Education Research* 12 no. 1 (2016): 15.

218   Ibid.

219   Ibid.

220   José Bidarra and Ellen Rusman, "Towards a Pedagogical Model for Science Education: Bridging Educational Contexts through a Blended Learning Approach," *Open Learning* 32 no. 1 (2017): 6.

221   Bridget M. Kuehn, "Virtual and Augmented Reality Put a Twist on Medical Education," *Journal of American Medical Association* 319 no. 8 (2018): 756-758.

222   Ibid.

223   Ibid.

224   Filip Górski, Pawel Bun, Radoslaw Wichniarek, Przemyslaw Zawadzki, Adam Hamrol, "Ef-

fective Design of Educational Virtual Reality Applications for Medicine Using Knowledge-Engineering Techniques," *EURASIA Journal of Mathematics, Science & Technology Education* 13 no. 2 (2017): 395.

225 Juan Mateu, María José Lasala, and Xavier Alamán, "Developing Mixed Reality Educational Applications: The Virtual Touch Toolkit," *Sensors* 15 no. 9 (2015): 21762.

226 Vincent Higgins, "Augmented & Virtual Reality: The Future of Work, Not Just Play," *Professional Safety* 62 no. 6 (2017): 86.

227 Ibid.

228 Ibid.

229 Ibid.

230 Eugenijus Kurilovas, "Evaluation of Quality and Personalisation of VR/AR/MR Learning Systems," *Behaviour & Information Technology* 35 no. 11 (2016): 1000.

231 Global Education Futures, "Global Education 2015-2035," *Global Education Futures Initiative*, accessed November 23, 2018, https://www.edu2035.org/images/people/Future%20of%20Global%20Education%20Map%20(2014)-ilovepdf-compressed.pdf

232 United States, Department of Education, "Secretary Betsy DeVos Announces 'Rethink School' Tour," *Press Release*, accessed December 2, 2018, https://www.ed.gov/news/media-advisories/secretary-betsy-devos-announces-rethink-school-tour

233 Arika Herron, "Education Secretary DeVos to Visit Indianapolis, Gary Schools Friday," *Indy Star*, September 13, 2017, https://www.indystar.com/story/news/education/2017/09/13/education-secretary-devos-visit-indianapolis-gary-schools-friday/663713001/

Tricia Harte, "Piloting Virtual Reality into the Classroom," *Fox 59*, August 23, 2017, https://fox59.com/2017/08/23/piloting-virtual-reality-into-the-classroom/

234 Victory VR, "Trump Administration Takes Virtual Reality Curriculum for a Test Drive," *Victory VR: Education, News, Technology,* September 18, 2017, http://www.victoryvr.biz/1519-2/

235 Ibid.

236 Ibid.

237 Emanuella Grinberg, "Would You Want Google Glass in Class?," *CNN*, February 11, 2014, https://www.cnn.com/2014/02/10/living/google-glass-in-schools/index.html

Eric Boykin, "Google Glass in the Class: Wearable Technology of the Educational Future," *Duke University Digital Initiative*, (2014), https://dukedigitalinitiative.duke.edu/google-glass-in-the-class-wearable-technology-of-the-educational-future

238 Jonathan Vanian, "Facebook Debuts Big Oculus Educational VR Push in Seattle, Taiwan, and Japan," *Fortune*, August 28, 2018, fortune.com/2018/08/28/facebook-oculus-vr-education/

239 Signe Brewster, "The Best VR Headset for Your Phone," *Wirecutter: A New York Times Company*, July 11, 2018, https://thewirecutter.com/reviews/best-vr-headset-for-your-phone/

240 Paul Lamkin, "The Best Smartphone Headsets for VR Apps: Gear VR, Daydream, Cardboard and More – iOS and Android Compatible Devices," *Wareable*, March 8, 2018, https://www.wareable.com/vr/best-smartphone-headsets-mobile-vr-apps-1655

241 Ray Kurzweil, *The Singularity Is Near: When Humans Transcend Biology* (New York: Viking, 2005), 337.

242 Eugenijus Kurilovas, "Evaluation of Quality and Personalisation of VR/AR/MR Learning Systems," *Behaviour & Information Technology* 35 no. 11 (2016): 998.

243 Mark Zuckerberg, "So What if You Could Type Directly from Your Brain," *Facebook*, April 19, 2017, https://www.facebook.com/zuck/videos/vb.4/10103661167577621/?type=2&theater

244 Aatif Sulleyman, "Mind-Reading Headset Allowing People to Control Computers with Their Thoughts Described in Microsoft Patent," *The Independent*, https://www.independent.co.uk/life-style/gadgets-and-tech/news/mind-reading-headset-computer-control-thoughts-microsoft-patent-a8163976.html

245 Sydney Johnson, "This Company Wants to Gather Student Brainwave Data to Measure 'Engagement,'" *EdSurge*, October 26, 2017, https://www.edsurge.com/news/2017-10-26-this-company-wants-to-gather-student-brainwave-data-to-measure-engagement

246 Ibid.

247 Ibid.

248 Ibid.

249 E. Paul Zehr, "The Potential Transformation of Our Species by Neural Enhancement," *Journal of Motor Behavior* 47 no. 1 (2015): 75

250 Ray Kurzweil, *The Singularity Is Near: When Humans Transcend Biology* (New York: Viking,

2005), 226-227.

251   Ibid, 316.

252   Ibid, 317.

253   2045 Strategic Social Initiative, "Ray Kurzweil about GF2045 and 'Avatar,'" *Global Future 2045 News*, March 19, 2012, http://2045.com/news/29620.html

254   Katie Drummond, "Russian Mogul to 'Forbes' Billionaires: Limitless Lifespans Can Be Yours," *Forbes*, July 19, 2012, https://www.forbes.com/sites/katiedrummond/2012/07/19/dmitry-itskov-avatar/#2bc083a257ad

255   2045 Strategic Social Initiative, "Global Future 2045 International Congress," *Russia 2045*, February 2012, quoted in Daniel Estulin, *TransEvolution: The Coming Age of Human Deconstruction* (Walterville, OR: Trine Day, 2014), 162.

256   Ibid, 165.

257   Ibid, 164.

258   Ibid, 165.

259   Dominic Gover, "Bilderberg 2.0: The Singularity, Google's Ray Kurzweil and the Ultimate Power," *International Business Times*, June 7, 2013, https://www.ibtimes.co.uk/google-conspiracy-bilderberg-singularity-476127

260   Ray Kurzweil, *The Singularity Is Near: When Humans Transcend Biology* (New York: Viking, 2005), 324-325.

261   Arjun Kharpal, "Elon Musk: Humans Must Merge with Machines or Become Irrelevant in AI Age," *CNBC*, February 13, 2017, https://www.cnbc.com/2017/02/13/elon-musk-humans-merge-machines-cyborg-artificial-intelligence-robots.html

262   Ibid.

263   Elon Musk, interview by Joe Rogan, "Joe Rogan Experience #1169," *Powerful JRE*, September 6, 2018, https://www.youtube.com/watch?v=ycPr5-27vSI

264   Ibid.

265   Rolfe Winkler, "Elon Musk Launches Neuralink to Connect Brains With Computers: Start-up from CEO of Tesla and SpaceX Aims to Implant Tiny Electrodes in Human Brains," *Wall Street Journal*, March 27, 2017, https://www.wsj.com/articles/elon-musk-launches-neuralink-to-connect-brains-with-computers-1490642652

266   John Thornhill, "The March of the Technocrats: There Are Lessons to Be Learnt Today from the 'Revolt of the Engineers' in the 1930s," *Financial Times*, February 19, 2018, https://www.ft.com/content/df695f10-154d-11e8-9376-4a6390addb44

267   Joseph C Keating Jr. and Scott Haldeman, "Joshua N Haldeman, DC: the Canadian Years, 1926-1950," *Journal of the Canadian Chiropractic Association* 39 no. 3 (1995): 172-186.

268   Ray Argyle, "The Last Utopians: Technocracy Promised Depression-Weary Canadians an End to Their Hardship. But the Offer Came with a Catch," *Canada's History Society*, January 1, 2018, https://www.canadashistory.ca/explore/politics-law/the-last-utopians

269   Ibid.

Endnotes – Chapter Eighteen

1   Max Tegmark, *Life 3.0: Being Human in the Age of Artificial Intelligence* (New York: Alfred A. Knopf, 2017), 167.

2   Ibid.

3   Ibid.

4   Ibid.

5   Ibid.

6   Ibid.

7   Ibid.

8   Ibid.

9   Ibid.

10   Ibid.

11   Ibid.

12   Ibid.

13   Ibid.

14   Warwick Ashford, "CIA and Google Invest in High-Tech Crystal Ball Technology: The CIA and Google Have Joined Forces to Fund a Start-up Company That Claims to Have the Technolo-

gy to Predict the Future Using Information Collected from the Internet," *Computer Weekly*, August 3, 2010, https://www.computerweekly.com/news/1280093436/CIA-and-Google-invest-in-high-tech-crystal-ball-technology

15   Bertrand Russell, *In Praise of Idleness, and Other Essays* (London: G. Allen & Unwin, 1958).

16   Editors of the Encyclopedia Britannica, "Taylorism: Scientific Management System," *Encyclopedia Britannica*, accessed December 6, 2018, https://www.britannica.com/science/Taylorism

17   Erik Loomis, "US Workers Were Once Massacred Fighting for the Protections Being Rolled Back Today," Moyers & Company, April 23, 2014, https://billmoyers.com/2014/04/23/us-workers-were-once-massacred-fighting-for-the-protections-being-rolled-back-today/

Sarah Jones, "The Pinkertons Still Never Sleep," *New Republic*, March 23, 2018, https://newrepublic.com/article/147619/pinkertons-still-never-sleep

18   Chester McArthur Destler, "Entrepreneurial Leadership Among the 'Robber Barons': A Trial Balance," *Journal of Economic History* 6 (1946): 28-49.

19   Carnegie Mellon University, "The Fourth Industrial Revolution," CMU News, January 20, 2016, https://www.cmu.edu/news/stories/archives/2016/january/the-fourth-industrial-revolution.html

20   David Rothkopf, *Superclass: The Global Power Elite and the World They Are Making* (London: Little, Brown, 2008).

21   Thomas Henry Huxley, "Letter to Anton Dohrn, July 7, 1871," The Huxley File, eds. Charles Blinderman and David Joyce (Clark University, 1998), https://mathcs.clarku.edu/huxley/letters/71.html#7jul1871

22   Yuval Noah Harari, *Homo Deus: A Brief History of Tomorrow* (London: Vintage, 2016), 409.

23   Mark Harris, "Inside the First Church of Artificial Intelligence," *Wired Magazine*, November 15, 2017, https://www.wired.com/story/anthony-levandowski-artificial-intelligence-religion/

24   Michael DePaul and Amelia Hicks, "A Priorism in Moral Epistemology," *Stanford Encyclopedia of Philosophy*, June 28, 2016, https://plato.stanford.edu/entries/moral-epistemology-a-priori/

Sean Carroll, "Science And Morality: You Can't Derive 'Ought' From 'Is,'" NPR, May 4, 2010, https://www.npr.org/sections/13.7/2010/05/04/126504492/you-can-t-derive-ought-from-is

25   Immanuel Kant, *Groundwork of the Metaphysic of Morals*, trans. H. J. Paton (New York: Harper & Row, 1948).

United States of America, Declaration of Independence, July 4, 1776, https://www.archives.gov/founding-docs/declaration-transcript

Endnotes – Chapter Nineteen

1   Antony C. Sutton, *America's Secret Establishment: An Introduction to the Order of Skull and Bones,* Updated Reprint (Walterville, OR: Trine Day, 2002), 111.

2   David Ruenzel, "The World According to Gatto," Education Week, March 1, 2001, https://www.edweek.org/tm/articles/2001/03/01/06gatto.h12.html

3   John Taylor Gatto, *An Underground History of American Education: An Intimate Investigation into the Prison of Modern Schooling* (New York: Oxford Village Press, 2006), 386.

4   Antony C. Sutton, *America's Secret Establishment: An Introduction to the Order of Skull and Bones,* Updated Reprint (Walterville, OR: Trine Day, 2002), 111.

5   Ibid, 387.

6   Charlotte Thomson Iserbyt, "Charter School Trap (Part 1 of 2)," News With Views, February 22, 2011, http://www.newswithviews.com/iserbyt/iserbyt107.htm

7   Ibid.

8   Ibid, "Death Sentence for Private and Home Education, Courtesy of Supreme Court," News With Views, July 8, 2002, https://www.newswithviews.com/iserbyt/iserbyt1.htm

9   Ibid, "Wake Up Homeschoolers: They're Coming for Your Children," News With Views, July 13, 2015, http://newswithviews.com/iserbyt/iserbyt139.htm

10   Ibid, "Charter School Trap (Part 1 of 2)," News With Views, February 22, 2011, http://www.newswithviews.com/iserbyt/iserbyt107.htm

11   Trisha Powell Crain, "Alabama Charter School Commission Adds New Charter, Expands Others," Advance Local: Alabama Media Group, February 4, 2019, https://www.al.com/news/2019/02/alabama-charter-school-commission-adds-new-charter-expands-others.html

Ibid, "Three Alabama Charter Schools Win $1 Million Each in Federal Education Grants," Advance Local: Alabama Media Group, October 9, 2018, https://www.al.com/news/2018/10/three_alabama_charter_schools.html

12   Sarah Peters, "Gadsden School Board Election to Take Place," Gadsden Messenger, April 5, 2019, https://gadsdenmessenger.com/2019/04/05/gadsden-school-board-election-to-take-place/

13   State of Missouri, Department of Elementary and Secondary Education, St. Louis Charter Schools (Jefferson City, MO: DESE, 2016), https://dese.mo.gov/sites/default/files/qs-charter-stl-charterschools_14.pdf

14   Ryan Delaney, "State School Board Ends Decade-Long Oversight of St. Louis Schools," St. Louis Public Radio, April 16, 2019, https://news.stlpublicradio.org/post/state-school-board-ends-decade-long-oversight-st-louis-schools#stream/0

15   Blythe Bernhard, "St. Louis Public Schools Expected to Return to Control of Elected Board," St. Louis Today: Post-Dispatch, April 5, 2019, https://www.stltoday.com/news/local/metro/st-louis-public-schools-expected-to-return-to-control-of/article_fdfb4fcb-8e73-50ab-9e7e-8e68340ca63e.html

16   Linh Tat, "Critics Fear Proposed Montclair Charter Will Upset District's Choice Program," Politico, September 7, 2016, https://www.politico.com/states/new-jersey/story/2016/09/montclair-charter-school-foes-to-urge-state-education-officials-to-reject-application-105226

Network for Public Education, "Save Our School NJ Cautiously Looks Forward to a Post Chris Christie New Jersey," NPE, December 18, 2017, https://networkforpubliceducation.org/save-school-nj-cautiously-looks-forward-post-chris-christie-new-jersey/

Winnie Hu, "Christie Says 23 Schools Get Charters," New York Times, January 18, 2011, https://www.nytimes.com/2011/01/19/education/19christie.html

17   Erin Roll, "Montclair Parents Debate Appointed vs. Elected School Board," Montclair Local News, April 4, 2019, https://www.montclairlocal.news/2019/04/04/montclair-appointed-elected-board-nj/

18   Paul Caine, "School Discontent Prompts Calls for an Elected School Board," WTTW News, January 24, 2019, https://news.wttw.com/2019/01/24/school-discontent-prompts-calls-elected-school-board

19   Dan Petrella, "Illinois House Approves Bill Creating Elected Chicago School Board — An Idea Mayor-Elect Lori Lightfoot Supports," Chicago Tribune, April 4, 2019, https://www.chicagotribune.com/news/local/politics/ct-met-illinois-house-elected-chicago-school-board-20190404-story.html

Pranathi Posa, "What Does an Elected School Board Mean for Chicago?," Chicago Maroon, April 29, 2019, https://www.chicagomaroon.com/article/2019/4/30/state-bill-elected-chicago-school-board-could-soon/

State of Illinois, General Assembly, House of Representatives, House Bill (HB) 2267, 101st Illinois General Assembly, April 4, 2019, http://ilga.gov/legislation/billstatus.asp?DocNum=2267&GAID=15&GA=101&DocTypeID=HB&LegID=118102&SessionID=108

20   Elaine Chen, "Mayor Appoints Booth Professor to Chicago's School Board," The Chicago Maroon, December 19, 2018, December 19, 2018, https://www.chicagomaroon.com/article/2018/12/20/mayor-appoints-booth-professor-chicagos-school-boa/

21   Charlotte Thomson Iserbyt, "Back to Basics Reform: Or . . . OBE Skinnerian International Curriculum?" (Barbara Morris Report, 1985), 34.

22   Ibid, "Wake Up Homeschoolers: They're Coming for Your Children," News With Views, July 13, 2015, http://newswithviews.com/iserbyt/iserbyt139.htm

23   Willard W. Garvey, "Letter to President Reagan," April 6, 1984, quote in Charlotte Thomson Iserbyt, "Wake Up Homeschoolers: They're Coming for Your Children," News With Views, July 13, 2015, http://newswithviews.com/iserbyt/iserbyt139.htm

24   Landon E. Beyer and Michael W. Apple, The Curriculum: Problems, Politics, and Possibilities (Albany, NY: State University of New York Press, 1988).

25   Douglas D. Noble, "Education, Technology, and Military," The Curriculum: Problems, Politics, and Possibilities, eds. Landon E. Beyer and Michael W. Apple (Albany, NY: State University of New York Press, 1988), 245-246.

26   Ibid, 246-245.

27   Liz Tausner, "Teachers Hear from Alfie Kohn, 'Case Against Grades,'" Dwight-Englewood School News Detail, September 12, 2012, https://www.d-e.org/news-detail?pk=635200

28   Alfie Kohn, Punished by Rewards: The Trouble with Gold Stars, Incentive Plans, A's, Praise, and Other Bribes (Boston: Houghton Mifflin, 2018), quoted in Valerie Strauss, "Why Dangling Rewards in Front of Students and Teachers Is Counterproductive," Washington Post, October 5, 2016,

https://www.washingtonpost.com/news/answer-sheet/wp/2016/10/05/why-dangling-rewards-in-front-of-students-and-teachers-is-counterproductive/?utm_term=.d2d3f8f7babc

29 Ibid.

30 Ibid.

31 Kenneth Goodman, "The President's Education Program: A Response," Support for Learning and Teaching of English 3 no. 2 (1978), quoted in Charlotte Thomson Iserbyt, "Back to Basics Reform: Or . . . OBE Skinnerian International Curriculum?" (*Barbara Morris Report*, 1985), 8.

32 Arizona Federation of Teachers Resolution, May 5, 1984, quoted in Charlotte Thomson Iserbyt, "Back to Basics Reform: Or . . . OBE Skinnerian International Curriculum?" (*Barbara Morris Report*, 1985), 3.

33 Charlotte Thomson Iserbyt,"Back to Basics Reform: Or . . . OBE Skinnerian International Curriculum?" (*Barbara Morris Report*, 1985), 4.

34 Lori Kay Baranek, "The Effect of Rewards and Motivation on Student Achievement," Grand Valley State University Masters Theses: Graduate Research and Creative Practice, no. 238 (Allendale, MI: Grand Valley State University, 1996), 21, https://scholarworks.gvsu.edu/cgi/viewcontent.cgi?article=1292&context=theses

35 Alfie Kohn, *Punished by Rewards: The Trouble with Gold Stars, Incentive Plans, A's, Praise, and Other Bribes* (Boston: Houghton Mifflin, 2018), quoted in Valerie Strauss, "Why Dangling Rewards in Front of Students and Teachers Is Counterproductive," Washington Post, October 5, 2016, https://www.washingtonpost.com/news/answer-sheet/wp/2016/10/05/why-dangling-rewards-in-front-of-students-and-teachers-is-counterproductive/?utm_term=.d2d3f8f7babc

36 Antony C. Sutton, *America's Secret Establishment: An Introduction to the Order of Skull and Bones*, Updated Reprint (Walterville, OR: Trine Day, 2002), 111.

37 Lori Kay Baranek, "The Effect of Rewards and Motivation on Student Achievement," Grand Valley State University Masters Theses: Graduate Research and Creative Practice, no. 238 (Allendale, MI: Grand Valley State University, 1996), 21-22, https://scholarworks.gvsu.edu/cgi/viewcontent.cgi?article=1292&context=theses

38 Michel Foucault, *Discipline and Punishment: The Birth of the Prison* (New York: Vintage Books, 1995).

Suzanne Gearhart,"Foucault's Response to Freud: Sado-Masochism and the Aestheticization of Power," *Psychoanalysis: Theory and Practice*, 29 no. 3 (1995): 389-403.

39 Jacques-Alain Miller and Richard Miller, "Jeremy Bentham's Panoptic Device," *MIT Press*, 41 (Summer, 1987): 3-29.

Michel Foucault, *Discipline and Punishment: The Birth of the Prison* (New York: Vintage Books, 1995).

Thomas McMullan, "What Does the Panopticon Mean in the Age of Digital Surveillance? The Parallel Between Jeremy Bentham's Panopticon and CCTV May Be Clear, but What Happens When You Step into the World of Data Capture?," *The Guardian*: US Edition, July 23, 2015, https://www.theguardian.com/technology/2015/jul/23/panopticon-digital-surveillance-jeremy-bentham

University College London, "Who Was Jeremy Bentham? The Panopticon," The Bentham Project, accessed May 23, 2019, https://www.ucl.ac.uk/bentham-project/who-was-jeremy-bentham/panopticon

40 Jacques-Alain Miller and Richard Miller, "Jeremy Bentham's Panoptic Device," *MIT Press*, 41 (Summer, 1987): 3-29.

Michel Foucault, *Discipline and Punishment: The Birth of the Prison* (New York: Vintage Books, 1995).

University College London, "Who Was Jeremy Bentham? The Panopticon," The Bentham Project, accessed May 23, 2019, https://www.ucl.ac.uk/bentham-project/who-was-jeremy-bentham/panopticon

41 Meriem El-Khattabi, "Mining for Success: Have Student Data Privacy and Educational Data-Mining Created a Legislative War Zone?," *Journal of Law Technology and Policy* no. 2 (2017): 511-538.

42 Mario Trujillo, "Public Wants 'Right to Be Forgotten' Online," The Hill, March 19, 2015, https://thehill.com/policy/technology/236246-poll-public-wants-right-to-be-forgotten-online

Rebecca Heilweil, "How Close Is an American Right-to-Be-Forgotten?," *Forbes*, March 4, 2018, https://www.forbes.com/sites/rebeccaheilweil1/2018/03/04/how-close-is-an-american-right-to-be-forgotten/#42cf6cdc626e

43 David Meyer, "The 'Right to Be Forgotten,' Globally? How Google Is Fighting

to Limit the Scope of Europe's Privacy Law," *Fortune*, September 10, 2018, http://fortune.com/2018/09/10/google-eu-court-justice-right-to-be-forgotten/

European Union, General Data Protection Regulations, EU Regulation 2016/679, EU Parliament and Council, April 27, 2016, https://eur-lex.europa.eu/legal-content/EN/TXT/?qid=1532348683434&uri=CELEX:02016R0679-20160504

44		Consumer Watchdog, "Consumer Rights Group Consumer Watchdog Files Complaint with FTC Over Google's Privacy," Consumer Watchdog: Expose. Confront. Change, July 7, 2016, https://www.consumerwatchdog.org/consumer-rights-group-consumer-watchdog-files-complaint-ftc-over-googleaeutms-privacy

45		Shaudee Dehghan, "How Does California's Erasure Law Stack Up Against the EU's Right to Be Forgotten?," *The International Association of Privacy Professionals*, April 17, 2018, https://iapp.org/news/a/how-does-californias-erasure-law-stack-up-against-the-eus-right-to-be-forgotten/

46		Joseph J. Lazzarotti, Jason C. Gavejian, and Maya Atrakchi, "State Law Developments in Consumer Privacy," *National Law Review*, March 15, 2019, https://www.natlawreview.com/article/state-law-developments-consumer-privacy

47		Jason C. Gavejian, Joseph J. Lazzarotti, Nathan W. Austin, and Mary T. Costigan, *National Law Review*, January 29, 2019, https://www.natlawreview.com/article/california-consumer-privacy-act-faqs-employers

48		Charlotte Thomson Iserbyt, "Back to Basics Reform: Or … OBE Skinnerian International Curriculum?" (*Barbara Morris Report*, 1985), 32.

49		United States, Department of Education, "Protection of Pupil Rights Amendment," Law & Guidance, February 17, 2005, https://www2.ed.gov/policy//gen/guid/fpco/ppra/index.html

50		Ibid.

51		C. S. Lewis, *The Abolition of Man: Or Reflection on Education with Special Reference to the Teaching of English in the Upper Forms of Schools* (New York: Macmillan, 1947).

52		Ibid, *The Abolition of Man: Or Reflection on Education with Special Reference to the Teaching of English in the Upper Forms of Schools* (New York: Macmillan, 1947).

53		Ibid, *That Hideous Strength: A Modern Fairytale for Grownups* (New York: Macmillan, 1946).

54		University of Oxford, "C. S. Lewis at Magdalene College," Libraries and Archives: Treasure of the Month (Magdalene College, November 21, 2013), http://www.magd.ox.ac.uk/libraries-and-archives/treasure-of-the-month/news/c-s-lewis/

55		C. S. Lewis, *The Abolition of Man: Or Reflection on Education with Special Reference to the Teaching of English in the Upper Forms of Schools* (New York: Macmillan, 1947).

56		University of Cambridge, "CS Lewis: 50 Years after His Death a New Scholarship Will Honour His Literary Career," Research: News, November 8, 2013), https://www.cam.ac.uk/research/news/cs-lewis-50-years-after-his-death-a-new-scholarship-will-honour-his-literary-career

57		C. S. Lewis, *The Discarded Image: An Introduction to Medieval and Renaissance Literature* (Cambridge: University of Cambridge Press, 1964), 185-186.

58		Joe R. Christopher, "Dorothy Sayers and the Inklings," *Mythlore*: A Journal of J. R. R. Tolkien, C. S. Lewis, Charles Williams, and Mythopoetic Literature 4 no. 1.13 (1976), Article 3.

59		Dorothy Sayers, "The Lost Tools of Learning," *Increasing Academic Achievement with the Trivium of Classical Education: Its Historical Development, Decline in the Last Century, and Resurgence in Recent Decades*, ed. Randall D. Hart (New York: iUniverse, 2006), 107.

60		Hamza Yusuf, "The Liberal Arts in an Illiberal Age: Freeing Thought from the Shackles of Feeling and Desire," *Renovatio*: The Journal of Zaytuna College December 19, 2018, https://renovatio.zaytuna.edu/article/the-liberal-arts-in-an-illiberal-age

John C. Scott, "The Mission of the University: Medieval to Postmodern Transformations," *Journal of higher Education* 77 no. 1 (2006).

Miriam Joseph, *The Trivium: The Liberal Arts of Logic, Grammar, and Rhetoric (Understanding the Nature and Function of Language)* (Philadelphia: Paul Dry Books, 2002), 24-26, 43, 53, 75, 101-103, 143-145, 158, 188, 194, 215, 226-230, 237-238, 275.

Randall D. Hart, *Increasing Academic Achievement with the Trivium of Classical Education: Its Historical Development, Decline in the Last Century, and Resurgence in Recent Decades* (New York: iUniverse, 2006), 12-56.

Richard E. Rubenstein, *Aristotle's Children : How Christians, Muslims, and Jews Rediscovered Ancient Wisdom and Illuminated the Middle Ages* (Orlando, FL: Harcourt, 2004).

61		"Authors: Hamza Yusuf," *Renovatio*: The Journal of Zaytuna College, accessed May 17,

2019, https://renovatio.zaytuna.edu/authors/hamza-yusuf

Hamza Yusuf, "The Liberal Arts in an Illiberal Age: Freeing Thought from the Shackles of Feeling and Desire," *Renovatio*: The Journal of Zaytuna College December 19, 2018, https://renovatio.zaytuna.edu/article/the-liberal-arts-in-an-illiberal-age

62   Benjamin G. Kohl, "The Changing Concept of the 'Studia Humanitatis' in the Early Renaissance," *Renaissance Studies* 6 no. 2 (1992): 185-209.

C. S. Lewis, *The Discarded Image: An Introduction to Medieval and Renaissance Literature* (Cambridge: University of Cambridge Press, 1964), 186.

G. Felicitas Munzel, "Kant on Moral Education, or 'Enlightenment' and the Liberal Arts," *The Review of Metaphysics* 57 no. 1 (2003): 43-73.

Hamza Yusuf, "The Liberal Arts in an Illiberal Age: Freeing Thought from the Shackles of Feeling and Desire," *Renovatio*: The Journal of Zaytuna College December 19, 2018, https://renovatio.zaytuna.edu/article/the-liberal-arts-in-an-illiberal-age

John C. Scott, "The Mission of the University: Medieval to Postmodern Transformations," *Journal of higher Education* 77 no. 1 (2006).

Richard E. Rubenstein, *Aristotle's Children: How Christians, Muslims, and Jews Rediscovered Ancient Wisdom and Illuminated the Middle Ages* (Orlando, FL: Harcourt, 2004).

63   Gavin P. Hendricks, "A Derridarean Critique of Logocentrism as Opposed to Textcentrism in John 1v1," Koers 79 no. 1 (2014): http://www.scielo.org.za/scielo.php?script=sci_arttext&pid=S2304-85572014000100010

Michael Harrison, "Logocentrism," *The Chicago School of Media Theory: Theorizing Media Since 2003*, accessed May 23, 2019, https://lucian.uchicago.edu/blogs/mediatheory/keywords/logocentrism/

64   Aristotle, *The Organon: Or Logical Treatises*, trans. Octavius Freire Owen, vol. I (London: Bohn's Classical Library, 1853).

Ibid, vol. II (London: Bohn's Classical Library, 1853).

Ibid, *The Metaphysics*, trans. John H. M'Mahon (London: George Bell and Sons, 1896).

Ibid, *The Physics*, trans. Philip H. Wicksteed and Francis M. Cornford, vol. I (New York: G. P. Putnam's Sons, 1934).

Ibid, vol. II (New York: G. P. Putnam's Sons, 1934).

Miriam Joseph, *The Trivium: The Liberal Arts of Logic, Grammar, and Rhetoric (Understanding the Nature and Function of Language)* (Philadelphia: Paul Dry Books, 2002), 24-26, 75, 275.

Paul Studtmann, "Aristotle's Categories," Stanford *Encyclopedia of Philosophy*, November 5, 2013, https://plato.stanford.edu/entries/aristotle-categories/

65   Hanne Andersen and Brian Hepburn, "Scientific Method," *Stanford Encyclopedia of Philosophy*, November 13, 2015, https://plato.stanford.edu/entries/scientific-method/

66   Antony C. Sutton, *America's Secret Establishment: An Introduction to the Order of Skull and Bones*, Updated Reprint (Walterville, OR: Trine Day, 2002), 111.

67   David Ruenzel, "The World According to Gatto," Education Week, March 1, 2001, https://www.edweek.org/tm/articles/2001/03/01/06gatto.h12.html

68   John Taylor Gatto, *An Underground History of American Education: An Intimate Investigation into the Prison of Modern Schooling* (New York: Oxford Village Press, 2006), 387.

69   David Ruenzel, "The World According to Gatto," Education Week, March 1, 2001, https://www.edweek.org/tm/articles/2001/03/01/06gatto.h12.html

70   John Taylor Gatto, *An Underground History of American Education: An Intimate Investigation into the Prison of Modern Schooling* (New York: Oxford Village Press, 2006), 387.

71   Ibid, 187.

72   Ibid, 188.

73   Ibid, 187.

74   Ibid, 308.

75   Ibid, 387.

76   C. S. Lewis, *The Discarded Image: An Introduction to Medieval and Renaissance Literature* (Cambridge: University of Cambridge Press, 1964), 185-186.

77   Ibid, 185-190.

78   Dorothy L. Sayers Society, "Sayer's Biography: About Dorothy L. Sayers," The Dorothy L. Sayers Society: The Official Site of the Renowned English Crime Writer Dorothy L. Sayers, accessed May 18, 2019, https://www.sayers.org.uk/biography

79   Randall D. Hart, *Increasing Academic Achievement with the Trivium of Classical Education: Its Historical Development, Decline in the Last Century, and Resurgence in Recent Decades* (New York:

iUniverse, 2006), 71-74.

80   Dorothy Sayers, "The Lost Tools of Learning," Increasing Academic Achievement with the *Trivium of Classical Education: Its Historical Development, Decline in the Last Century, and Resurgence in Recent Decades,* ed. Randall D. Hart (New York: iUniverse, 2006), 107.

81   Ibid, 107-108.

82   Miriam Joseph, *The Trivium: The Liberal Arts of Logic, Grammar, and Rhetoric (Understanding the Nature and Function of Language)* (Philadelphia: Paul Dry Books, 2002), 3.

83   Ibid.

84   Ibid.

85   Aristotle, *Historia Animalium*, trans. D'arcy Wentworth Thompson, eds. J. A. Smith and W. D. Ross (Oxford: Clarendon Press, 1910).

Editors of the Columbia Electronic Encyclopedia, "Alcuin," *Columbia Electronic Encyclopedia*, 6th ed., http://eds.a.ebscohost.com/ehost/detail/detail?vid=13&sid=faa463ef-ae-fa-44bb-9e84-bc0f28bb47ce%40sessionmgr4010&bdata=JkF1dGhUeXBlPXNoaWImc2l0ZT1laG-9zdC1saXZl#AN=134480414&db=a9h

Editors of the Encyclopedia Britannica, "Divine Right of Kings: Political Doctrine," March 22, 2017, https://www.britannica.com/topic/divine-right-of-kings

Ibid, "Government: Middle Ages," Encyclopedia Britannica, accessed May 18, 2019, https://www.britannica.com/topic/government/The-Middle-Ages

Evina Steinova, "Psalmos, Notas, Cantus: On the Meanings of Nota in the Carolingian Period," *Speculum* 90 no 2 (2015): 424-457.

Jack Richard Censer and Lynn Hunt, *Liberty, Equality, Fraternity: Exploring the French Revolution* (University Park, PA: Pennsylvania State University Press, 2001).

John Agnew, "Deus Vult: The Geopolitics of the Catholic Church," *Geopolitics* 15 no. 1 (2010): 39-61, https://www.geog.ucla.edu/sites/default/files/users/jagnew/391.pdf

Paul W. Fox, "Louis XIV and the Theories of Absolutism and Divine Right," *The Canadian Journal of Economics and Political Science 26 no. 1 (1960): 128-142.*

Plato, *The Republic*, trans. B. Jowett (New York: Modern Library, 1941).

86   David A. Thomas, "John Wycliff: Morningstar of the Reformation," *Journal of the Tennessee Speech Communication Association* 4 no. 1 (1978): 12-15.

Joseph P. Tomain, "Introduction to Law in Literature and Philosophy," University of Cincinnati College of Law Faculty Scholarship and Publications 330 (2016): 14, https://scholarship.law.uc.edu/cgi/viewcontent.cgi?article=1331&context=fac_pubs

87   David A. Thomas, "John Wycliff: Morningstar of the Reformation," *Journal of the Tennessee Speech Communication Association* 4 no. 1 (1978): 12-15.

Diana Schaub, "Montesquieu's Popular Science," *The New Atlantis: A Journal of Technology and Society* no. 20 (2008): 37-46, https://www.thenewatlantis.com/publications/montesquieus-popular-science

Editors of the Encyclopedia Britannica, "Divine Right of Kings: Political Doctrine," March 22, 2017, https://www.britannica.com/topic/divine-right-of-kings

Edward J. Woell, "The Public Sphere of Past and Present, and the Place of the Liberal Arts," Western Illinois University Lecture Archive, September 1, 2016, http://www.wiu.edu/news/lecture_archive/liberalArts16.php

Joseph P. Tomain, "Introduction to Law in Literature and Philosophy," University of Cincinnati College of Law Faculty Scholarship and Publications 330 (2016): 14, https://scholarship.law.uc.edu/cgi/viewcontent.cgi?article=1331&context=fac_pubs

Joseph Wilhelm, "Jan Hus," *Catholic Encyclopedia* vol. 7 (New York: Robert Appleton Company, 1910), http://www.newadvent.org/cathen/07584b.htm

Michael Lind, "Why the Liberal Arts Still Matter," *Wilson Quarterly* (Autumn 2006), http://archive.wilsonquarterly.com/essays/why-liberal-arts-still-matter

Opinion/Letters, "Praise for the Real Liberal Arts, If You Can Find Them: Very Few Modern Liberal-Arts Programs Resemble the Education Thomas Jefferson Received—One Grounded in the Great Books of the Western World," *Wall Street Journal*, April 2, 2015, https://www.wsj.com/articles/praise-for-the-real-liberal-arts-if-you-can-find-them-letters-to-the-editor-1428008843

Steven C. Bahls, "Liberal Arts Education and Courageous Servant Leadership," President's Office of Augustana College: Speeches and Statements (2003), https://digitalcommons.augustana.edu/cgi/viewcontent.cgi?referer=https://www.google.com/&httpsredir=1&article=1001&context=presidentsstatements

88   Andrew Fleming West, "The Seven Liberal Arts," *Alcuin and the Rise of the Christian Schools*, ed. Christopher A. Perrin (Classical Academic Press, 2010), http://classicalsubjects.com/resources/TheSevenLiberalArts.pdf

Editors of the Columbia Electronic Encyclopedia, "Alcuin," *Columbia Electronic Encyclopedia*, 6th ed., http://eds.a.ebscohost.com/ehost/detail/detail?vid=13&sid=faa463ef-ae-fa-44bb-9e84-bc0f28bb47ce%40sessionmgr4010&bdata=JkF1dGhUeXBlPXNoaWImc2l0ZT1laG-9zdC1saXZl#AN=134480414&db=a9h

Michael Lind, "Why the Liberal Arts Still Matter," *Wilson Quarterly* (Autumn 2006), http://archive.wilsonquarterly.com/essays/why-liberal-arts-still-matter

James R. Muir, "Overestimating Plato and Underestimating Isocrates: The Example of Thomas Jefferson," *Journal of Thought* 49 no. 3 & 4 (2015): http://journalofthought.com/wp-content/uploads/2016/02/06muir.pdf

Randall D. Hart, *Increasing Academic Achievement with the Trivium of Classical Education: Its Historical Development, Decline in the Last Century, and Resurgence in Recent Decades* (New York: iUniverse, 2006), 21-31.

Takeshi Sasaki, "Plato and *Politeia* in Twentieth-Century Politics," *Platonic Studies* 9 (2012): https://journals.openedition.org/etudesplatoniciennes/281

W. H. Cowley, "The Seven Liberal Arts Hoax," *Improving College and University Teaching* 26 no. 1 (1978): 97-99.

89   Claire Fallon, "When Booting Dead White Guys Off Reading Lists Is A Good Idea," *Huffington Post*, October 27, 2017, https://www.huffpost.com/entry/when-booting-dead-white-guys-off-reading-lists-is-a-good-idea_n_59f29887e4b03cd20b80a874

Devon Black, "Reconstructing the Canon," *Harvard Political Review*, April 25, 2018, https://harvardpolitics.com/culture/thecanon/

Patricia Hagen, "Review: 'Dead White Guys,' by Matt Burriesc; in Defense of the Western Canon," *Star Tribune*, July 28, 2015, http://www.startribune.com/review-dead-white-guys-by-matt-burriesci-in-defense-of-the-western-canon/318906491/

90   Miriam Joseph, *The Trivium: The Liberal Arts of Logic, Grammar, and Rhetoric (Understanding the Nature and Function of Language)* (Philadelphia: Paul Dry Books, 2002), 45.

91   Ibid, 47.

92   Dorothy Sayers, "The Lost Tools of Learning," *Increasing Academic Achievement with the Trivium of Classical Education: Its Historical Development, Decline in the Last Century, and Resurgence in Recent Decades*, ed. Randall D. Hart (New York: iUniverse, 2006), 113-114.

93   C. S. Lewis, *The Discarded Image: An Introduction to Medieval and Renaissance Literature* (Cambridge: University of Cambridge Press, 1964), 186.

94   Ibid, 185-186.

95   John Taylor Gatto, *An Underground History of American Education: An Intimate Investigation into the Prison of Modern Schooling* (New York: Oxford Village Press, 2006), 11-12.

96   Antony C. Sutton, *America's Secret Establishment: An Introduction to the Order of Skull and Bones*, Updated Reprint (Walterville, OR: Trine Day, 2002), 71-76, 83, 107-109.

97   Ibid, 71-76, 107-109.

98   Ibid, 71-76, 83, 107-109.

99   Ibid.

John Taylor Gatto, *An Underground History of American Education: An Intimate Investigation into the Prison of Modern Schooling* (New York: Oxford Village Press, 2006), 61-74.

100   George Orwell, "Politics and the English Language," 75 *Arguments: An Anthology*, ed. Alan Ainsworth (Boston: McGraw Hill, 2008).

Patrick Groff, "The New Anti-Phonics," *Elementary School Journal* 77 no. 4 (1977): 323-332.

Robert Emans, "History of Phonics," *Elementary English* 45 no. 5 (1968): 602-608.

101   Bernard Crick, *George Orwell: A Life* (Boston: Little, Brown, 1980).

102   George Orwell, "Politics and the English Language," 75 *Arguments: An Anthology*, ed. Alan Ainsworth (Boston: McGraw Hill, 2008), 11.

103   Ibid, 21.

104   Ibid, *1984* (London: Signet Classics, 1949).

105   Ibid, 7.

106   Ibid, 246-247.

107   Sonia Campos-Rivera and David Rattray, "Start Early and Finish Strong," *National Civic Review* 100 no. 4 (2011): 52.

108   Louis G. Denti and Gilbert Guerin, "Dropout Prevention: A Case for Enhanced Early Literacy Efforts," *Clearing House: A Journal of Educational Strategies* 72 no. 4 (1999): 232.
109   George Orwell, *1984* (London: Signet Classics, 1949), 246.
110   Ibid, "Politics and the English Language," 75 *Arguments: An Anthology*, ed. Alan Ainsworth (Boston: McGraw Hill, 2008), 21.
111   Dorothy Sayers, "The Lost Tools of Learning," *Increasing Academic Achievement with the Trivium of Classical Education: Its Historical Development, Decline in the Last Century, and Resurgence in Recent Decades*, ed. Randall D. Hart (New York: iUniverse, 2006), 115.
112   Ibid.
113   Editors of Encyclopaedia Britannica, "Laws of Thought: Logic," *Encyclopaedia Britannica*, April 8, 2019, https://www.britannica.com/topic/laws-of-thought
    Miriam Joseph, *The Trivium: The Liberal Arts of Logic, Grammar, and Rhetoric (Understanding the Nature and Function of Language)* (Philadelphia: Paul Dry Books, 2002), 71-89, 109-129.
114   Ibid, 121.
    José Veríssimo Teixeira da Mata, "Epicurus, Vasiliev and Aristotle on the Law of the Excluded Third," *Studies in Epistemology, Logic, Methodology, and Philosophy of Science* 387 (2017): 79-82.
    Thomas L. Saaty, "The Three Laws of Thought, Plus One: The Law of Comparisons," *Axioms* 3 (2014): 46-49.
115   Miriam Joseph, *The Trivium: The Liberal Arts of Logic, Grammar, and Rhetoric (Understanding the Nature and Function of Language)* (Philadelphia: Paul Dry Books, 2002), 109-186.
116   Ibid, 9.
117   Ibid, 209-265.
118   Ibid, 187-202, 204-205
119   Ibid, 202-204.
120   Ibid, 203-205.
121   Dorothy Sayers, "The Lost Tools of Learning," *Increasing Academic Achievement with the Trivium of Classical Education: Its Historical Development, Decline in the Last Century, and Resurgence in Recent Decades*, ed. Randall D. Hart (New York: iUniverse, 2006), 110.
122   British Broadcasting Corporation, "George Orwell at the BBC: The Writer of 'Nineteen Eighty-Four' Holds True to His Ideals," BBC Archives, accessed May 20, 2019, http://www.bbc.co.uk/archive/orwell/
    C. Fleay and M. L. Sanders, "Looking into the Abyss: George Orwell at the BBC," *Journal of Contemporary History* 24 no. 3 (1989): 503-518.
    George Orwell, "Memo from Orwell to the Eastern Service Director," BBC Archives, October 15, 1942, http://www.bbc.co.uk/archive/orwell/7422.shtml
    Mark Lawson, "George Orwell and the BBC," BBC, January 24, 2013, https://www.bbc.co.uk/blogs/aboutthebbc/entries/d3a46264-89b5-3198-8143-5158da7ff20b
    Telegraph Reporters, "Andrew Marr: George Orwell Would Have 'Sneered and Spat' on His Statue Unveiled by BBC," *Telegraph*, November 7, 2017, https://www.telegraph.co.uk/news/2017/11/07/andrew-marr-george-orwell-would-have-sneered-spat-statue-unveiled/
123   George Orwell, "Politics and the English Language," 75 *Arguments: An Anthology*, ed. Alan Ainsworth (Boston: McGraw Hill, 2008), 20.
124   Dorothy Sayers, "The Lost Tools of Learning," *Increasing Academic Achievement with the Trivium of Classical Education: Its Historical Development, Decline in the Last Century, and Resurgence in Recent Decades*, ed. Randall D. Hart (New York: iUniverse, 2006), 113.
125   Ibid, 116.
126   Ibid.
127   Ibid.
128   Ibid, 116.
129   American Historical Association, *Conclusions and Recommendations for the Social Studies* (New York: Charles Scribner's Sons, 1934) quoted in Charlotte Thomson Iserbyt, *The Deliberate Dumbing Down of America: A Chronological Paper Trail* (Parkman, OH: Conscience Press, 1999), 24.
130   Ibid.
131   Ibid.
132   Randall D. Hart, *Increasing Academic Achievement with the Trivium of Classical Education: Its Historical Development, Decline in the Last Century, and Resurgence in Recent Decades* (New York: iUniverse, 2006), 81-82.
133   Ibid, 82.

134   Ibid.
135   Eastern University, "Stephen R. Turley, Ph.D.," College of Arts and Sciences: Music Department, accessed May 20, 2019, https://www.eastern.edu/stephen-turley
Stephen R. Turley, *Classical vs. Modern Education: A Vision from C. S. Lewis* (USA: Turley Talks, 2016), 37.
136   Ibid, 27.
137   "Authors: Hamza Yusuf," *Renovatio*: The Journal of Zaytuna College, accessed May 17, 2019, https://renovatio.zaytuna.edu/authors/hamza-yusuf
138   Hamza Yusuf, "The Liberal Arts in an Illiberal Age: Freeing Thought from the Shackles of Feeling and Desire," *Renovatio*: The Journal of Zaytuna College December 19, 2018, https://renovatio.zaytuna.edu/article/the-liberal-arts-in-an-illiberal-age
139   Stephen Dafoe, "Masonic Biographies: Albert Mackey," accessed November 18, 2018, The Masonic Dictionary, http://www.masonicdictionary.com/mackey.html
140   Albert G. Mackey, *An Encyclopedia of Freemasonry and Its Kindred Societies Comprising the Whole Range of Arts, Sciences, and Literature as Connected with the Institution*, eds. William J. Hughan and Edward L. Hawkins, New and Revised Ed. (New York: Masonic History Company, 1914).
141   Mortimer J. Adler, "Mortimer J. Adler Papers 1914-1995," University of Chicago Special Collections Research Center (University of Chicago Library), accessed May 20, 2019, https://www.lib.uchicago.edu/e/scrc/findingaids/view.php?eadid=ICU.SPCL.ADLERM
142   Ibid, *The Paideia Proposal: An Educational Manifesto* (New York: MacMillan, 1982).
143   Ibid, "Mortimer J. Adler Papers 1914-1995," University of Chicago Special Collections Research Center (University of Chicago Library), accessed May 20, 2019, https://www.lib.uchicago.edu/e/scrc/findingaids/view.php?eadid=ICU.SPCL.ADLERM
144   Randall D. Hart, *Increasing Academic Achievement with the Trivium of Classical Education: Its Historical Development, Decline in the Last Century, and Resurgence in Recent Decades* (New York: iUniverse, 2006), 81-90.
William Grimes, "Mortimer Adler, 98, Dies; Helped Create Study of Classics," *New York Times*, June 29, 2001, https://www.nytimes.com/2001/06/29/nyregion/mortimer-adler-98-dies-helped-create-study-of-classics.html
145   Edwin McDowell, "'Great Books' Takes in Moderns and Women," *New York Times*, October 25, 1990, https://www.nytimes.com/1990/10/25/books/great-books-takes-in-moderns-and-women.html
Mortimer J. Adler, *The Great Conversation: A Reader's Guide to Great Books of the Western World* (Chicago: Encyclopedia Britannica, 1994).
Ibid, *The Great Ideas: A Syntopicon of Great Books of the Western World*, vol. II (Chicago: Encyclopedia Britannica, 1955).
Ibid, vol. II (Chicago: Encyclopedia Britannica, 1955).
Ibid, "Philosophy Is Everybody's Business," *Center for the Study of the Great Ideas: A Syntopical Approach to the Great Books and Practical Philosophy*, accessed May 20, 2019, https://www.thegreatideas.org/greatideas1.html
Moyers & Company, "Six Great Ideas with Bill Moyers and Mortimer Adler," Public Square Media, accessed May 20, 2019, https://billmoyers.com/series/six-great-ideas-bill-moyers-mortimer-adler/
146   Jan Irvin, interview by Tony Meyers, Tragedy and Hope: Independent Publishers of Free Knowledge and Priceless Wisdom; Re-Contextualizing History, One Episode at a Time, November 30, 2011, https://tragedyandhope.com/th-films/logic-fallacies-and-the-trivium/
Logos Media, "Trivium Education: Trivium Study," Logos Media: Formerly Gnostic Media, accessed May 20, 2019, https://logosmedia.com/triviumstudy
Tragedy and Hope Media, "Biography and Resume: Richard Grove," Tragedy and Hope: Independent Publishers of Free Knowledge and Priceless Wisdom; Re-Contextualizing History, One Episode at a Time, https://tragedyandhope.com/contact/biography-and-resume/
Ibid, "Trivium: Resources for the Trivium Method of Critical Thinking and Creative Problem Solving, useful to the Peace Revolution curriculum," Tragedy and Hope: Independent Publishers of Free Knowledge and Priceless Wisdom; Re-Contextualizing History, One Episode at a Time, accessed May 20, 2019, https://tragedyandhope.com/trivium/
147   Great Hearts Academies, "Core Purpose and Values: To Cultivate the Minds and Hearts of Students through the Pursuit of Truth, Goodness, and Beauty," accessed April 25, 2019, https://www.greatheartsamerica.org/great-hearts-core-purpose/
148   Ibid, "Board of Directors," accessed May 20, 2019, https://www.greatheartsamerica.org/

people/board-of-directors/

149   Stephen R. Turley, *Classical vs. Modern Education: A Vision from C. S. Lewis* (USA: Turley Talks, 2016), 28.

150   Ibid, 29.

151   Ibid.

152   Immanuel Kant, *Groundwork of the Metaphysic of Morals*, trans. H. J. Paton (New York: Harper & Row, 1948).

153   Aristotle, *The Metaphysics*, trans. John H. M'Mahon (London: George Bell and Sons, 1896).

Ibid, *The Physics*, trans. Philip H. Wicksteed and Francis M. Cornford, vol. I (New York: G. P. Putnam's Sons, 1934).

Ibid, vol. II (New York: G. P. Putnam's Sons, 1934).

Eric Entrican Wilson and Lara Denis, "Kant and Hume on Morality," *Stanford Encyclopedia of Philosophy*, March 29, 2018, https://plato.stanford.edu/entries/kant-hume-morality/

David Hume, *A Treatise of Human Nature: Being an Attempt to Introduce the Experimental Method of Reasoning into Moral Subjects*, ed. L. A. Selby-Bigge (Oxford: Clarendon Press, 1888).

Immanuel Kant, *Prolegomena to Any Future Metaphysics*, ed. Paul Carus, 3rd ed. (Chicago: Open Court Publishing, 1912).

154   David Noonan, "Meet the Two Scientists Who Implanted a False Memory into a Mouse: In a Neuroscience Breakthrough, the Duo Pioneered a Real-Life Version of Inception," *Smithsonian Magazine*, November 2014, https://www.smithsonianmag.com/innovation/meet-two-scientists-who-implanted-false-memory-mouse-180953045/

155   Jeff Blagdon, "Monkey Mentally Controls Robot 7,000 Miles Away," *The Verge*, February 22, 2013, https://www.theverge.com/2013/2/22/4016570/monkey-mentally-controls-robot-7000-miles-away

156   Rachel Lerman, "Be Wary of Robot Emotions; 'Simulated Love Is Never Love,'" Associated Press News, April 26, 2019, https://www.apnews.com/99c9ec8ebad242ca88178e22c7642648

157   Elsevier, "Discovery of Quantum Vibrations in 'Microtubules' inside Brain Neurons Supports Controversial Theory of Consciousness," *ScienceDaily*, January 16, 2014, https://www.sciencedaily.com/releases/2014/01/140116085105.htm

Stuart Hameroff and Roger Penrose, "Consciousness in the Universe: A Review of the 'Orch OR' Theory," *Physics of Life Reviews* 11 no. 1 (2014): 39-78.

158   Dirk K.F. Meijer and Hans J.H. Geesink, "Consciousness in the Universe Is Scale Invariant and Implies an Event Horizon of the Human Brain," *NeuroQuantology*: An Interdisciplinary Journal of Neuroscience and Quantum Physics 15 no. 3 (2017): 41-79.

Harald Atmanspacher, "Quantum Approaches to Consciousness," *Stanford Encyclopedia of Philosophy*, June 2, 2015, https://plato.stanford.edu/entries/qt-consciousness/

159   Yuval Noah Harari, *Homo Deus: A Brief History of Tomorrow* (London: Vintage, 2016), 125-126.

160   Ibid, 136.

161   Leonid I. Perlovsky, "Computational Complexity and the Origin of Universals," *Philosophy of Mind: Twentieth World Congress of Philosophy,* August 1998, https://www.bu.edu/wcp/Papers/Mind/MindPerl.htm

162   Ray Kurzweil, *The Singularity Is Near: When Humans Transcend Biology* (New York: Viking, 2005), 326.

163   Immanuel Kant, *Critique of Pure Reason*, trans. Norman Kemp Smith (London: MacMillan, 1929).

164   Ibid, *Prolegomena to Any Future Metaphysics*, ed. Paul Carus, 3rd ed. (Chicago: Open Court Publishing, 1912).

165   Andrew Brook, "Kant's View of the Mind and Consciousness of Self," *Stanford Encyclopedia of Philosophy*, January 22, 2013, https://plato.stanford.edu/entries/kant-mind/

Immanuel Kant, Critique of Pure Reason, trans. Norman Kemp Smith (London: MacMillan, 1929).

166   C. Stephen Evans, "Kant and Kierkegaard on the Possibility of Metaphysics," *Kant and Kierkegaard on Religion*, eds. D. Z. Phillips and T. Tessin (London: Palgrave Macmillan, 2000), 3-24.

Michael Wheeler, "Martin Heidegger," *Stanford Encyclopedia of Philosophy*, October 12, 2011, https://plato.stanford.edu/entries/heidegger/

Paul Redding, "Georg Wilhelm Friedrich Hegel," *Stanford Encyclopedia of Philosophy*, August 4, 2015, https://plato.stanford.edu/entries/hegel/

167

168   Amita Chatterjee, "Naturalism in Classical Indian Philosophy," *Stanford Encyclopedia of Philosophy*, October 27, 2017, https://plato.stanford.edu/entries/naturalism-india/

C. S. Lewis, *The Abolition of Man: Or Reflection on Education with Special Reference to the Teaching of English in the Upper Forms of Schools* (New York: Macmillan, 1947).

Edwin McDowell, "'Great Books'Takes in Moderns and Women," New York Times, October 25, 1990, https://www.nytimes.com/1990/10/25/books/great-books-takes-in-moderns-and-women.html

Lao Tzu, *Tao Te Ching*, trans. John H. McDonald and John Baldock (London: Sirius, 2017).

Luke T. Lee and Whalen W. Lai, "The Chinese Conceptions of Law: Confucian, Legalist, and Buddhist," *Hastings Law Journal* 29 no. 6 (1978): 1307-1329.

Harvard Divinity School, "The Dharma: The Teachings of the Buddha," Religious Liberty Project, accessed May 21, 2019, https://rlp.hds.harvard.edu/religions/buddhism/dharma-teachings-buddha

Mortimer J. Adler, *The Great Conversation: A Reader's Guide to Great Books of the Western World* (Chicago: Encyclopedia Britannica, 1994).

Ibid, *The Great Ideas: A Syntopicon of Great Books of the Western World*, vol. II (Chicago: Encyclopedia Britannica, 1955).

Ibid, vol. II (Chicago: *Encyclopedia Britannica*, 1955).

Ibid, "Philosophy Is Everybody's Business," Center for the Study of the Great Ideas: A Syntopical Approach to the Great Books and Practical Philosophy, accessed May 20, 2019, https://www.thegreatideas.org/greatideas1.html

Moyers & Company, "Six Great Ideas with Bill Moyers and Mortimer Adler," Public Square Media, accessed May 20, 2019, https://billmoyers.com/series/six-great-ideas-bill-moyers-mortimer-adler/

Ṛig-Veda Sanhitá, trans. H. H. Wilson (London: N. Trübner and Co., 1866).

Siddhārtha Gautma, *Four Noble Truths*, trans. Viranjeewa Weerakkody, eds. Re'rukāne' Chandawimala and Mahanayaka Thera (Sri Lanka, Polgasowita: Sri Chandawimala Dhamma Treatises Preservation Board, 2003).

169   Yuval Noah Harari, *Homo Deus: A Brief History of Tomorrow* (London: Vintage, 2016), 134-135.

170   Aristotle, *The Metaphysics*, trans. John H. M'Mahon (London: George Bell and Sons, 1896).

Ibid, *The Physics*, trans. Philip H. Wicksteed and Francis M. Cornford, vol. I (New York: G. P. Putnam's Sons, 1934).

Ibid, vol. II (New York: G. P. Putnam's Sons, 1934).

171   David Hume, *A Treatise of Human Nature: Being an Attempt to Introduce the Experimental Method of Reasoning into Moral Subjects*, ed. L. A. Selby-Bigge (Oxford: Clarendon Press, 1888).

Julian Baggini, "Hume on Religion, Part 7: Soul-Searching," *The Guardian*: US Edition, March 23, 2009, https://www.theguardian.com/commentisfree/belief/2009/mar/20/philosophy-religion-hume

172   Aristotle, *The Metaphysics*, trans. John H. M'Mahon (London: George Bell and Sons, 1896).

Ibid, *The Physics*, trans. Philip H. Wicksteed and Francis M. Cornford, vol. I (New York: G. P. Putnam's Sons, 1934).

Ibid, vol. II (New York: G. P. Putnam's Sons, 1934).

David Hume, *A Treatise of Human Nature: Being an Attempt to Introduce the Experimental Method of Reasoning into Moral Subjects*, ed. L. A. Selby-Bigge (Oxford: Clarendon Press, 1888).

173   René Descartes, *Discourse on the Method of Rightly Conducting One's Reason and of Seeking Truth in the Sciences*, trans. John Veitch (New York: E. P. Dutton & Co., 1912).

Ibid, *Meditations on First Philosophy in Which the Existence of God and the Immortality of the Soul Are Demonstrated*, trans. Laurence J. Lafleur (Indianapolis: Bobbs-Merrill Company, 1951).

Yuval Noah Harari, *Homo Deus: A Brief History of Tomorrow* (London: Vintage, 2016), 134-135.

174   Ibid, 134.

175   C. S. Lewis, *The Abolition of Man: Or Reflection on Education with Special Reference to the Teaching of English in the Upper Forms of Schools* (New York: Macmillan, 1947).

G. S. Kirk and J. E. Raven, *The Pre-Socratic Philosophers: A Critical History with a Selection of Texts* (Cambridge: University of Cambridge Press, 1957).

John 1:1-21:25 (KJV)

Lao Tzu, *Tao Te Ching*, trans. John H. McDonald and John Baldock (London: Sirius, 2017).

176   Auguste Comte, *The Positive Philosophy of Auguste Comte*, trans. Harriet Martineau (New

York: D Appleton, 1853).

Larry A. Hickman, "Dewey, Pragmatism, Technology," *The Oxford Handbook of Dewey*, ed. Steven Fesmire (November 2017), DOI: 10.1093/oxfordhb/9780190491192.013.18

William James, *Pragmatism, a New Name for Some Old Ways of Thinking: Popular Lectures on Philosophy* (New York: Longmans, Green, and Co., 1928).

177   Allan Stormon, "Unlock the Remarkable Power of Pragmatic AI: How a Readily Deployable form of AI is Transforming Today's Enterprise," *Huffington Post*, June 22, 2017, https://www.huffpost.com/entry/unlock-the-remarkable-power-of-pragmatic-ai_b_594c1e56e4b0f078efd97fe2

Nick Bostrom, "Transhumanist Values," *Ethical Issues for the Twenty-First Century* (Philosophy Documentation Center, 2005), 3-14.

178   Ayn Rand, *Introduction to Objectivist Epistemology*, trans. Leonard Peikoff and Harry Binswanger (New York: New American Library, 1990).

Ibid, *The Virtue of Selfishness: A New Concept of Egoism*, trans. Nathaniel Branden, 50th Anniversary Ed. (Charlotte, NC: Paw Prints, 2016).

Henri Lefebvre, *Dialectical Materialism*, trans. John Sturrock (Minneapolis: University of Minnesota Press, 1968).

Karl Marx and Friedrich Engels, *The German Ideology*, trans. C. J. Arthur (New York: International Publishers, 1947).

179   Alex Pearlman, "The Opposing Leaders of the Transhumanist Movement Got Salty in a Debate: Transhumanist Point-Counterpoint," *Vice*, April 25, 2016, https://www.vice.com/en_us/article/jpg577/transhumanist-debate

Friedrich Wilhelm Nietzsche, *The Antichrist*, trans. H. L. Mencken (New York: Alfred A. Knopf, 1920).

Joshua Fox, "Unintended Consequences: 19th Century Socialism and 21st Century Transhumanism," *Humanity+ Magazine*, July 7, 2011, https://hplusmagazine.com/2011/07/07/unintended-consequences-19th-century-socialism-and-21st-century-transhumanism/

Zoltan Istvan, "The Growing World of Libertarian Transhumanism," *The American Conservative*, August 8, 2017, https://www.theamericanconservative.com/articles/the-growing-world-of-libertarian-transhumanism/

180   Barbara C. Scholz, Francis Jeffry Pelletier, and Geoffrey K. Pullum, "Philosophy of Linguistics," *Stanford Encyclopedia of Philosophy*, January 1, 2015, https://plato.stanford.edu/entries/linguistics/

Bertrand Russell, "On Denoting," *Mind* 14 no. 56 (1905): 479-493.

Ferdinand de Saussure, *Course in General Linguistics*, trans. Roy Harris, Reprint (London: Bloomsbury, 2016).

Ludwig Wittgenstein, *Philosophical Investigations,* trans. G. E. M. Anscombe, P. M. S. Hacker, and Joachim Schulte, Revised 4th Ed. (Alden, MA: Wiley-Blackwell, 2009).

181   Ludwig Feuerbach, *The Essence of Christianity*, trans. George Eliot (Buffalo, N.Y.: Prometheus Books, 1989).

Ibid, *Principles of the Philosophy of the Future*, trans. Manfred Vogel (Indianapolis: Hackett Publishing, 1986).

Marylin Chapin Massey, "Censorship and the Language of Feuerbach's 'Essence of Christianity' (1841)," *Journal of Religion* 65 no. 2 (1985): 173-195.

Paul Bishop, "'Elementary Aesthetics,' Hedonist Ethics: The Philosophical Foundations of Feuerbach's Late Works," *History of European Ideas* 34 no. 3 (2008): 298-309.

Todd Gooch, "Ludwig Andreas Feuerbach," *Stanford Encyclopedia of Philosophy*, December 9, 2013, https://plato.stanford.edu/entries/ludwig-feuerbach/

182   "Robots in Our Brains Will Make Us 'Godlike' Says Google," BBC, October 2, 2015, http://www.bbc.co.uk/newsbeat/article/34427570/robots-in-our-brains-will-make-us-godlike-says-google

Yuval Noah Harari, *Homo Deus: A Brief History of Tomorrow* (London: Vintage, 2016).

183   Albert Camus, *Lyrical and Critical Essays*, trans. Ellen Conroy Kennedy, ed. Philip Thody (New York: Knopf, 1968).

Ibid, *The Myth of Sisyphus and Other Essays,* trans. Justin O'Brien (London: Hamish Hamilton, 1955).

Jean-Paul Sartre, *Existentialism and Humanism*, trans. Philip Mairet (London: Mcthuen, 1948).

John Foley, *Albert Camus: From the Absurd to Revolt* (Stocksfield, ENG: Acumen, 2008).

Martin Heidegger, *Being and Time*, trans. John Macquarrie and Edward Robinson, 35th Reprint

(Malden, MA: Blackwell, 2013).

Ronald Aronson, "Albert Camus," *Stanford Encyclopedia of Philosophy*, April 10, 2017, https://plato.stanford.edu/archives/sum2017/entries/camus/

184   Beth Singler, "Existential Hope and Existential Despair in AI Apocalypticism and Transhumanism," *Zygon: Journal of Religion and Science* 54 no. 1 (2019): 156-176.

Fabio Fossa, "Nihilism, Existentialism, – and Gnosticism? Reassessing the Role of the Gnostic Religion in Hans Jonas's Thought," *Philosophy and Social Criticism* (2019): https://doi.org/10.1177/0191453719839455.

Leon Culbertson, "Sartre on Human Nature: Humanness, Transhumanism and Performance-Enhancement," Sports, *Ethics, and Philosophy*: The Official Journal of the British Philosophy of Sport Association 5 no. 3 (2011): 231-244.

Patrícia Vieira, "Is Existentialism a Posthumanism?," Philosophical Salon: A Los Angeles Review of Books Channel, November 2, 2015, https://thephilosophicalsalon.com/is-existentialism-a-posthumanism/

Steven Crowell, "Existentialism," *Stanford Encyclopedia of Philosophy*, March 9, 2015, https://plato.stanford.edu/entries/existentialism/

185   J. P. Babbage, "Fracking: Fire Water (But Not the Kind You Drink)," *The Economist*, June 25, 2013, https://www.economist.com/babbage/2013/06/25/fire-water

Editors of the Encyclopedia Britannica, "Dust Bowl: Region, United States," accessed May 25, 2019, https://www.britannica.com/place/Dust-Bowl

Emily Dixon, "Nuclear Fuel Rods from Fukushima Disaster Reactor 3 Are Now Being Painstakingly Removed," CNN, April 15, 2019.

Sarah Zielinski, "The Colorado River Runs Dry: Dams, Irrigation and Now Climate Change Have Drastically Reduced the Once-Mighty River. Is It a Sign of Things to Come?," *Smithsonian Magazgine*, October 2010, https://www.smithsonianmag.com/science-nature/the-colorado-river-runs-dry-61427169/

186   Adrian Rodriguez, "Marin Activists Rally Against 5G," *Marin Independent Journal*, May 15, 2019, https://www.marinij.com/2019/05/15/marin-activists-rally-against-5g/

Mike Elgan, "Who's Slowing Down Fast 5G? Forget America's Opposition to Huawei. The Real Threat to 5G Nirvana Lies Elsewhere. (Hint: Conspiracy Theories Are Involved)," Computer World, May 18, 2019, https://www.computerworld.com/article/3396179/who-s-slowing-down-fast-5g.html

Ryan Collins, "Group Protests 5G, Doesn't Want It on Kauai," *The Garden Island*: Kauai's Newspaper Since 1901, May 16, 2019, https://www.thegardenisland.com/2019/05/16/hawaii-news/group-protests-5g-doesnt-want-it-on-kauai/

Shennekia Grimshaw, "Activists Protest Against 5G Towers: A Group Says They Are Nervous Because of Potential Health Risks Linked to 5G," WDVM Local News: Bethesda, https://www.localdvm.com/news/i-270/activists-protest-against-5g-towers/2004392639

187   Jim Puzzanghera, "Is 5G Technology Dangerous? Early Data Shows a Slight Increase of Tumors in Male Rats Exposed to Cellphone Radiation," *Los Angeles Times*, August 8, 2016, https://www.latimes.com/business/la-fi-cellphone-5g-health-20160808-snap-story.html

Julia Belluz, "A Comprehensive Guide to the Messy, Frustrating Science of Cellphones and Health: With 5G Networks Coming, Understanding the Health Effects of Radio-Frequency Radiation Is More Urgent Than Ever," *Vox*, November 2, 2018, https://www.vox.com/2018/7/16/17067214/cellphone-cancer-5g-evidence-studies

188   Agostino Di Ciaula, "Towards 5G Communication Systems: Are There Health Implications?," *International Journal of Hygiene and Environmental Health* 221 no. 3 (2018): 367.

189   Andryanna Sheppard, "Group Rallies Against New 5G Technology Rollout," ABC News: KDRV TV, May 15, 2019, https://www.kdrv.com/content/news/Group-rallies-against-new-5G-technology-roll-out-510001741.html

190   Ryan Collins, "Group Protests 5G, Doesn't Want It on Kauai," *The Garden Island*: Kauai's Newspaper Since 1901, May 16, 2019, https://www.thegardenisland.com/2019/05/16/hawaii-news/group-protests-5g-doesnt-want-it-on-kauai/

191   Adrian Rodriguez, "Marin Activists Rally Against 5G," *Marin Independent Journal*, May 15, 2019, https://www.marinij.com/2019/05/15/marin-activists-rally-against-5g/

192   Rob Hughes, "Petition Circulating to Stop 5G from Coming to Charlotte: 5G Promises Faster Internet Speeds, but That's Just Part of the Equation. It Could Also Allow for Smart Stoplights, Automated Cars and Even Hologram Video conferencing," NBC News: WCNC TV, May 9, 2019, https://www.wcnc.com/article/tech/petition-circulating-to-stop-5g-from-coming-to-char-

lotte/275-4613b9a4-8244-426c-aa68-f695f168e023

193   Julia Moro, "Long Islanders Join Nationwide Anti-5G Rally," *Long Island Press*, May 16, 2019, https://www.longislandpress.com/2019/05/16/long-islanders-join-nationwide-anti-5g-rally/

194   Emily Burkhard, "Albany Residents Debate Safety of 5G," NBC News: WNYT TV, May 16, 2019, https://wnyt.com/news/albany-residents-debate-safety-of-5g/5356550/

195   Paul Kirby, "Protesters Call on Woodstock to Block 5G Wireless Installation," *Daily Freeman*, May 15, 2019, https://www.dailyfreeman.com/news/local-news/protesters-call-on-woodstock-to-block-g-wireless-installation/article_21df1904-7743-11e9-baa8-cbe50257f5da.html

196   Karen Wynn, "Local Group Rallies in Asheville as Part of National Protest Over 5G Technology," ABC News: WLOS TV, May 15, 2019, https://wlos.com/news/local/local-group-rallies-in-asheville-as-part-of-national-protest-over-5g-technology

Patti and Doug. "Stopping 5G Microwave Radiation: The May 15th National Day of Action," Centre for Research on Globalization, May 4, 2019, https://www.globalresearch.ca/stopping-5g-microwave-radiation-the-may-15th-national-day-of-action/5676493

DIAGRAMS FROM
AMERICA'S SECRET ESTABLISHMENT

The Americanization Of Wilhelm Wundt

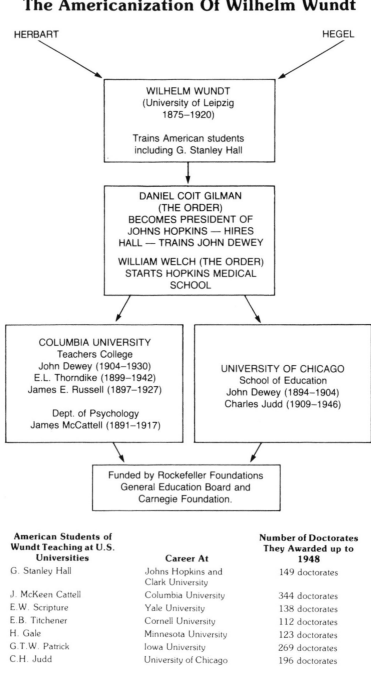

HERBART   HEGEL

WILHELM WUNDT
(University of Leipzig
1875–1920)

Trains American students
including G. Stanley Hall

DANIEL COIT GILMAN
(THE ORDER)
BECOMES PRESIDENT OF
JOHNS HOPKINS — HIRES
HALL — TRAINS JOHN DEWEY

WILLIAM WELCH (THE ORDER)
STARTS HOPKINS MEDICAL
SCHOOL

COLUMBIA UNIVERSITY
Teachers College
John Dewey (1904–1930)
E.L. Thorndike (1899–1942)
James E. Russell (1897–1927)

Dept. of Psychology
James McCattell (1891–1917)

UNIVERSITY OF CHICAGO
School of Education
John Dewey (1894–1904)
Charles Judd (1909–1946)

Funded by Rockefeller Foundations
General Education Board and
Carnegie Foundation.

American Students of Wundt Teaching at U.S. Universities	Career At	Number of Doctorates They Awarded up to 1948
G. Stanley Hall	Johns Hopkins and Clark University	149 doctorates
J. McKeen Cattell	Columbia University	344 doctorates
E.W. Scripture	Yale University	138 doctorates
E.B. Titchener	Cornell University	112 doctorates
H. Gale	Minnesota University	123 doctorates
G.T.W. Patrick	Iowa University	269 doctorates
C.H. Judd	University of Chicago	196 doctorates

478

Achievements Of The Troika

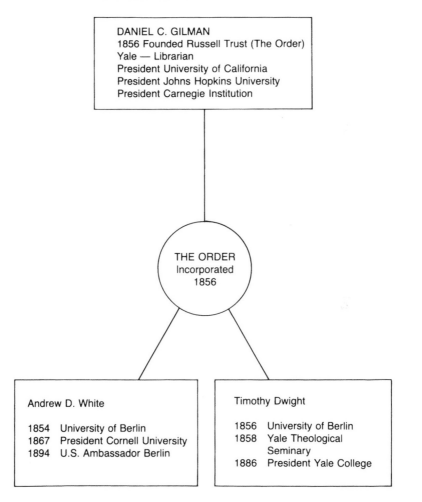

DANIEL C. GILMAN
1856 Founded Russell Trust (The Order)
Yale — Librarian
President University of California
President Johns Hopkins University
President Carnegie Institution

THE ORDER
Incorporated
1856

Andrew D. White

1854　University of Berlin
1867　President Cornell University
1894　U.S. Ambassador Berlin

Timothy Dwight

1856　University of Berlin
1858　Yale Theological
　　　Seminary
1886　President Yale College

APPENDIX TO MEMORANDUM NUMBER ONE:
THE ORDER IN THE YALE FACULTY

Member	Date Initiated	Position at Yale
BEEBE, William	1873	Professor of Mathematics (1882-1917)
BEERS, Henry A.	1869	Professor of English Literature (1874-1926)
BELLINGER, Alfred R.	1917	Professor of Greek (1926-
DAHL, George	1908	Professor Yale Divinity School (1914-1929)
DARLING, Arthůr B.	1916	Professor of History (1925-1933)
DAY, Clive	1892	Professor of Economic History (1902-1938)
DEXTER, Franklin B.	1861	Secretary, Yale University (1869-99)
DWIGHT, Timothy	1849	President of Yale University (1886-98)
FARNAM, Henry	1874	Professor of Economics (1880-1933)
FARNAM, William	1866	Trustee Sheffield Scientific School (1894-1923)
FRENCH, Robert D.	1910	Professor of English (1919-1950)
GILMAN, Daniel C.	1852	See text.
GRAVES, Henry S.	1892	Dean, Yale School of Forestry (1900-1939)
GRUENER, G.	1884	Professor of German (1892-1928)
HADLEY, Arthur T.	1876	President of Yale (1899-1921)
HILLES, Frederick W.	1922	Professor of English (1931-
HOLDEN, Reuben A.	1940	Assistant to President (1947-
HOPPIN, James M.	1840	Professor of History of Art (1861-99)
INGERSOLL, James W.	1892	Professor of Latin (1897-1921)
JONES, Frederick S.	1884	Dean, Yale College 1909-1926)
LEWIS, Charlton M.	1886	Professor of English (1898-1923)
LOHMAN, Carl A.	1910	Secretary, Yale University (1927-
LYMAN, Chester	1837	Professor of Mechanics (1859-1890)
McLAUGHLIN, Edward T.	1883	Professor of English (1890-93)
NORTHROP, Cyrus	1857	Professor of English (1863-84)
PACKARD, Lewis R.	1856	Professor of Greek (1863-84)
PECK, Tracy	1861	Professor of Latin (1889-1908)
PERRIN, Bernadotte	1869	Professor of Greek (1893-1909)
PIERCE, Frederick E.	1904	Professor of English (1910-35)
ROOT, Reginald D.	1926	Yale football coach (1933-48)
SCHWAB, John C.	1886	Professor of Political Economy (1893-1906)
SEYMOUR, Charles	1908	Professor of History (1915-37) President (1936-1950)
SEYMOUR, Charles Jr.	1935	Professor of Art (1949-
SILLIMAN, Benjamin Jr.	1837	Professor of Chemistry (1846-85)
STOKES, Anson P.	1896	Secretary of Yale (1899-1921)
SUMNER, William G.	1863	Professor of Economics (1872-1909)
TAFT, William H.	1878	Professor of Law (1913)
TARBELL, Frank B.	1873	Professor of Greek (1882-87)
THACHER, Thomas A.	1835	Professor of Latin (1842-86)
THOMPSON, John R.	1938	Professor of Law (1949-
WALKER, Charles R.	1916	Assistant Secretary (1943-45)
WOOLSEY, Theodore S.	1872	Professor of International Law (1878-1929)
WRIGHT, Henry B.	1898	Professor of History (1907-11)
WRIGHT, Henry P.	1868	Professor of Latin (1871-1918) Dean, Yale College (1884-1909)

Members Of The Order In Education
(For Yale University see list at end of Memorandum Number One)

Name	Date Initiated	Affiliations
BURTT, Edwin A.	1915	Professor of Philosophy, University of Chicago (1924-1931) and Cornell University (1931-1960)
ALEXANDER, Eben	1873	Professor of Greek and Minister to Greece (1893-97)
BLAKE, Eli Whitney	1857	Professor of Physics, Cornell (1868-1870) and Brown University (1870-95)
CAPRON, Samuel M.	1853	Not known
CHAUVENET, William	1840	U.S. Naval Academy (1845-59) and Chancellor Washington University (1862-9)
COLTON, Henry M.	1848	Not known
COOKE, Francis J.	1933	New England Conservatory of Music
COOPER, Jacob	1852	Professor of Greek, Center College (1855-1866), Rutgers University (1866-1904)
CUSHING, William	1872	Not known
CUSHMAN, Isaac LaFayette	1845	Not known
CUTLER, Carroll	1854	President, Western Reserve University (1871-1886)
DALY, Frederick J.	1911	Not known
DANIELS, Joseph L.	1860	Professor of Greek, Olivert College, and President (1865-1904)
EMERSON, Joseph	1841	Professor of Greek, Beloit College (1848-1888)
EMERSON, Samuel	1848	Not known
ESTILL, Joe G.	1891	Connecticut State Legislature (1932-1936)
EVANS, Evan W.	1851	Professor of Mathematics, Cornell University (1868-1872)

EWELL, John L.	1865	Professor of Church History, Howard University (1891-1910)
FEW SMITH, W.	1844	Not known
FISHER, Irving	1888	Professor of Political Economy, Yale (1893-1935)
FISK, F.W.	1849	President, Chicago Theological Seminary (1887-1900)
GREEN, James Payne	1857	Professor of Greek, Jefferson College (1857-59)
GRIGGS, John C.	1889	Vassar College (1897-1927)
GROVER, Thomas W.	1874	Not known
HALL, Edward T.	1941	St. Mark's School Southborough, Mass.
HARMAN, Archer	1913	St. Paul's School, Concord, N.H.
HARMAN, Archer, Jr.	1945	St. Paul's School, Concord, N.H.
HEBARD, Daniel	1860	Not known
HINCKS, John H.	1872	Professor of History, Atlanta University (1849-1894)
HINE, Charles D.	1871	Secretary, Connecticut State Board of Education (1883-1920)
HOLLISTER, Arthur N.	1858	Not known
HOPKINS, John M.	1900	Not known
HOXTON, Archibald R.	1939	Episcopal High School
HOYT, Joseph G.	1840	Chancellor, Washington University (1858-1862)
IVES, Chauncey B.	1928	Adirondack-Florida School
JOHNSON, Charles F.	1855	Professor of Mathematics, U.S. Naval Academy (1865-1870), Trinity College (1884-1906)
JOHNSTON, Henry Phelps	1862	Professor of History, N.Y. City College (1883-1916)
JOHNSTON, William	1852	Professor of English Literature, Washington & Lee (1867-1877) and Louisiana State University (1883-1889)
JONES, Theodore S.	1933	Institute of Contemporary Art
JUDSON, Isaac N.	1873	Not known
KELLOGG, Fred W.	1883	Not known
KIMBALL, John	1858	Not known
KINGSBURY, Howard T.	1926	Westminster School
KINNE, William	1948	Not known
KNAPP, John M.	1936	Princeton University
KNOX, Hugh	1907	Not known
LEARNED, Dwight Whitney	1870	Professor of Church History, Doshiba College, Japan (1876-1928)
McCLINTOCK, Norman	1891	Professor of Zoology, University of Pittsburgh (1925-30), Rutgers (1932-6)
MACLEISH, Archibald	1915	Library of Congress (1939-1944), UNESCO, State Dept., OWI, Howard University

MACLEISH, William H.	1950	Not known
MACLELLAN, George B.	1858	Not known
MOORE, Eliakim H.	1883	Professor of Mathematics, University of Chicago (1892-1931)
MORSE, Sidney N.	1890	Not known
NICHOLS, Alfred B.	1880	Professor of German, Simmons College (1903-1911)
NORTON, William B.	1925	Professor of History, Boston Univ.
OWEN, Edward T.	1872	Professor of French, University of Wisconsin (1879-1931)
PARSONS, Henry McI	1933	Columbia University
PERRY, David B.	1863	President, Douana College (1881-1912)
PINCKARD, Thomas C.	1848	Not known
POMEROY, John	1887	Professor of Law, University of Illinois (1910-1924)
POTWIN, Lemuel S.	1854	Professor, Western Reserve University (1871-1906)
REED, Harry L.	1889	President, Auburn Theological Seminary (1926-1939)
RICHARDSON, Rufus B.	1869	Director of American School of Classical Studies, Athens (1893-1903)
RUSSELL, William H.	1833	Collegiate School, Hartford
SEELY, Wm. W.	1862	Dean, Medical Faculty, University of Cincinnati (1881-1900)
SHIRLEY, A.	1869	Not known
SOUTHWORTH, George CS	1863	Bexley Theological Seminary (1888-1900)
SPRING, Andrew J.	1855	Not known
STAGG, Amos A.	1888	Director Physical Education, University of Chicago
STILLMAN, George S.	1935	St. Paul's School
SUTHERLAND, Richard O.	1931	Not known
THACHER, William L.	1887	Not known
TIGHE, Lawrence G.	1916	Treasurer of Yale
TWICHELL, Charles P.	1945	St. Louis Country Day School
TYLER, Charles M.	1855	Professor of History, Cornell University (1891-1903)
TYLER, Moses Coit	1857	Professor at Cornell (1867-1900)
VOGT, T.D.	1943	Not known
WALKER, Horace F.	1889	Not known
WATKINS, Charles L.	1908	Director, Phillips Art School
WHITE, John R.	1903	Not known
WHITNEY, Emerson C.	1851	Not known
WHITNEY, Joseph E.	1882	Not known
WILLIAMS, James W.	1908	Not known
WOOD, William C.	1868	Not known
YOUNG, Benham D.	1848	Not known
YARDLEY, Henry A.	1855	Berkeley Divinity School (1867-1882)

Index